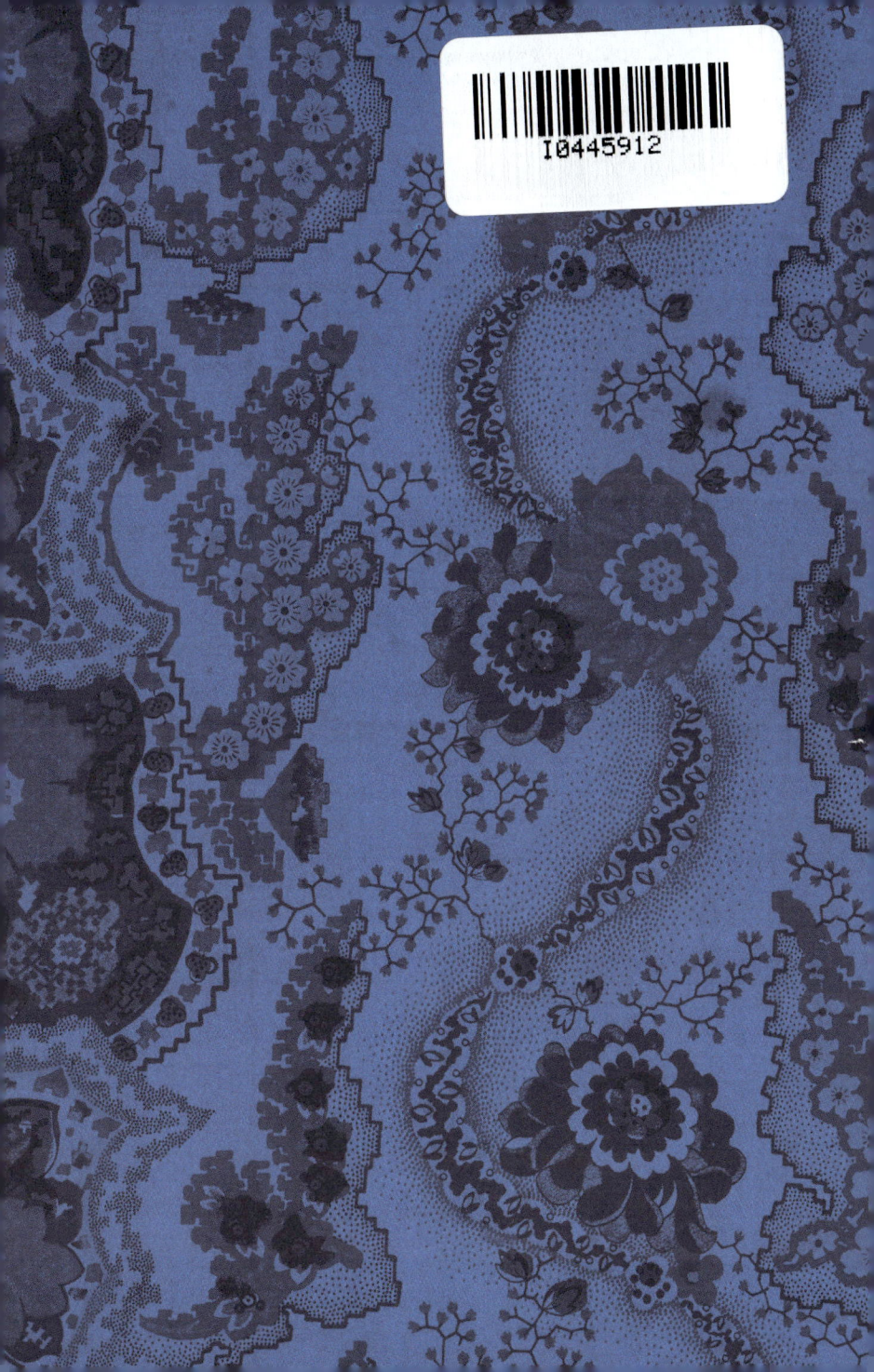

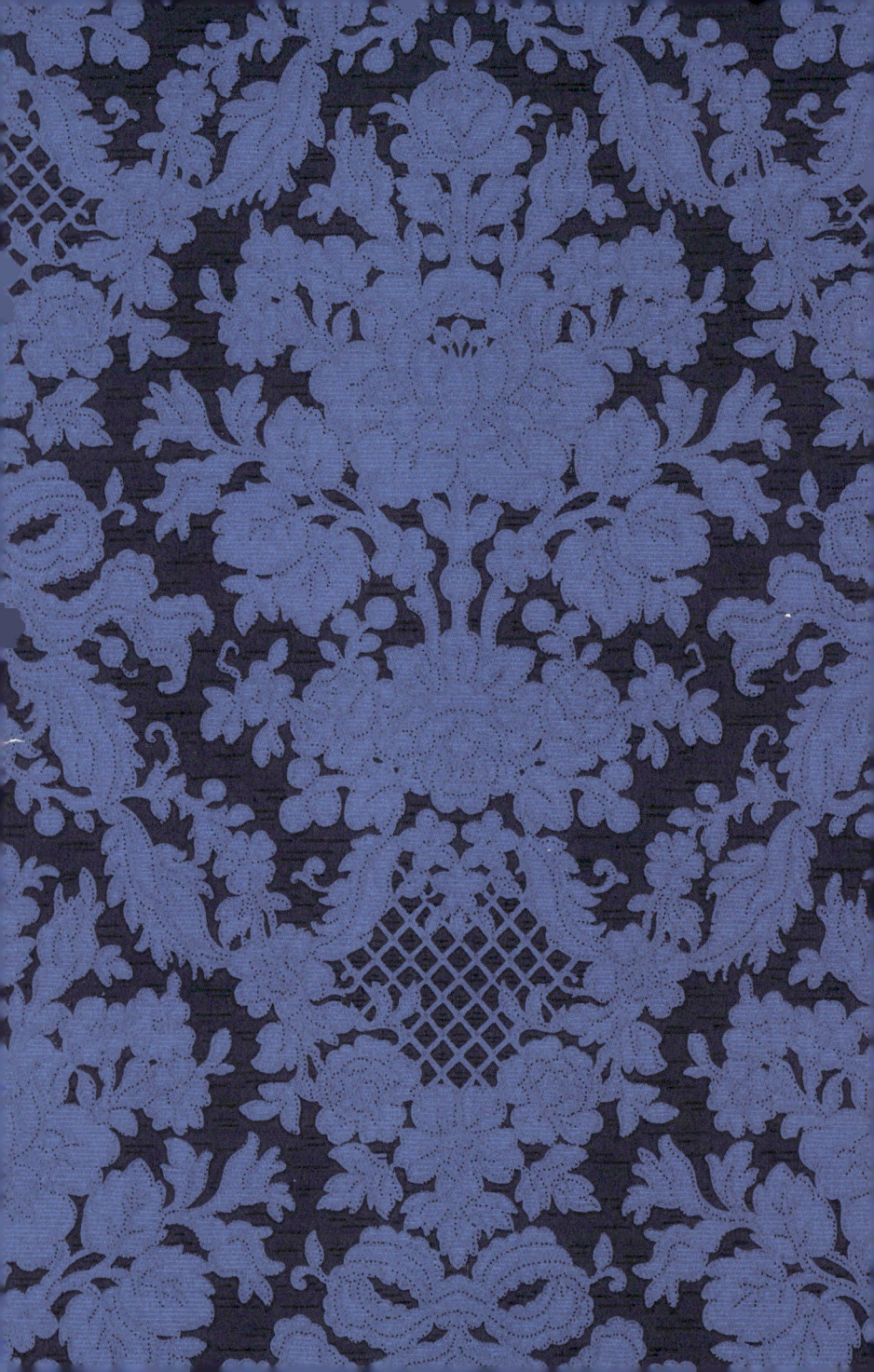

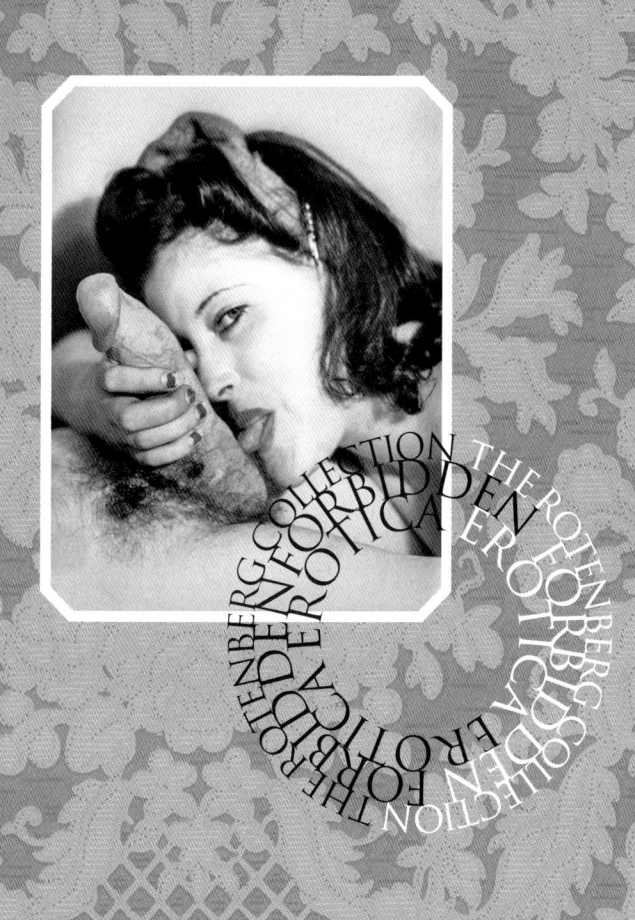

THE ROTENBERG COLLECTION FORBIDDEN EROTICA

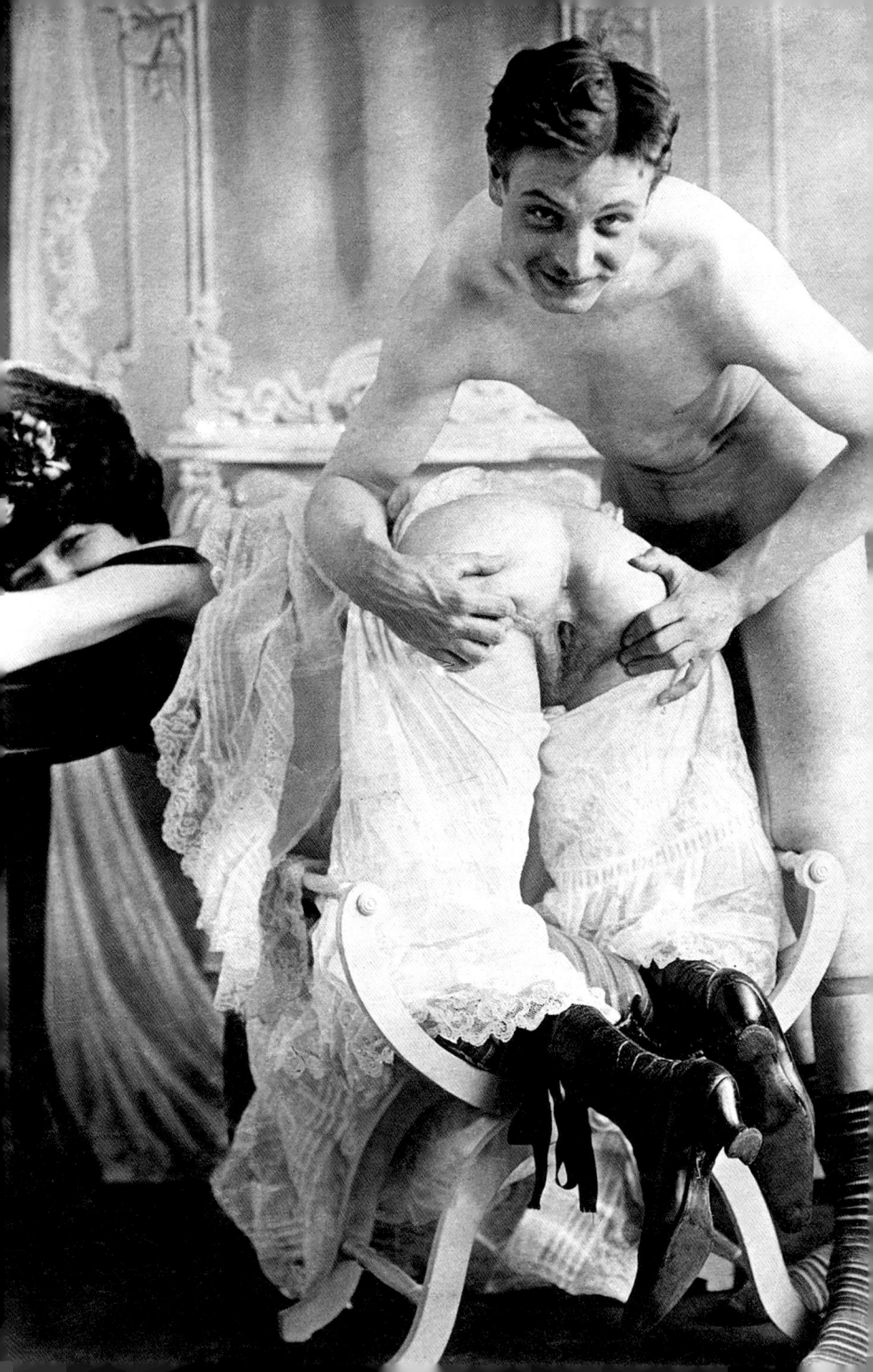

THE ROTENBERG
COLLECTION

FORBIDDEN
EROTICA

TASCHEN
Bibliotheca Universalis

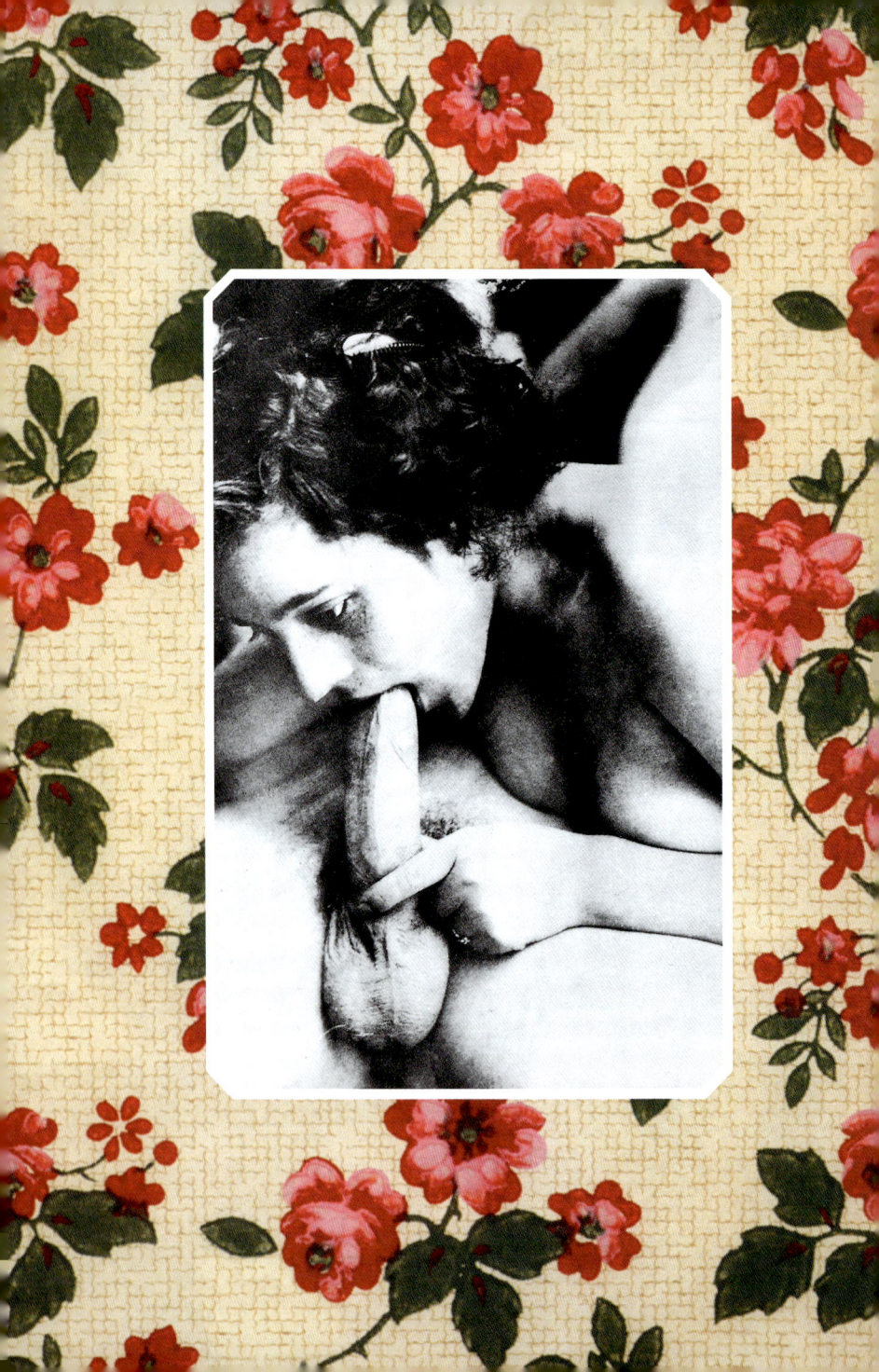

FORBIDDEN EROTICA: INTRODUCTION

The nude is and always has been one of the most popular subjects for photography. No one knows exactly when the first nude photographs were taken, but they seem to have first turned up in Paris around 1845 at opticians, instrument makers and art dealers.[1] The content of these images ranged widely, from nudes seen altogether decently from the back, in the manner of classical "academy figures", all the way through to brazen displays of genitalia, from sex between lesbians to heterosexual coitus.

By far the greater proportion of the pictures was produced by men, for men. Thus they are representative of the general masculine erotic imagination, or at least what the photographers assumed that to be. To appeal to that male audience, many pictures were taken which portray fellatio. Lesbian activity features less than it would today, but male homosexual imagery is as explicit as it would be now, even though male homosexual acts were considered criminal at the time. Of course, the most popular subject of all is heterosexual intercourse in all its myriad configurations. For the photographer who could capture such scenes, there was then, as there is today, considerable money to be made.

The identity of very few, if any, of the models who posed for the pictures in *Forbidden Erotica* is known. Many of the models were prostitutes. In view of the situation faced by most of them – a lifetime of suffering, privation and pointless drudgery – posing for pornographic photographs must have seemed like a lucky break. There is also evidence that a small number of the models were mental patients with little to no knowledge of what they were doing posing for the photos.

The names of the photographers who took these pictures have not survived, either. The photos were produced outside the pale of formal artistic circumstances, and intended for popular consumption. The producers, often anonymous, were not professional artists with extensive training or discipline.

The earliest pictures in *Forbidden Erotica* date from the 1870s and 1880s. By that time, processes had been invented for developing photographs from negatives, enabling them to be mass-produced. (Earlier formats, such as daguerreotypes, tintypes and ambrotypes, were one-off, direct positives which could not be mass-produced.) The most recent images in the book date from the 1940s. The photographic formats include gelatin silver prints, albumen prints, real-photo post-cards, hand-tinted real-photo postcards and sepia-tone photographs and postcards, plus a small number of lithographs. Multiple generations of duplicate photos were made from the same originals. In some copies one can clearly see that the picture was thumb-tacked to a wall to be shot again. The book also features a small selection of illustrated pornographic postcards.

The picture postcard, coming on the scene in the 1870s, did much to hasten the popularization and dissemination of erotic/pornographic photography. The heyday of the erotic postcard reached from the 1890s through the 1930s. In France alone, between 1919 and 1939, over 20 million nude postcards were produced. These erotic and pornographic postcards, which were never intended to be sent through the post, are often more outspoken than today's pornography. It was, for instance, not uncommon for minors to take part in erotic posings, and there are many postcards showing dogs copulating with women. Today laws prohibit the publication of such imagery.

From the first, the authorities did everything possible to prevent the production of "obscene" photography. The Society for the Suppression of Vice had been formed in Britain in 1802 to protect the public from blasphemous publications, obscene books and prints, and brothels. Much of the photographic pornography that was created after 1850 was suppressed, confiscated and destroyed. To take just one instance, in 1874 a visit by the London police to the shipping department of a certain Henry Hayler yielded 130,248 "lewd" prints, which were confiscated on the spot.[2] The United States, a country steeped in Puritanism from its founding, had as a major late 19th-century enforcer of censorship one Anthony Comstock, a special agent of the U.S. Post Office and secretary of the New York Society for the Suppression of Vice. Comstock was instrumental in the crackdown on the dissemination of pornography via the U.S. mail.

It is no accident that the production of pornography flourished during a time of outward repression. As Paul Tabori writes in *Secret and Forbidden: The Moral History of the Passions of Mankind*, "pornography can only be rampant in the soil manured by prudery, and in an age where the contrast of spirit and flesh is the strongest."[3] Indeed, "terms such as 'obscene' or 'lewd' reflect the sexually repressive attitudes which became more widespread, interestingly enough, at the very time photography itself was being discovered and adopted."[4] *The Compact Edition of the Oxford English Dictionary* lists the first appearance of the word "pornographer" as 1850;[5] the invention of the photographic process dates from about 1839.

Even so, despite the laws against them and attempts to stop their output and distribution, photos like those in *Forbidden Erotica* were turned out by the thousands and sold all over the world. Clearly these photographs were mass-produced for a mass market. Cuba, France, England, Japan, and the United States have a long documented history of their production.

For the most part, the photographs in *Forbidden Erotica* represent the most hardcore and graphic examples in The Rotenberg Collection of erotic photography. Indeed, the term "erotic", which suggests sexuality that is dreamy, soft-focus, graceful, stylish, coquettish, charming, dainty and demure, really implies everything that the pictures in this book are *not*. Behind the prudery of the Victorian era, a romantic, veiled eroticism flourished. Beyond *that* was a boom in outright pornography. There is a vast difference between the artistic, the erotic and the pornographic photograph. "Artistic nudes make no promises, erotic nudes make a few, and obscene or pornographic works so completely fulfill them all that many viewers find them offensive rather than exciting."[6]

Many collections have been published celebrating the pre-Raphaelite and Art Nouveau-inspired erotic photographs of *la belle époque*. The photographic images in *Forbidden Erotica* were created further backstage. They have no pretensions to art. They are explicit and may be shocking, perhaps even frightening, to some. Today, most people are not used to seeing photographs of naked people who are not beautiful. They show the plain simple truth of the sexual act in nearly infinite variety. They bear little resemblance to the rarefied, exotic work of erotic artists of *la belle époque* such as Aubrey Beardsley, Félicien Rops, Gustav Klimt or Franz von Bayros. They come closer to illustrating two classics of Victorian pornographic literature: *My Secret Life* and *The Pearl*.

My Secret Life, an anonymous underground non-fiction work published circa 1890, is the sexually graphic diary of a wealthy English gentleman. The author reports on a lifetime of amatory experience in language which is neither expurgated nor embellished. Beginning with early memories of sexual abuse by his nursemaid, he goes on to relate his peeks at the household servant girls as they urinate (or "piddle" – his word); his partaking of the favors of these same servant girls despite his mother's instructions to leave them alone; his deflowering of countless virgins; and his random couplings with country girls in the lane. As he grows older, his appetites take him into more adventurous territory. He provides straightforward depictions of bondage, domination, flagellation, prostitution, orgies, cross-dressing, homosexuality, even rape.

All manner of sexual activity is rendered in exhaustive, almost clinical detail: from simple intercourse, to fellatio and cunnilingus (both of which the author terms "gamahuching"), sodomy, masturbation, etc. The following short passage is as good as any other in conveying the tenor of *My Secret Life*:

I laid him on the bed and putting his prick in my mouth began to suck it, first with the skin on, then gently with the skin off … It took effect directly … It was stiffened by the time Sarah got back … With cock stiff he got on to her in a minute. … His prick up to the roots was up her cunt … I had frigged him three times and he'd fucked thrice – I had fucked six times – I had fucked in his spunk, and had sucked his prick – Sarah had been fucked quite eight times. … [She] said, "I'm clean fucked out." Then paying them I left.[7]

In *My Secret Life*, the implication is conveyed that in Victorian society the "lower classes" were fair game for sexual exploitation by their social "betters". Servants and the poor were objectified, at times treated like animals, regarded almost as a separate species. Weary of sex with prostitutes, the anonymous author of *My Secret Life* writes: "I wanted a change, and began to look out for a nice, fresh servant. … They are clean, well-fed, full-blooded, … ready, yielding, hot-arsed, lewd and lubricious."[8] And if it was open season on these women – and men – as far as seduction or outright sexual abuse was concerned, it naturally follows that these individuals would be regarded as perfect specimens for photographing in all manner of compromising positions.

The underground magazine *The Pearl: A Journal of Facetiae and Voluptuous Reading*, published from July 1879 to December 1880, covers territory similar to that of *My Secret Life*, but in a very different tone. Whereas *My Secret Life* is stark and exudes an everyday carnality, *The Pearl* is heightened and dramatic, humorous and fanciful. In *The Pearl*, several stories were serialized monthly, among them: "Sub-Umbra, or Sport Among the She-Noodles", "Miss Coote's Confession, or The Voluptuous Experiences of An Old Maid; In a Series of Letters to a Lady Friend", and "Lady Pokingham, or They All Do It".

The Pearl seems to place a particularly strong emphasis on flagellation. Ralph Ginzburg writes in *An Unhurried View of Erotica*: "Flagellomania in 18th and 19th-century England had been cultivated to a degree never before or since equalled by humankind. … This pastime was known on the Continent as 'le vice anglais'".[9] A passage from *The Pearl*, a fragment of "Miss Coote's Confession", will serve as illustration:

Miss Flaybum's face shows the depth of her indignation, whilst her fat, plump bottom writhes at every stroke. … the flagellatrix and her friends are getting quite excited at the spectacle …, [which] seems to afford them exquisite voluptuous sensations, many of the elder girls being stretched on the floor together, or in other positions of sensual enjoyment.[10]

(The author of *My Secret Life* also relates his adventures visiting a flagellation parlor, the owner of which was traditionally called "the abbess".)

Many passages in *The Pearl* wield the titillating power of déshabillé and the relatively novel allure of undergarments. (It is interesting to note that women's underwear had only just come into fashion in the 1850s, about thirty years previous to the first publication of *The Pearl*.) The following example indicates the Victorian fascination with women "d'un certain âge" as well.

Maria gradually strips her mistress, who is a fine looking woman of the fat, fair and forty class. … She presently stands with only chemise and drawers, the latter so well filled out as to give promise of a splendid bottom within, and the ends beautifully trimmed with expensive lace, below which are seen a fine pair of plump legs, in flesh-coloured silk stockings, and high-heeled shoes, with jewelled buckles …[11]

Taken together, *My Secret Life* and *The Pearl* go a long way toward revealing the secret, repressed sexuality of the Victorian era. The images in *Forbidden Erotica* might be viewed as photographic illustrations of this sexuality. Both the clinical tone of *My Secret Life* and the playful spirit of *The Pearl* can be found in the photographs in this book. Certain photos match or surpass the stark tone of *My Secret Life*. While most of the models seem to be having a good time posing, grinning or leering knowingly at the camera, some stare blankly into the distance. The effect chills the soul. Then there are the close-up shots of apparently disembodied, gaping vulvae, huge erect penises, and insertions which leave nothing at all to the imagination. Except for their sepia tone or faded quality, these pictures are utterly timeless.

Spurred, perhaps, by the novelty of the photographic medium, or by the fact that the subject matter was forbidden, early photographers seem to have been determined, like the author of *My Secret Life*, to record every conceivable sexual act. No doubt, also, they were discovering the monetary advantages to be gained in feeding as many different sexual fantasies and fetishes as possible. There are shots of *ménages à trois*, *quatre* and more – men with men, women with women – in every possible permutation. Every race is represented. There are fanciful collages of orgies. There is an astounding abundance of images depicting fellatio and cunnilingus – *My Secret Life*'s "gamahuching".

There are pictures of gentlemen having their way with scullery maids in the kitchen. Other gentlemen are depicted taking country lasses for a roll in the hay. The viewer can peep through the keyhole, as it were, at three women merrily urinating together. "Piddling" seems to be a favorite subject generally. Enemas were also administered for the camera. Early pornographic photographers, like the authors of pornographic literature, took the opportunity to defy every taboo possible. A favorite theme is the depiction of clergymen and women – priests and nuns especially – performing all manner of licentious acts – from simple coitus to flagellation and "gamahuching".

Myriad props and sexual toys were put to use, from the mundane penis-shaped dildo – which, one may be surprised to discover, has been around for thousands of years – to cigars, cigarettes, wine, beer and champagne bottles, telephones, salamis, gourds, broomsticks, pool cues, hammers, maracas and an insect sprayer. The ultimate dildo in the history of the French postcard must be the mini Eiffel Tower shown inserted into a woman's derrière. Several photos show a man teeing off his golf swing from a woman's vagina. Sexual acrobatics are also a popular motif. A woman bends backwards or hangs upside down over a man's shoulders, a table, or a chair. She stands on one leg, the other over his shoulder. Or she stands on her head while he holds her upside down and inserts himself into her. Or he rests her legs on his shoulders while she hangs her head down and takes his penis in her mouth.

As in *My Secret Life* and *The Pearl*, the Victorian fascination with bondage, domination and flagellation is amply represented in the photographs. The present-day conception of the dominatrix, with mask, leather boots and whip, was well established by the late 19th century; several of her ilk can be found in *Forbidden Erotica*. There are also many shots of victims – chained, manacled and beaten with whips, willow switches or birch rods. A good number of models in the photos do not conform to the present day preoccupation with the erotic desirability of youth. Indeed, some photographs show men disporting with women who look young enough to be their mothers, or even their grandmothers. Numerous models are posed half-dressed or in underwear. Their frilled garters, stockings, high-button shoes, lace corsets, petticoats, bloomers and bonnets were as wildly arousing to late 19th and early 20th-century observers as they may appear quaint and silly to us. (Though it's hard to imagine that the photos of men and women attired in matching military hats, jackets, shoes – and nothing else – were not meant to elicit giggles, even then.)

Many "dirty jokes" were posed for the camera. One woman wears nothing but an open, fur-collared coat, to match her open, furry vagina. A smart-looking woman lounges about in déshabillé, reading a magazine entitled *Smart Sex*. A favorite prank depicts a woman about to cut into a plateful of a man's penis – a human sausage, of course – with a knife and fork. Three women pose together, spread-eagled; they're labeled "Faith, Hope and Charity". One woman breastfeeds a doll. There are some truly hilarious silly disguises: particularly the funny hats and false facial hair on the men, some of which was applied with grease paint in the manner of Groucho Marx.

Interestingly, the models in some of the later photos seem more ashamed of their actions than their earlier counterparts. At any rate, more of these later models appear to be trying to hide their identities, especially the men. Both sexes can be seen wearing dark glasses, big hats, blindfolds or masks, or turning their faces away from the camera. Many more men than women seem to be trying to retain their anonymity. Since most of these shots were taken for the enjoyment of male viewers, it was probably considered more important to be able to see the faces of the female models. Sometimes it is clear that the photographer deliberately excluded the models' heads from the shots. One can just hear what he might have said to them: "I promise; no one will know that it's you."

Why would the sense of embarrassment or shame at posing for pornography have increased in the years between the 1870s and the 1940s? Perhaps it was because photography itself was no longer novel and exciting. The thrill of being around this wonderful new invention was no longer a factor. Or perhaps the gulf between classes was no longer as large as in earlier days, or because the economic lot of the poor not quite so dire. Conditions were not as miserable, so if one were posing for pornographic photos, it meant one was not needy, but depraved, and therefore ought to feel ashamed.

The illustrated pornographic postcards in the book are altogether different from the photographs; they are lighter and more delicate. Like animated cartoons, they depict scenarios that would be impossible in reality. Many express a whimsical yet devilish sense of humor. One card shows two women playing a game, "Le vi-abolo" (a pun on the game "diabolo"), bouncing disembodied penises on strings and using them as dildos. On another, a woman uses the penises of two clowns – one black, one white – as a circus trapeze. The cards often provide a canvas for sly social commentary. On one, a woman straddles a huge penis which spouts semen, in the form of gold coins, into her purse. Other postcards sport droll little jokes. A card depicts a banquet with diners feasting on penises drizzled with seminal fluid. Their dish is dubbed "asperges sauce blanches" (asparagus in white sauce).

Over the past 150 years, most of the many thousands of vintage pornographic photos and postcards produced were suppressed, outlawed, seized and destroyed by the authorities – or by disapproving private citizens – until the entire output was nearly wiped out. A few rare examples have survived. Some of them can be found in the pages of *Forbidden Erotica*.

Laura Mirsky

For further information please contact:
www.vintagenudephotos.com

1) Michael Koetzle, 1000 Nudes, TASCHEN, Cologne 1994, p. 9.
2) Ibid., p. 228.
3) Paul Tabori, Secret and Forbidden: The Moral History of the Passions of Mankind, Signet Books, New York 1971, p. 105.
4) Koetzle, op. cit., p. 228.
5) The Compact Edition of the Oxford English Dictionary, Volume 2, Oxford University Press, United States 1971, p. 2242.
6) Koetzle, op. cit., p. 17.
7) Anonymous, My Secret Life, Grove Press, Inc., New York 1966, p. 454.
8) Anonymous, "My Secret Life", in: Steven Marcus, The Other Victorians: A Study of Sexuality and Pornography in Mid-Nineteenth-Century England, Basic Books, New York 1966, p. 133.
9) Ralph Ginzburg, An Unhurried View of Erotica, The Helmsman Press, New York 1958, p. 54.
10) Anonymous, The Pearl: A Journal of Facetiae and Voluptuous Reading, Grove Press, Inc., New York 1968, pp. 155–156.
11) Ibid., p. 154.

FORBIDDEN EROTICA: AN INTERVIEW

Mark Rotenberg talks to Laura Mirsky about
The Rotenberg Collection of erotica and pornography.

L.M. How did you start your collection of erotica and pornography?

M.R. About twenty years ago, in Brooklyn Heights, New York, I noticed a lot of activity outside a house two doors down from where I lived; and I saw a man's body being carted away. About two weeks later, some people hired by the city started throwing things away from the inside of his house into a huge dumpster. I started looking in the dumpster. The first day, the dumpster was knee-deep in girlie magazines. It piqued my interest. I kept looking in the dumpster for the next few days and started seeing newspapers from the Civil War, bits and pieces of erotica, lots of photos – old photos – some of the oldest photos in my collection.

L.M. How old is that?

M.R. I'd say the earliest photos that I pulled out of that original dumpster find were from the 1870s – old sepia-colored prints, albumen prints …

L.M. About how many photos were in that dumpster?

M.R. There were about fifteen hundred images, from as early as the 1870s going right through to the end of the 1950s, with some simple cheesecake photos. Many of the early photos that were discovered in that dumpster were very graphic, very hardcore images. That included sample sheets as well as full-size prints from the 1870s through the 1930s. After the 1930s the material seemed to be a bit more tame. There was obviously a period in the teens and the twenties when the French postcard – the simple nudes and hand-tinted images – were very widely produced and distributed; those were also represented in this original dumpster find.

L.M. How do you determine the age of the photographs?

M.R. Very often it's by the style depicted in the pictures – whether it's hairstyles or lingerie or backdrops. That's pretty much the only clue you have to identifying what period an image is from when there's very little in the way of clothing around. Sometimes you'd see rolled up stockings and high-button shoes or boots …

L.M. How about when the people in the photographs are completely nude? Then how do you determine the age of the photograph?
M.R. It's very, very tough. There's no real way to know. It's not likely any of the models are still around to take part in an interview, and photographers are certainly not known for most of the erotic photography that appears in this book.

L.M. Continue with your dumpster story.
M.R. After finding a lot of erotica and various other bits and pieces of art, I started doing a lot of research on it …

L.M. Where did you research nude photography?
M.R. I started spending some time with people in the publishing industry in New York – Milky Way Productions, also known as *Screw* magazine – Al Goldstein's little domain; and people at *Cheri* magazine …

L.M. You just called them up and asked them to help you identify the photographs?
M.R. I called them up and said that I had vintage material and asked if they would care to see any of it for possible use in any of their publications. I would go in and visit the editors or art directors at these publications, and they would ooh and ahh and exclaim that they had never seen

images that old of that type. They were only dealing with new material. They loved the idea of using the old images. I began to learn more and more about them as a result of speaking with these people. I learned, for example, that the material was really very rare. I learned that much of it was distributed in sort of underground ways, not sold in public venues, certainly not available in postcard shops, unless one knew the right word to say …

L.M. What was the "right" word to say?
M.R. Well, in America, I think "French postcards" became a pseudonym for erotica …

L.M. Who sold these things? How did one buy them?
M.R. I think that there were vendors of this material perhaps in drug stores, later on in gas stations. But originally, in Europe, I know that postcard dealers certainly did purvey erotica. They had sample sheets to show clients of the different images they had in print. Some of these sample sheets are included in the book. They would depict anywhere from four to as many as sixteen or thirty-two images on a small, basically hand-sized photo print, which was a sampler of the images that were available either in a series or individually. This is how much of the material was distributed in what was more a less a public venue.

L.M. Somebody would walk into a postcard shop and say the magic words and the dealer would pull out these sample sheets?

M.R. Yes, that's true. And then [clients] could look through the sample sheets to determine which set or sets they wanted to buy, or individual images if they were available that way, and come away with a nice little collection that tickled his or her fancy.

L.M. When did you decide to start collecting vintage erotica in earnest?

M.R. As soon as I brought the images to the various publication offices in New York and they indicated a willingness to reprint them and pay me, and return my originals to me, I decided that it was a good reason to collect more images. I would provide them with a wider base to choose from, so that they could custom-tailor specific layouts for a certain sexual theme or any other theme they could think of. I began attending shows where I knew this sort of material would be available, particularly photography fairs in New York City and paper collectible shows in Connecticut, New York, New Jersey [and] Pennsylvania. I began to ask friends if they knew of anyone who had related material, and then I began to run ads in print across America in various weekly or monthly publications.

L.M. When you were at any of these shows looking for this kind of material, did you ever come across people who were scandalized or found it objectionable that you were looking for it?

M.R. Well, yes. But not with anyone who ever had a severe problem with me individually, but rather with people who, upon my asking them if they had erotica, would say, "No, no, no, no, no. We never carry that. We wouldn't do that."

L.M. Did you find a lot of vintage erotica?

M.R. Yes. When I began collecting, the material seemed to be plentiful, and at any show I went to I was guaranteed to find a nice assortment of early material from the 1870s right up through the 1950s.

L.M. Did people have it right out on display?

M.R. Some did, but most of the material that I would be shown at one of these shows would only come out from boxes that were hidden under the table after I asked. Graphic images – what one would typically call hardcore or pornographic – were rarely on display and to this day are rarely on display at any one of these venues.

L.M. You said you started to run ads. What did you say in the ads?

M.R. "Wanted, erotica. Original images: 1860s to 1950s. Condition important."

L.M. Did any publications ever have a problem running your ads?

M.R. There were publications in the Midwest section of the U.S. that refused to run my ad. They claimed that they would not support the trade of any of this type of material.

L.M. Did you get any responses to your ads?

M.R. Yes, yes. I was receiving responses on a very regular basis from people all over the country, in all walks of life – whether they were young and were renovating a house and had found a shoebox full of erotica in a wall or in an old, sealed-up fireplace, or in an attic or a garage; or whether they were older folks who were selling off stuff in their house and who had stashed away a small packet of French postcards or Tijuana Bibles or some other erotica or decks of cards in a bedside table drawer. I heard from many, many different people, from doctors, to lawyers, to students – anyone.

L.M. Did you ever have to travel anywhere to see these things?

M.R. Yes, very often. I've spent many hours in the car driving to distant locations – maybe hundreds of miles away – after a large lot of quality material has been described to me over the phone or has been listed in a letter. Very often people are reluctant to send the material through the mail, fearing that it is illegal and that they could be arrested for the dissemination of erotica or pornography.

L.M. Is that true?

M.R. That is not true. I advertise openly for this material and, providing the material does not include images that are indeed patently illegal, such as images of underage persons or images of bestiality, virtually anything else is acceptable and is legal to send through the mail, especially if the sender and the recipient are over twenty-one years of age.

L.M. Can you recall any specific trips that you took?

M.R. Not too long ago, I made a trip out to central Pennsylvania, say, a three- or four-hour ride in each direction, to meet some people who had contacted me over the telephone about some early 20th-century images …

L.M. Where did you meet?

M.R. We agreed to meet at a specified time in a parking lot at McDonald's restaurant. Each one told the other what kind of car to expect to see and at the specified moment we met. I sat down in my own car with this person selling the images and we looked through the images …

L.M. Did they seem at all leery of you?

M.R. No, not really, not leery of me, but everyone was very guarded about their behavior and there was nothing untoward, nothing unseemly.

L.M. Have you ever felt that a moral judgment was being made about you for buying this material by the person selling it to you?

M.R. No. At the point when people will call me and offer the material or write and offer the material, we've both proceeded beyond the moral judgment. Anyone who would encounter this sort of material and had a moral problem with it, would certainly, in my opinion, not want to disseminate the material, or continue to allow it to even exist.

L.M. You think they'd just throw it away?

M.R. I believe that much of the material that is discovered by people who did not originally purchase it with the intent of looking at it and savoring it and preserving it – I believe that many of the people who eventually come upon it destroy it, simply by throwing it away. And there are a lot of people who will do that rather than sell it because they are embarrassed, or they are morally opposed to it, or both.

L.M. Any stories about finding some of the more "graphic" material?

M.R. Yes, yes. Several years ago I heard through a friend, a fellow-collector of magazines and the like, who had heard, in turn, from another friend that this other friend had gone to the house of an inventor …

L.M. There's a network of people who collect this sort of thing?

M.R. Yes, yes. Throughout the United States – I guess worldwide – there are numerous collectors, not only of original photographic images, but of novelty items, of folk art, primitive art, of all manner of erotica – from statues, to film, to calendars, to magazines, to books – anything with erotic themes, no matter whether it's an image or printed matter, text, illustrations. There's a very strong market for erotica. And whenever it becomes available, there [are] sure to be people actively trying to buy it and perhaps competing against one another to acquire it.

L.M. O.K., so more about this story …

M.R. Through a friend of a friend in New Jersey, in an urban area, there turned out to be a large collection of magazines and photographs that this person had been given by a neighbor: some of the most graphic material I have seen to date, spanning the period from the 1870s through the 1930s. Twenty-five hundred images in all, glued neatly into accountant's ledger books, from which everything had to be removed.

L.M. Do you know to whom these photos belonged originally?

M.R. After meeting with the individual who had been given all of these magazines and photos, I learned that the entire collection had come originally from his neighbor, who had a private workshop built into his house, a workshop into which his wife and children never went. Included in this workshop was a cabinet where he had all of his magazines and photos stored. During the last few months of his life, he knew that upon his death his family would go through the workshop and would discover the material that none of them ever knew about. Rather than have them be shocked to learn that he'd had this incredible collection of pornography, the man had decided that he would give it to his neighbor to keep or sell or destroy, however he saw fit. This neighbor is the man I met with, and he had thousands of magazines and thousands of photos. The photos are now in my archive.

L.M. Can you talk about some other places you've travelled to meet people?

M.R. Parking lots are always very good. They're neutral, and one doesn't feel trapped, especially if one remains in one's vehicle.

L.M. So, there's a sense of danger, always?

M.R. Well, it's erotica; it's not as if you're meeting to discuss the sale of a collectible doll. It's material that not everyone is thrilled to have or is thrilled to see or is thrilled to sell. There's a bit of a scandalous – and let's say somewhat illegal – feeling, even though the material isn't strictly speaking illegal, when it's in the possession of adults.

L.M. Have you ever had people who seemed fearful during the experience of selling you this material?

M.R. Yes, yes. On another occasion I had been contacted by a dentist in response to one of my ads.

He claimed to have an array of vintage hardcore photographs and hardcore playing cards and some French postcards he had found in an old lamp. We got together in a large suburban shopping mall in southern New Jersey, in an open venue called the Food Court, in an open seating area, right in the center. We went to a table and sat down. I was handed a knapsack, and I proceeded to witness extreme paranoia set in on the part of the seller. He was afraid that upon my opening a small plastic bag inside his knapsack, that some of the mall security patrol would come by, see the images I was looking at and promptly arrest me and him for possession of erotica. He was very, very paranoid – so paranoid that he did not want to sit at the same table with me. He joined his wife, whom he had left safely at another table; and from there he watched me as I looked through the material, to make certain that I would not run off with it or do anything else.

L.M. Have you always been interested in erotica?

M.R. Yes, since I was very little. Kissing girls when I was four, and looking at erotic early pin-up type magazines …

L.M. Were they in your house?

M.R. No, they weren't in my house, but my father had a luncheonette/candy store/stationery store with a full magazine rack. I would look through the magazines there, which included some early men's magazines from the 1950s into the 1960s. They featured the nude models in them. But there was nothing pornographic there, nothing even remotely nasty. They were basically just topless shots – very pretty.

L.M. When did you see your first – what you would call – pornography?

M.R. I think I must have been around nine years old. I remember finding a piece of 8 mm film – maybe twenty feet of film – on a reel. I found this in a parking lot outside my father's store. It seemed odd to me that somebody would leave what I assumed was a home movie – because I had only ever seen 8 mm home movies that were shot of my family and our trips and things like that. When I saw this small reel with a bit of film on it, I just assumed that it was somebody's home movie. So I took it home and put it on our 8 mm projector; and I noticed two people in very, very intimate contact, moving quite ferociously.

L.M. How did you feel when you saw this?

M.R. I felt as if I was seeing something that people do but I'd never witnessed before. It occurred to me at that time that this is something that everyone does, probably. The people looked happy when

17

they were doing it, and nobody seemed to be forcing them into this strange position. It seemed as if it was quite exciting! I was seeing something that I don't think I'd ever seen or heard about before! And I wanted to know more about it. I wanted to know what it was about, what it felt like, what it did, what the purpose was. They looked rather happy and tired, at the end of all the movement. And then I remember looking in a drawer underneath my father's butcher block table where he kept all kinds of things – more or less private territory. There were some magazines and photos. These showed full frontal nudity, where women's legs were wide open and their charms exposed.

L.M. How did you feel when you saw those for the first time?

M.R. Oh, I thought they were great; I thought they were great! Some of the photos were, in fact, hardcore; they were amateur photos. Maybe I should credit my father with starting my collection of erotica, for having had the magazines in his store. Then again, I was a randy little bastard when I was four. It had nothing to do with magazines or film or any of it.

L.M. Do you find vintage pornography more exciting than new pornography?

M.R. Yeah. It's not as uniform as new pornography. Not everyone looked the same, as they do now. They're not all polished as they are now. They were never pumped up with silicone. There were no implants in any parts of the body. The focus now is to make every aspect of a woman's body the most engorged and the most stretched and the most stupendous and the blondest and the most shaved. Today's erotica is boring in comparison with vintage erotica, where women could wear bloomers, rolled-up stockings and high button boots and shawls and hats and jewelry. Photos could be taken in a classical setting, with pretty backdrops or wonderful old pieces of furniture with terrific rugs and animal skins scattered about. There is just a huge difference.

L.M. How about the models in these old photographs? Do you find them attractive?

M.R. Some models were attractive, and some models were not attractive, much the same as in real life. You walk down the street and not everyone is going to look like Pamela Anderson Lee. And thank God! But when you see new erotica, especially in magazines, every single model is the same as the one on the page before.

L.M. How do you think most people will respond to seeing the collection in this book?

M.R. I hope their jaws drop! I think that even in the circle of publishers that I deal with, when I bring them the vintage material there is immediately a crowd around me. People stand there in disbelief. They think that erotica was created very recently, for them, by them, in certain cases. They have very little in the way of reference for early erotica.

L.M. How do you think the average citizen will respond to seeing this collection of photographs?

M.R. When they see images that are seventy, eighty, ninety, a hundred or more years older than they are, they're amazed! They're amazed! Over the years, I've collected over a hundred thousand photos. There was a private, secret underground wave that began from the time the first photograph was taken. It was a complete documentation of sexual behavior from the first snap of the shutter: stereo daguerreotypes, salt prints, calotypes, tintypes, magic lantern slides, stereopticon views, whether they're glass images or on photo paper, or cards, or transparencies, or film. Every format of photography has its fair share of erotica and pornography.

L.M. How do you differentiate between erotica and pornography?

M.R. I think that pornography is an appropriate title for material that gets one's juices flowing.

If it gets your temperature cooking a little bit and your blood pressure goes up a point or two – changes the flow of some juices in your body – then you can call it pornography.

L.M. Do you think that this book is mostly pornography?

M.R. Yes. I defy anyone to look at this book and not have some sort of traceable reaction.

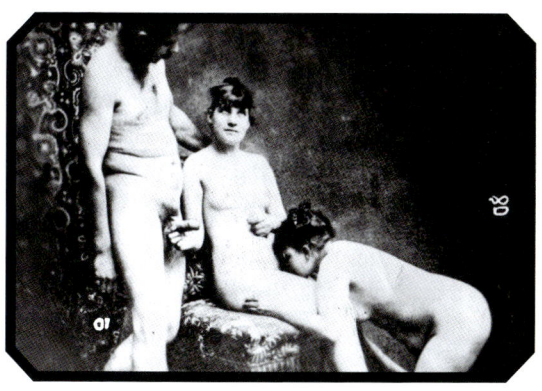

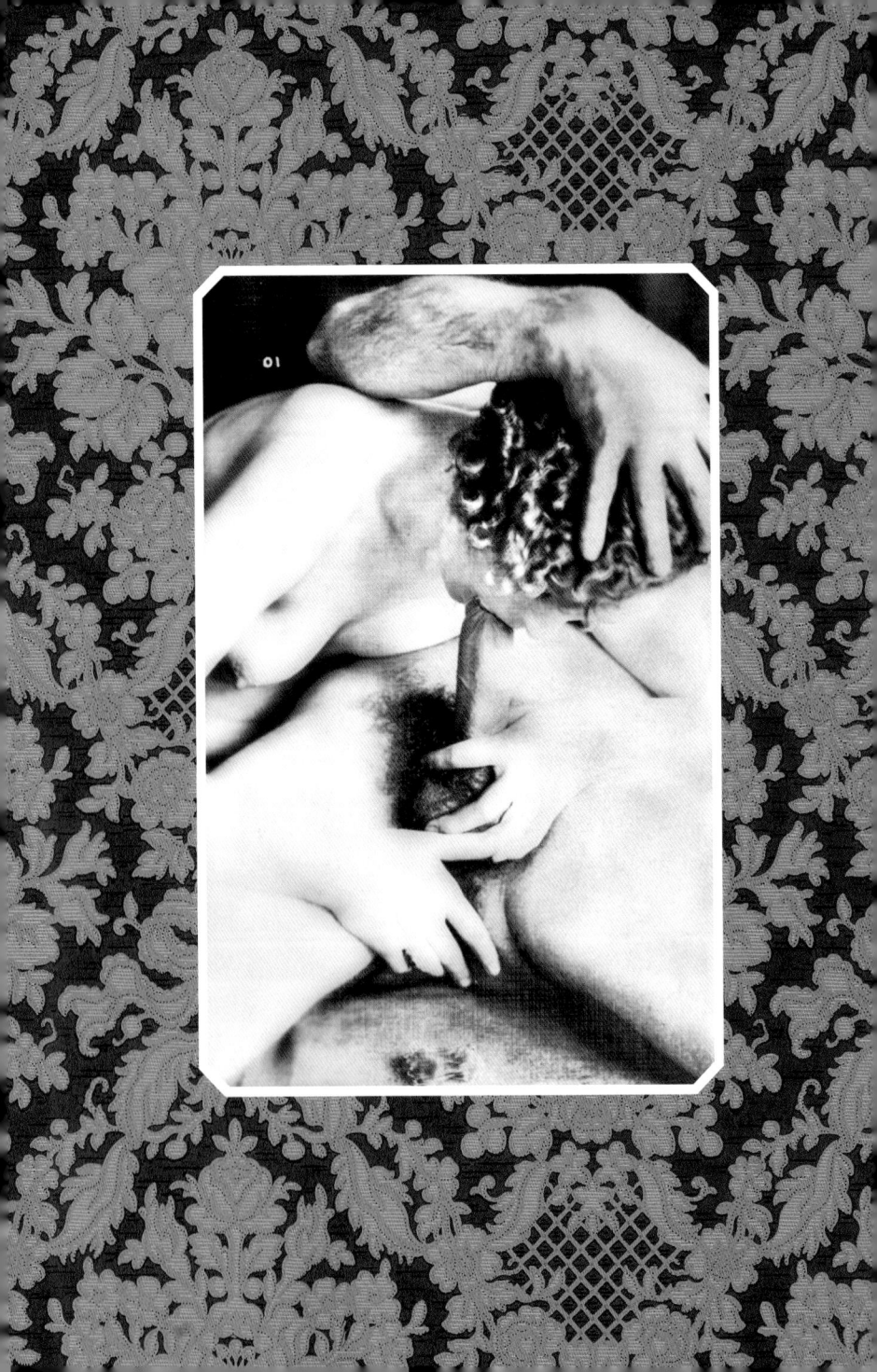

THE ROTENBERG
COLLECTION

FORBIDDEN EROTICA
THE
COLLECTION

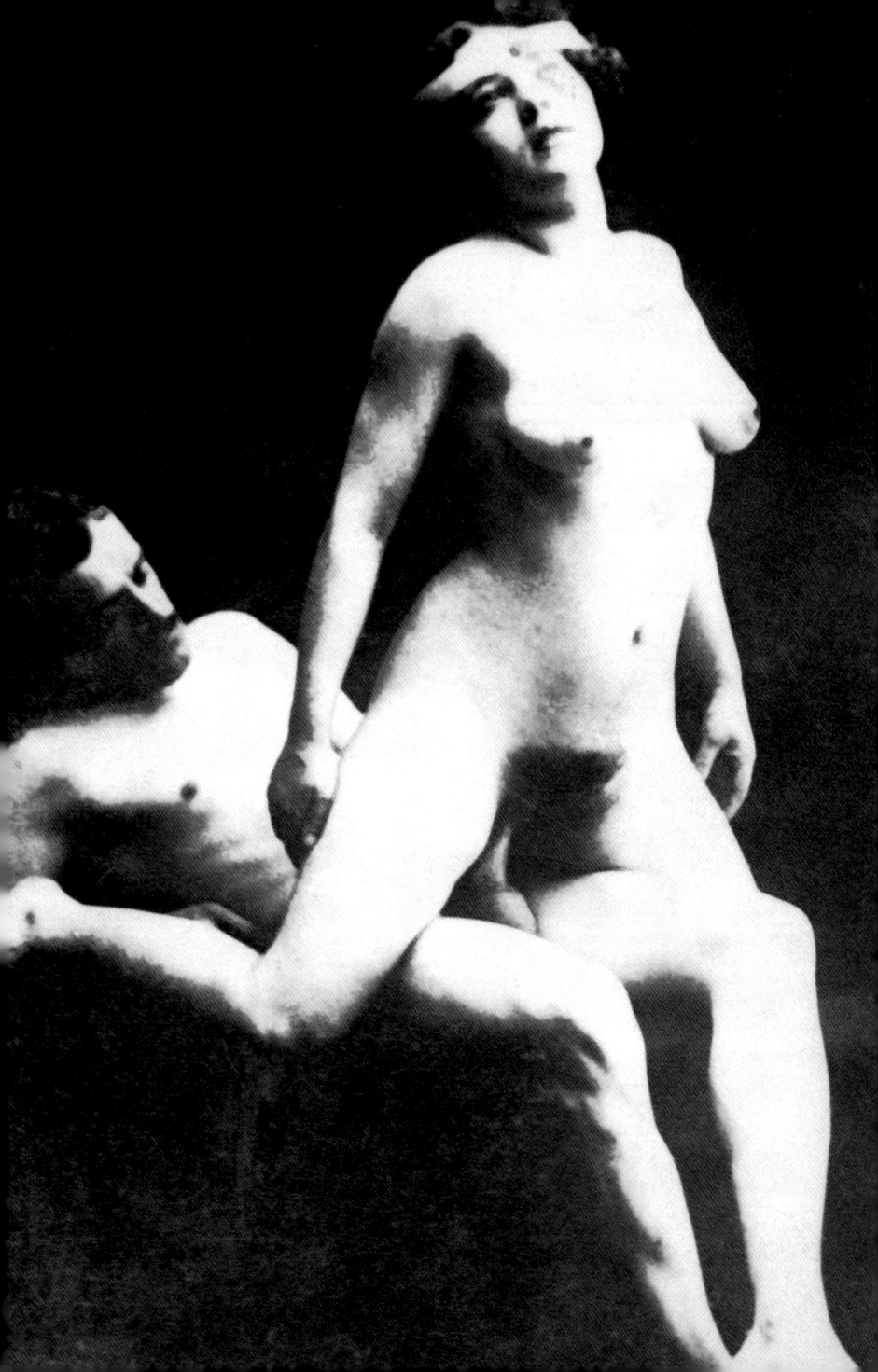

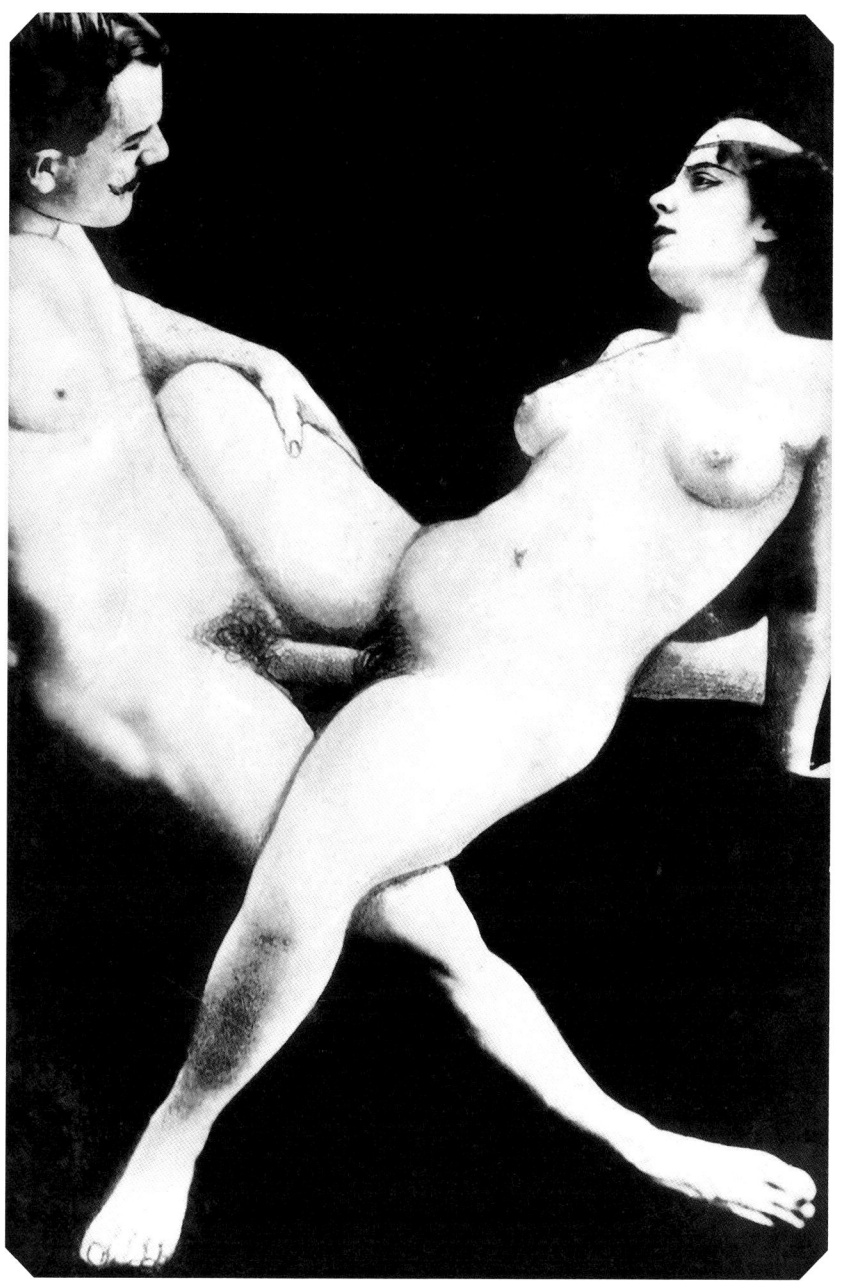

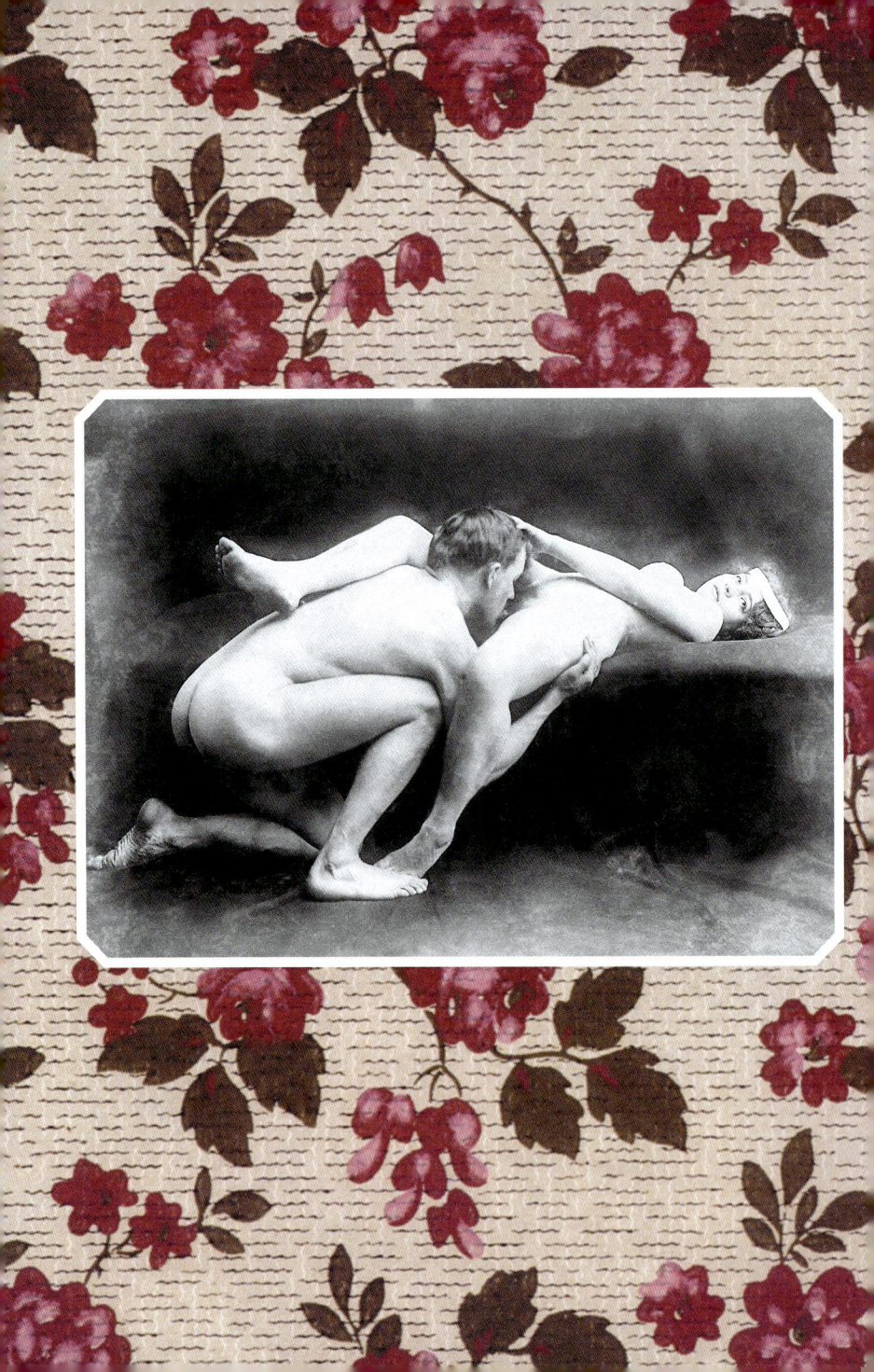

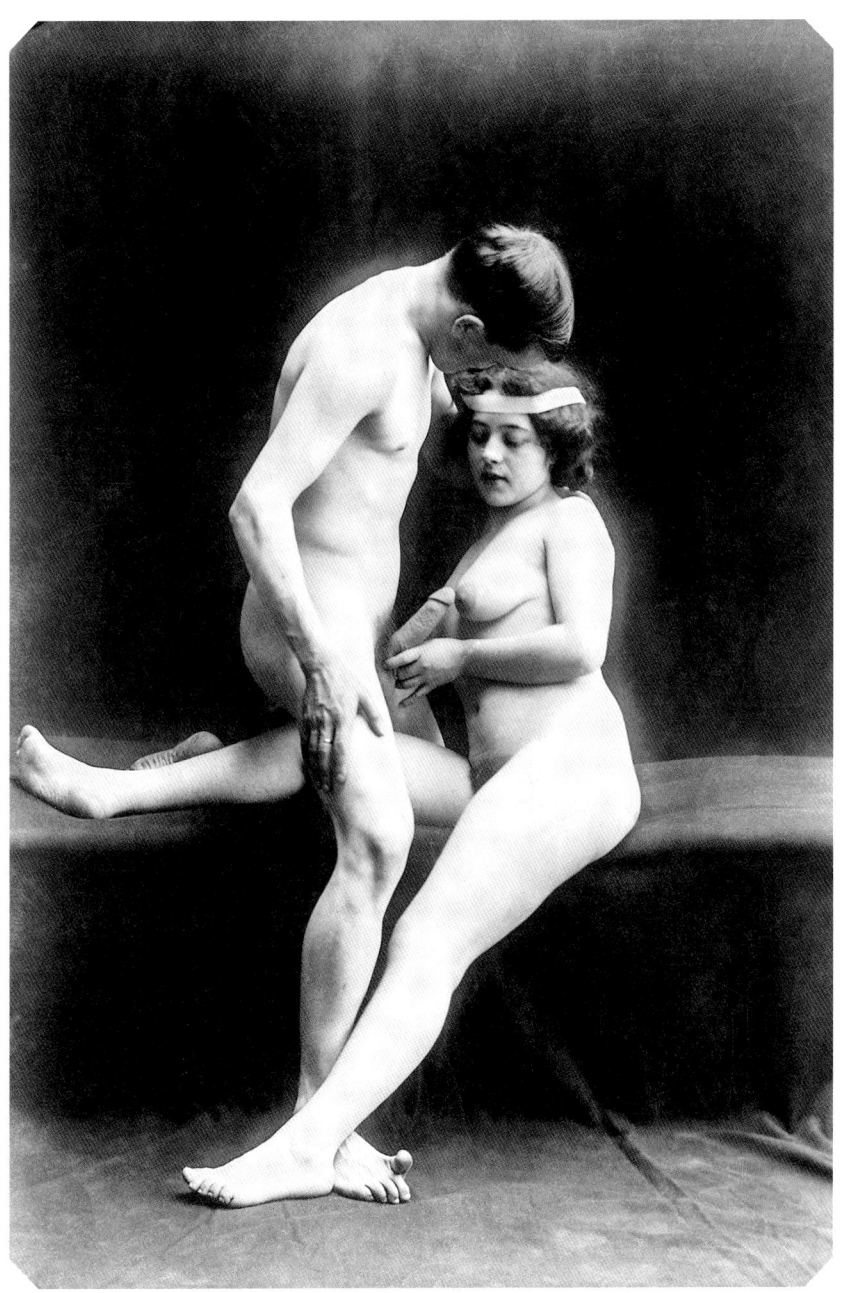

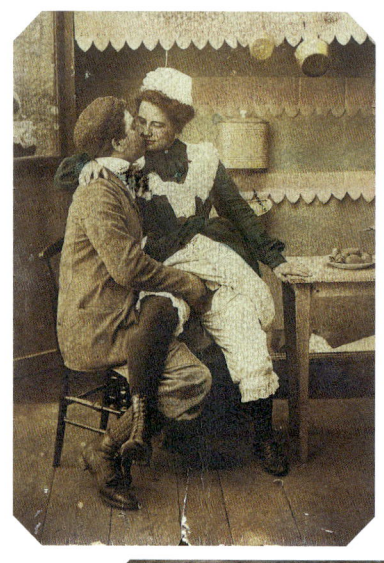

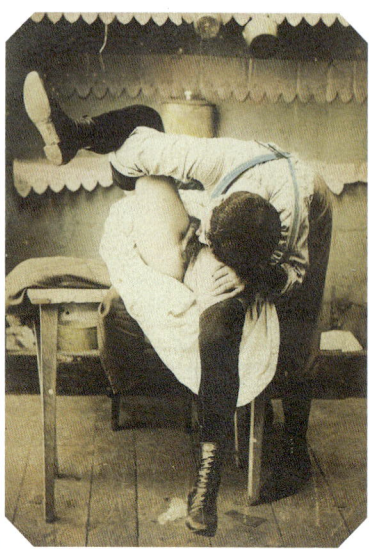

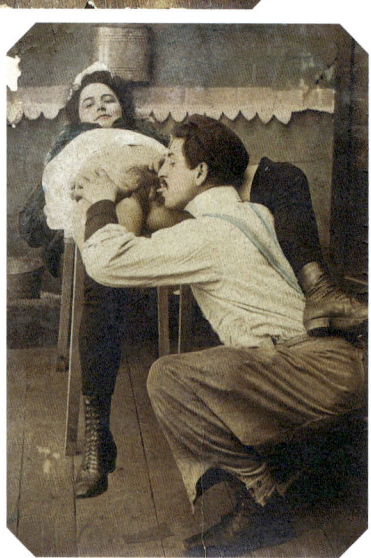

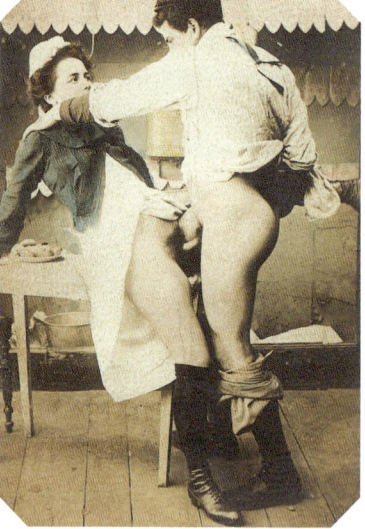

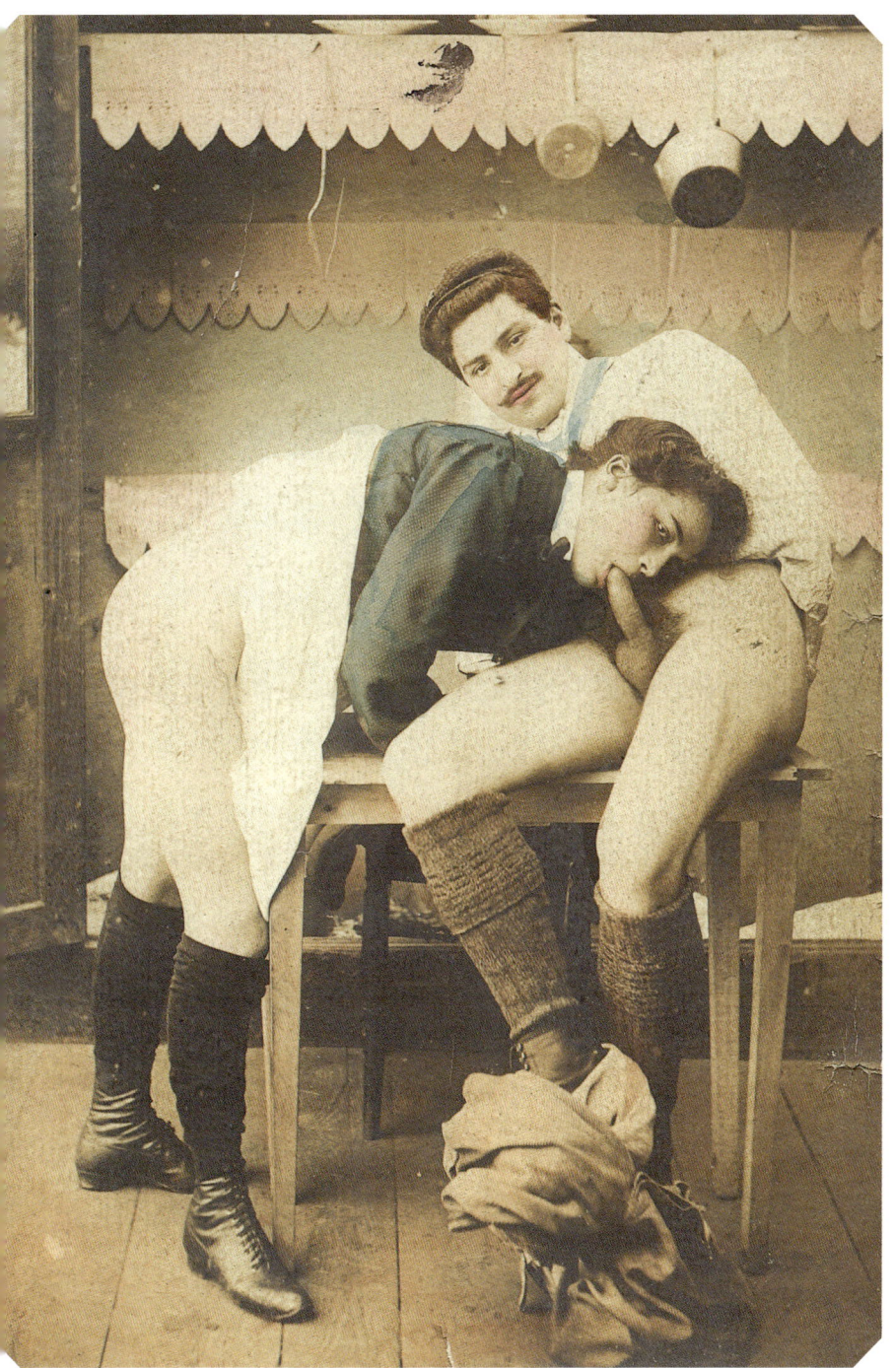

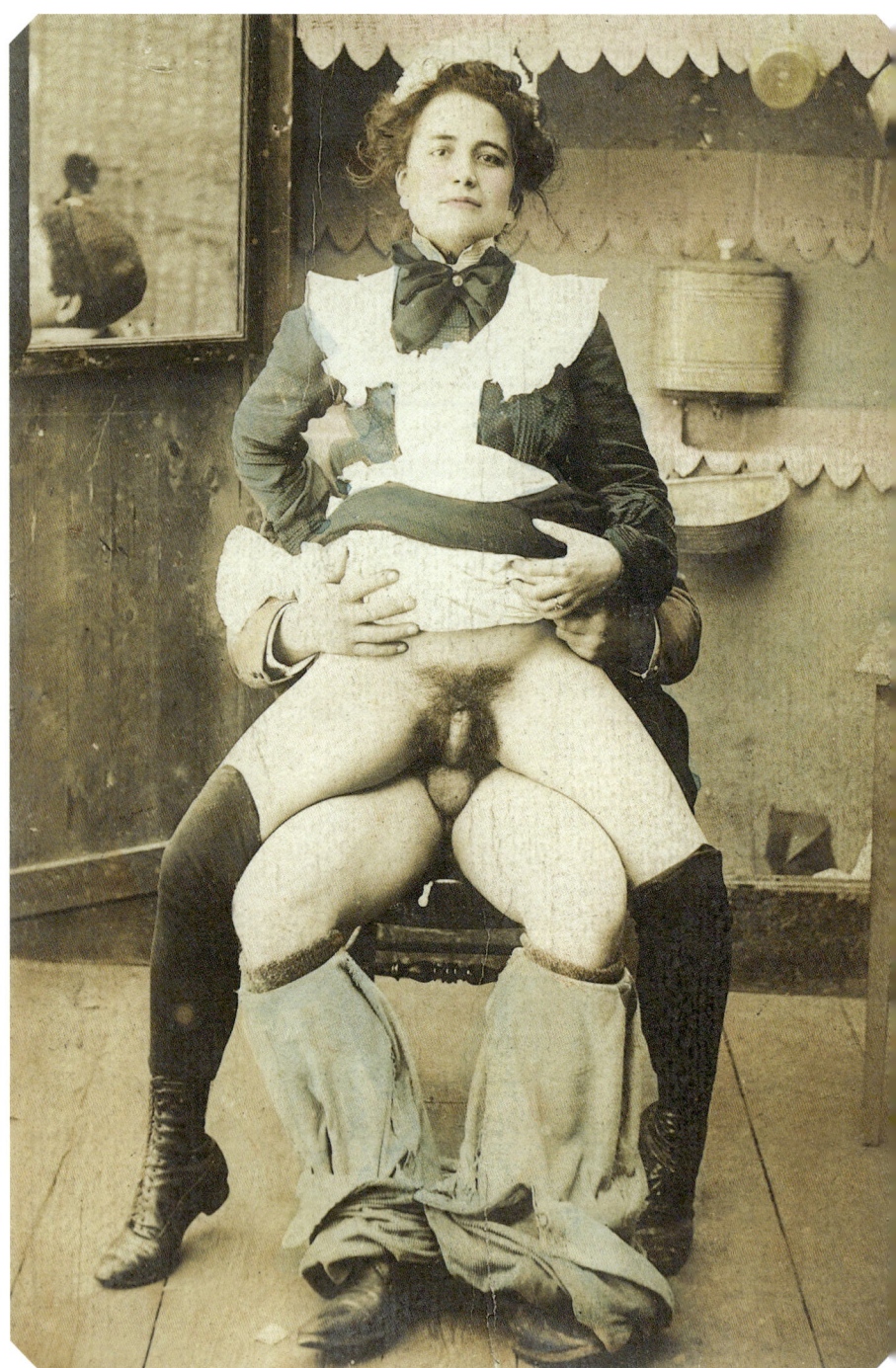

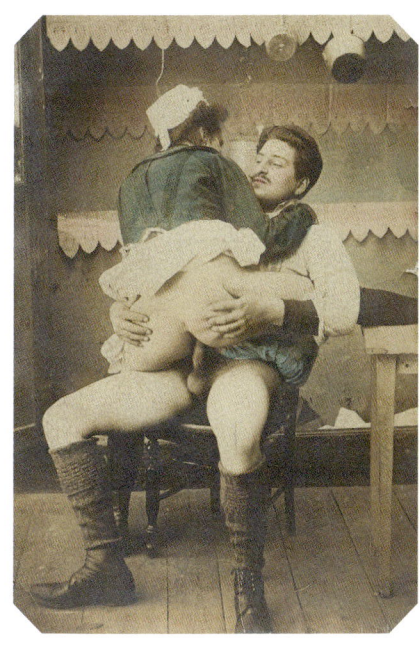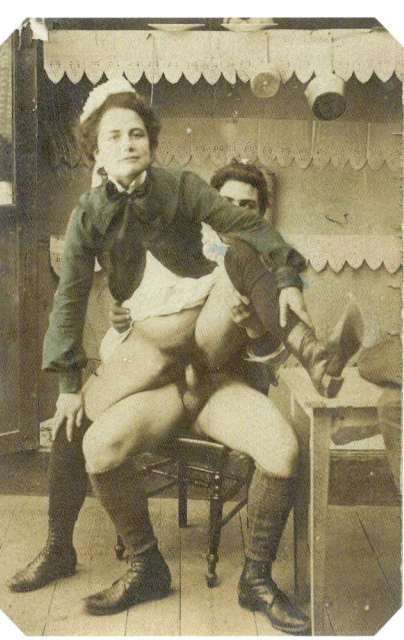

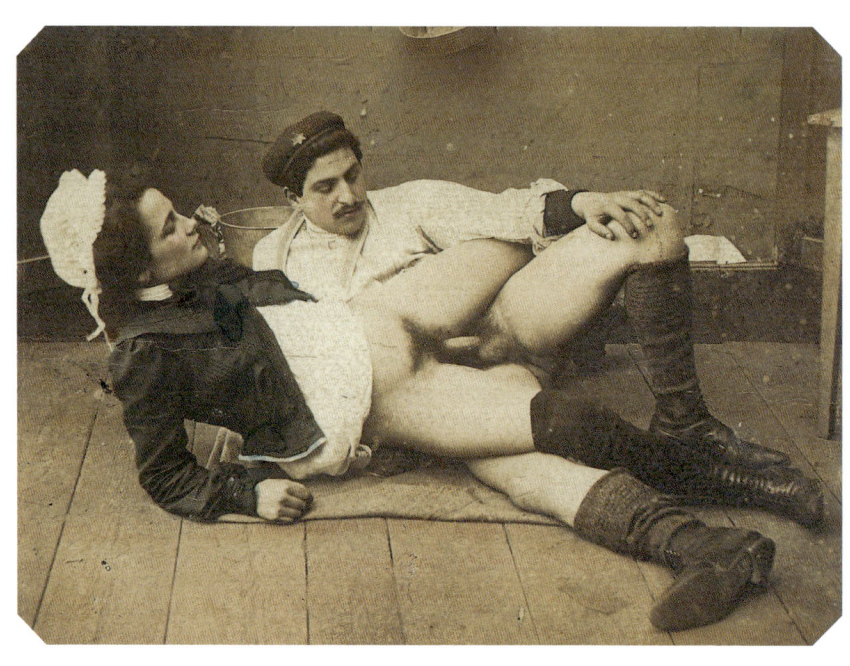

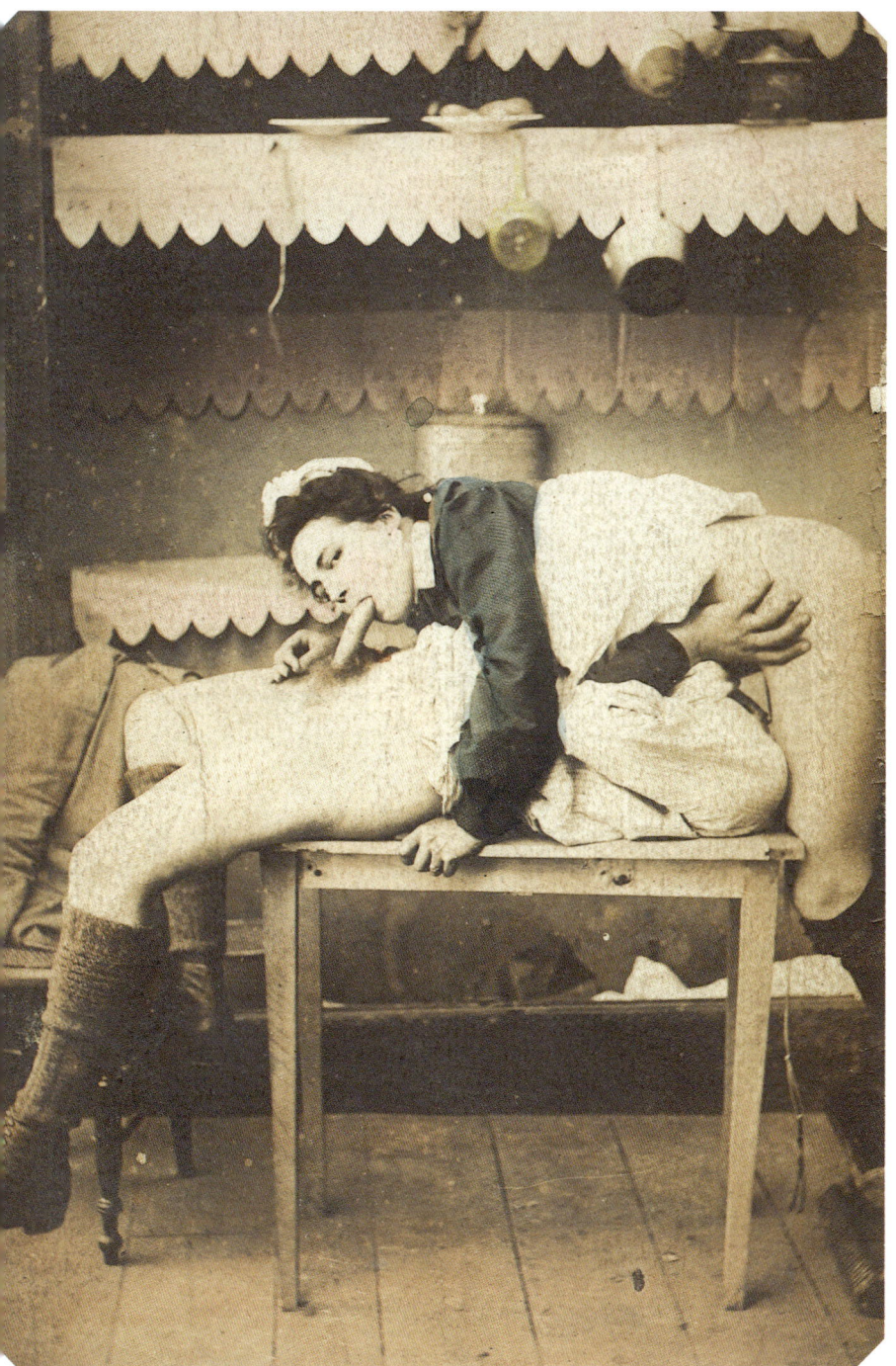

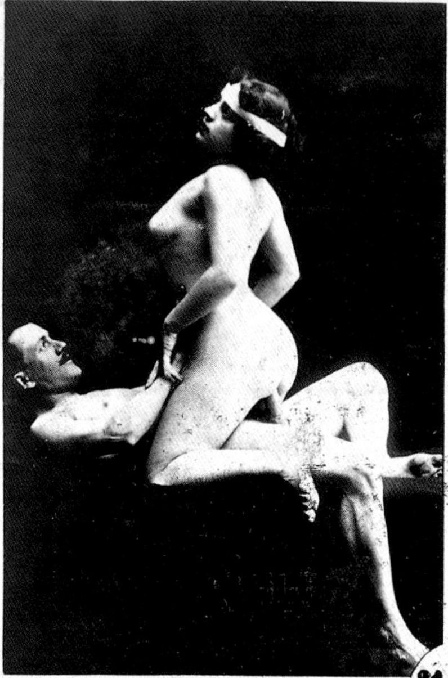

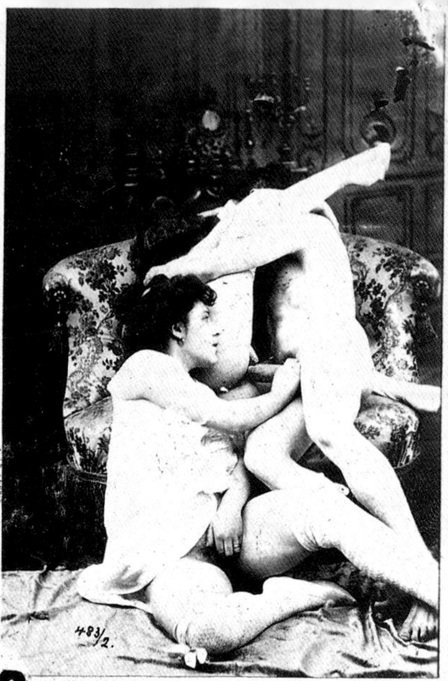

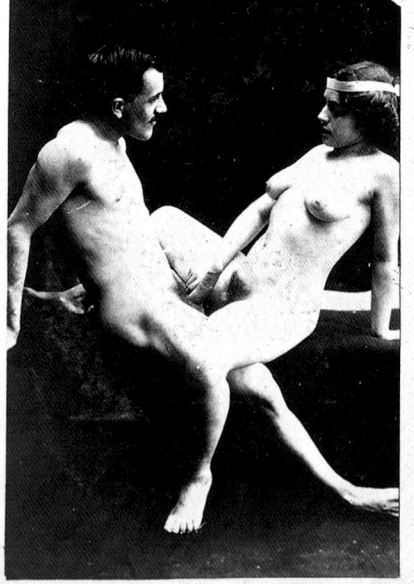
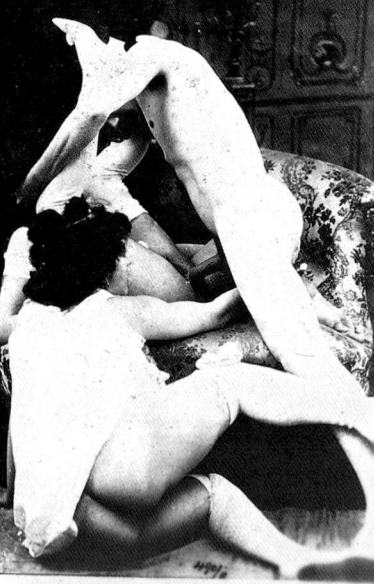

430

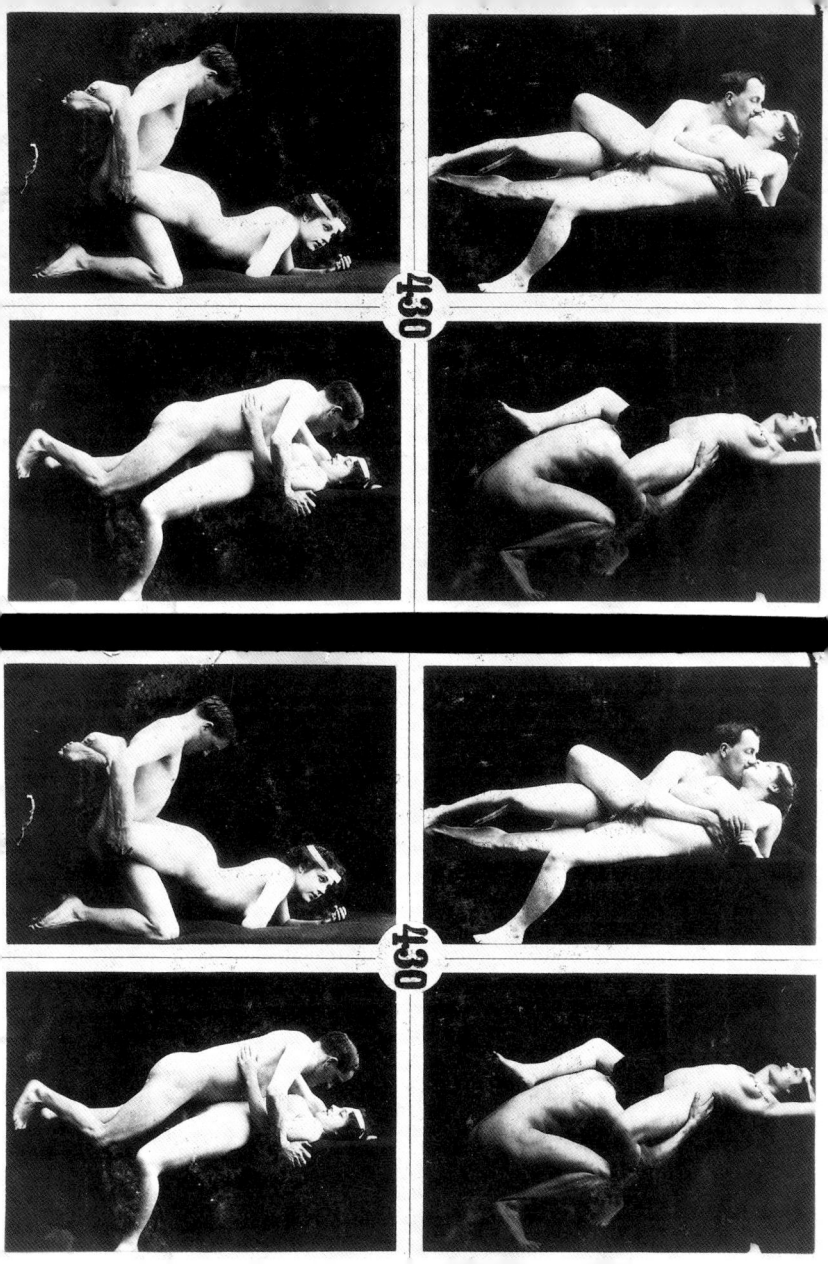

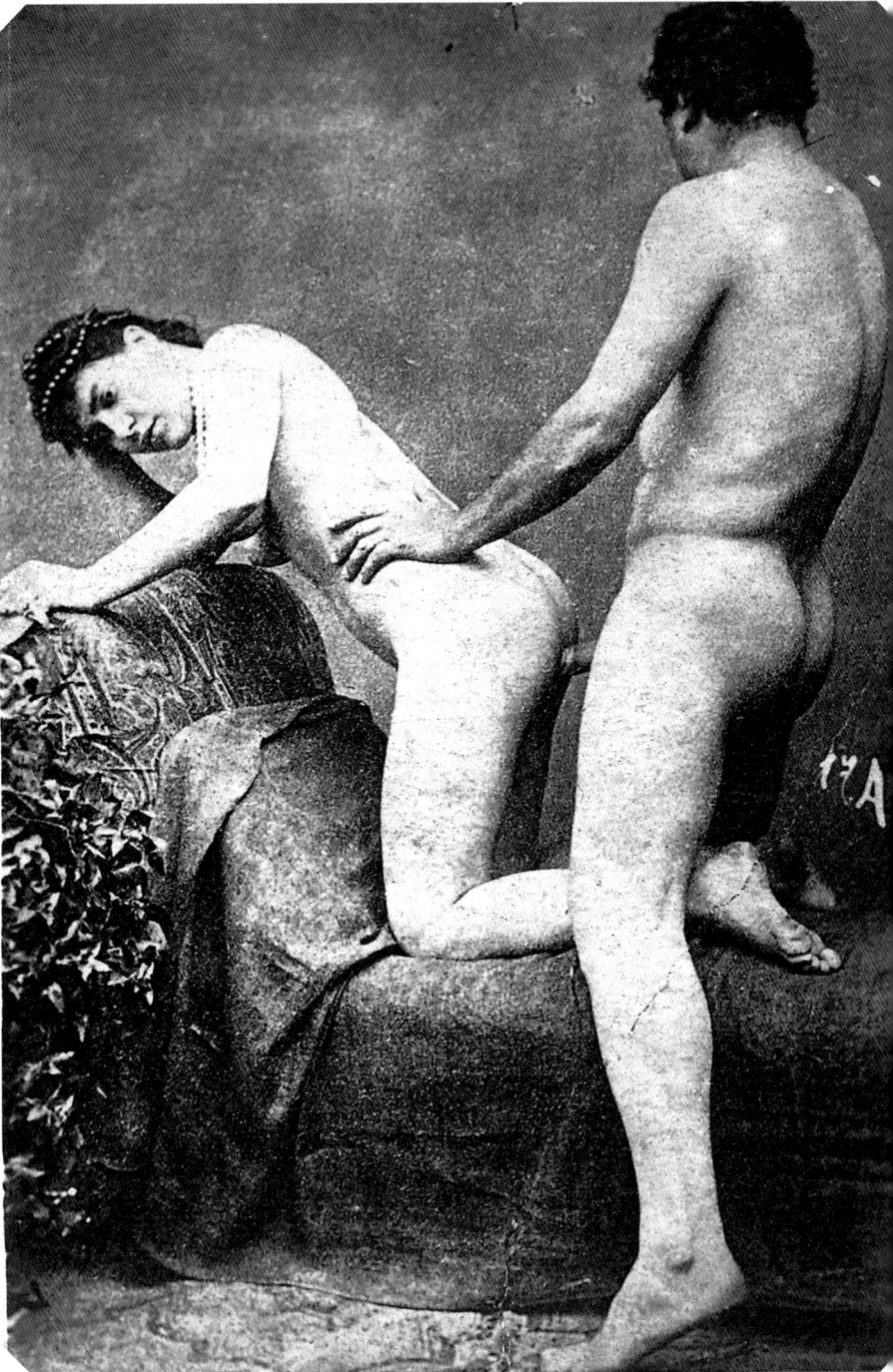

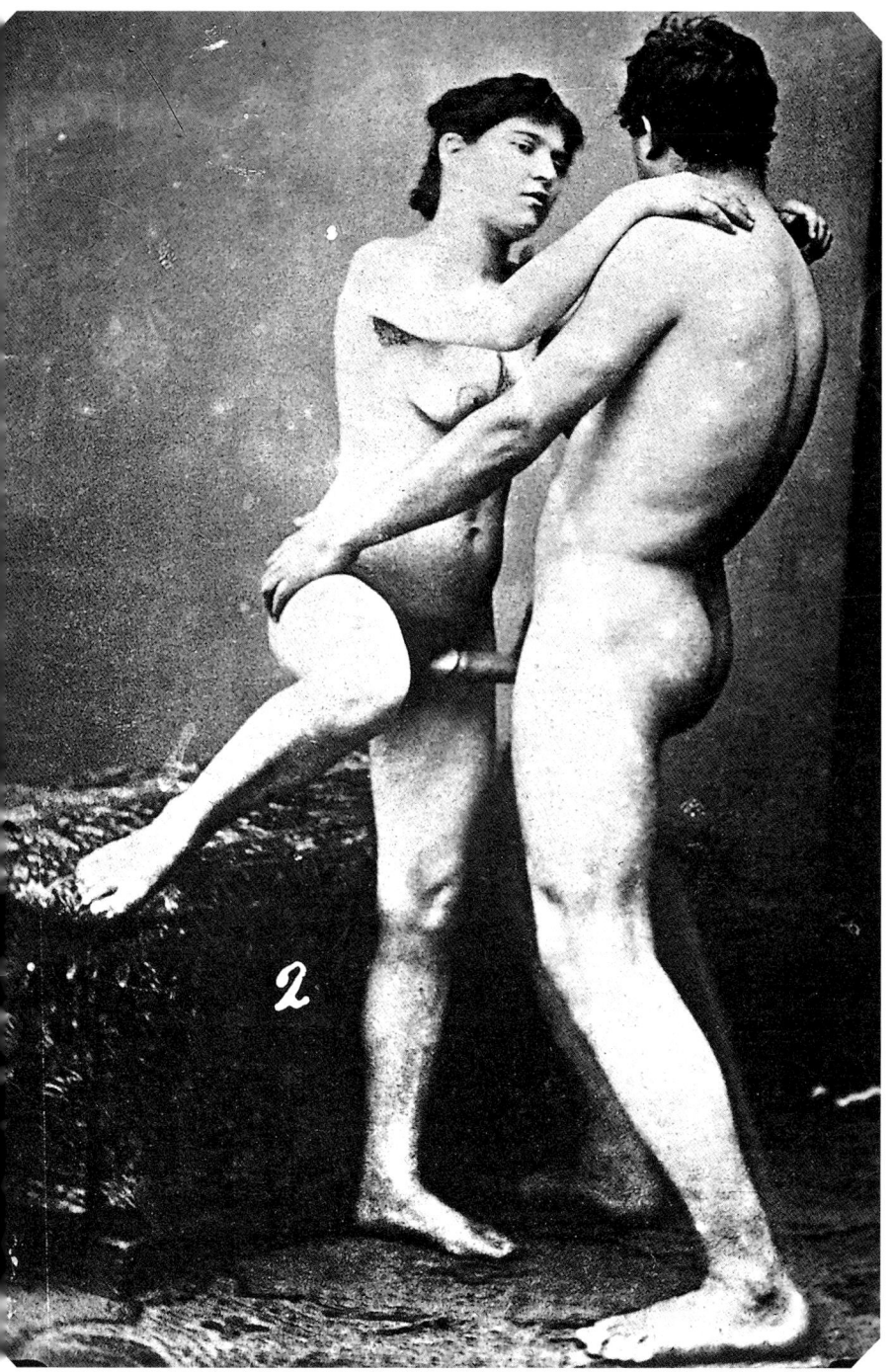

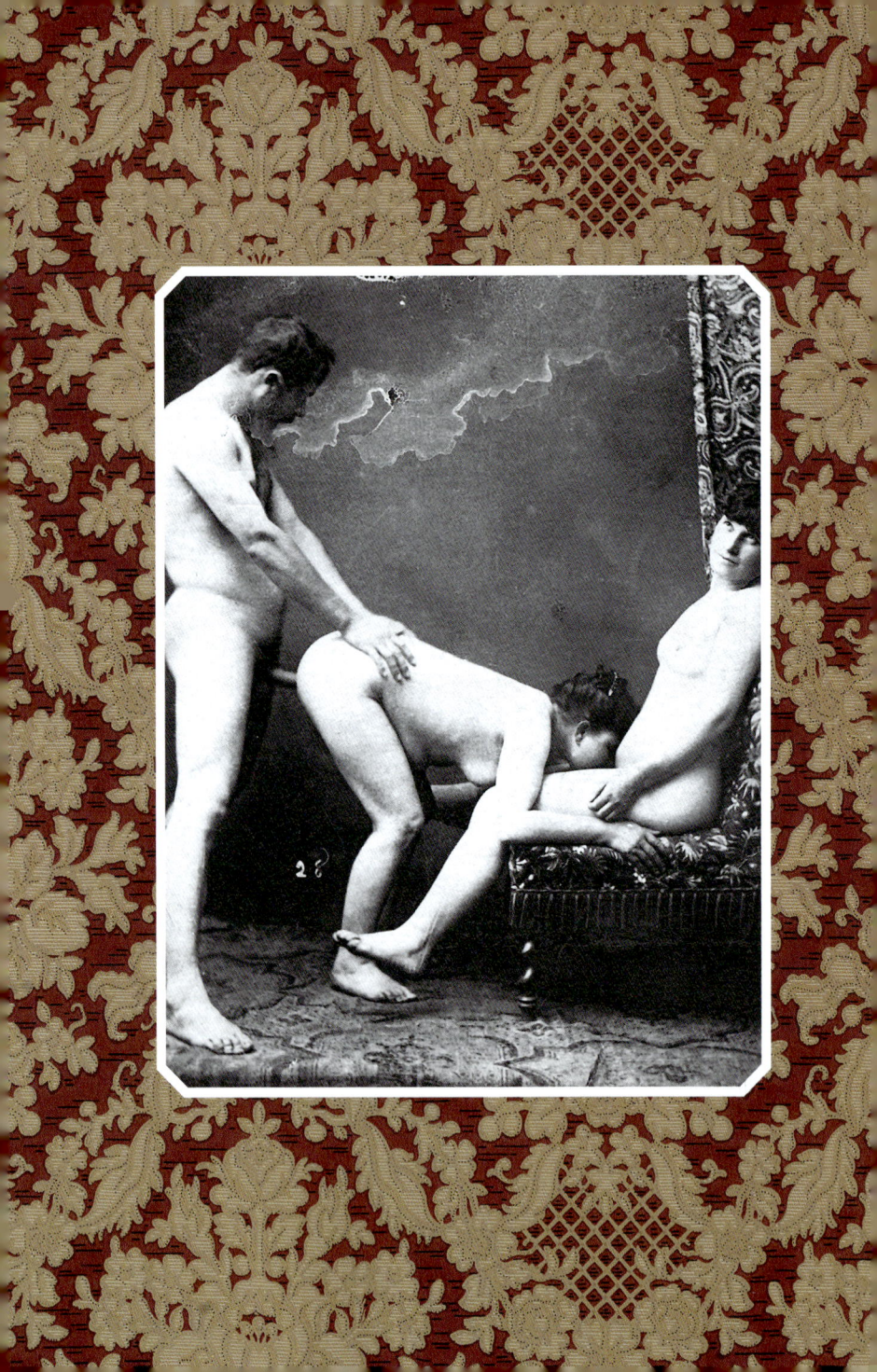

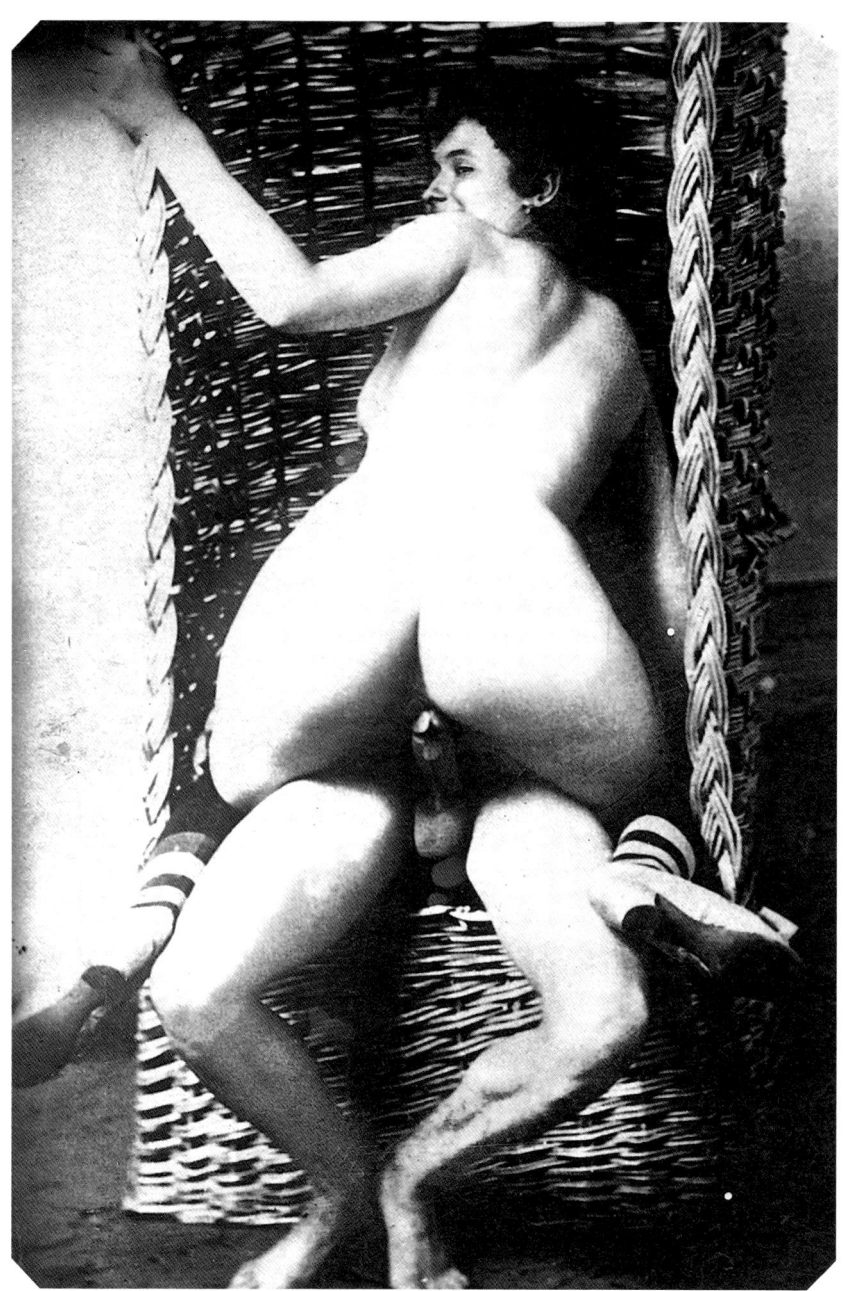

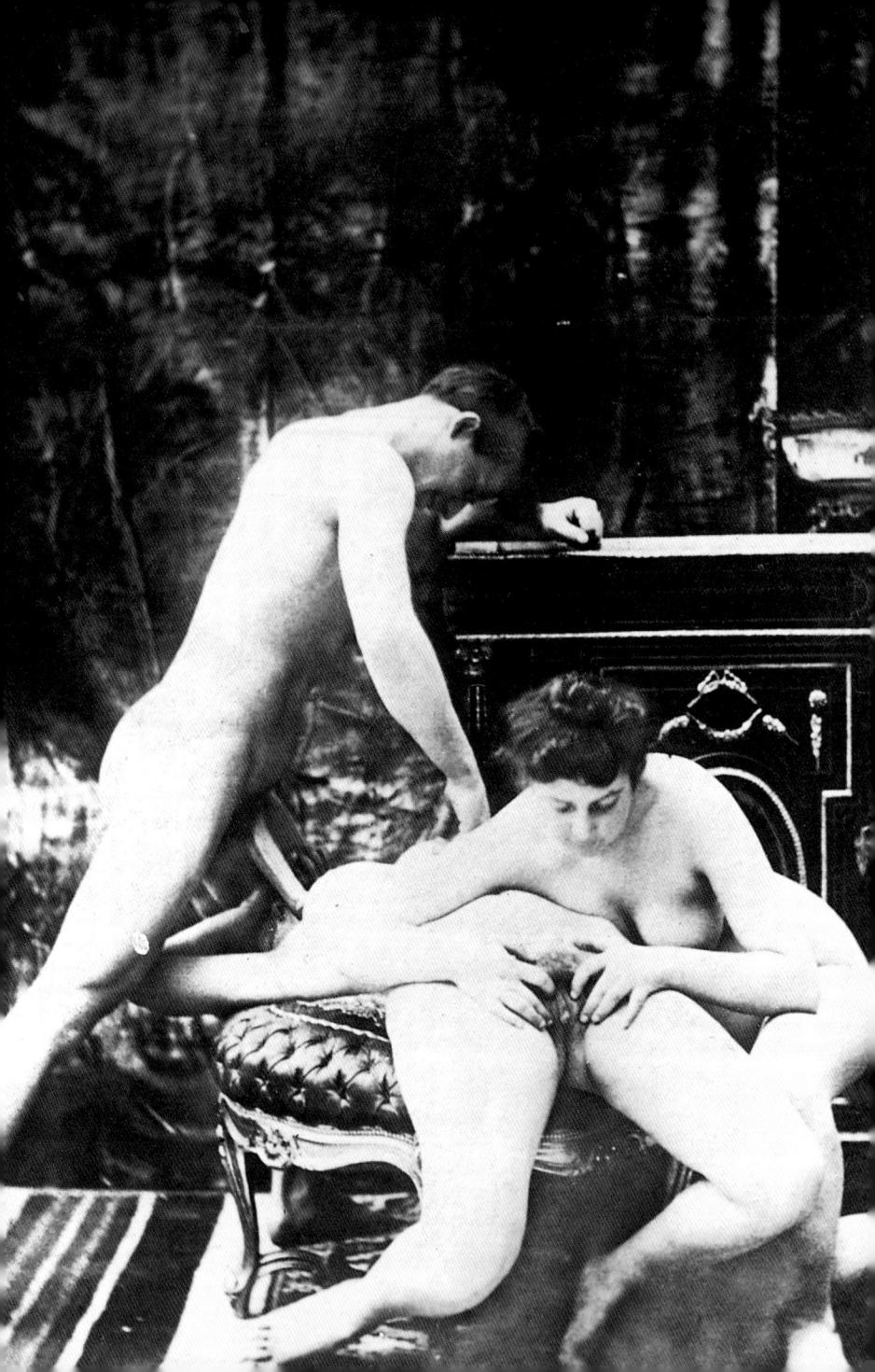

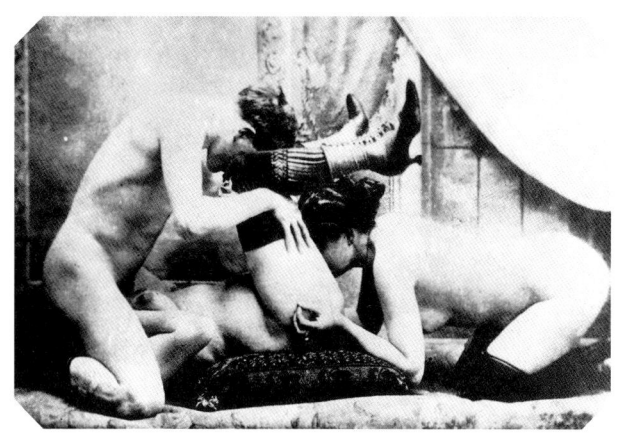

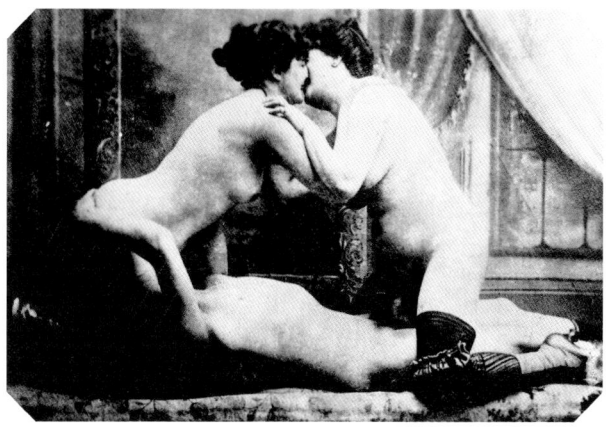

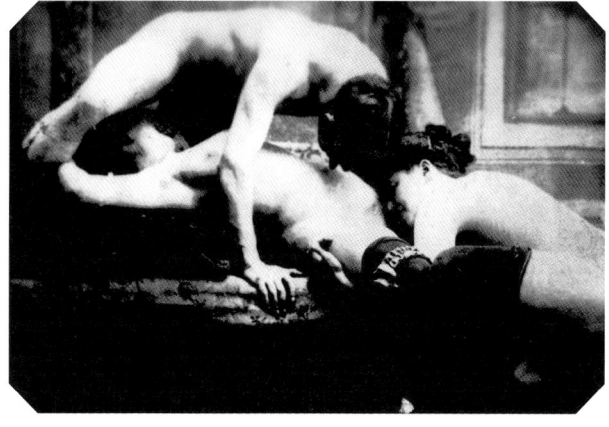

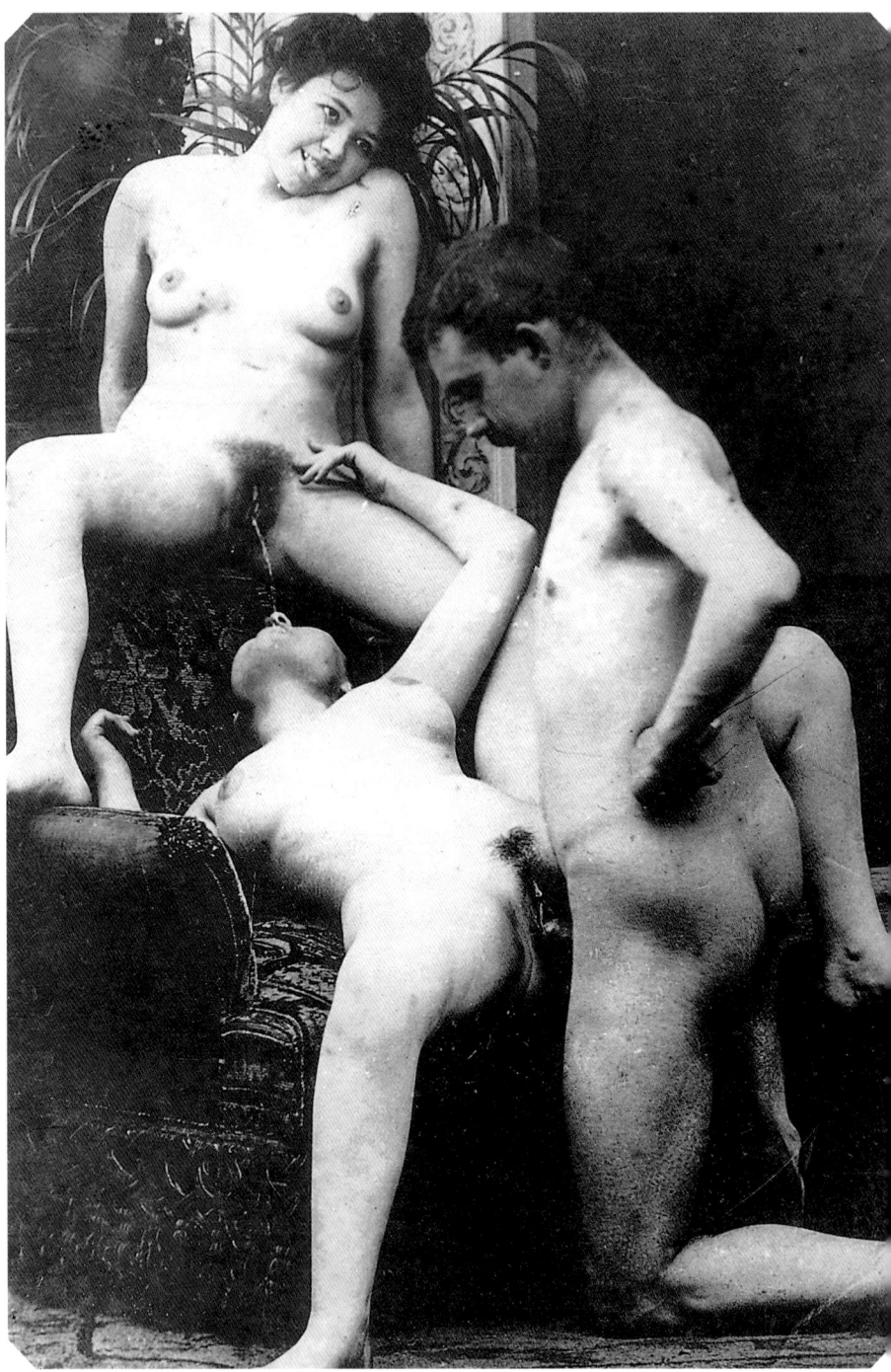

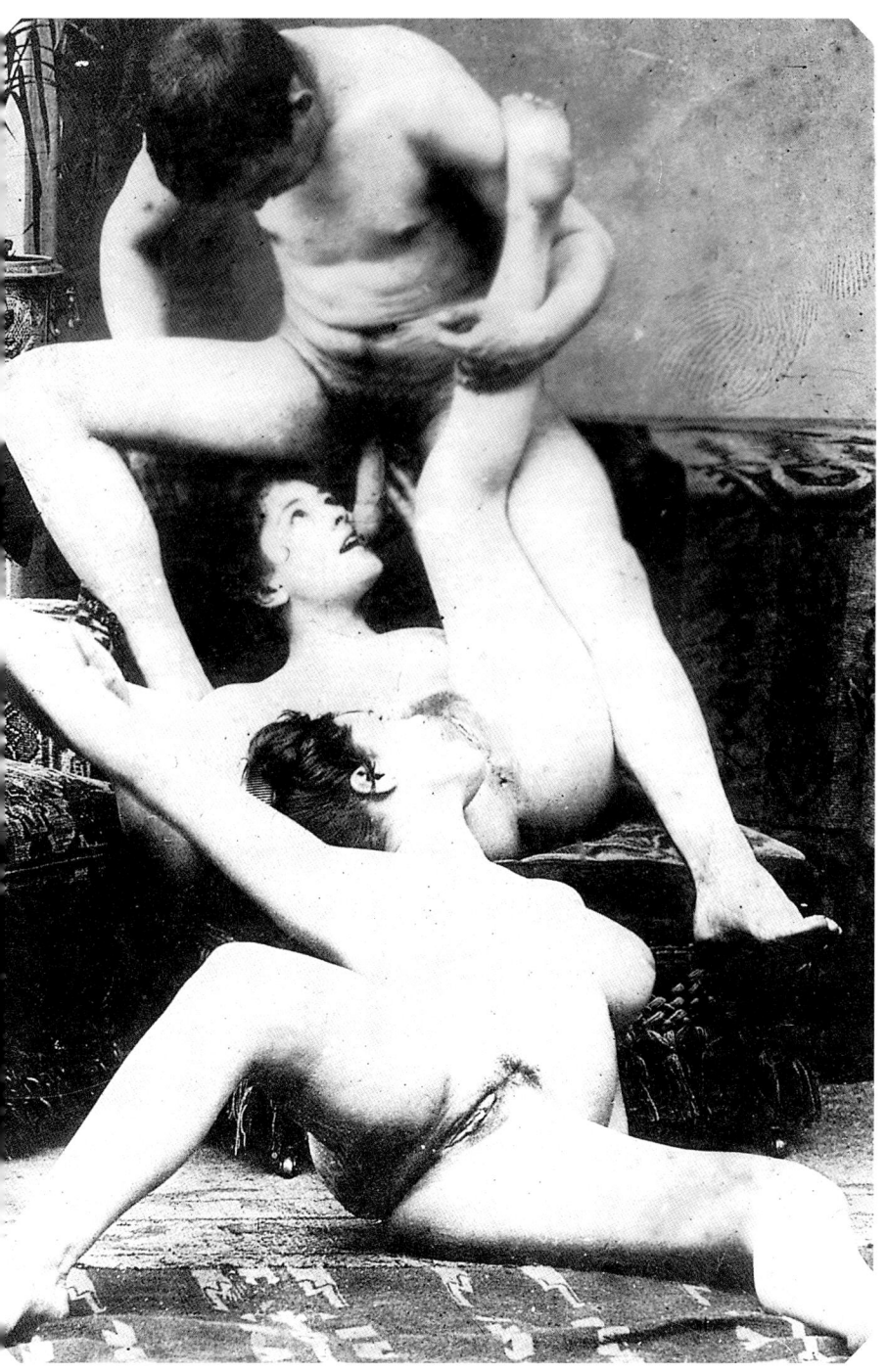

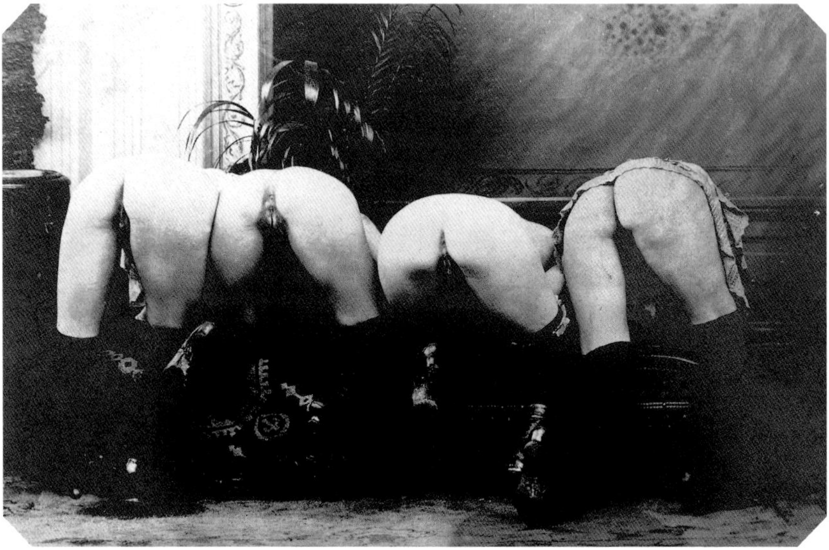

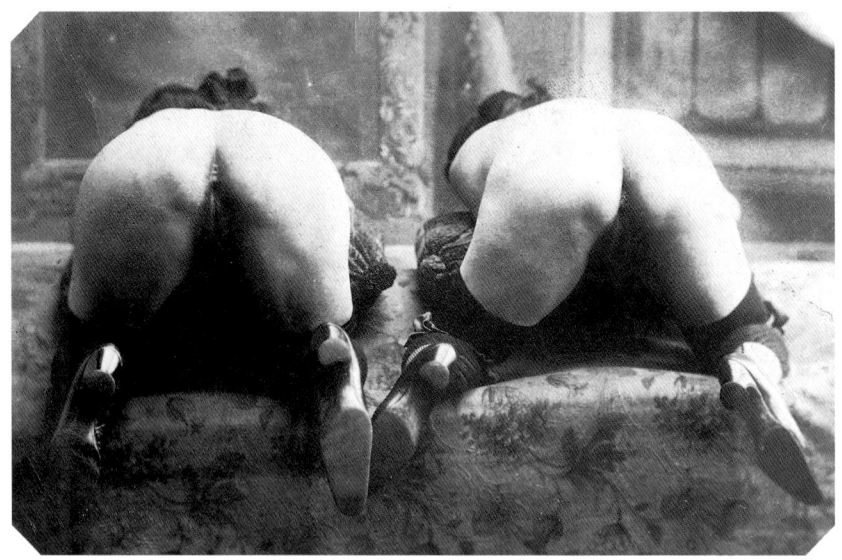

42

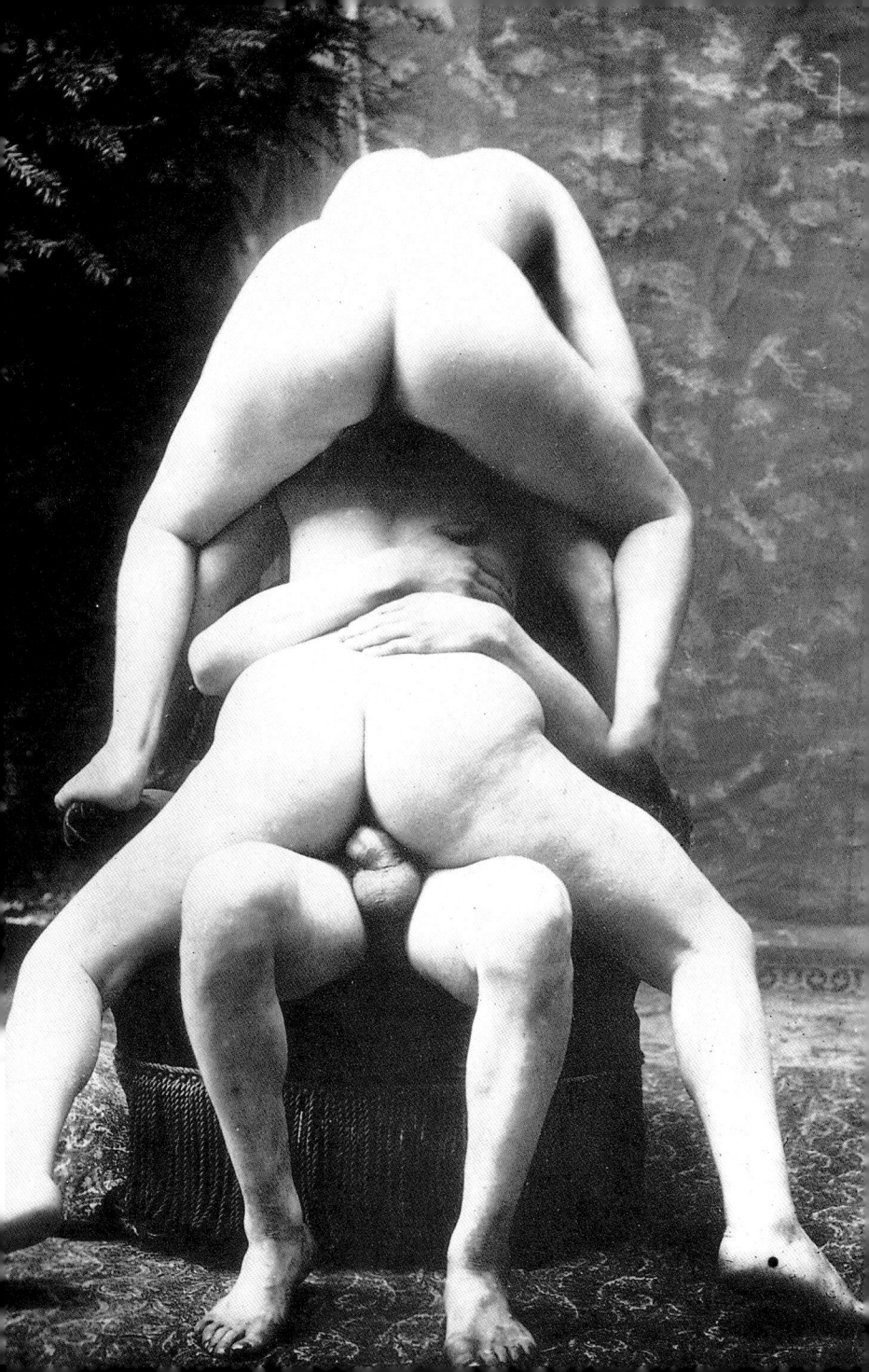

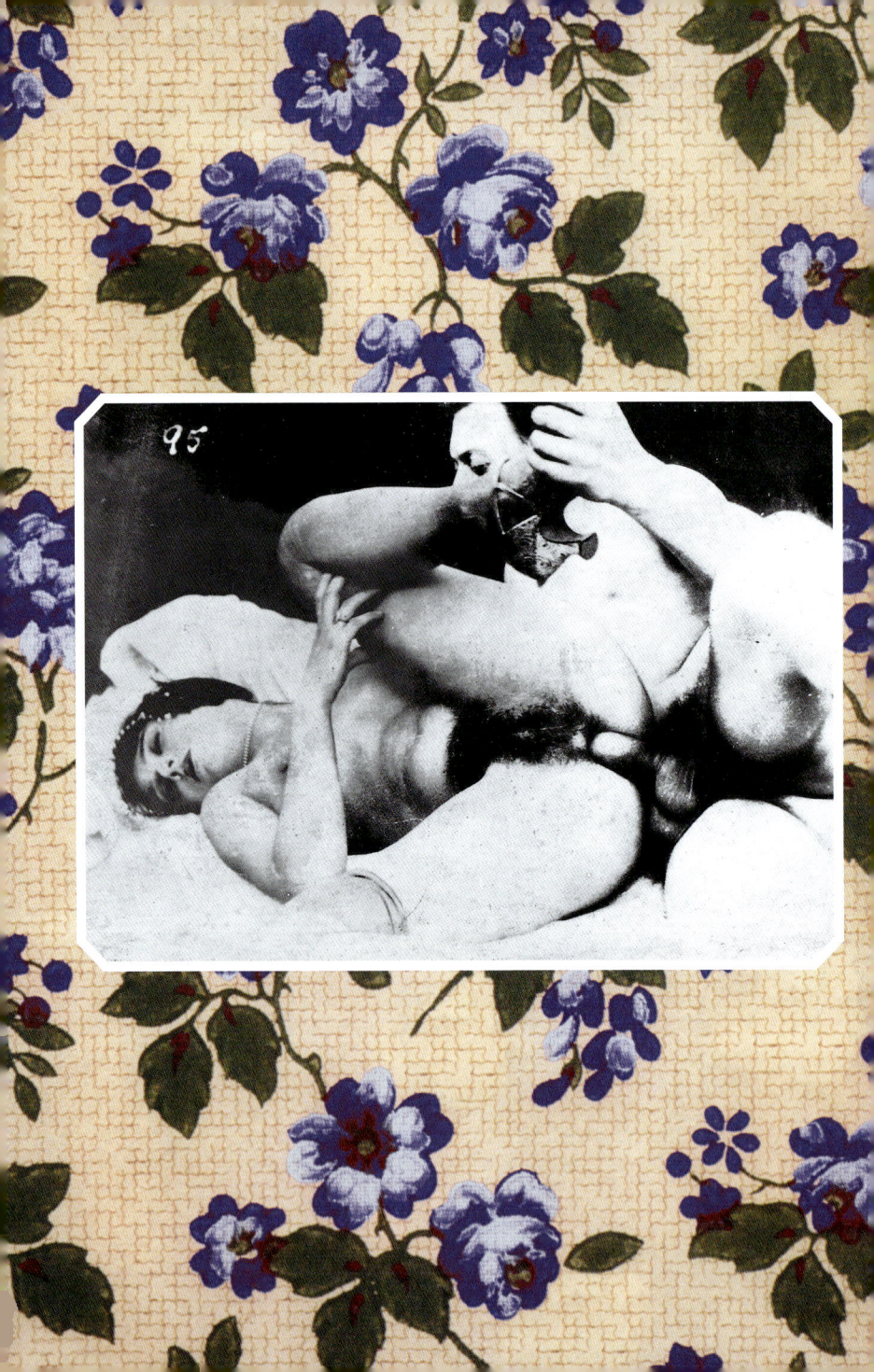

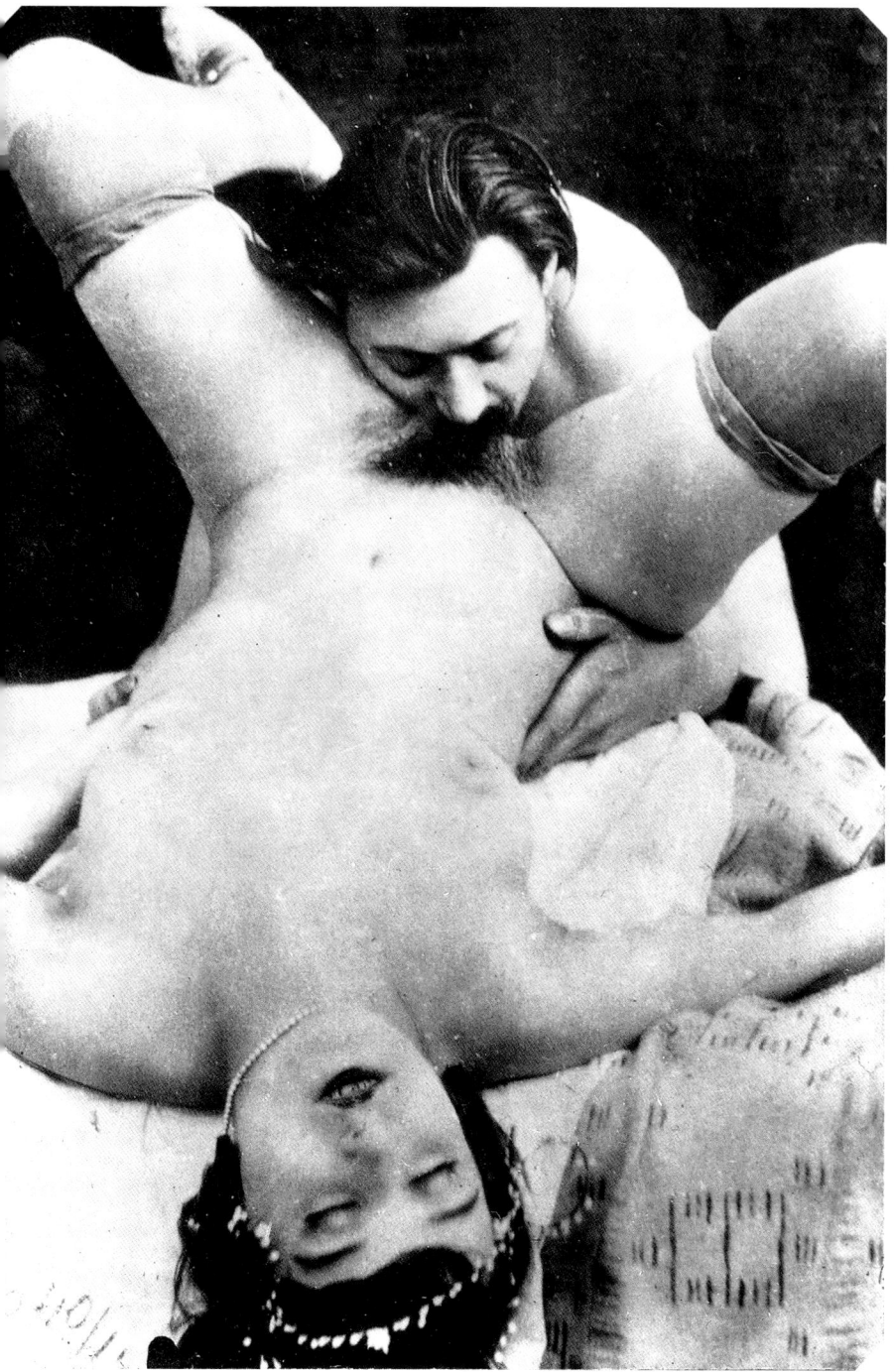

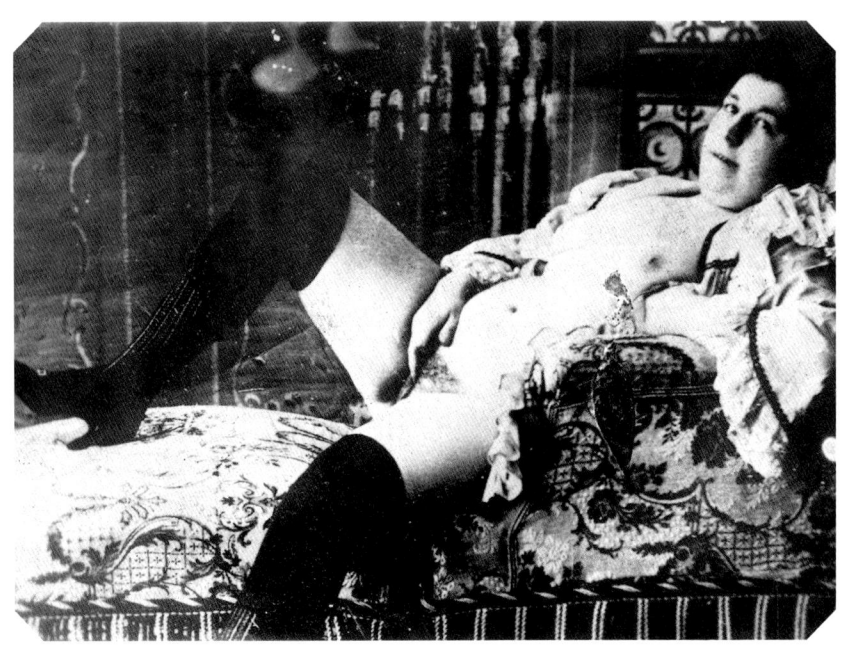

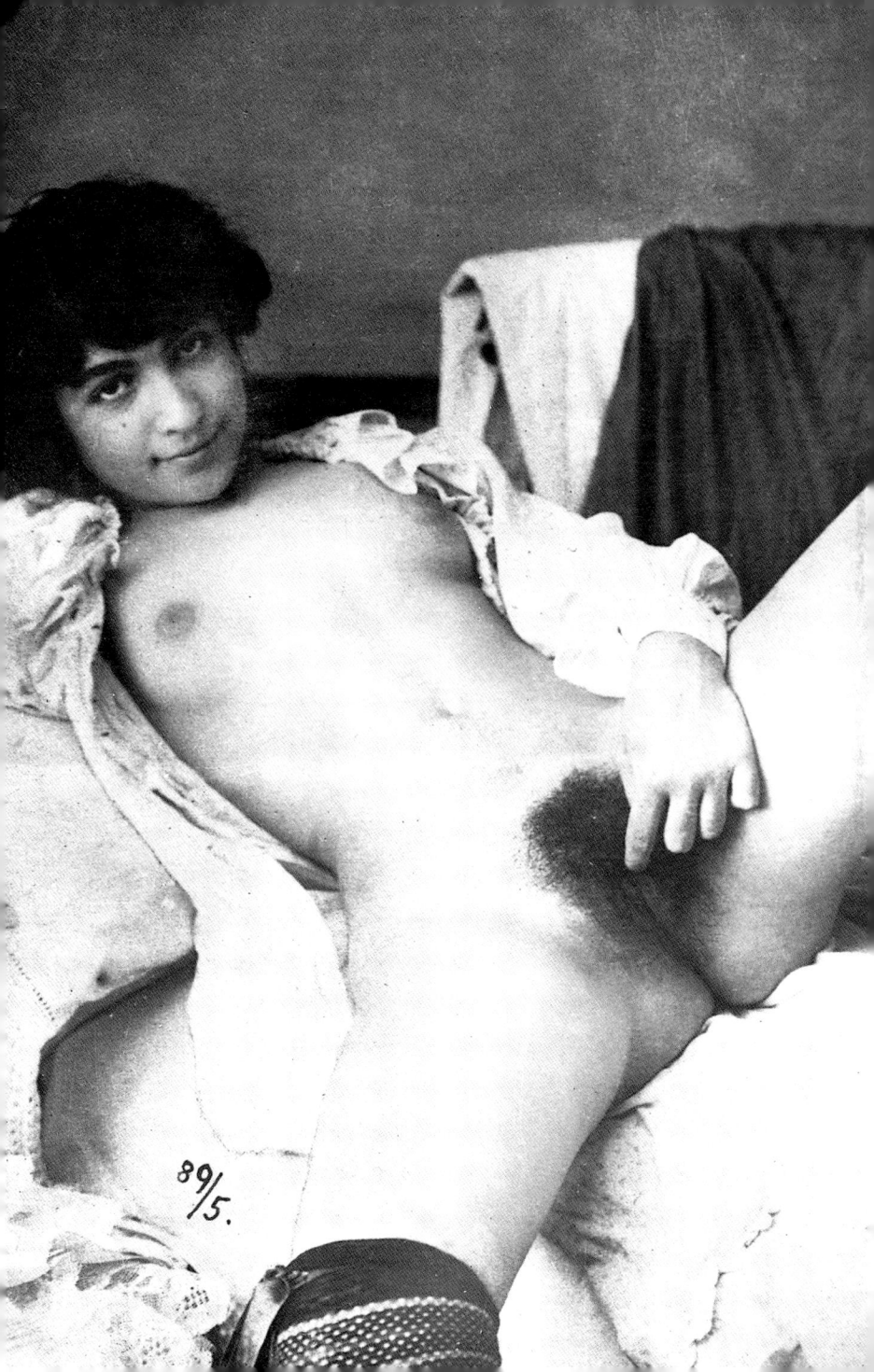

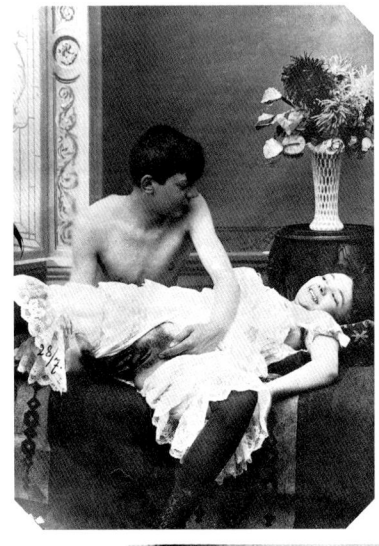

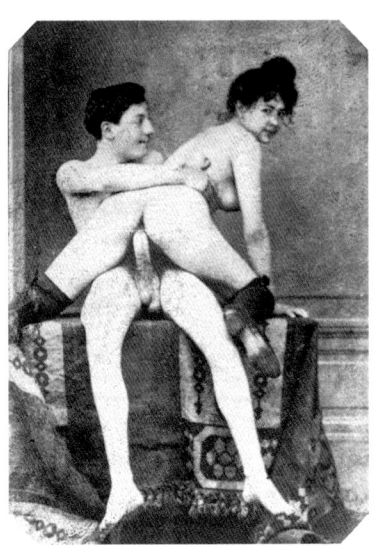

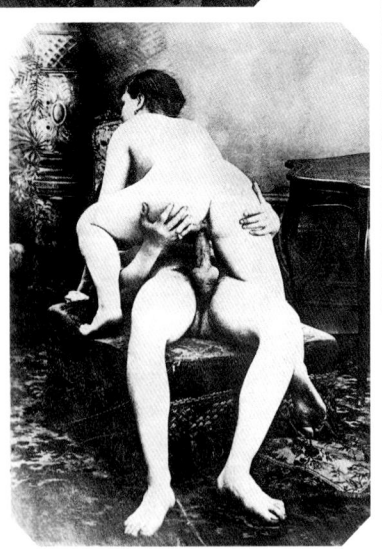

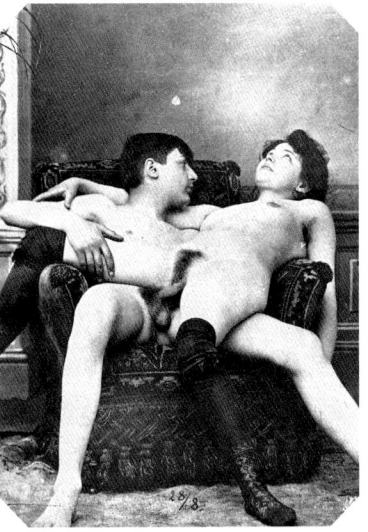

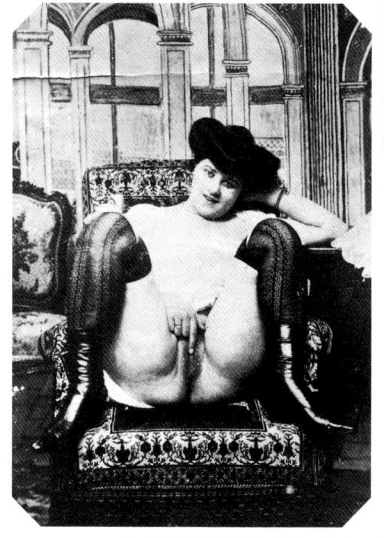
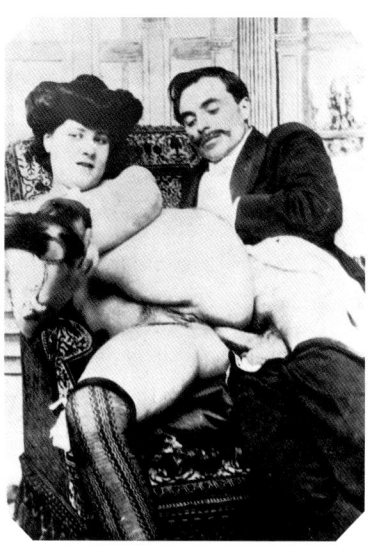
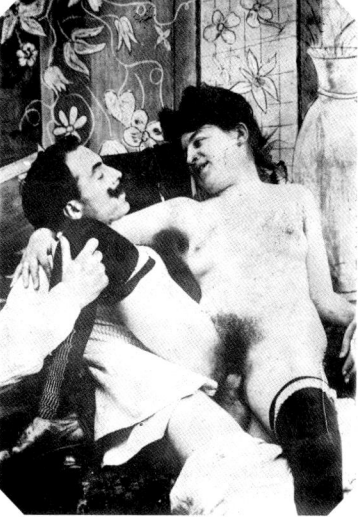
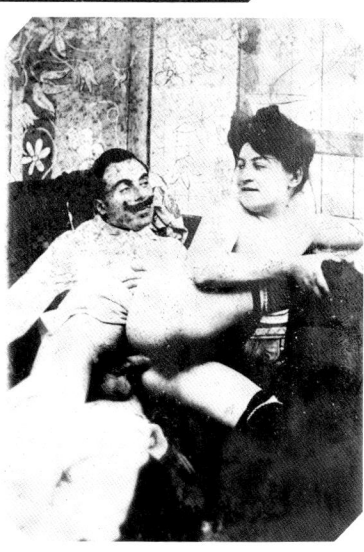

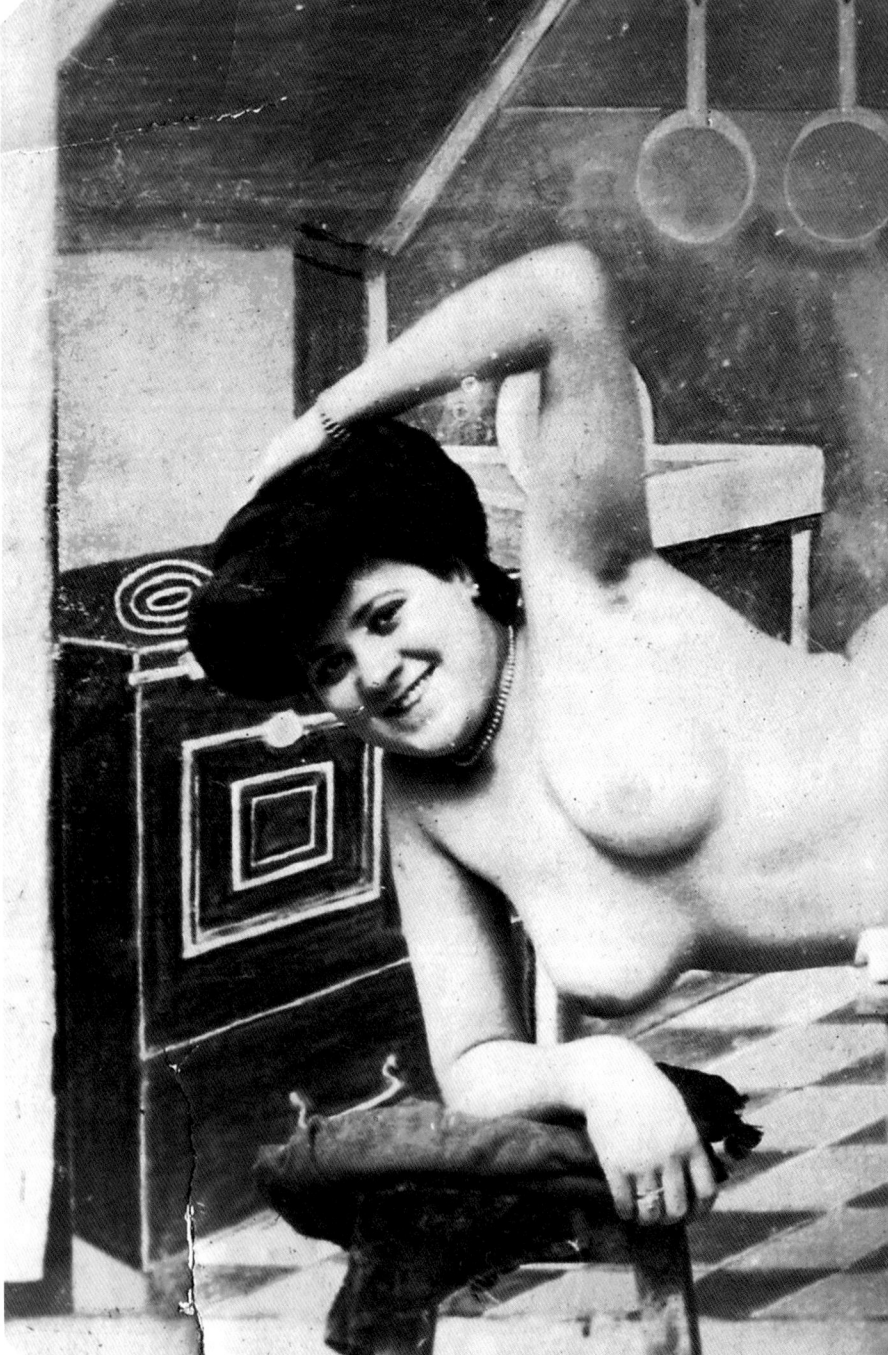

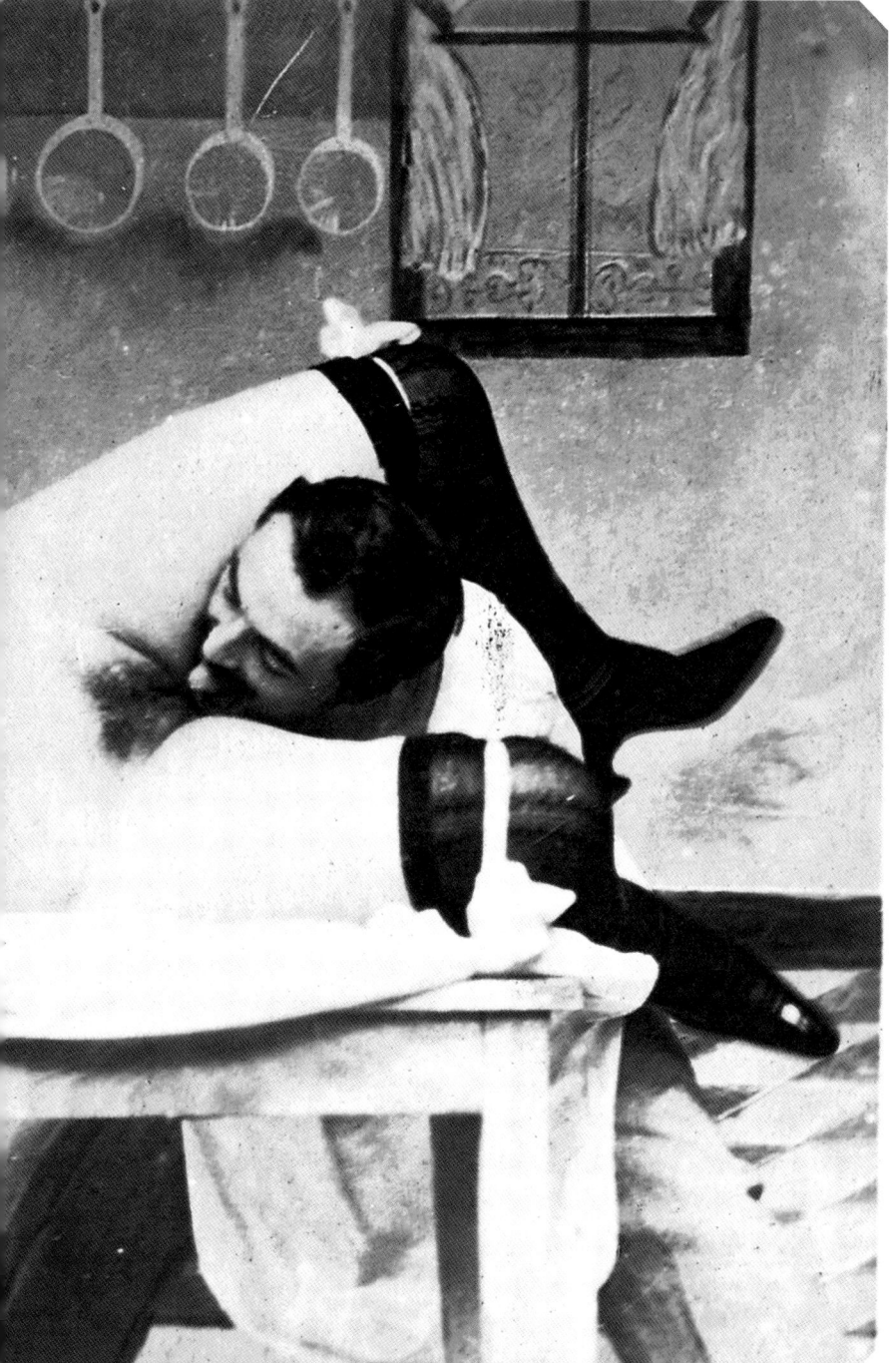

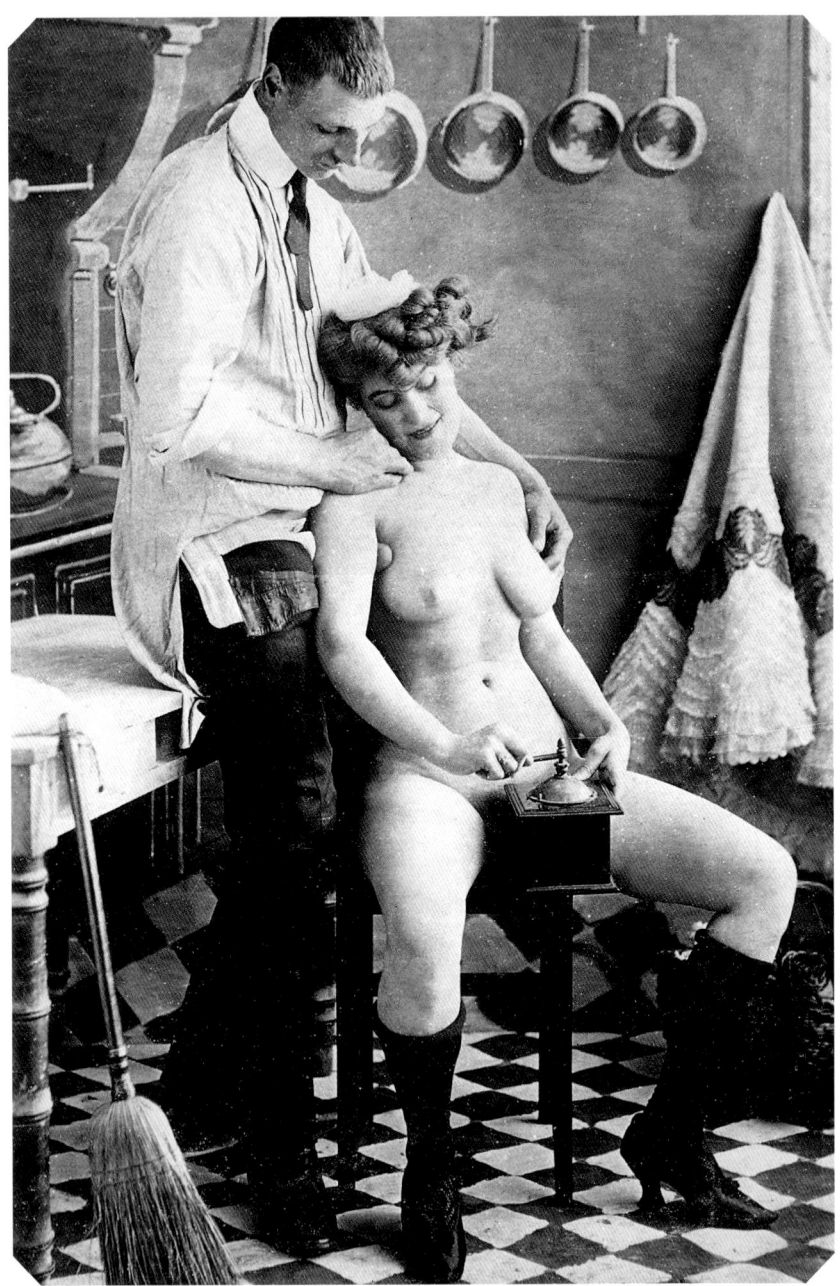

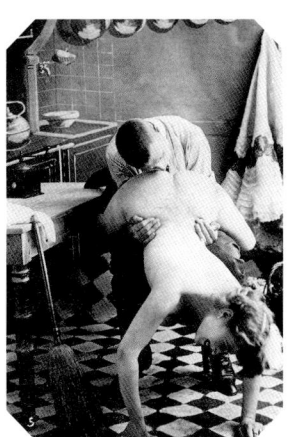

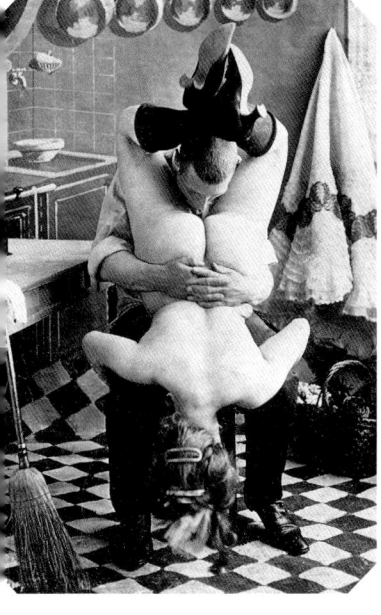

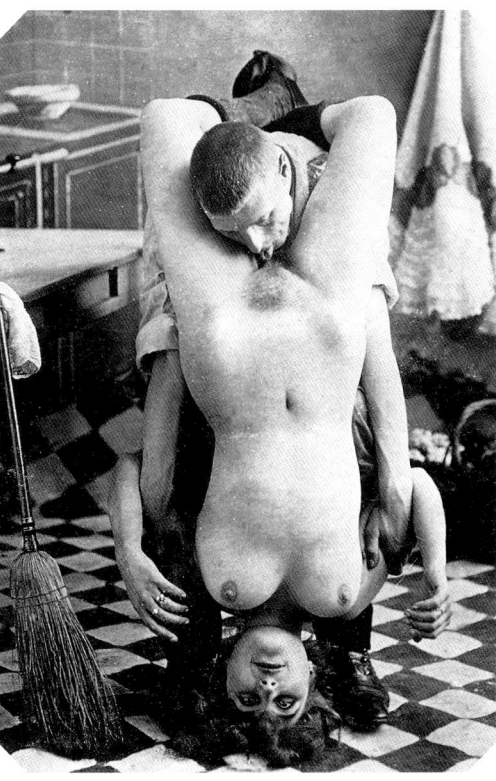

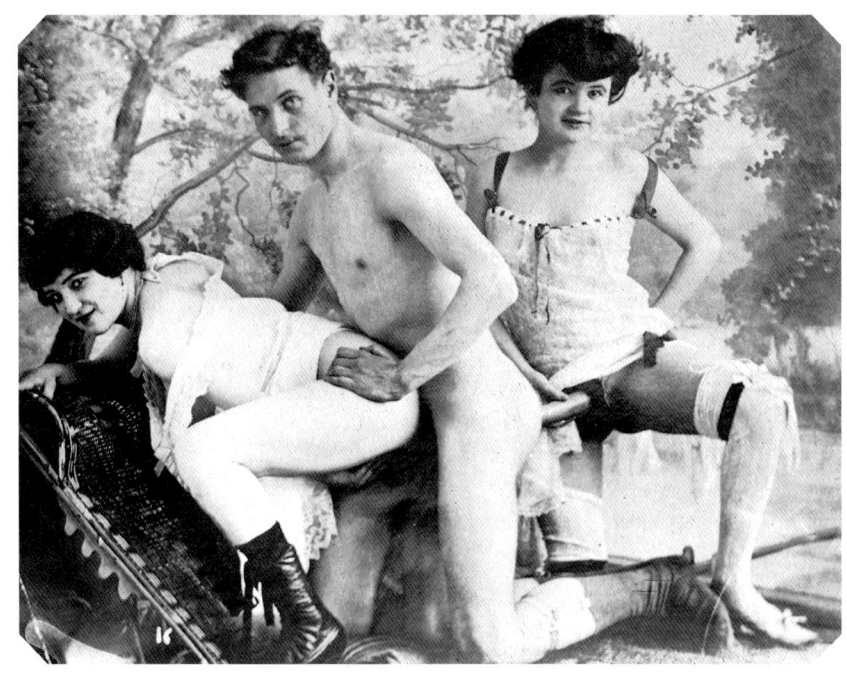

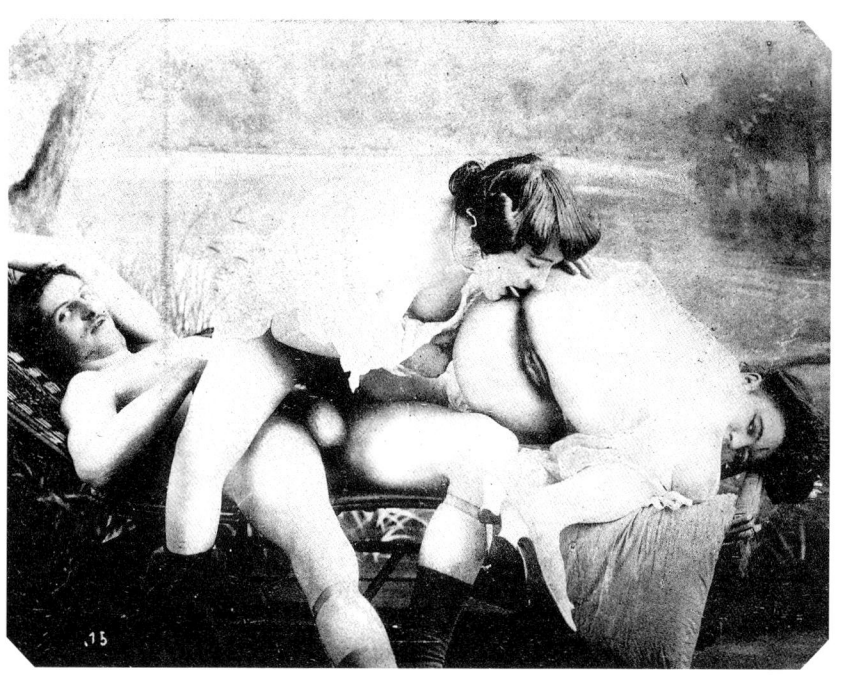

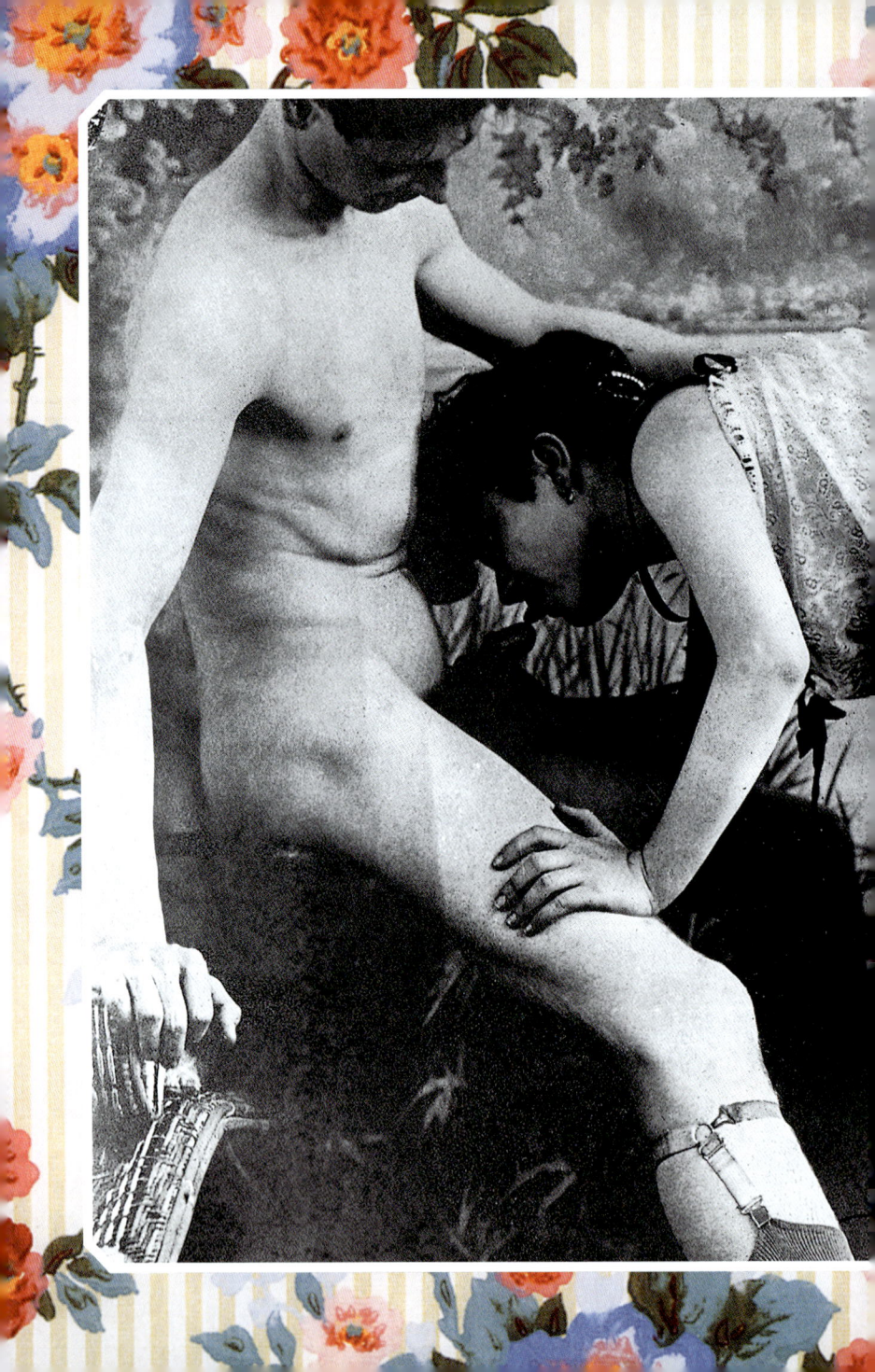

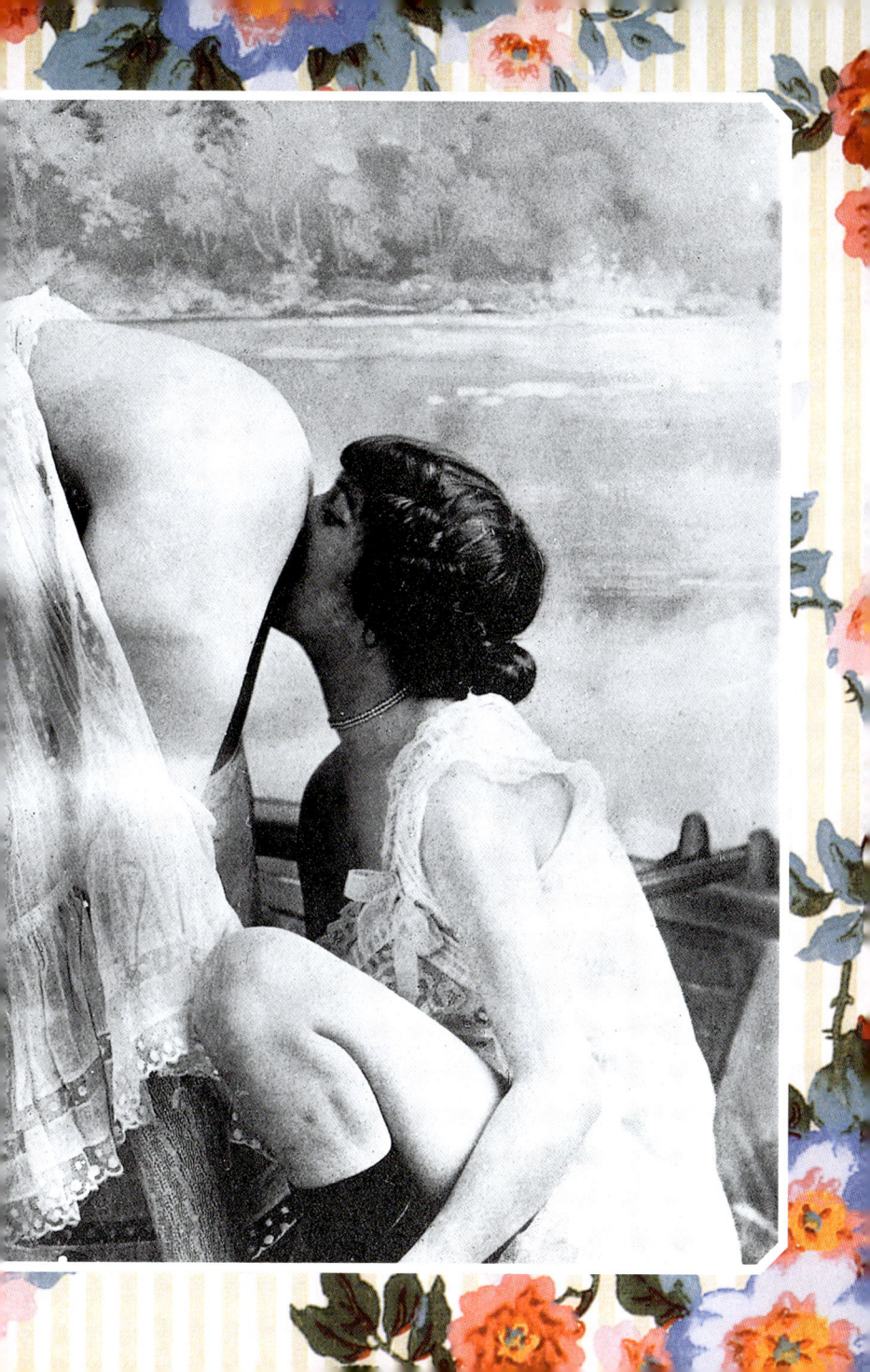

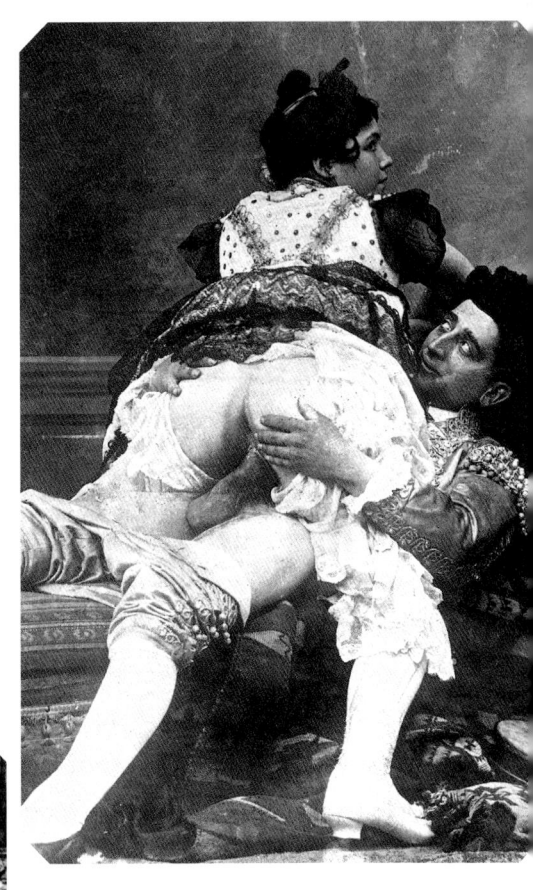

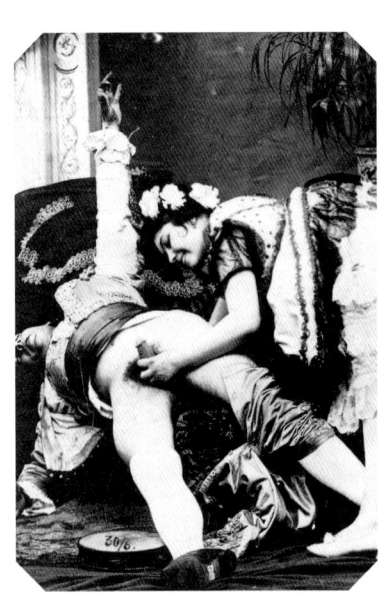

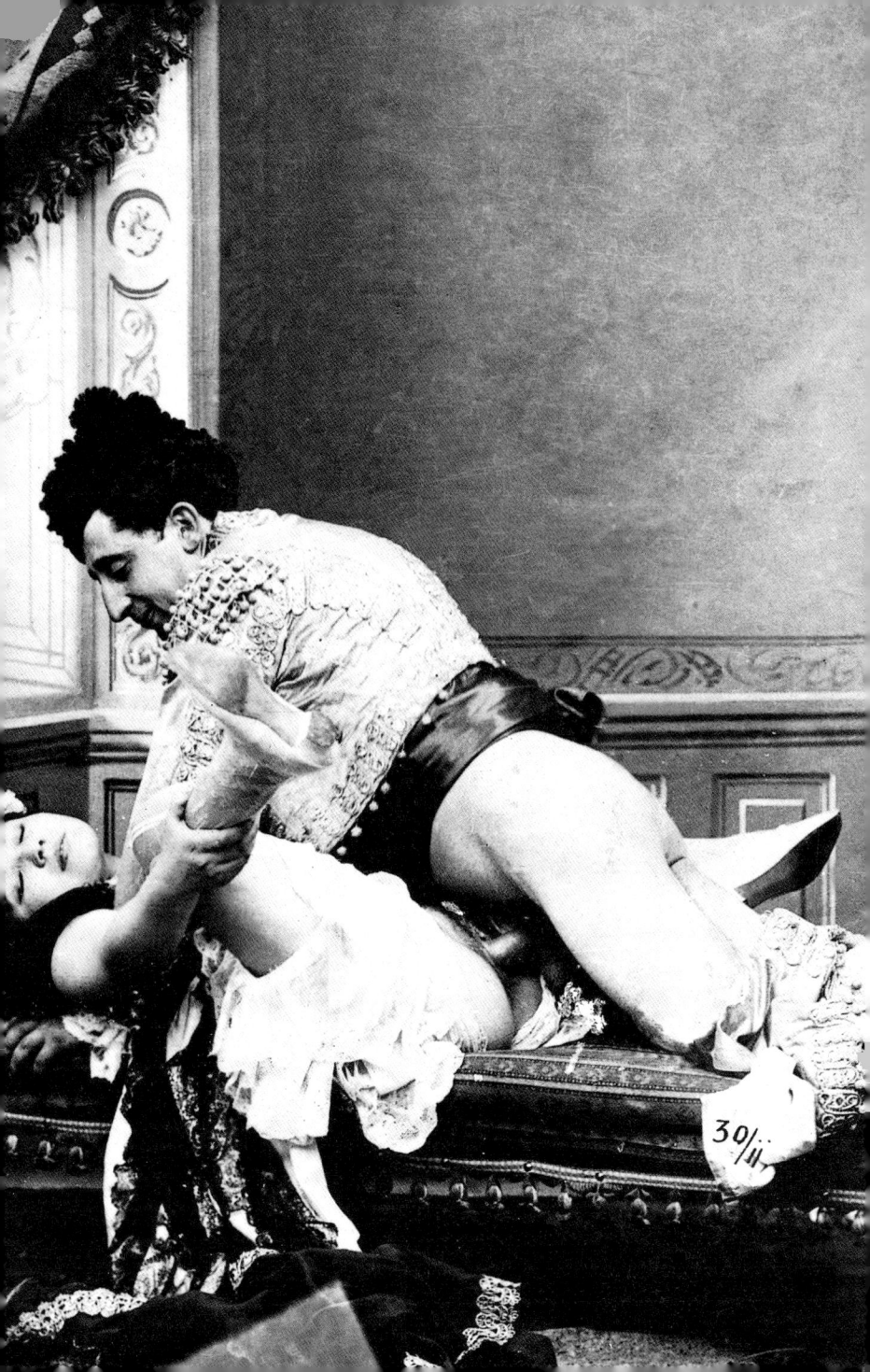

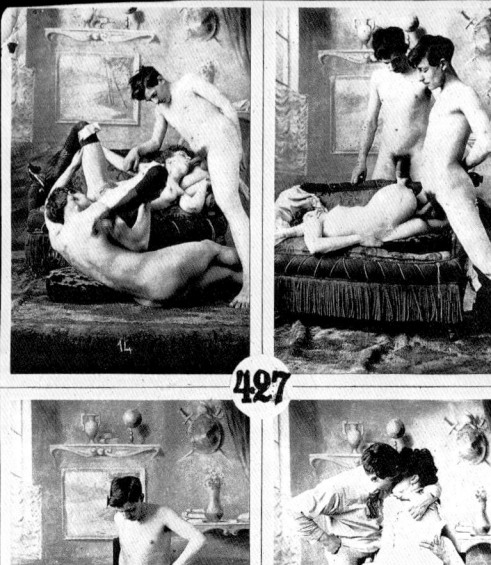

427

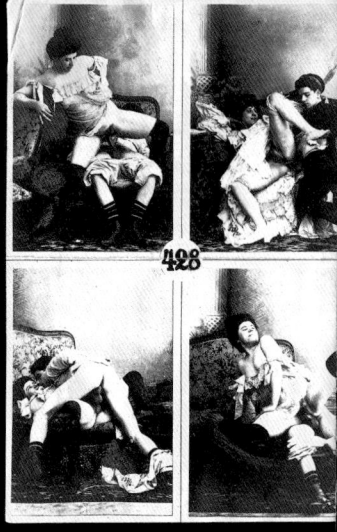

428

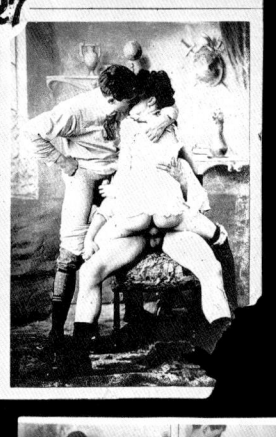

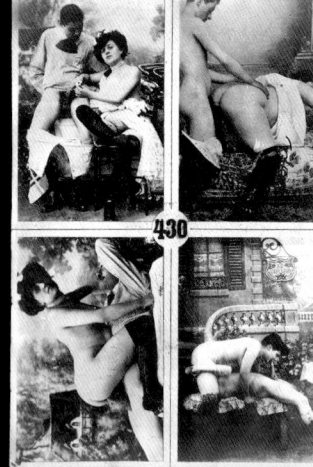

430

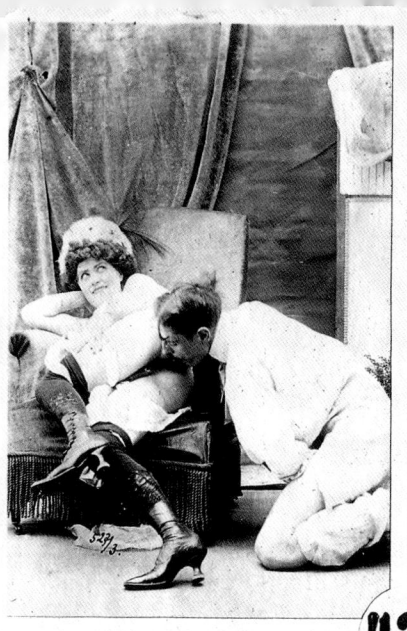

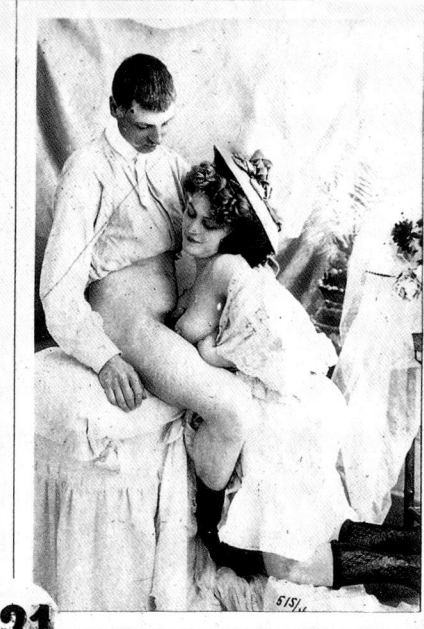

431

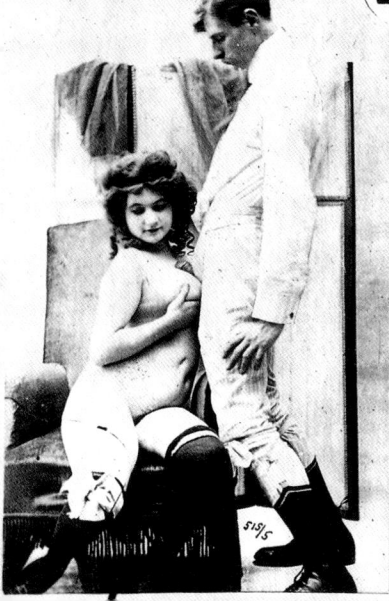

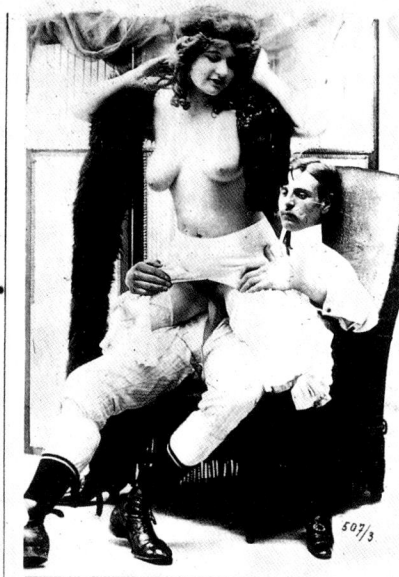

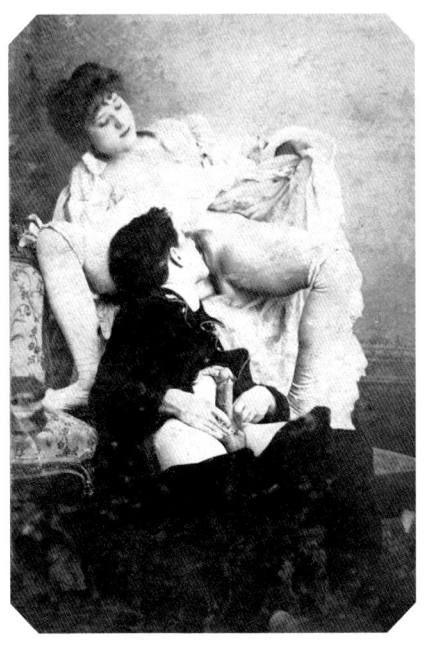
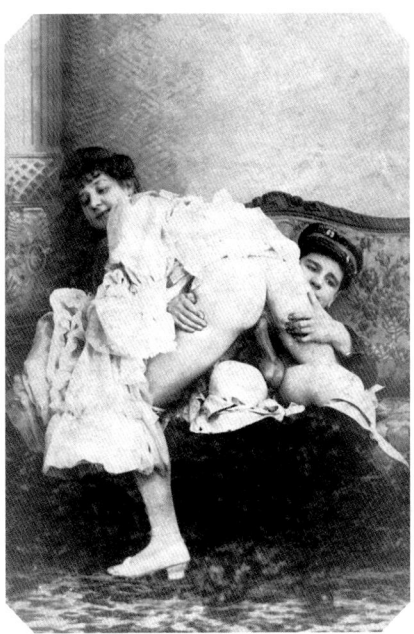

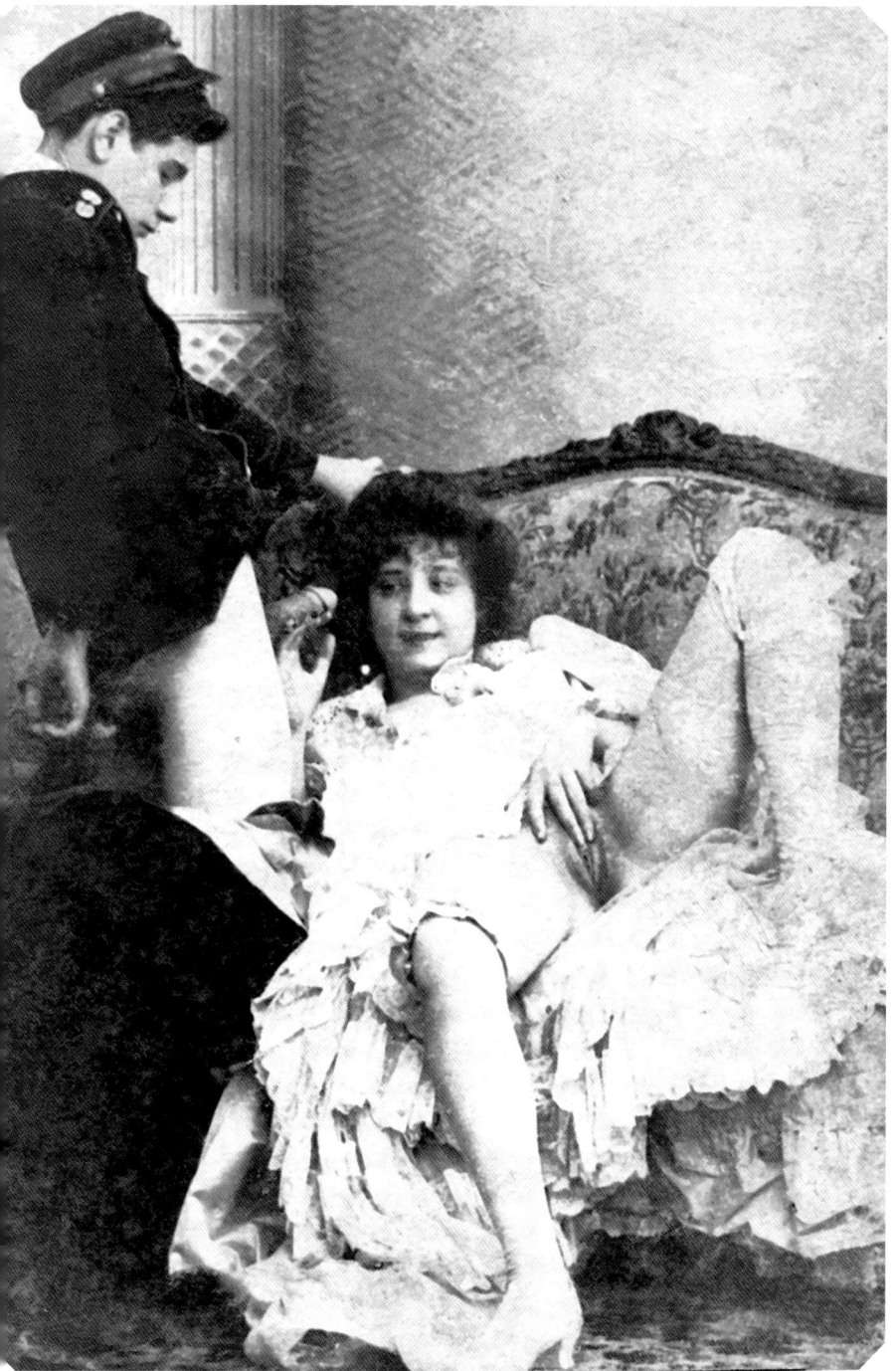

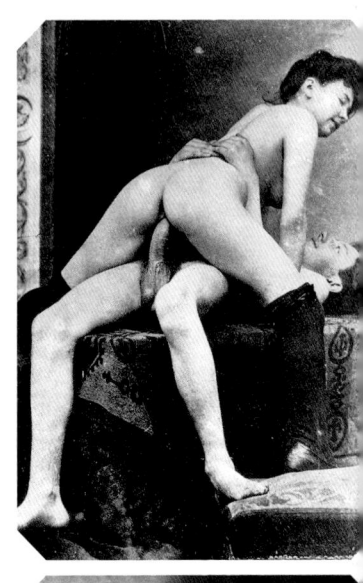
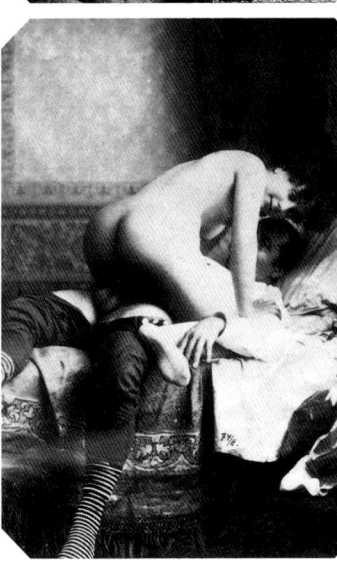
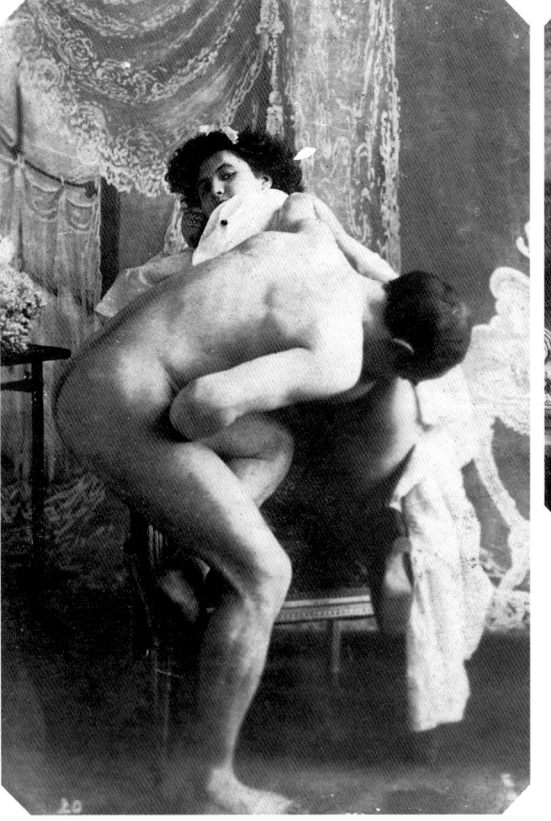

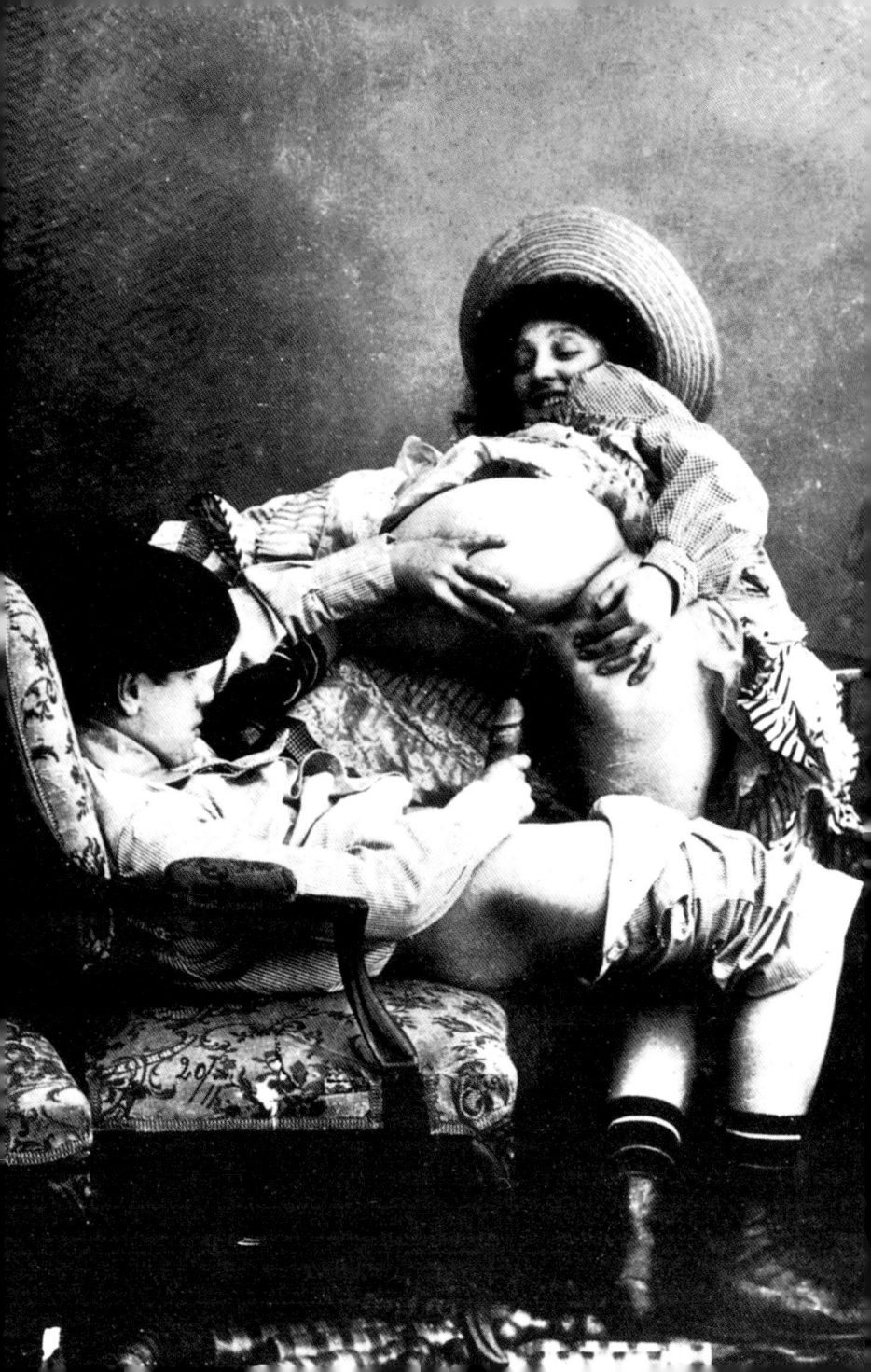

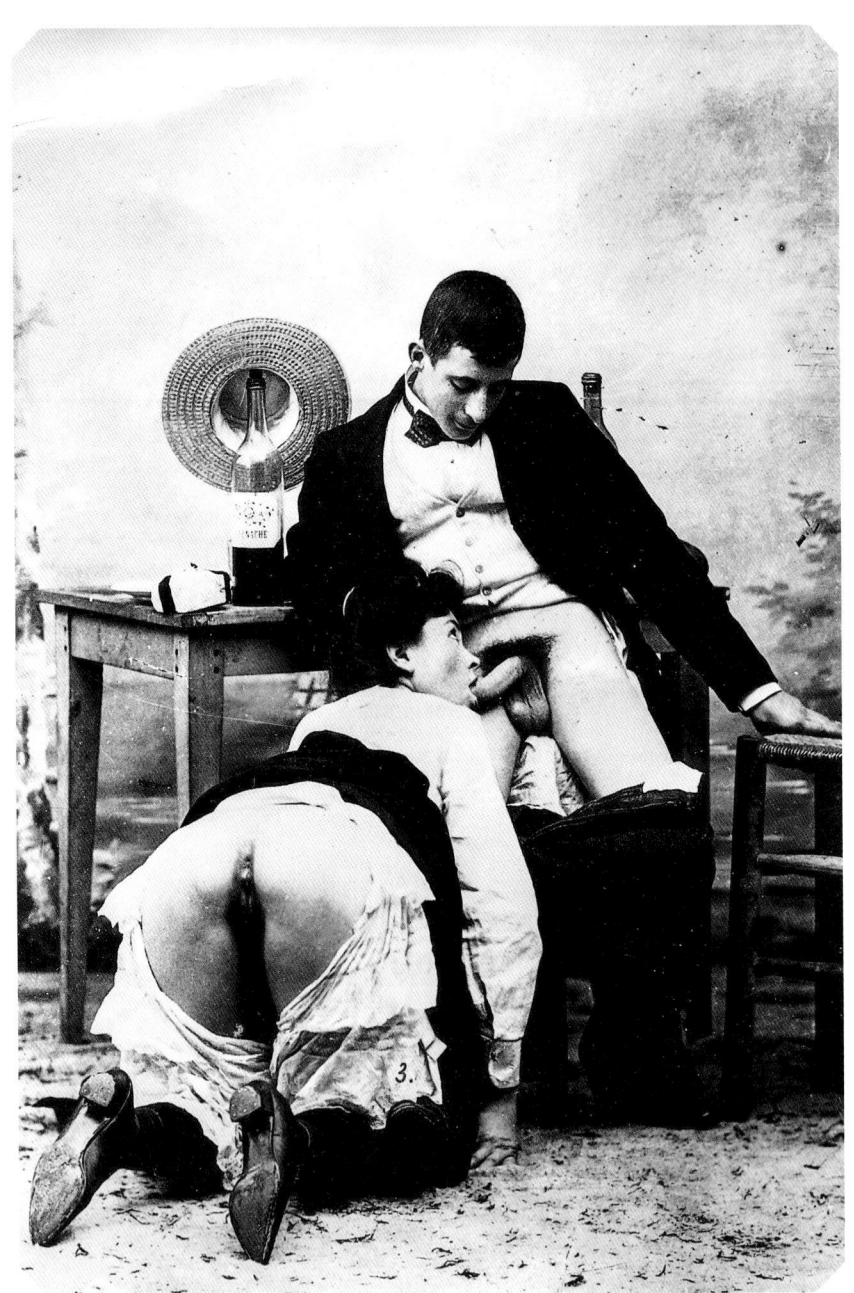

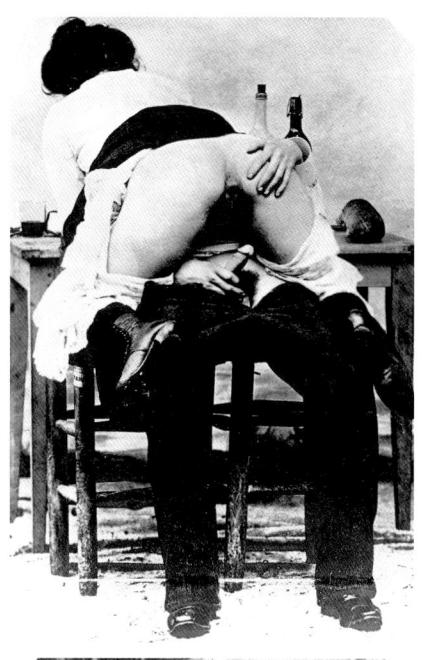
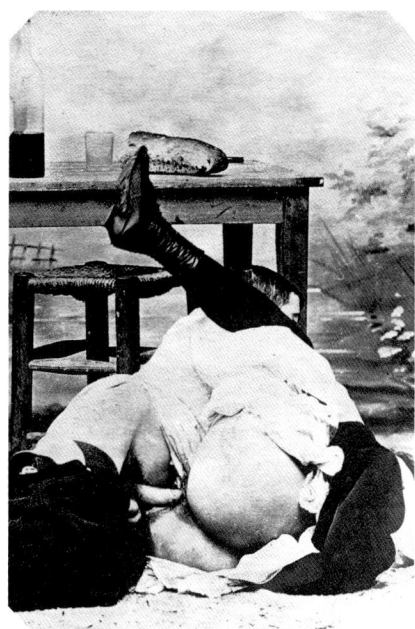
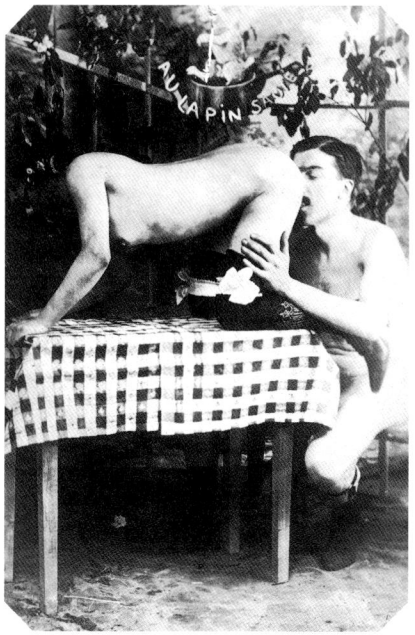
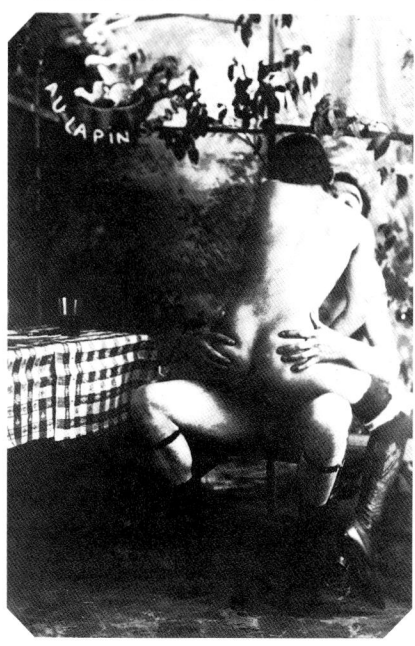

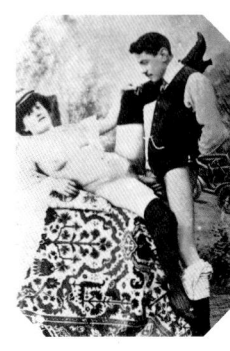
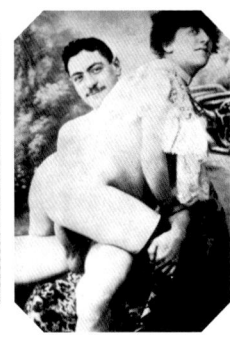
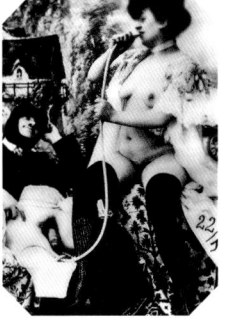
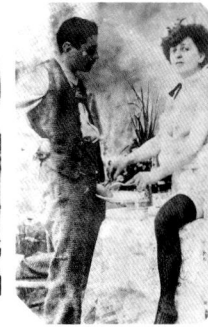
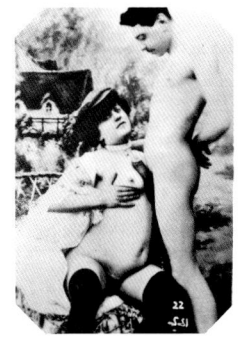
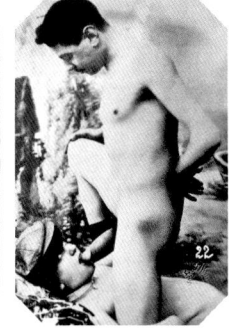
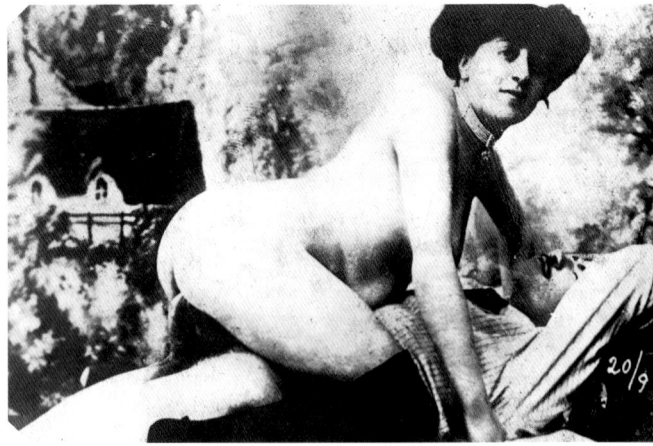

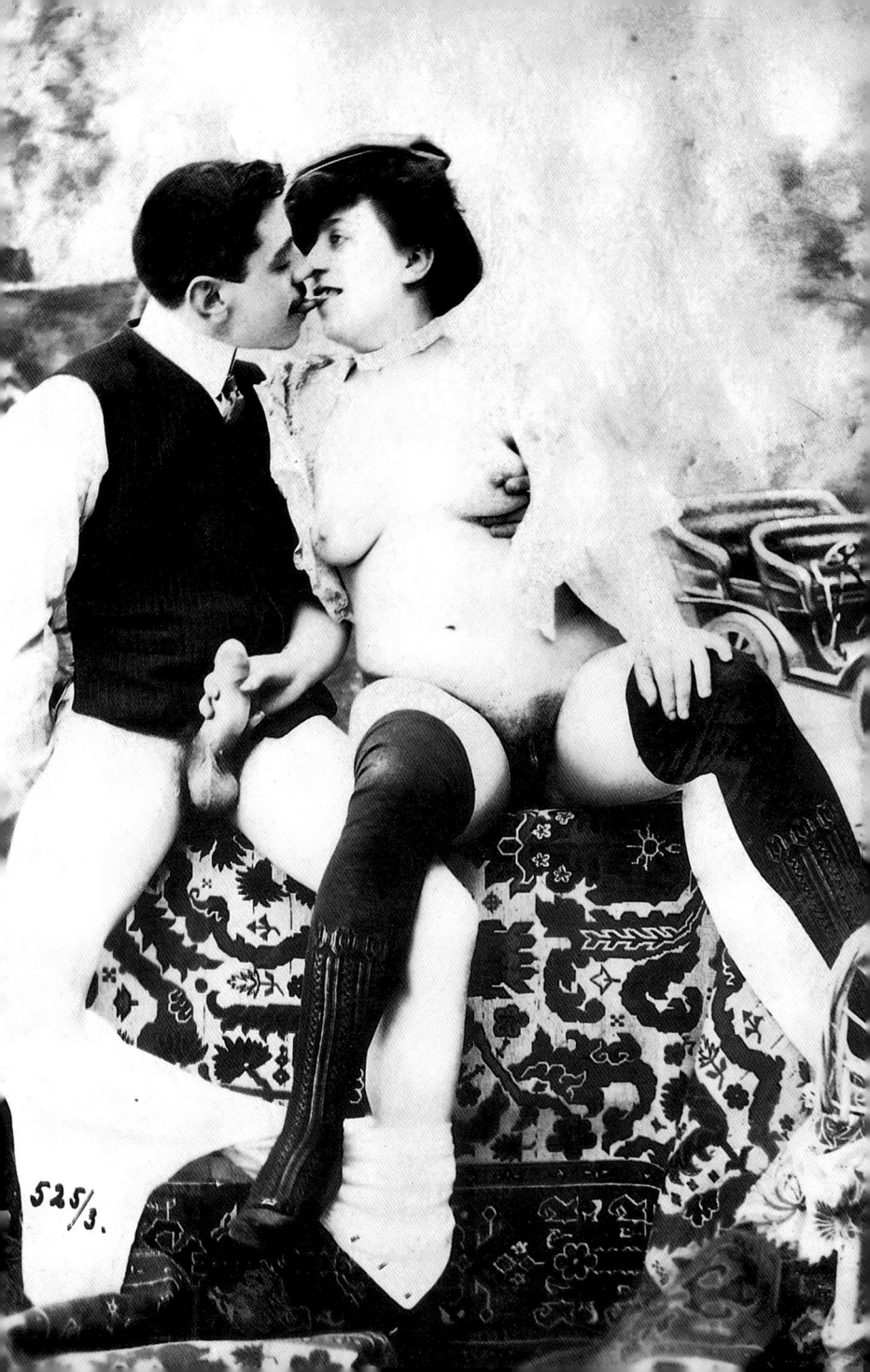

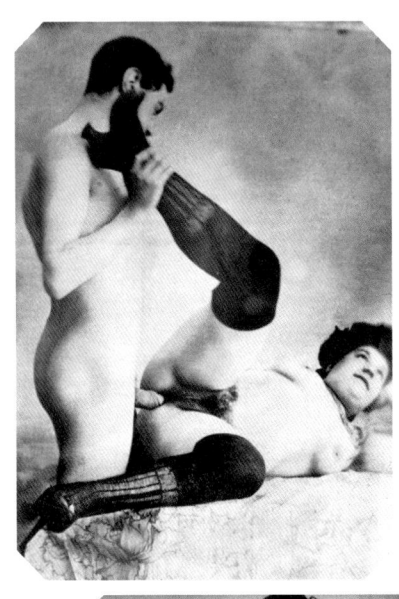

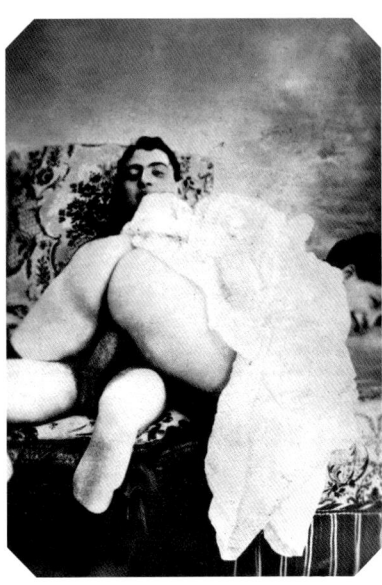

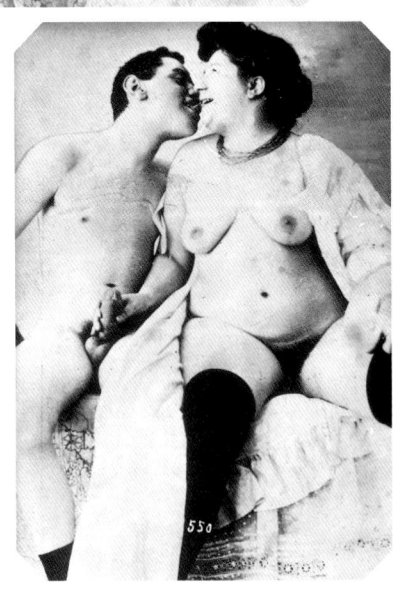

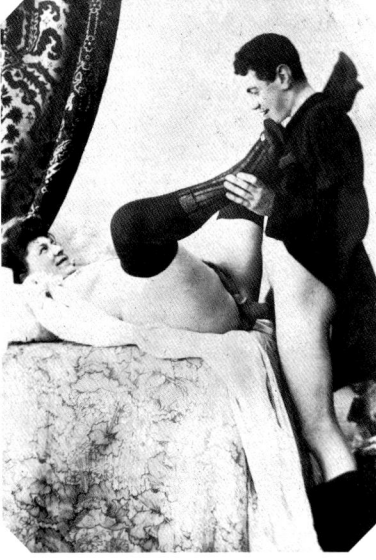

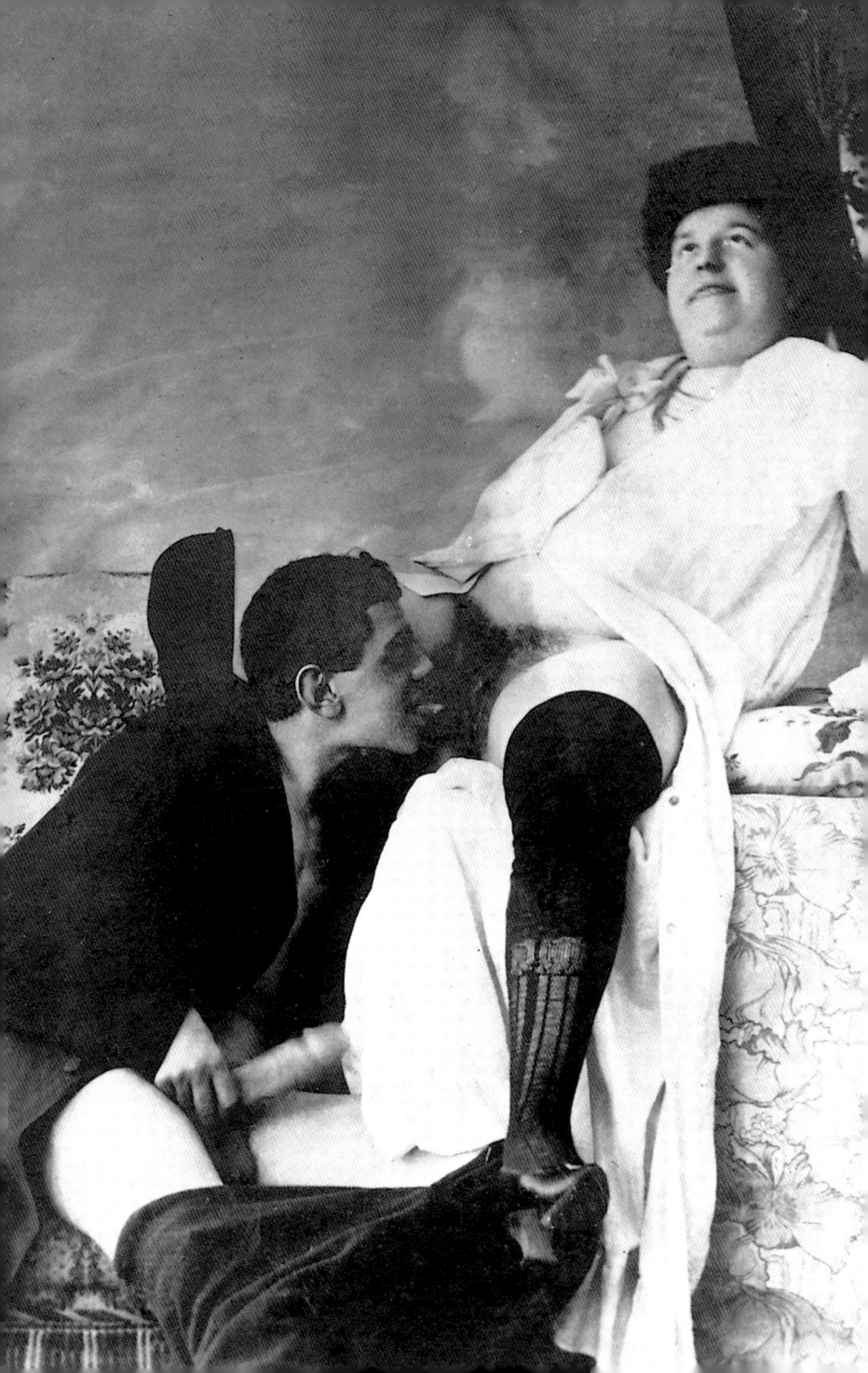

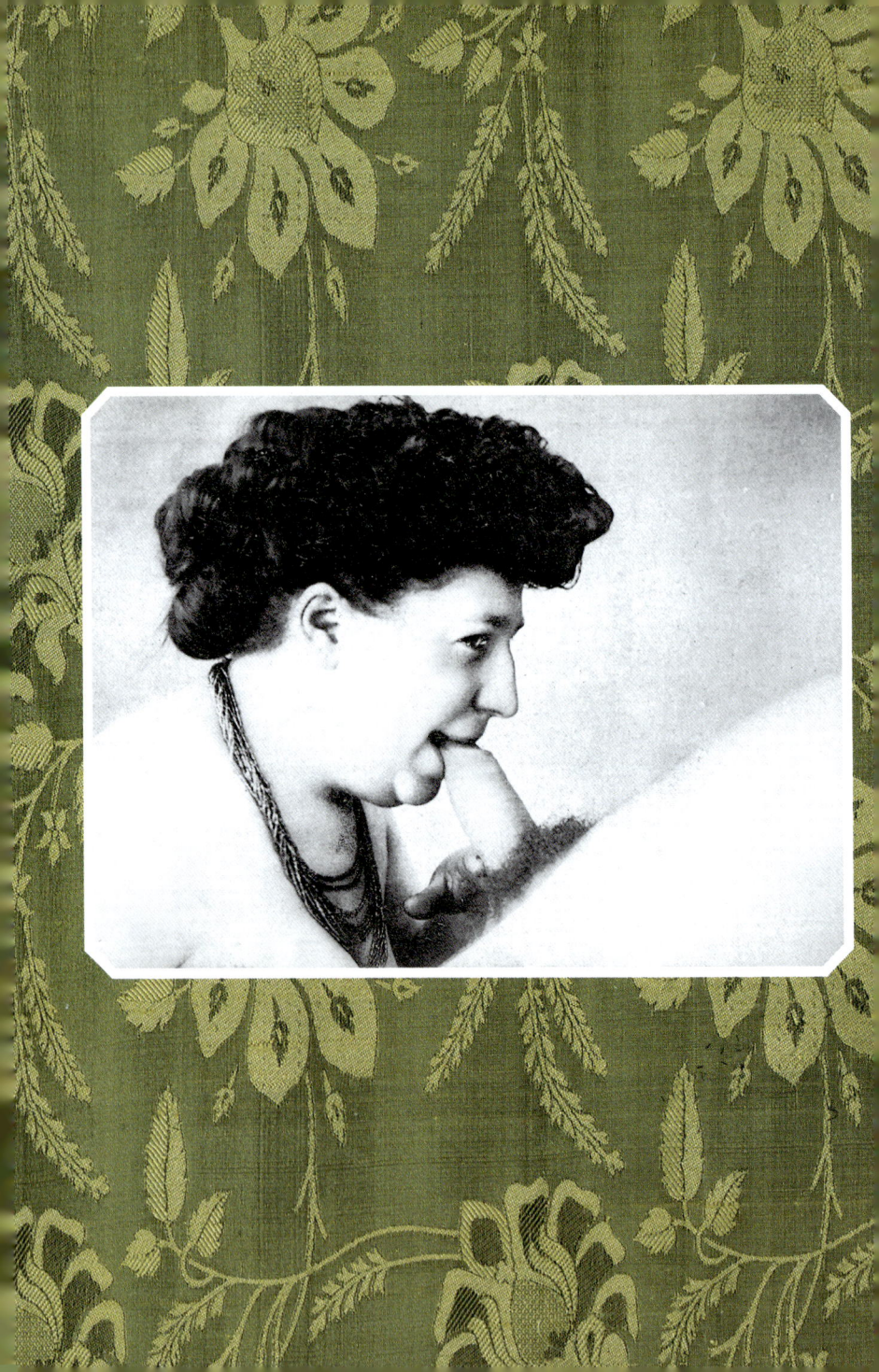

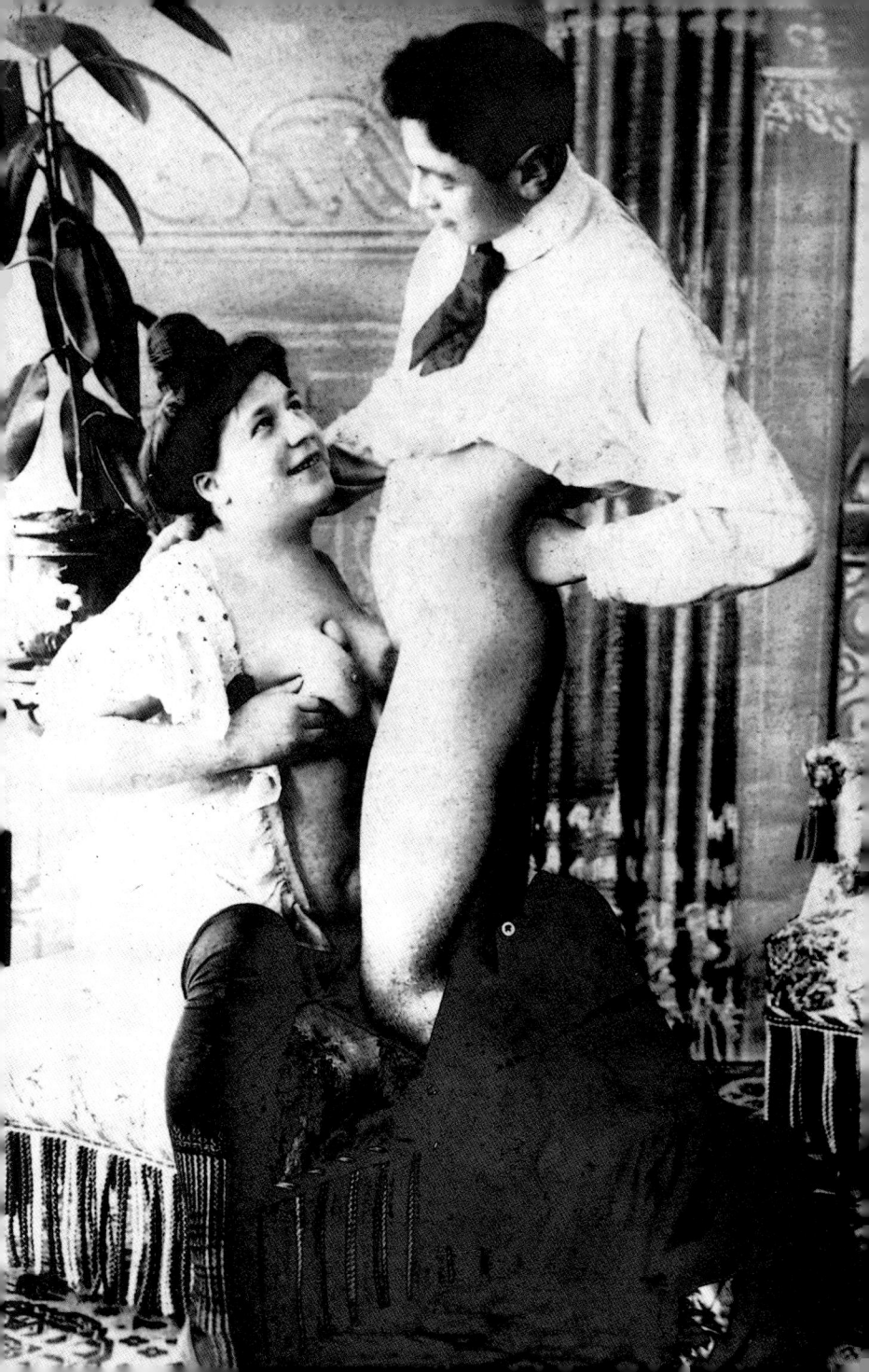

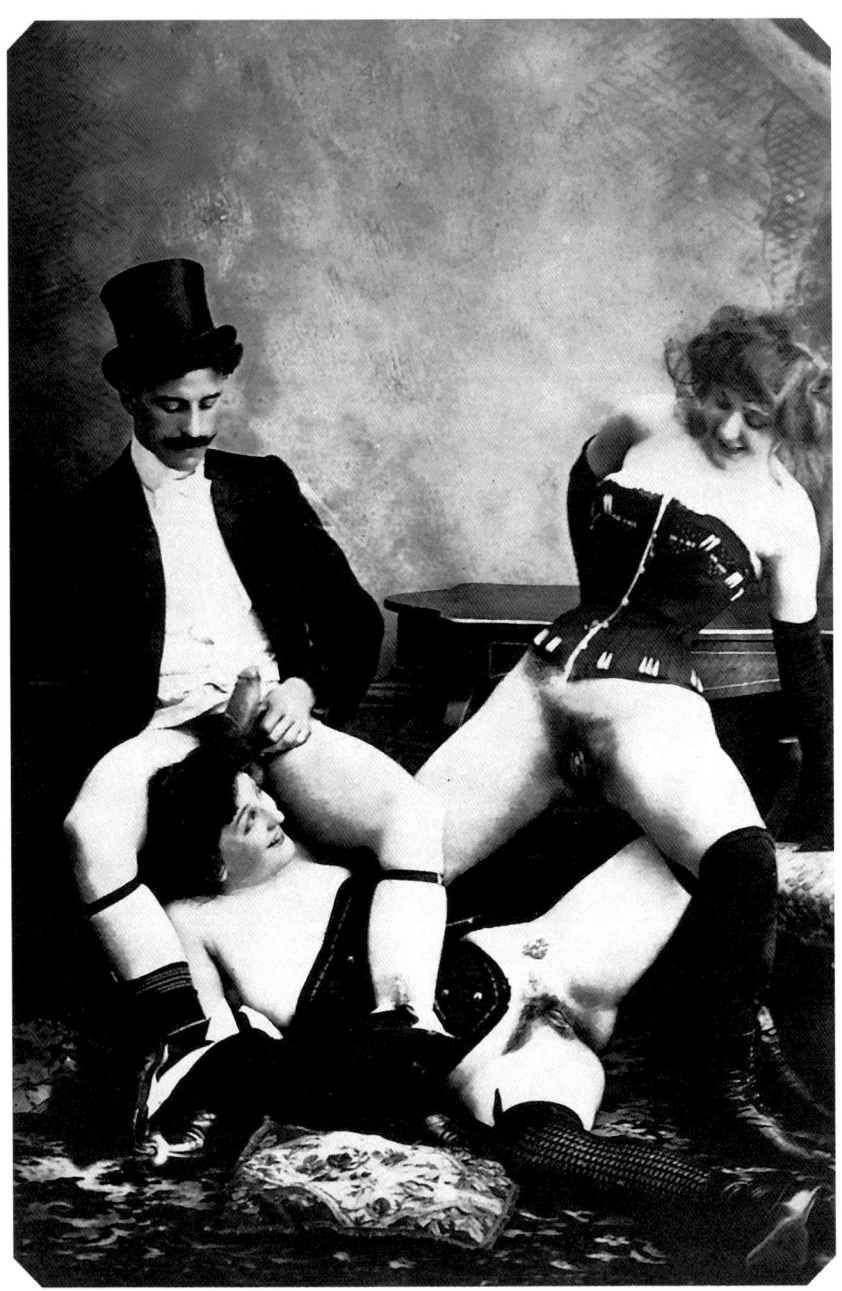

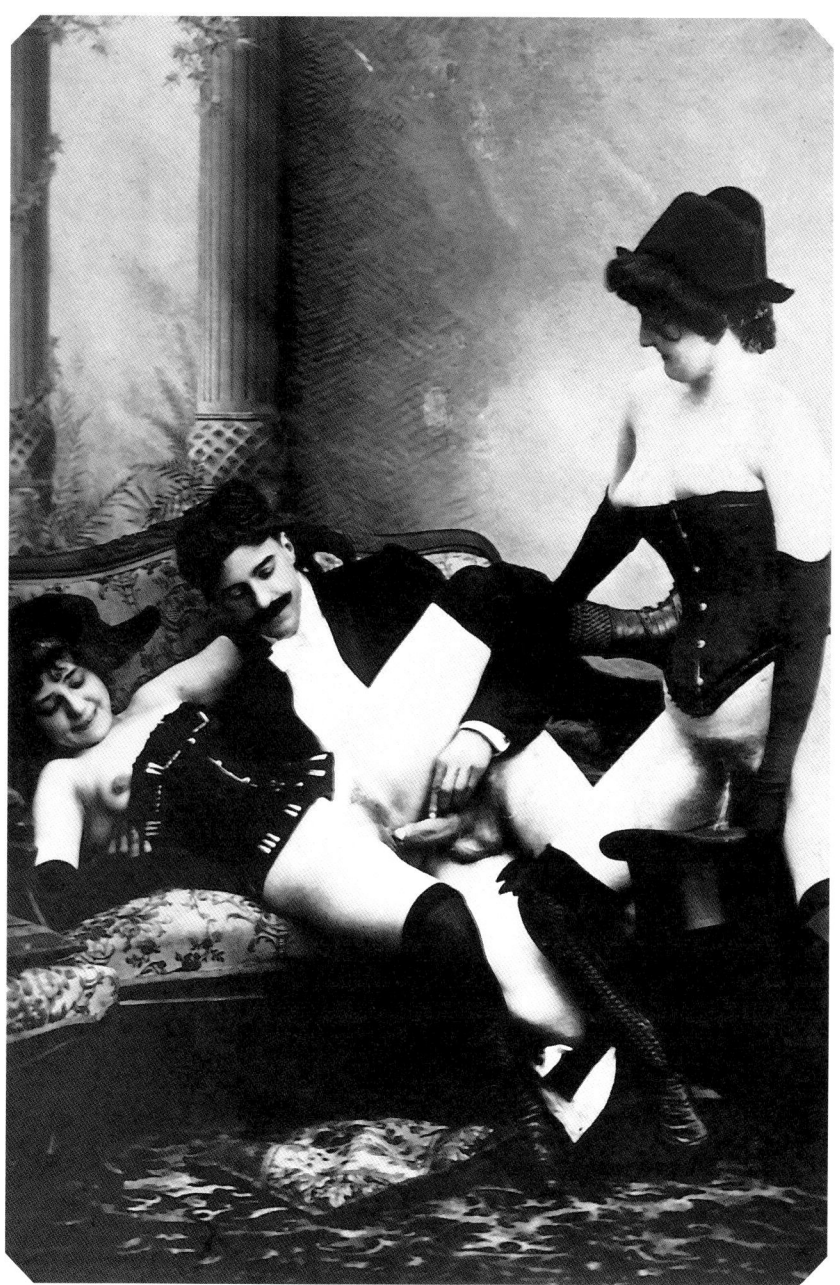

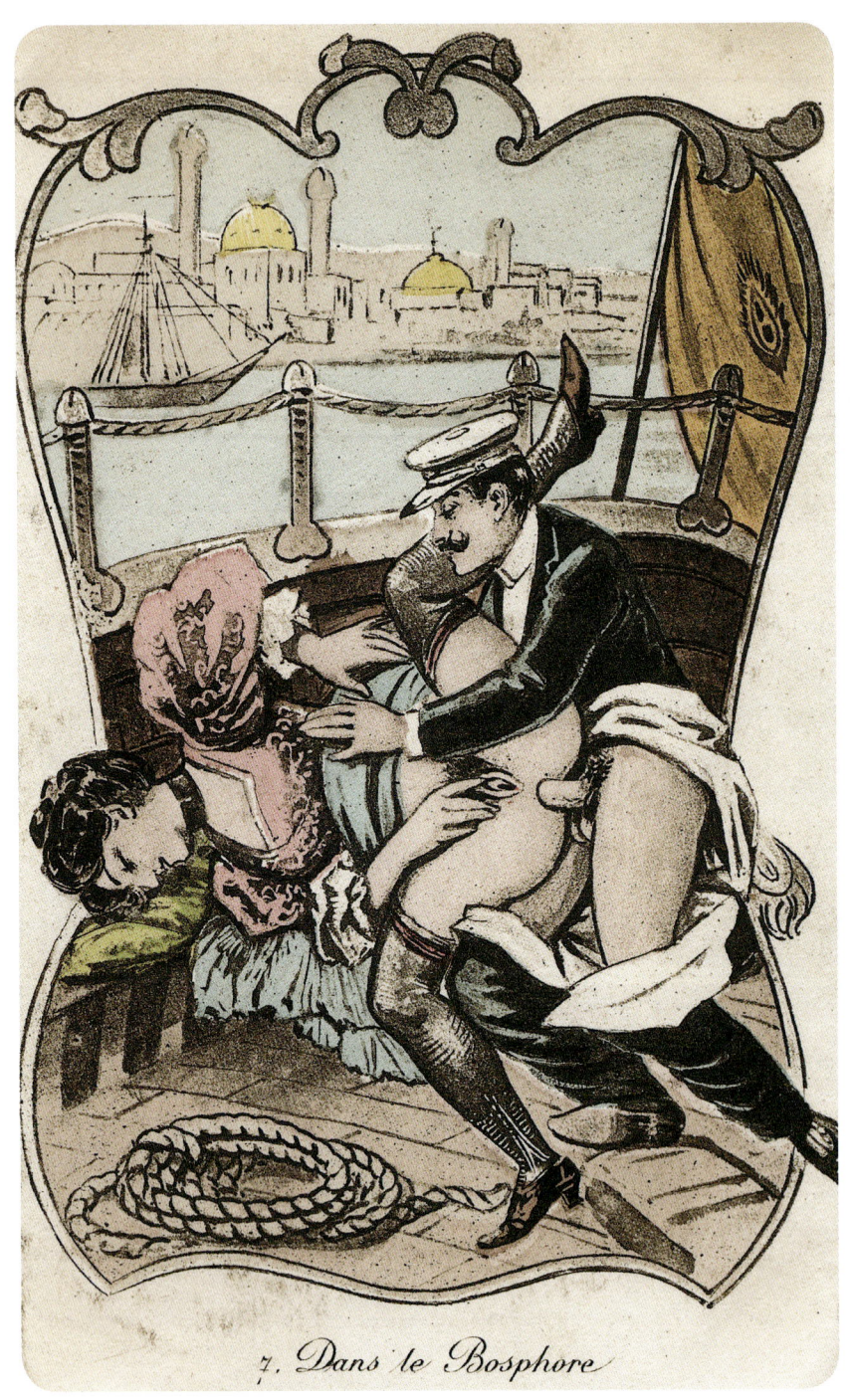

7. Dans le Bosphore

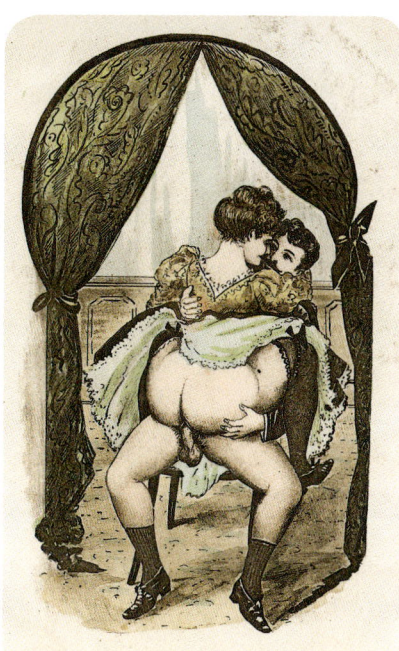

30. Haute école _ Riders' fashion

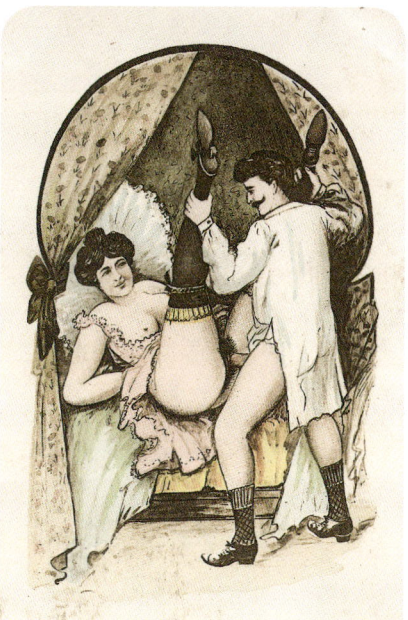

31. Enviander les brancards _ Between the shafts

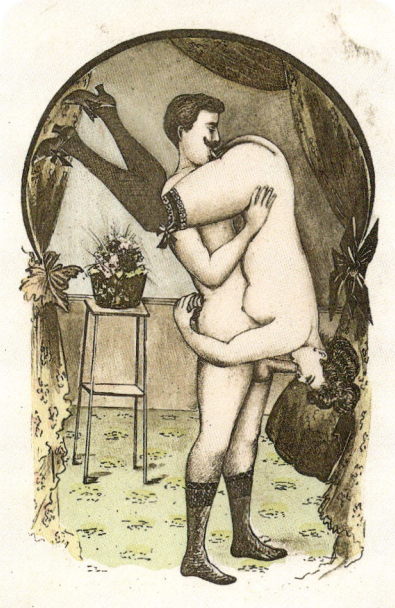

32. En Athlète _ Athletic fashion

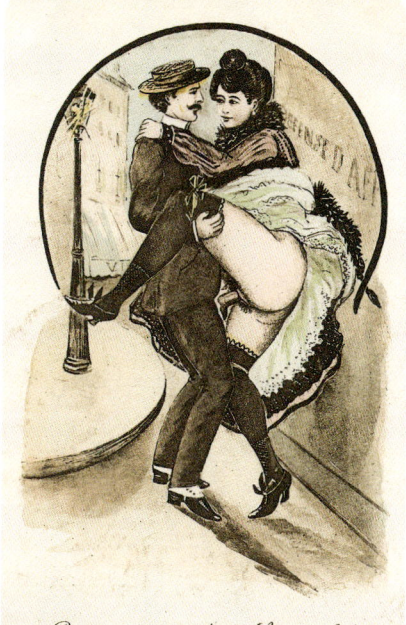

29. Position du tireur debout _ Standing fashion

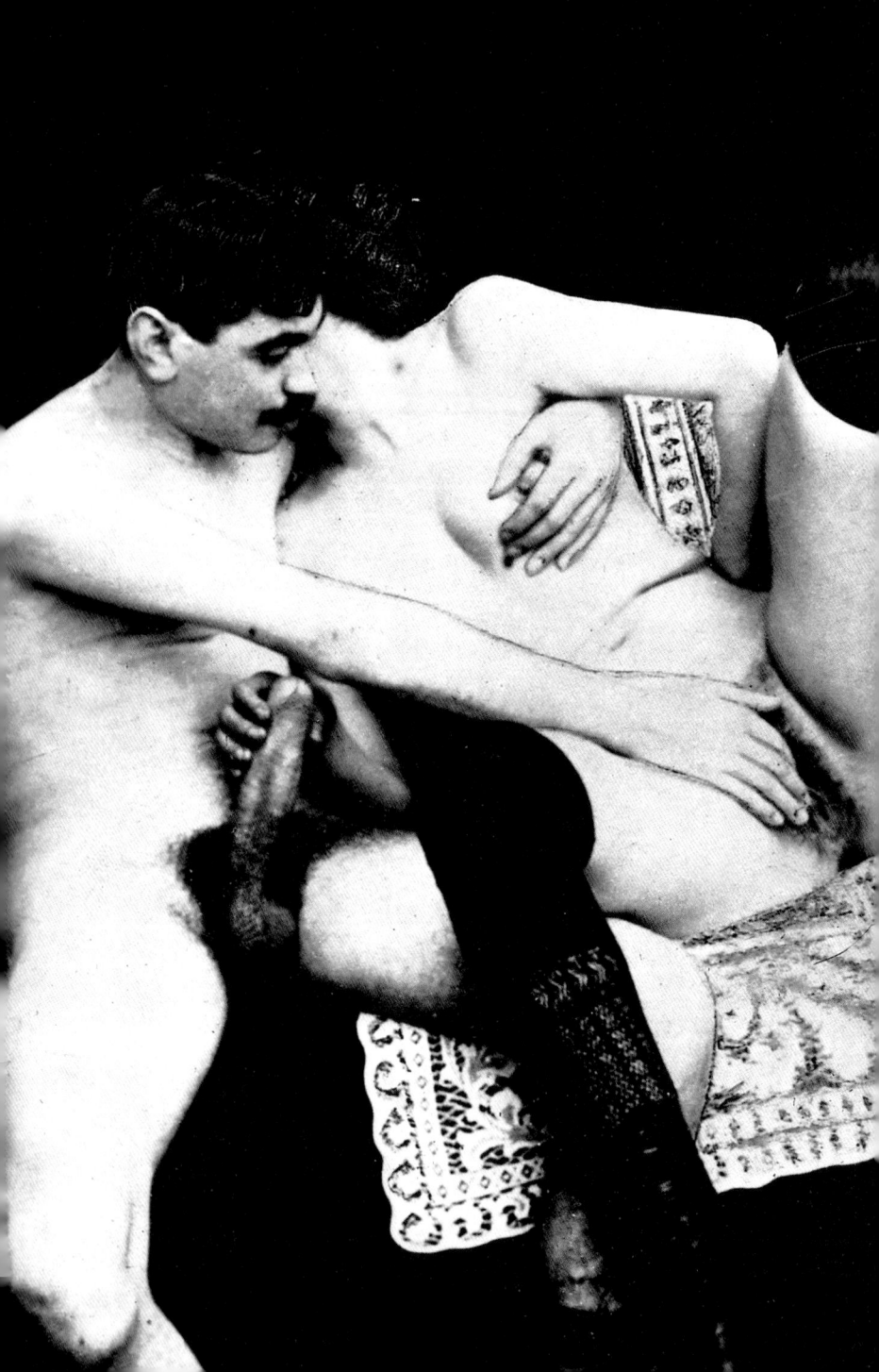

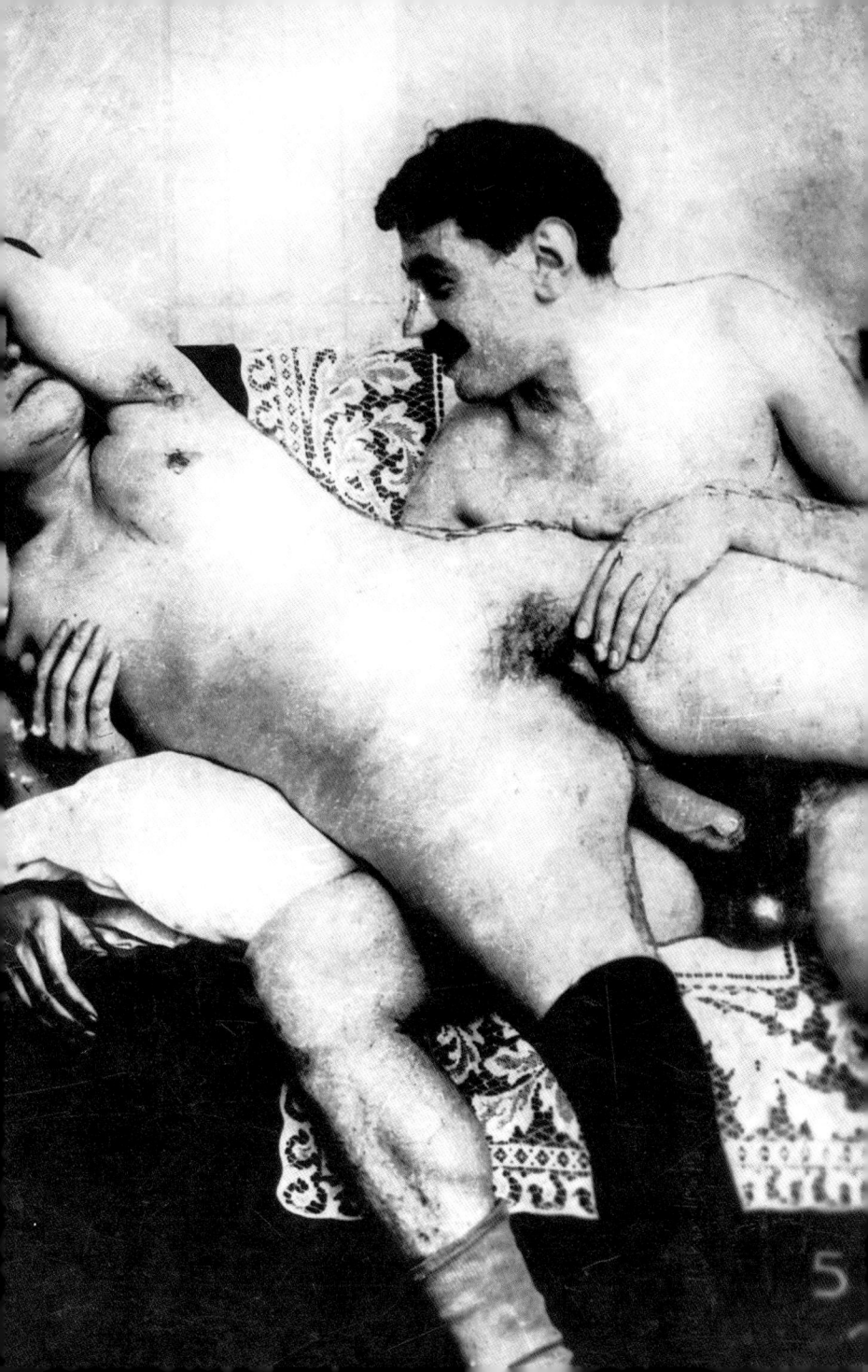

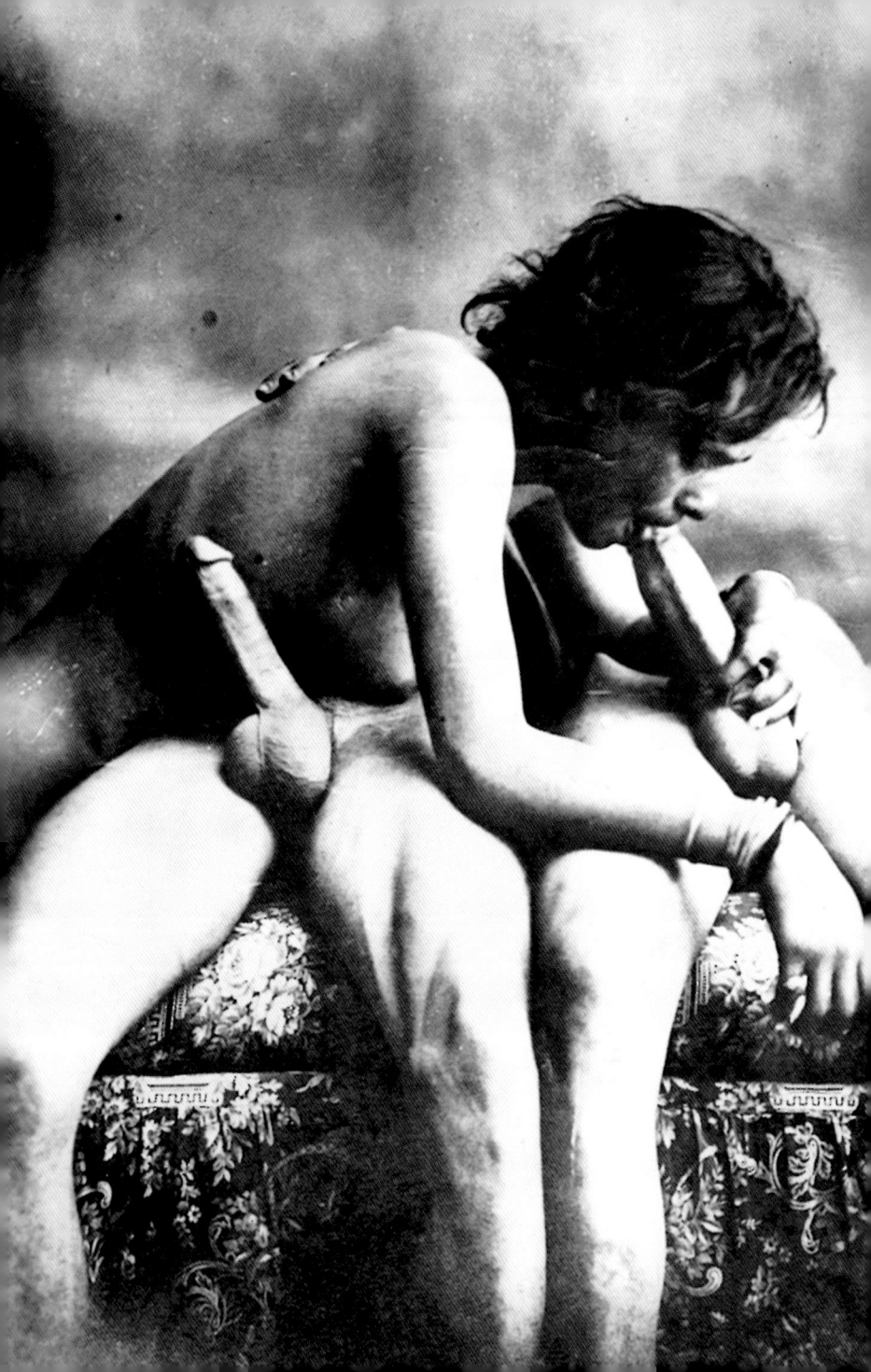

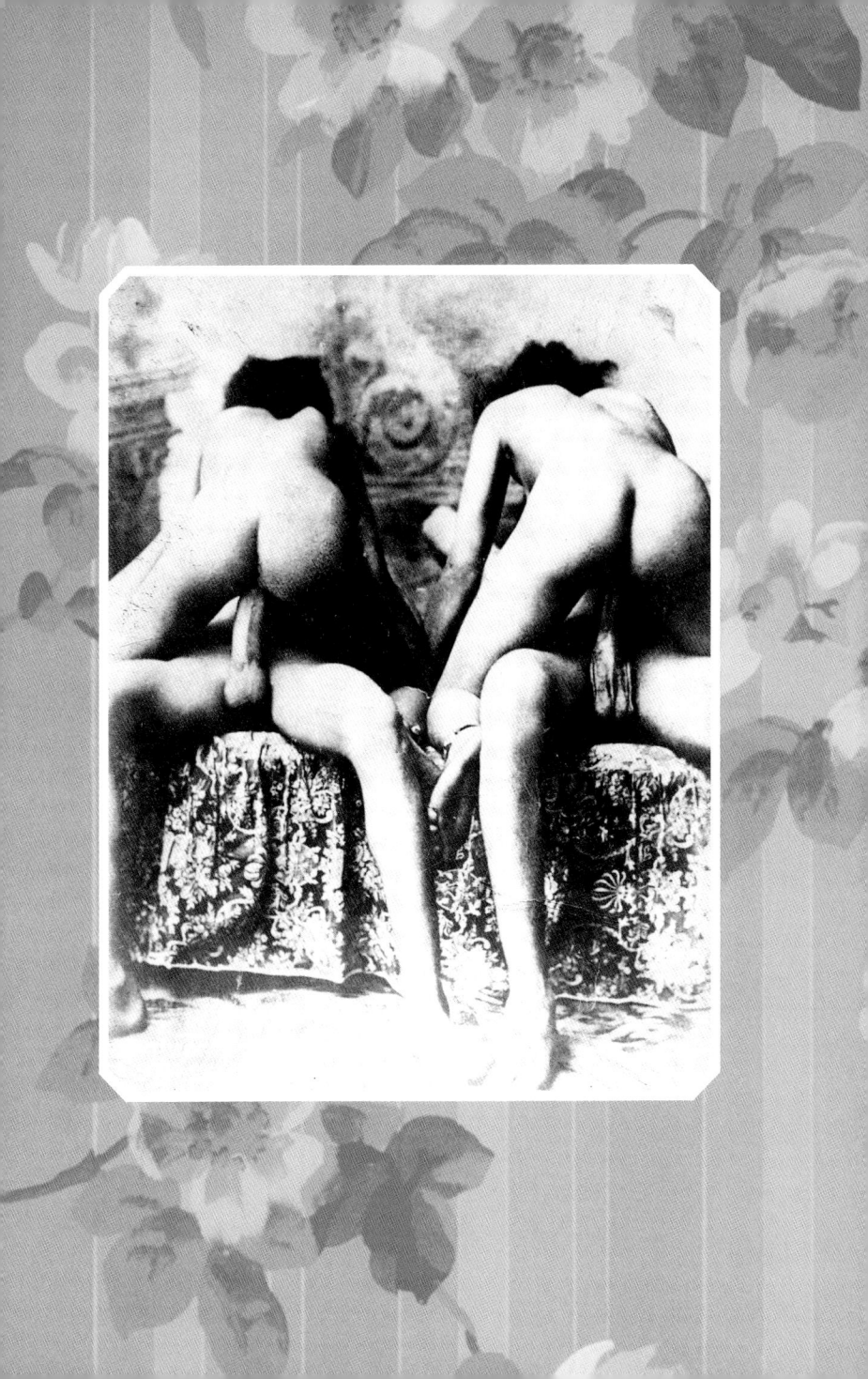

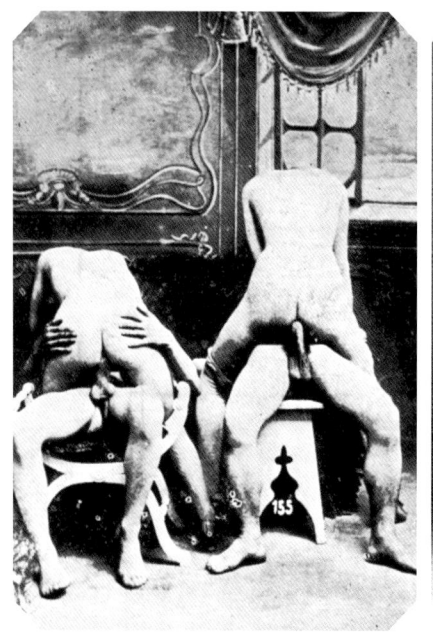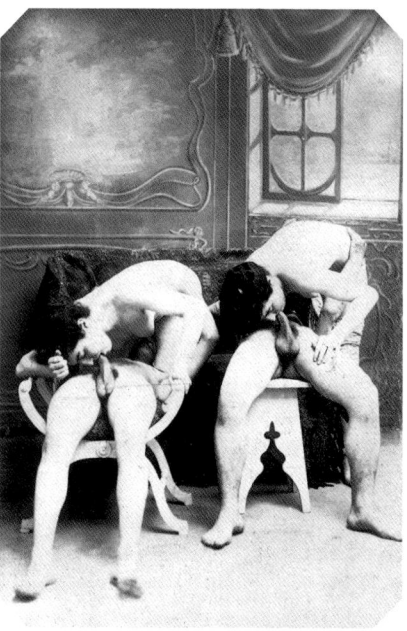

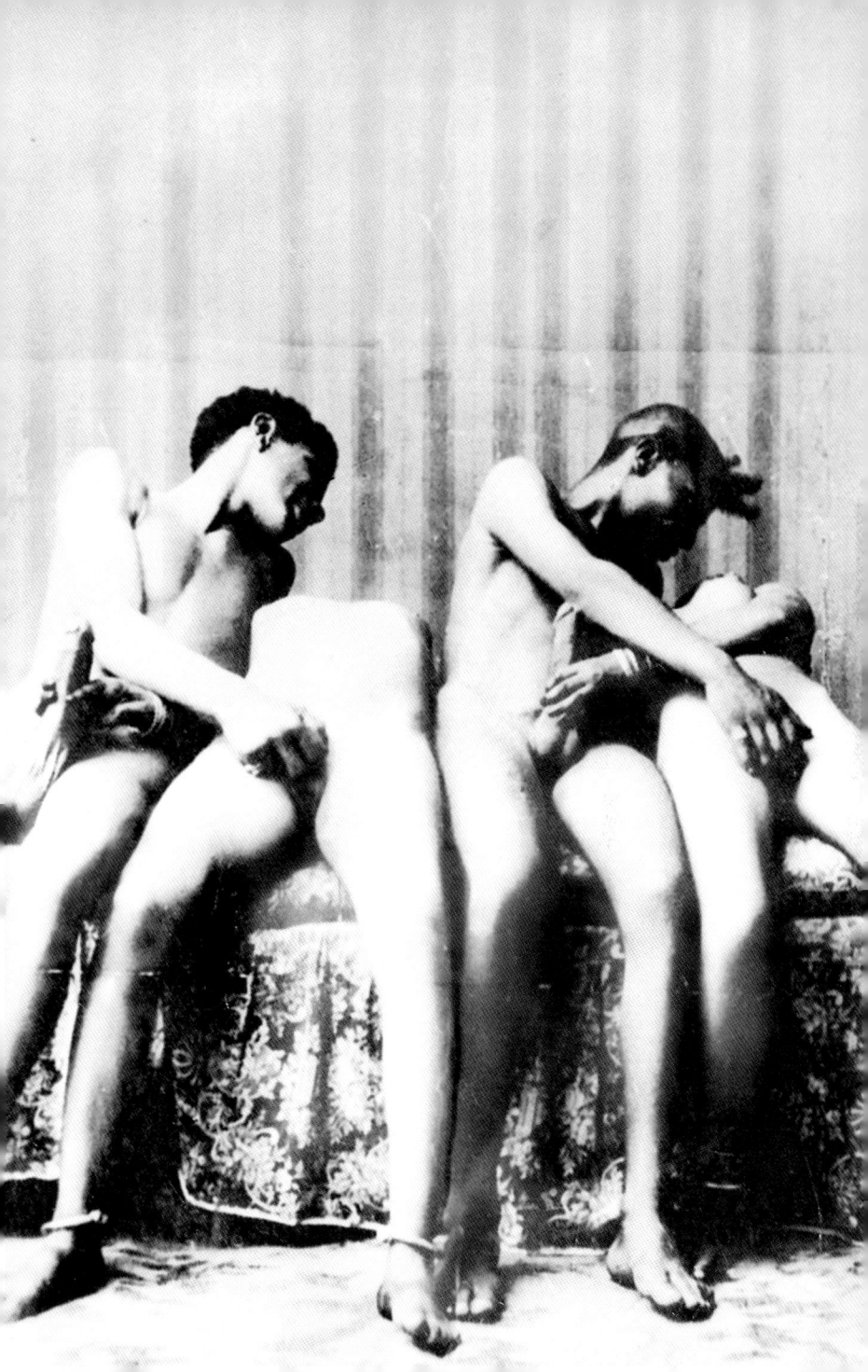

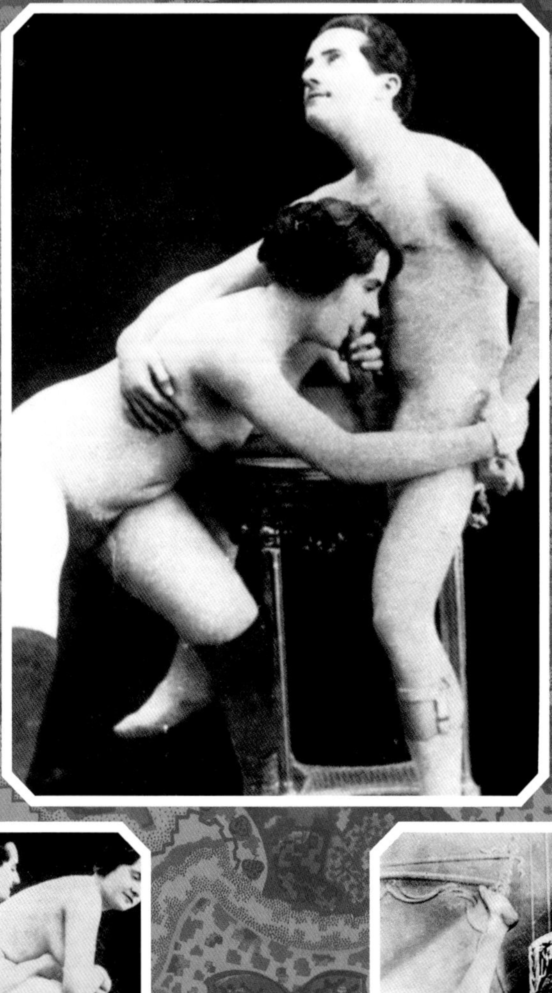

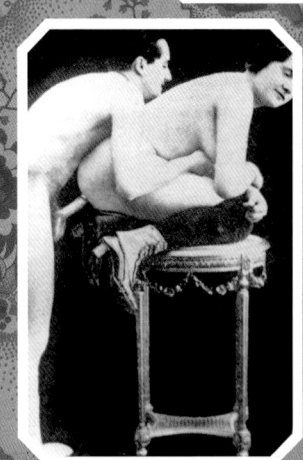
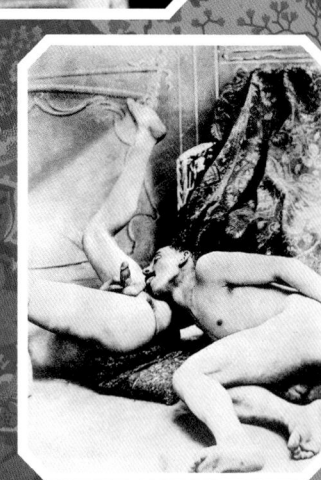

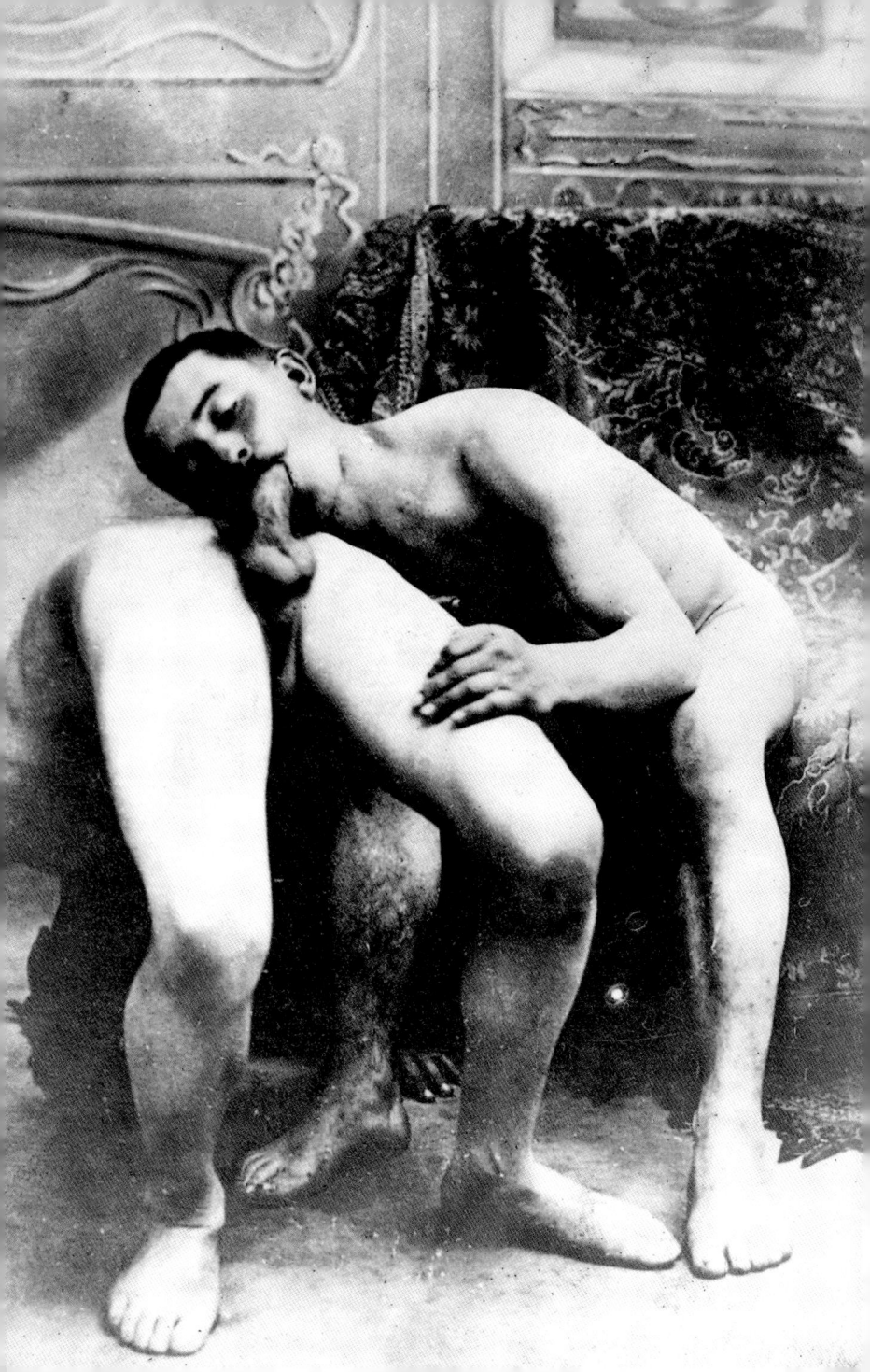

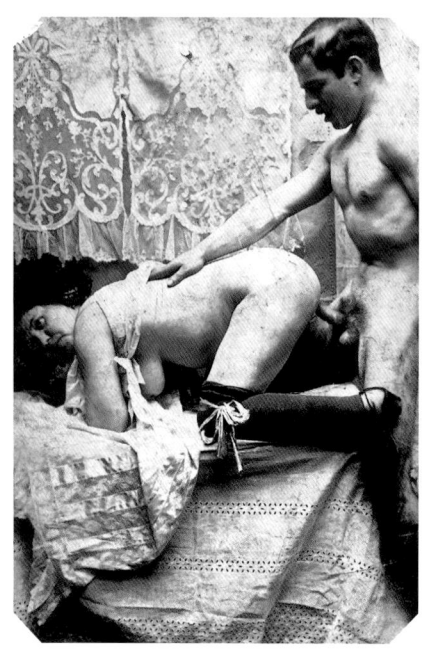

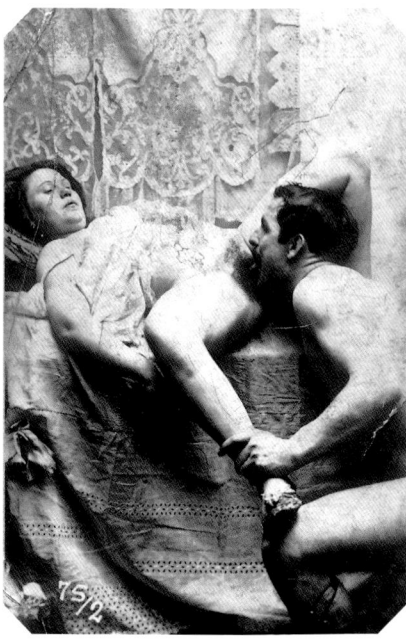

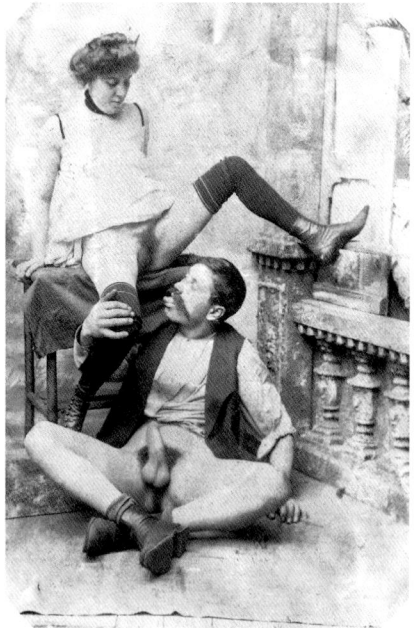

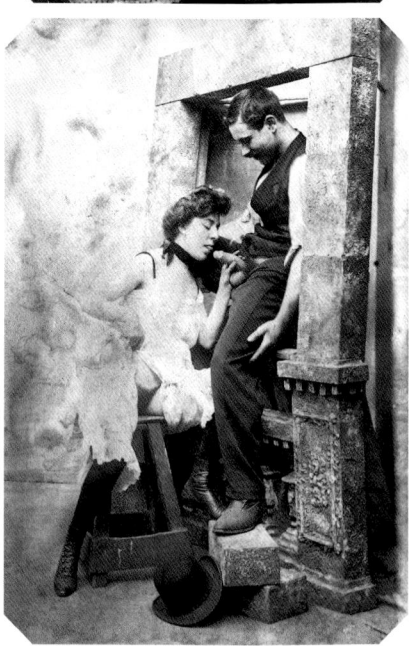

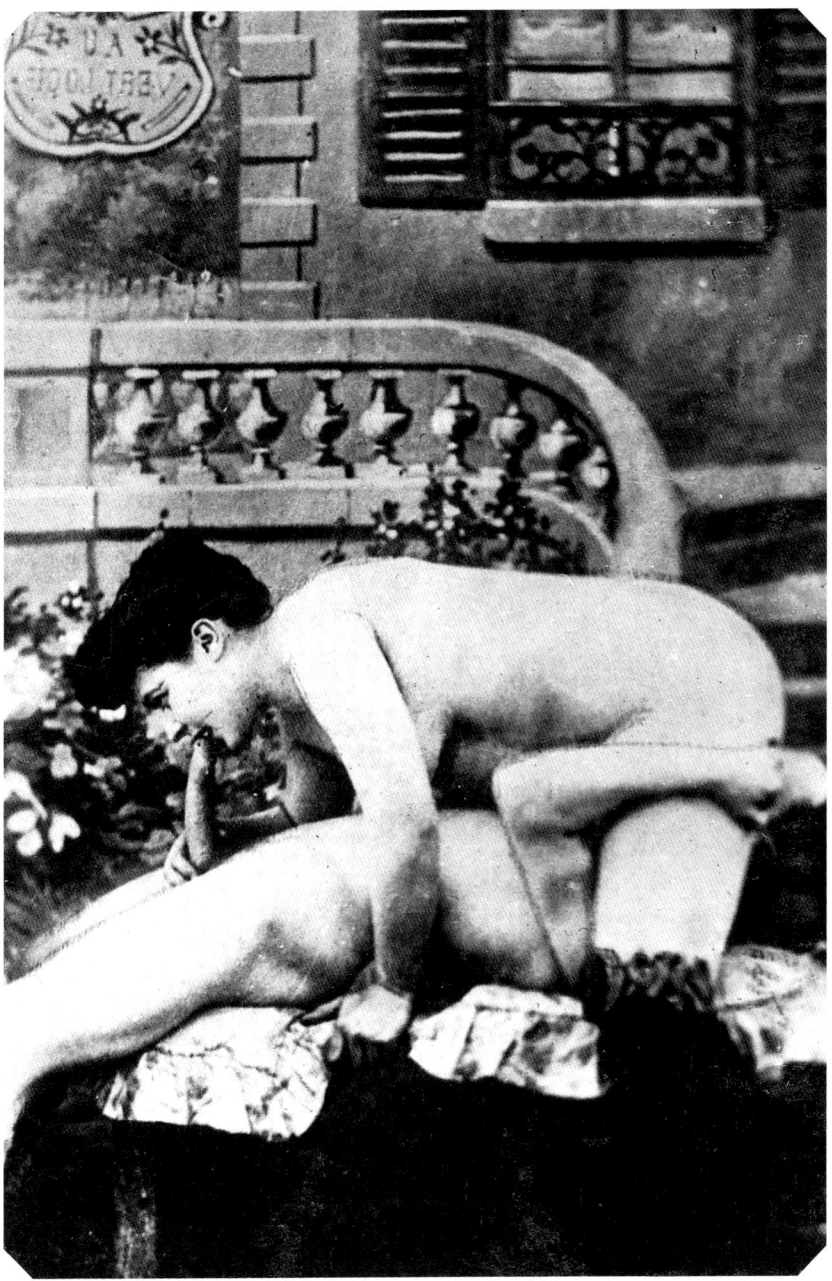

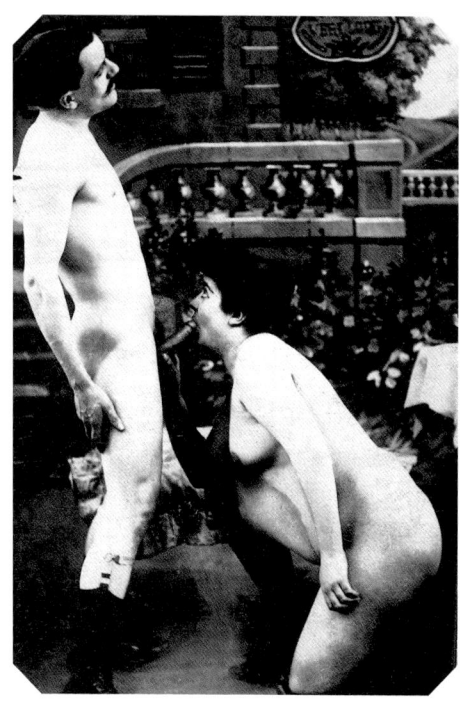
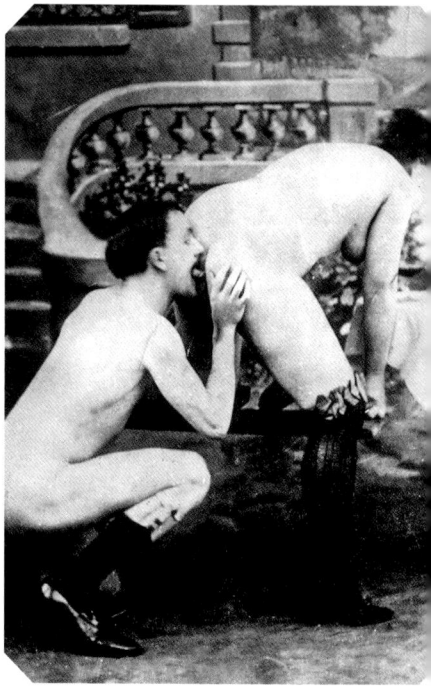

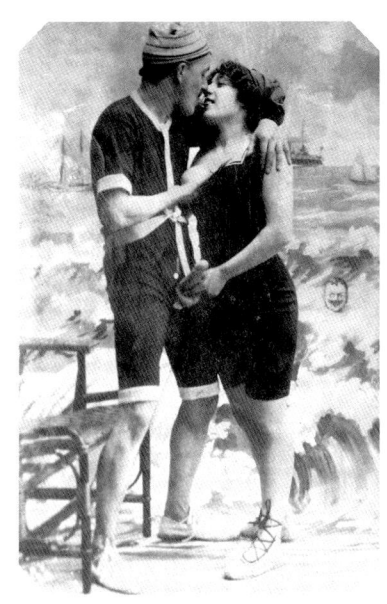

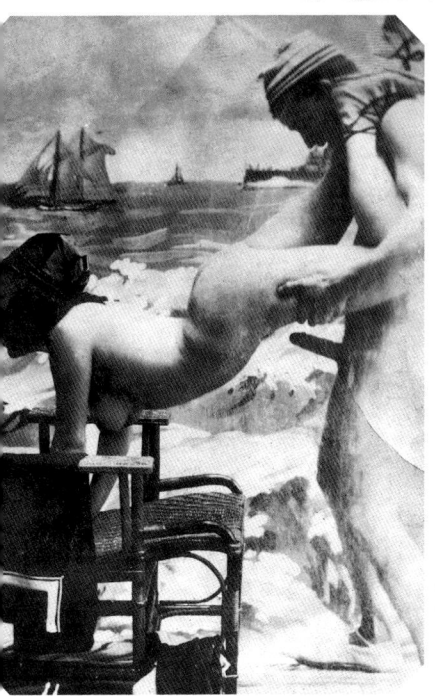

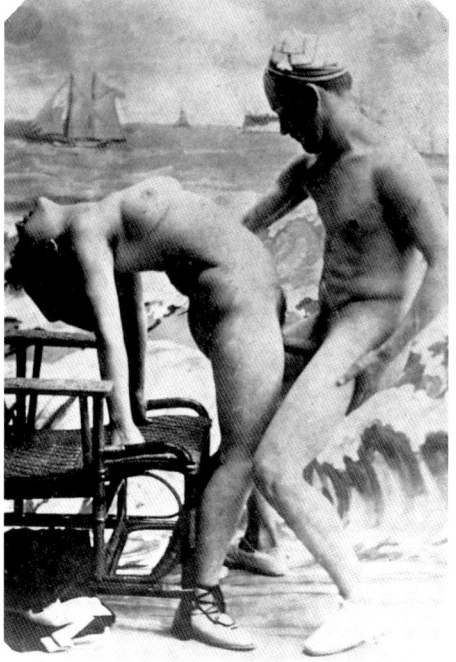

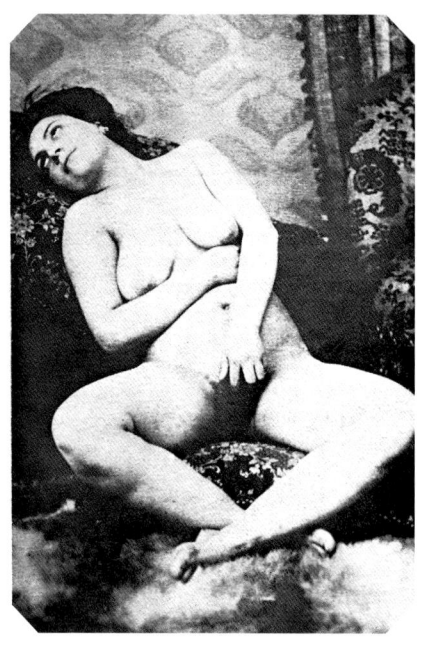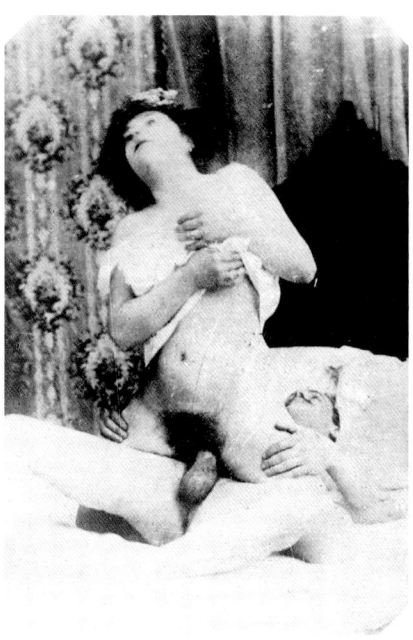

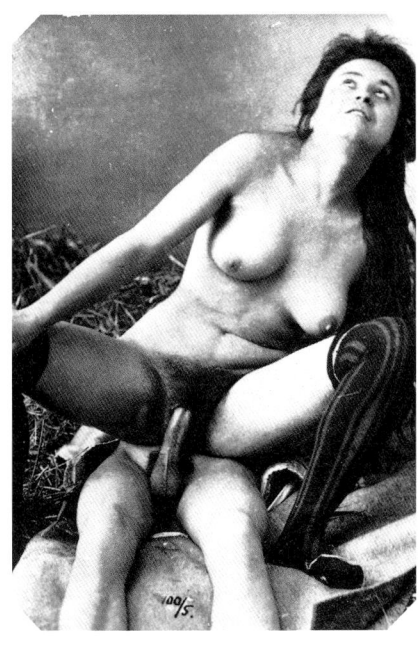 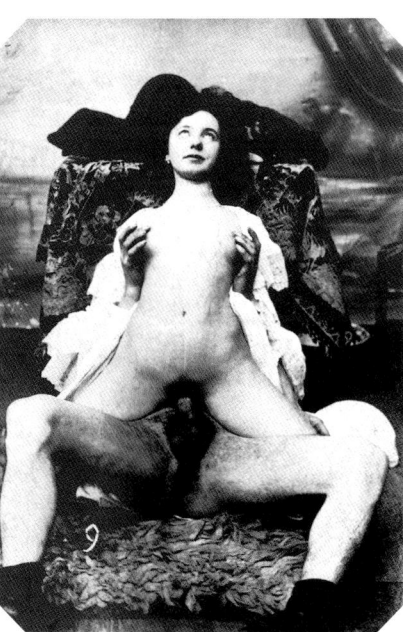

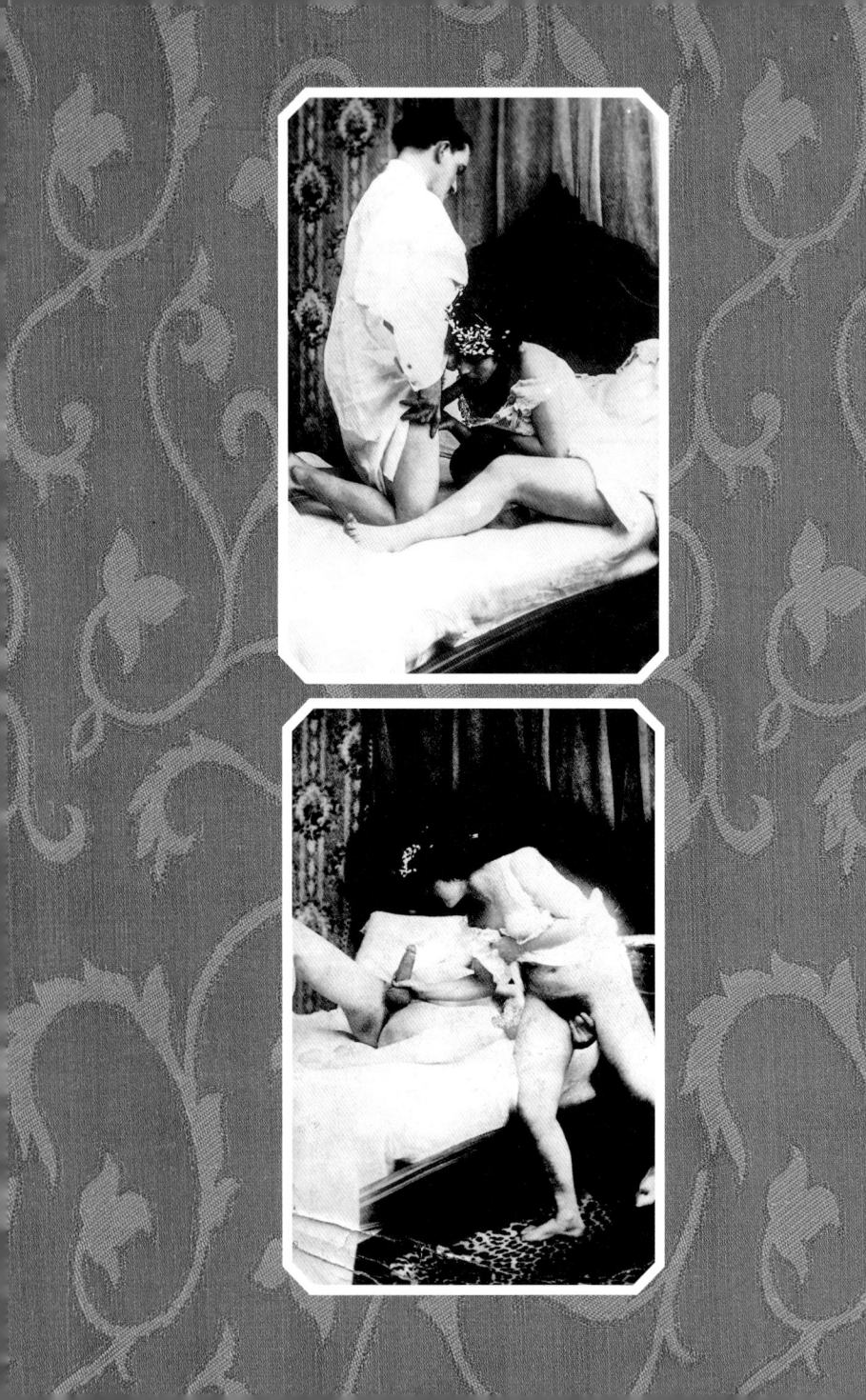

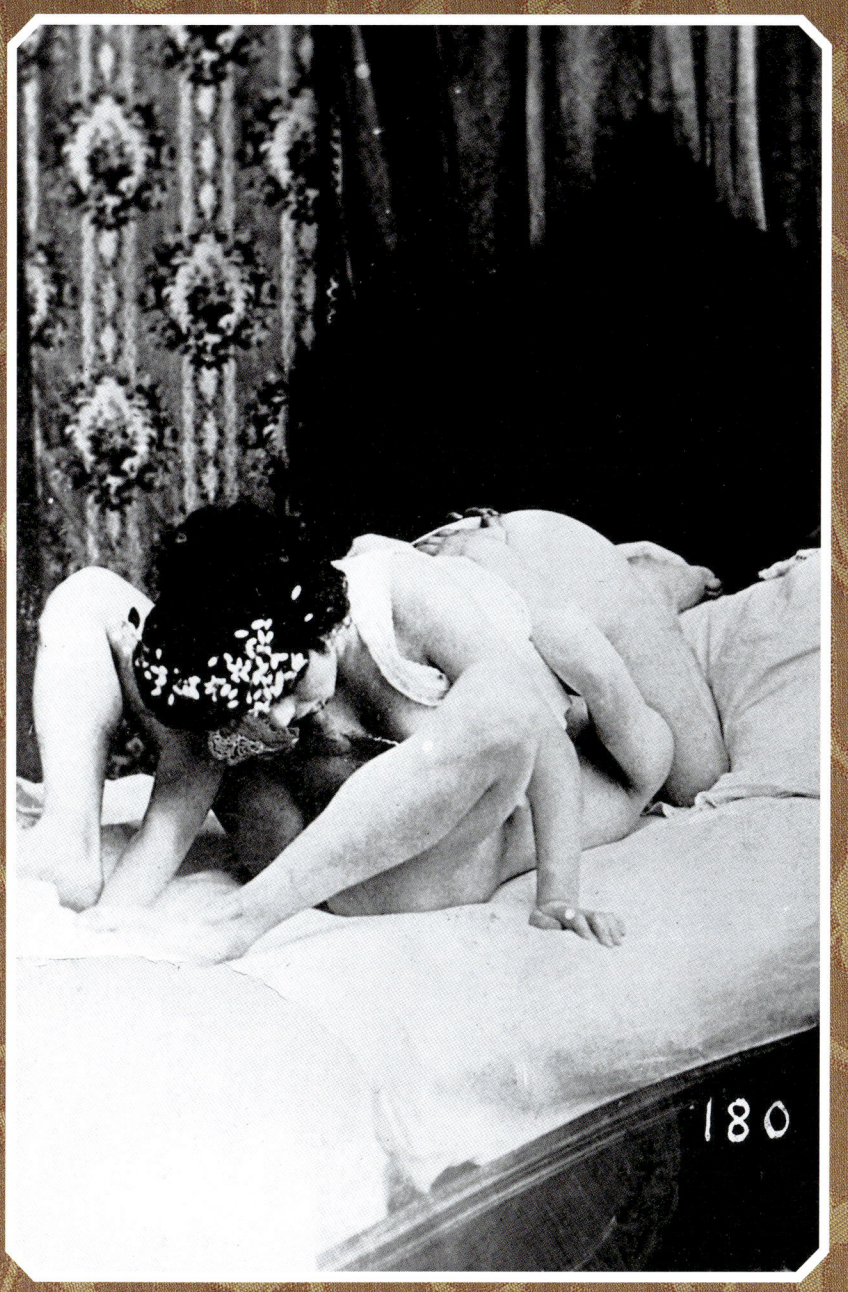

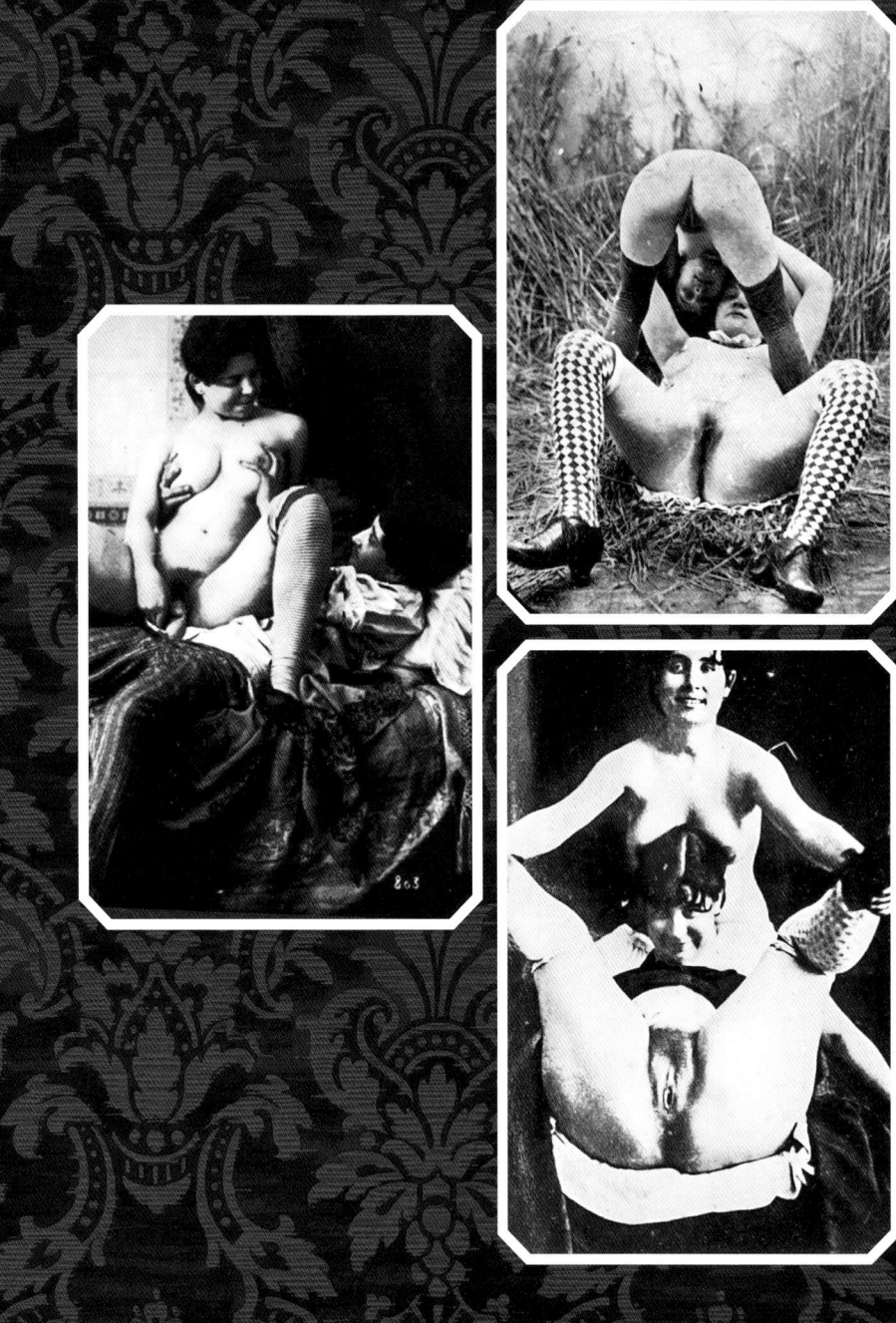

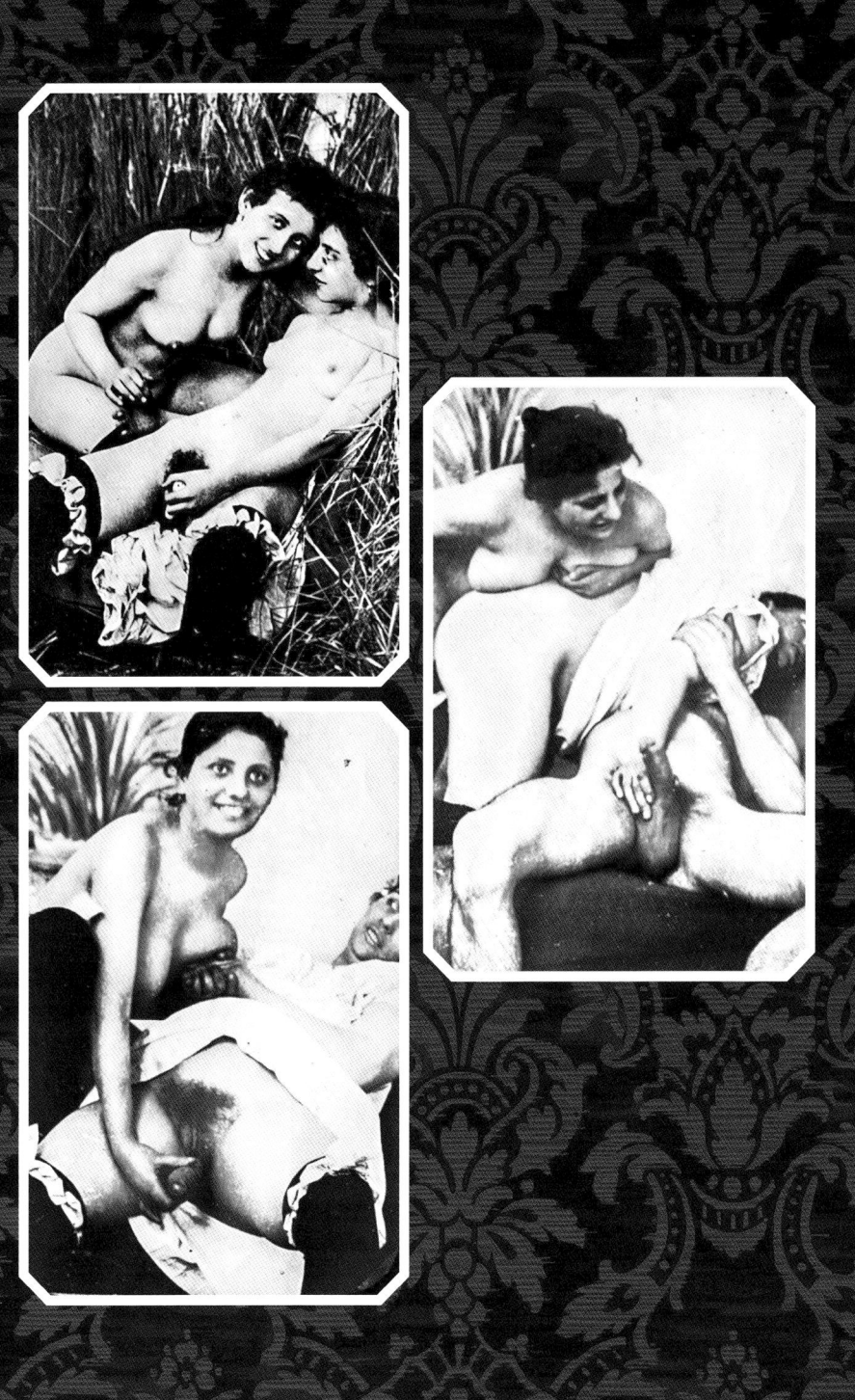

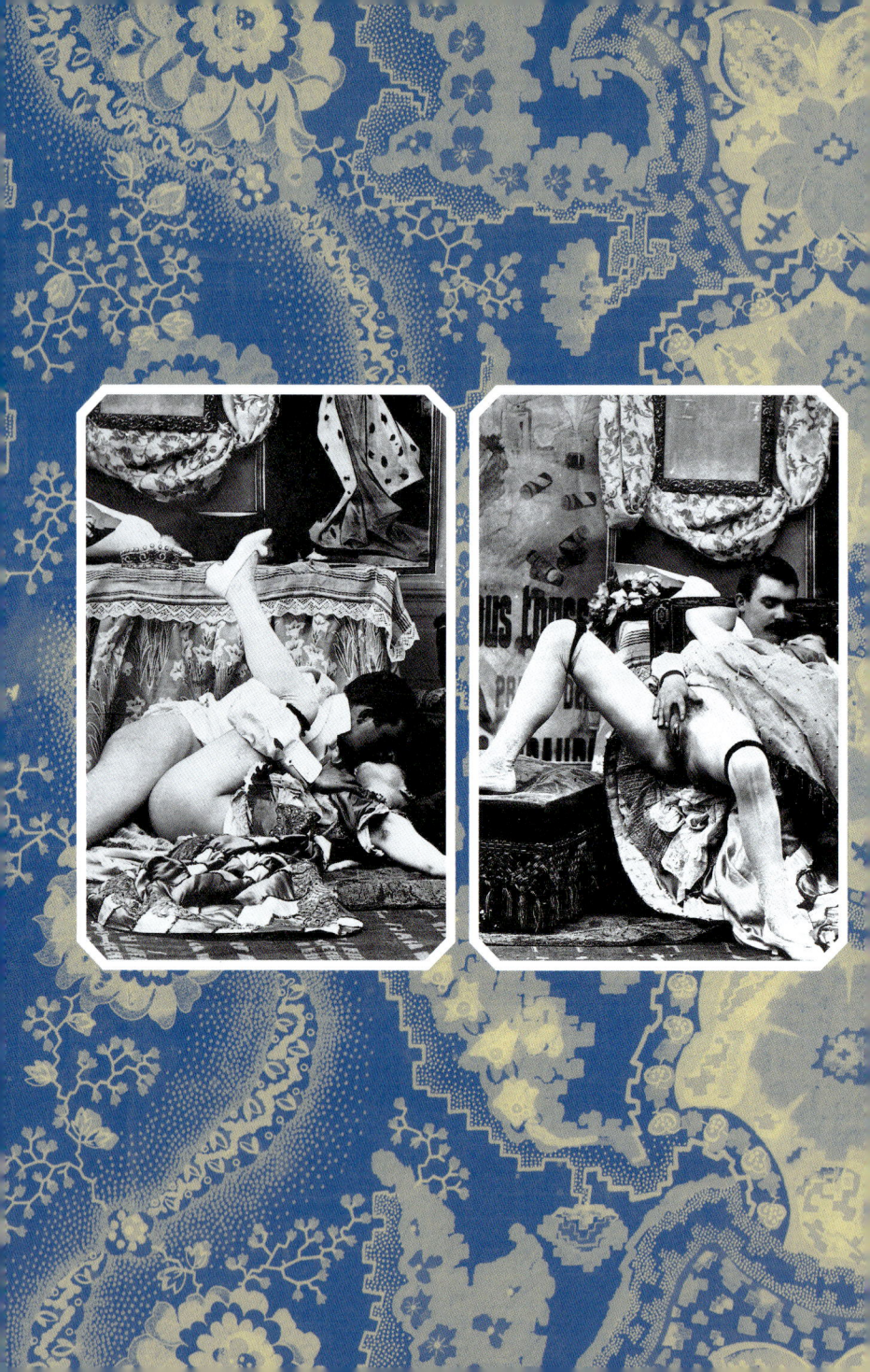

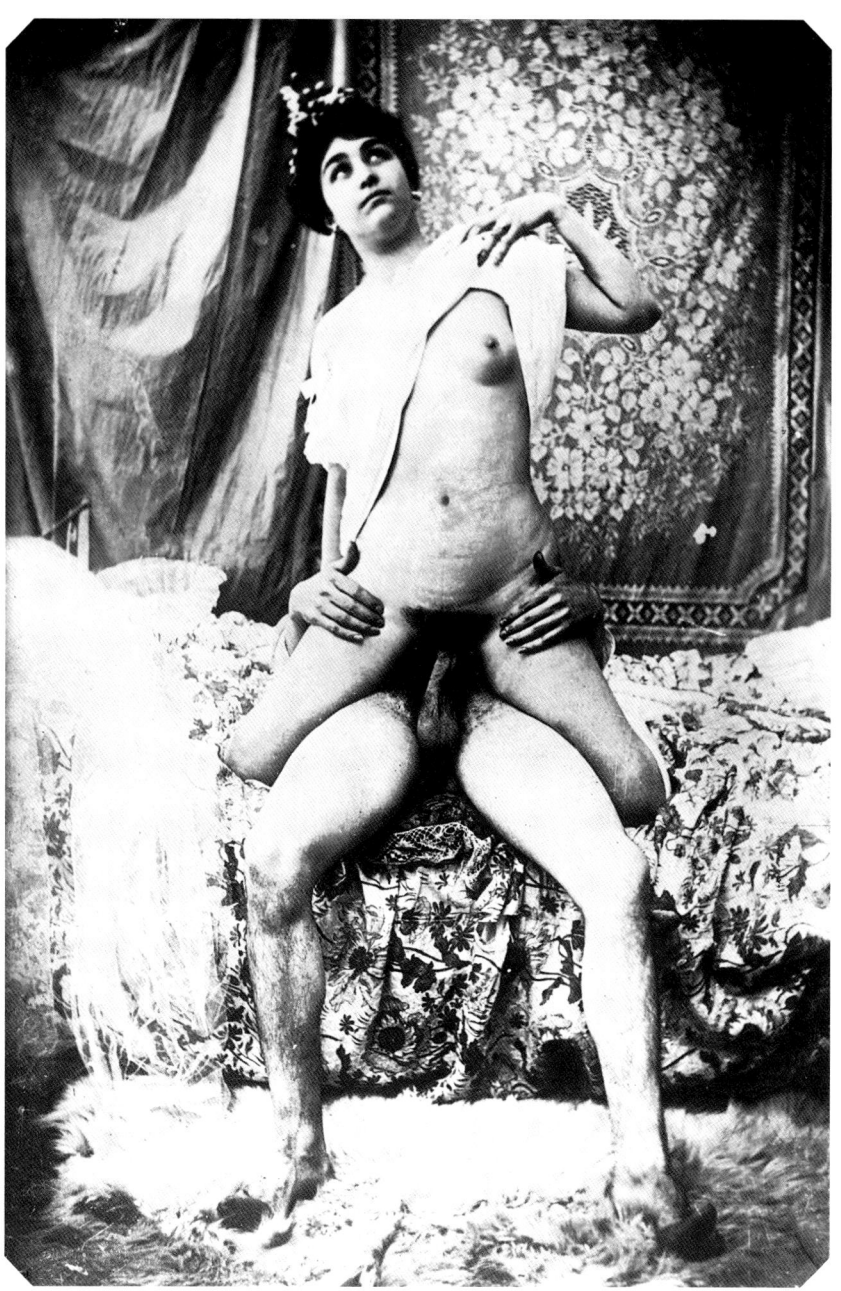

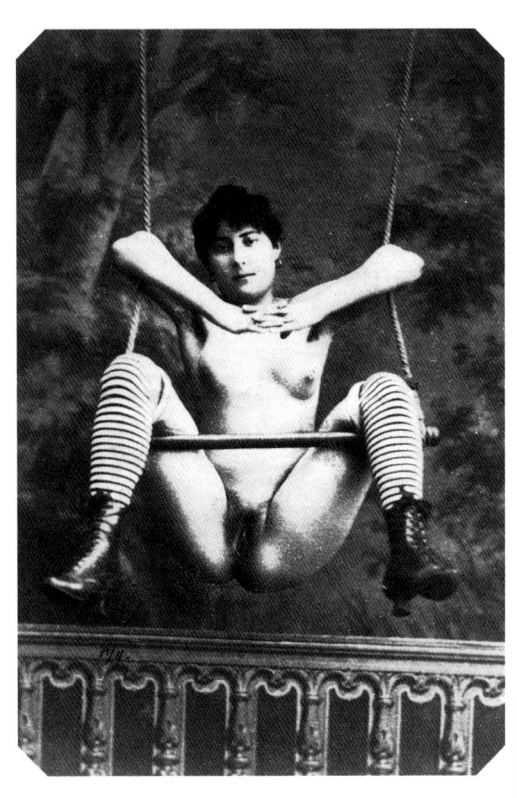

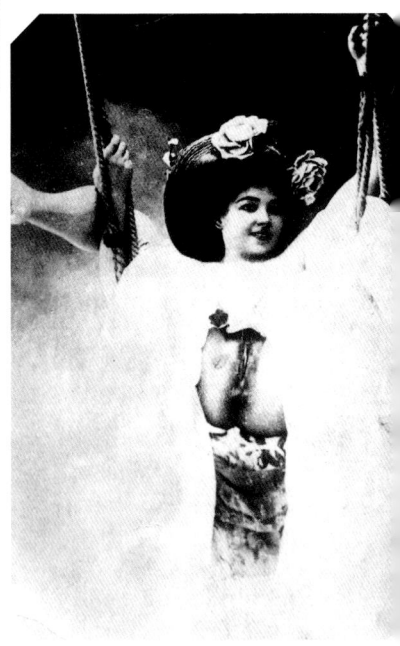

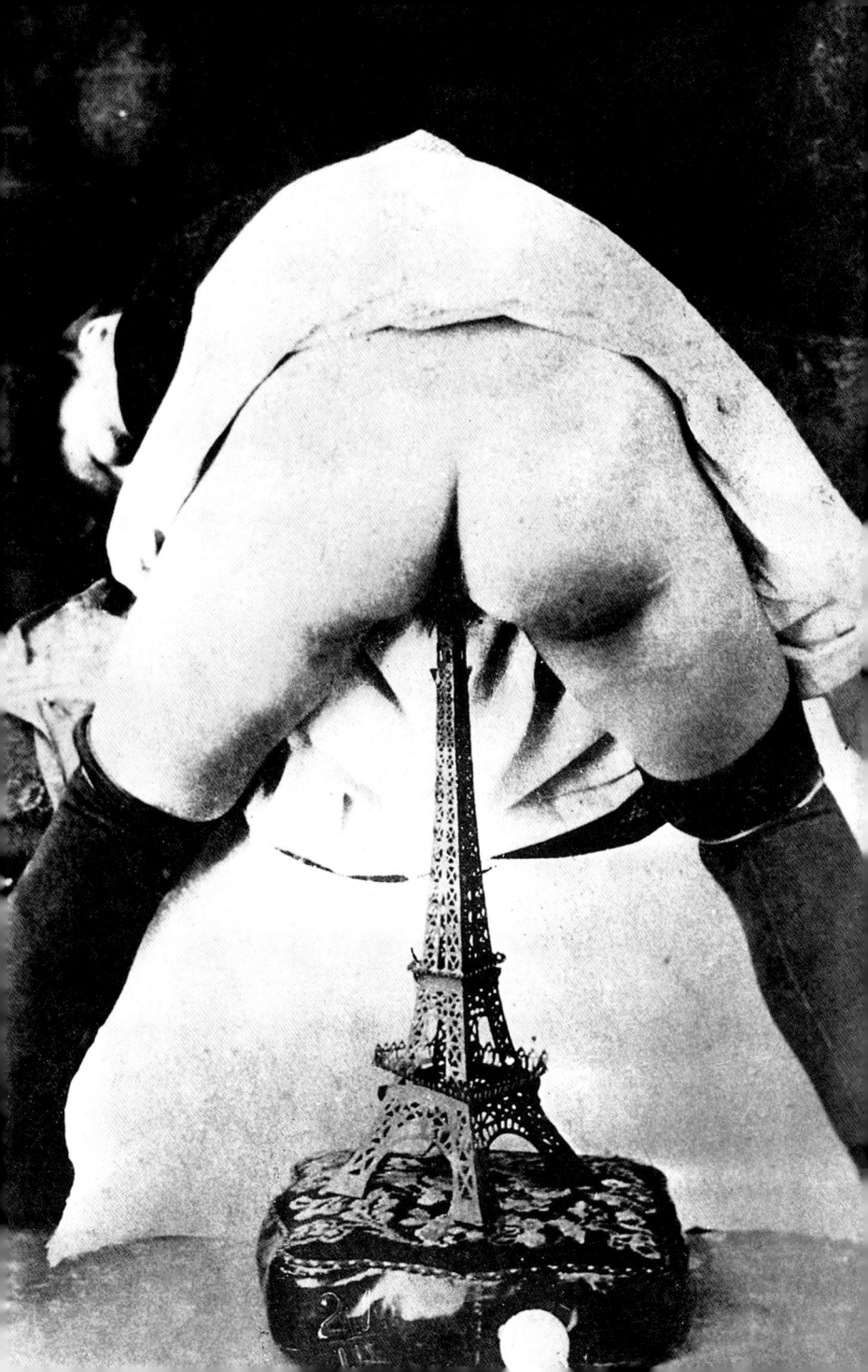

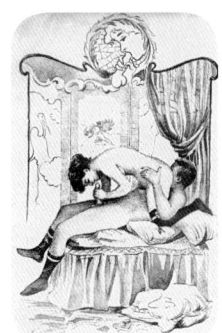

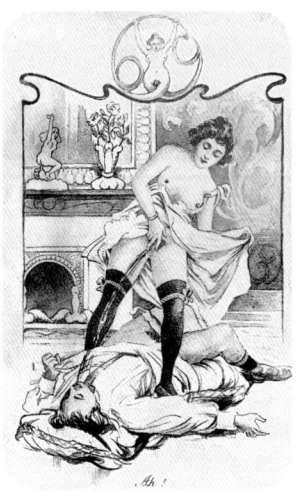

Ah !

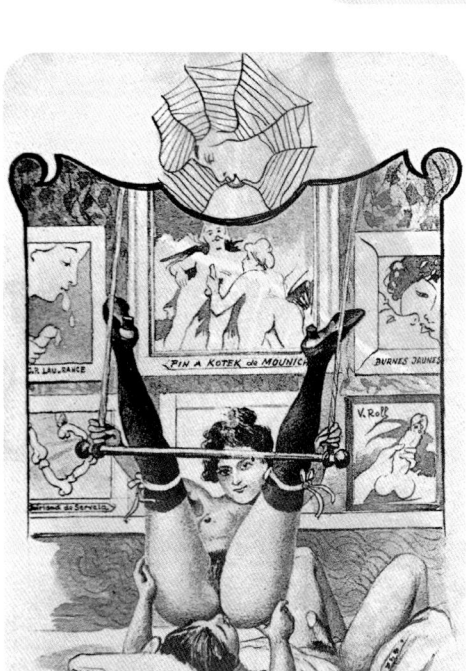

Fontaine

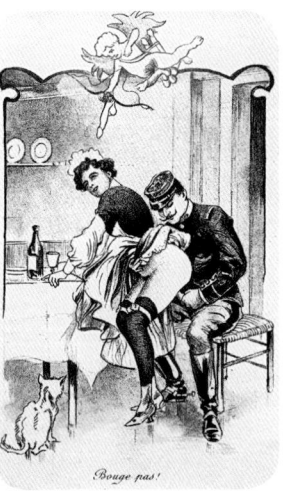

Bouge pas !

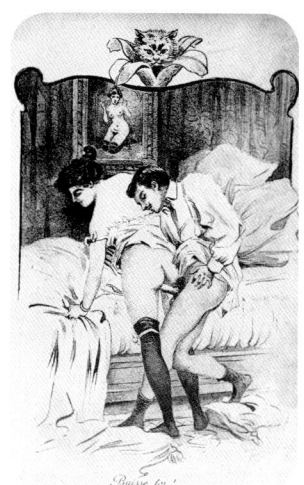

Baisse toi

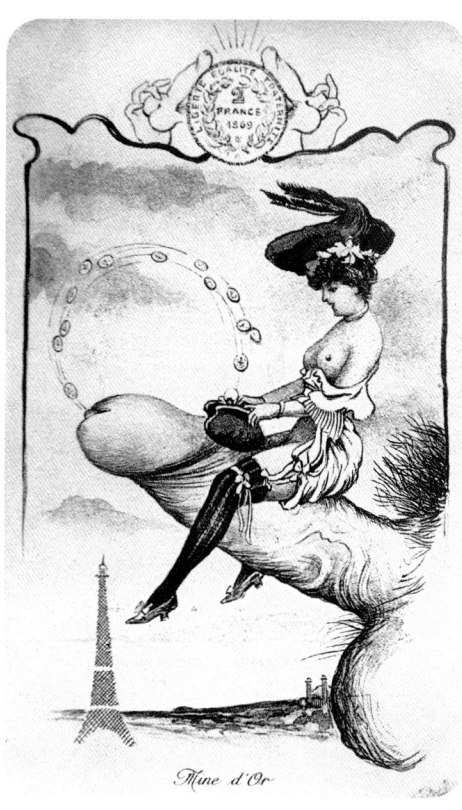

Mine d'Or

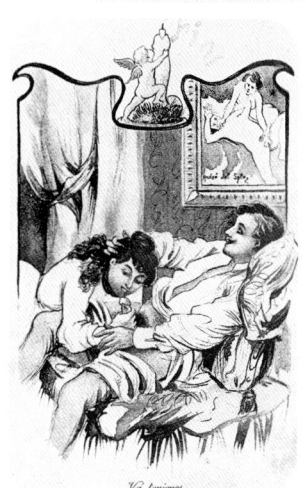

Va toujours

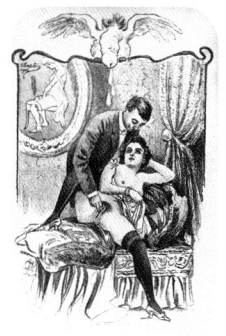

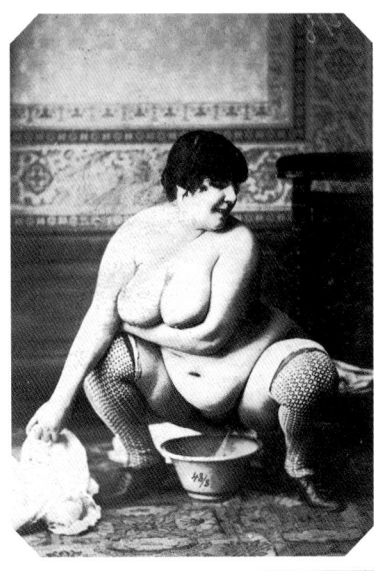

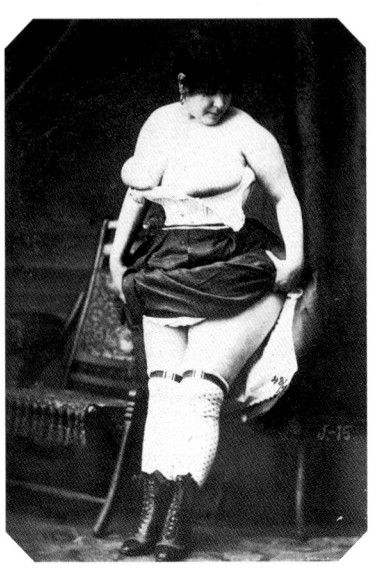

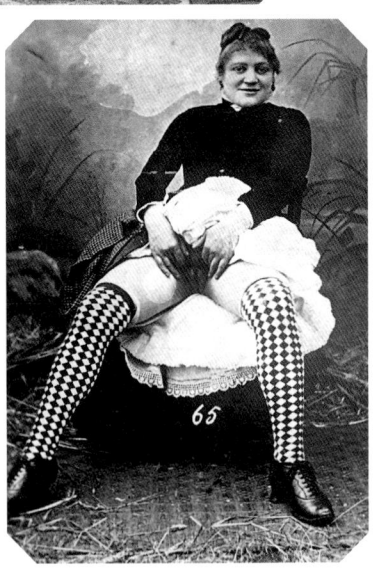

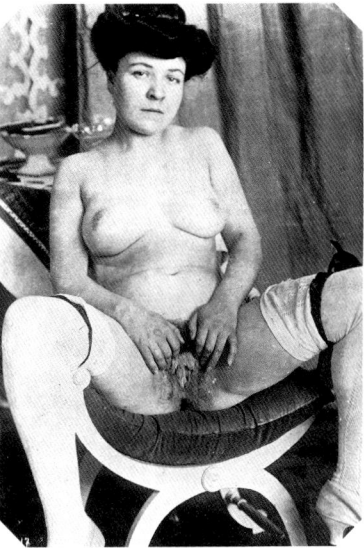

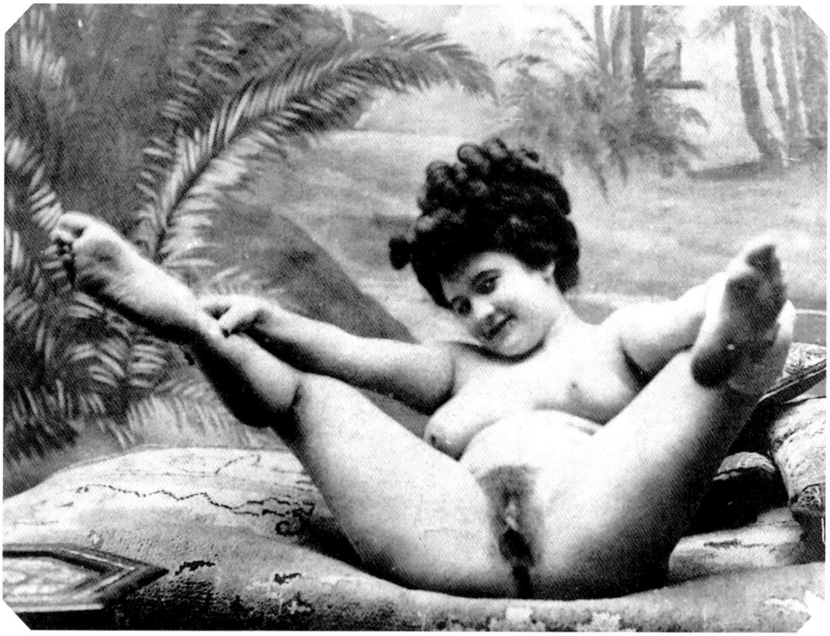

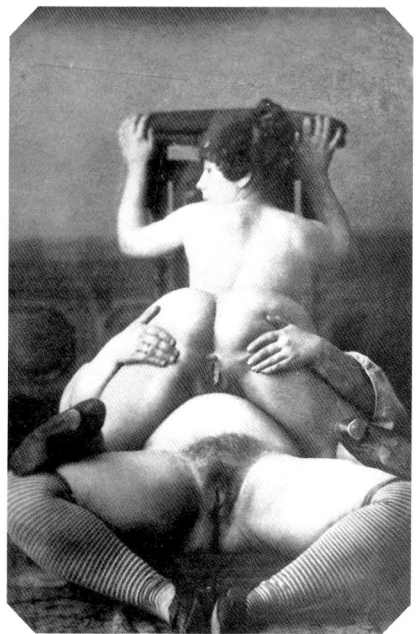
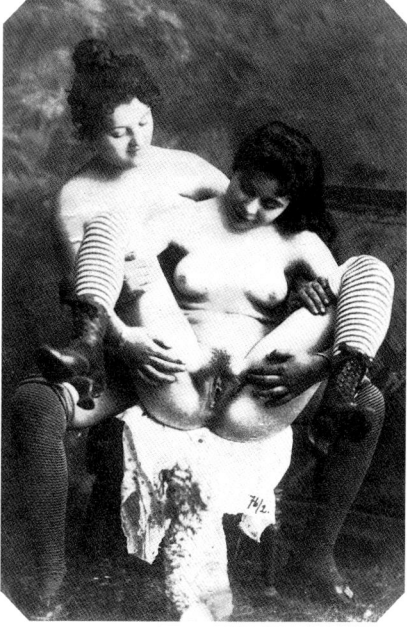

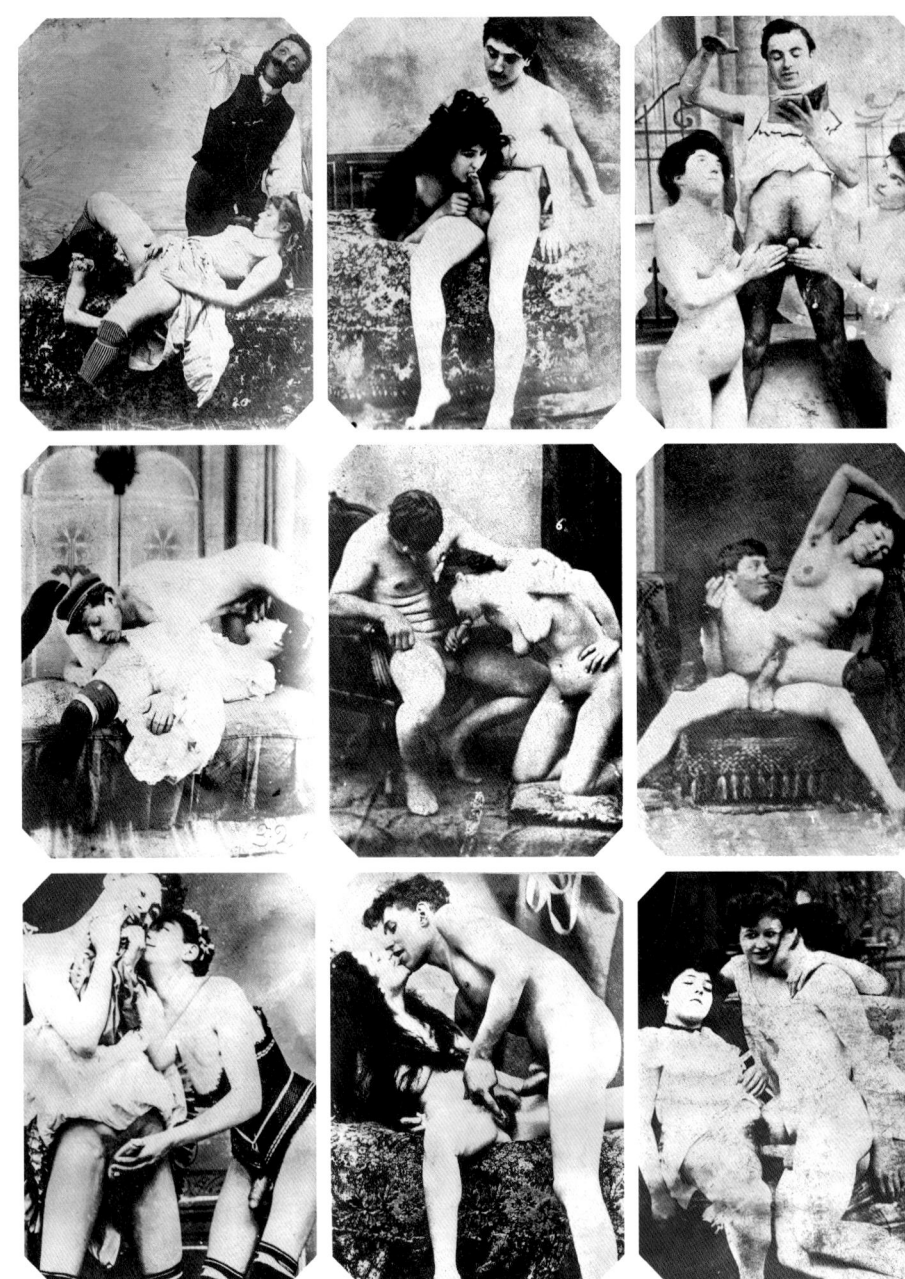

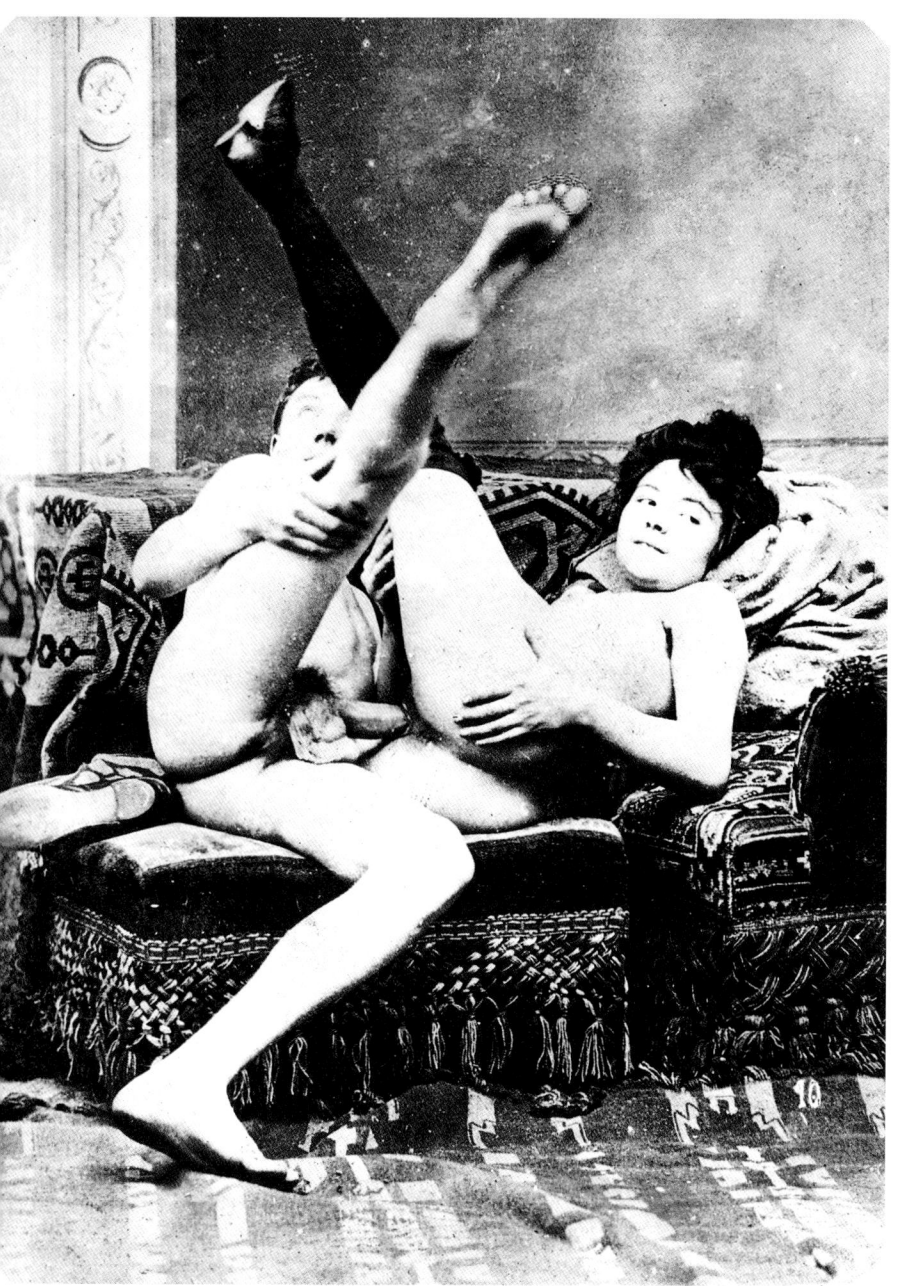

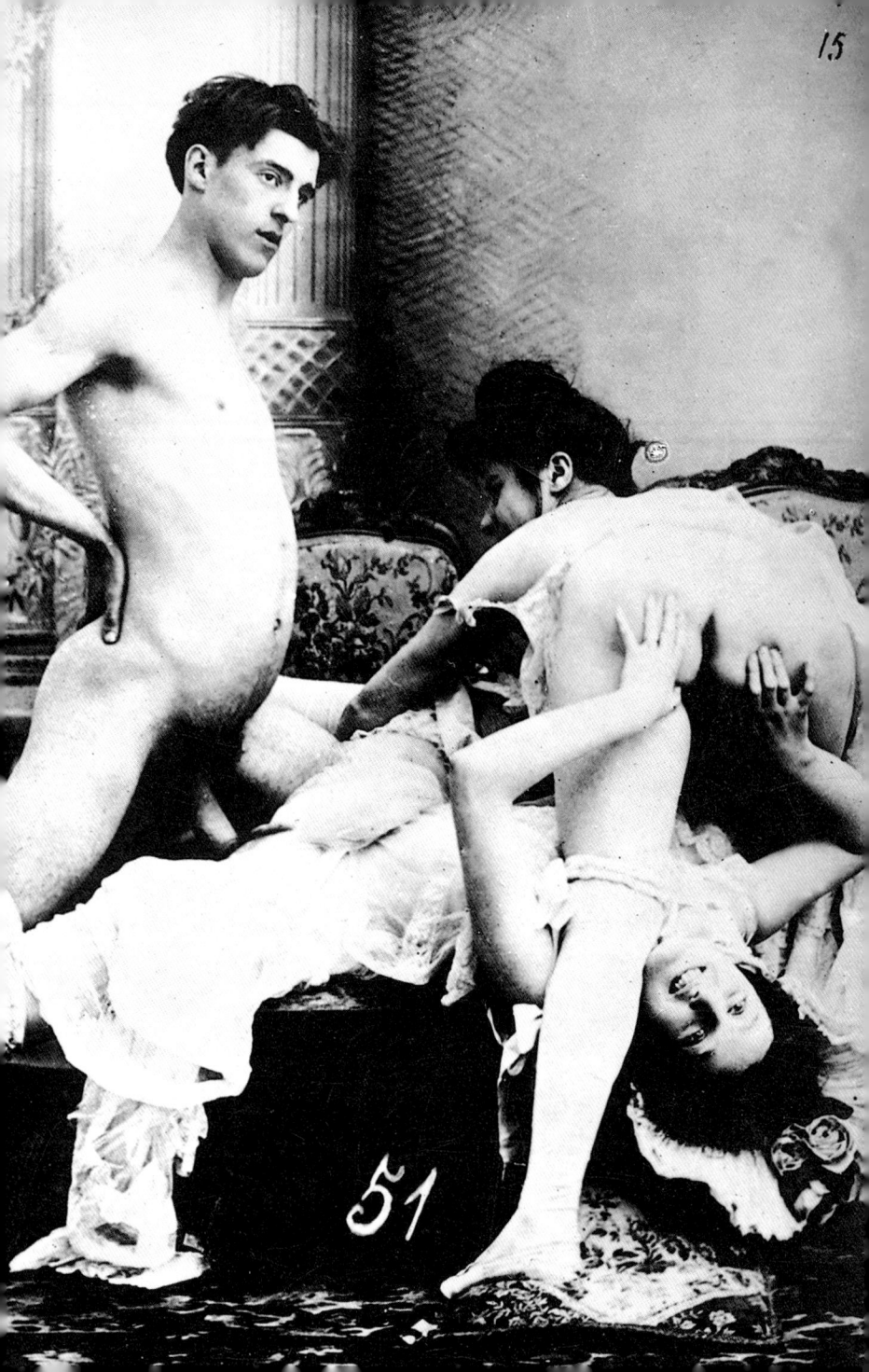

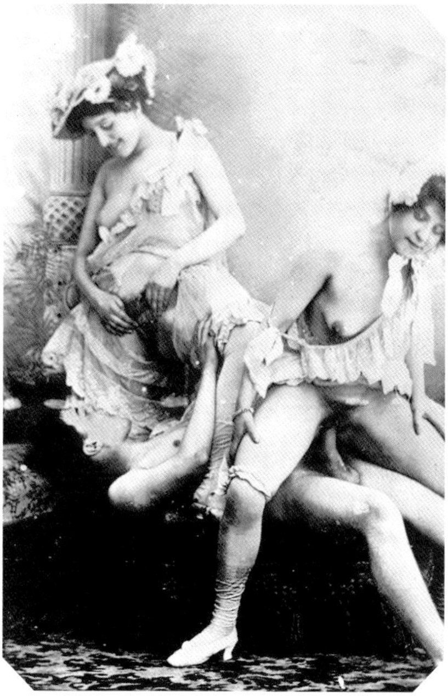

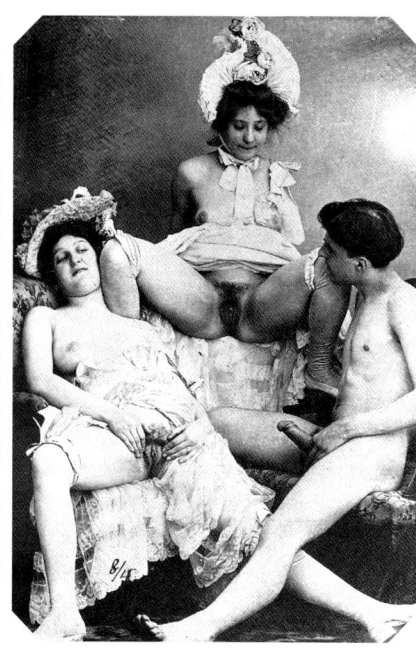

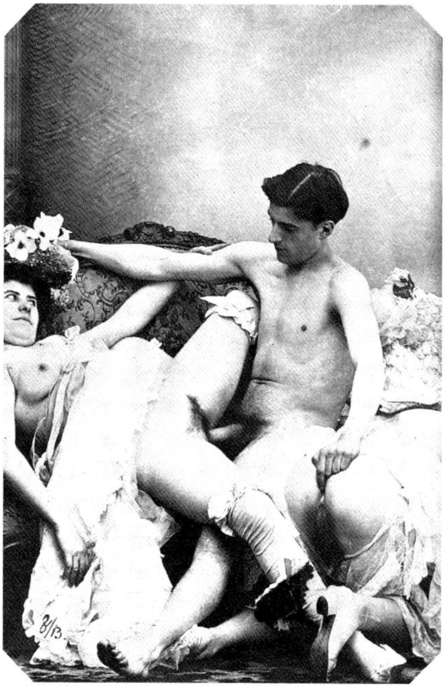

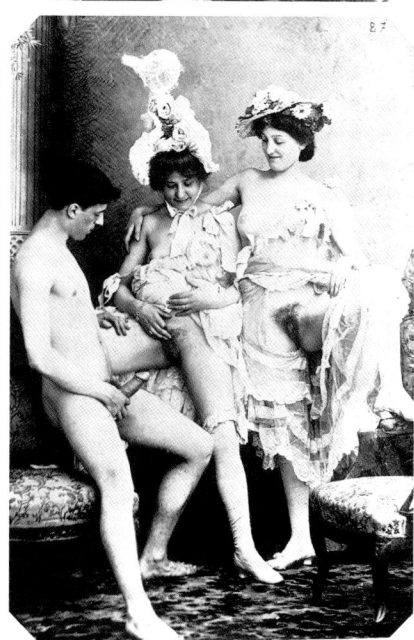

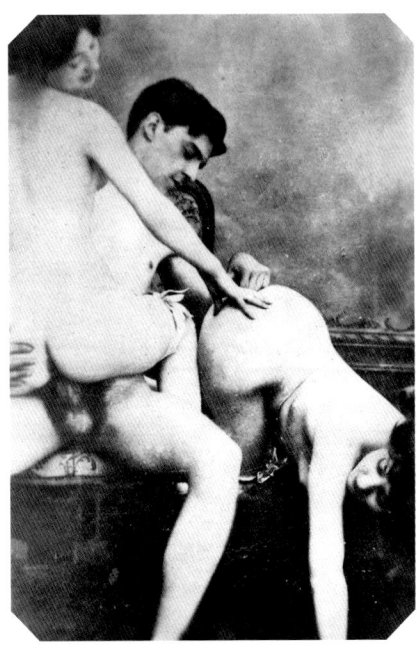

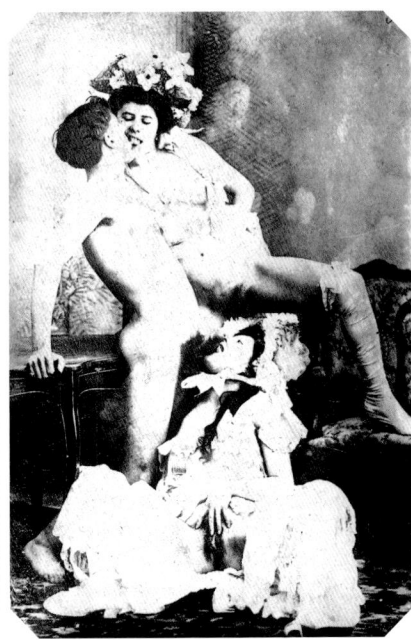

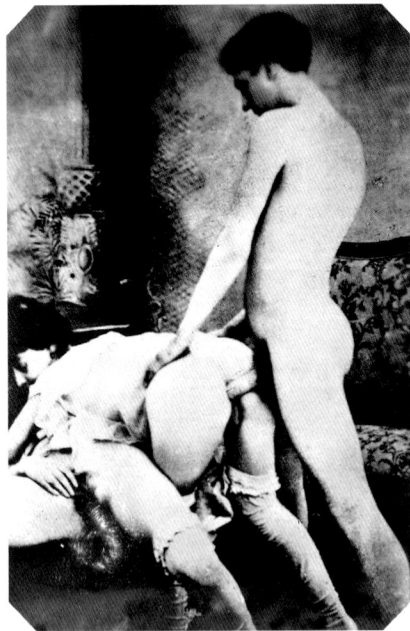

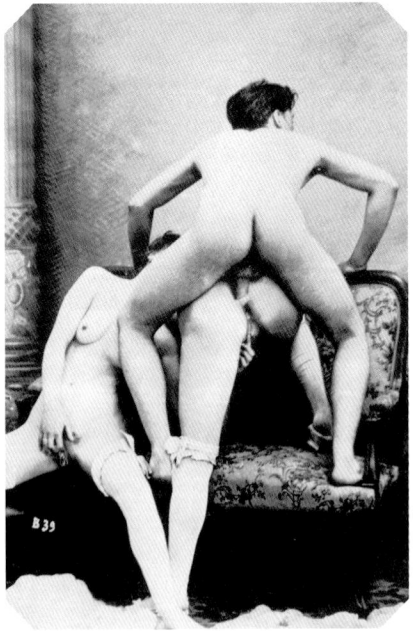

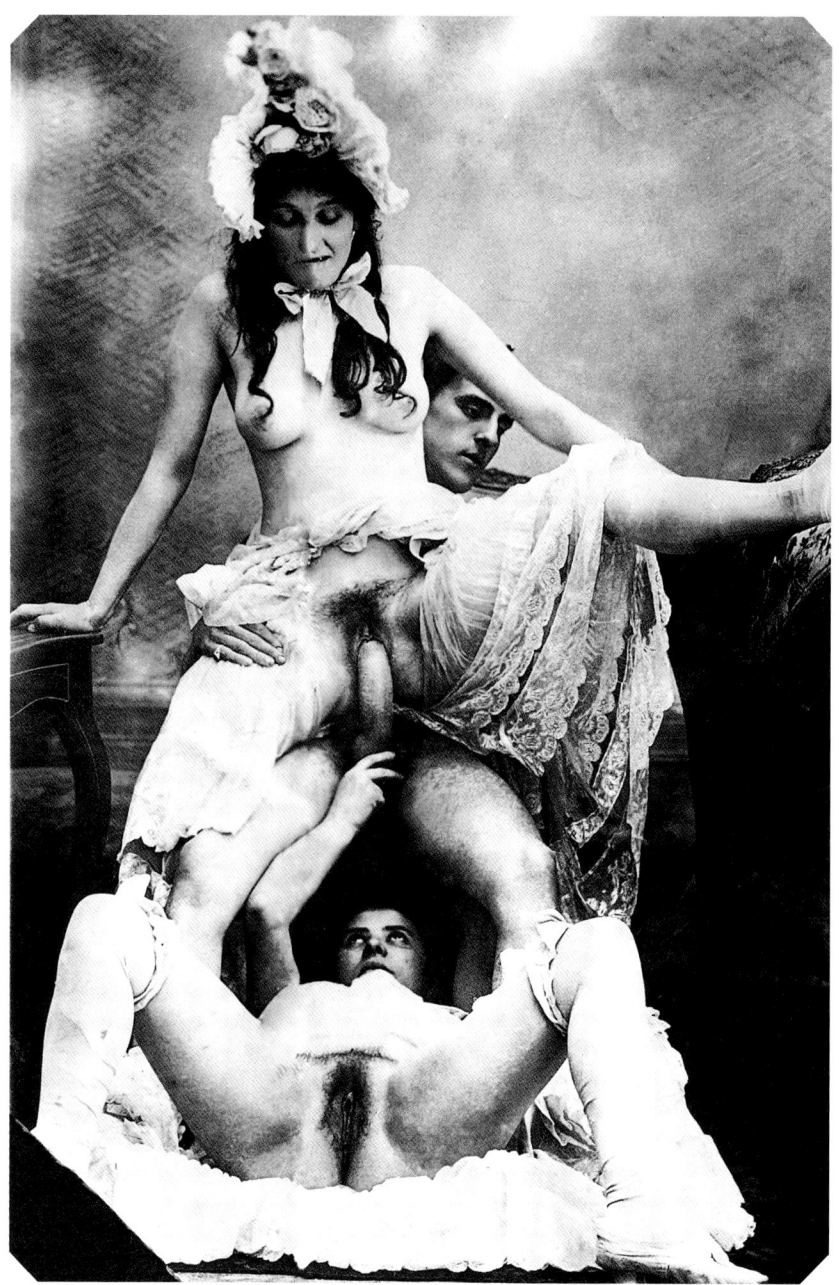

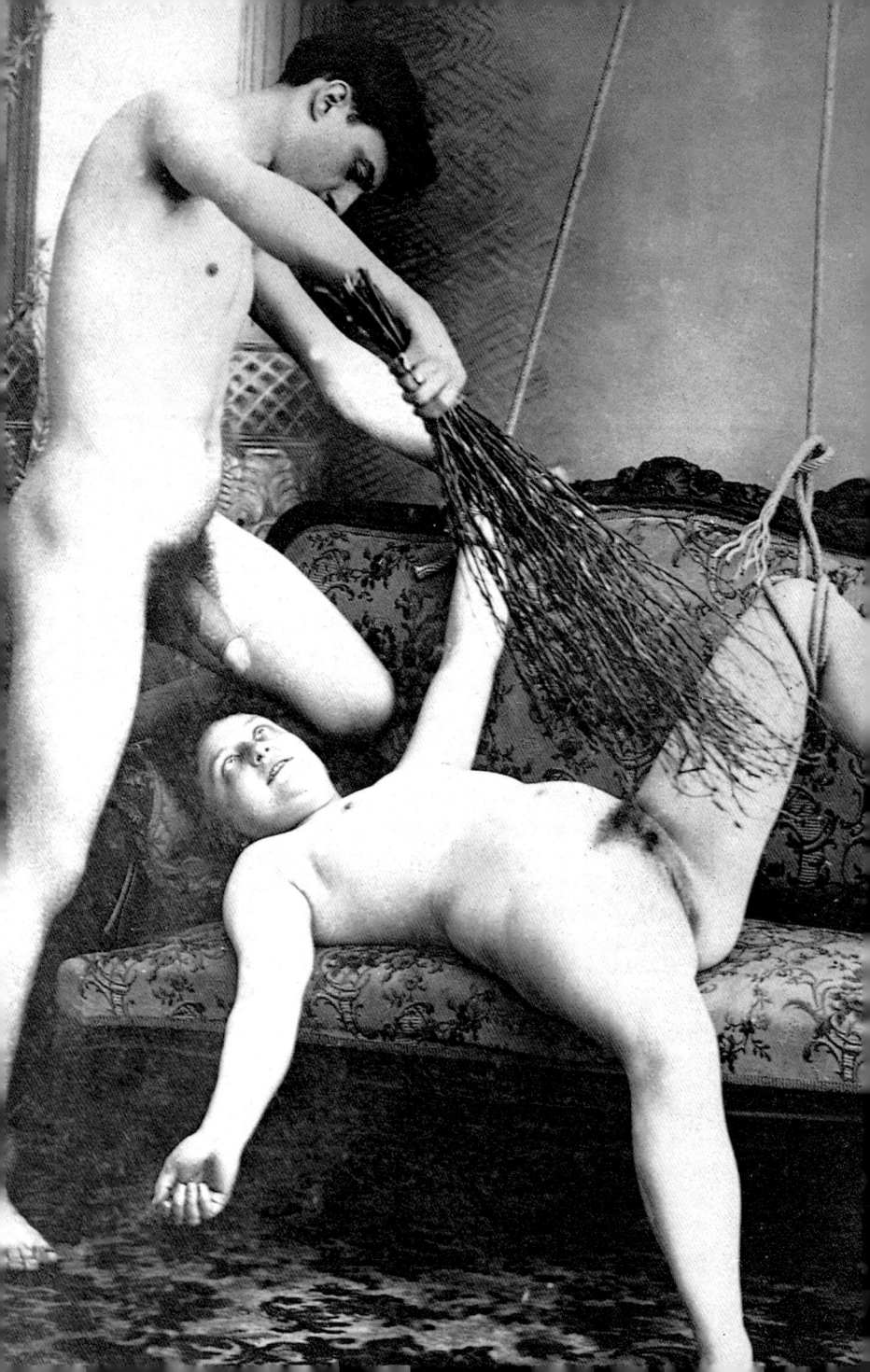

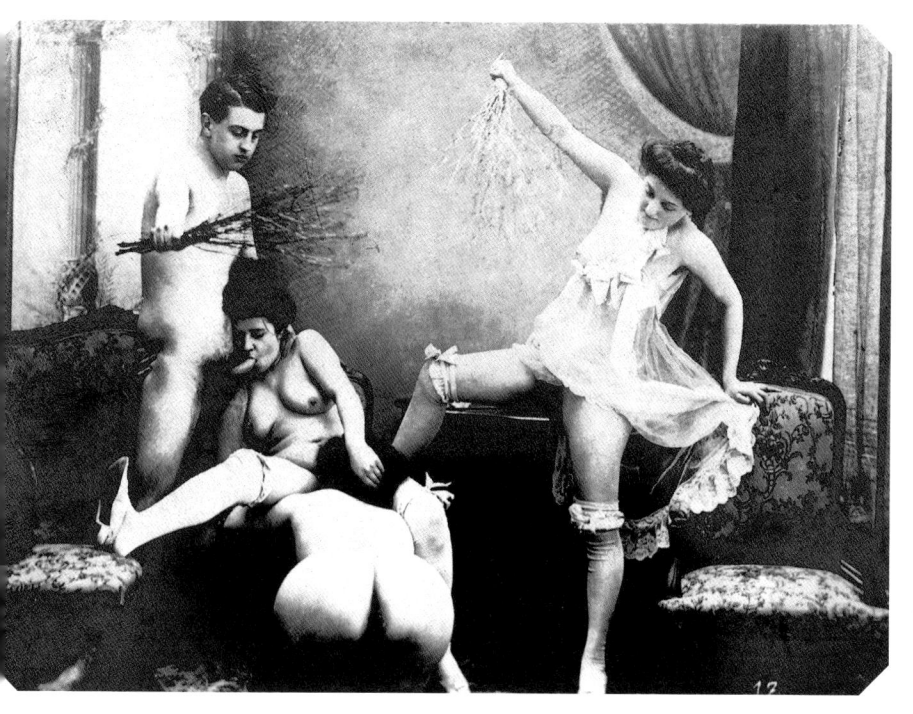

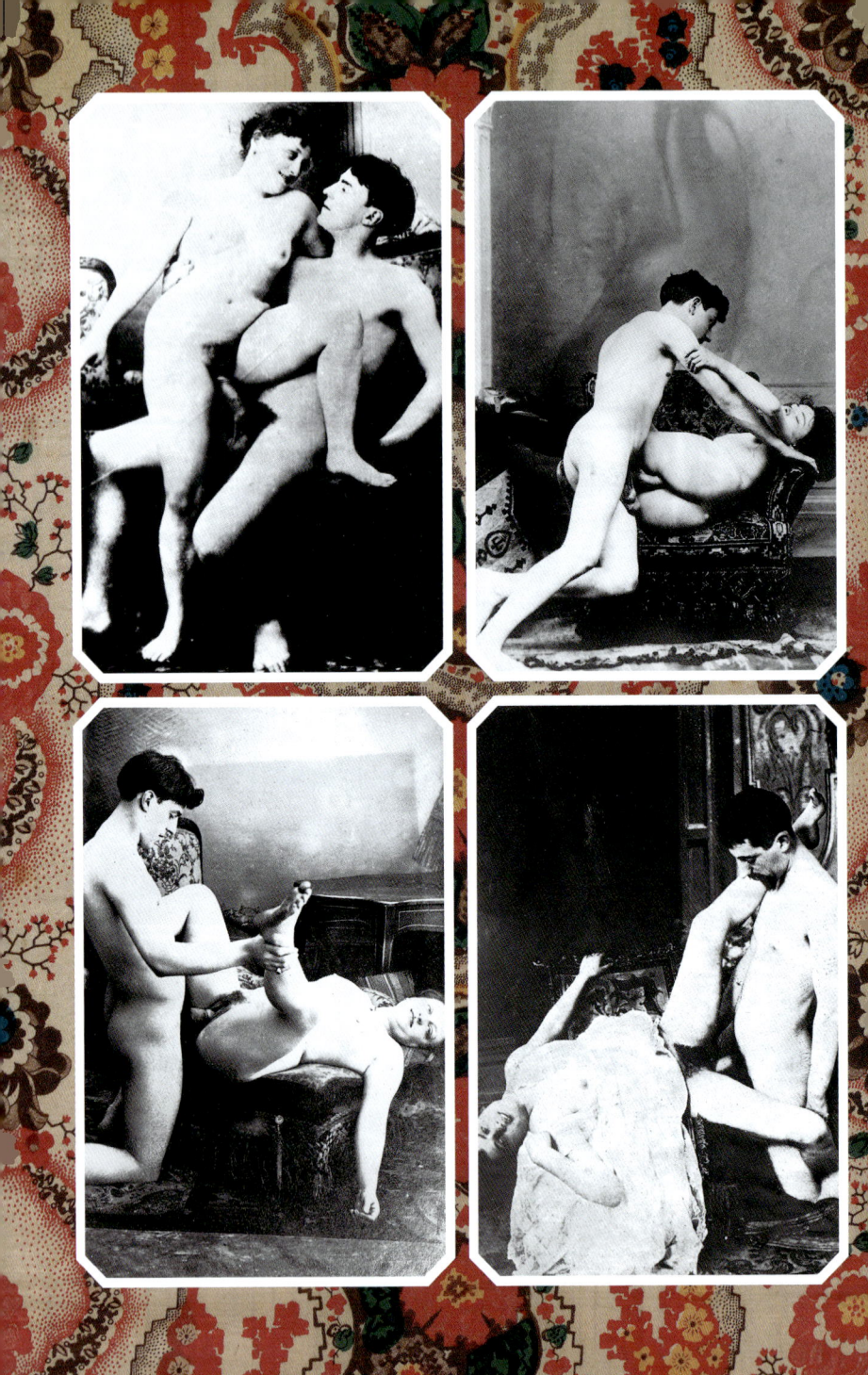

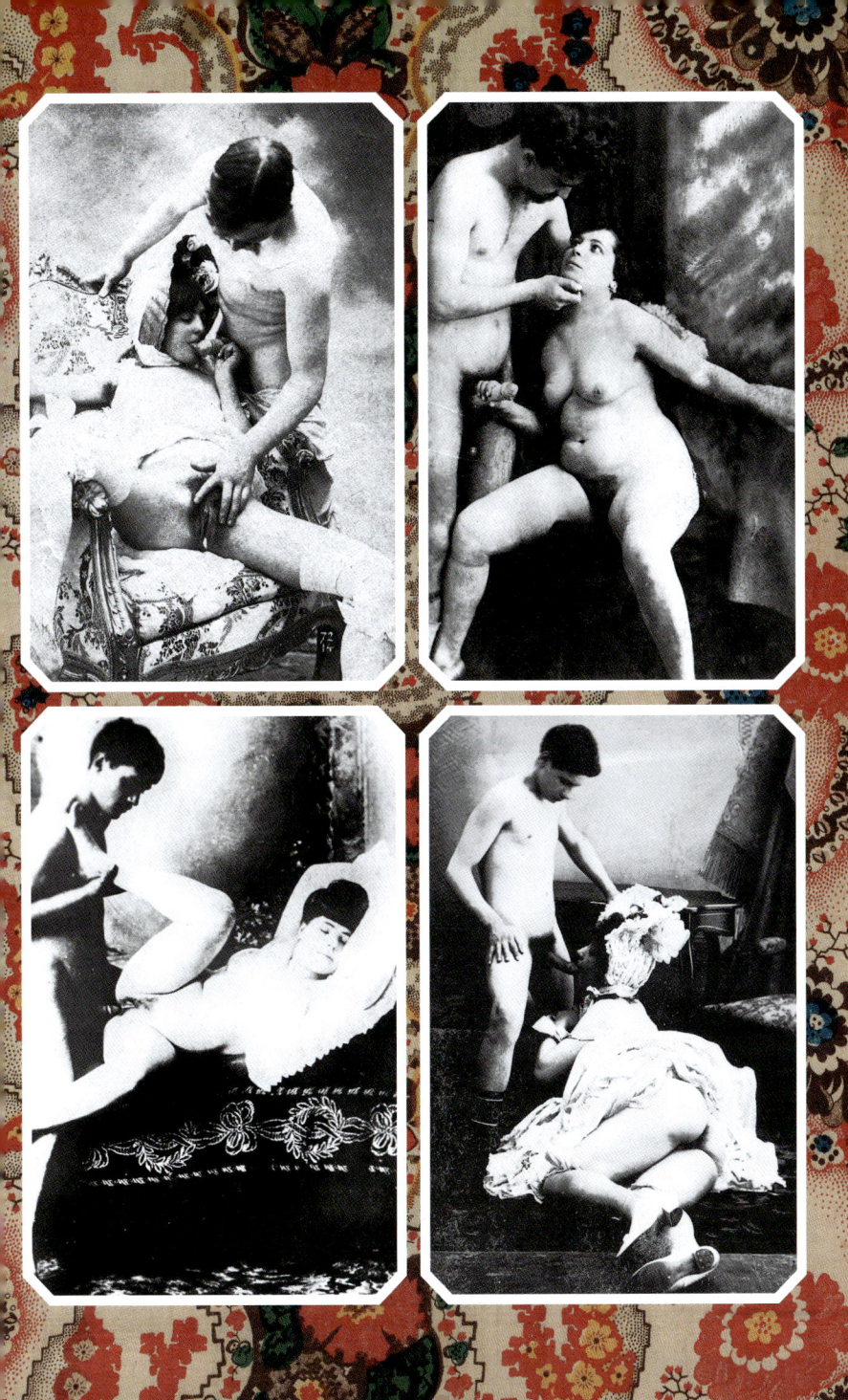

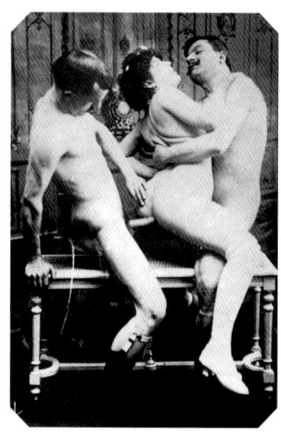

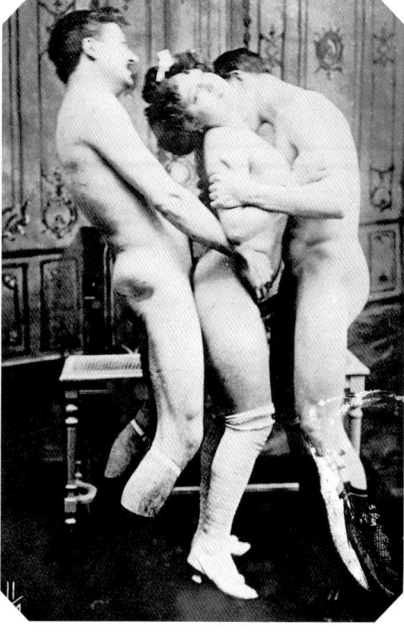

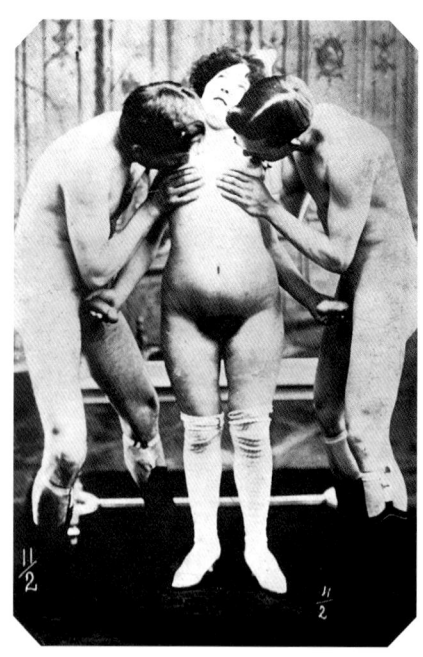

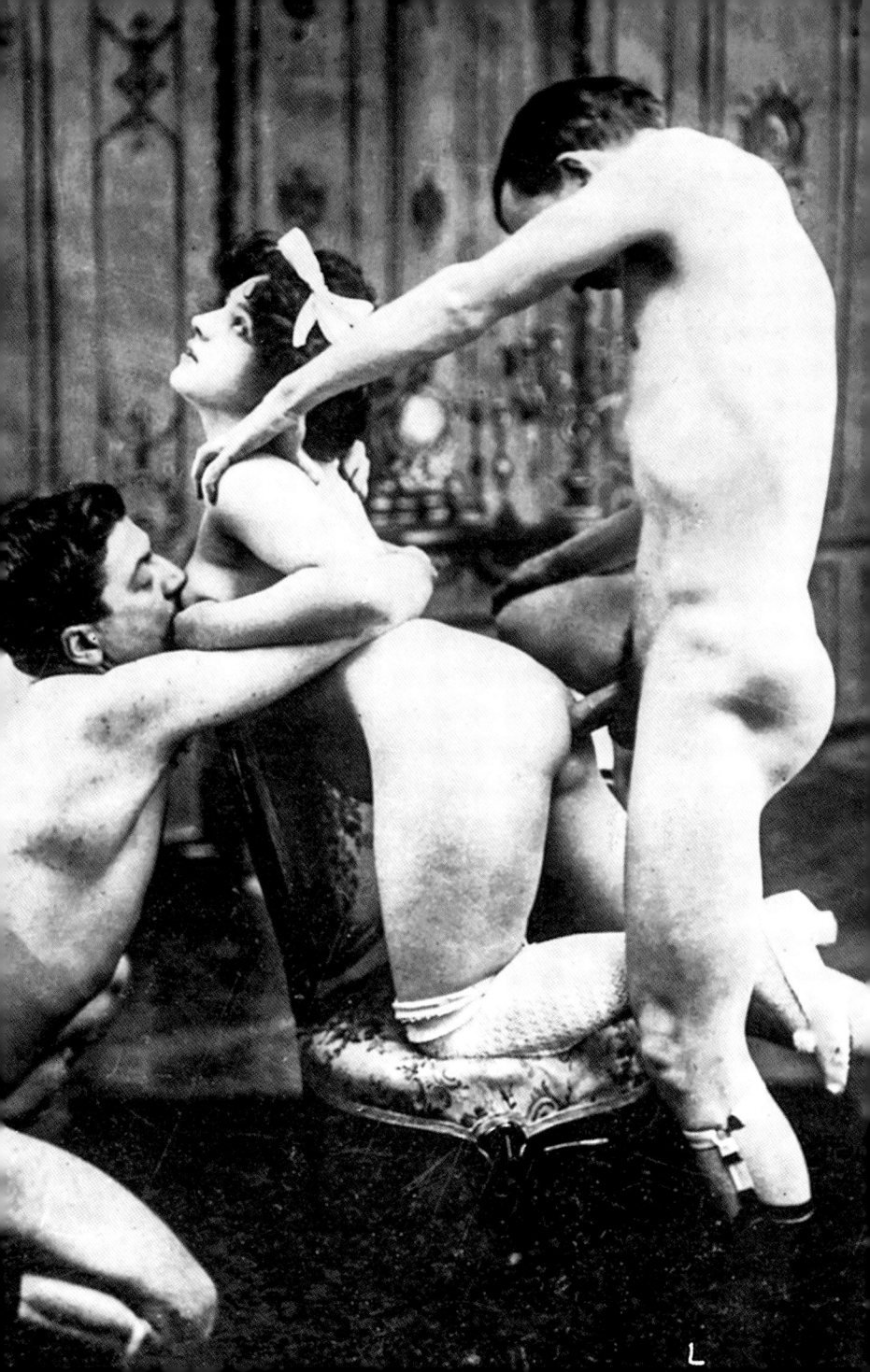

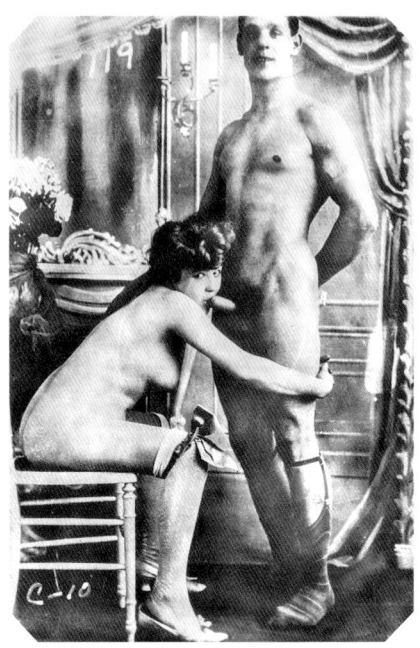
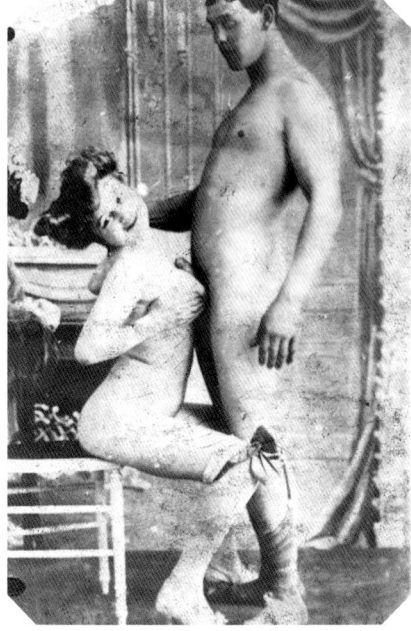
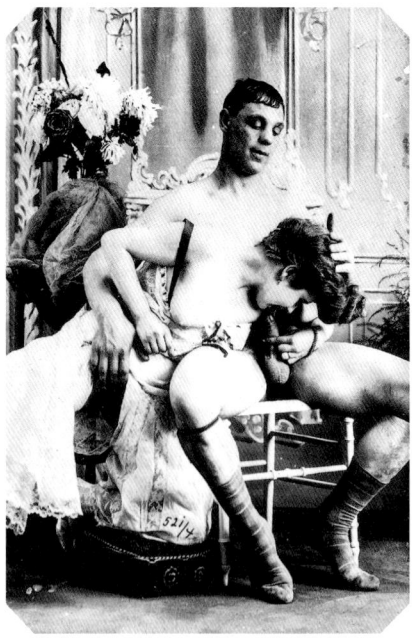
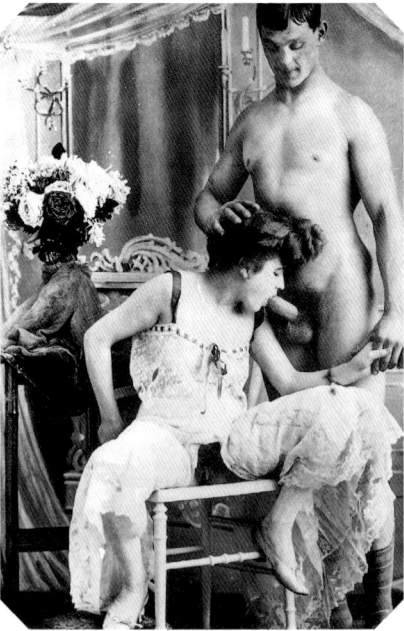

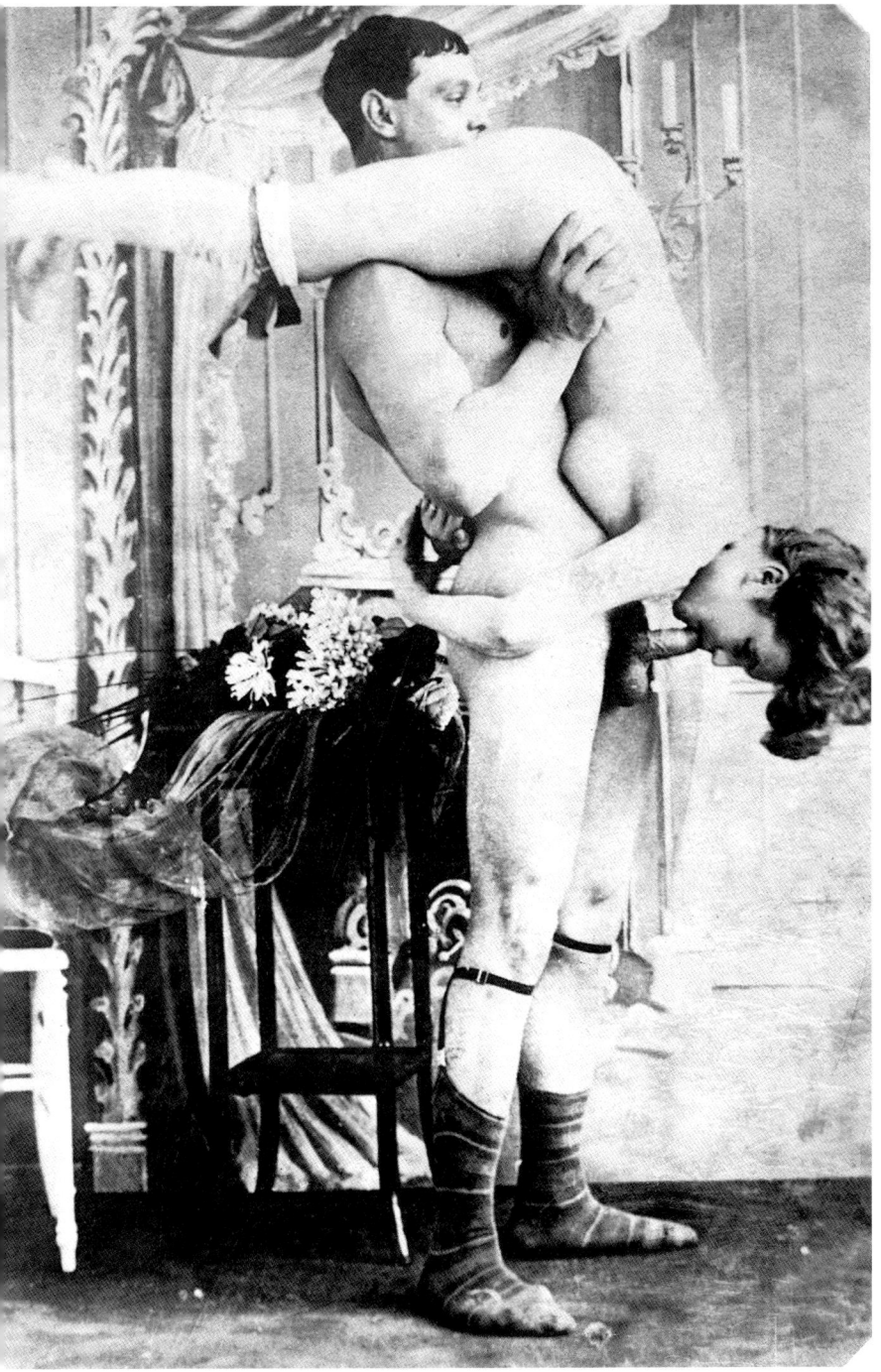

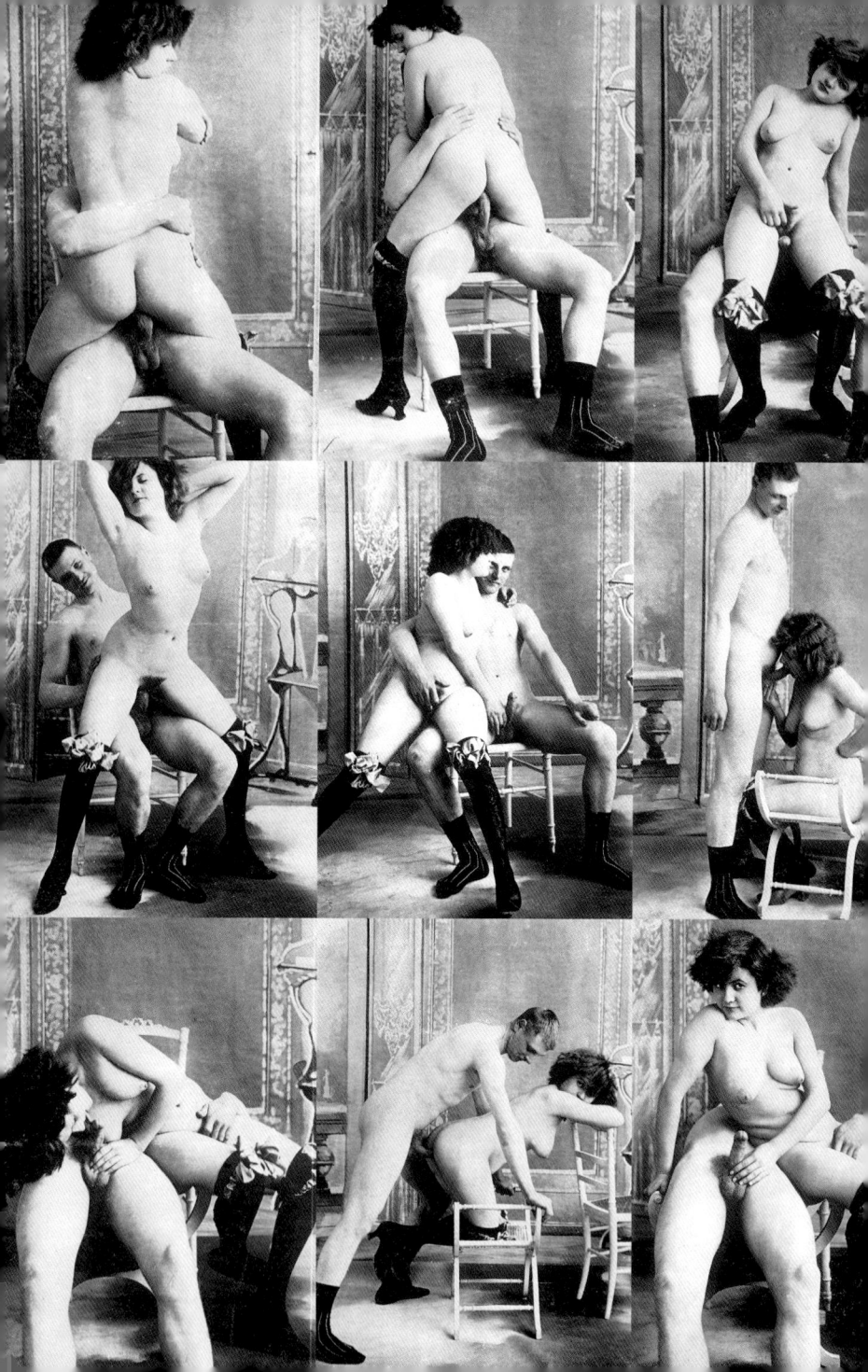

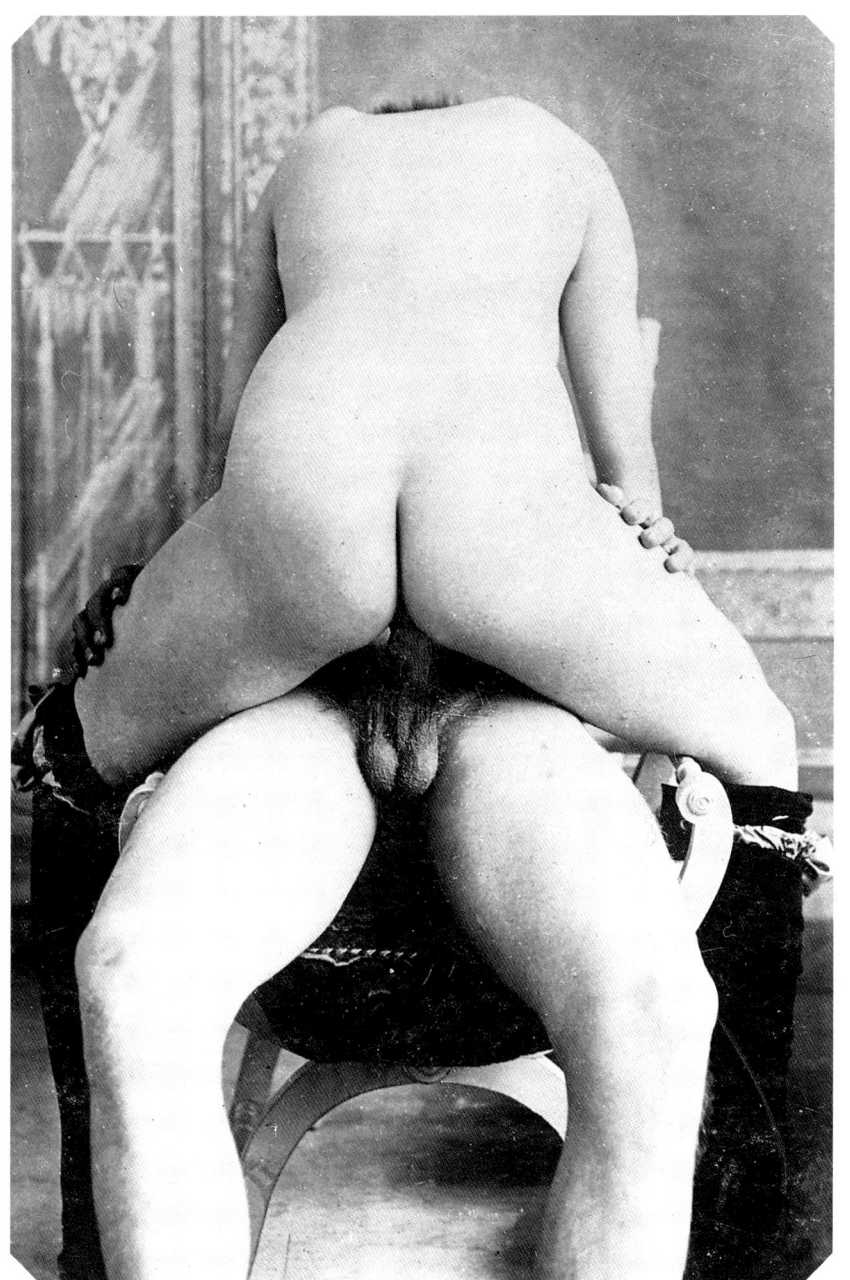

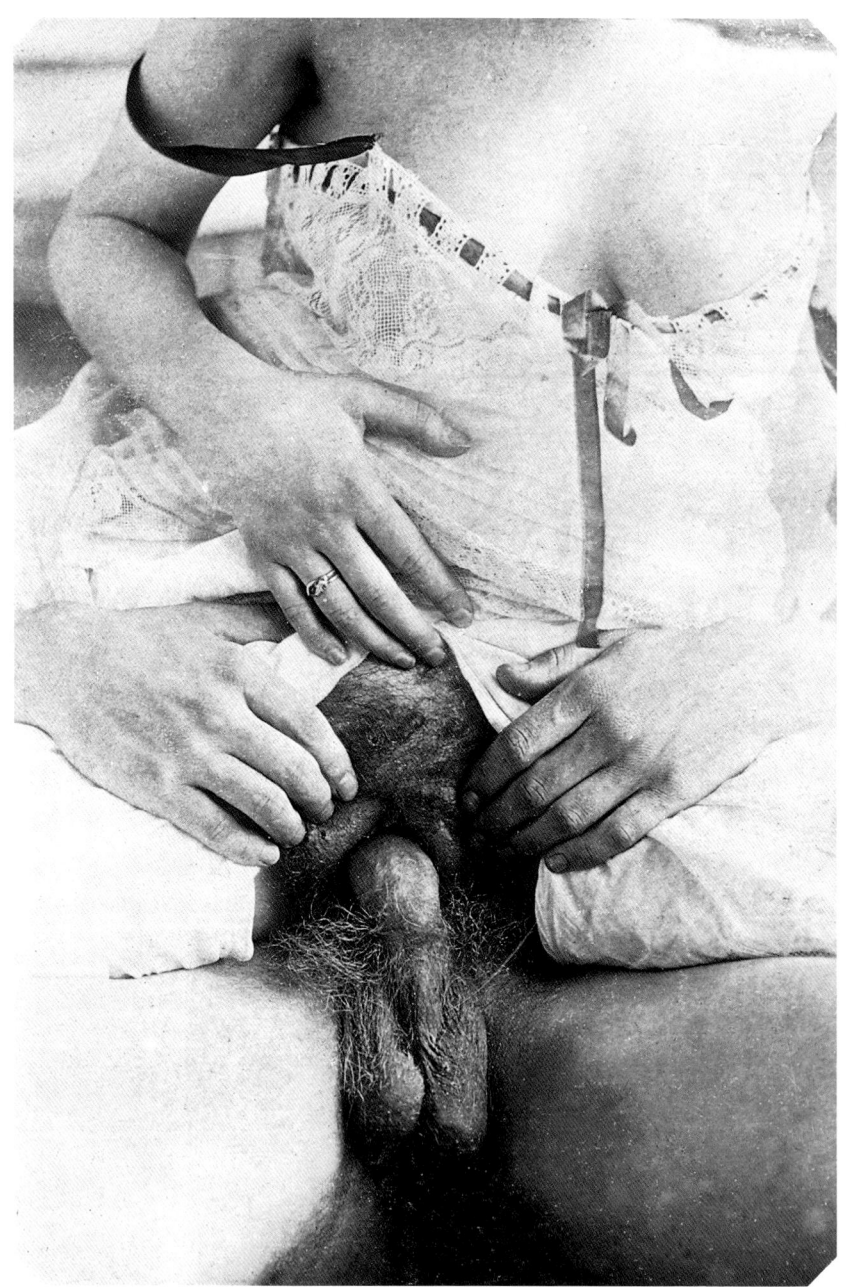

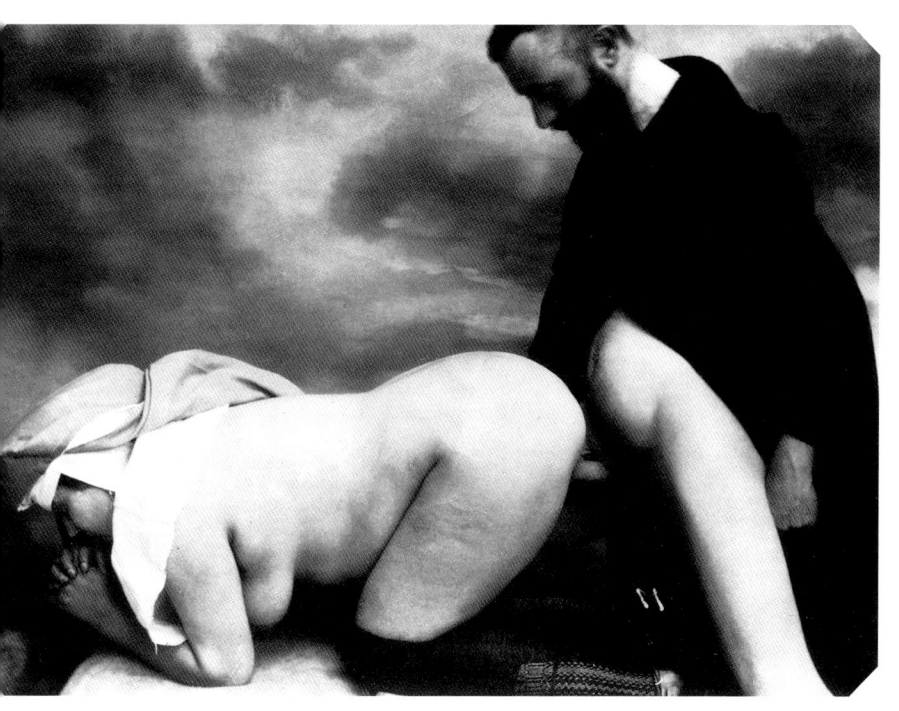

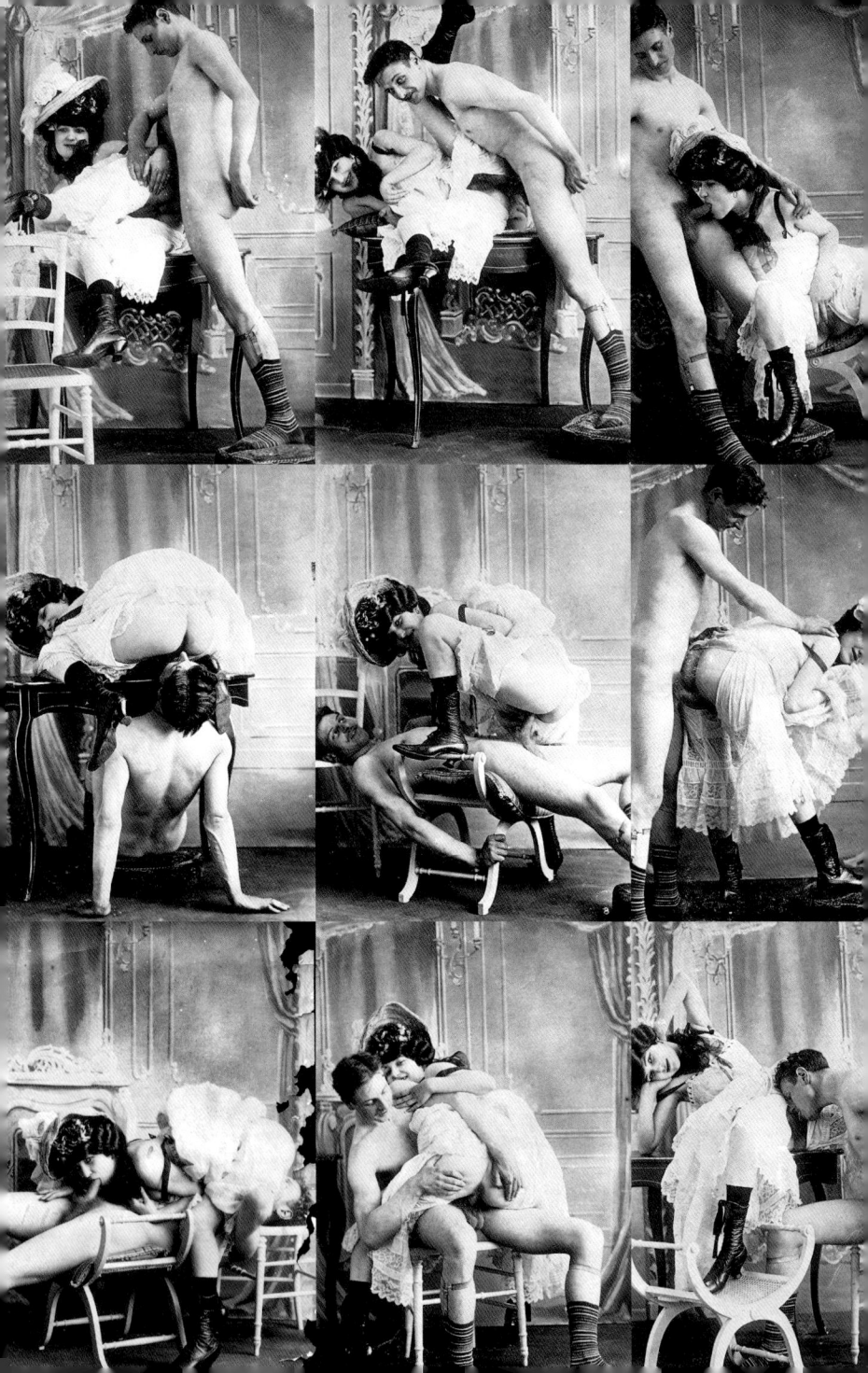

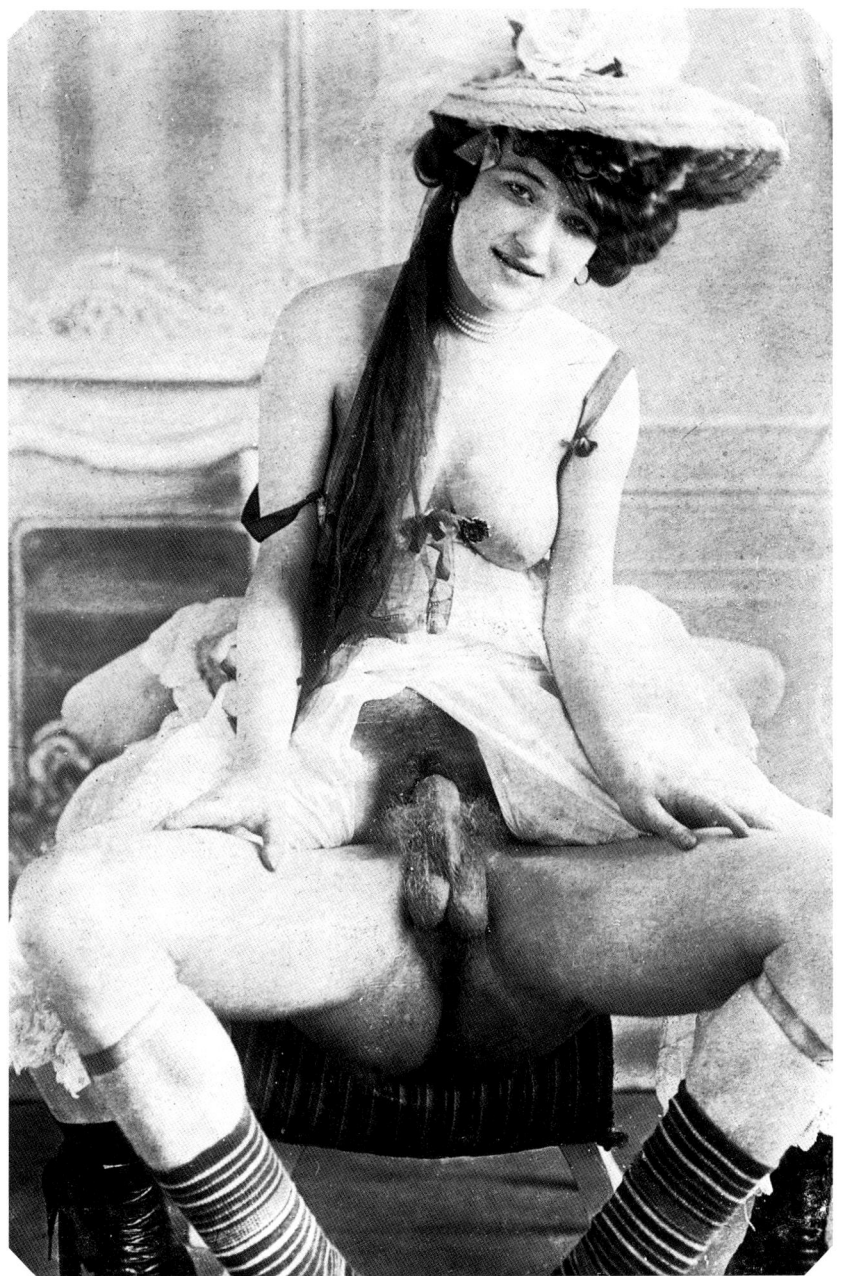

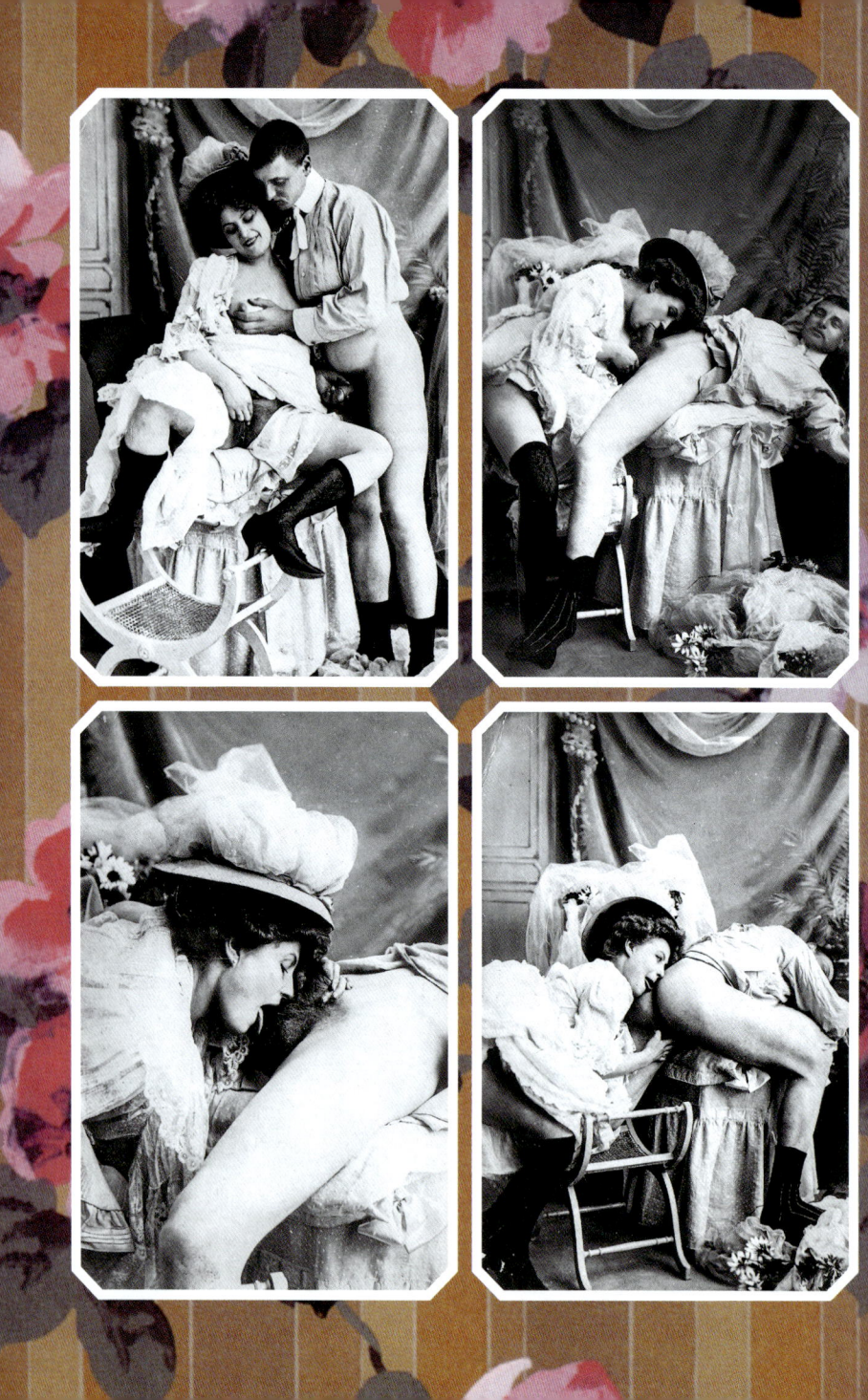

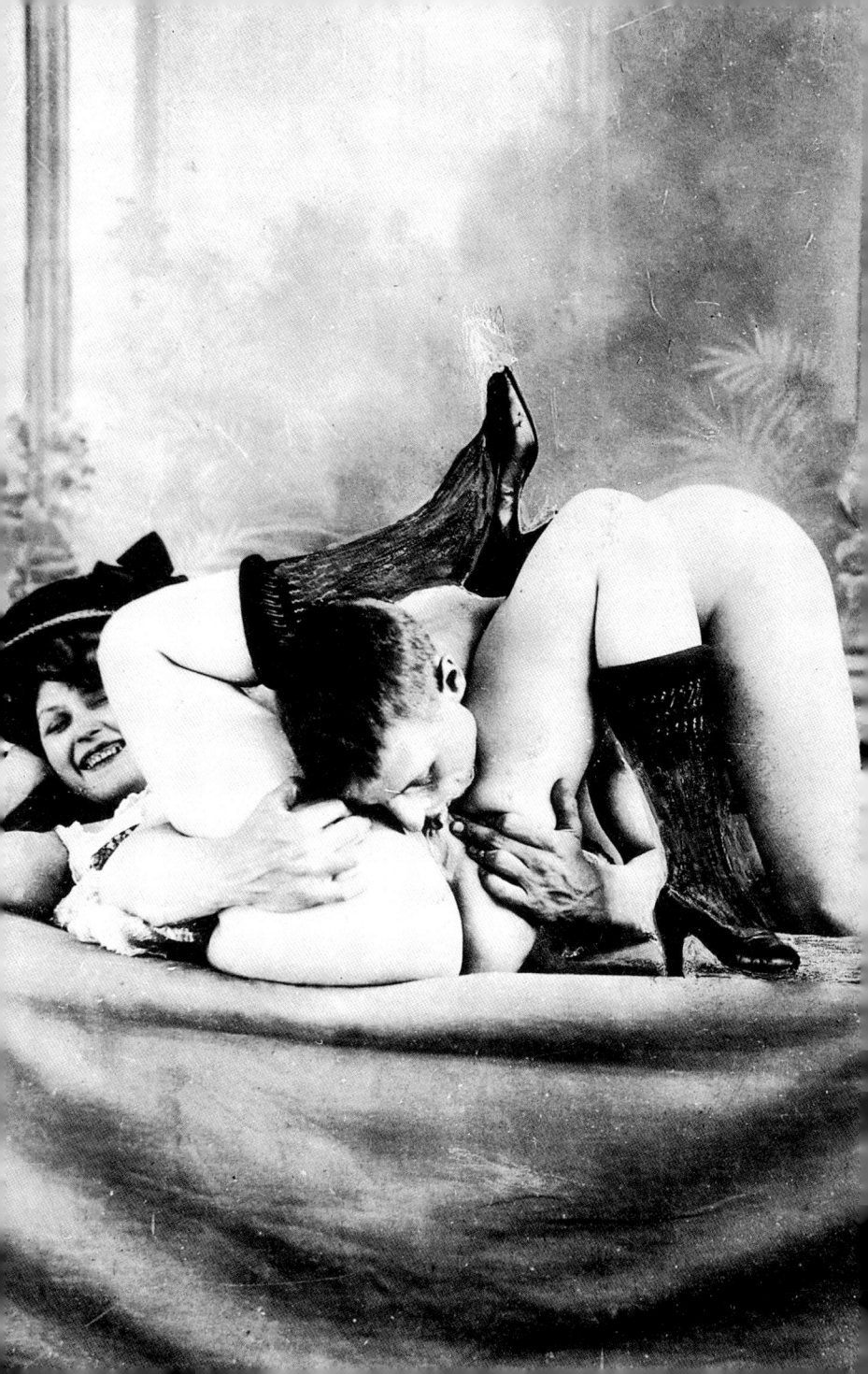

BIJOUX

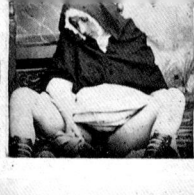

SERIE 182

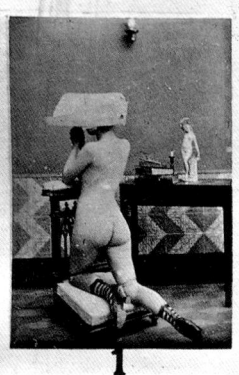

1

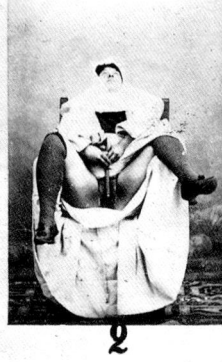

2

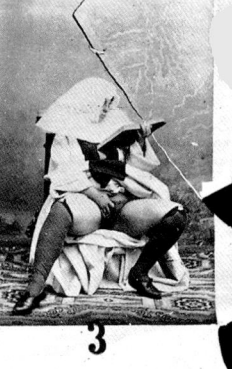

3

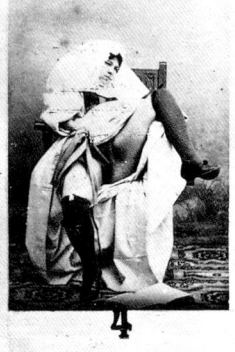

4

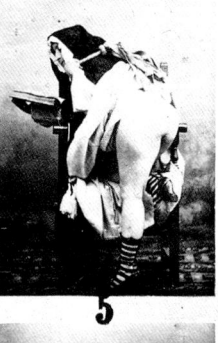

5

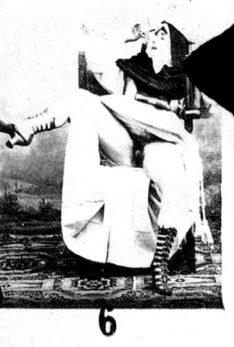

6

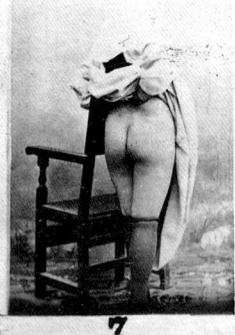

7

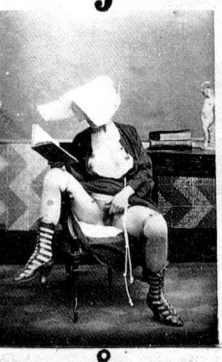

8

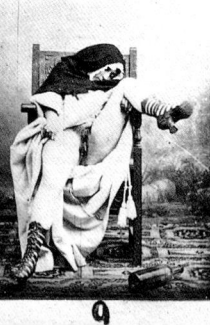

9

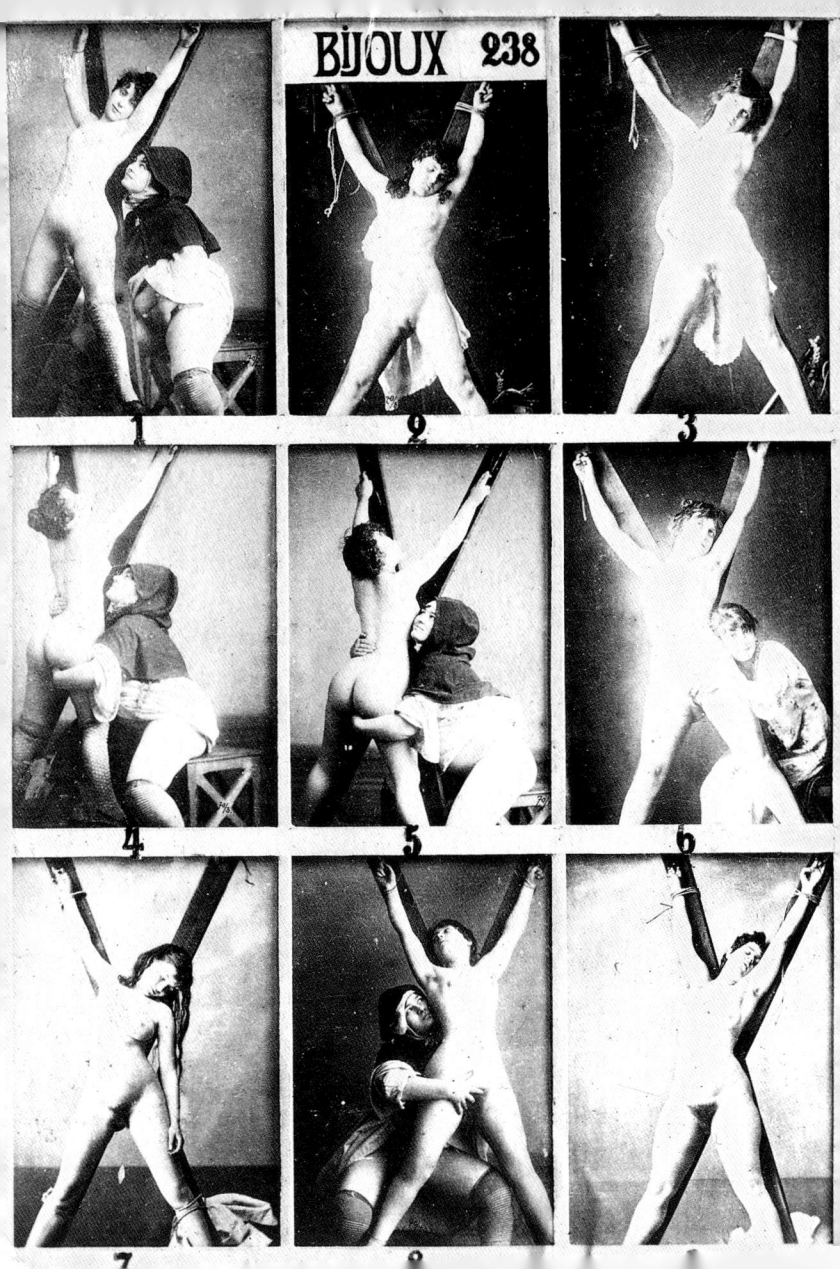

BIJOUX 238

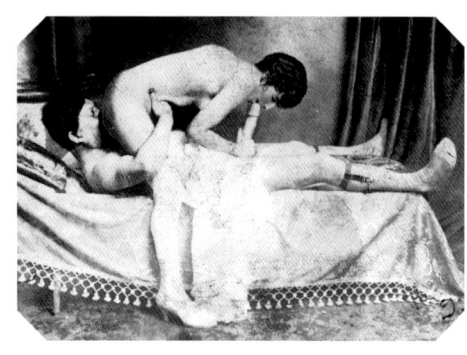

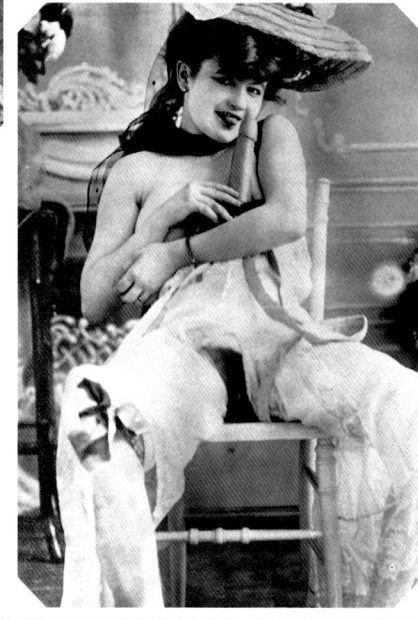

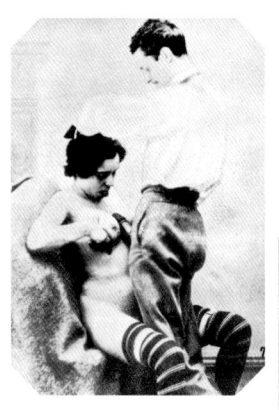

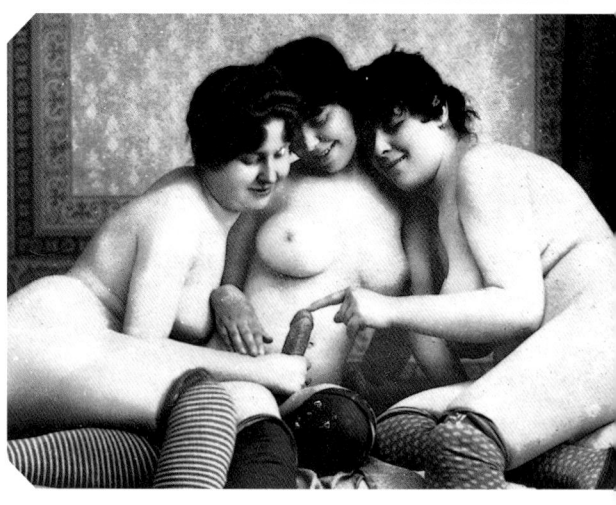

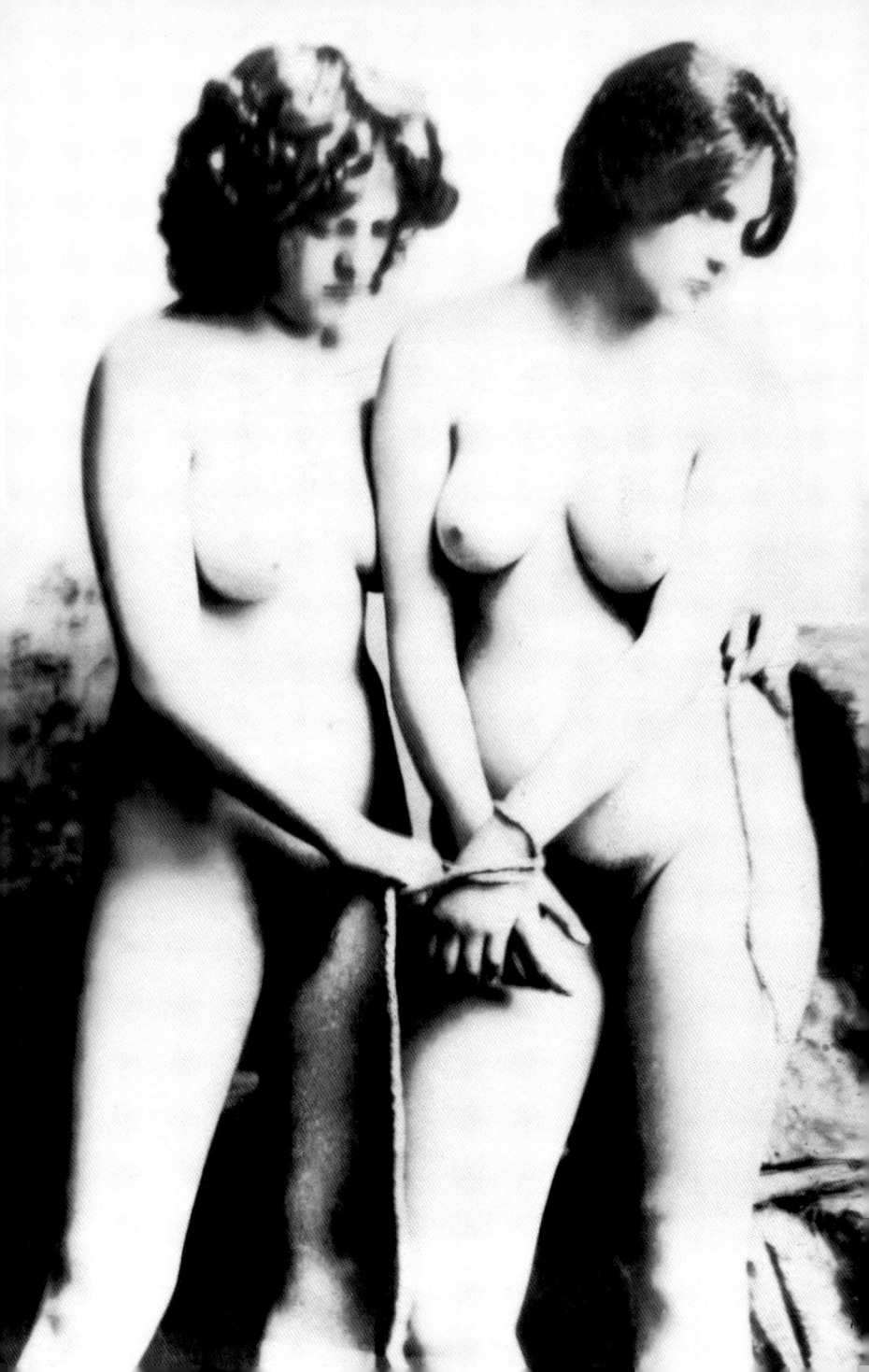

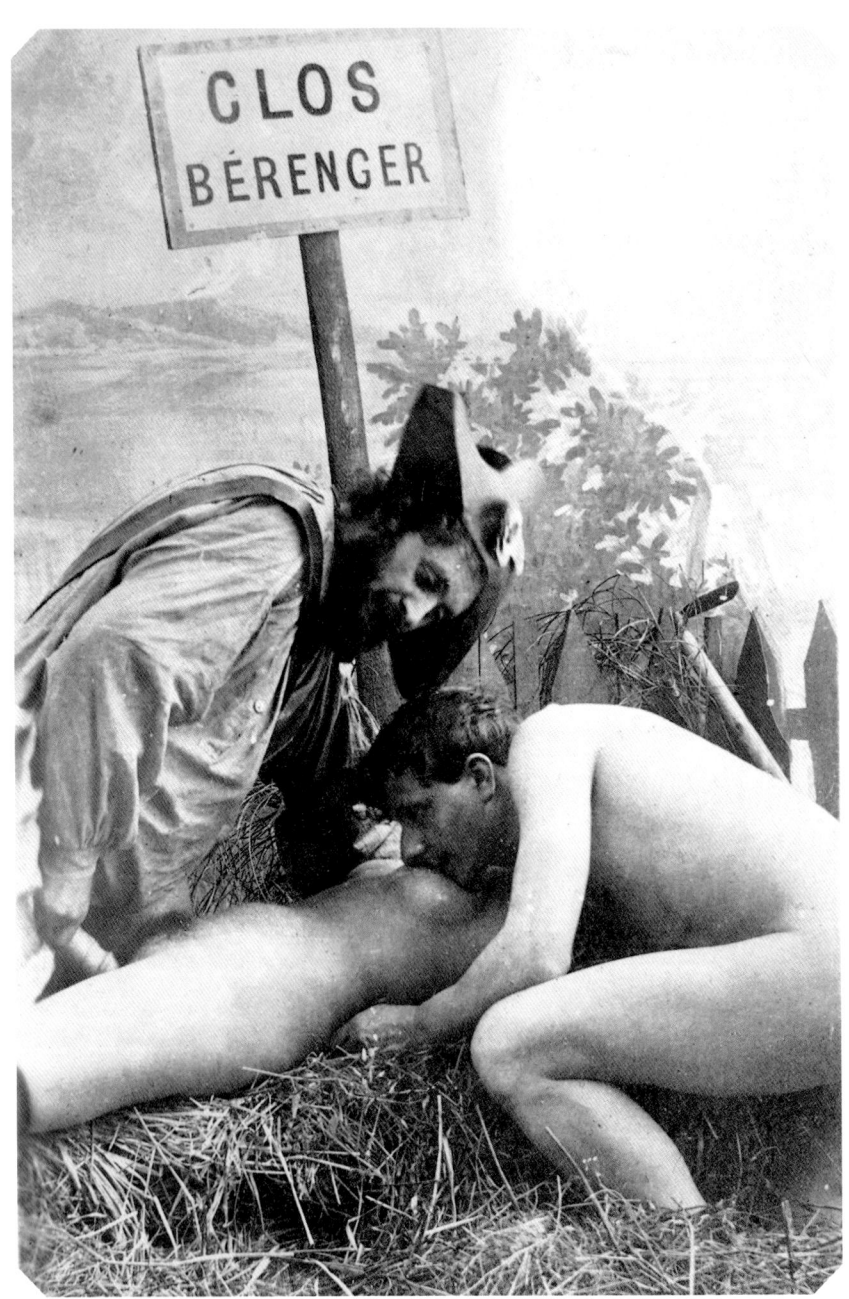

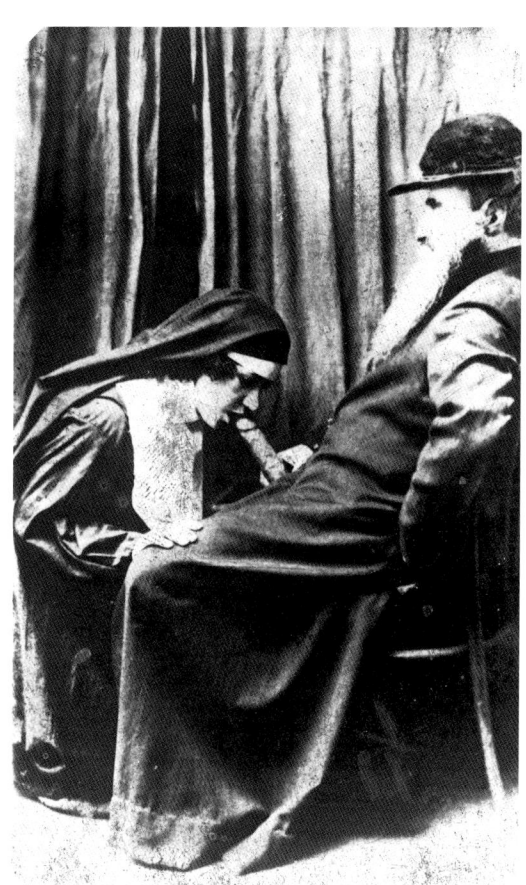

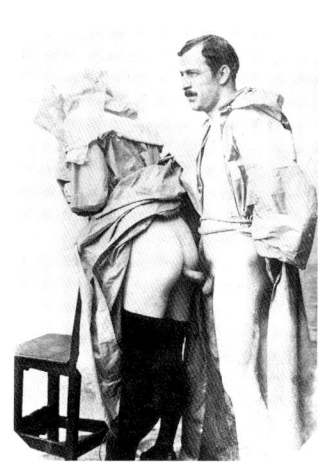

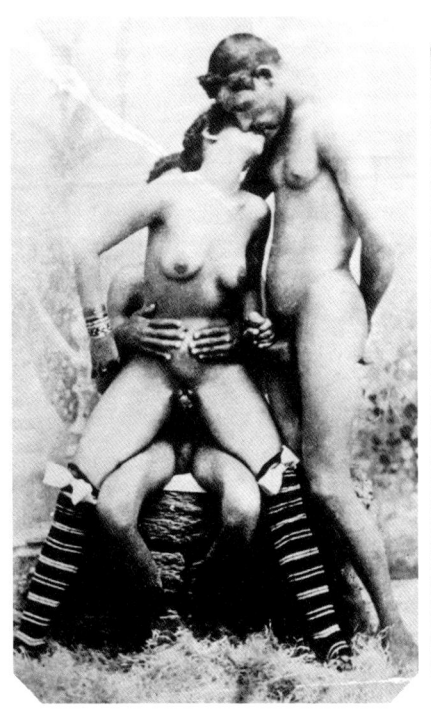

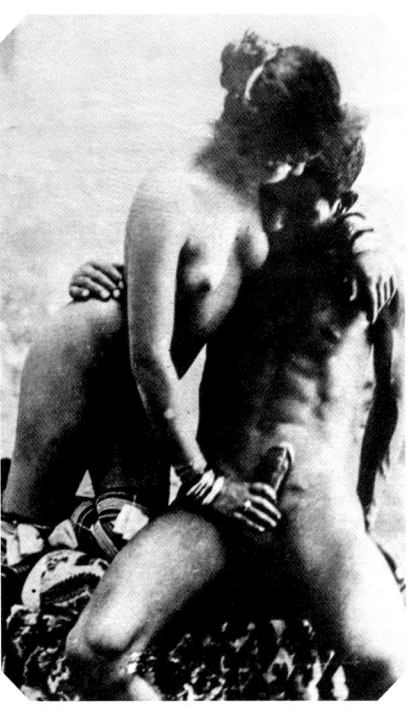

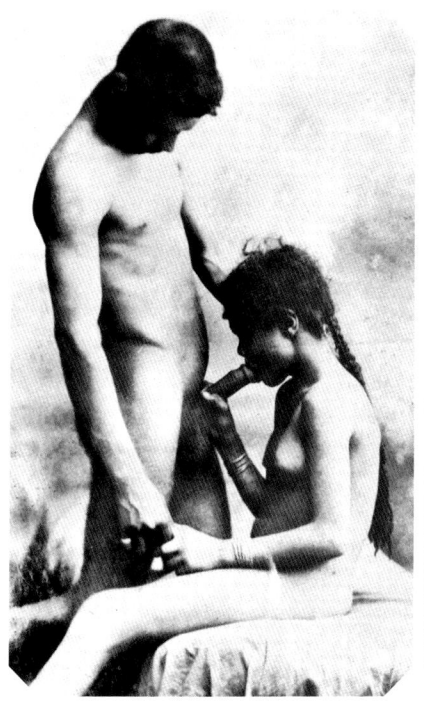
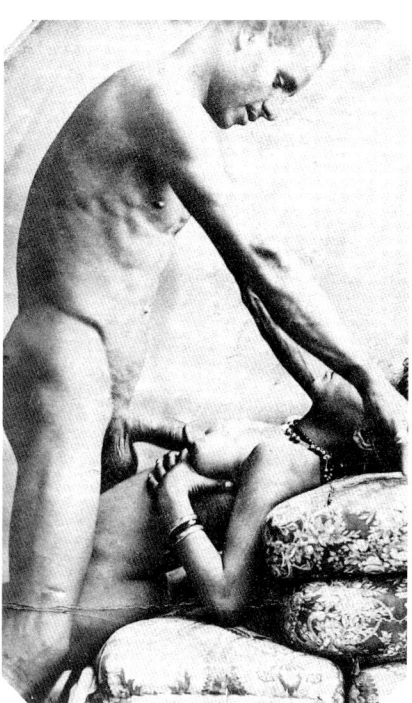

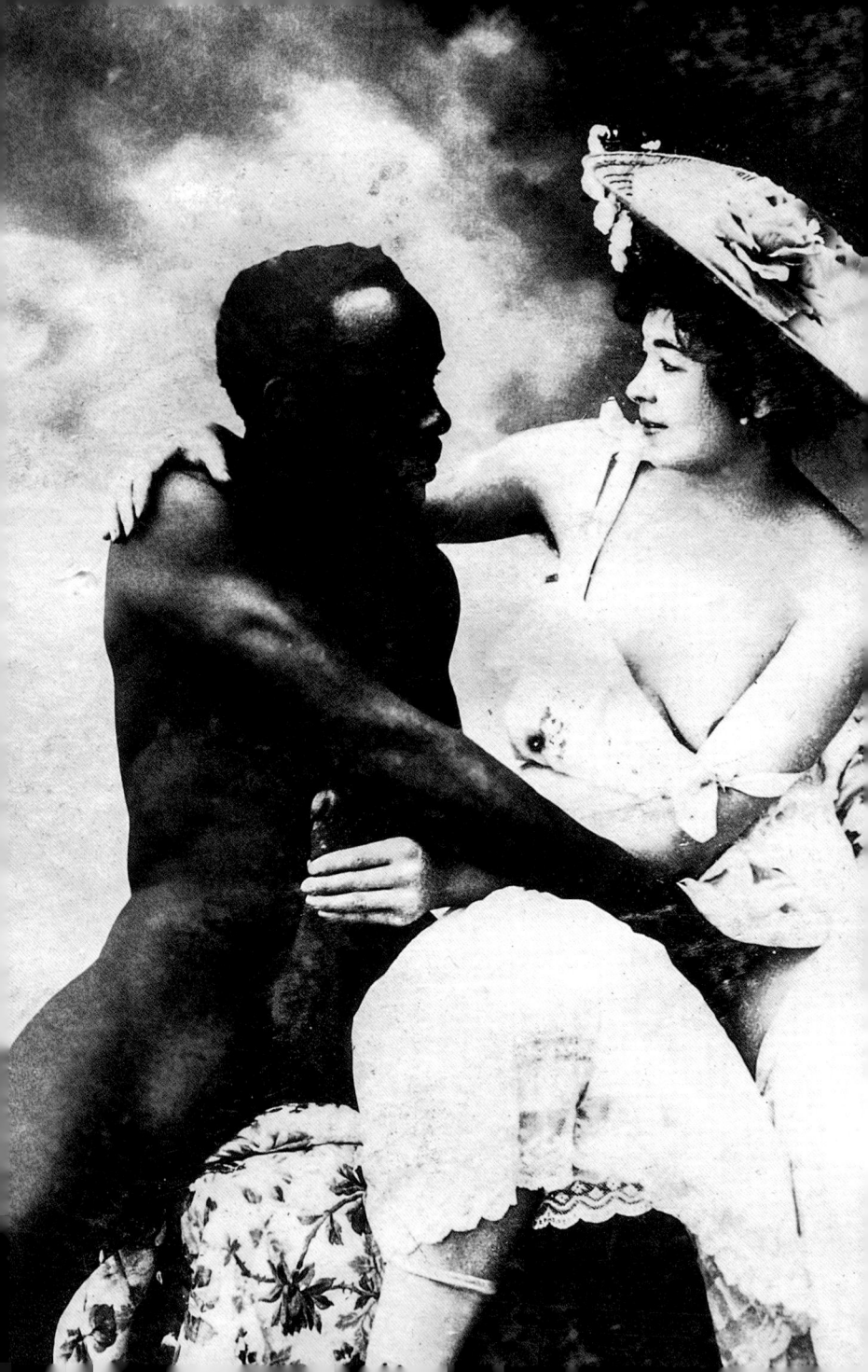

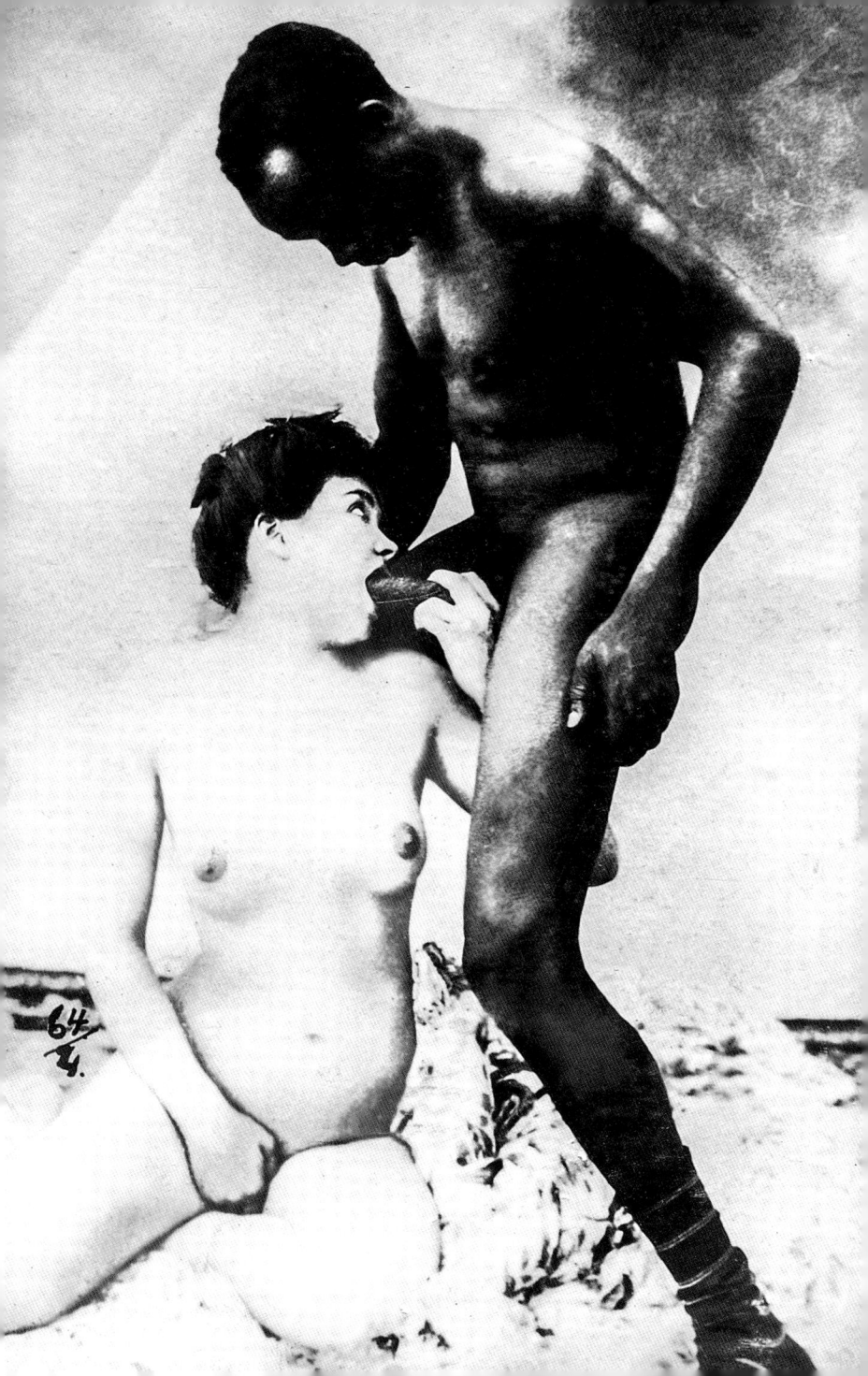

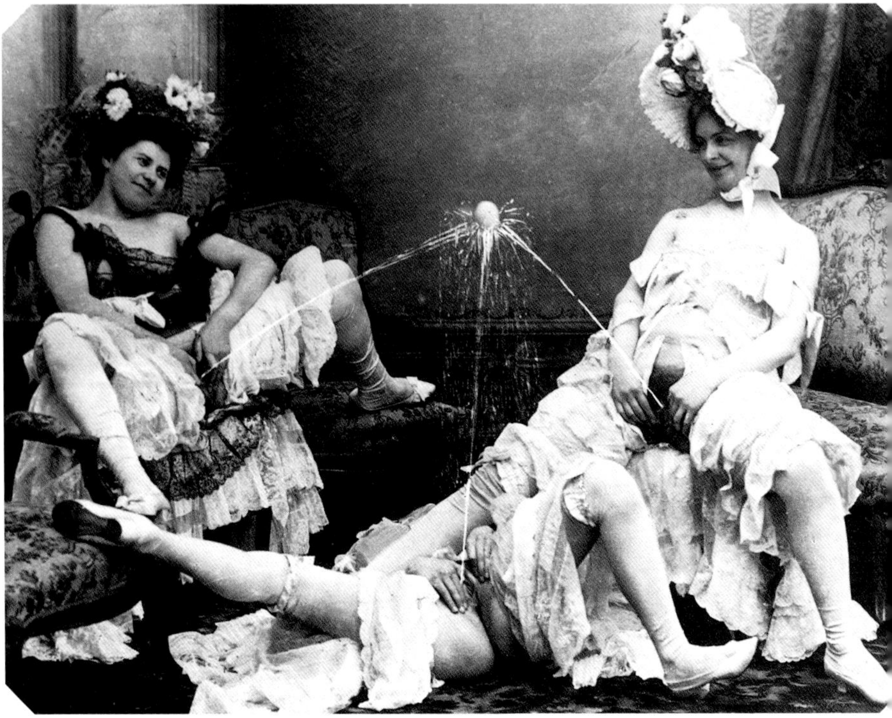

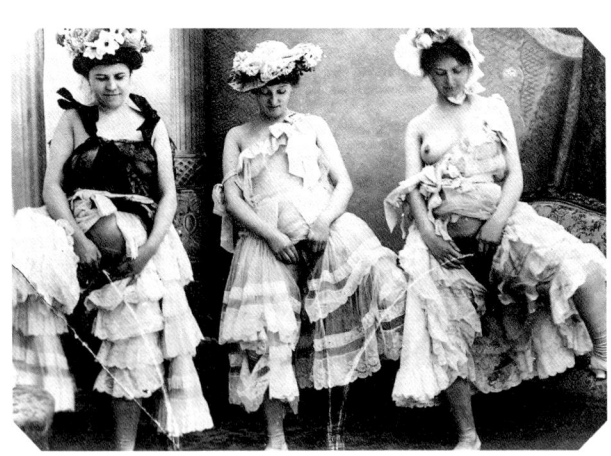

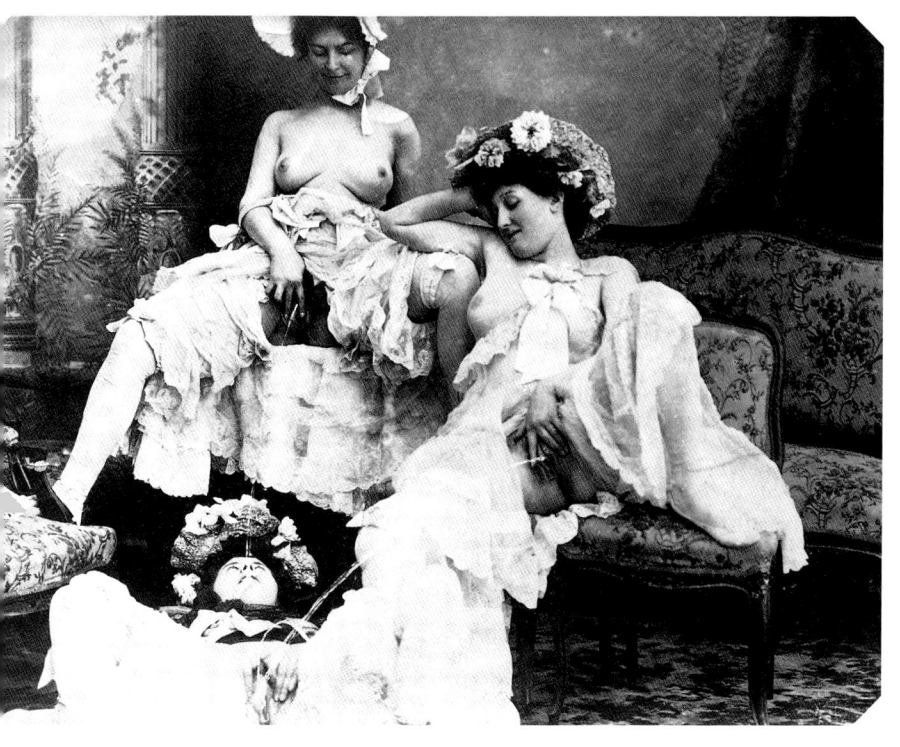

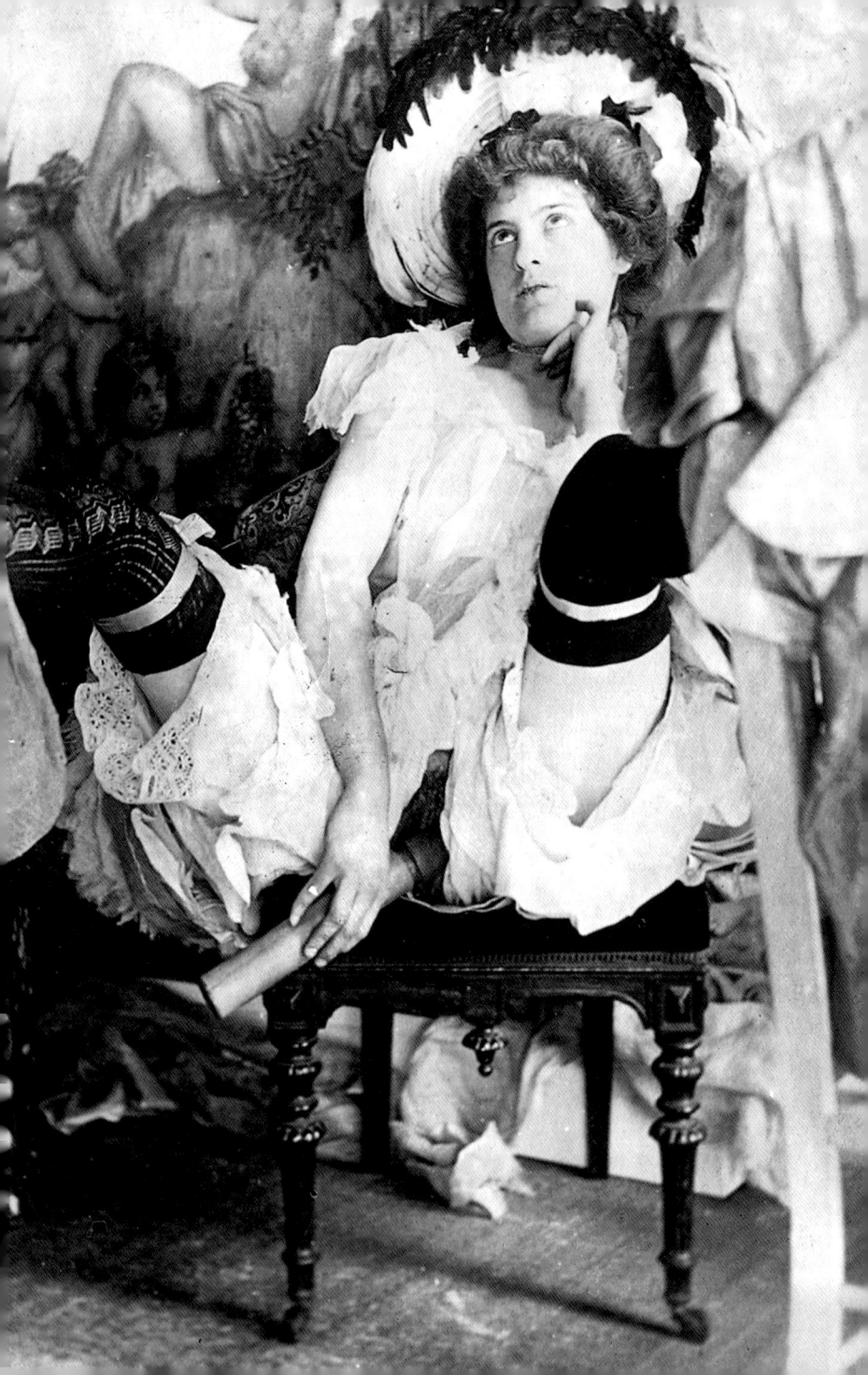

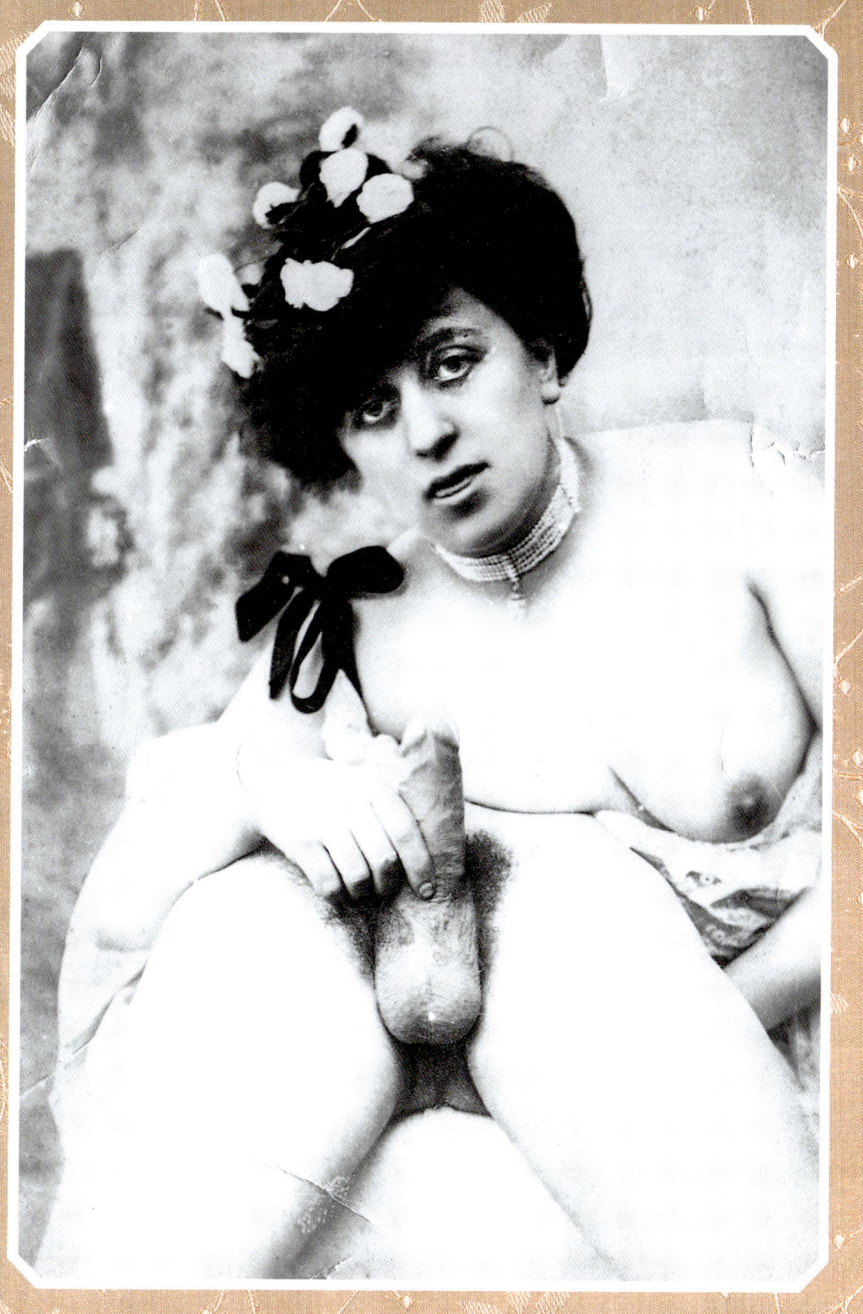

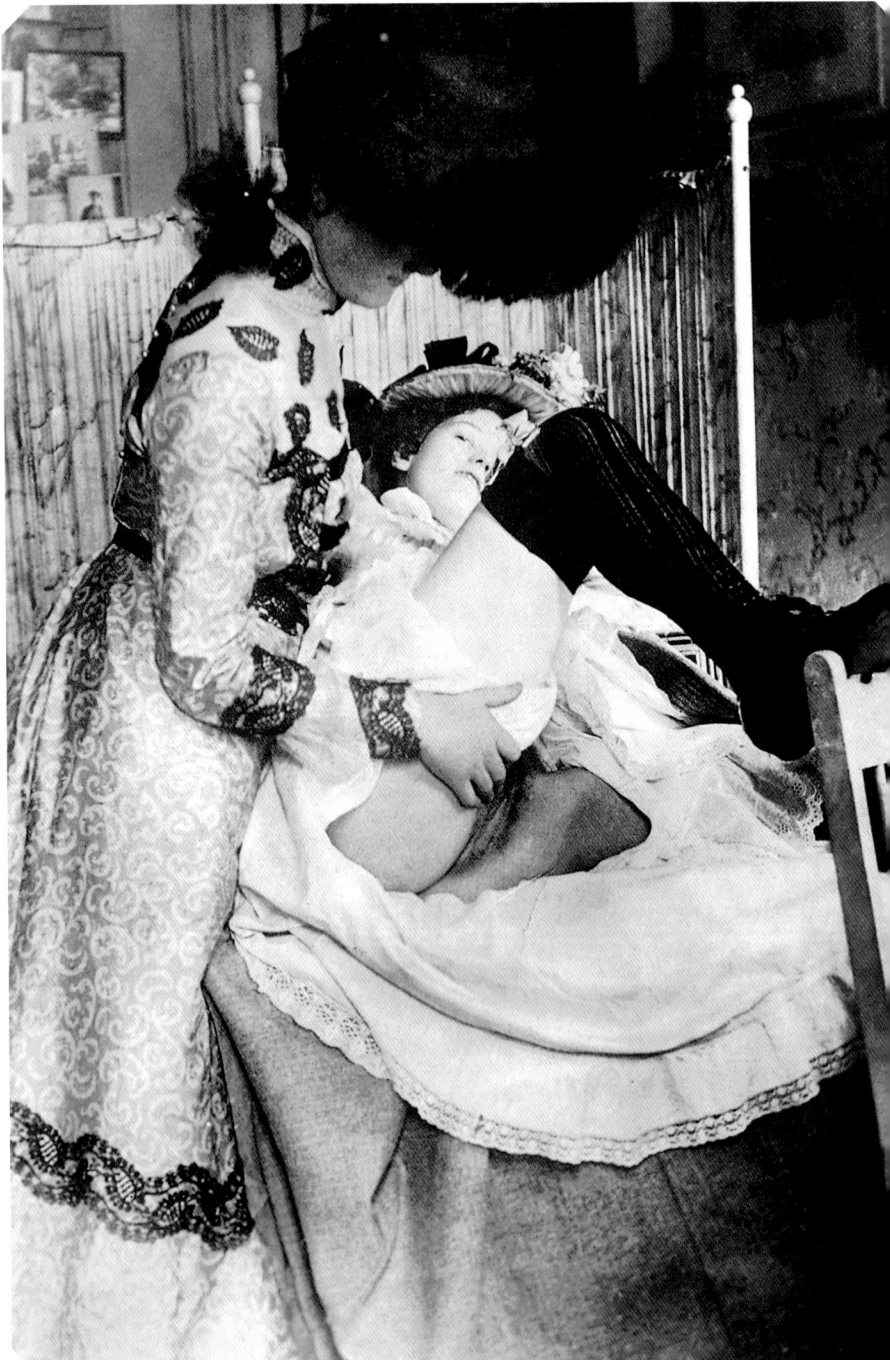

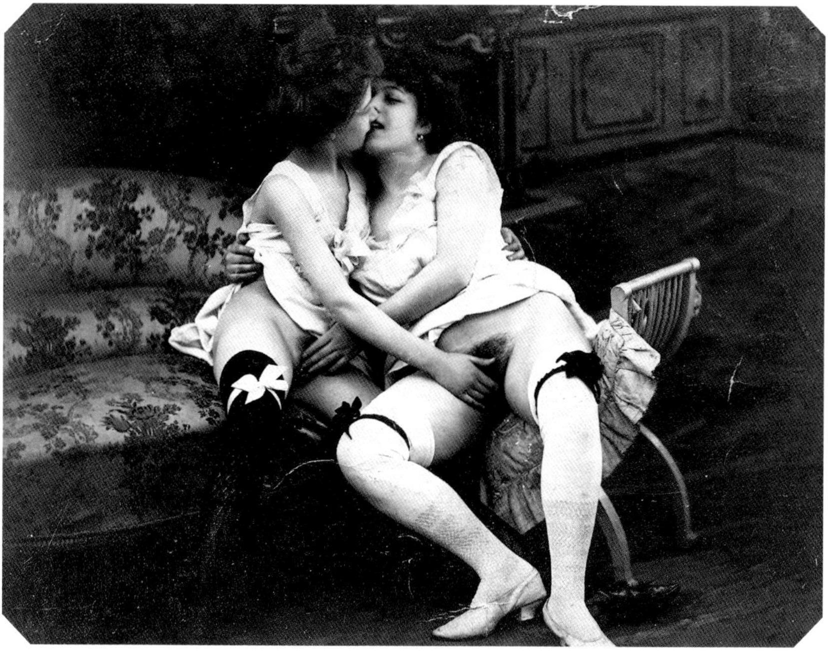

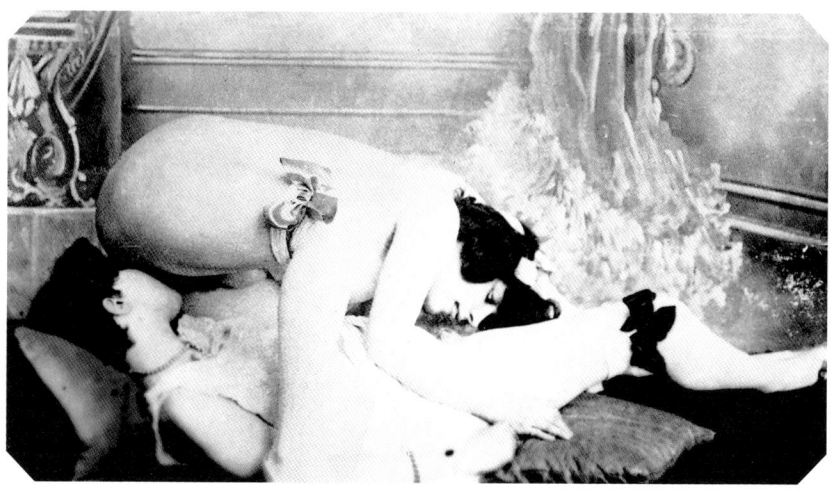

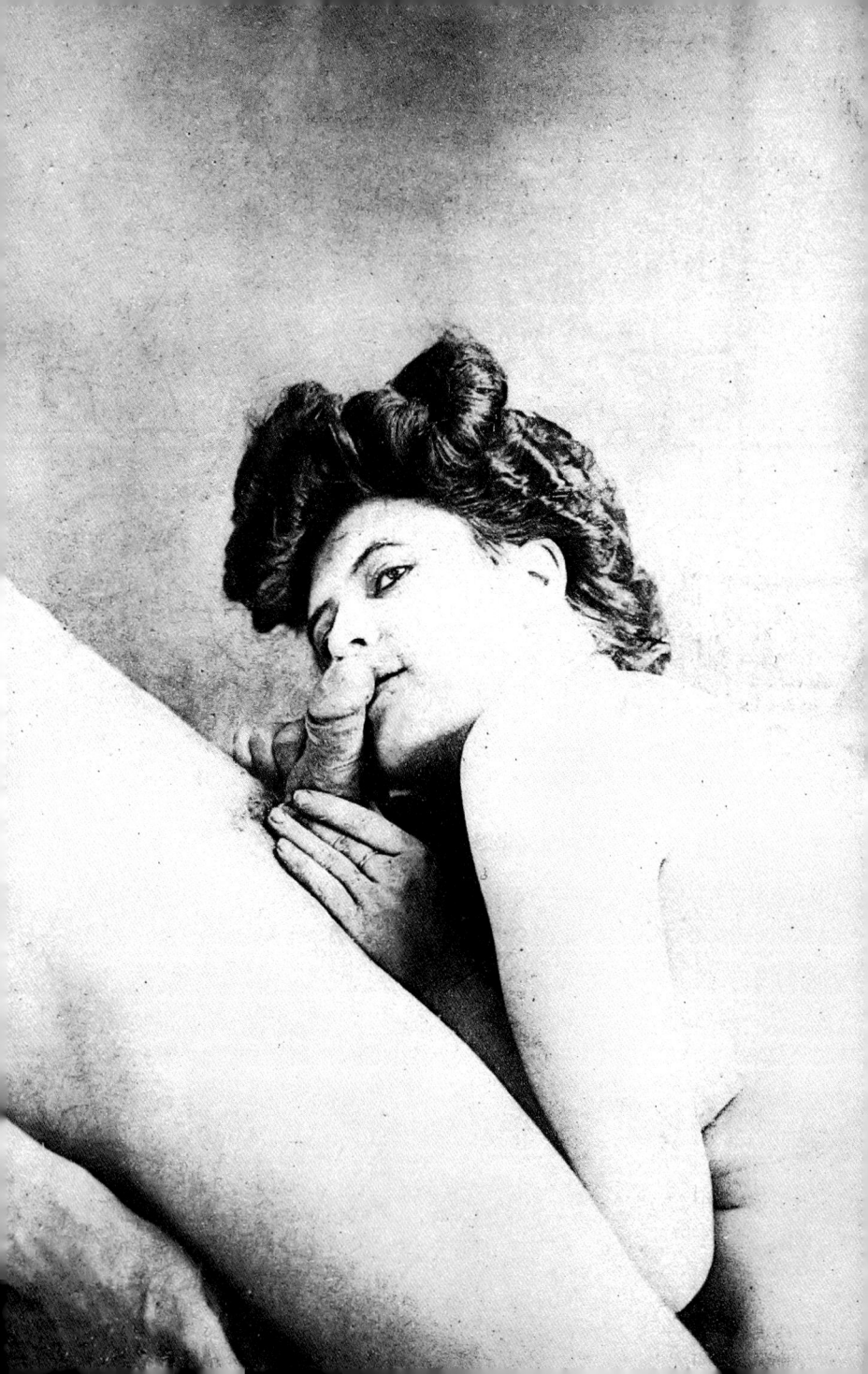

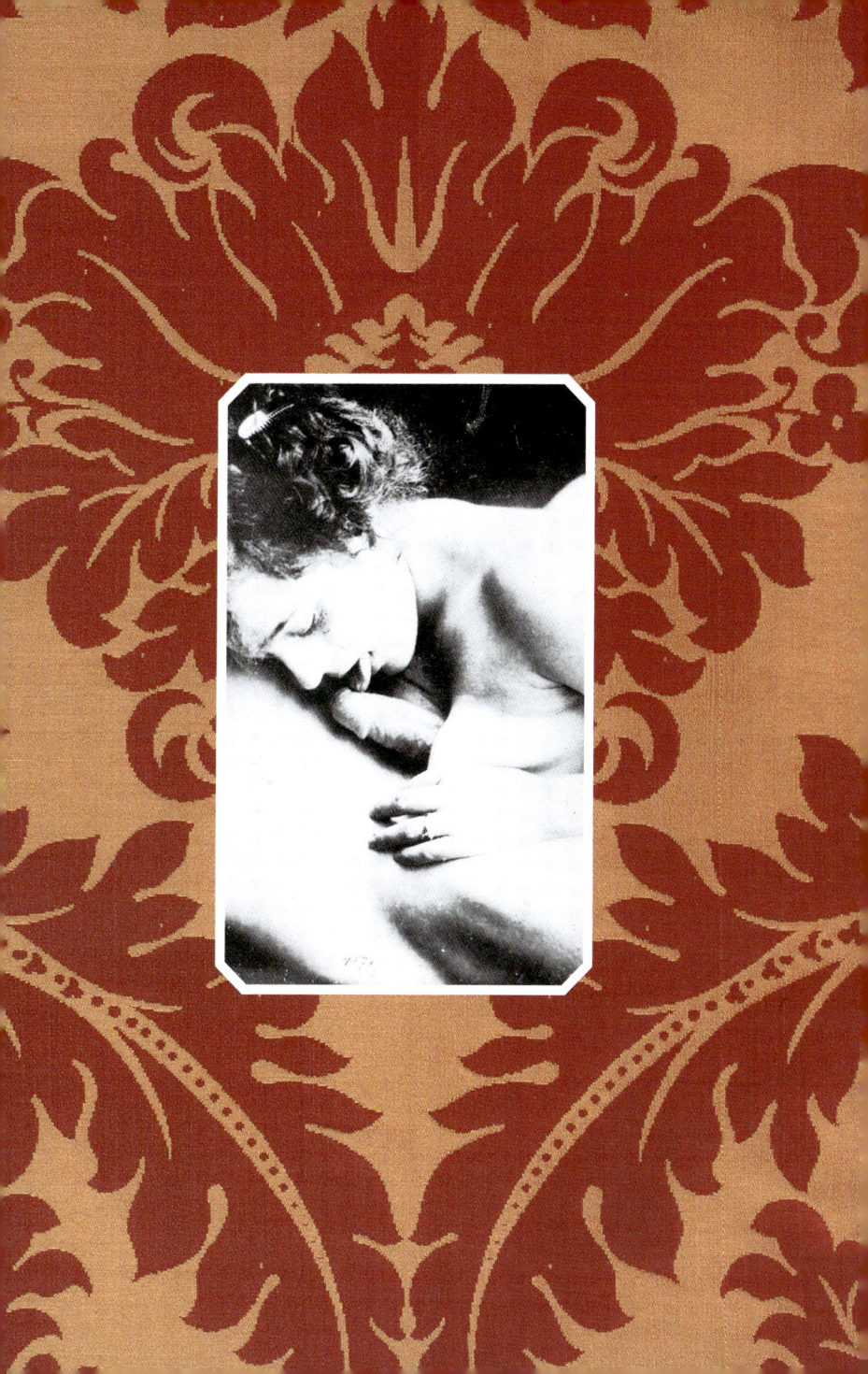

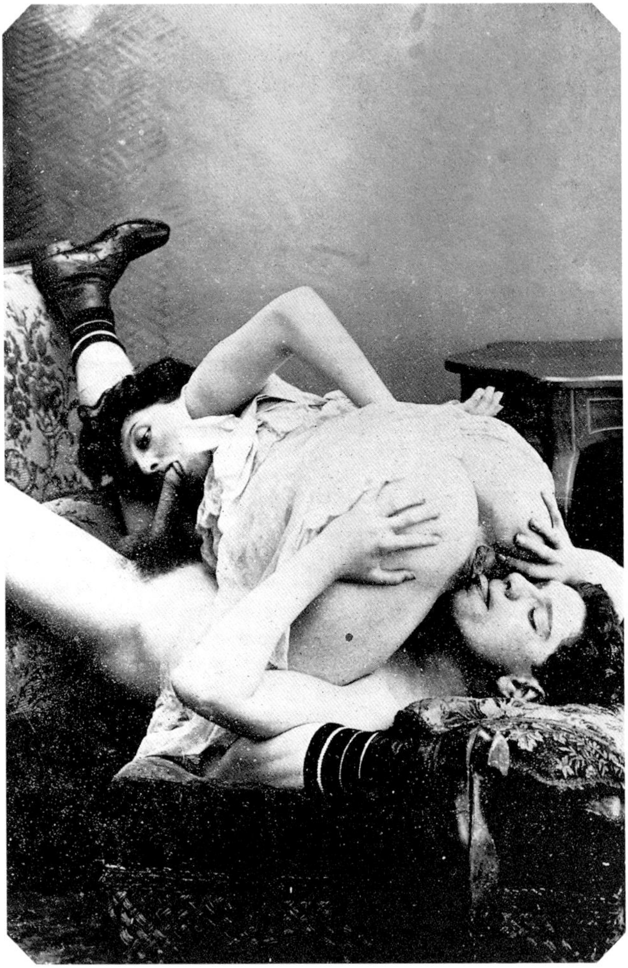

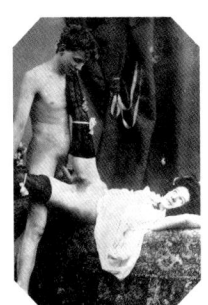

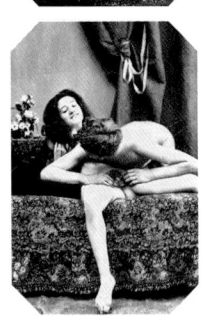

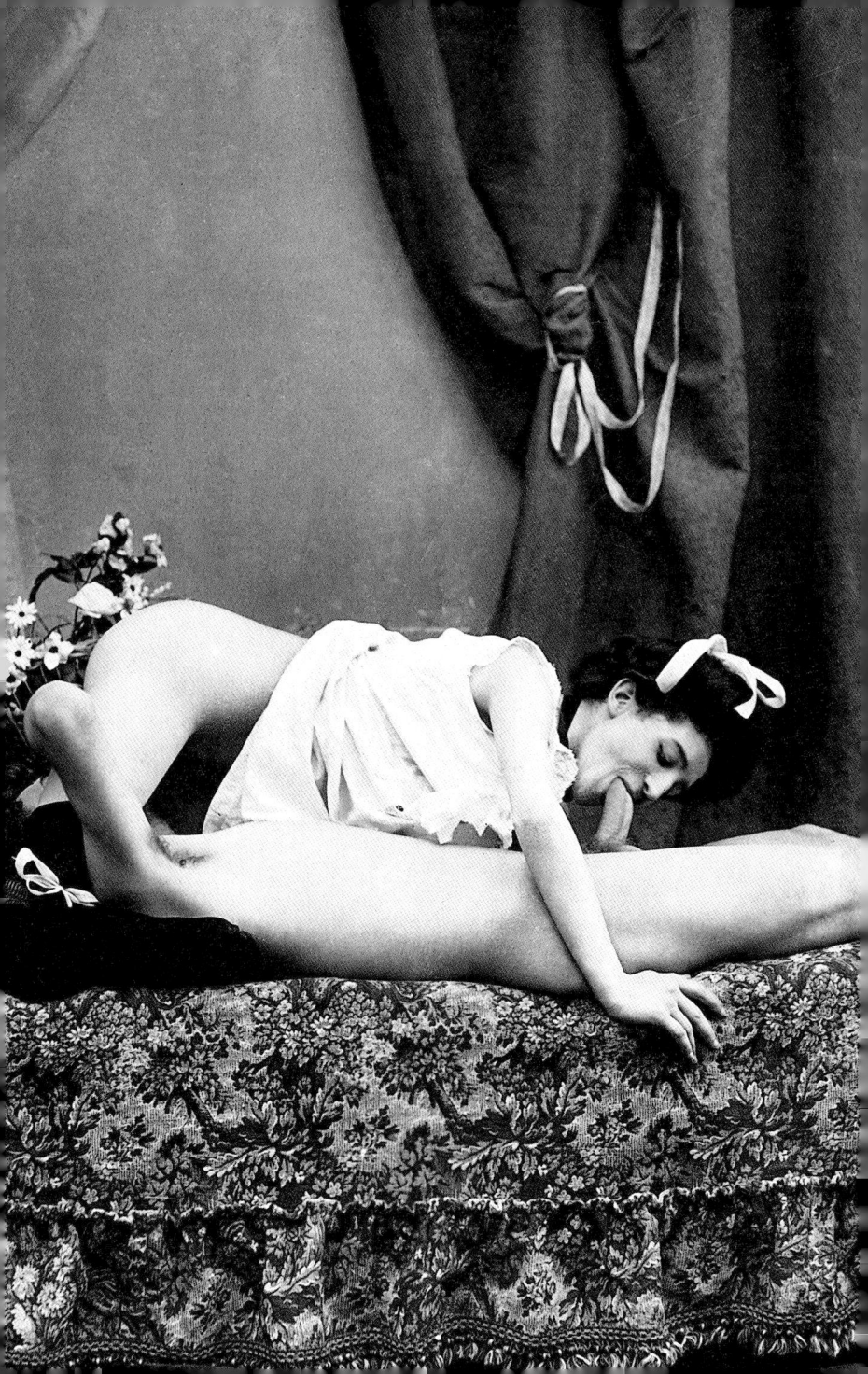

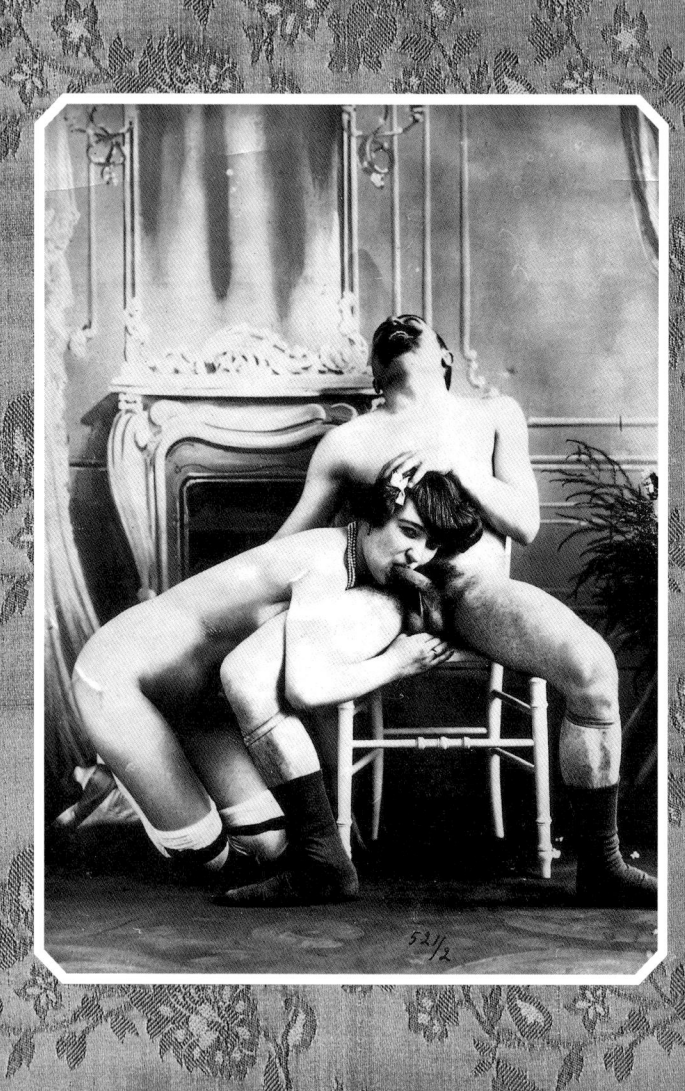

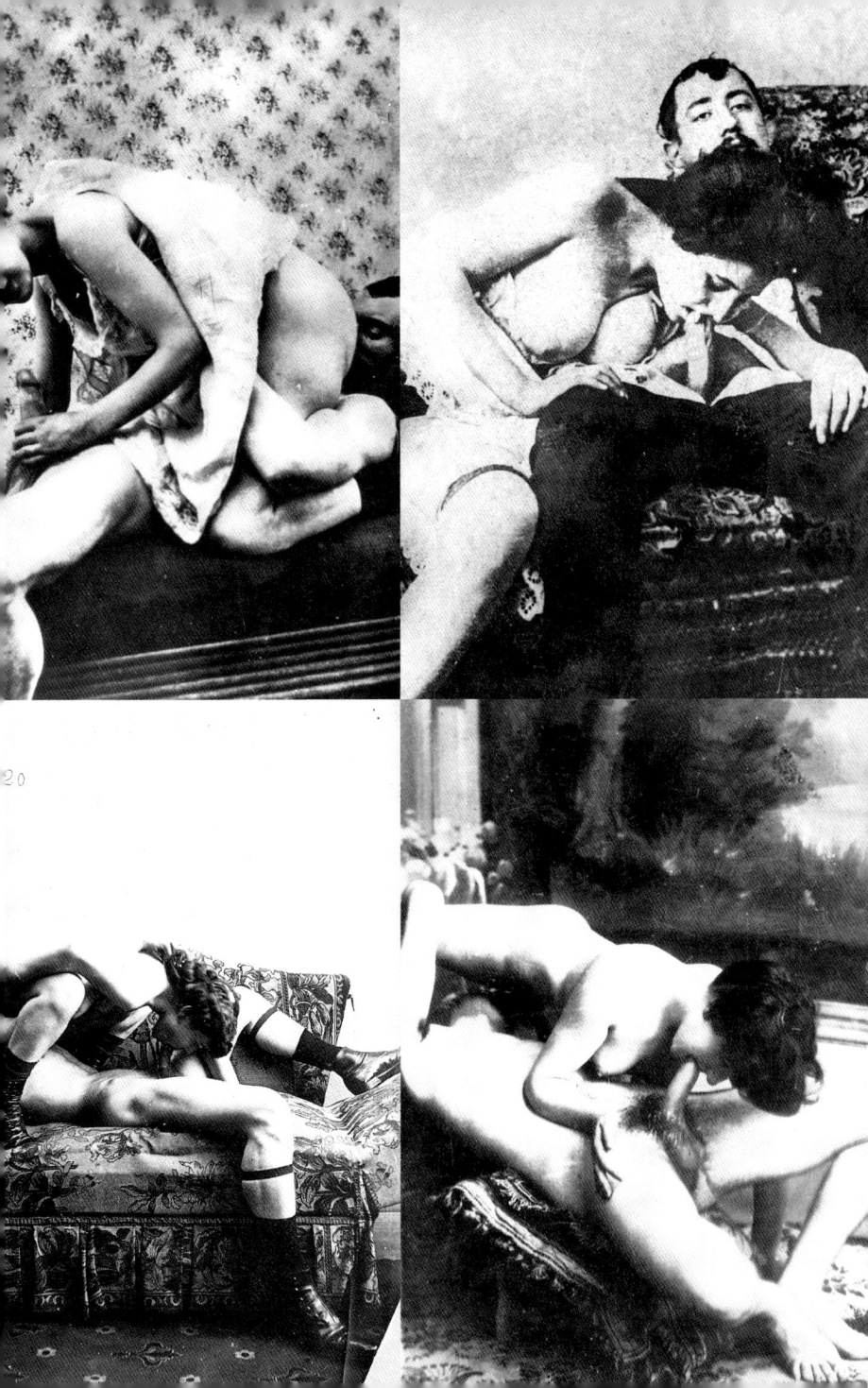

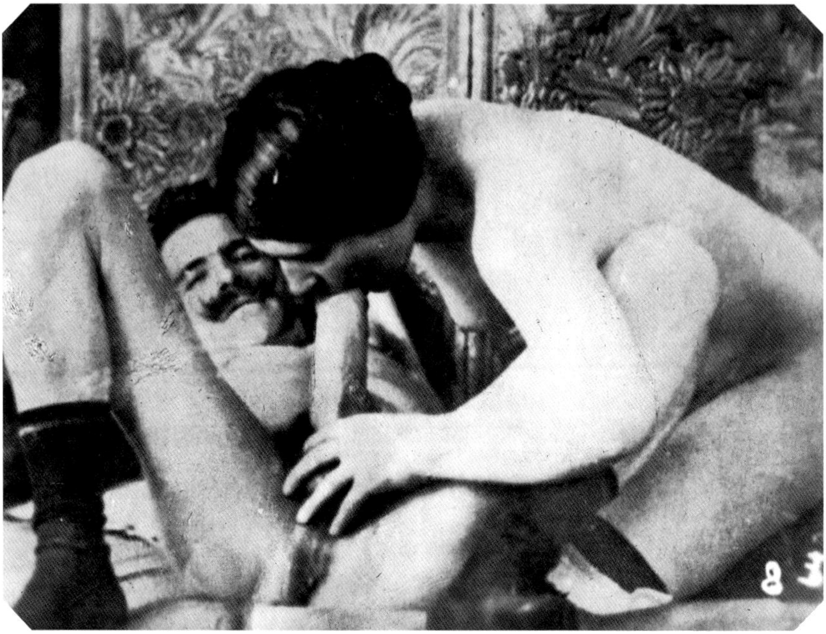

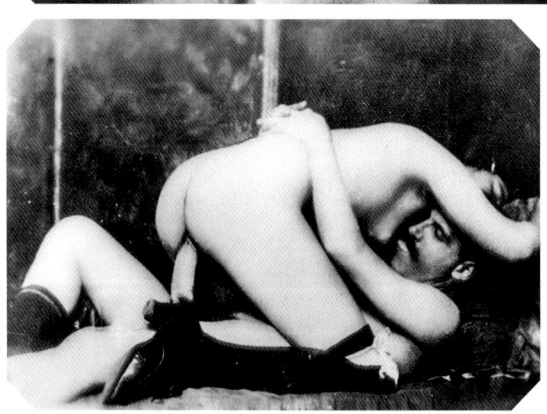

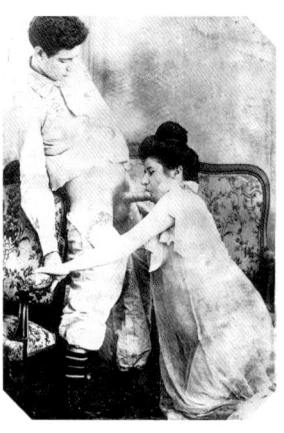

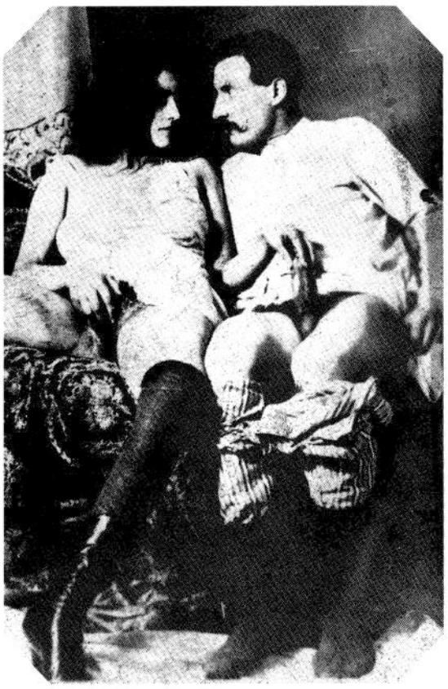

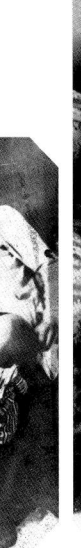

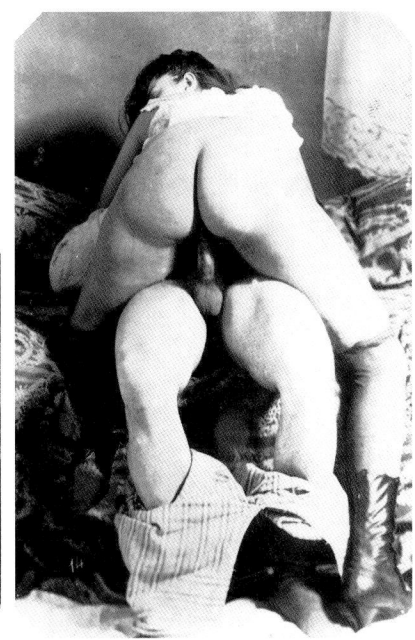

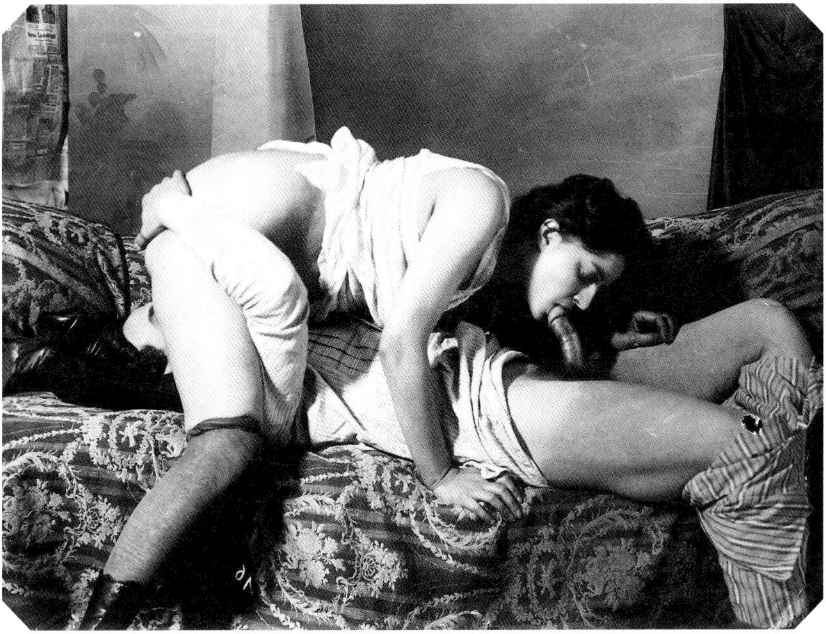

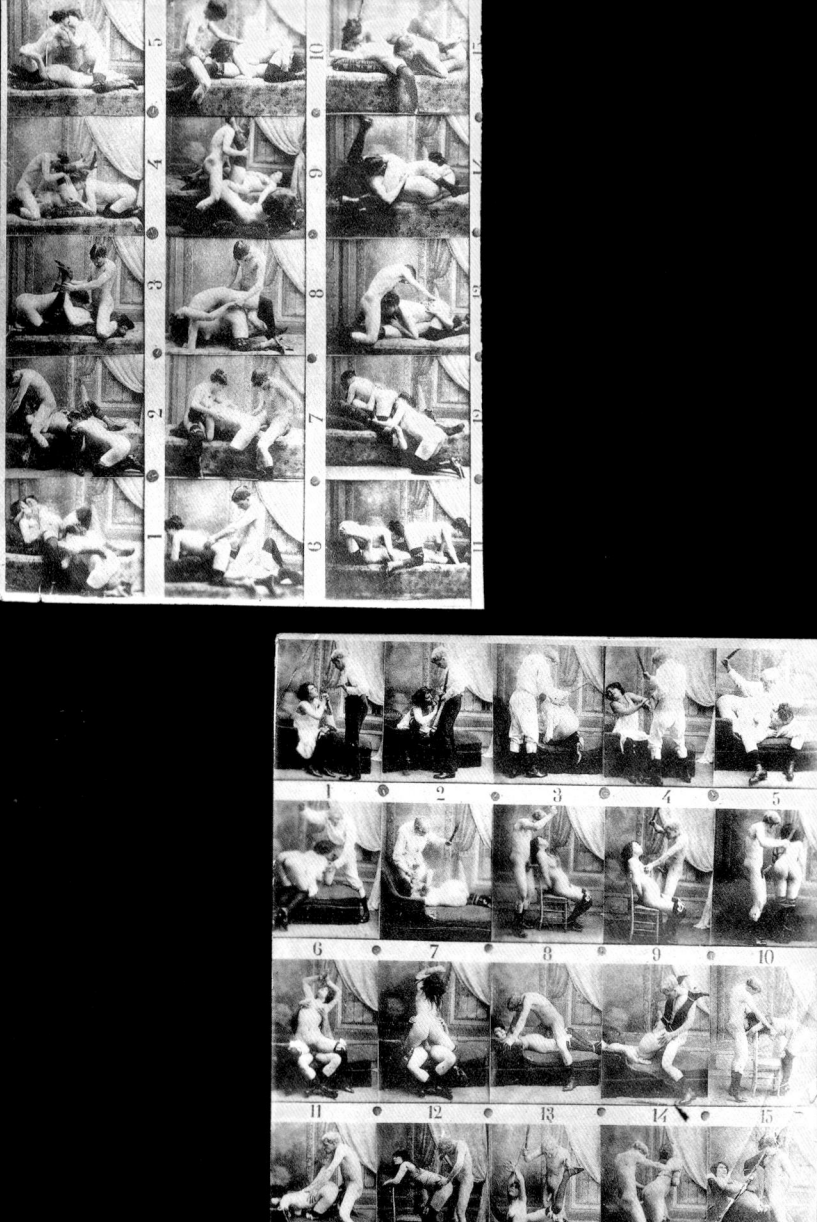

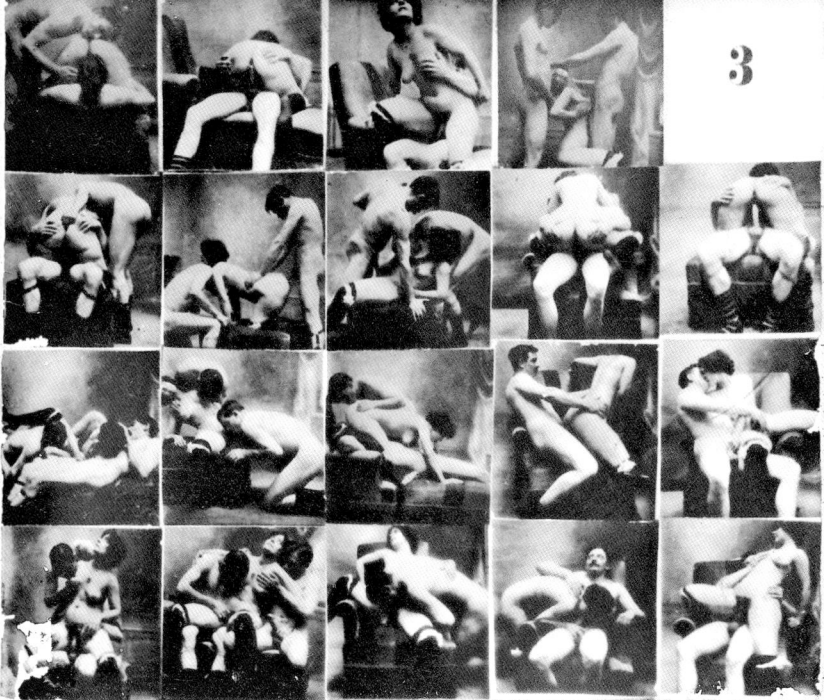

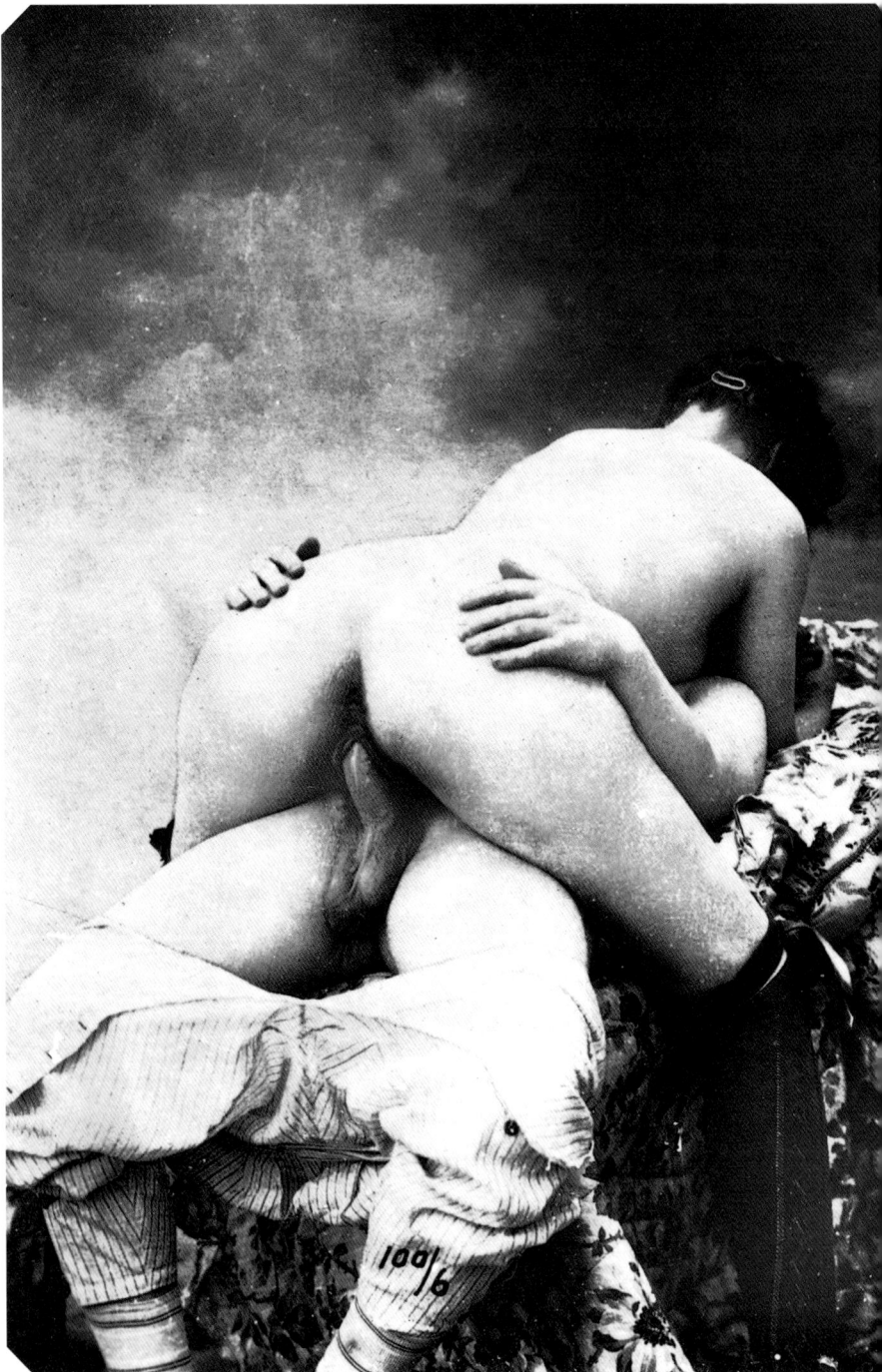

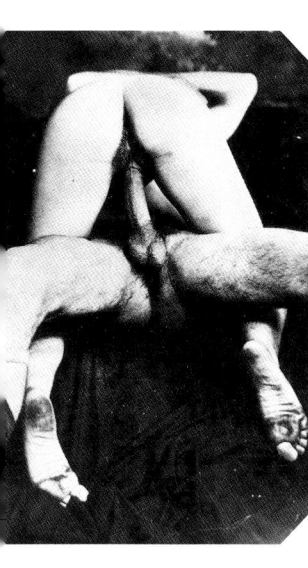

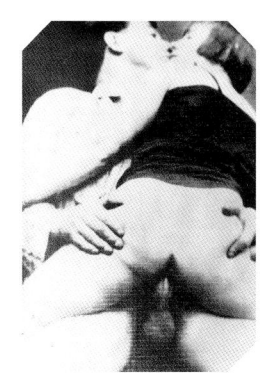

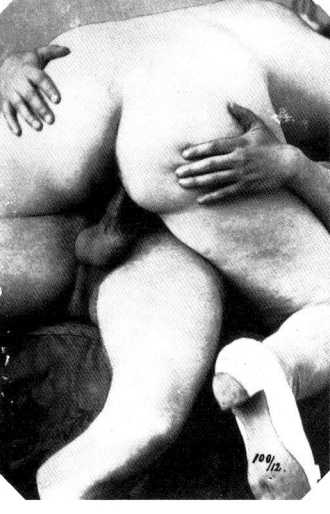

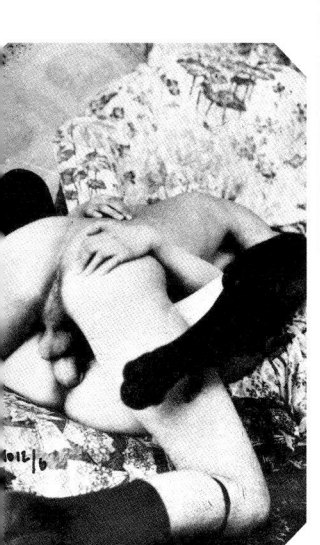

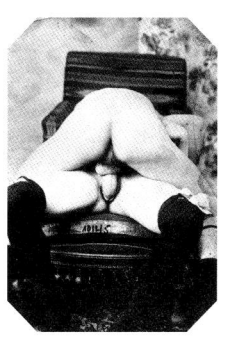

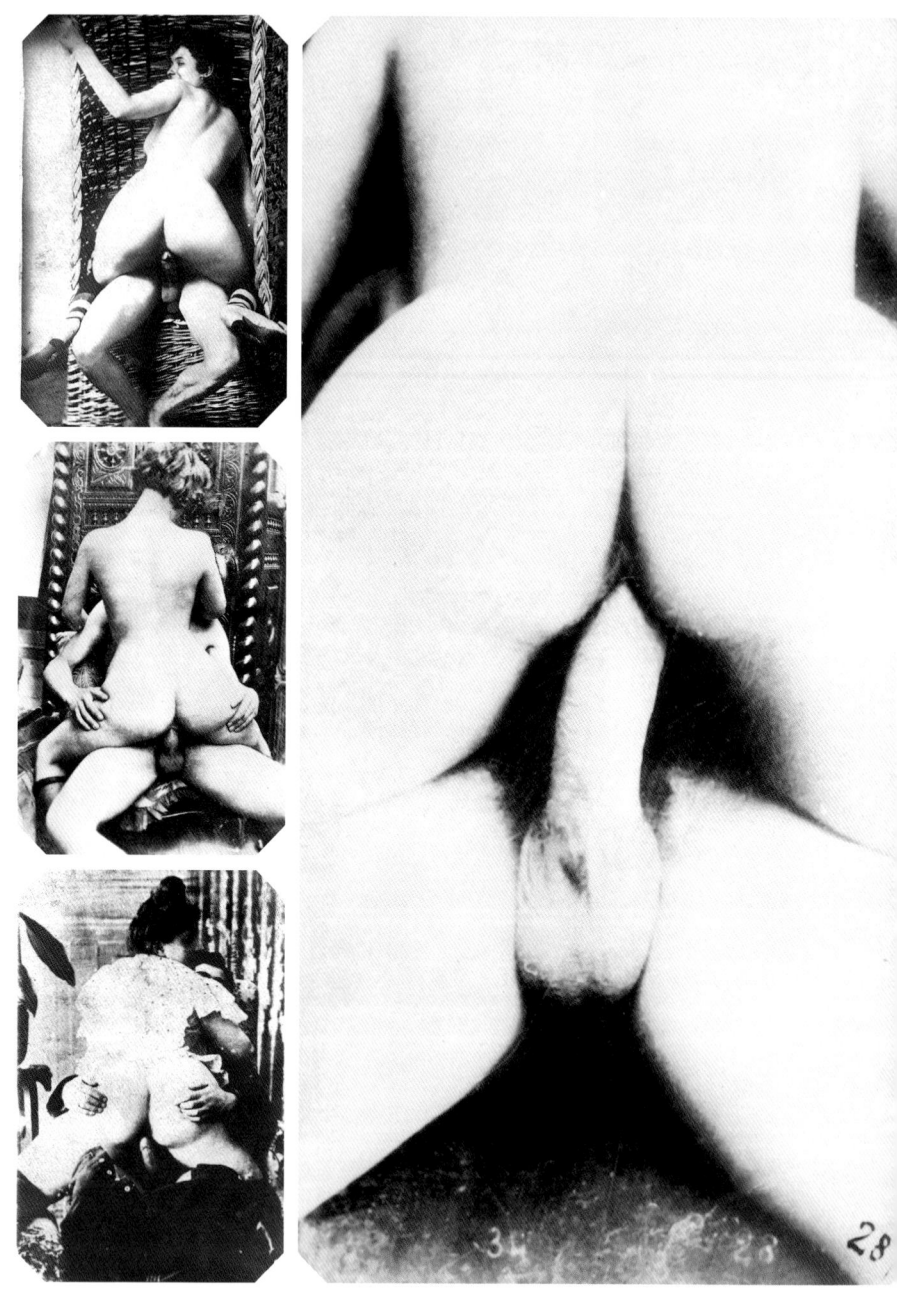

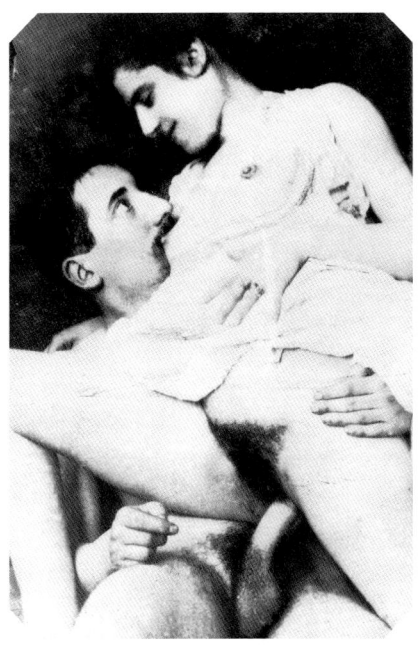
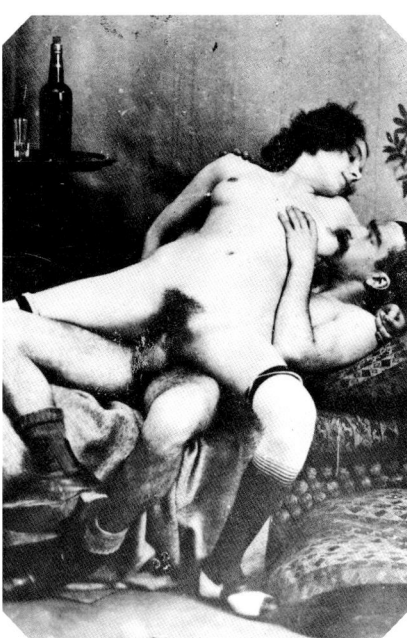
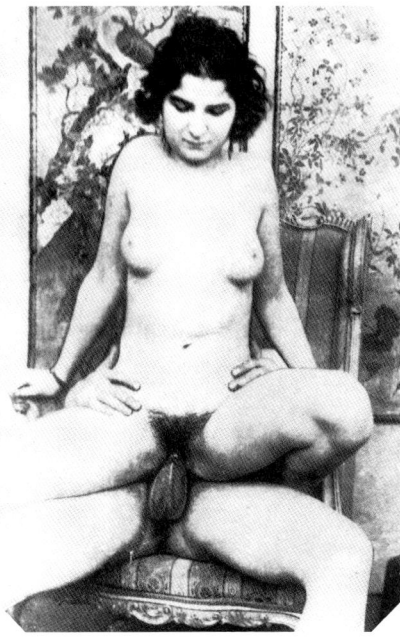
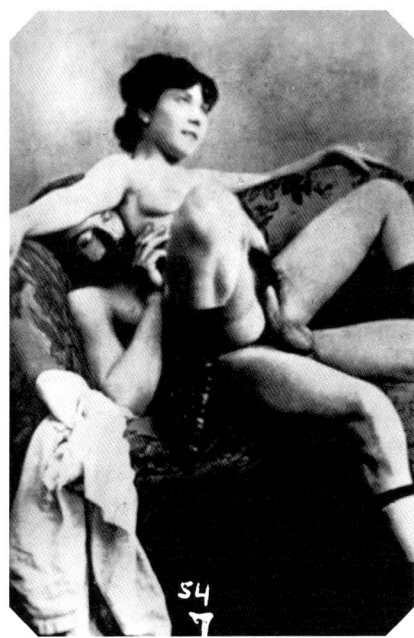

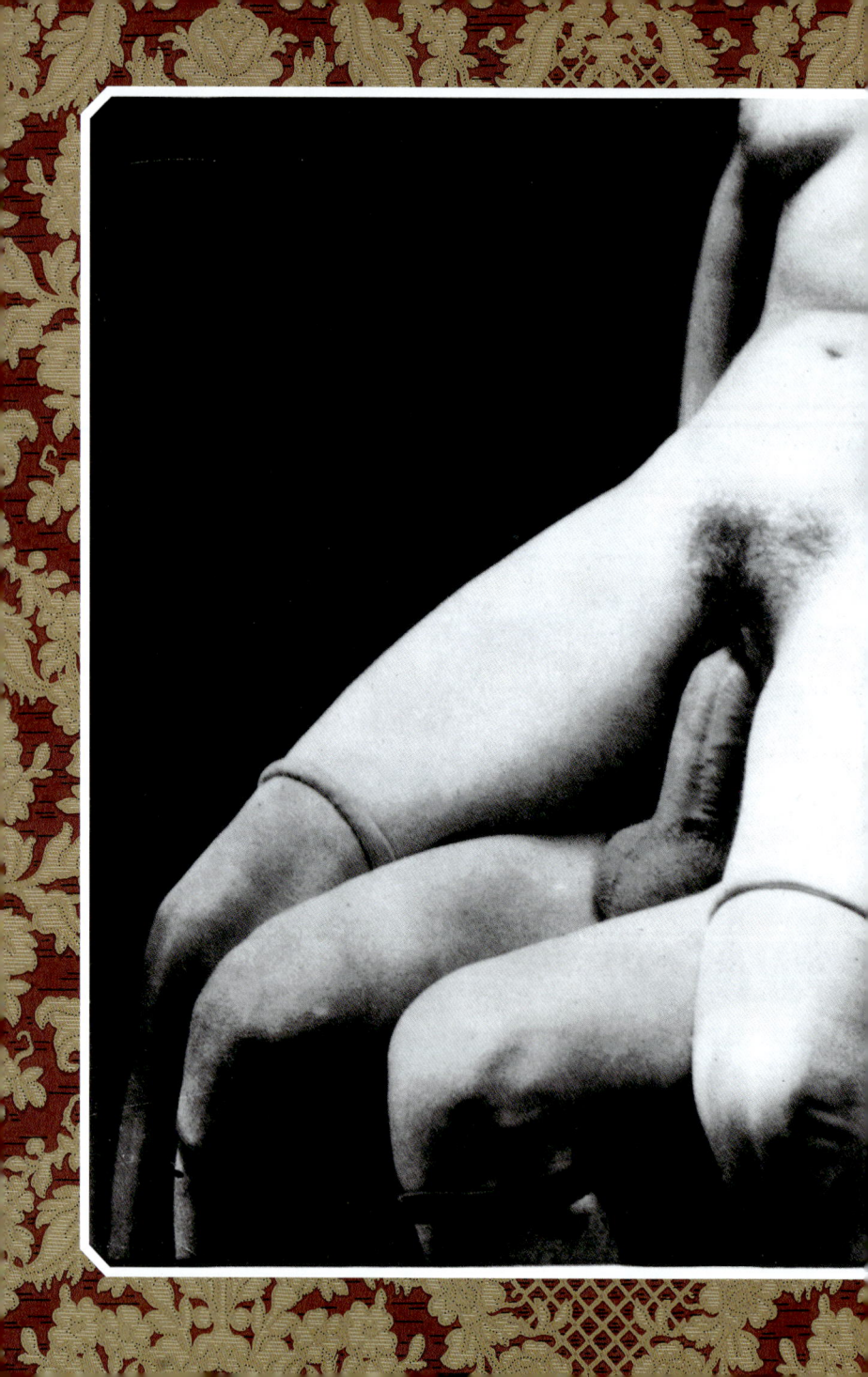

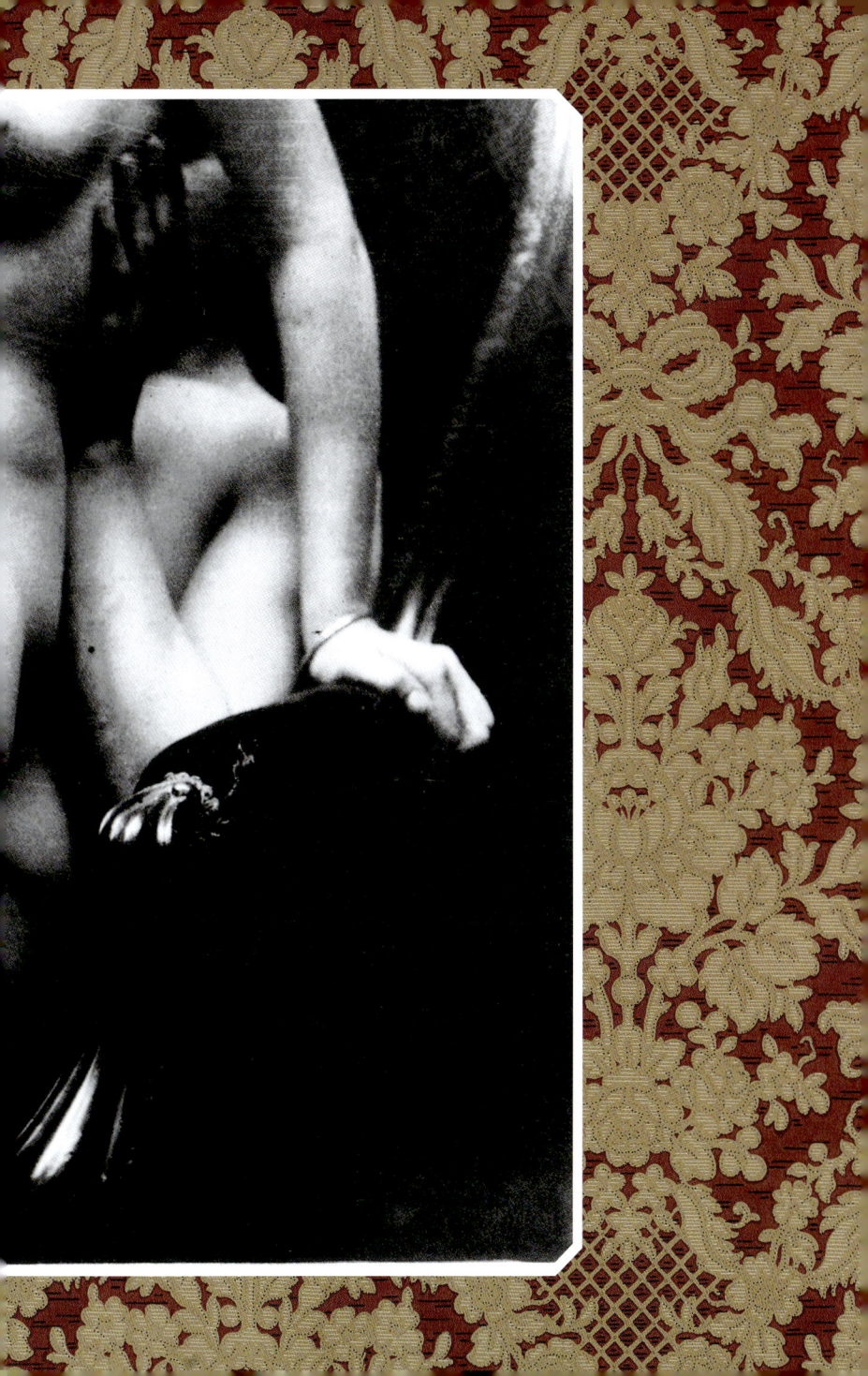

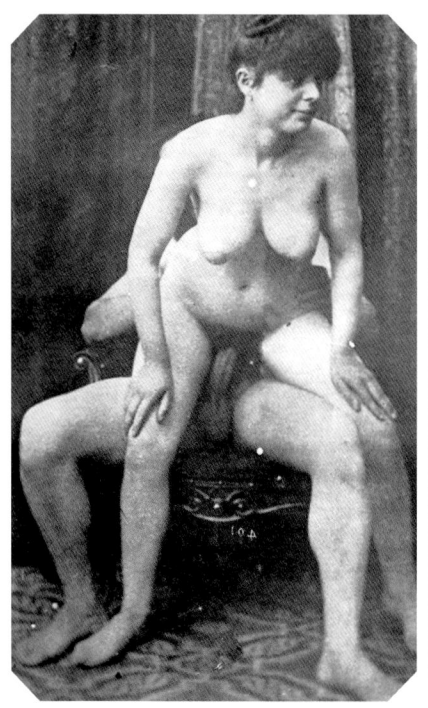 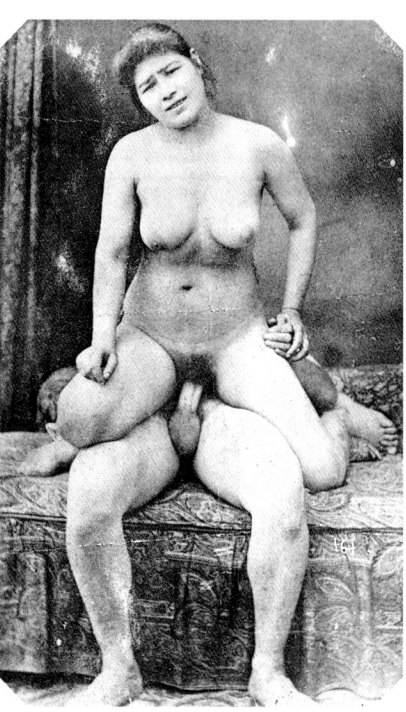

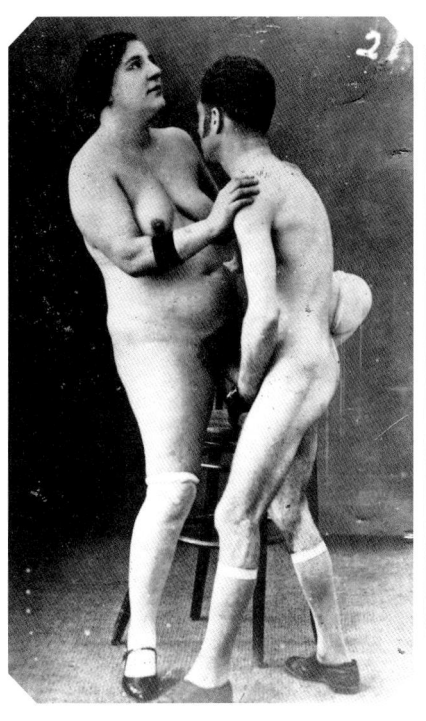 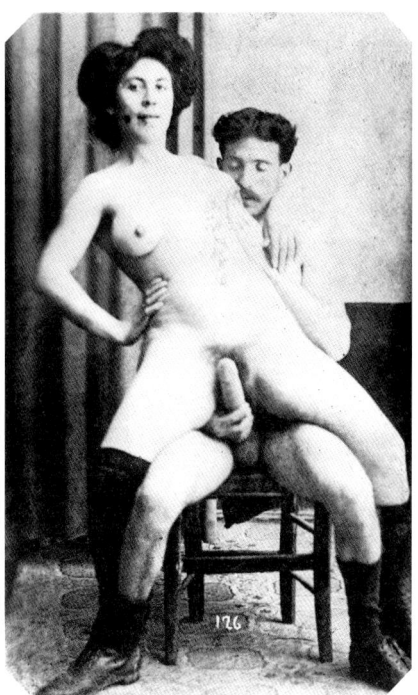

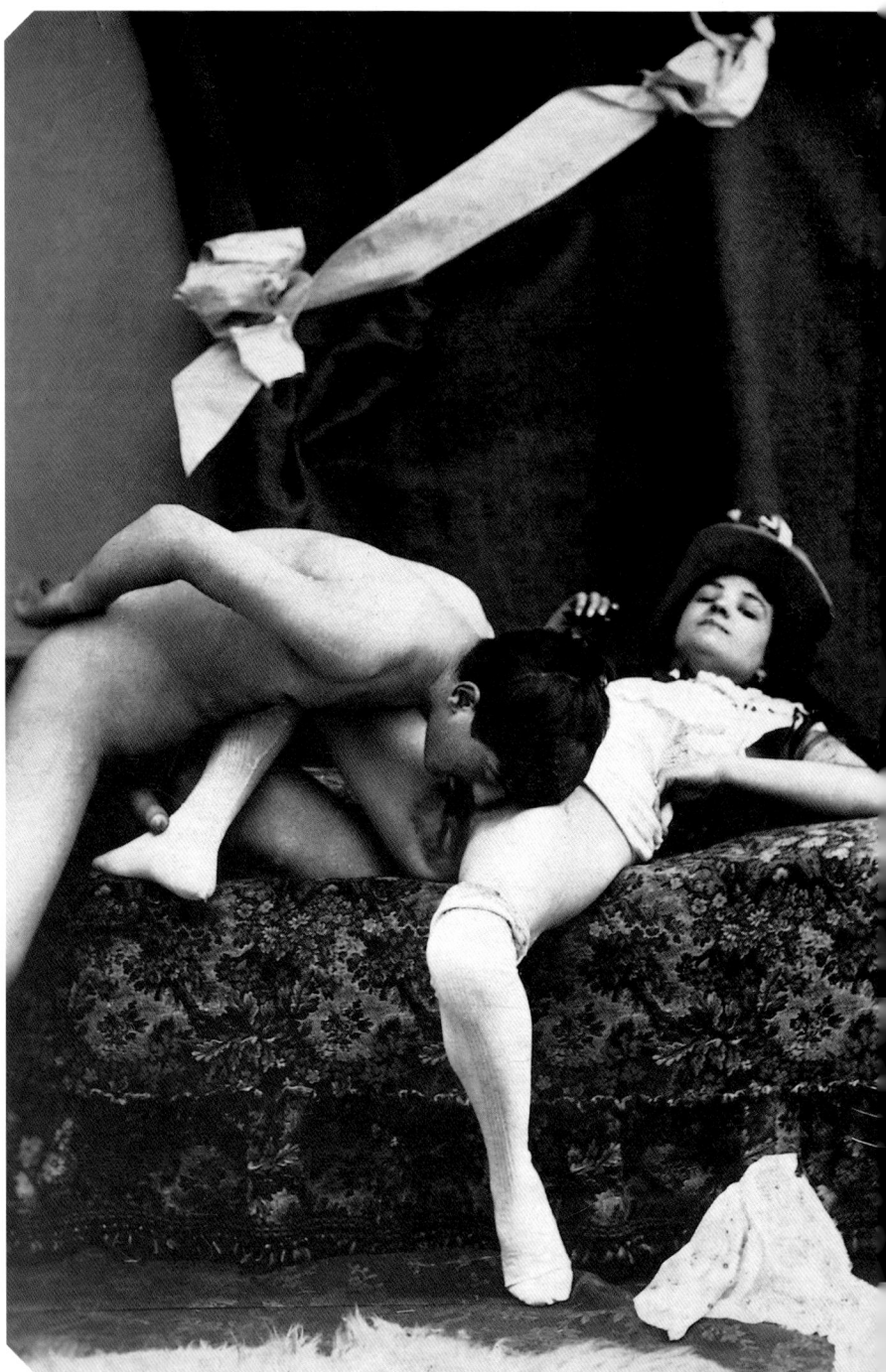

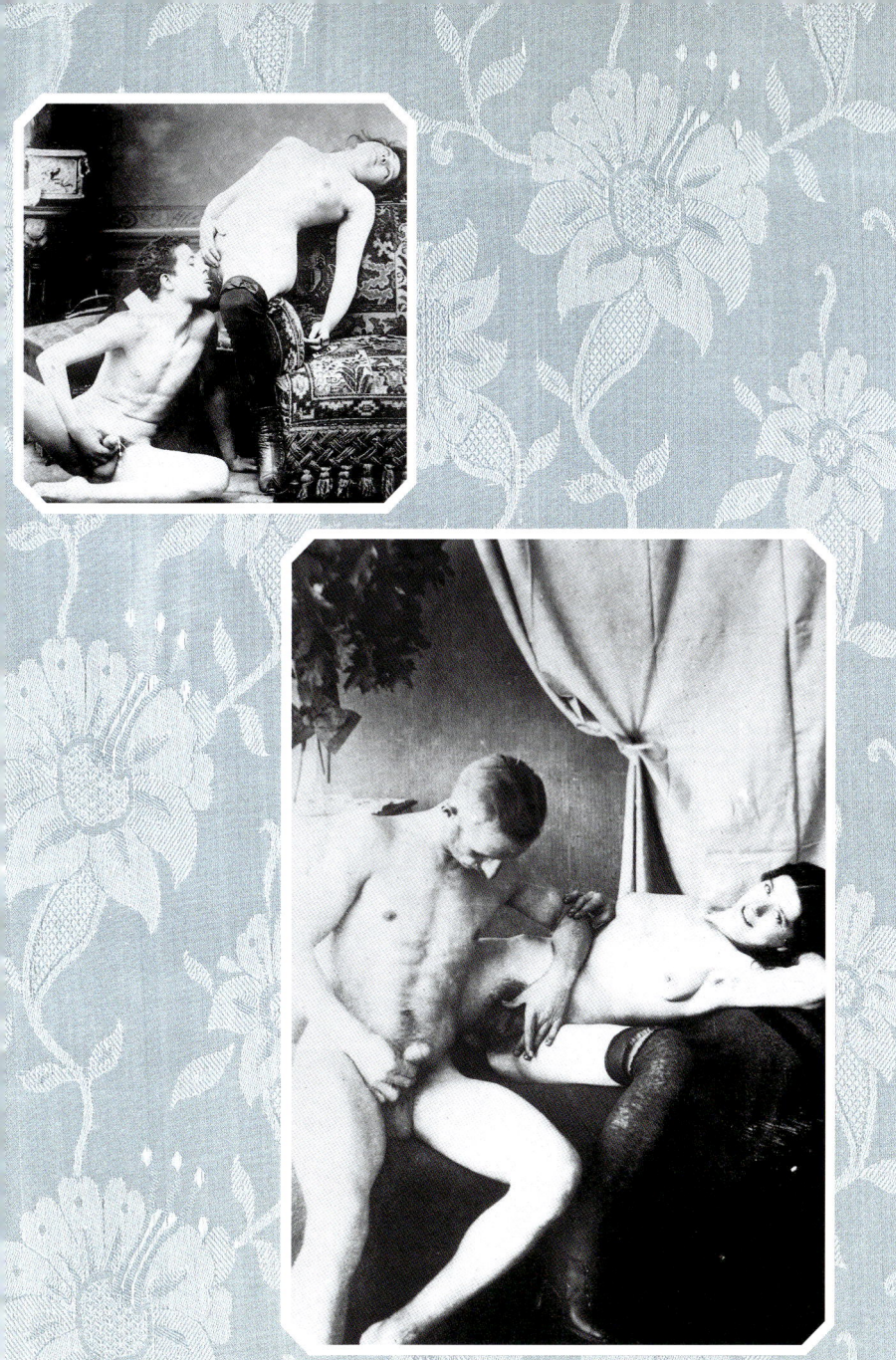

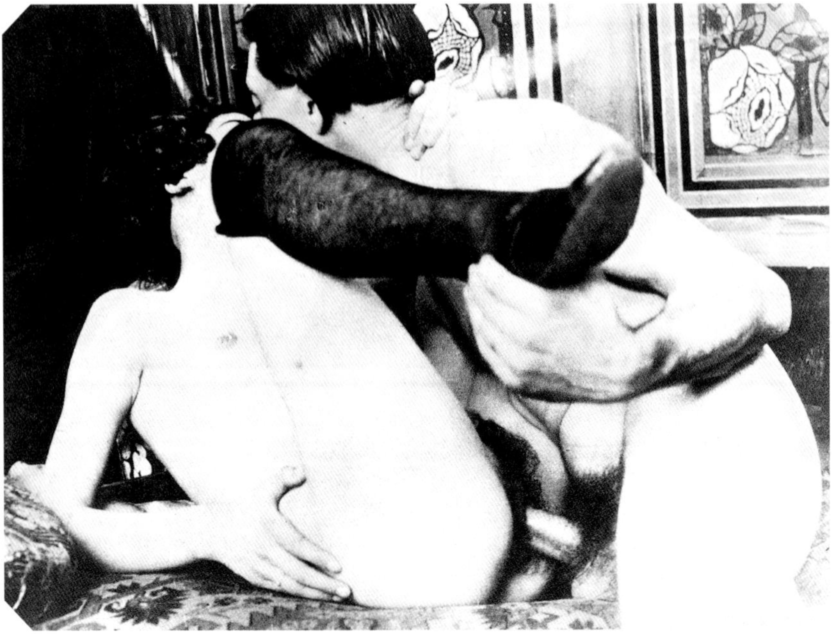

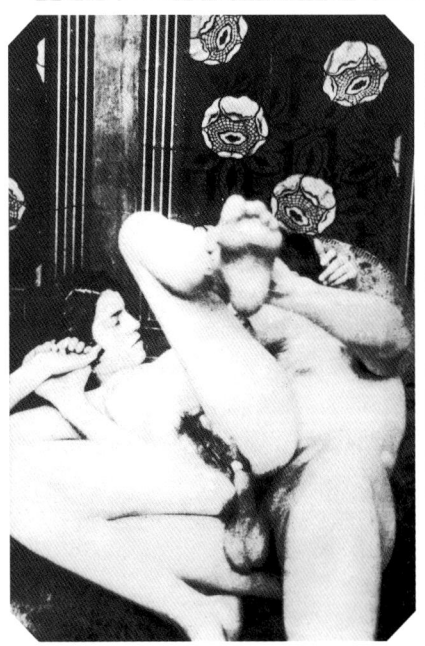
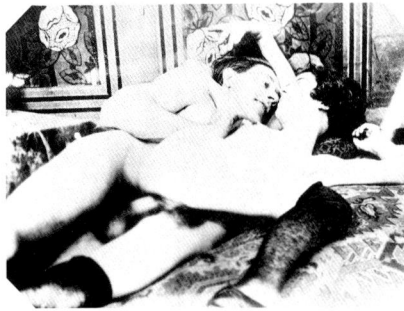
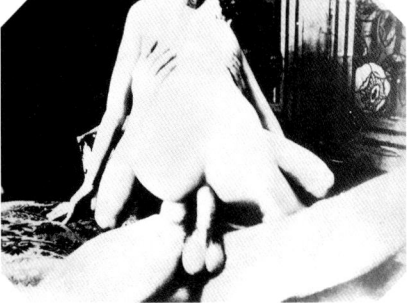

162

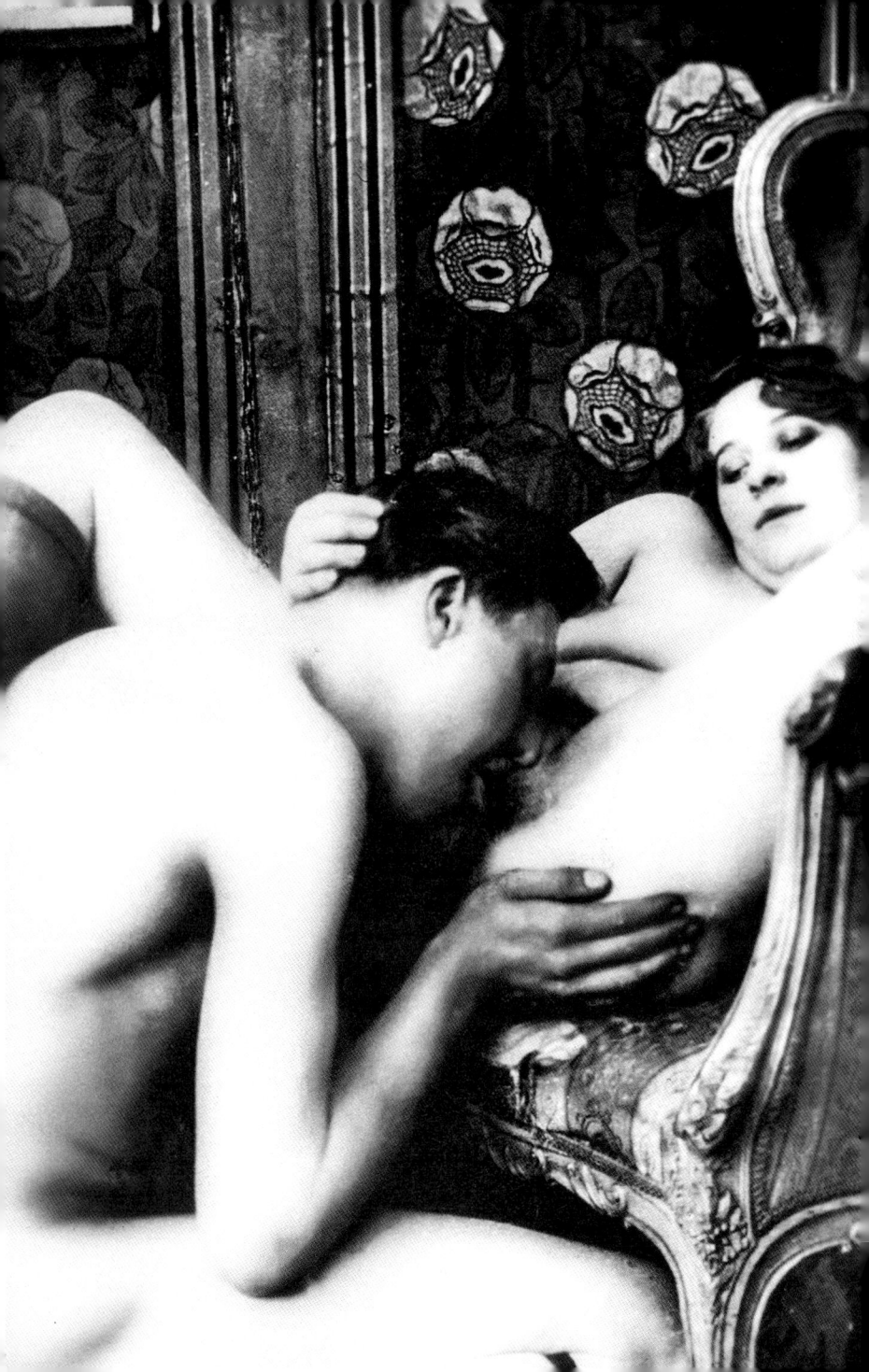

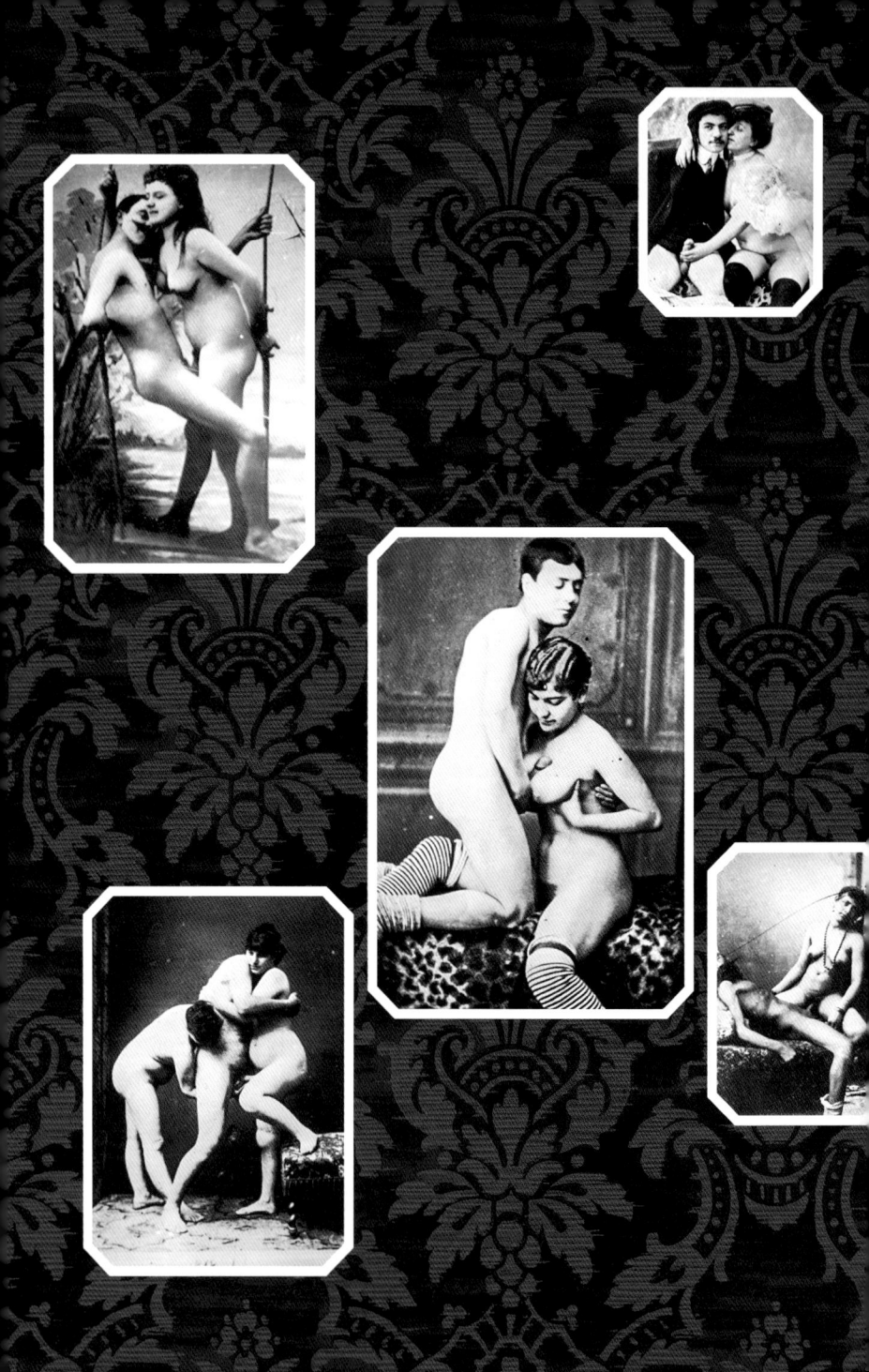

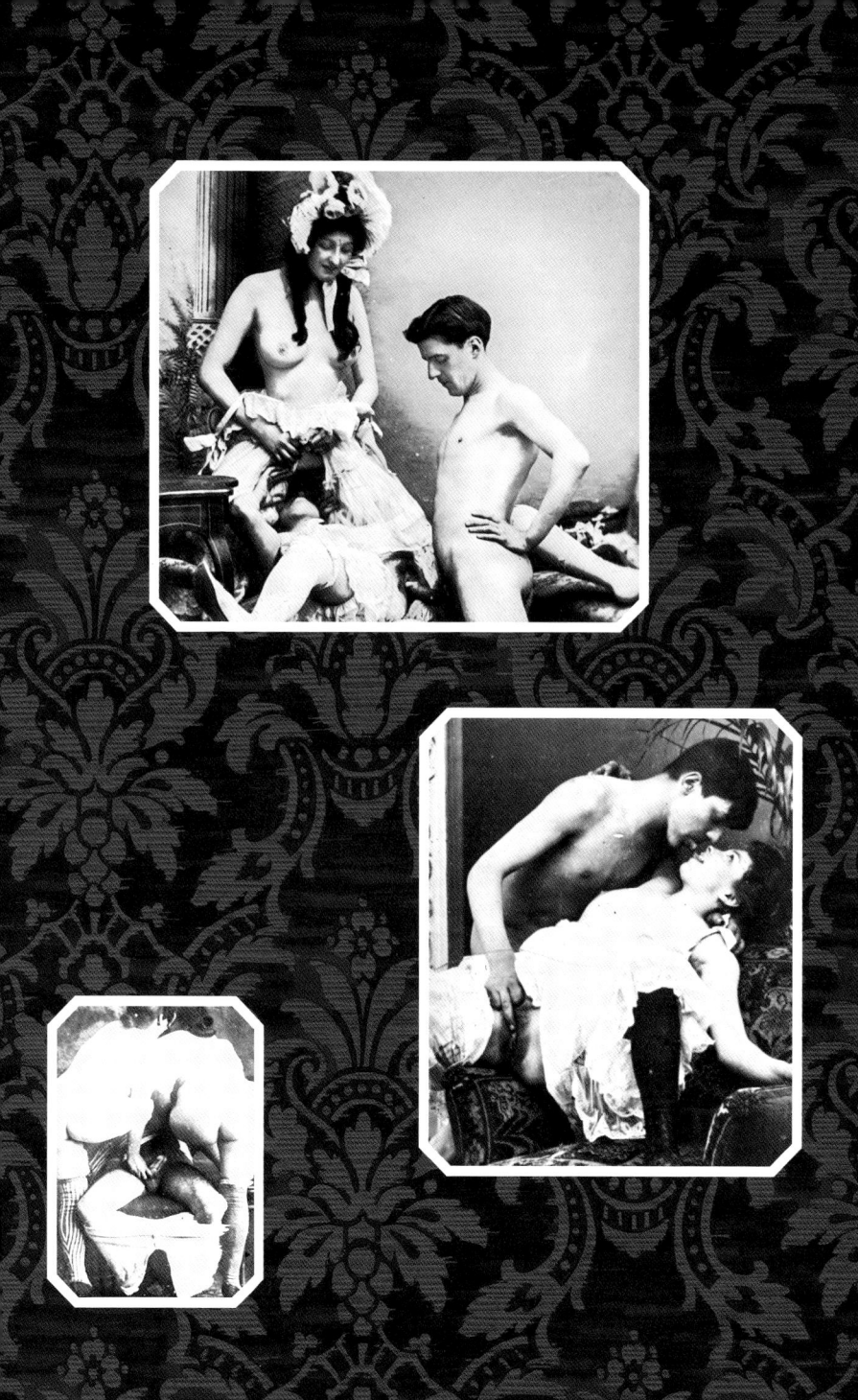

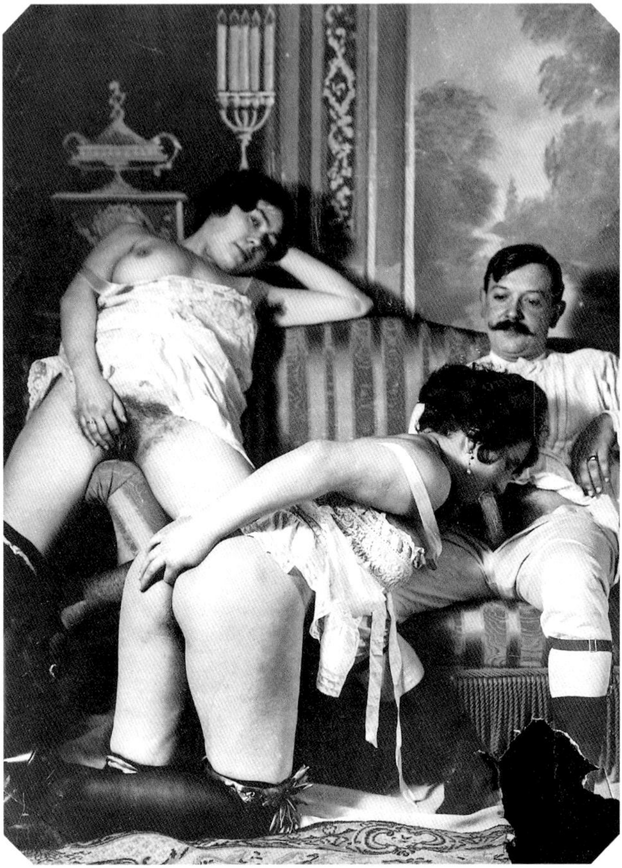

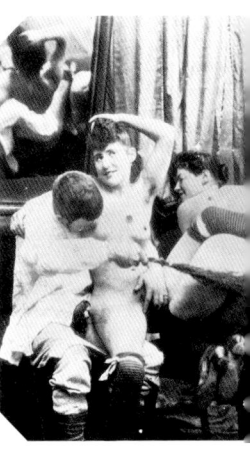

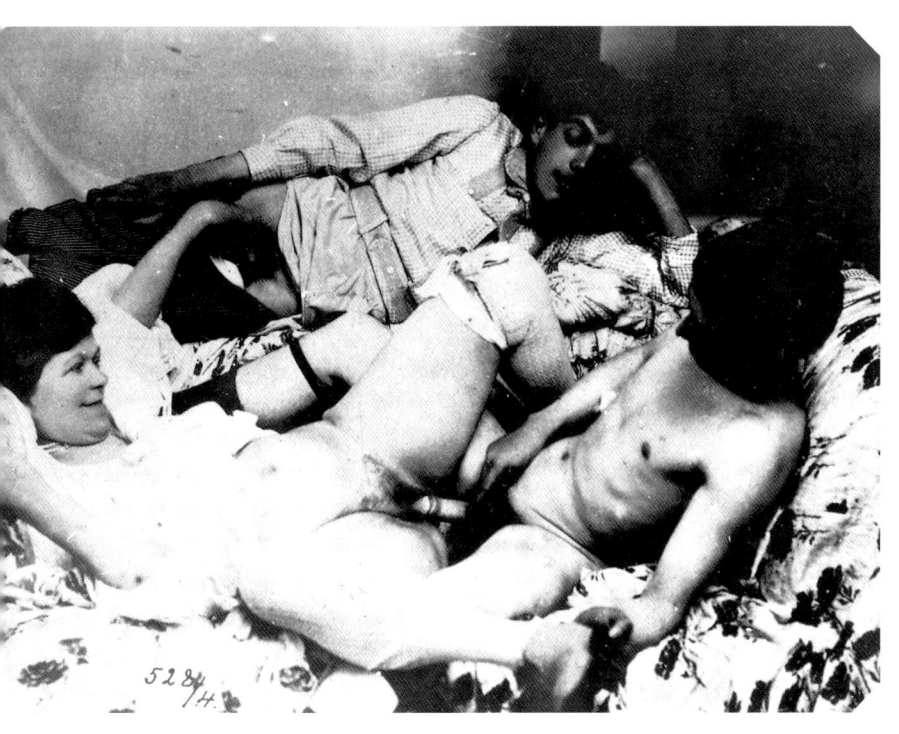

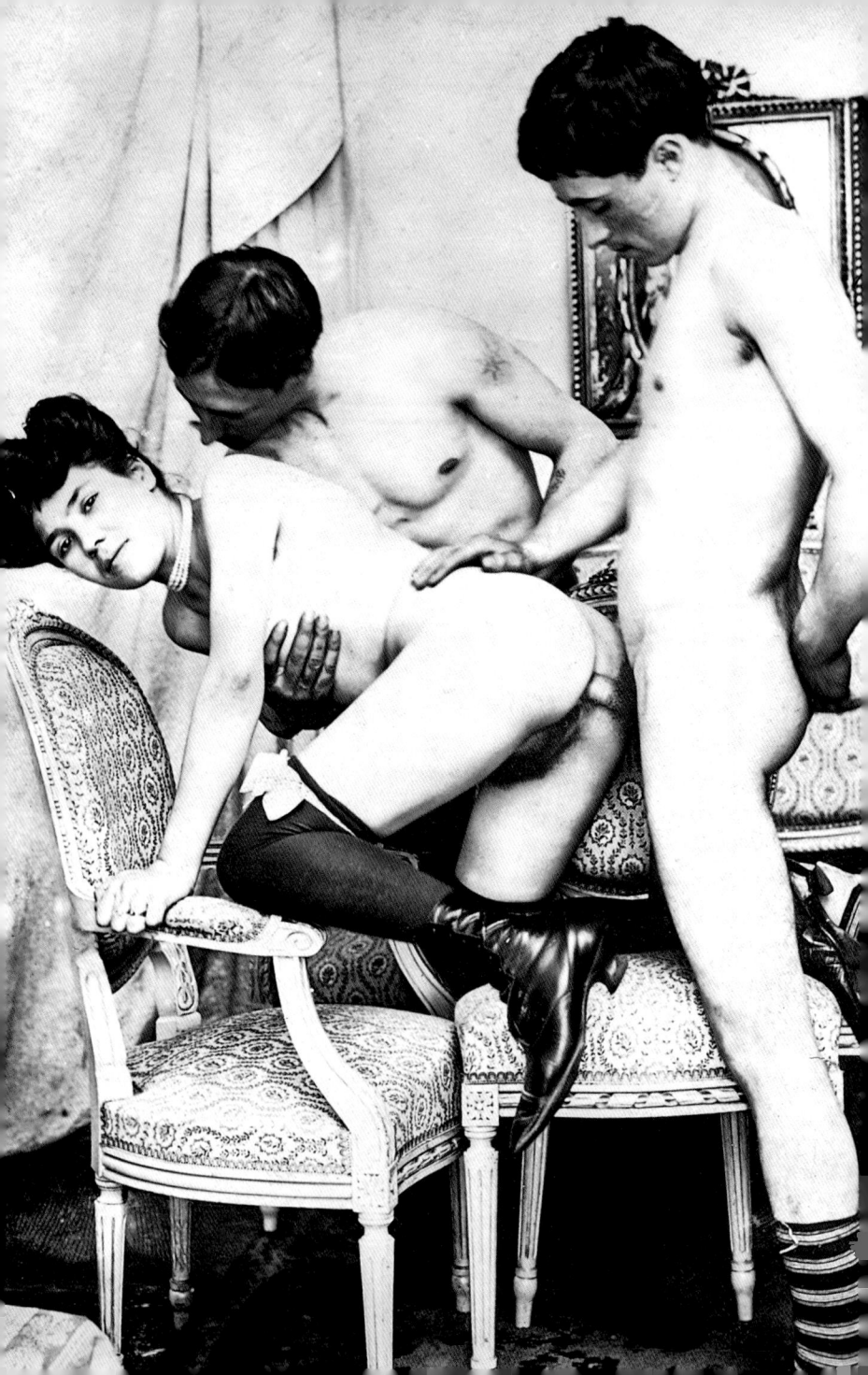

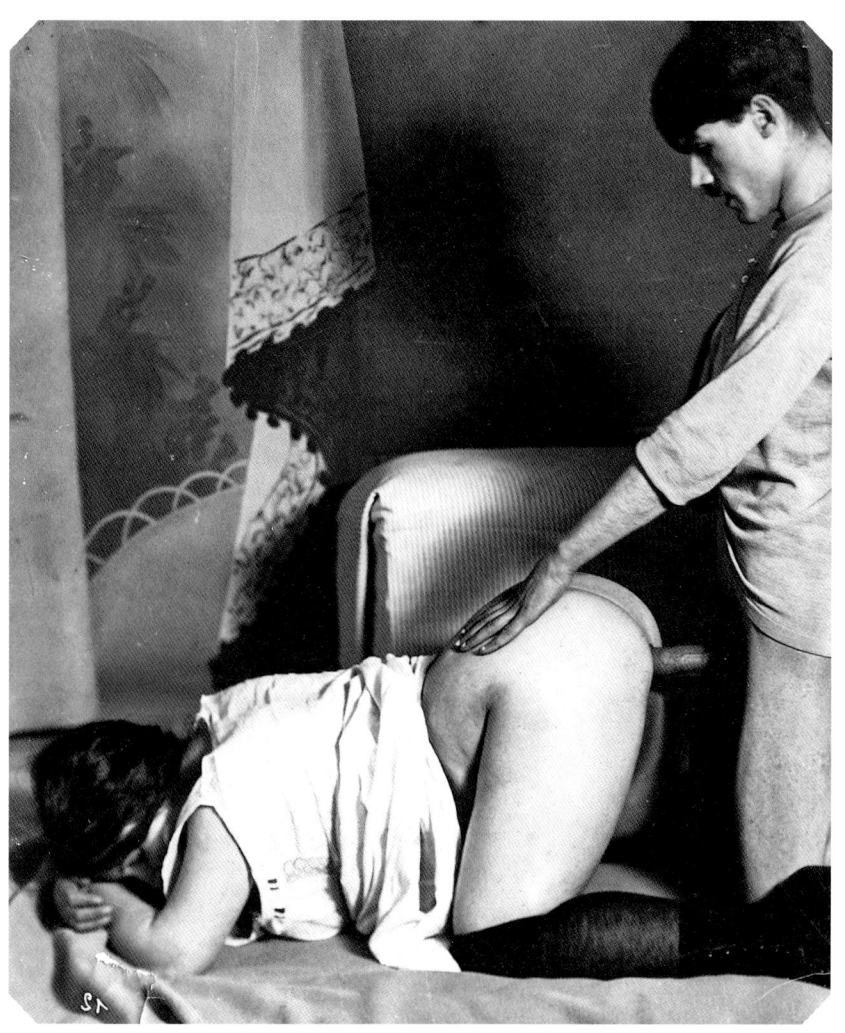

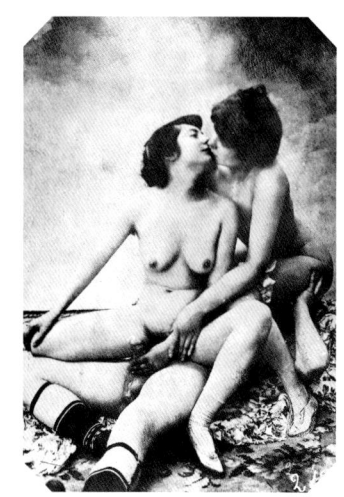

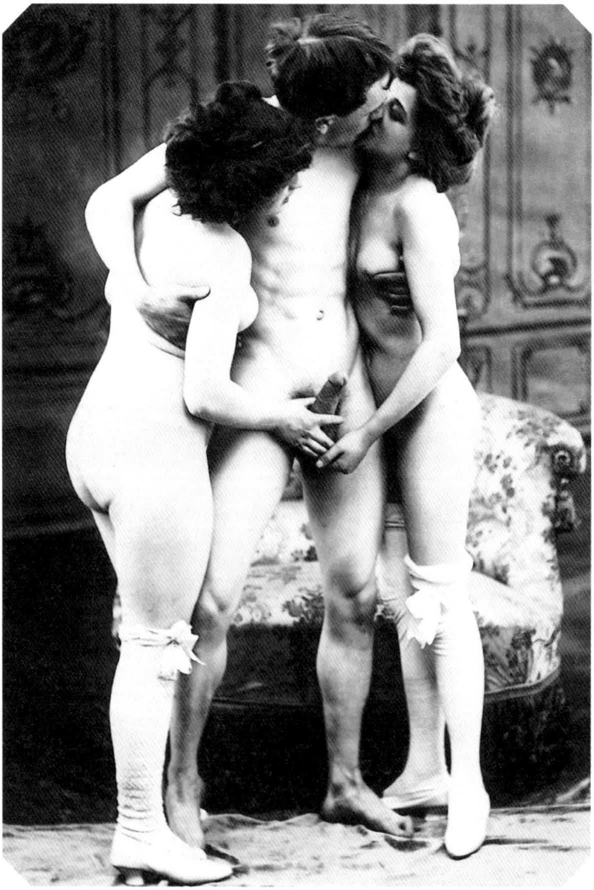

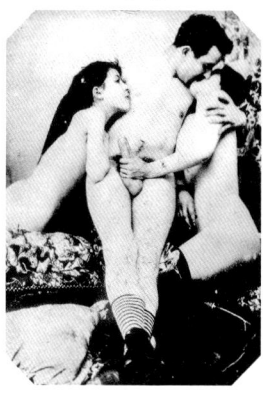

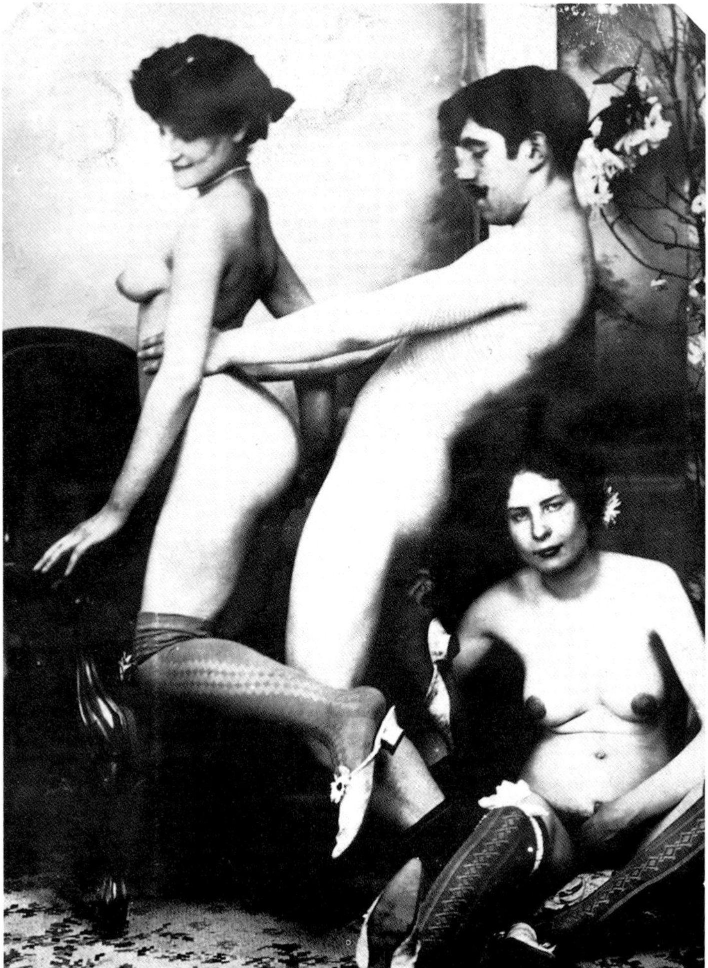

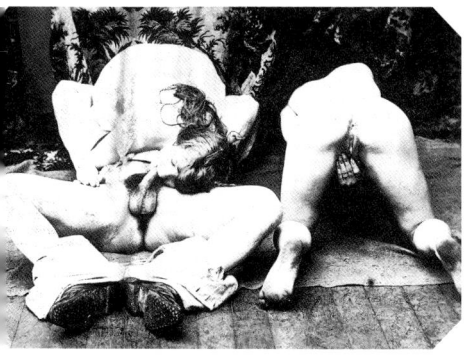

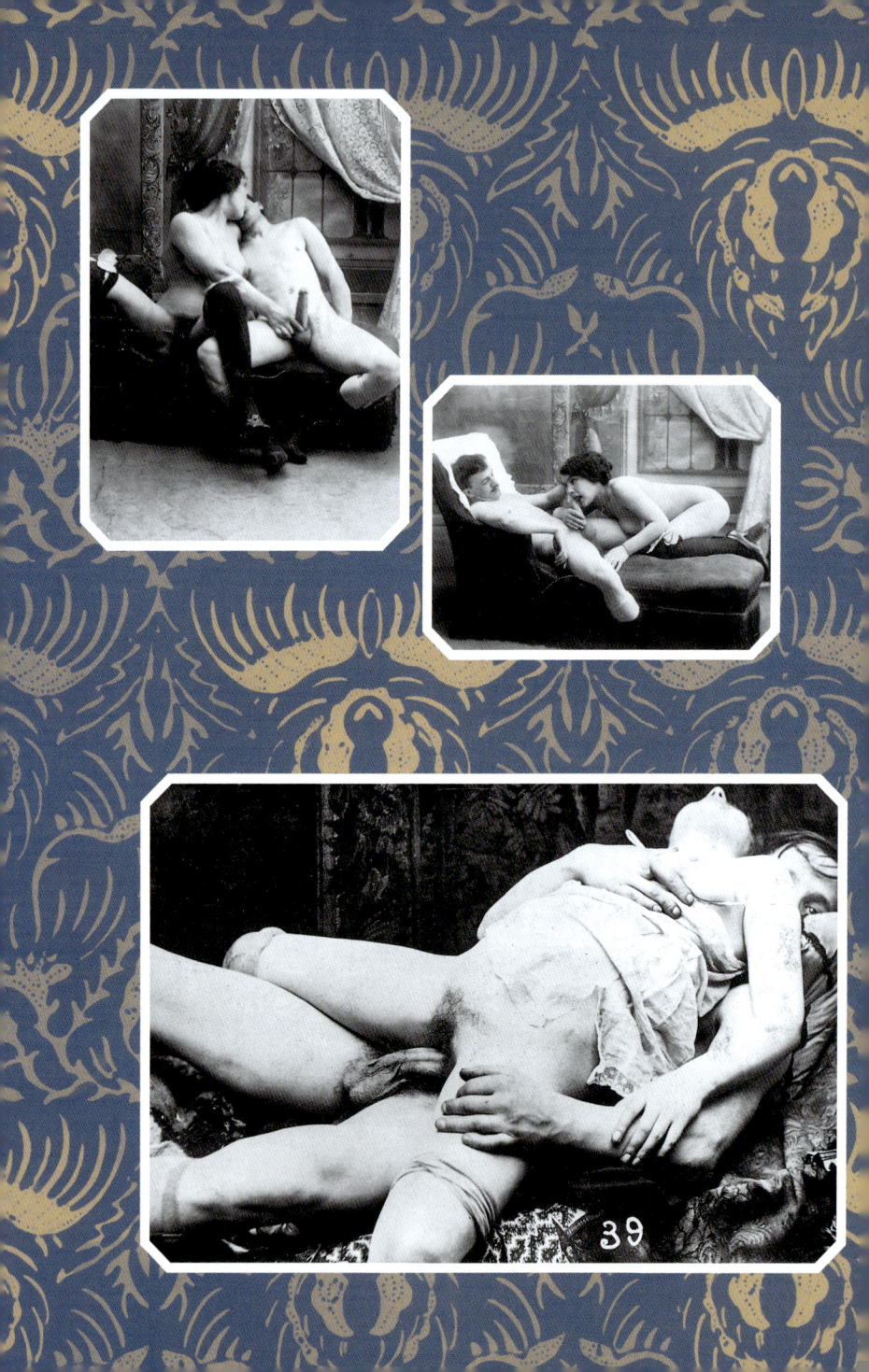

39

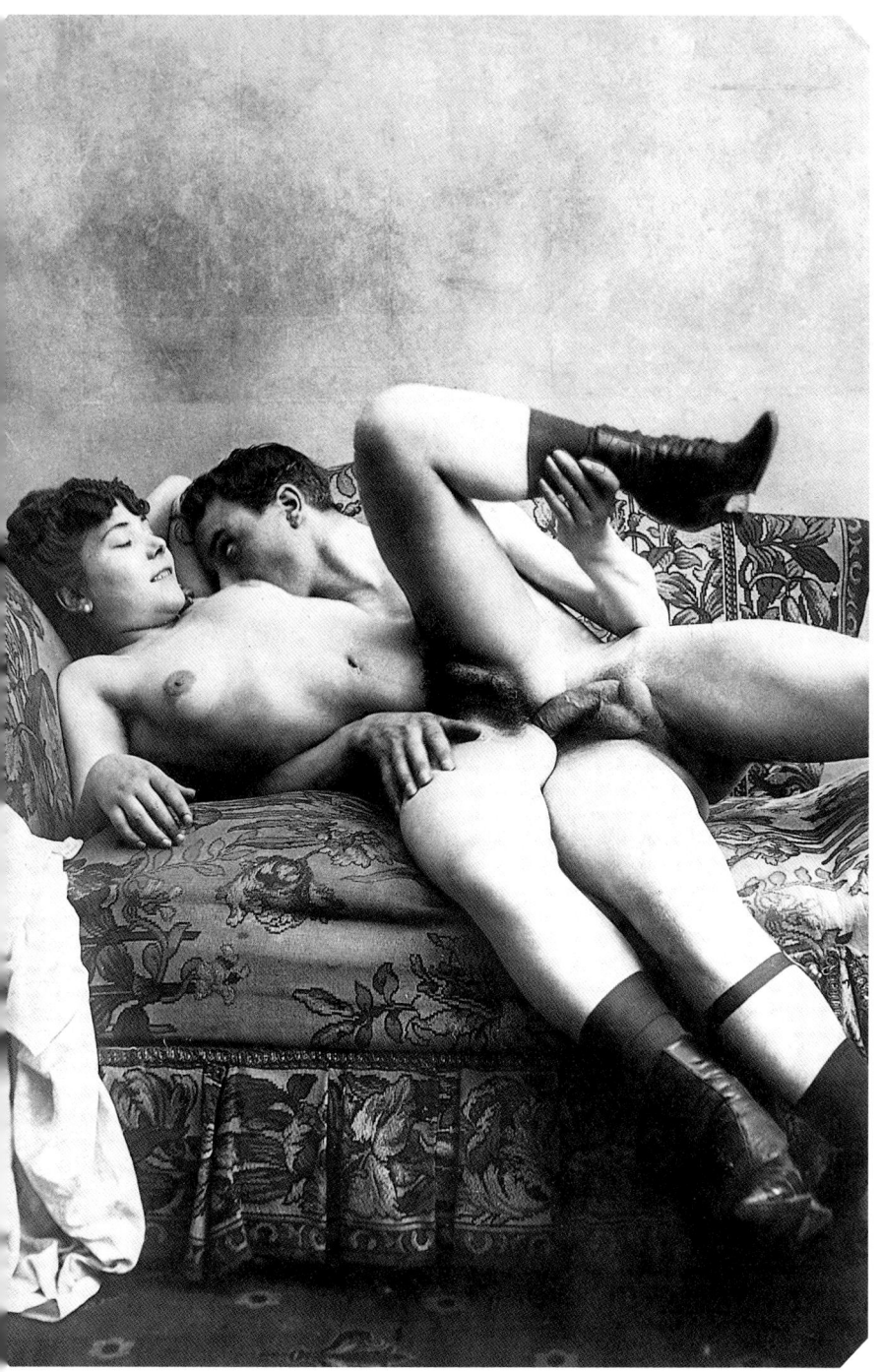

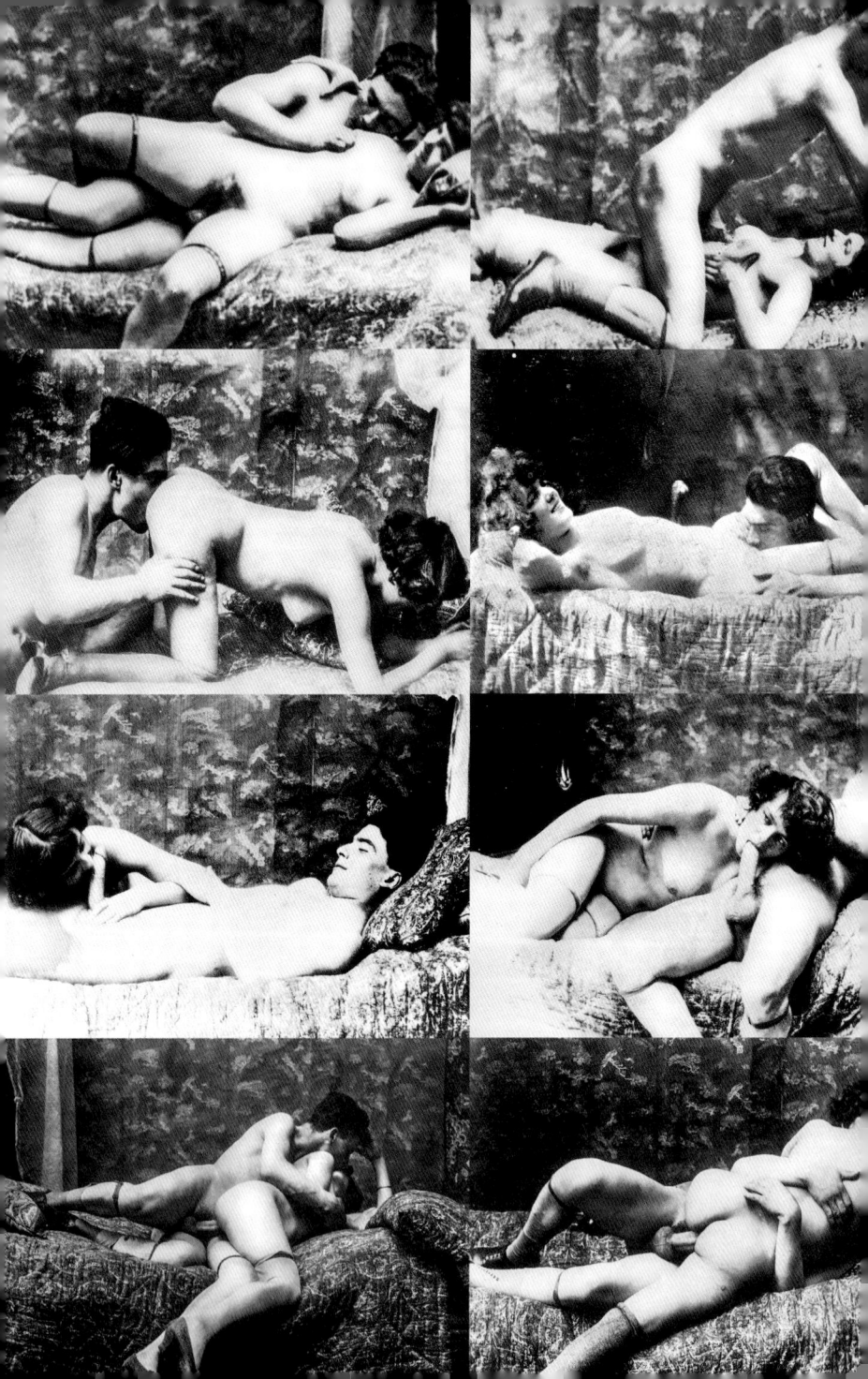

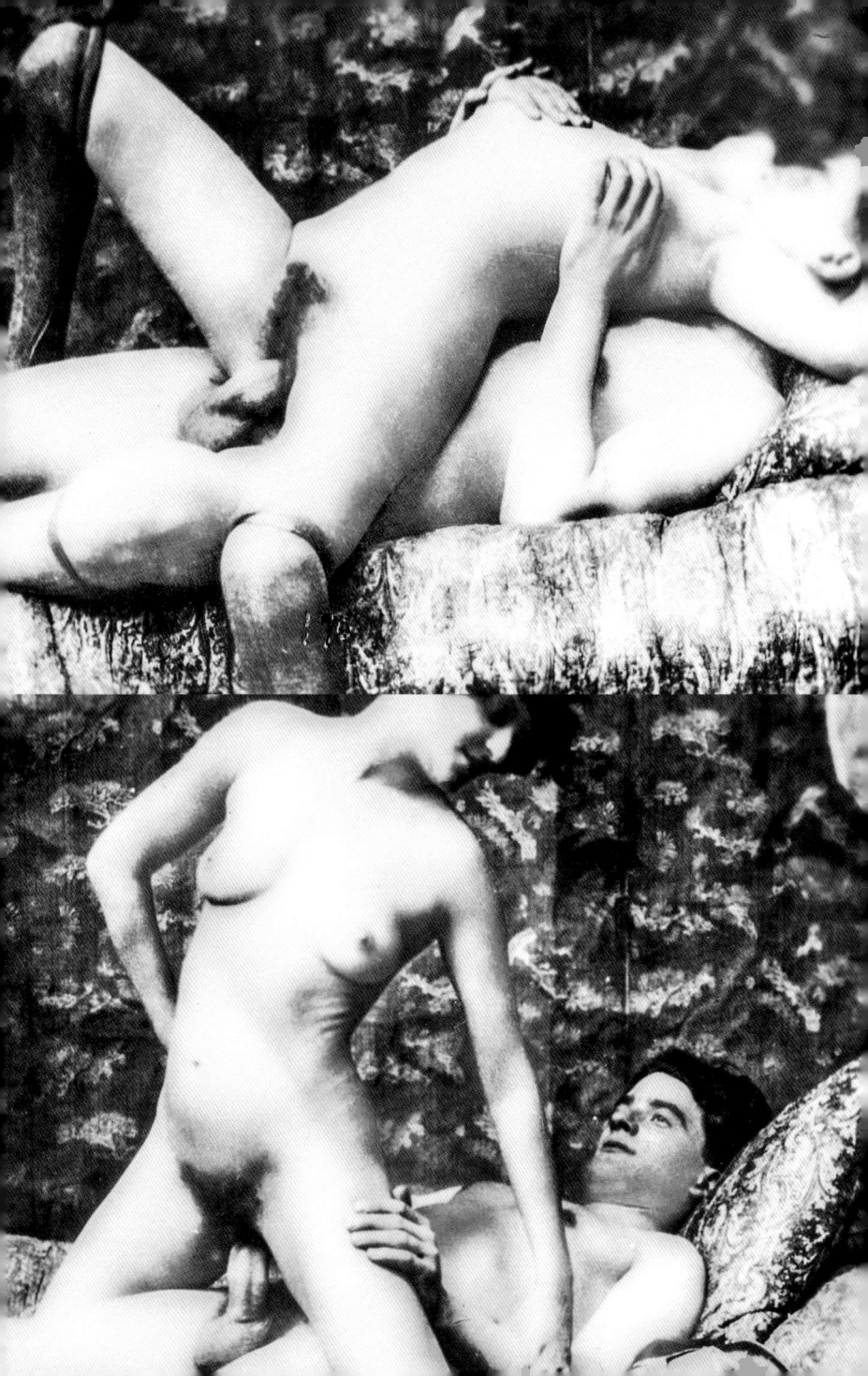

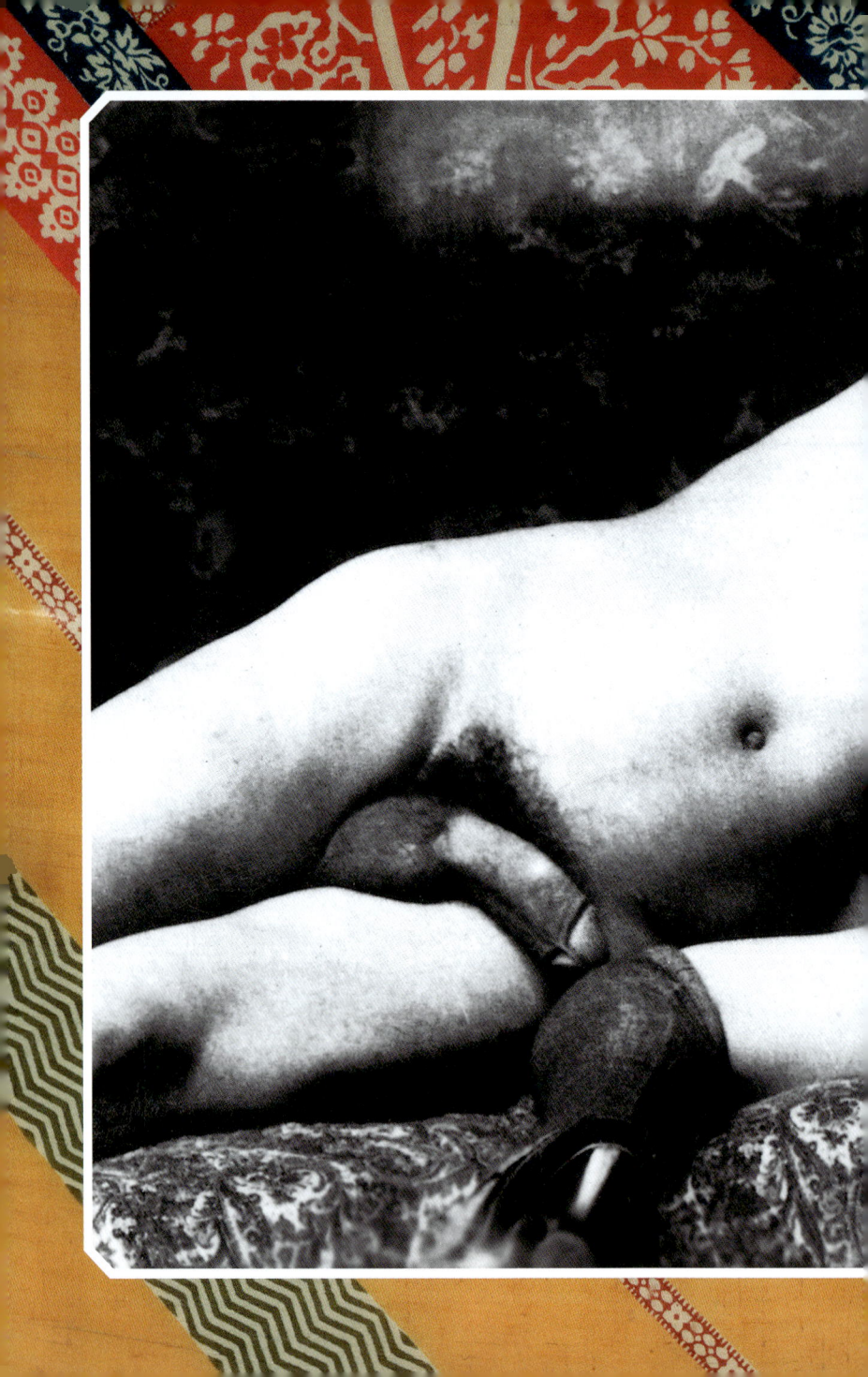

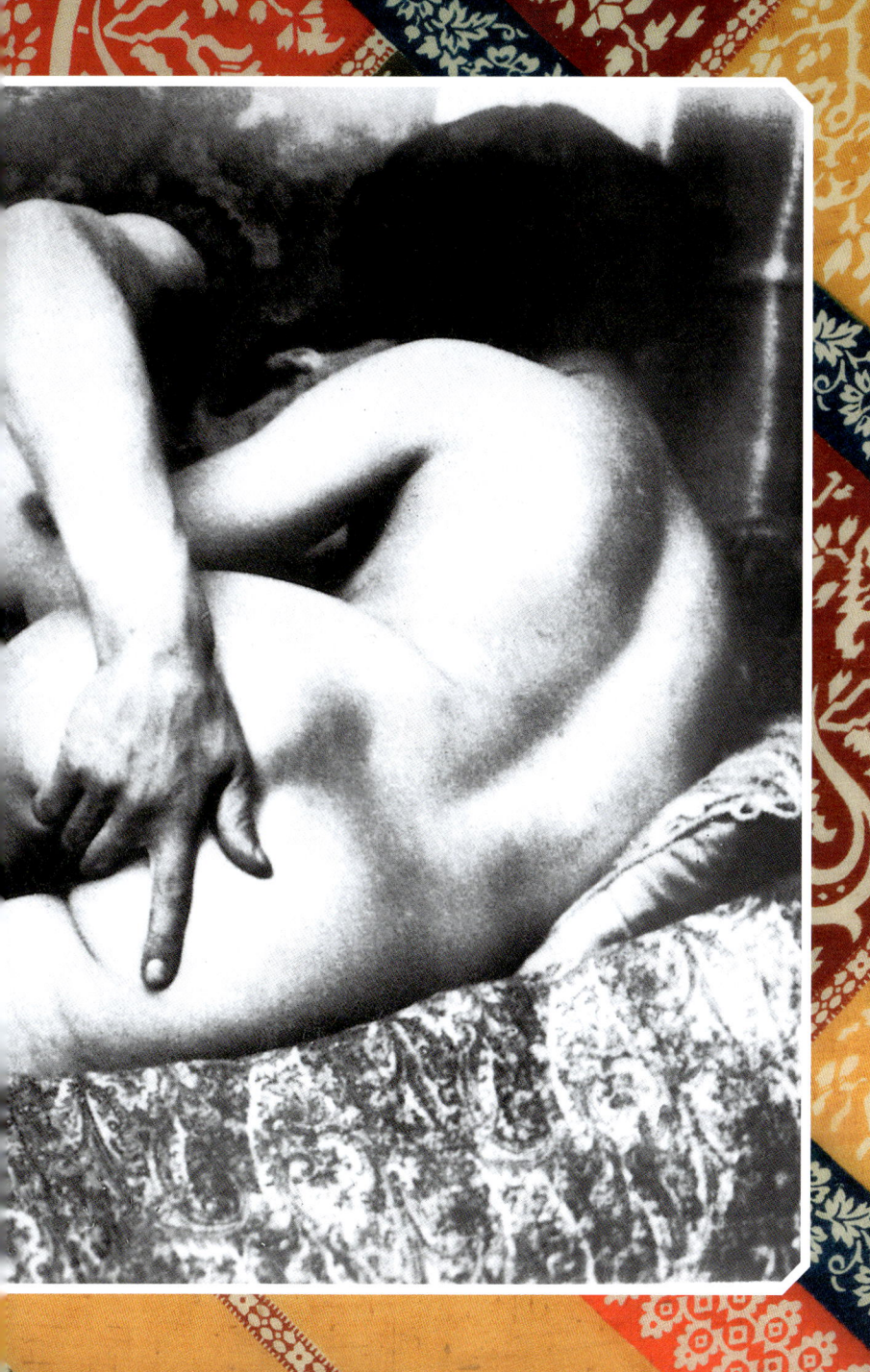

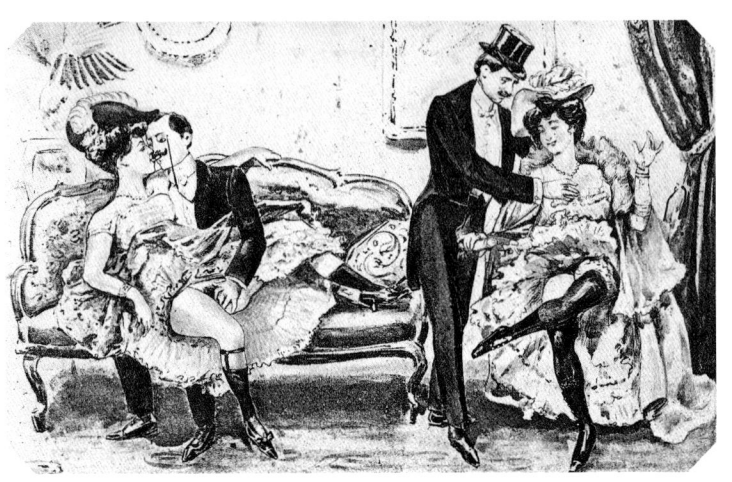

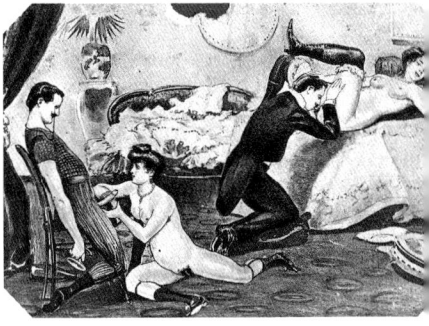

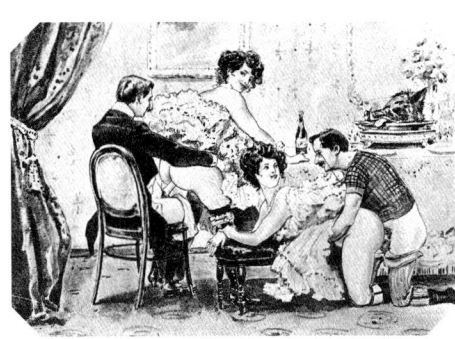

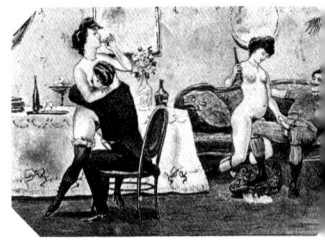

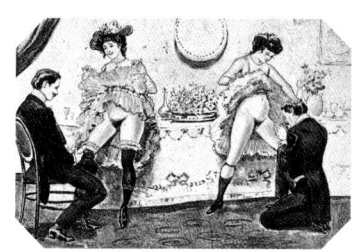

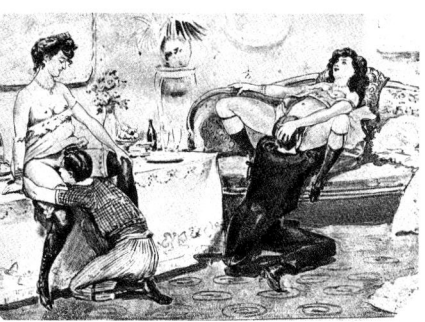

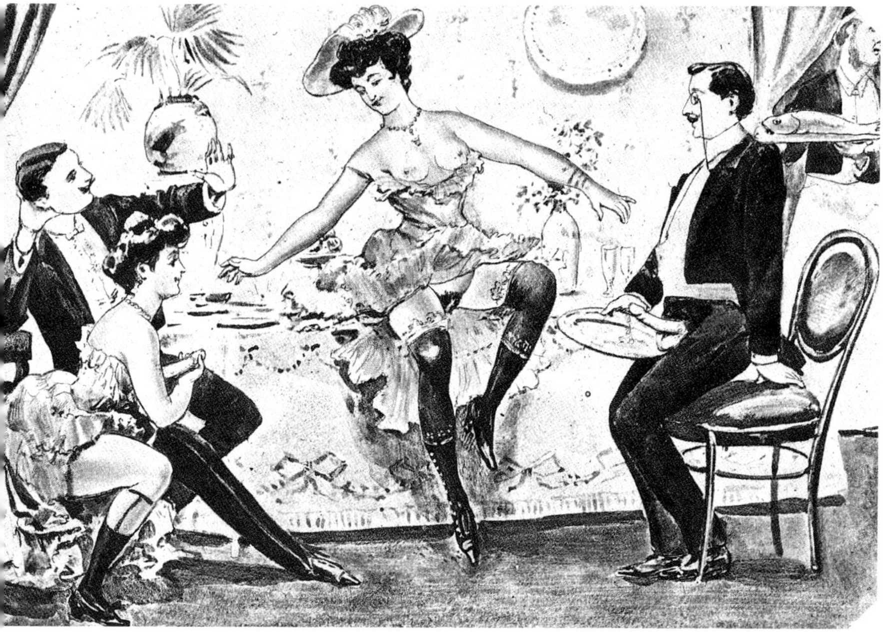

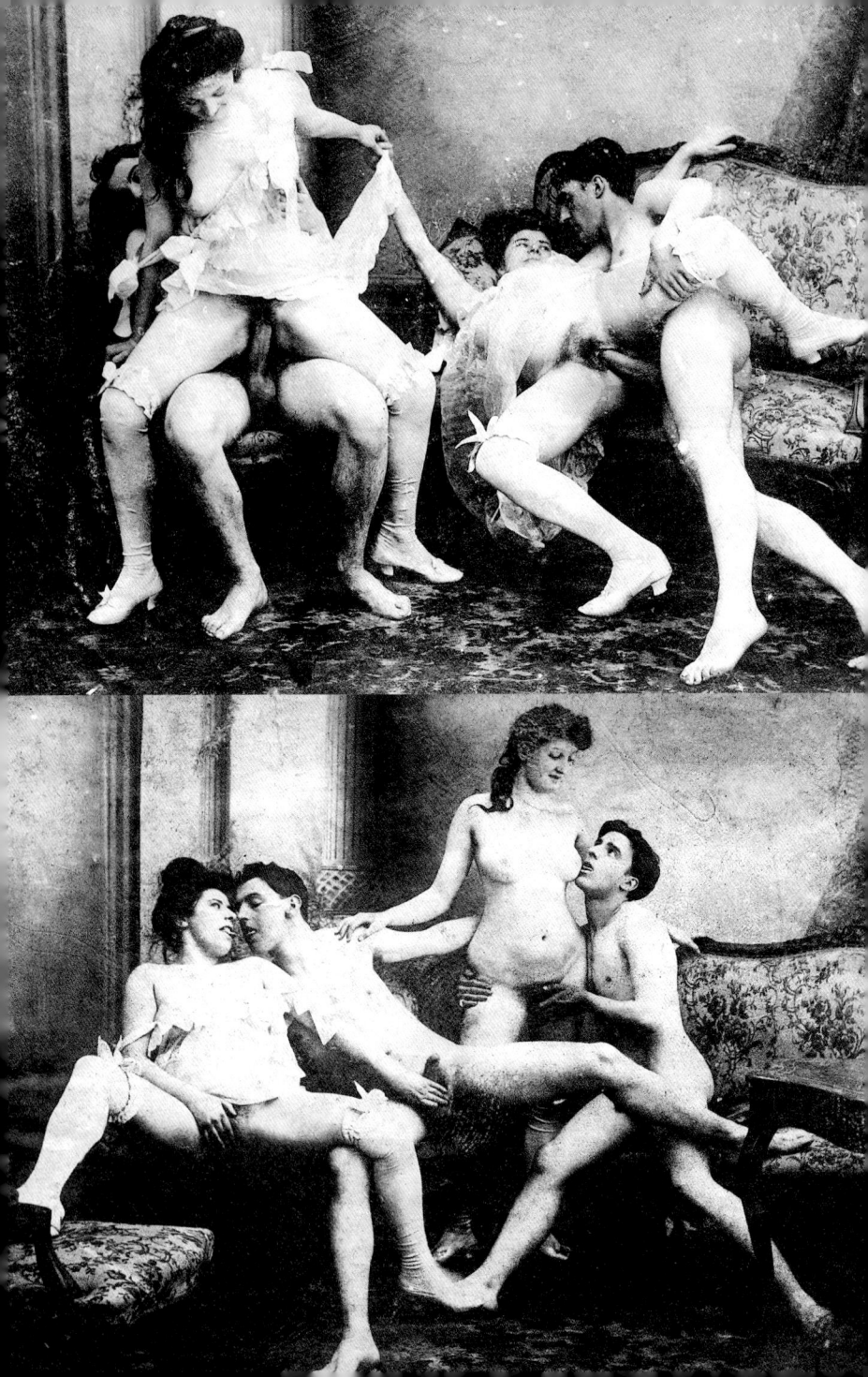

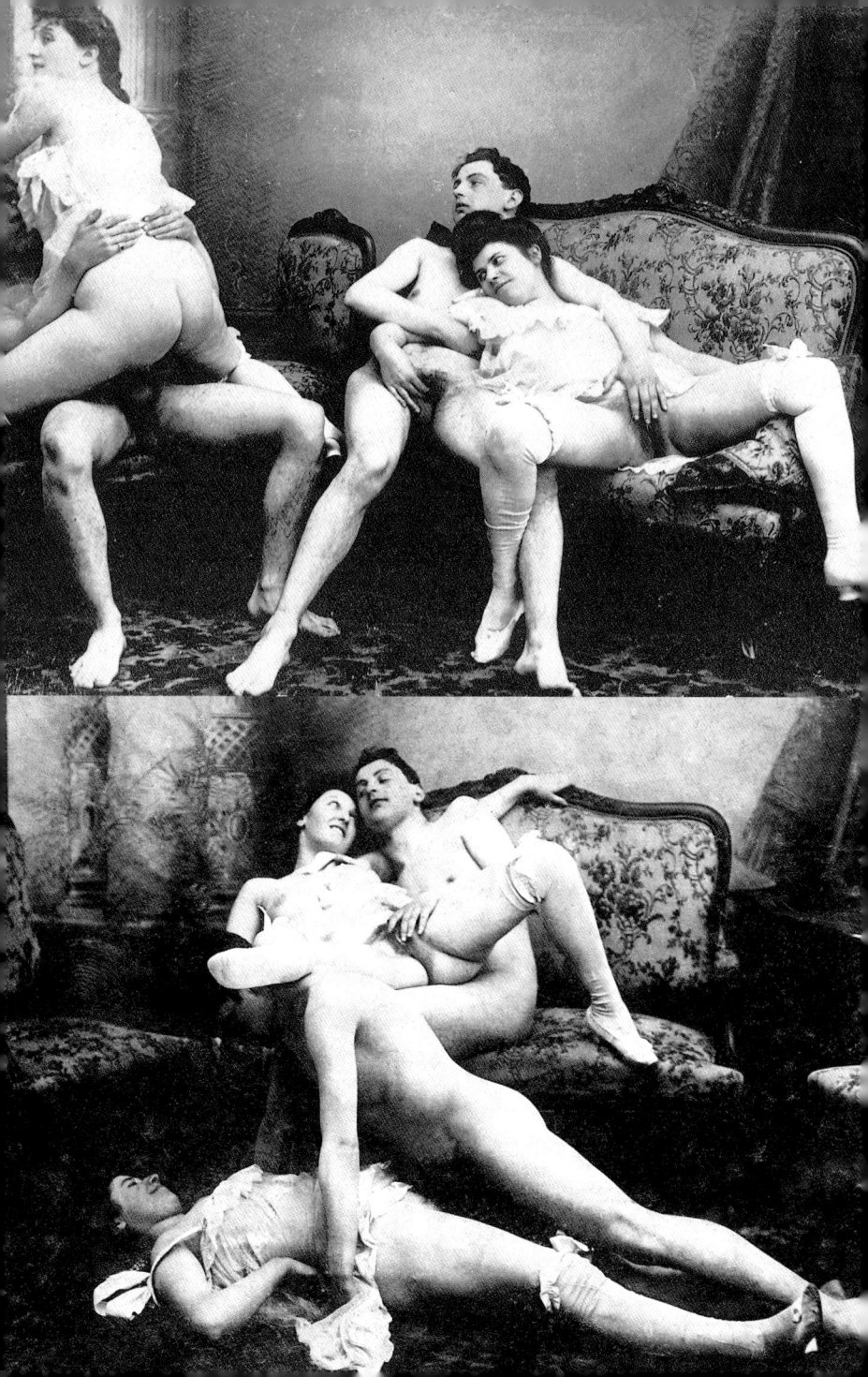

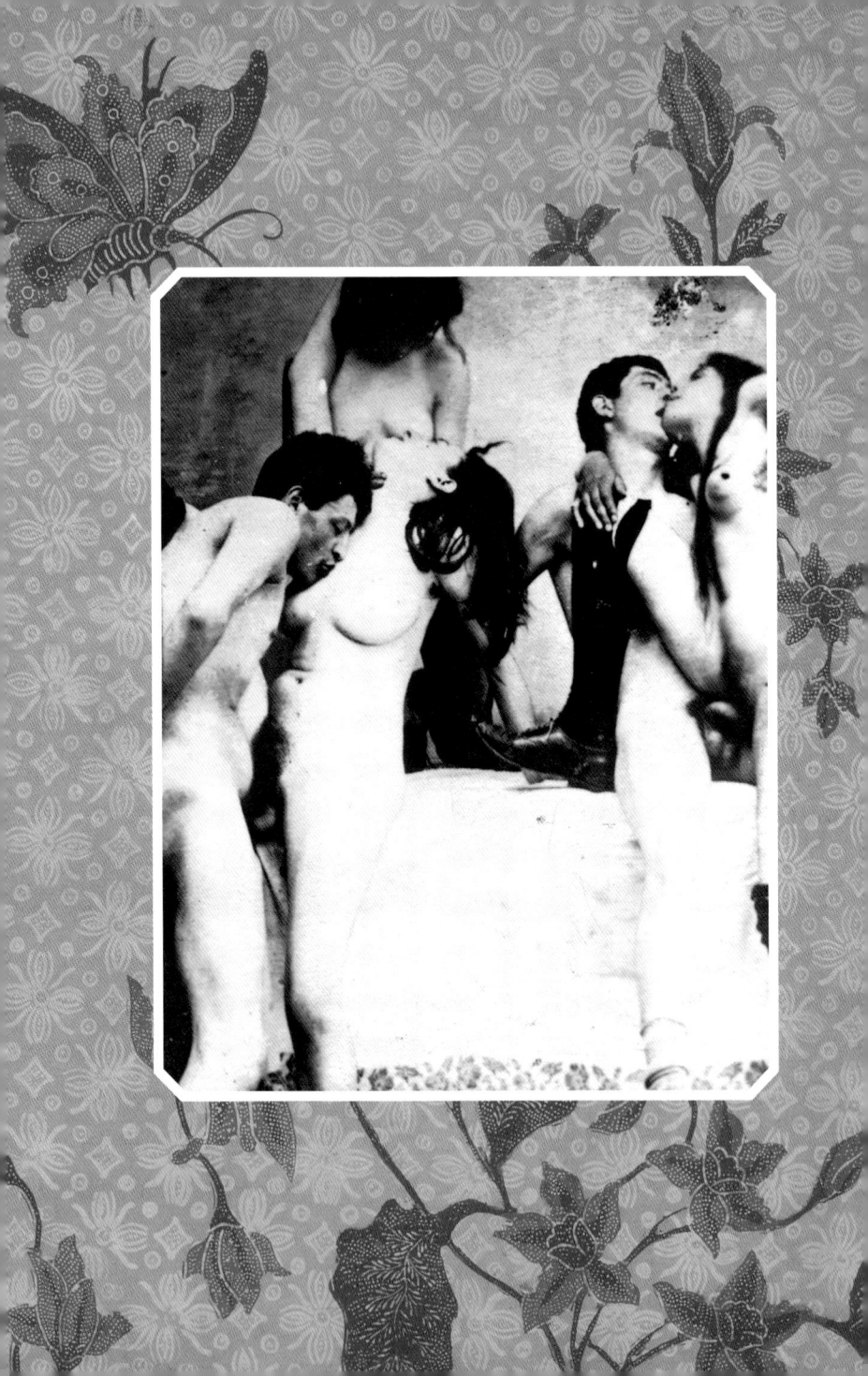

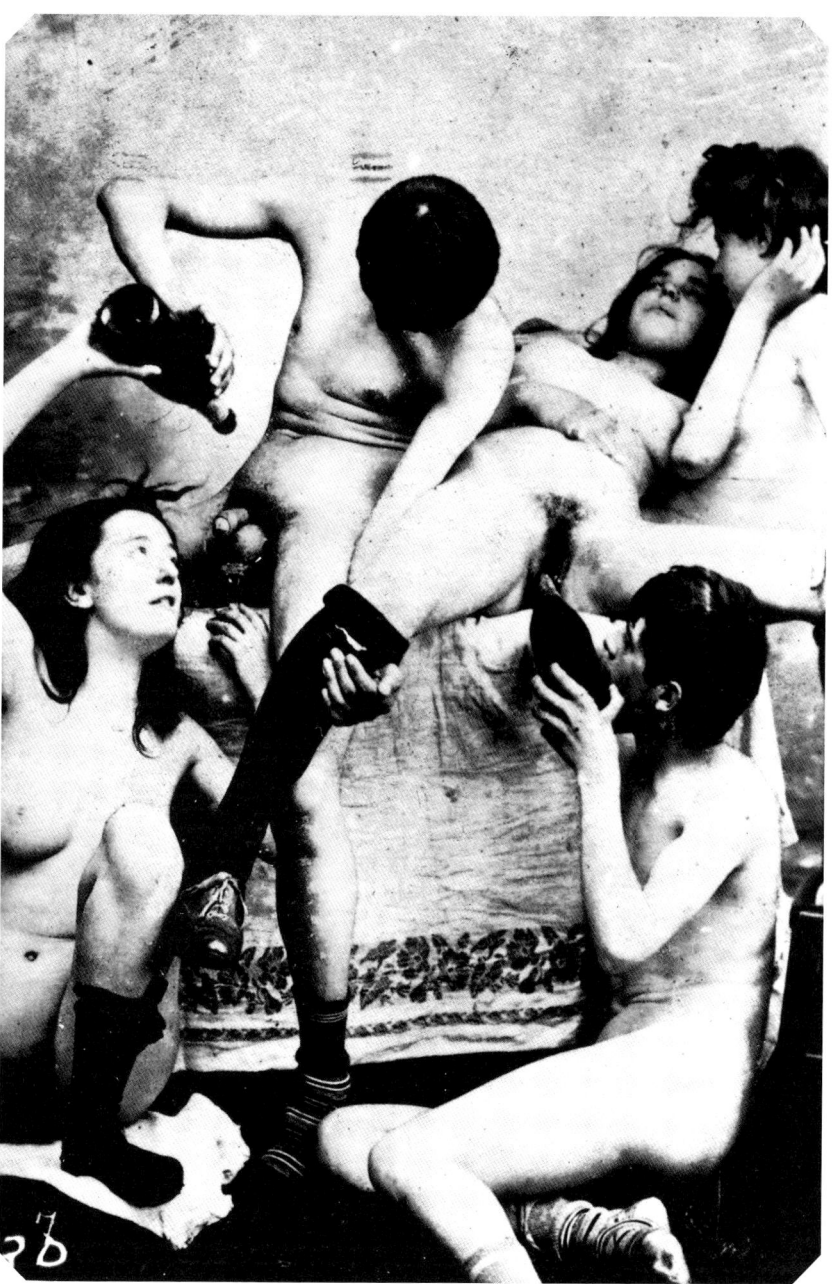

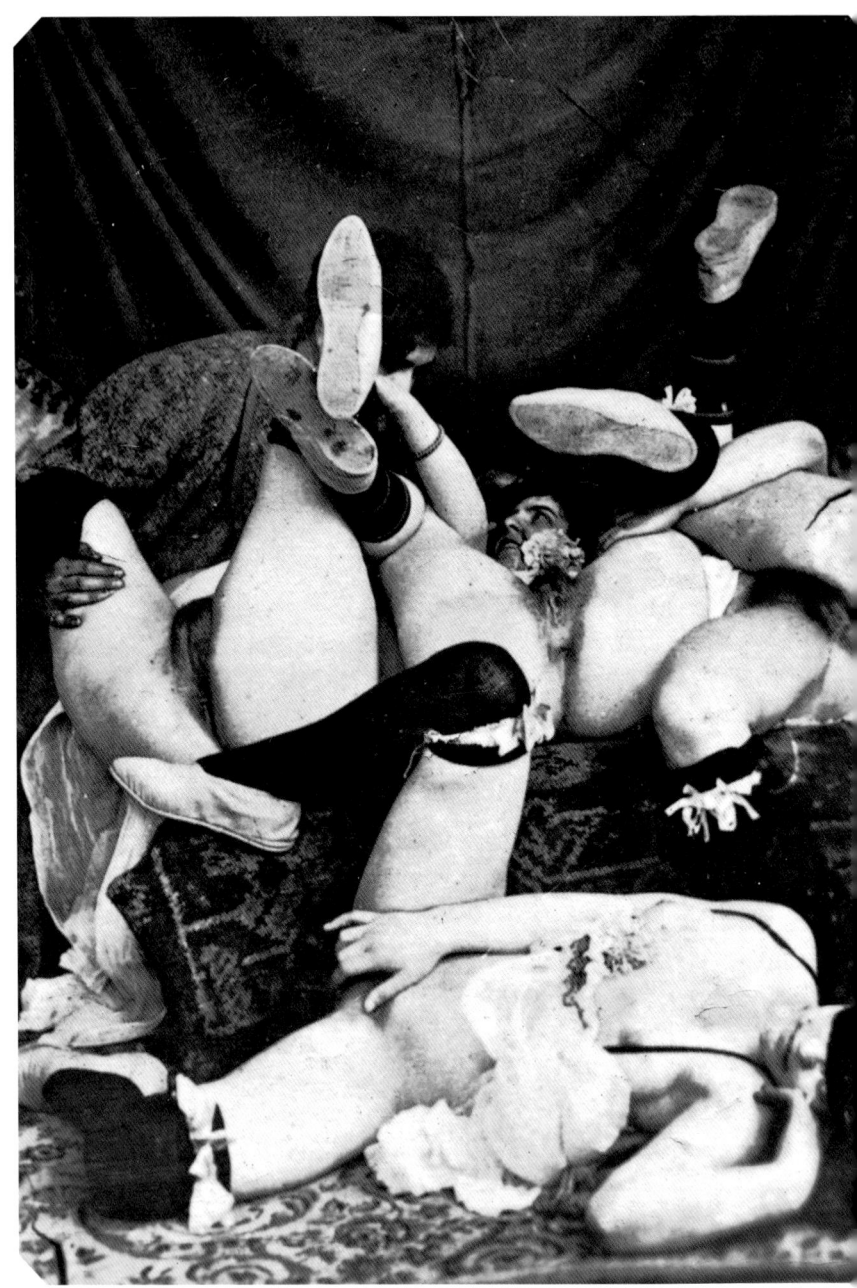

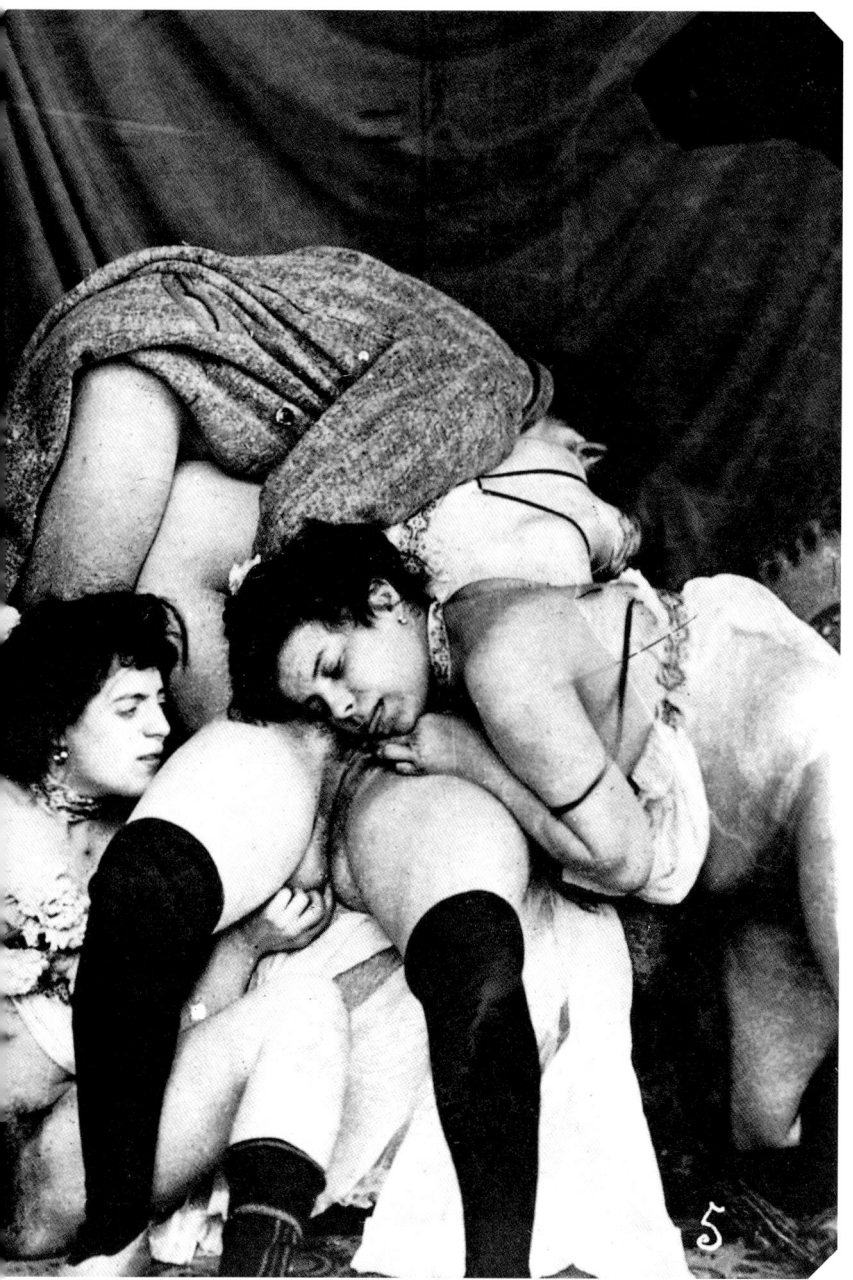

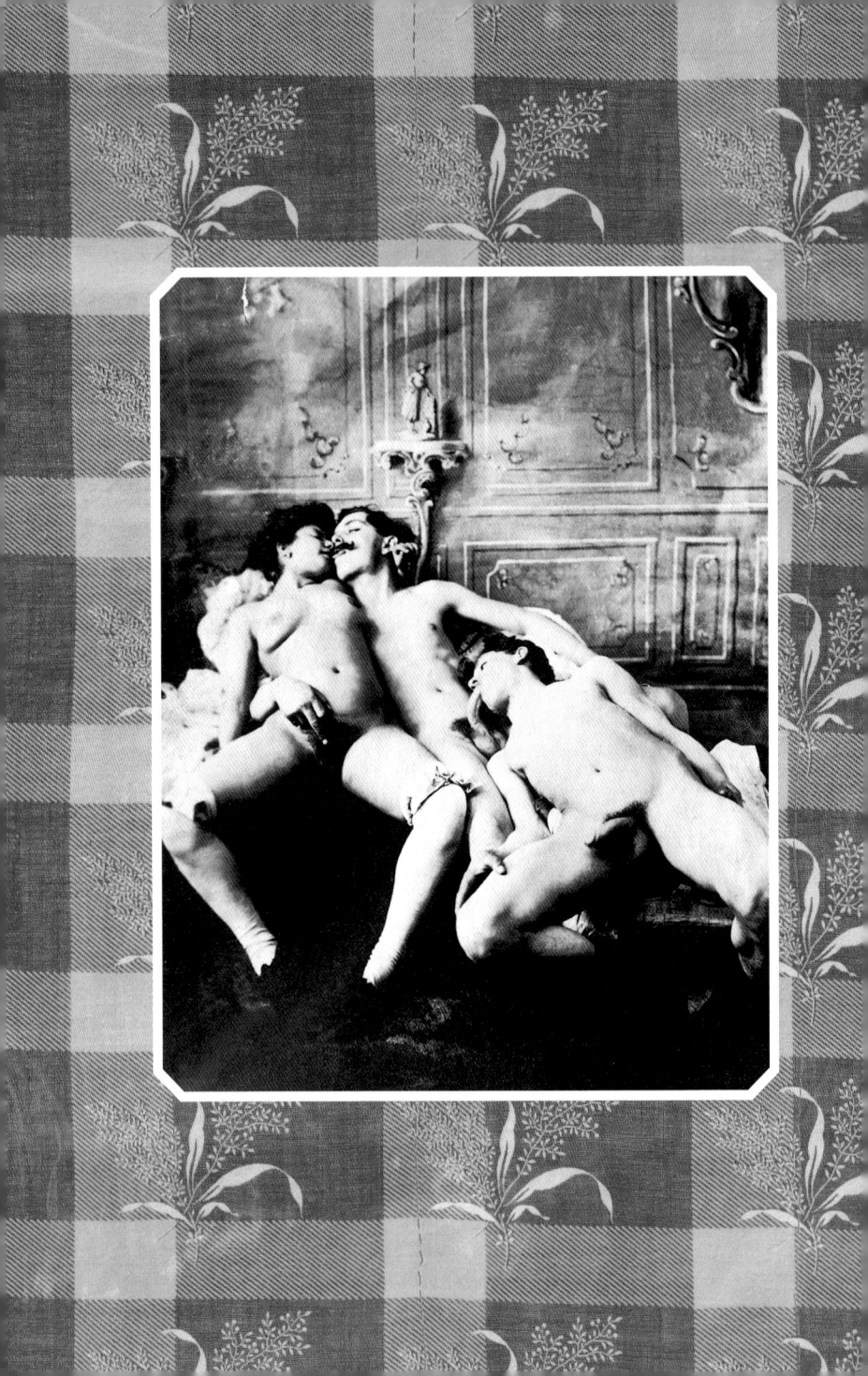

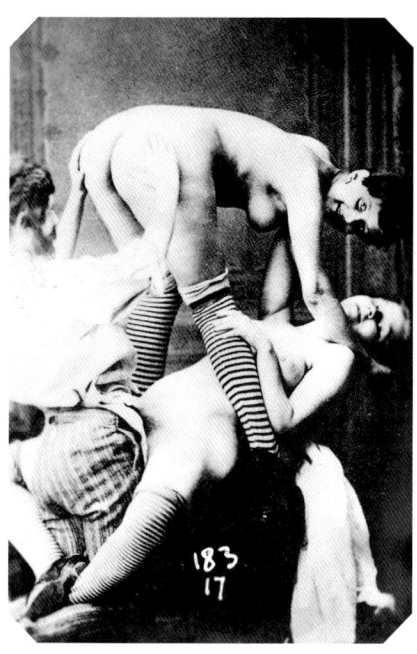

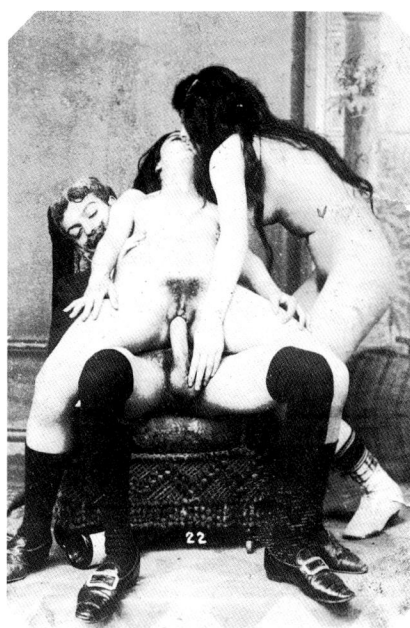

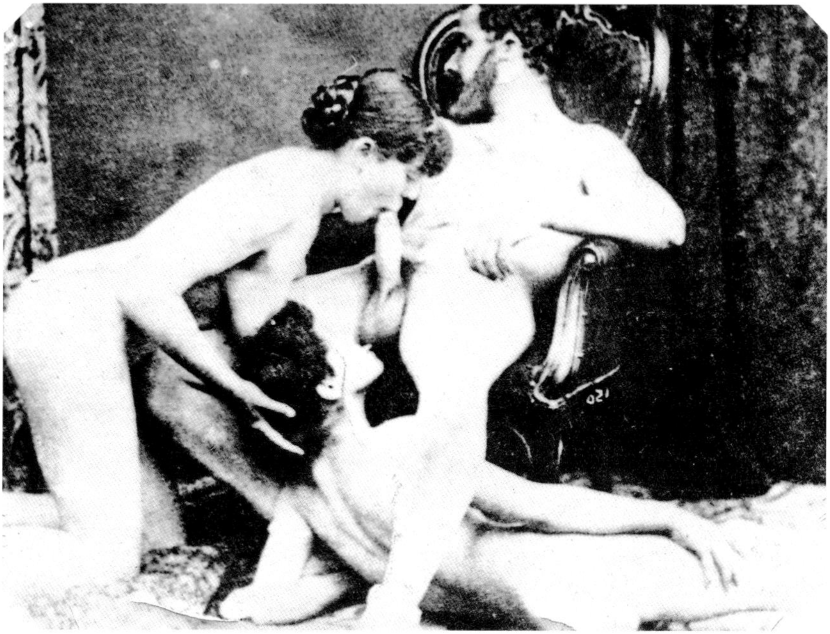

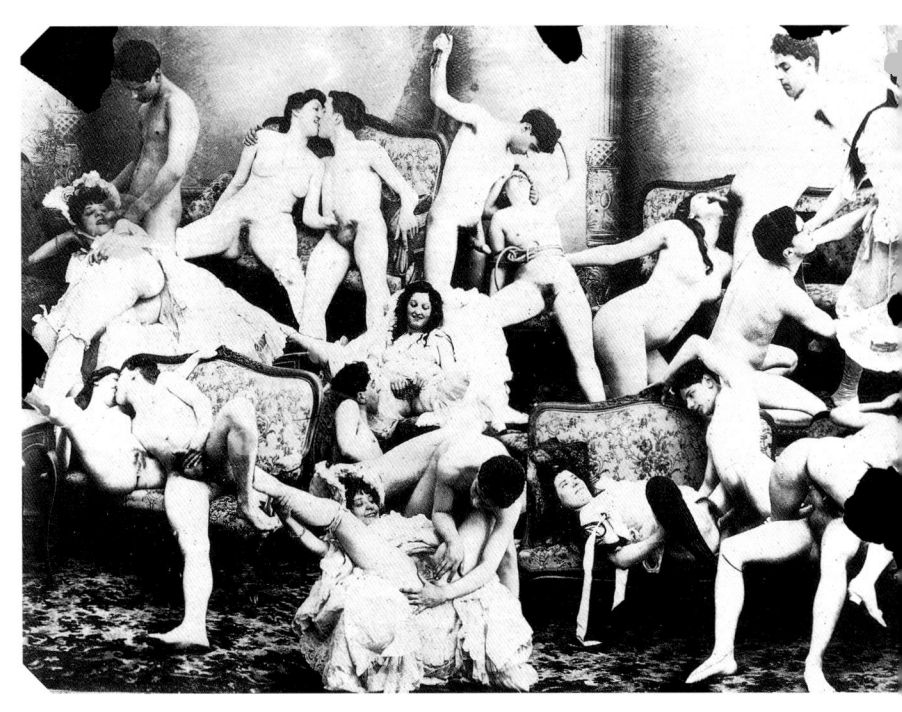

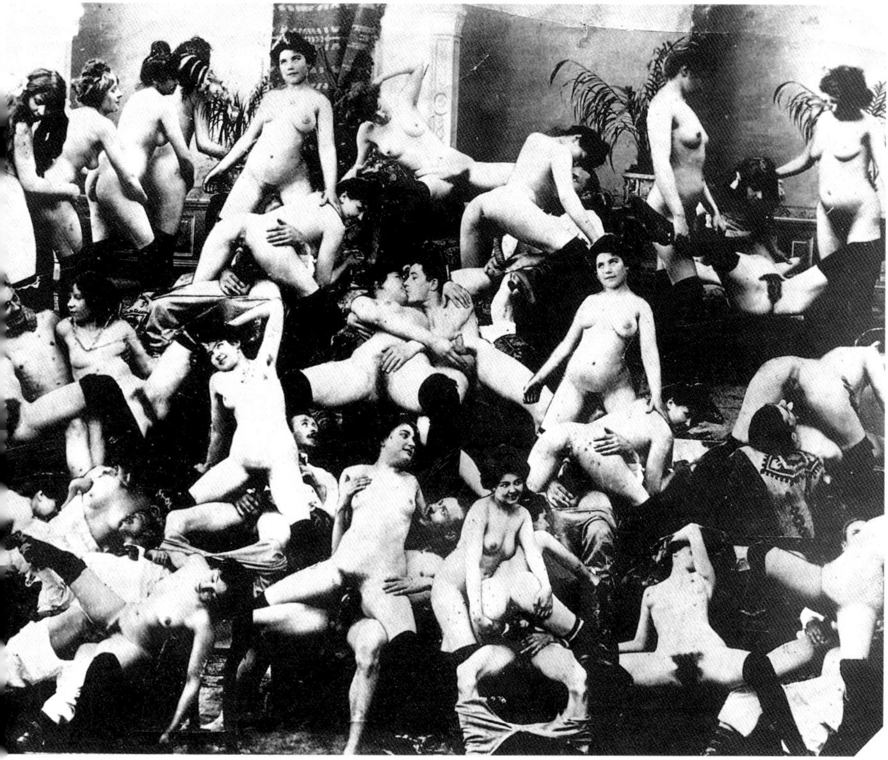

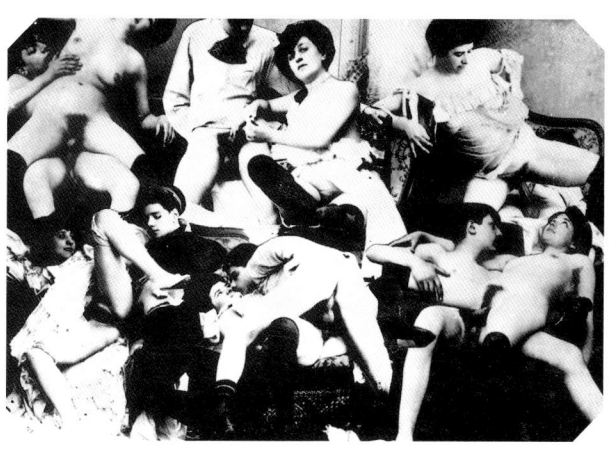

189

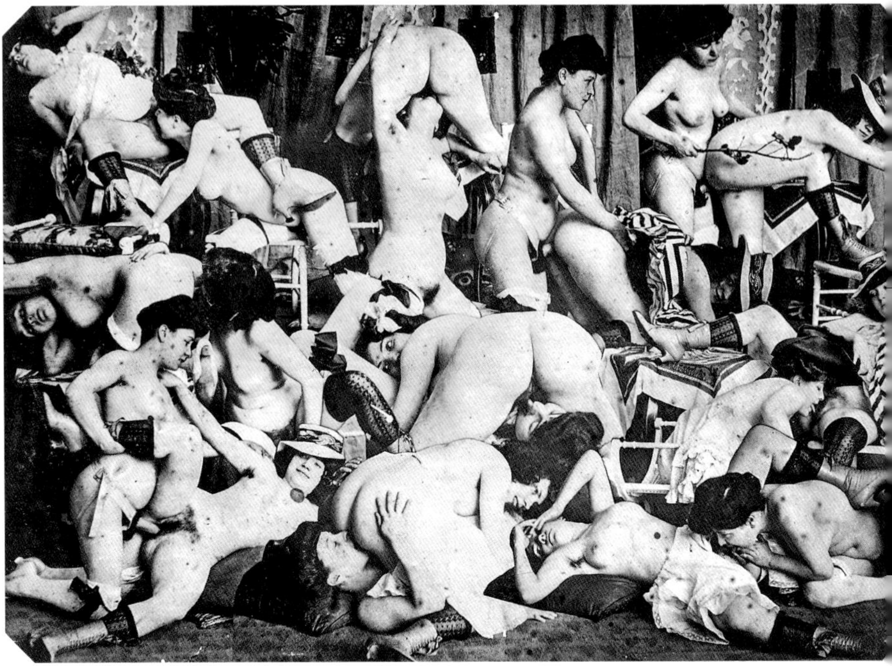

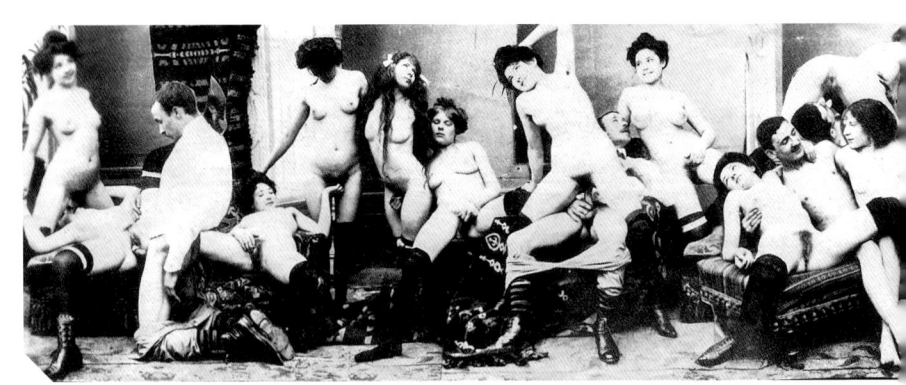

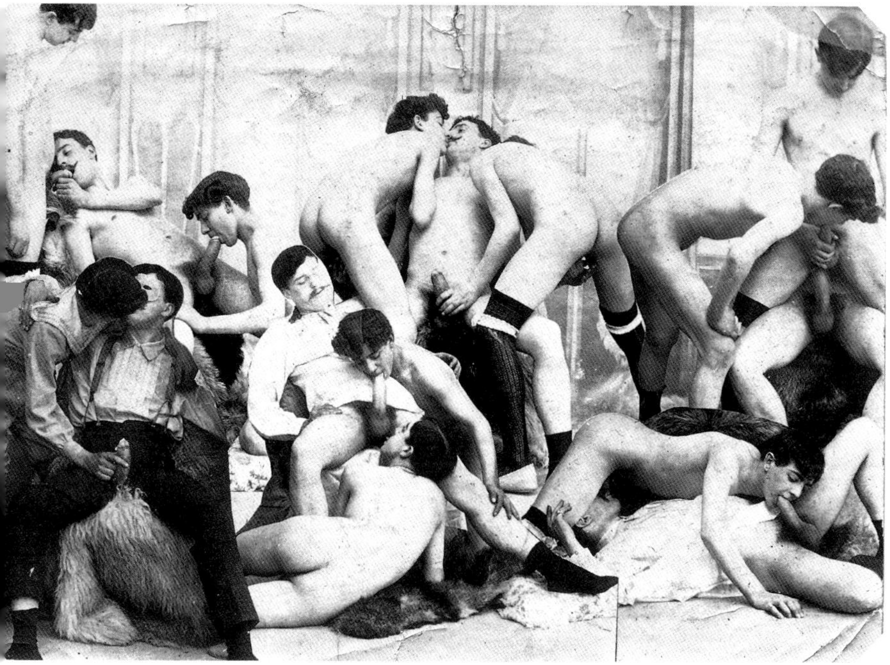

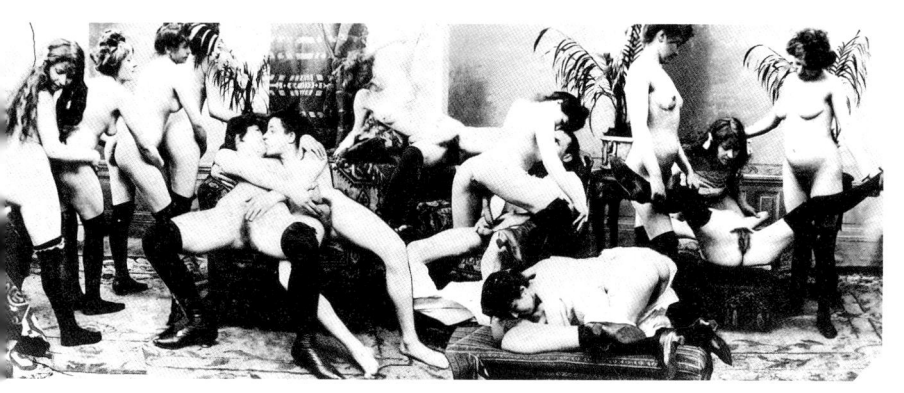

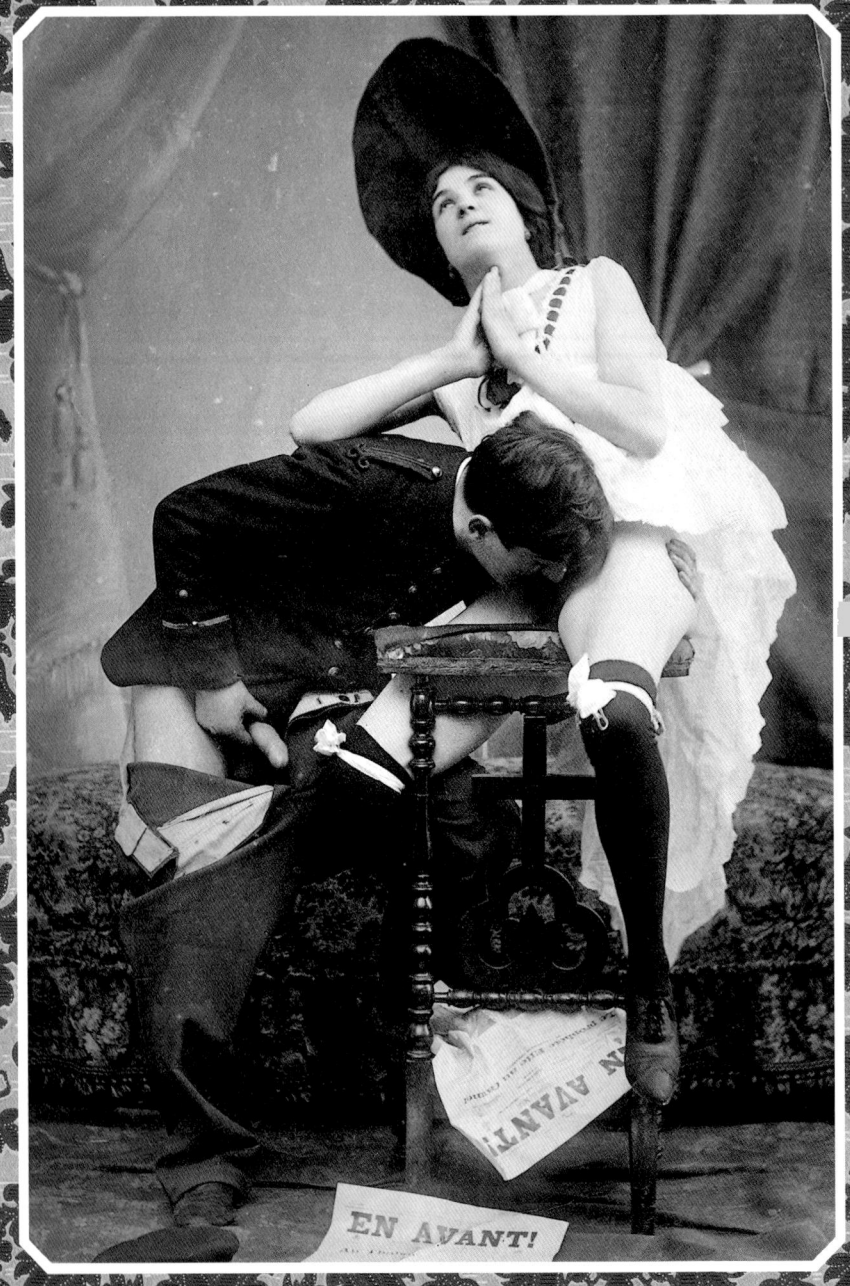

EN AVANT!

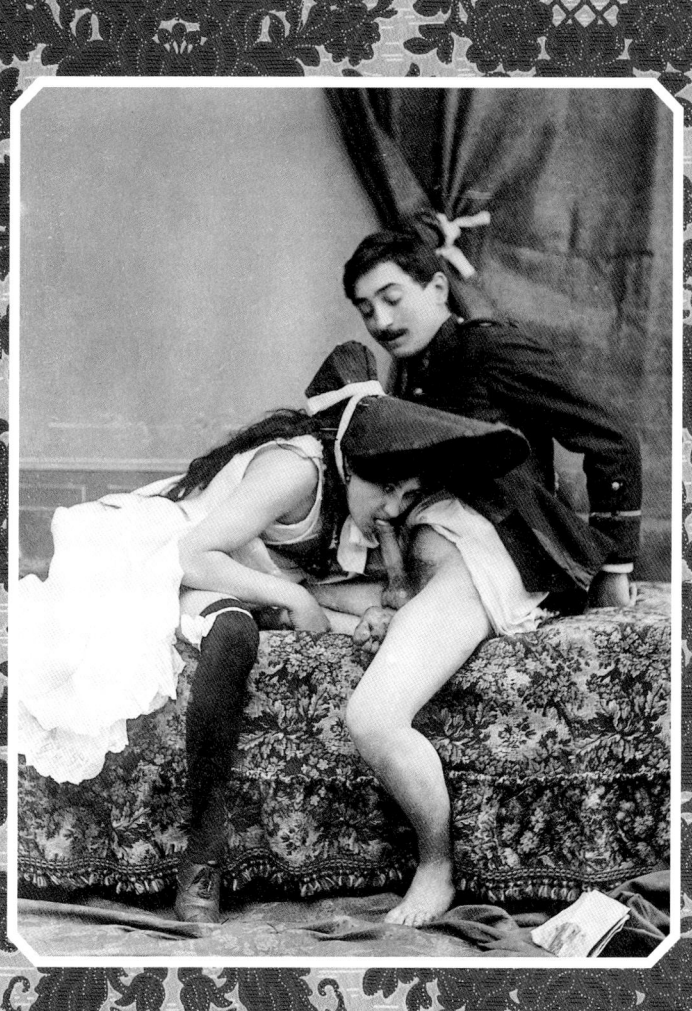

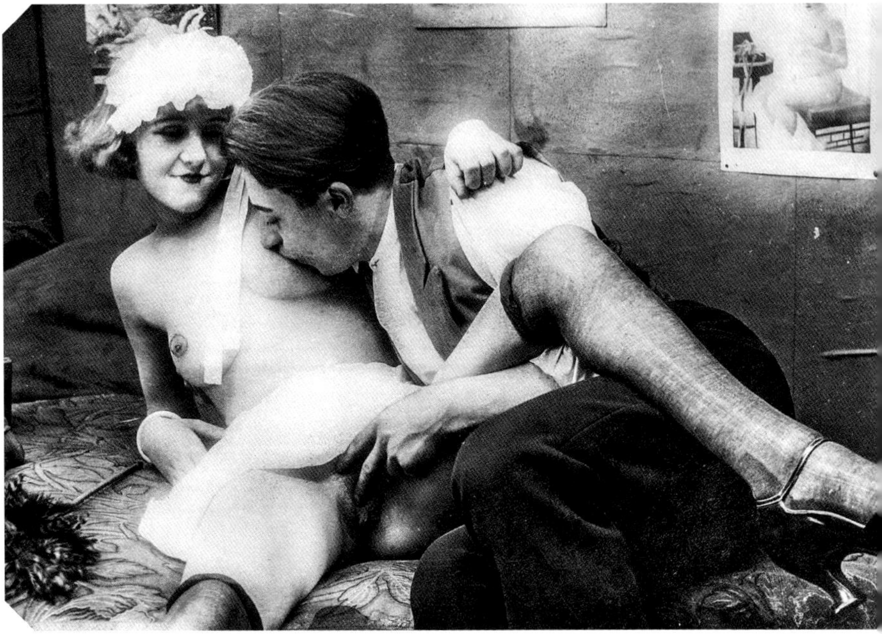

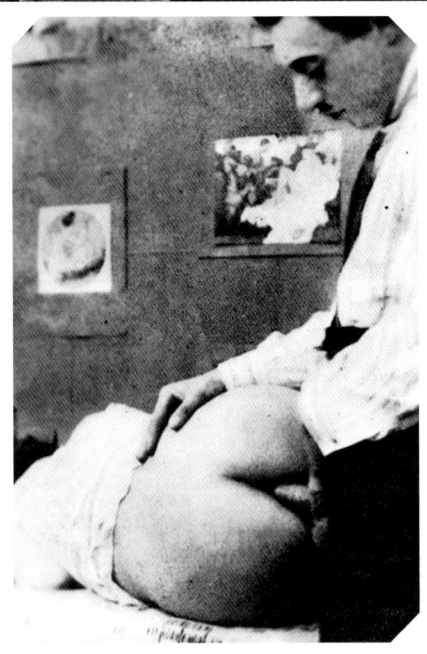

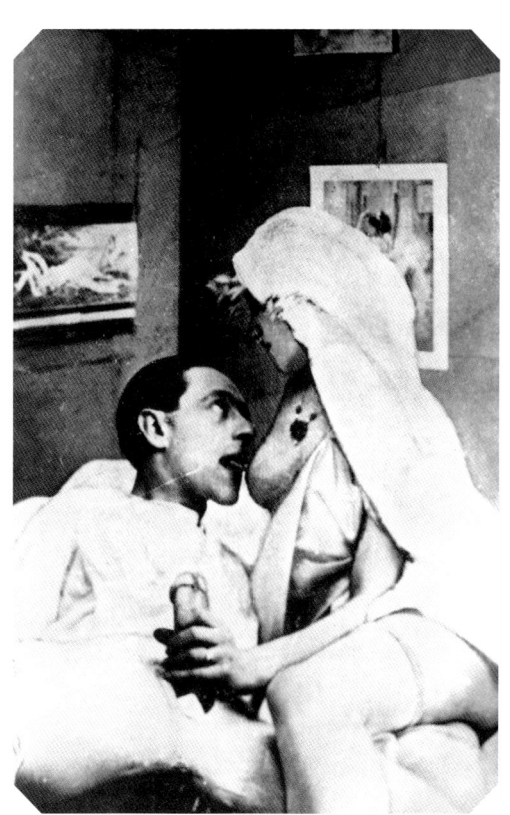

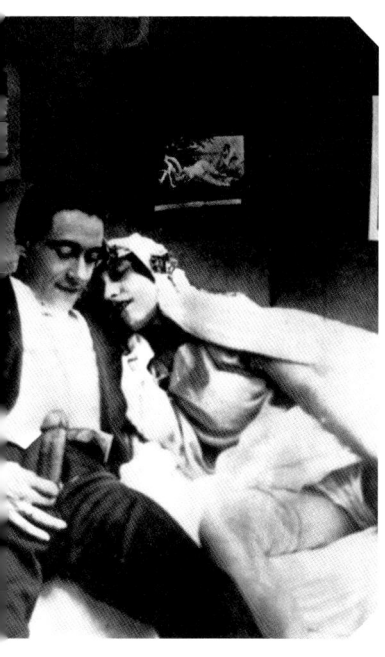

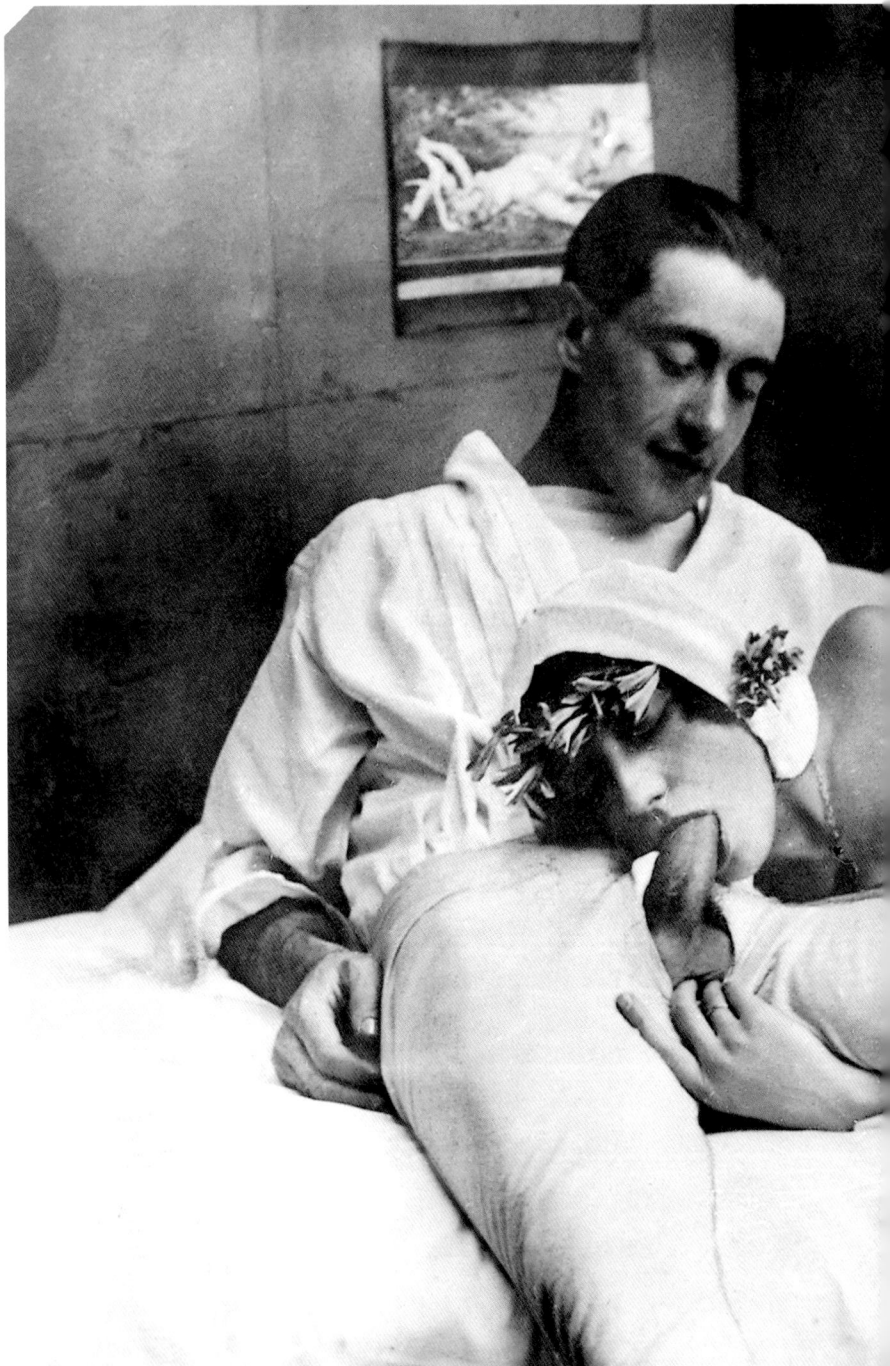

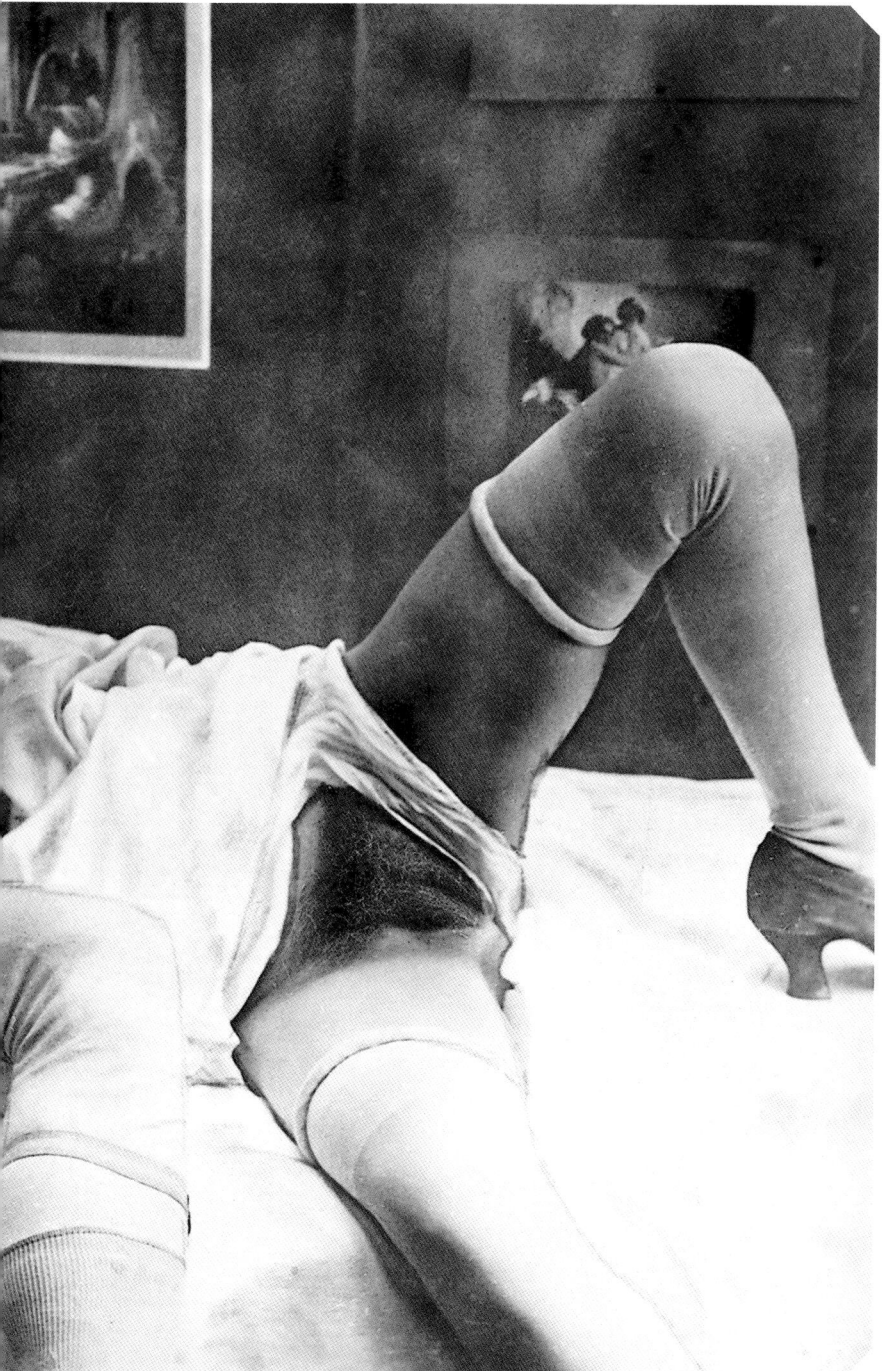

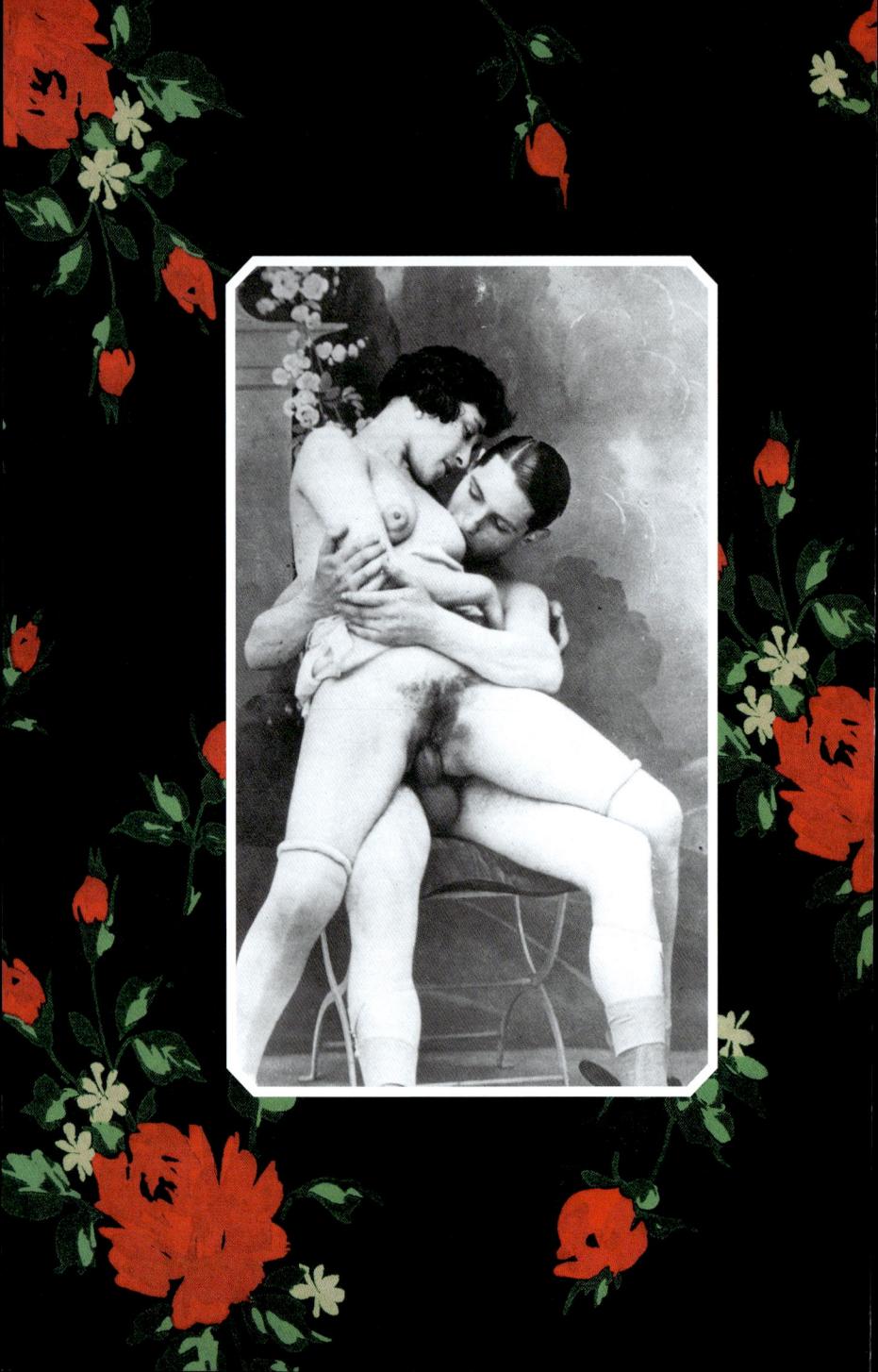

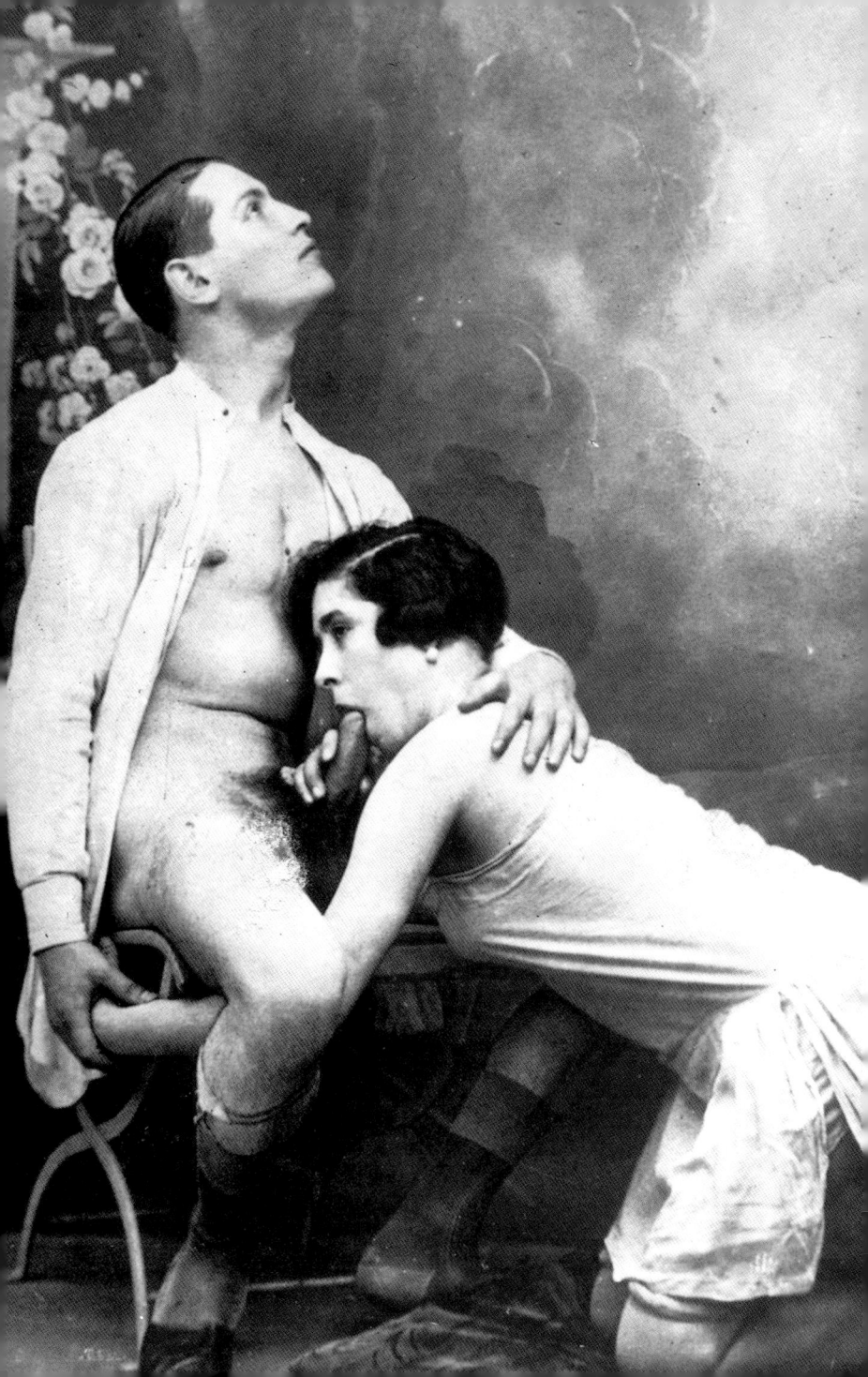

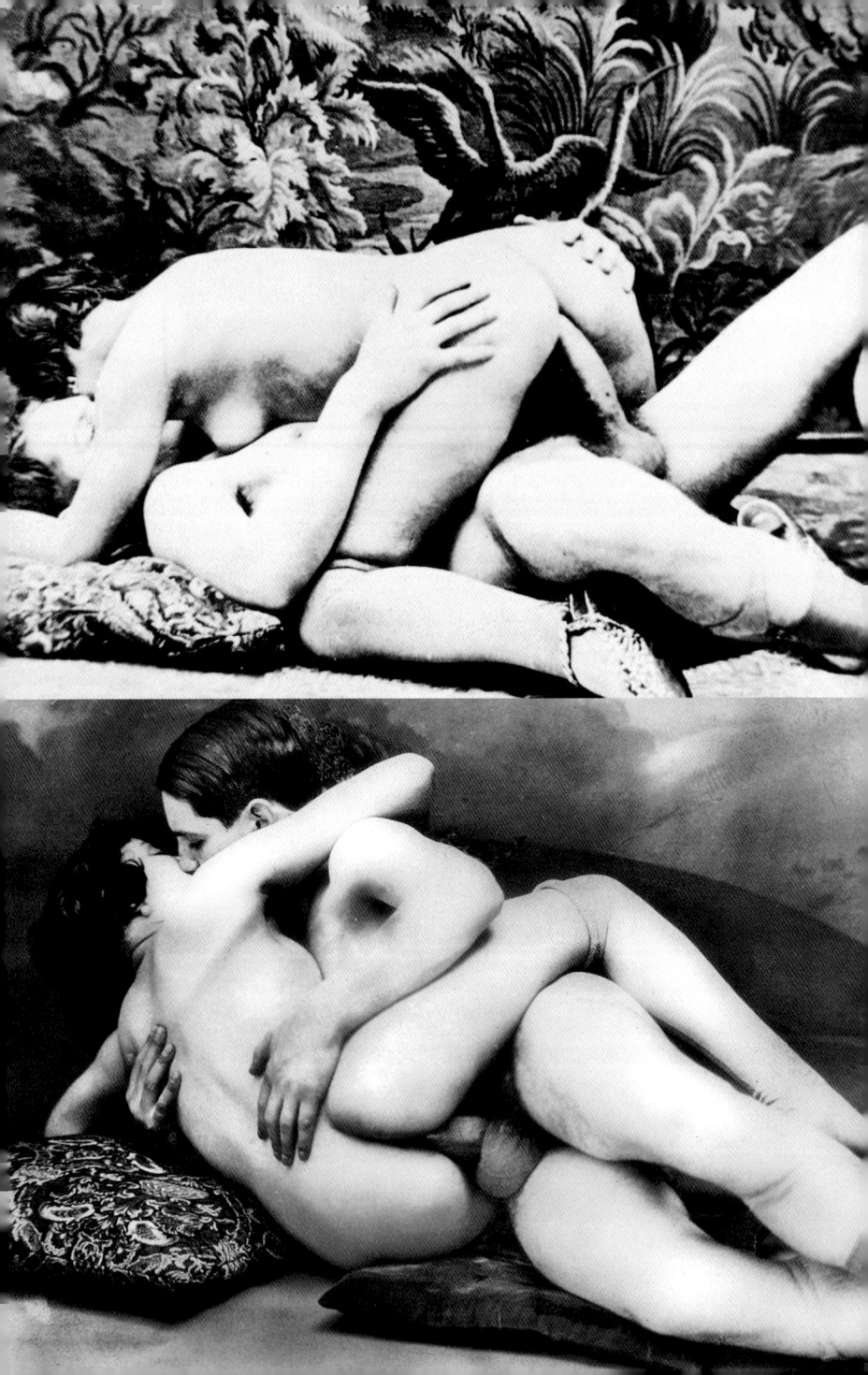

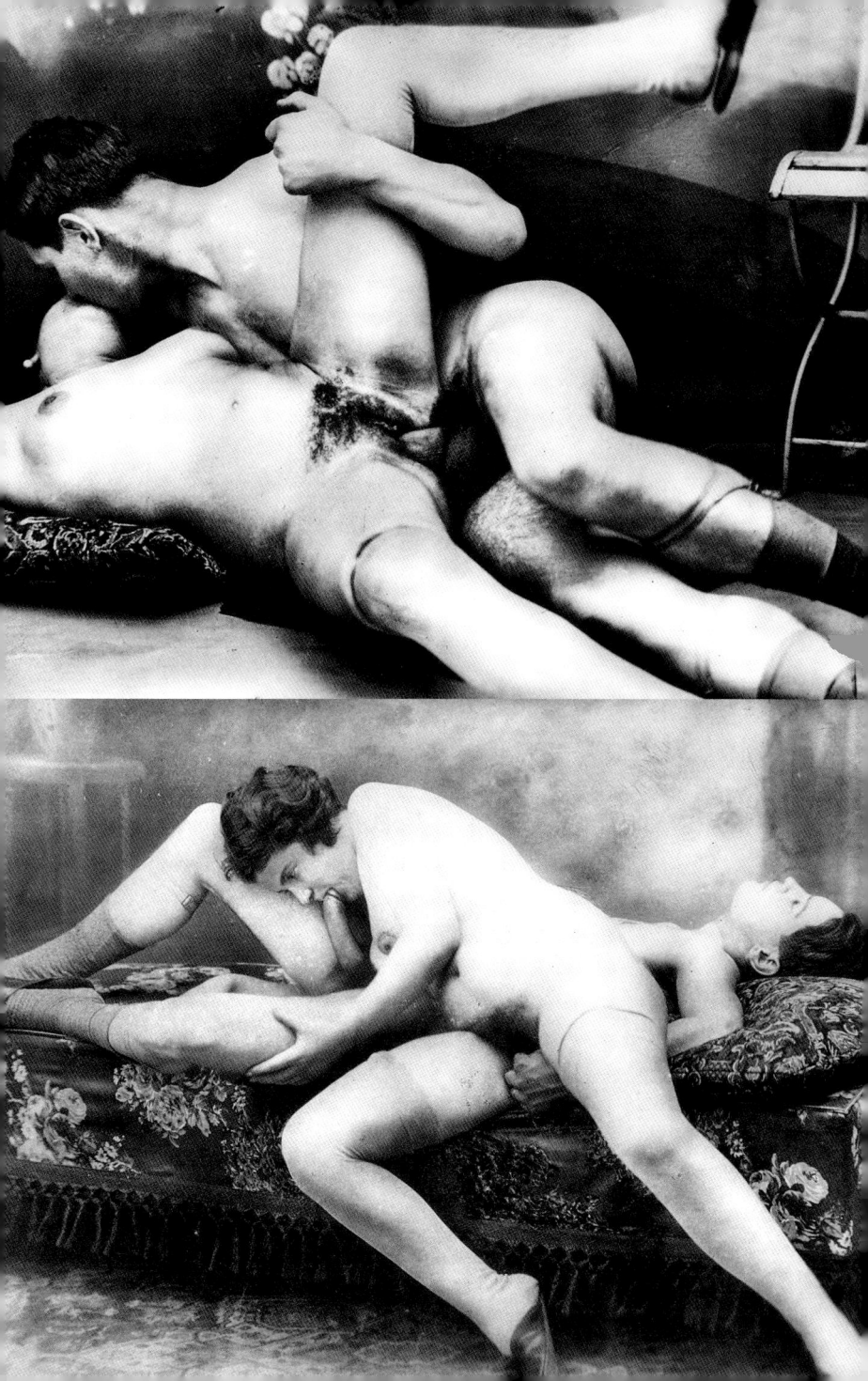

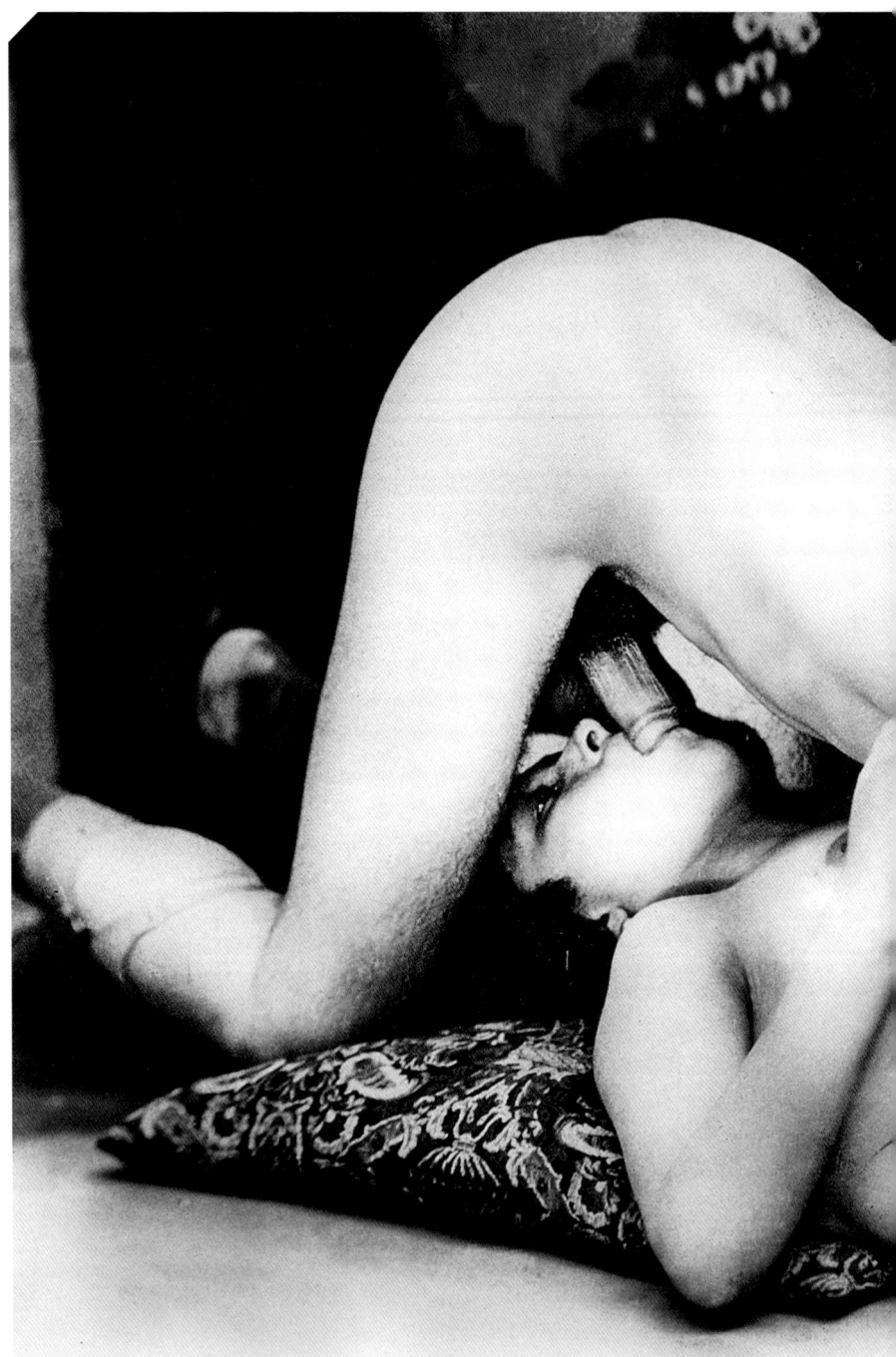

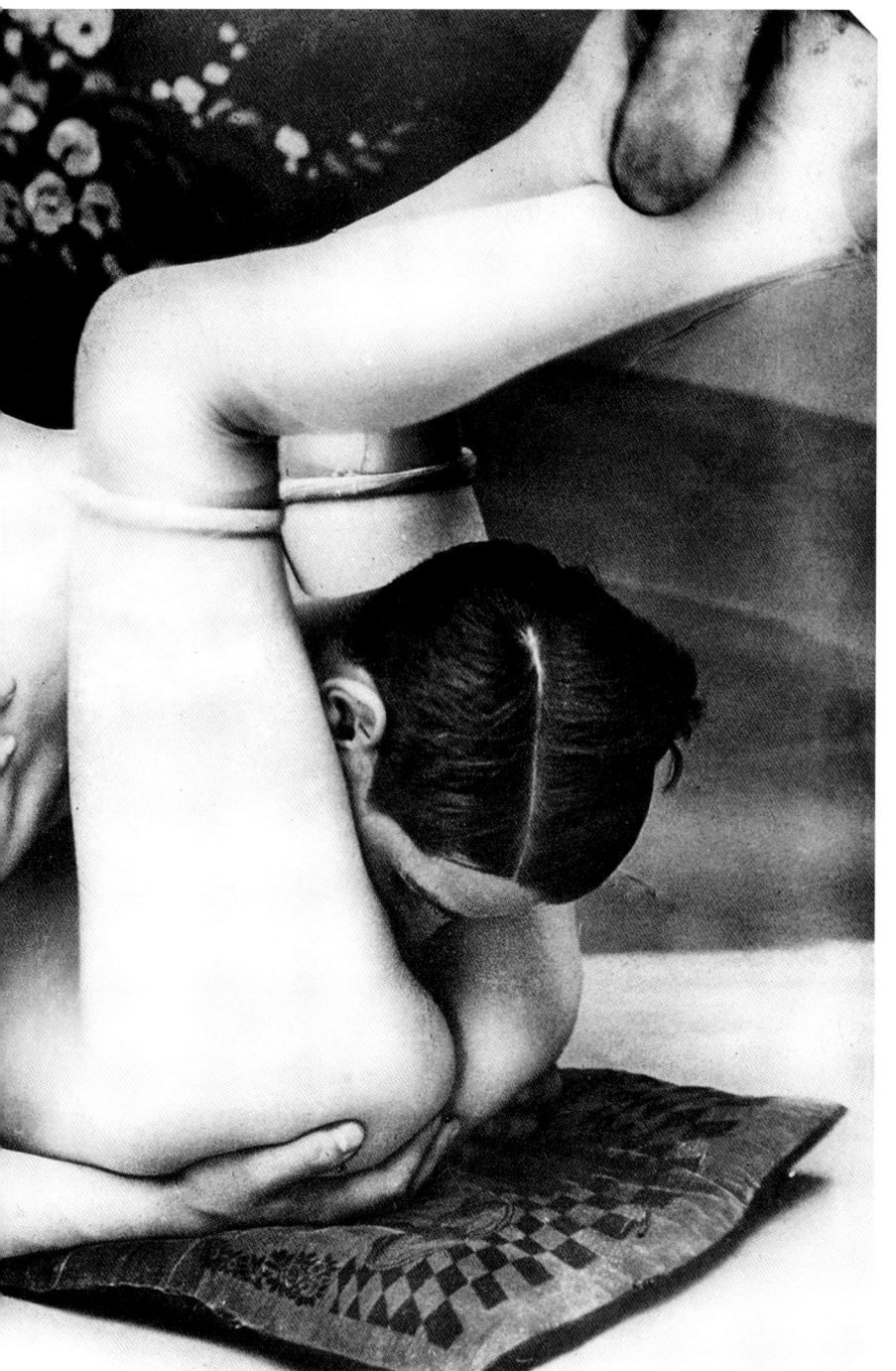

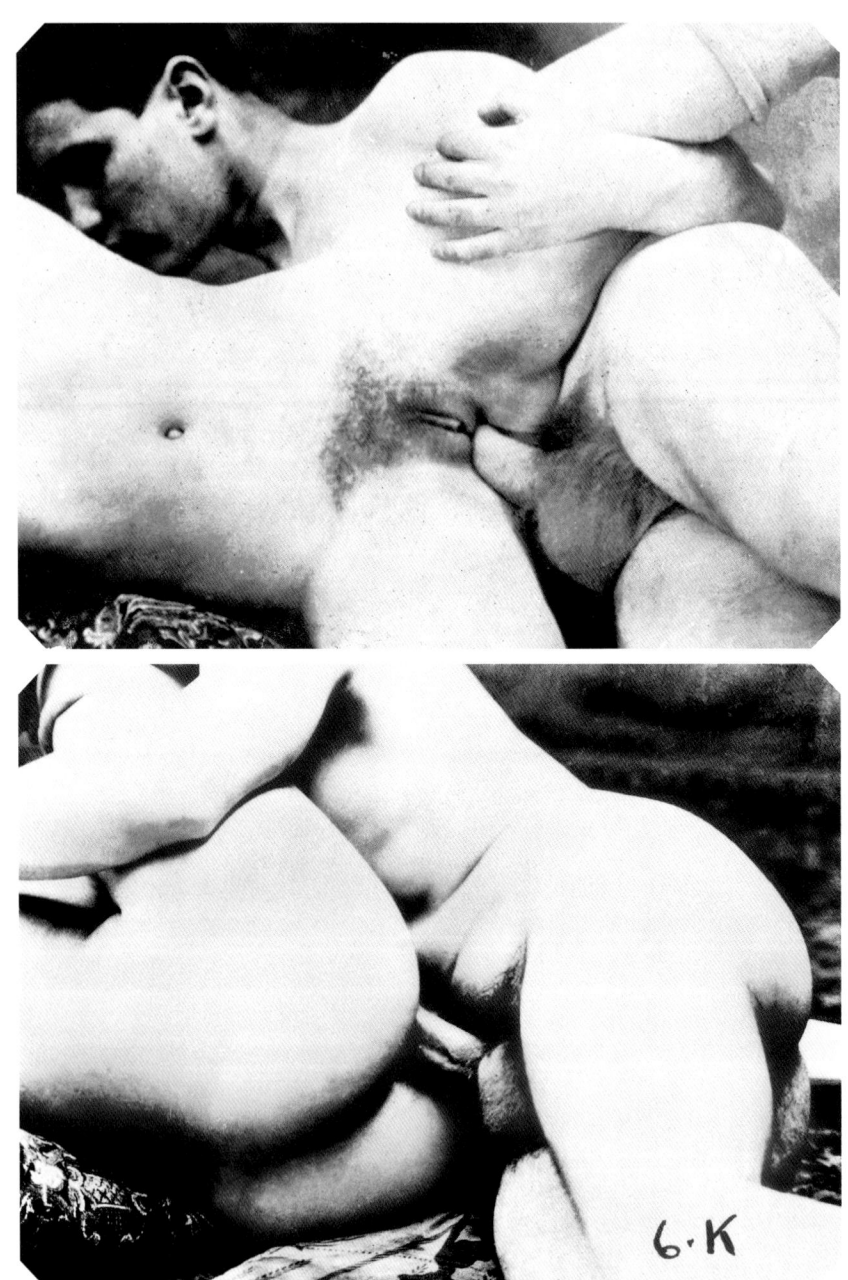

6·K

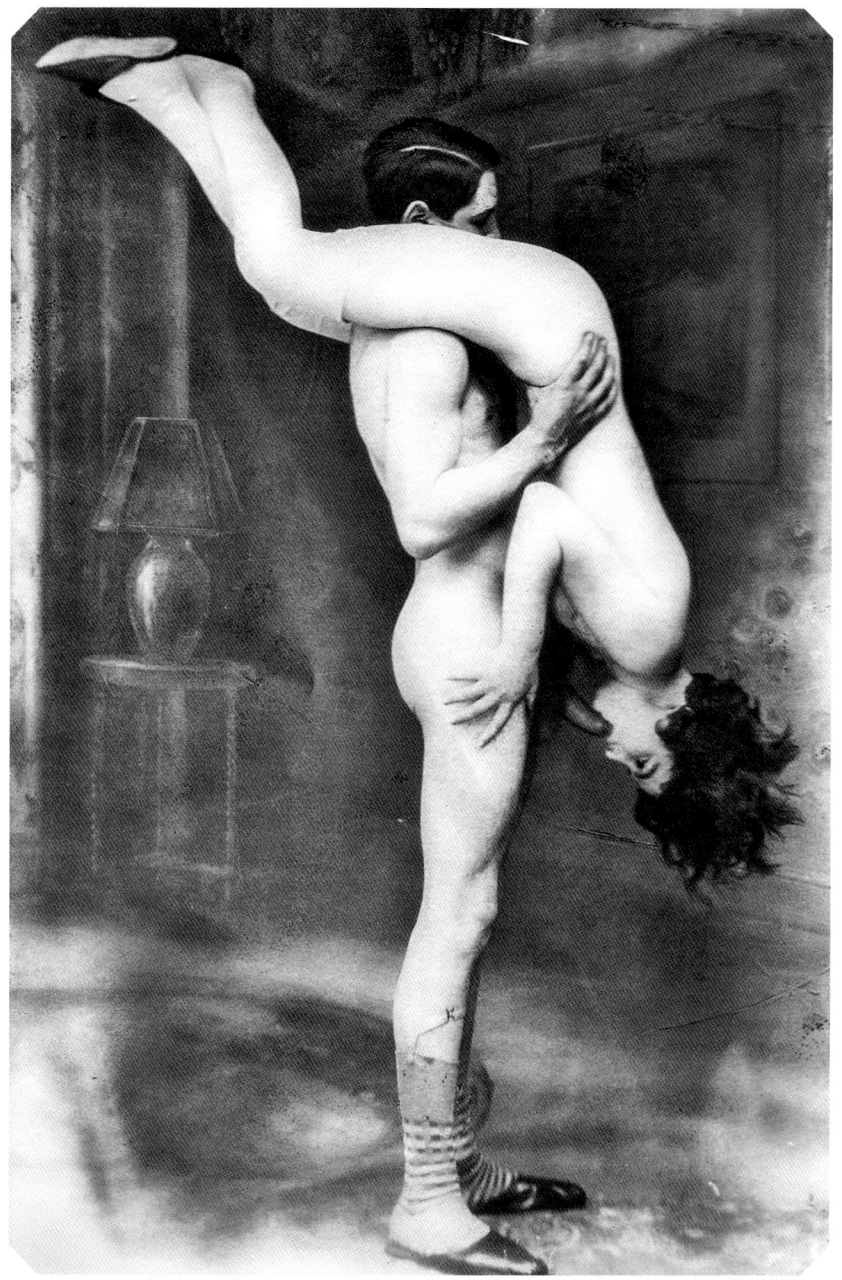

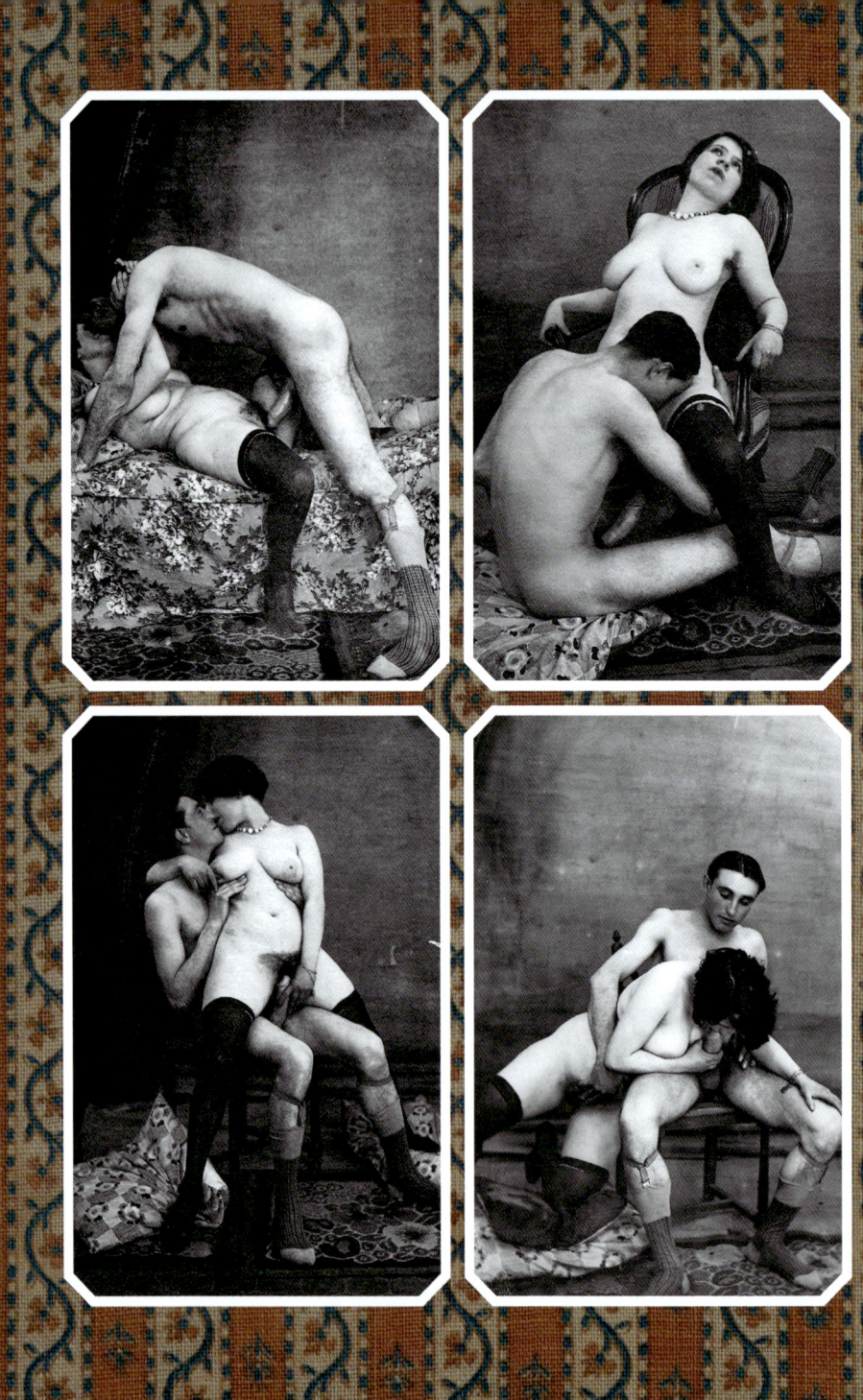

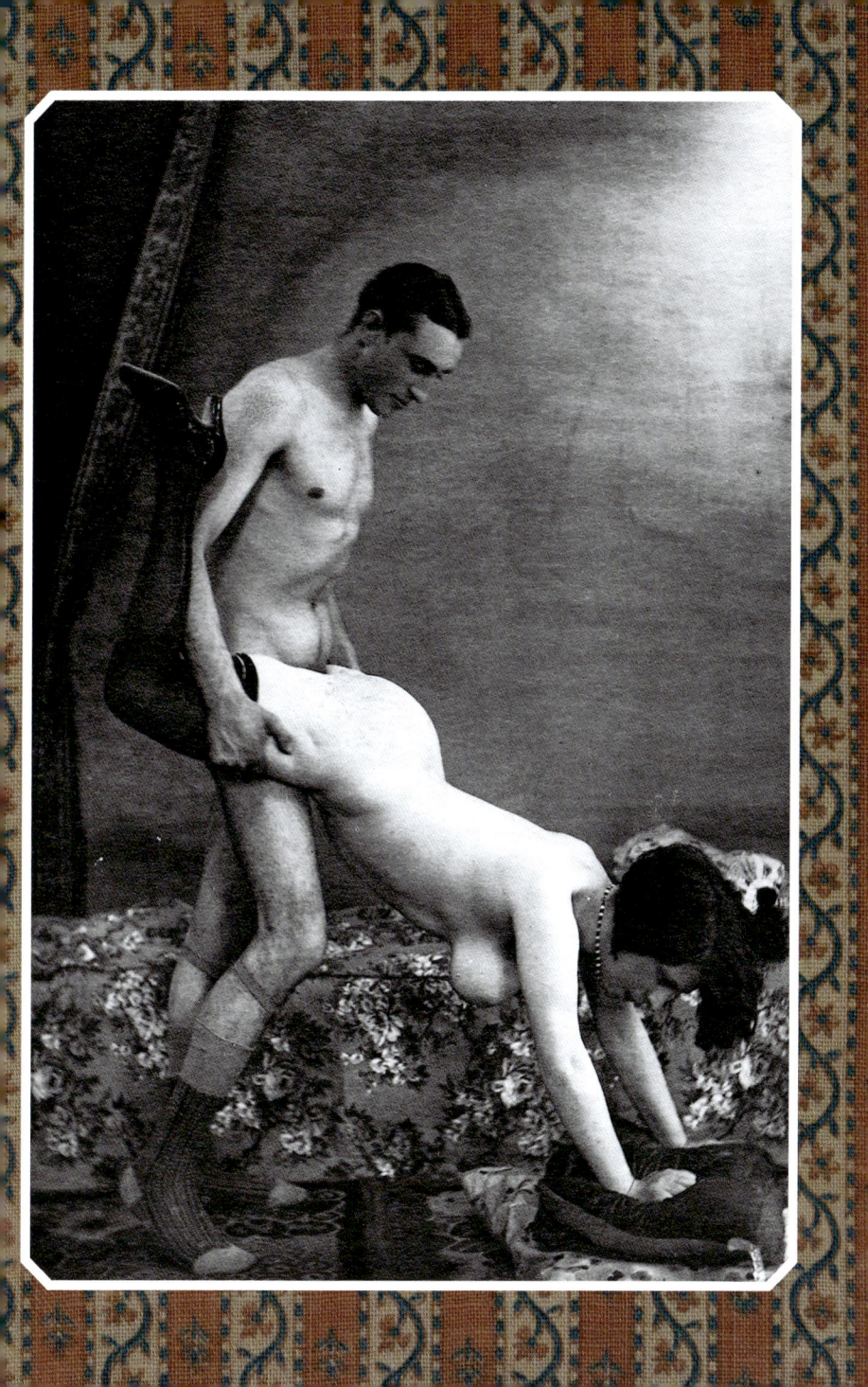

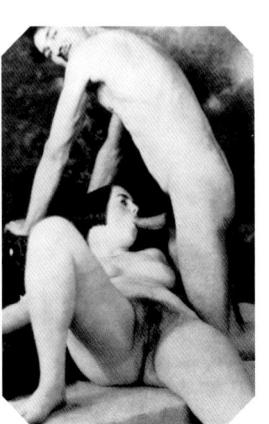

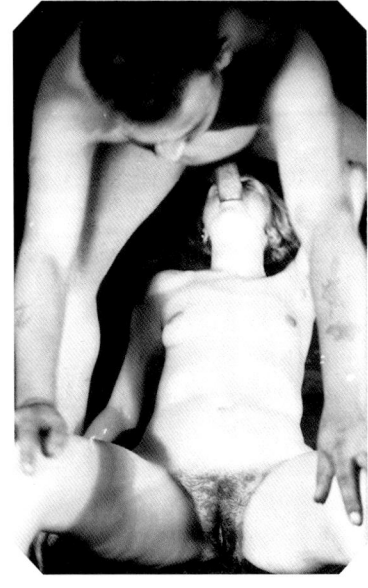

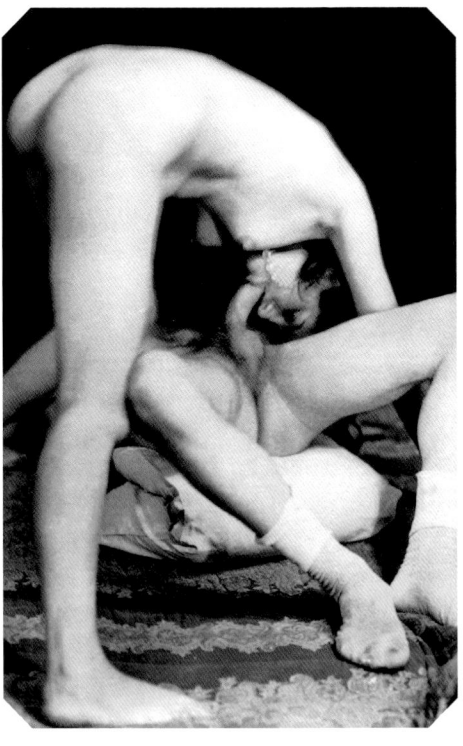

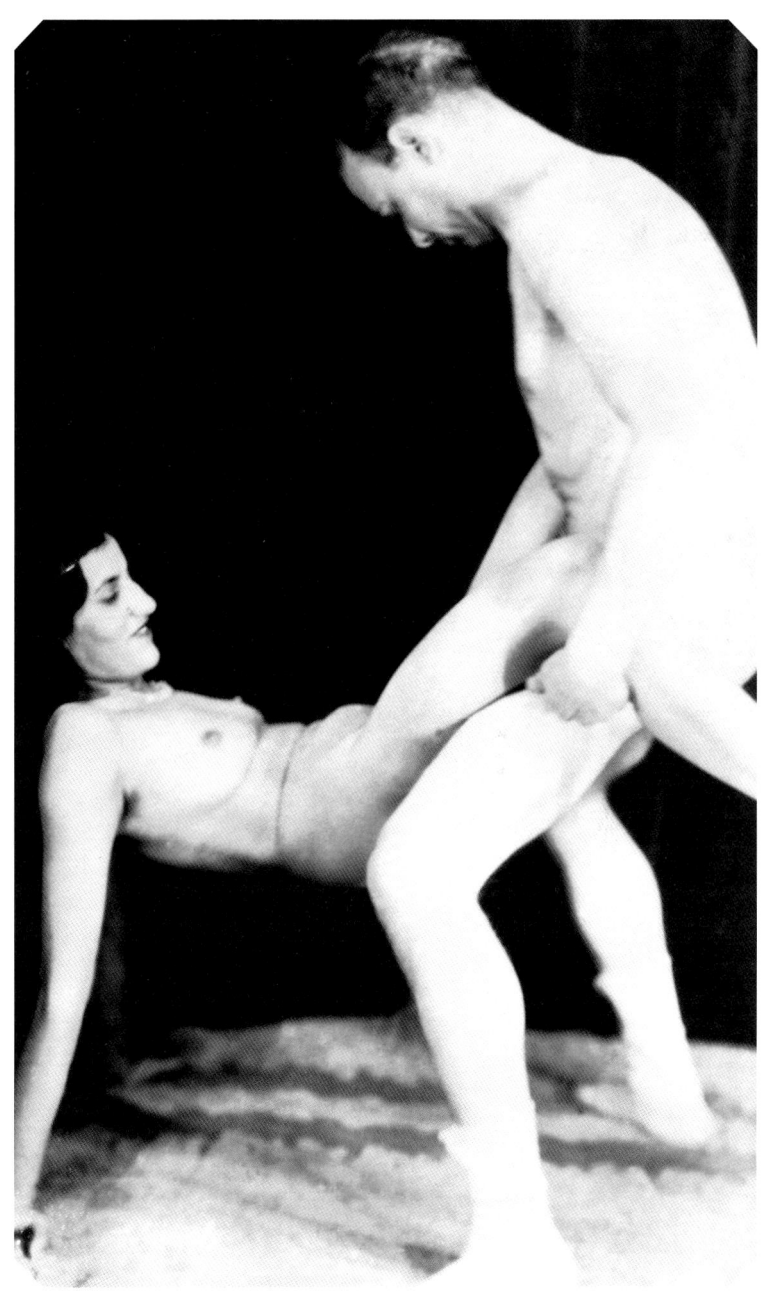

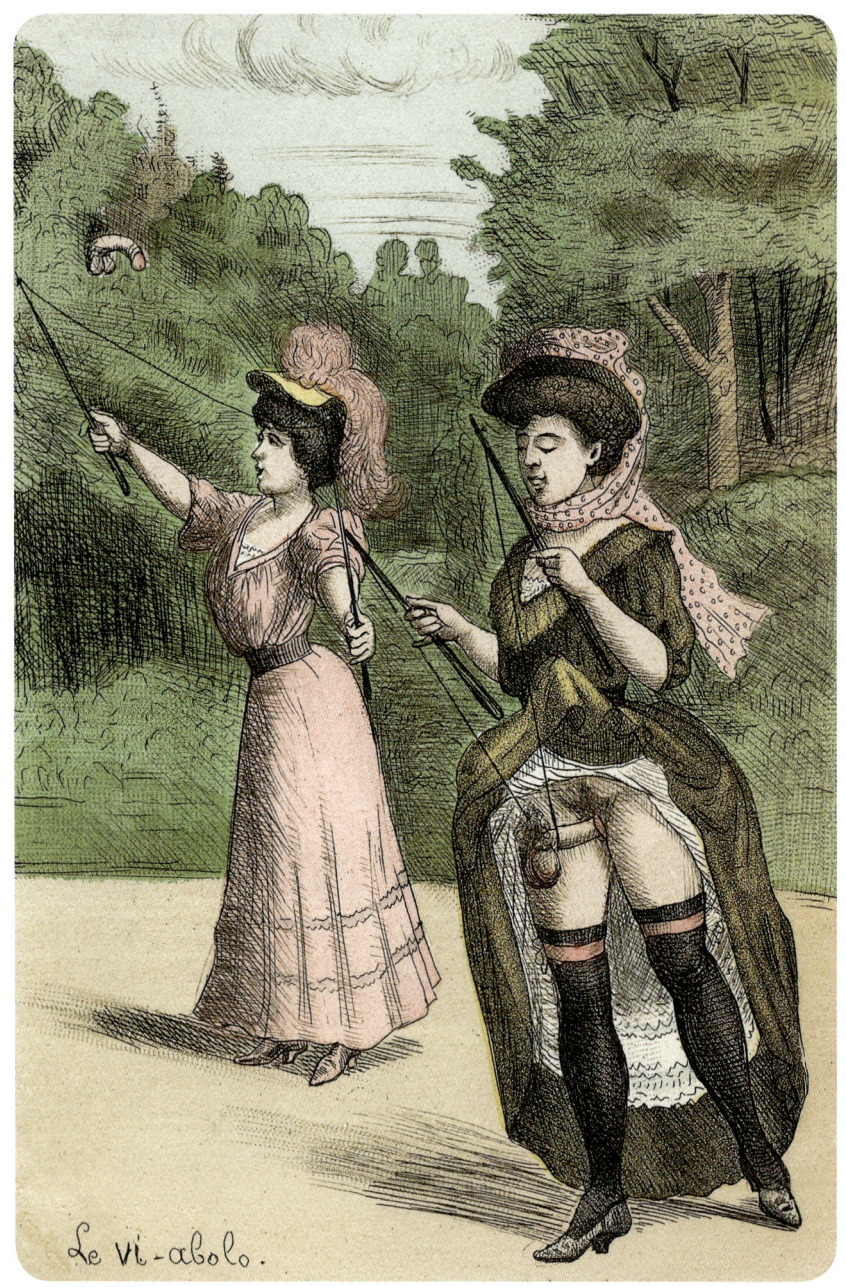

Le vi-abolo.

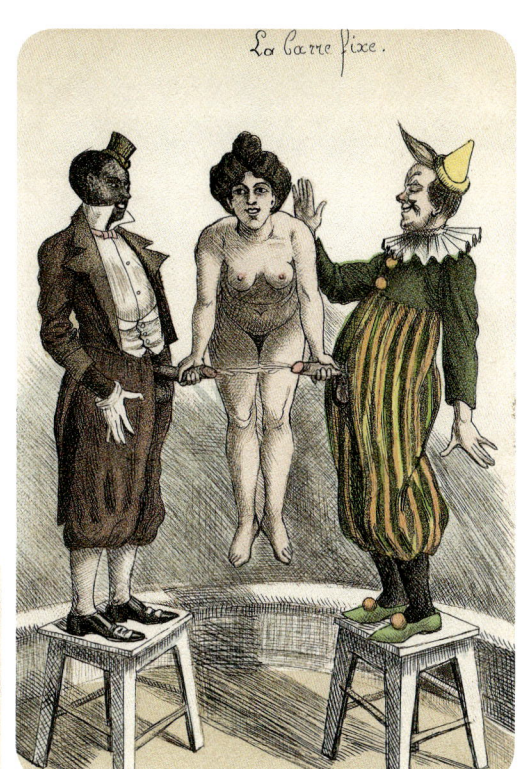

La barre fixe.

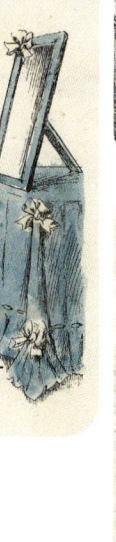

Méditation ?

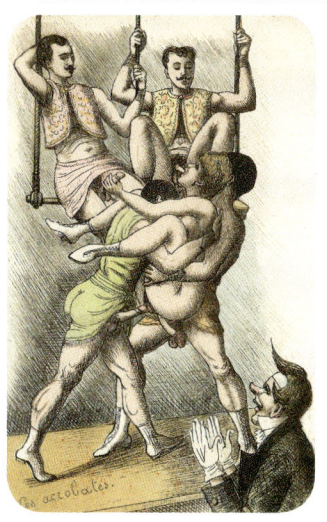

Les acrobates.

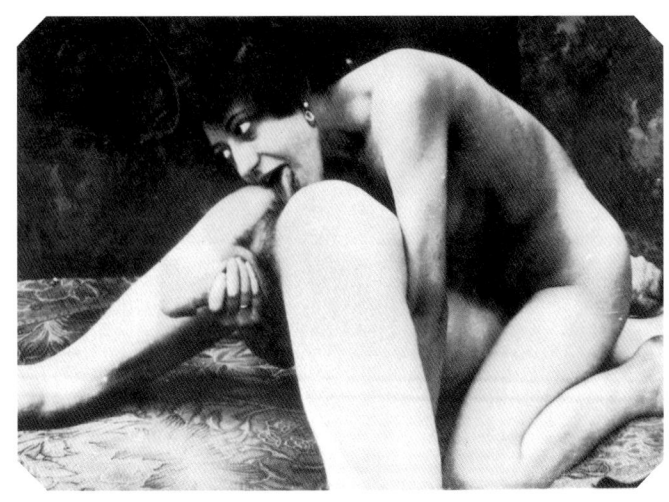

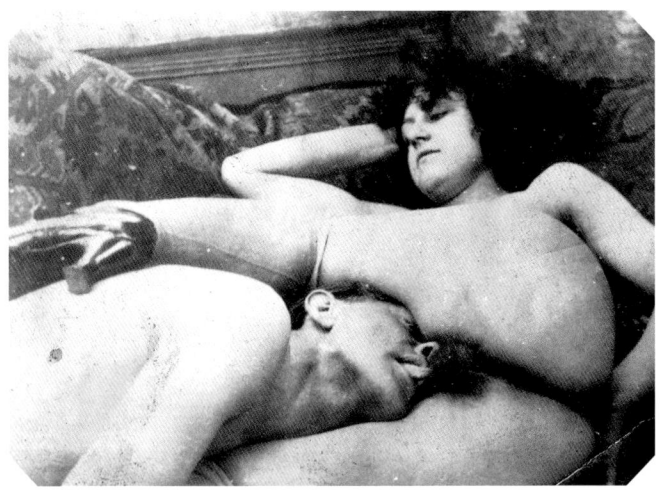

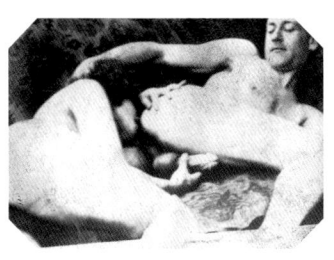

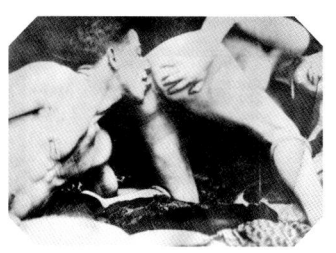

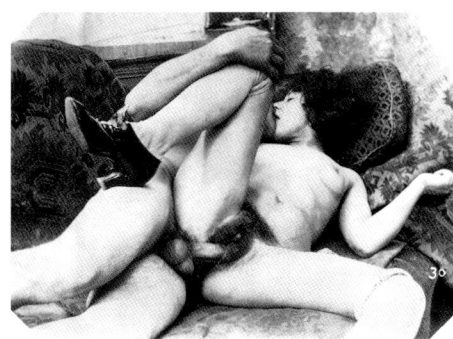

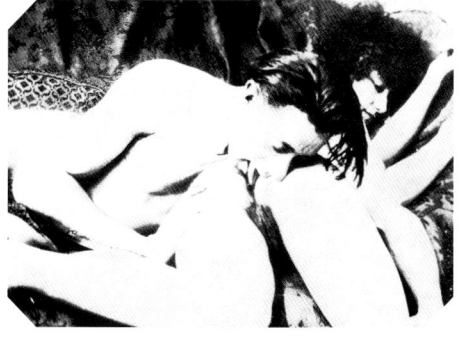

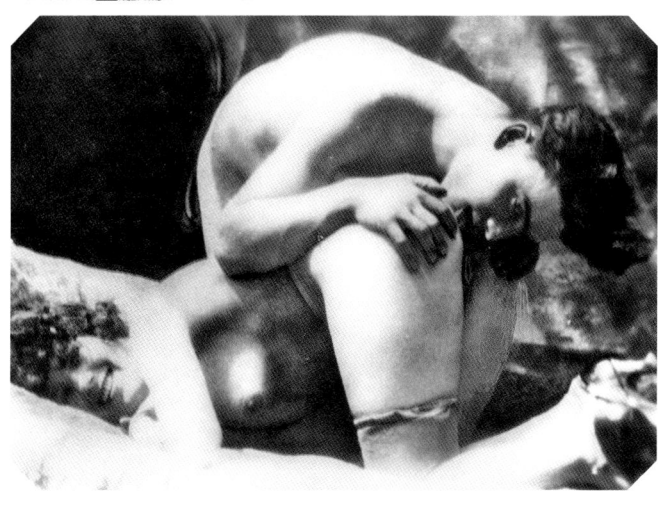

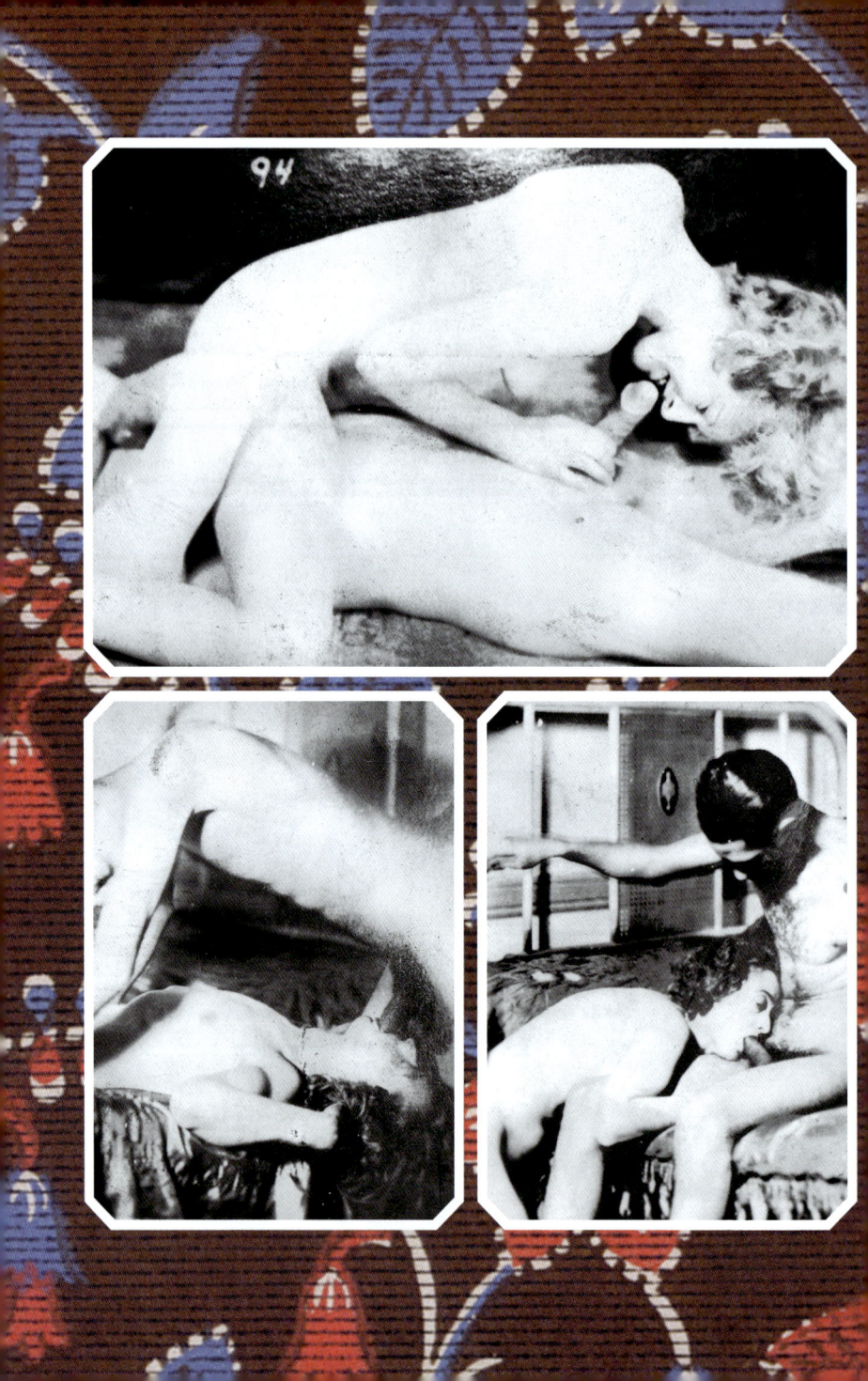

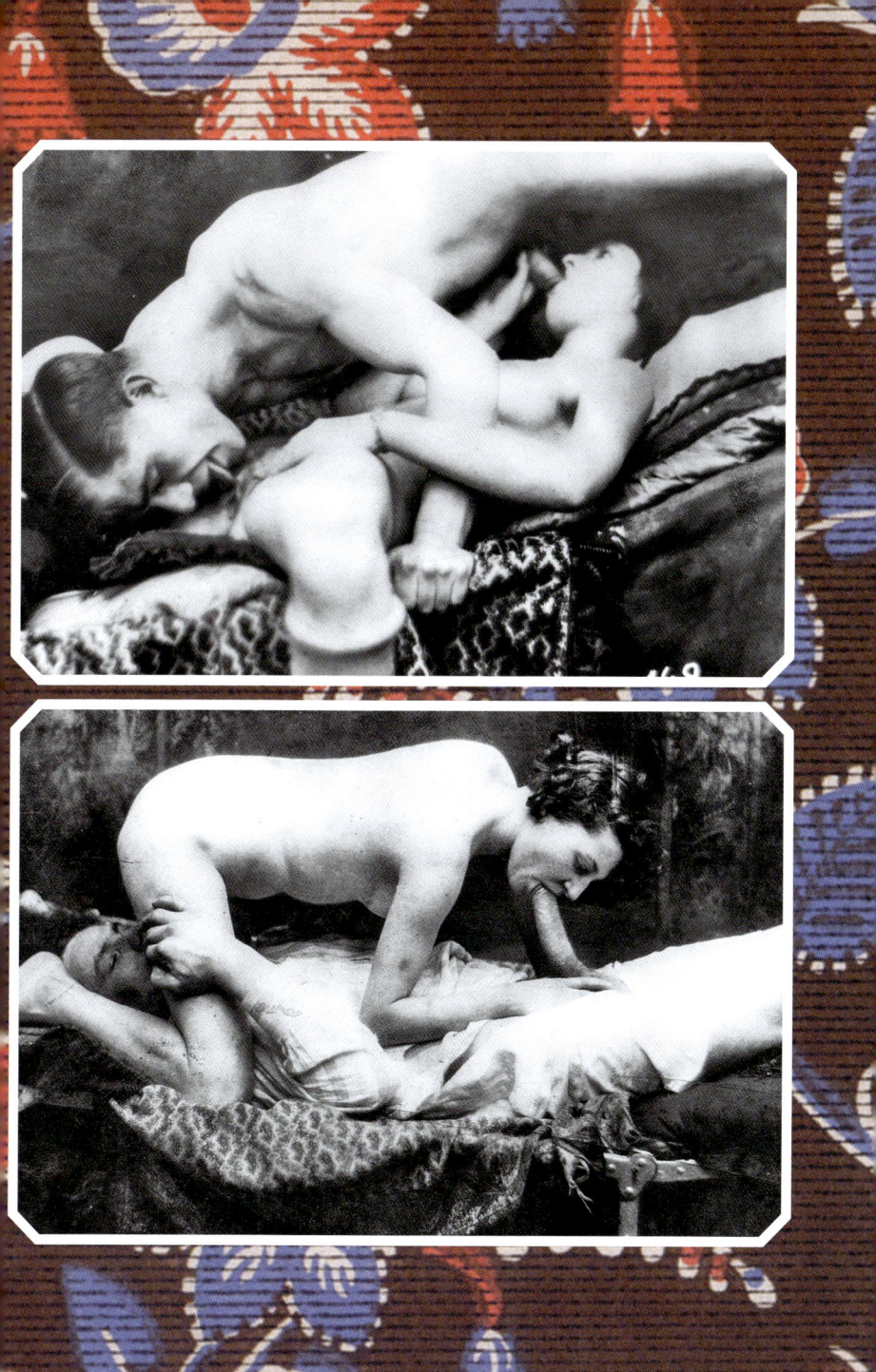

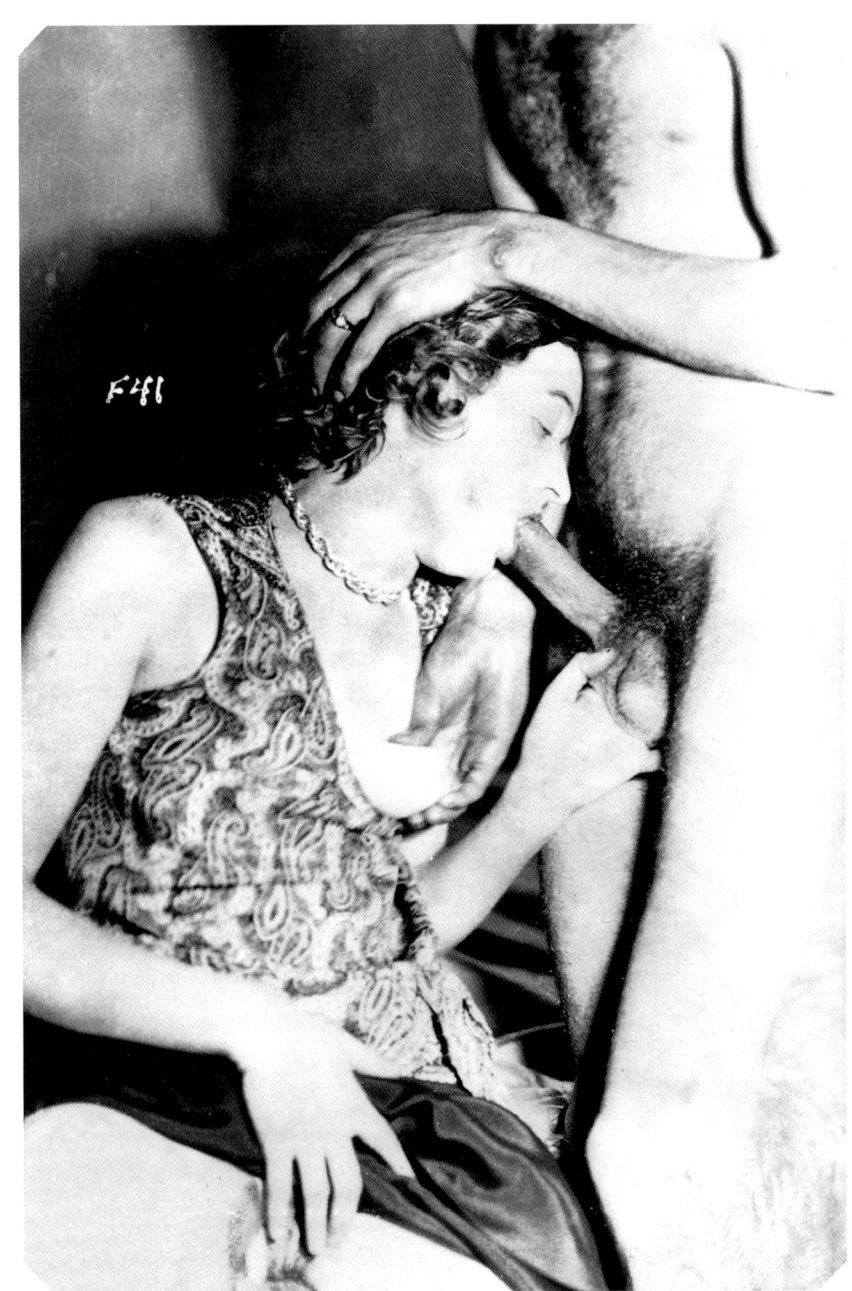

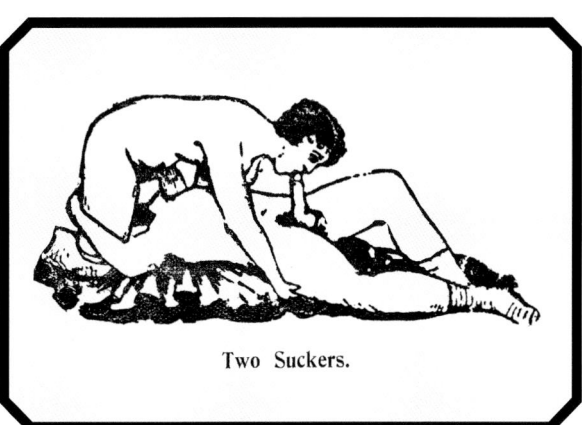

Two Suckers.

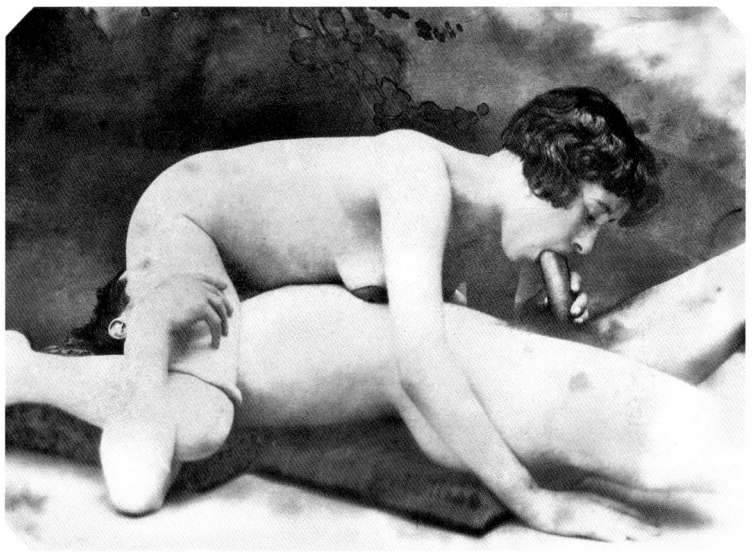

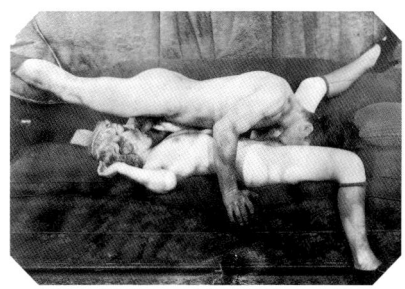

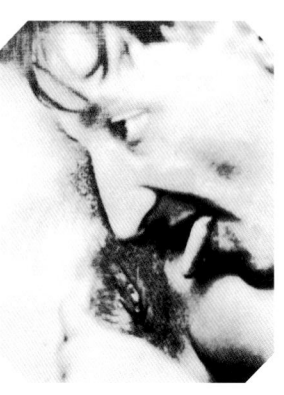

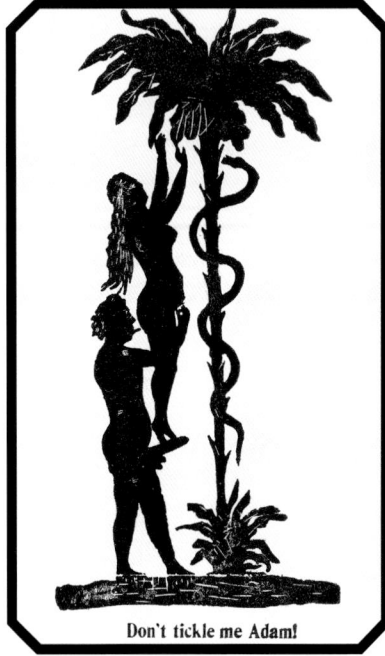

Don't tickle me Adam!

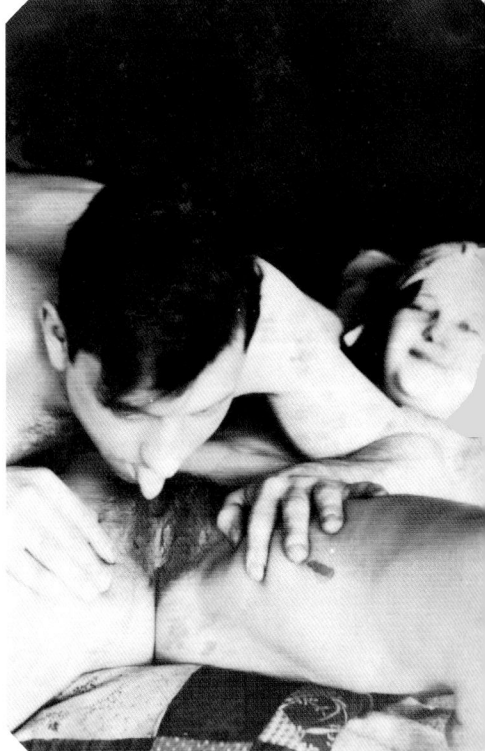

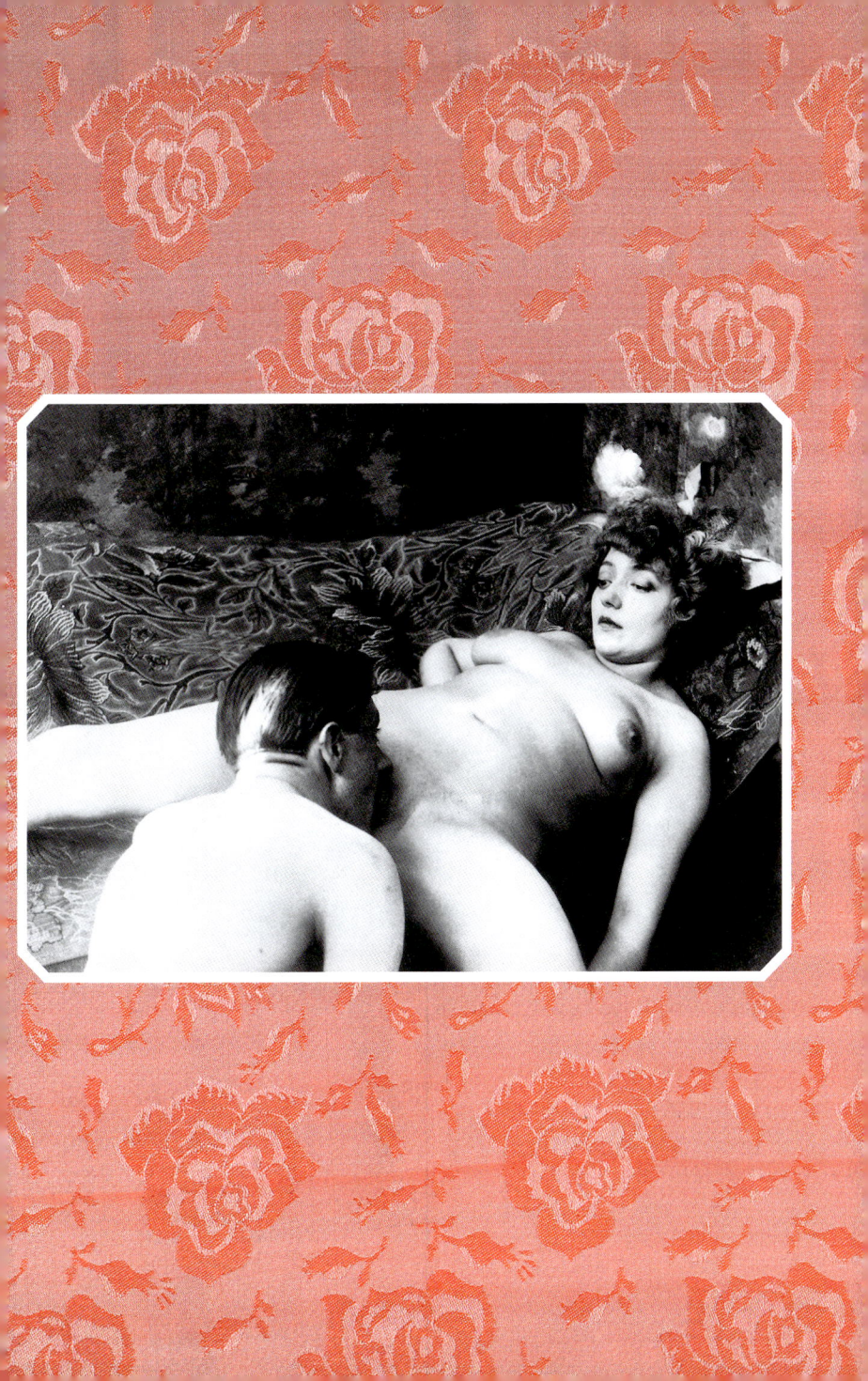

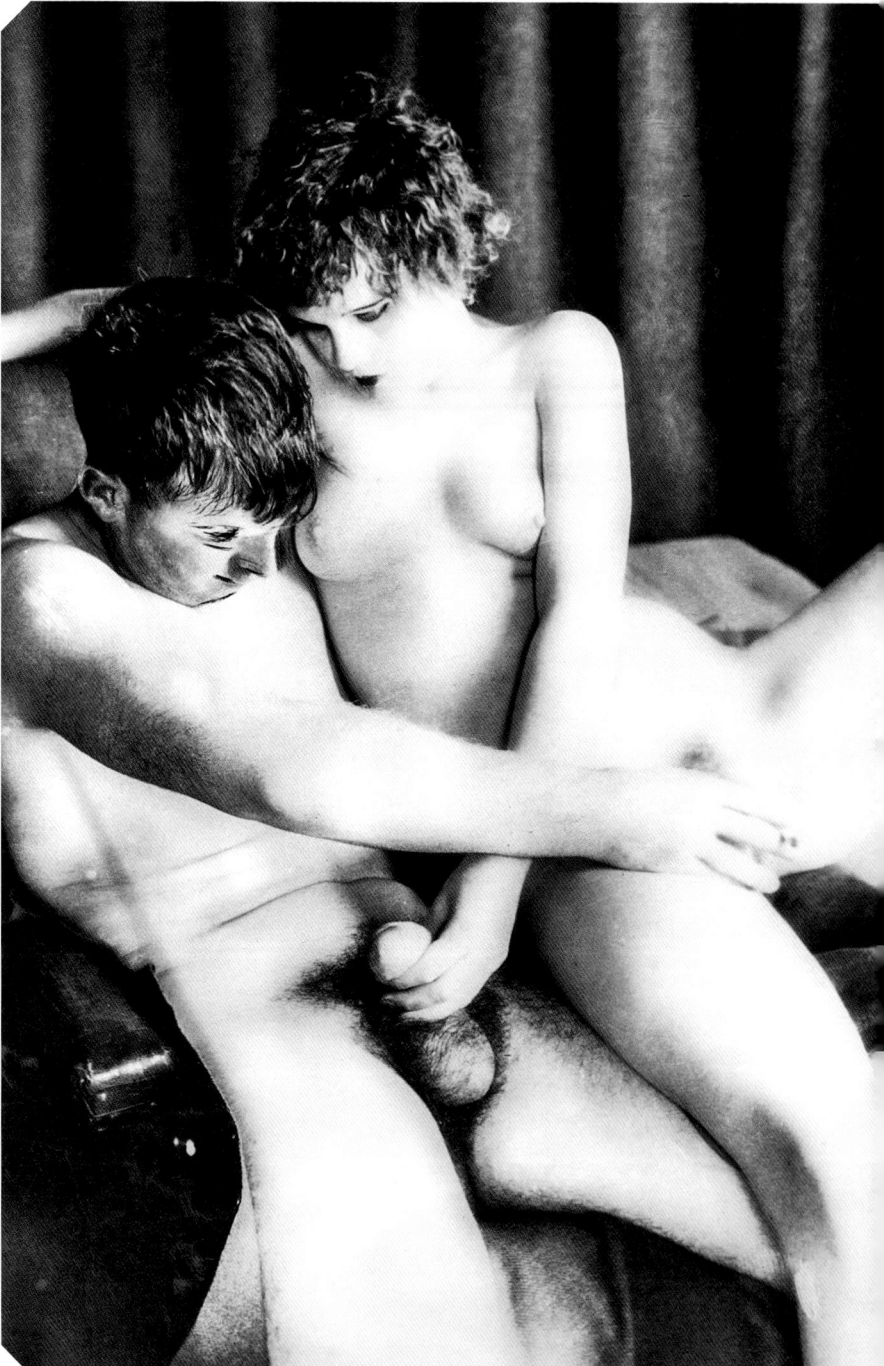

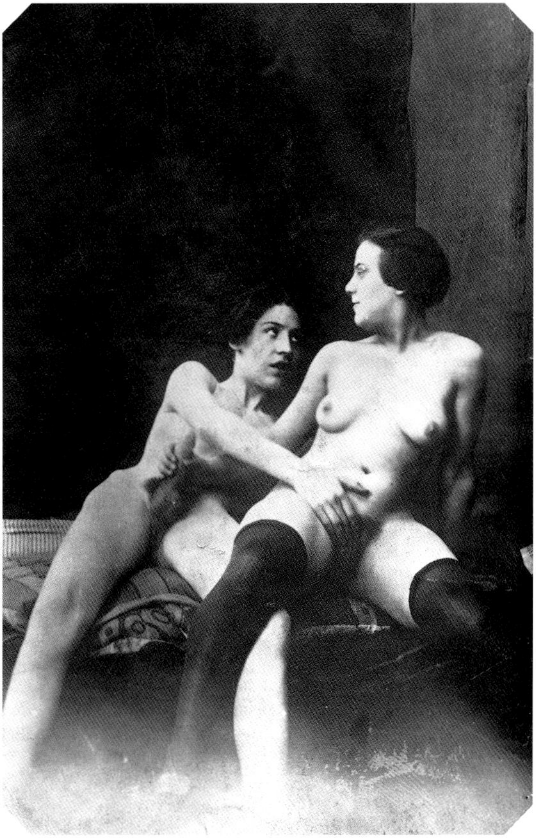

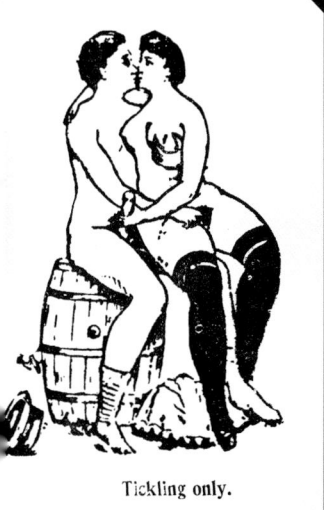

Tickling only.

221

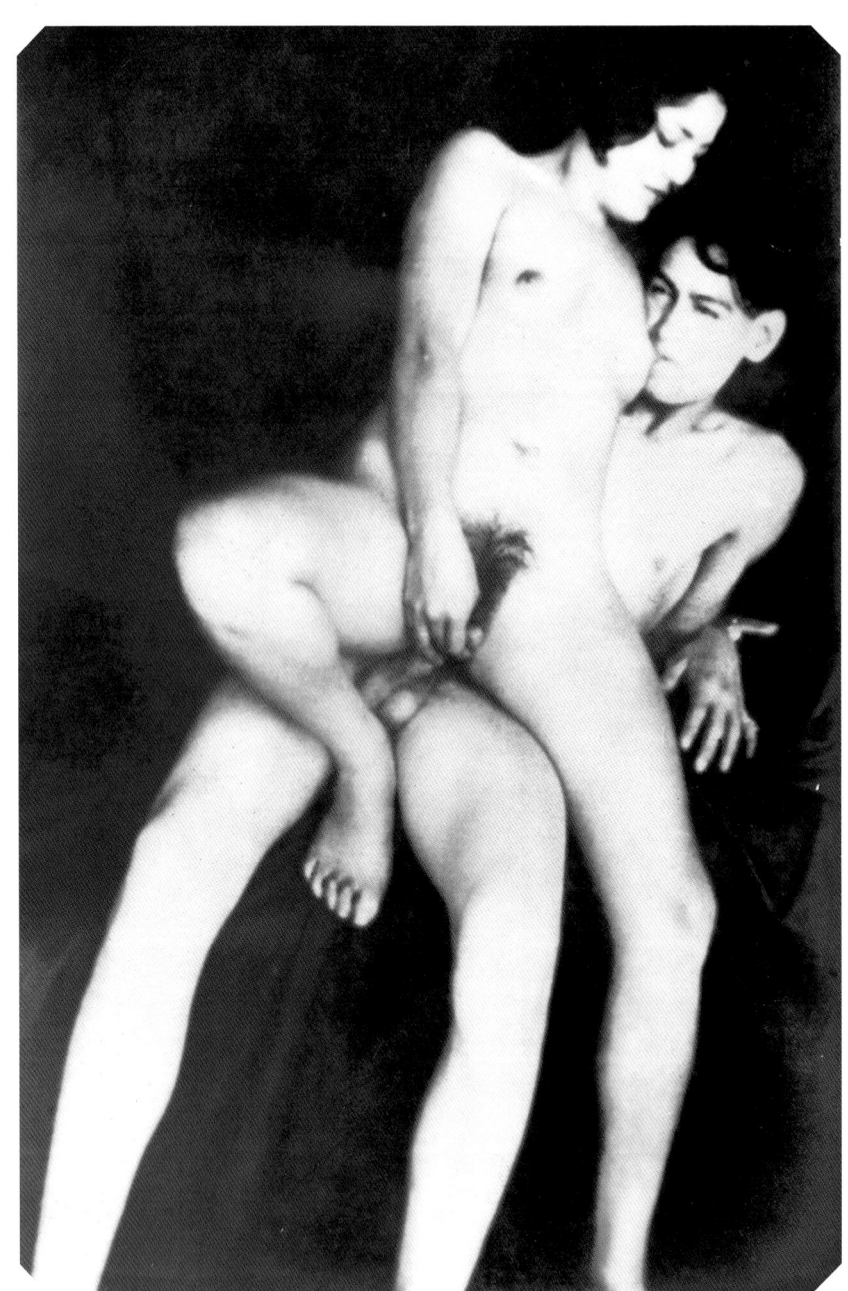

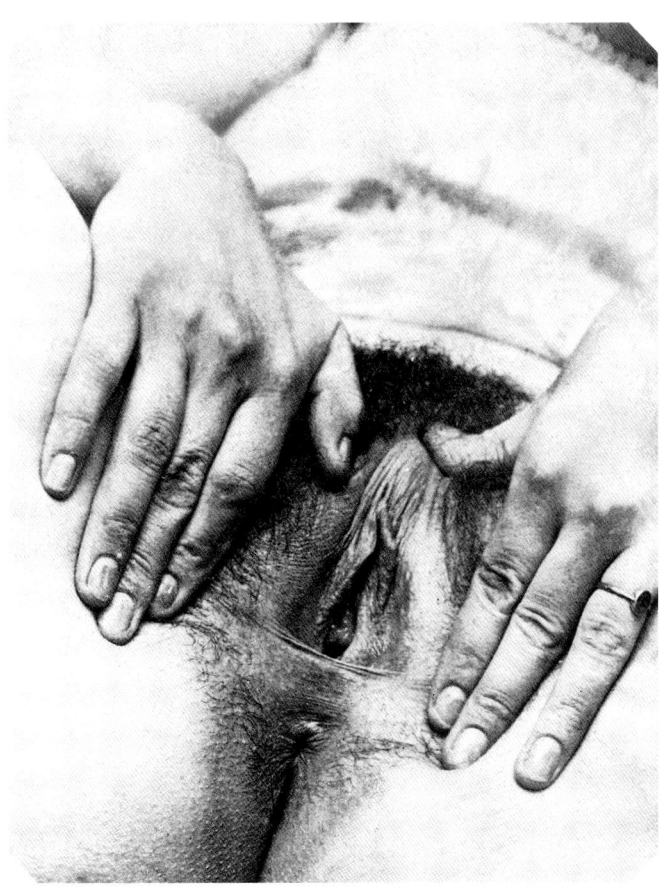

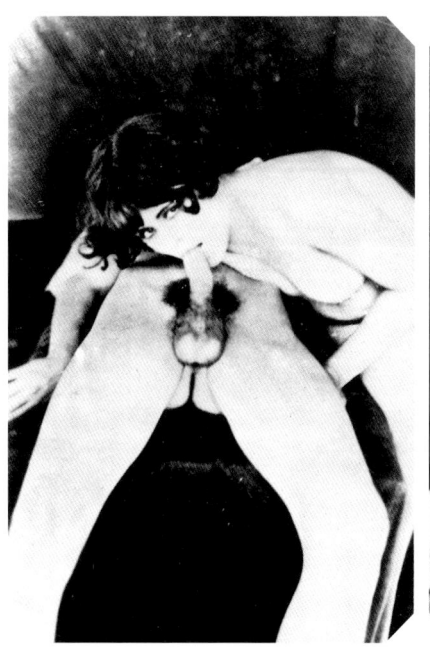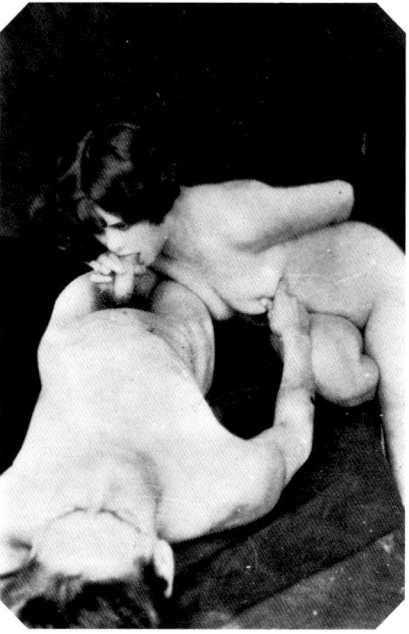

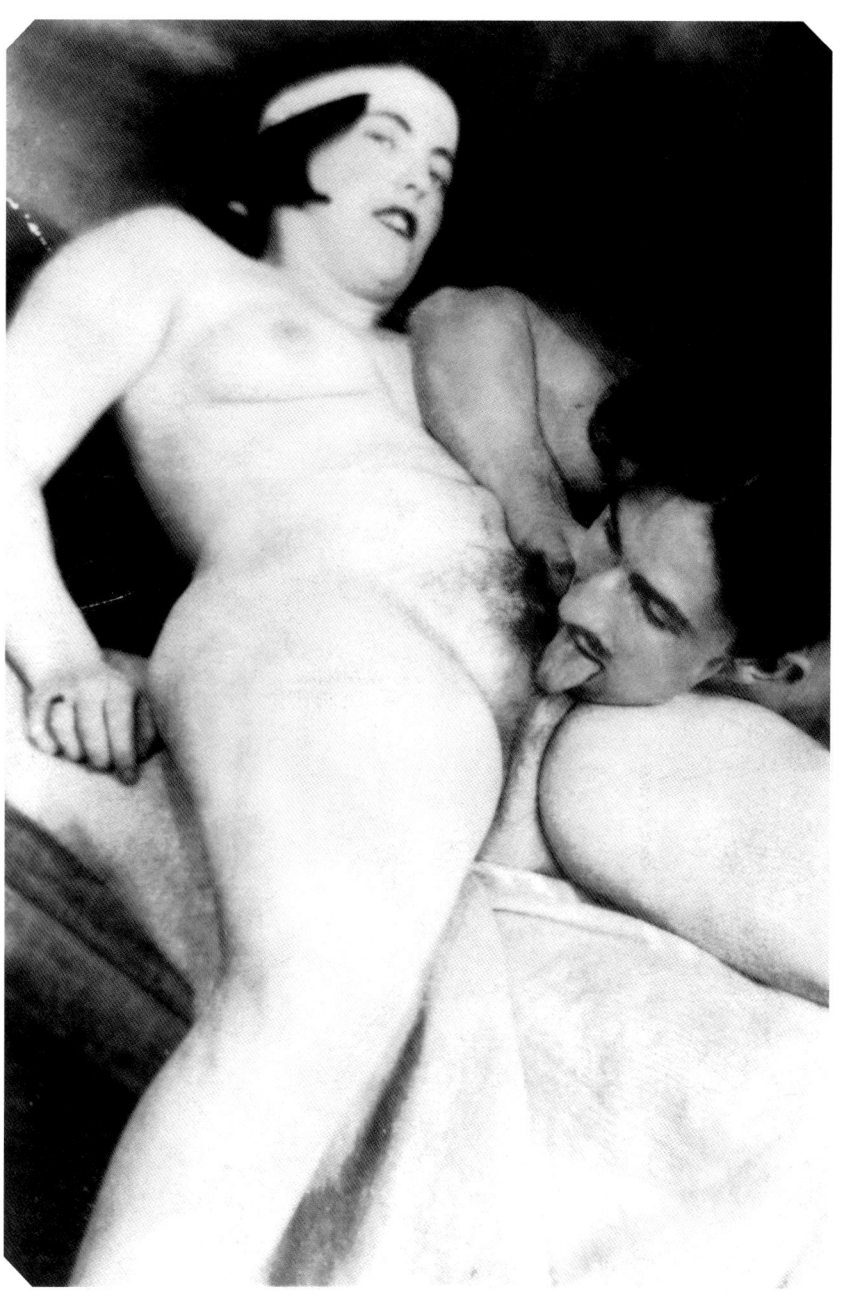

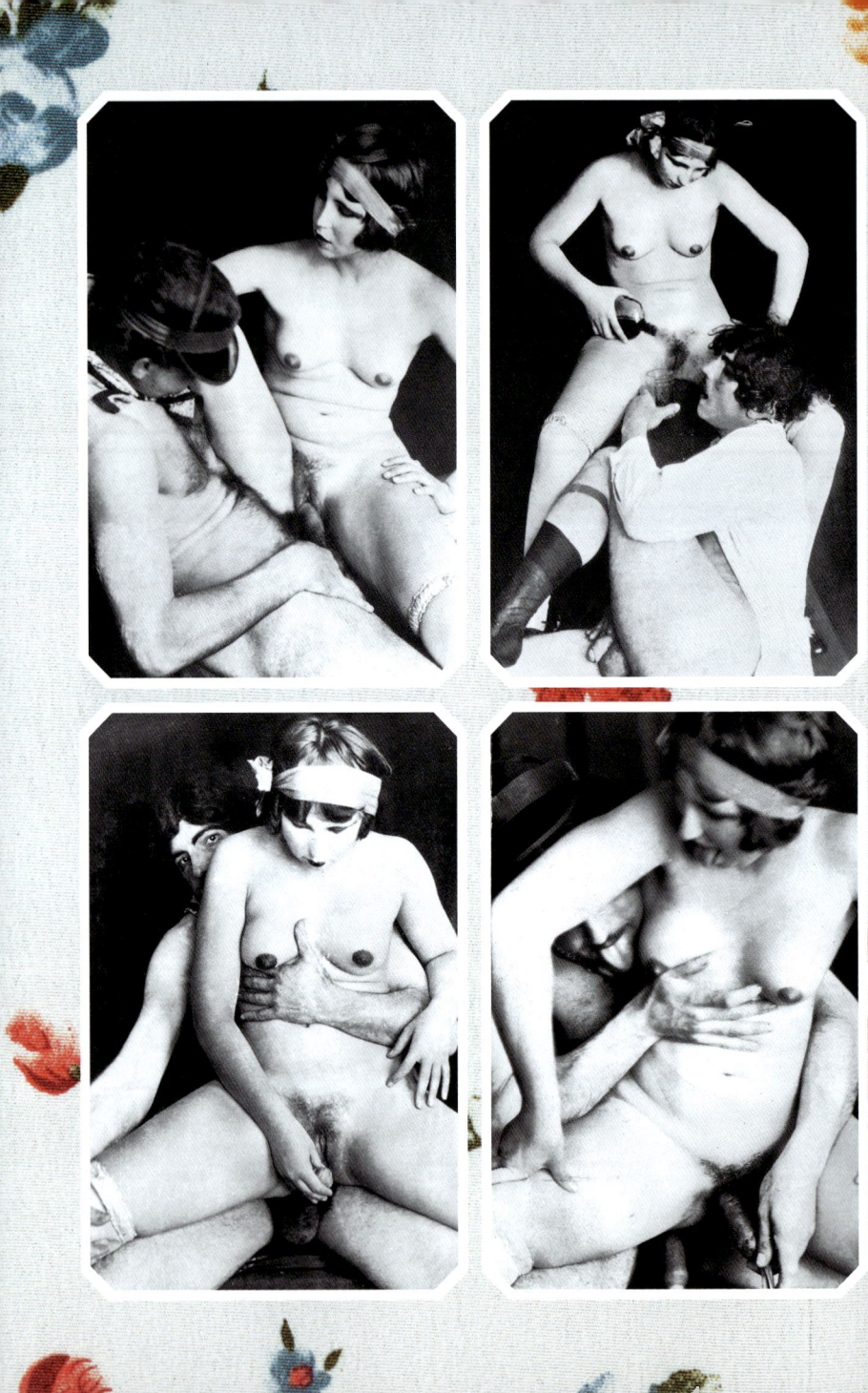

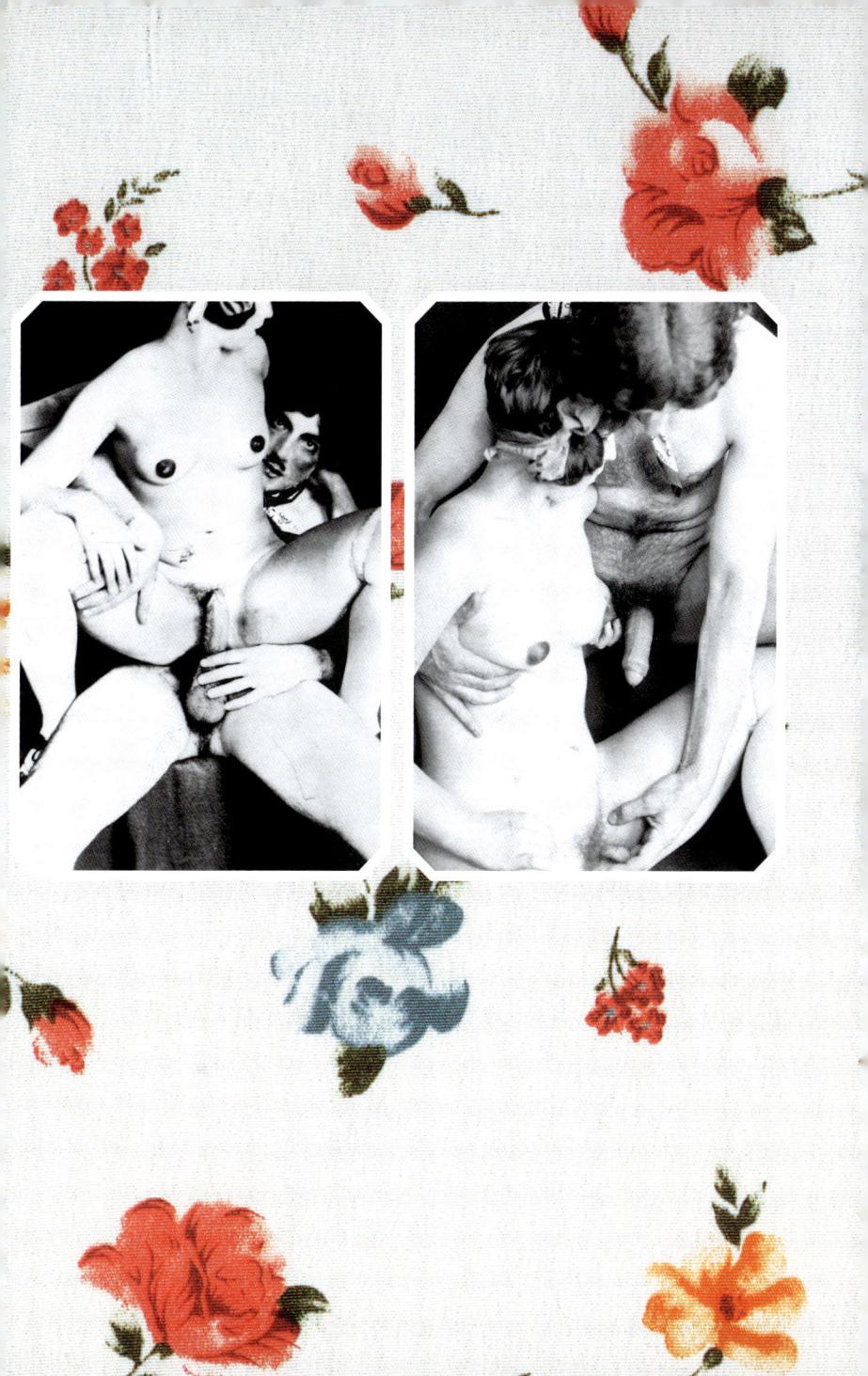

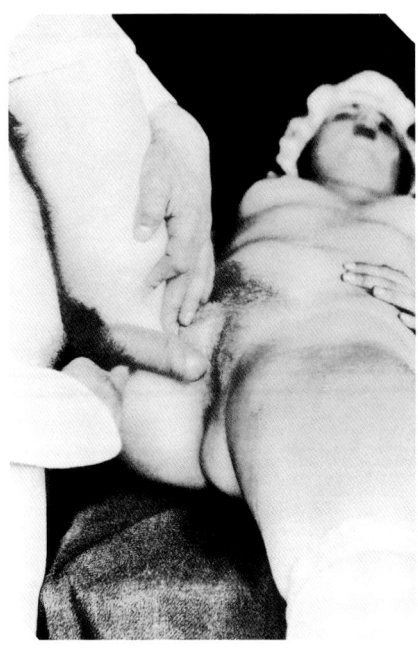

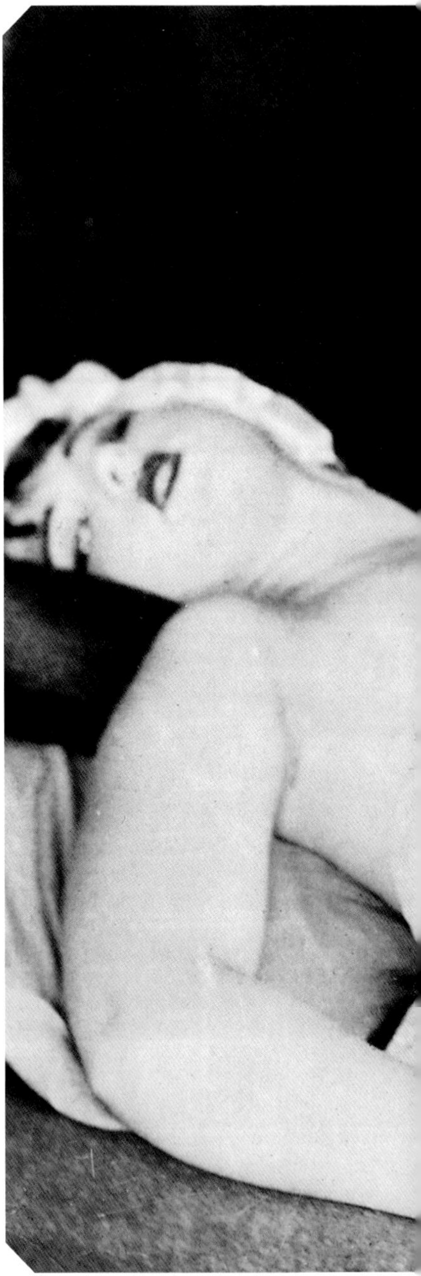

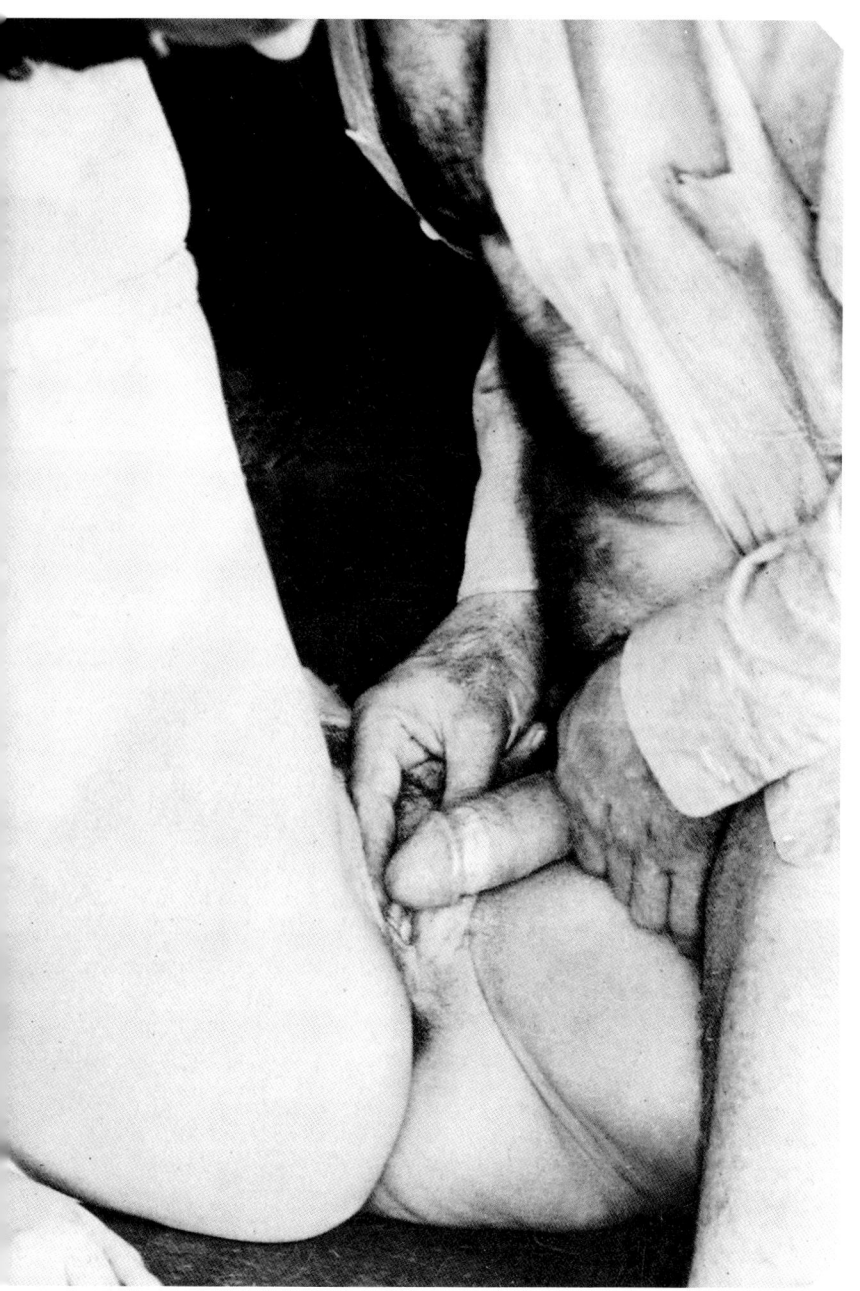

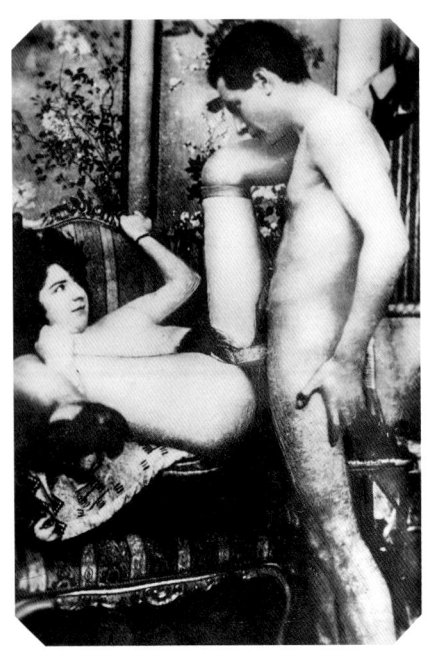

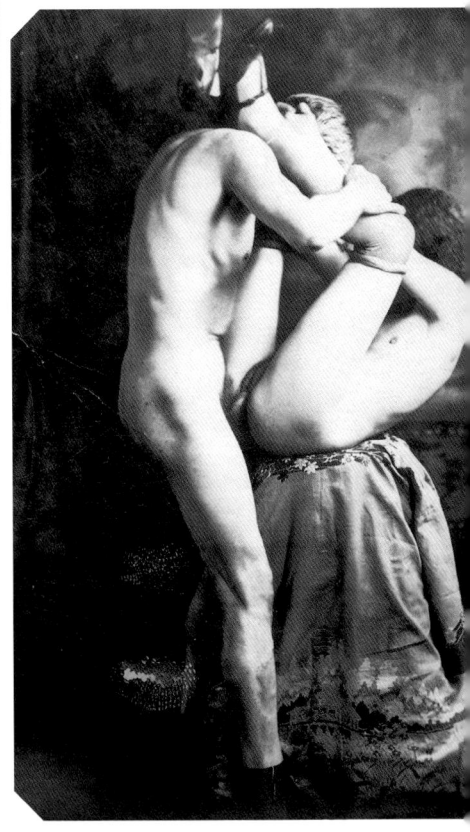

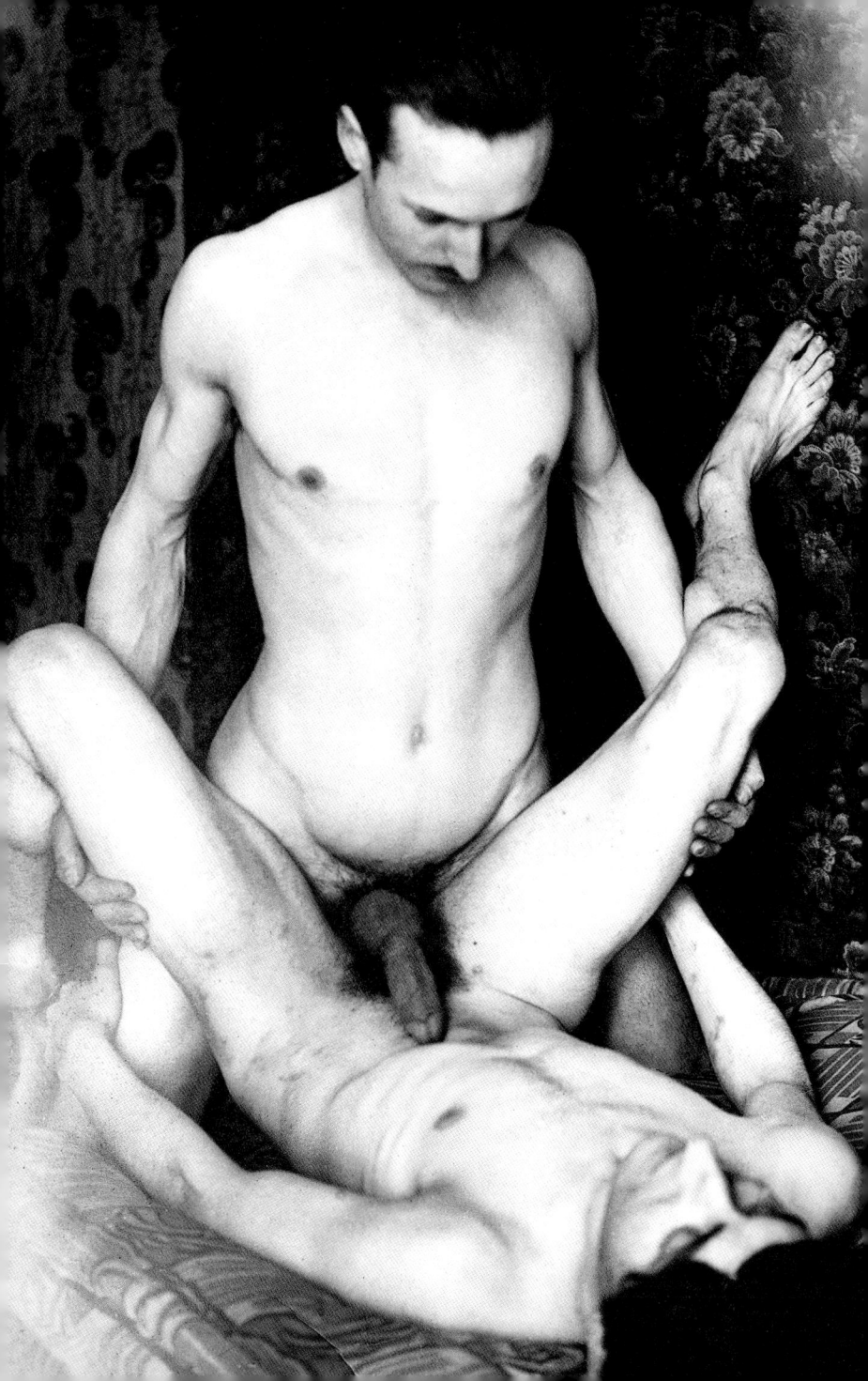

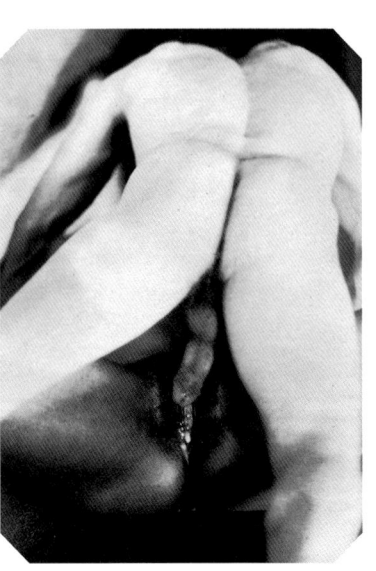

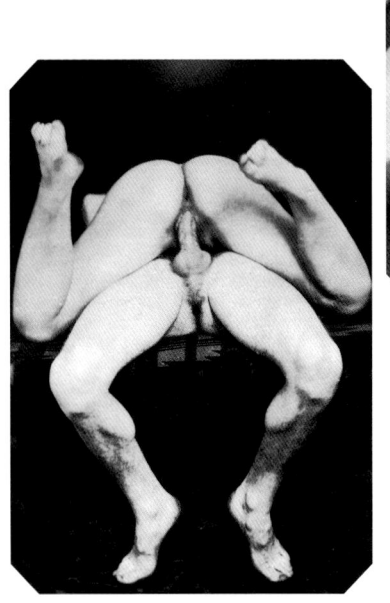

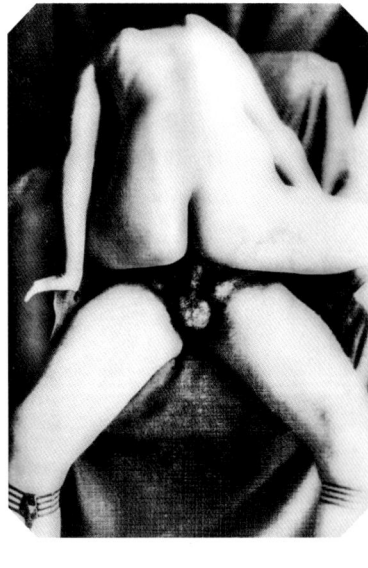

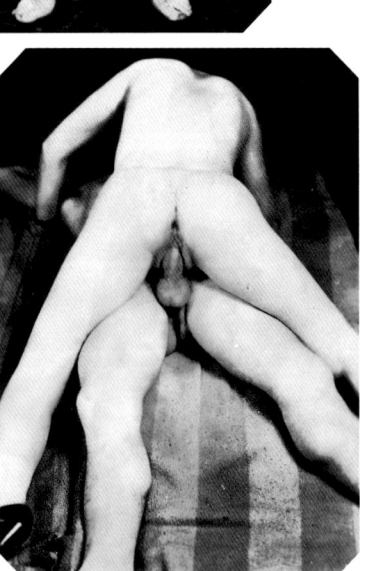

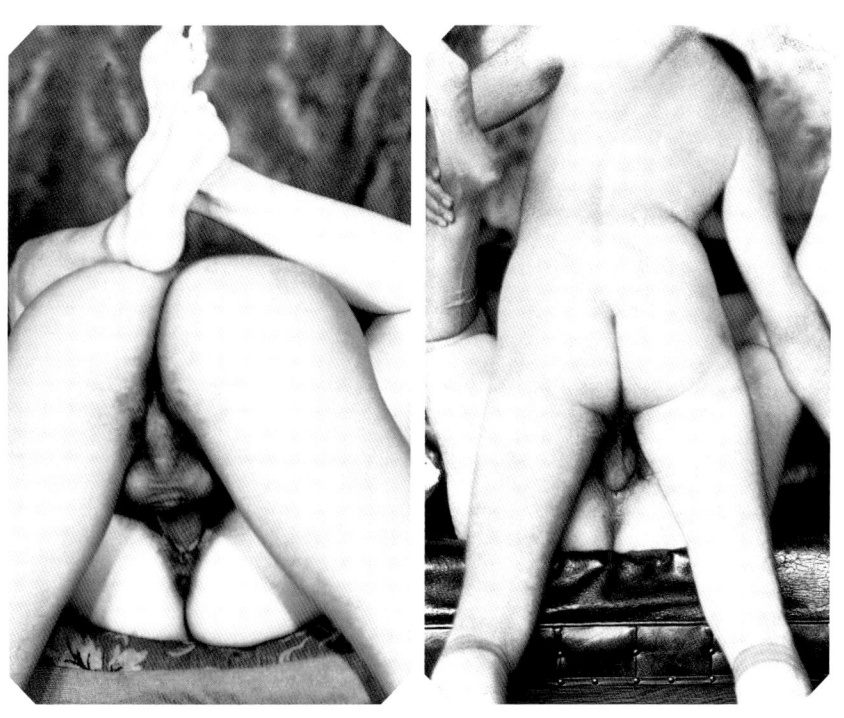

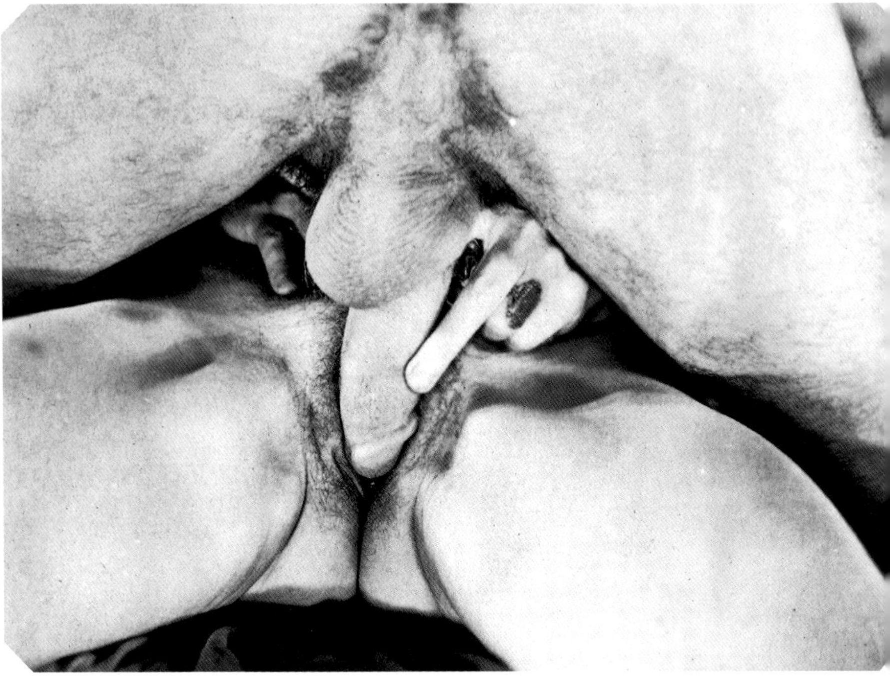

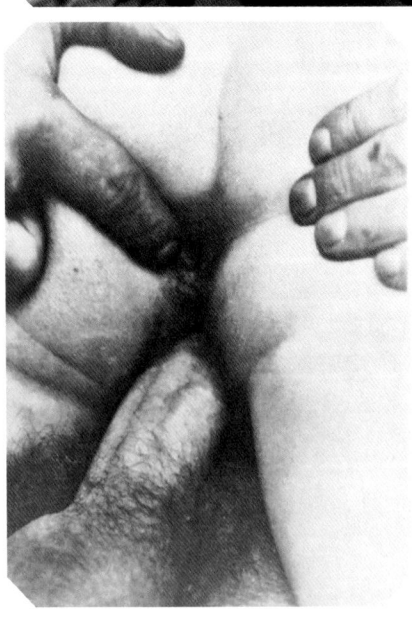

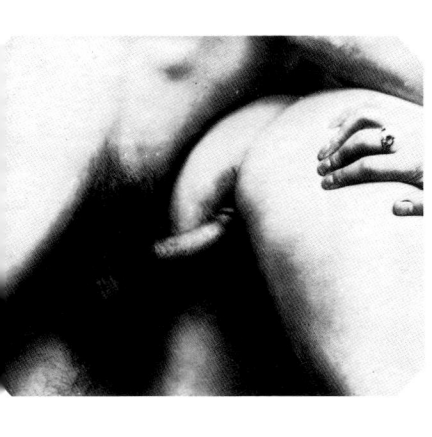

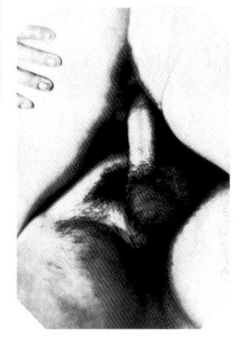

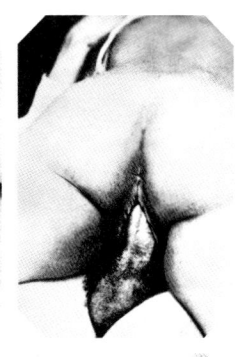

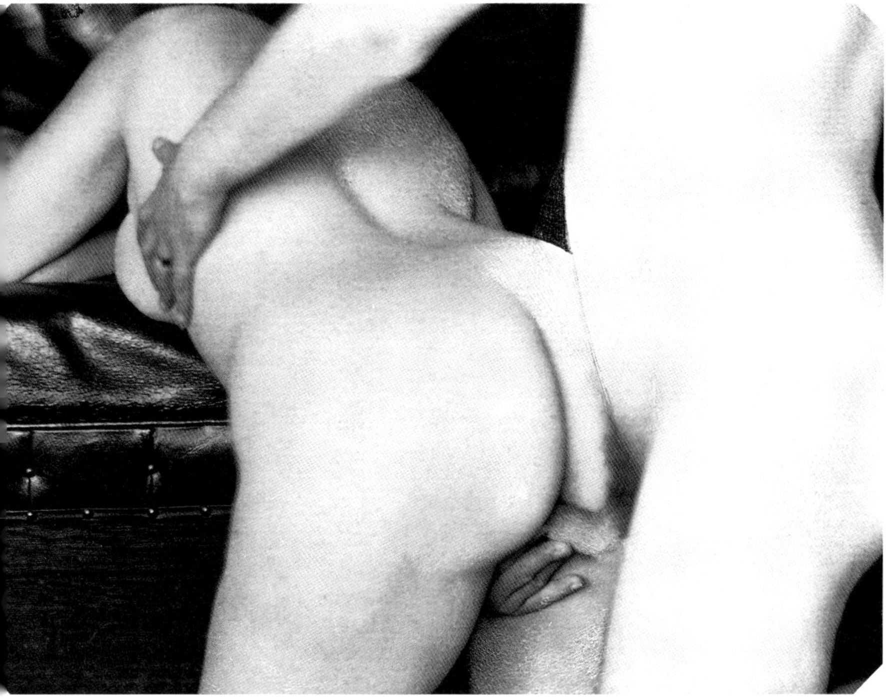

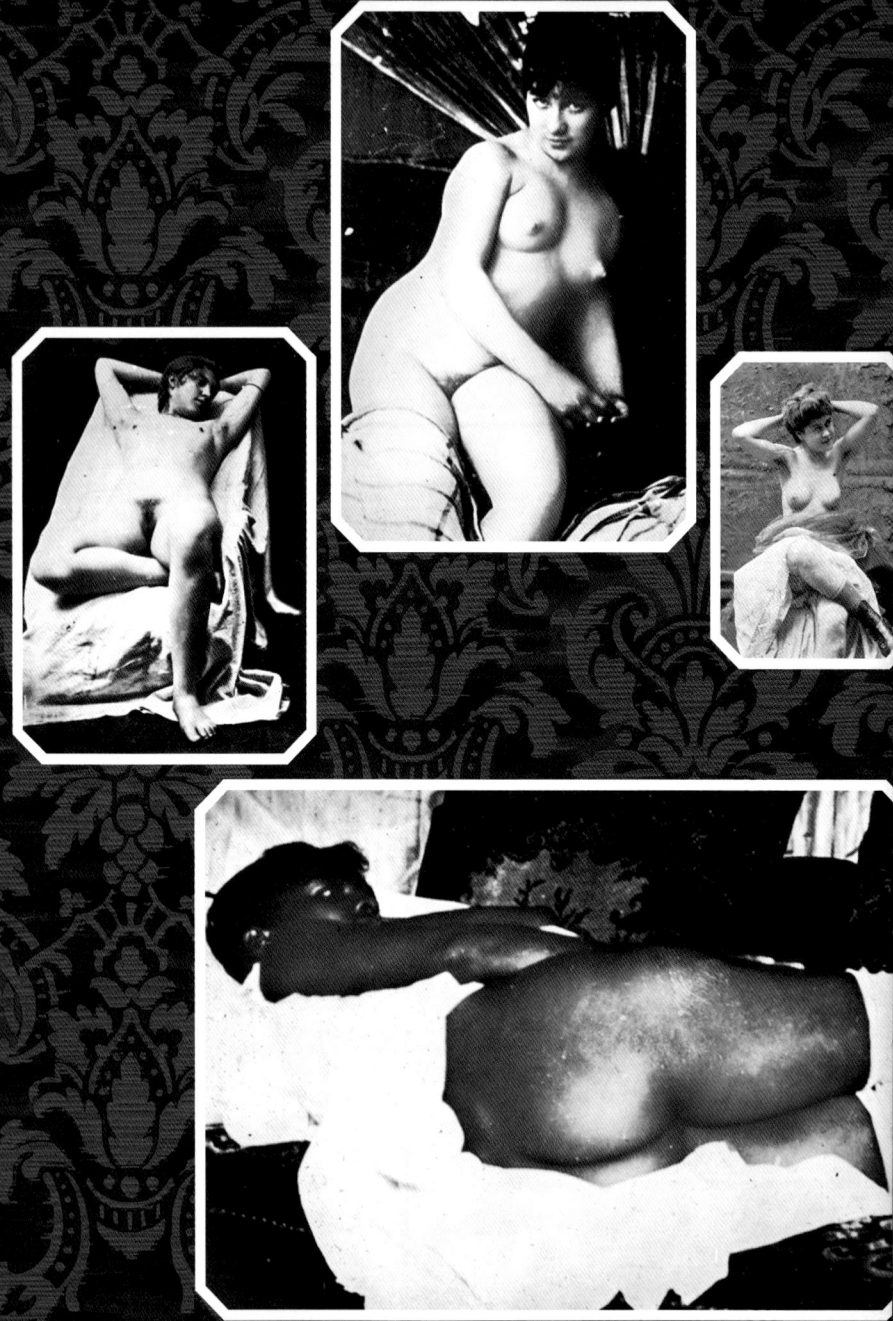

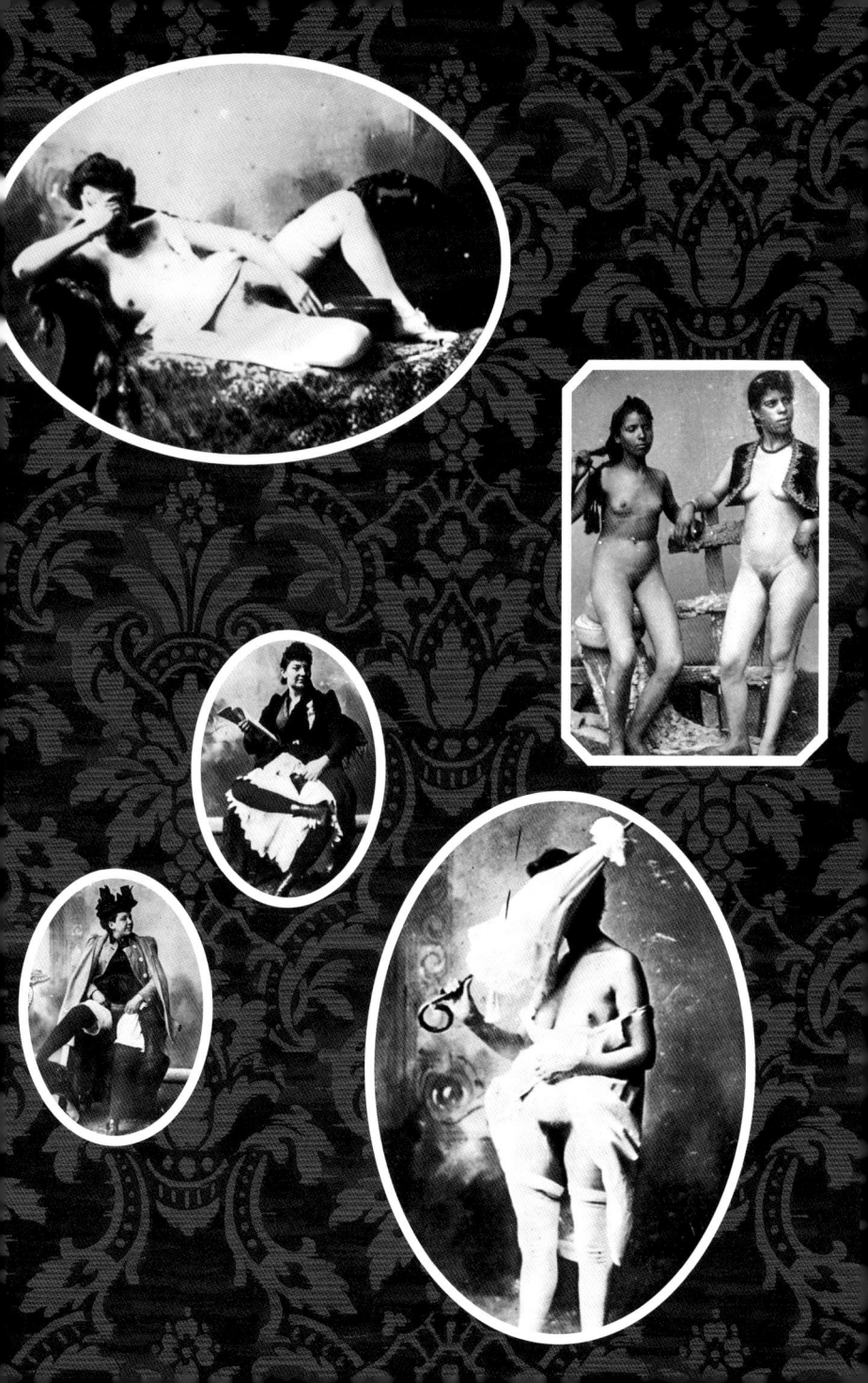

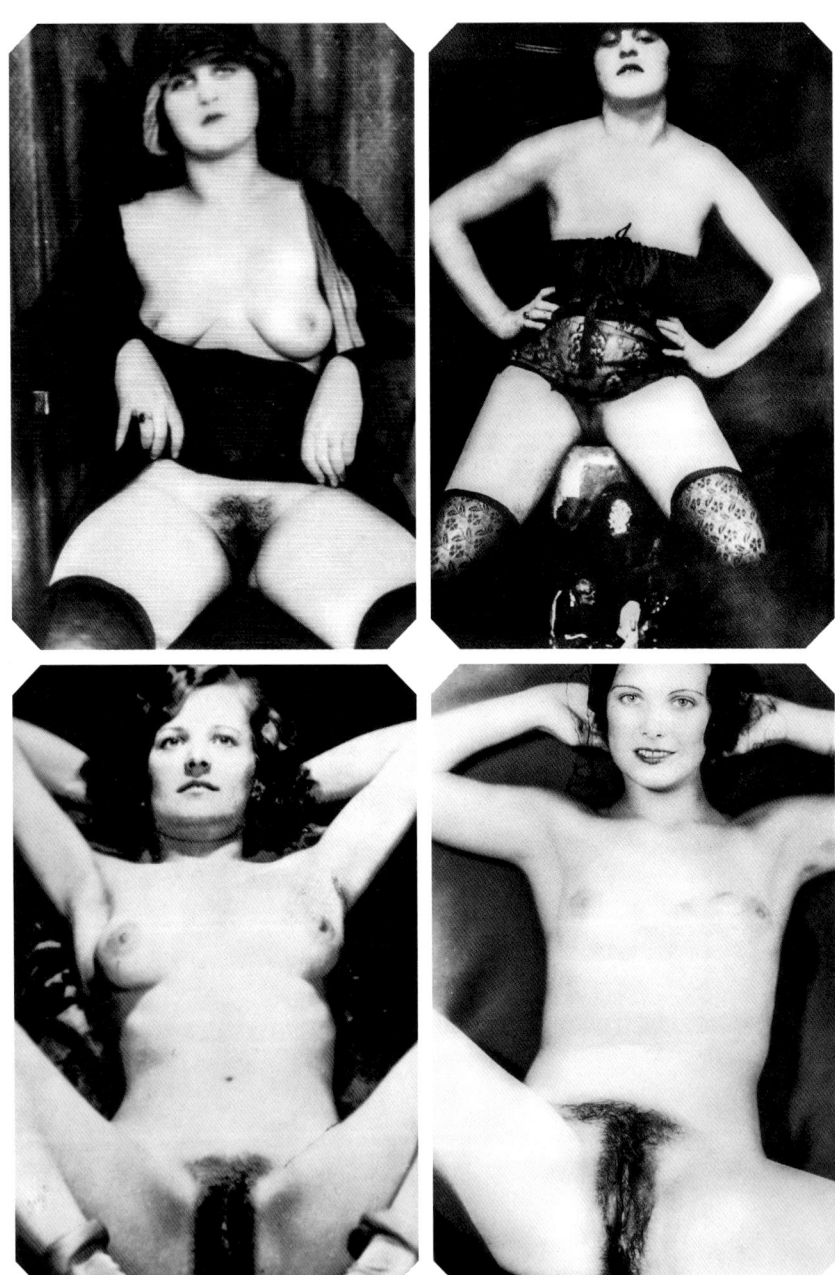

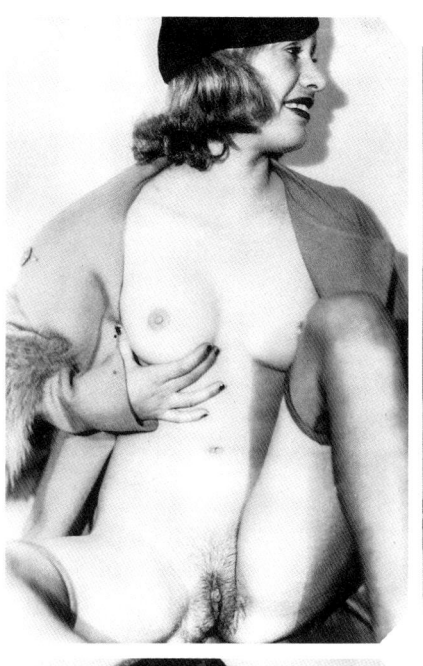
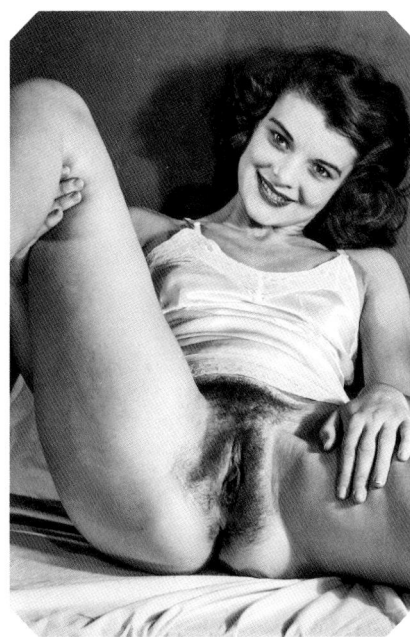
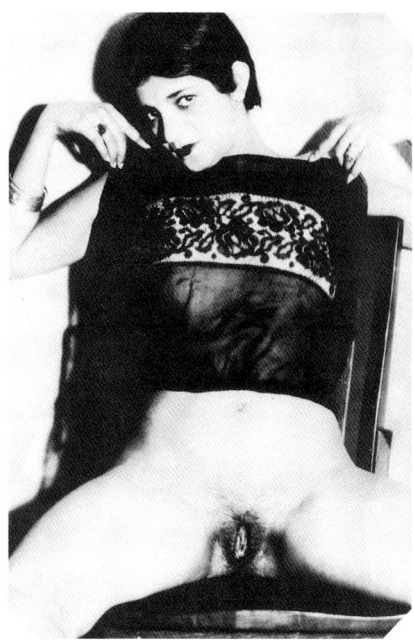
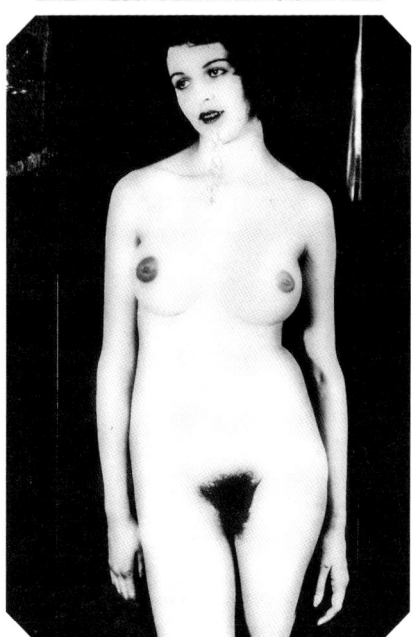

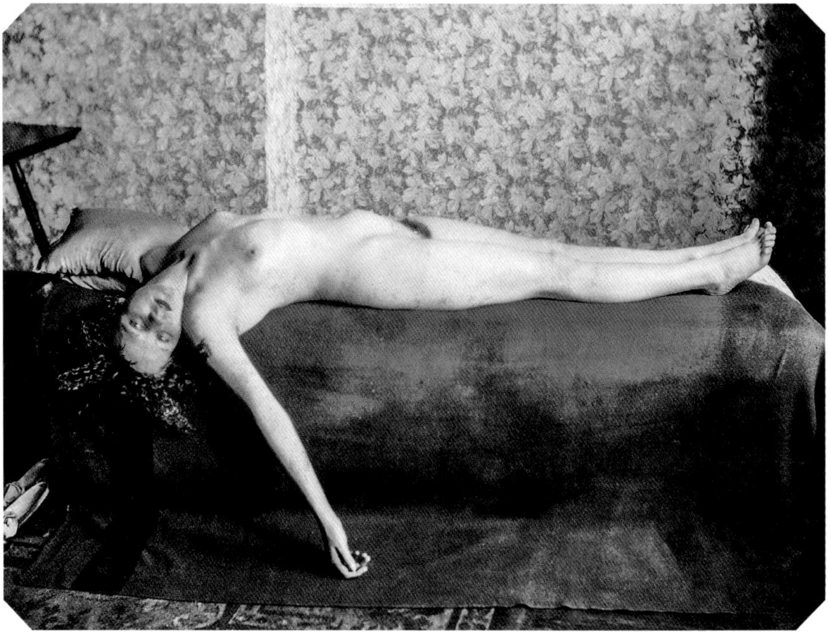

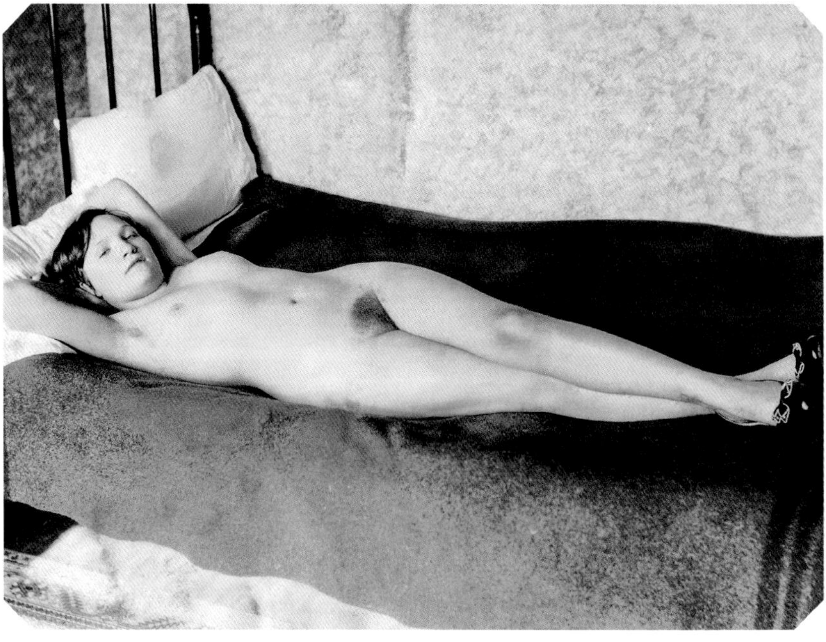

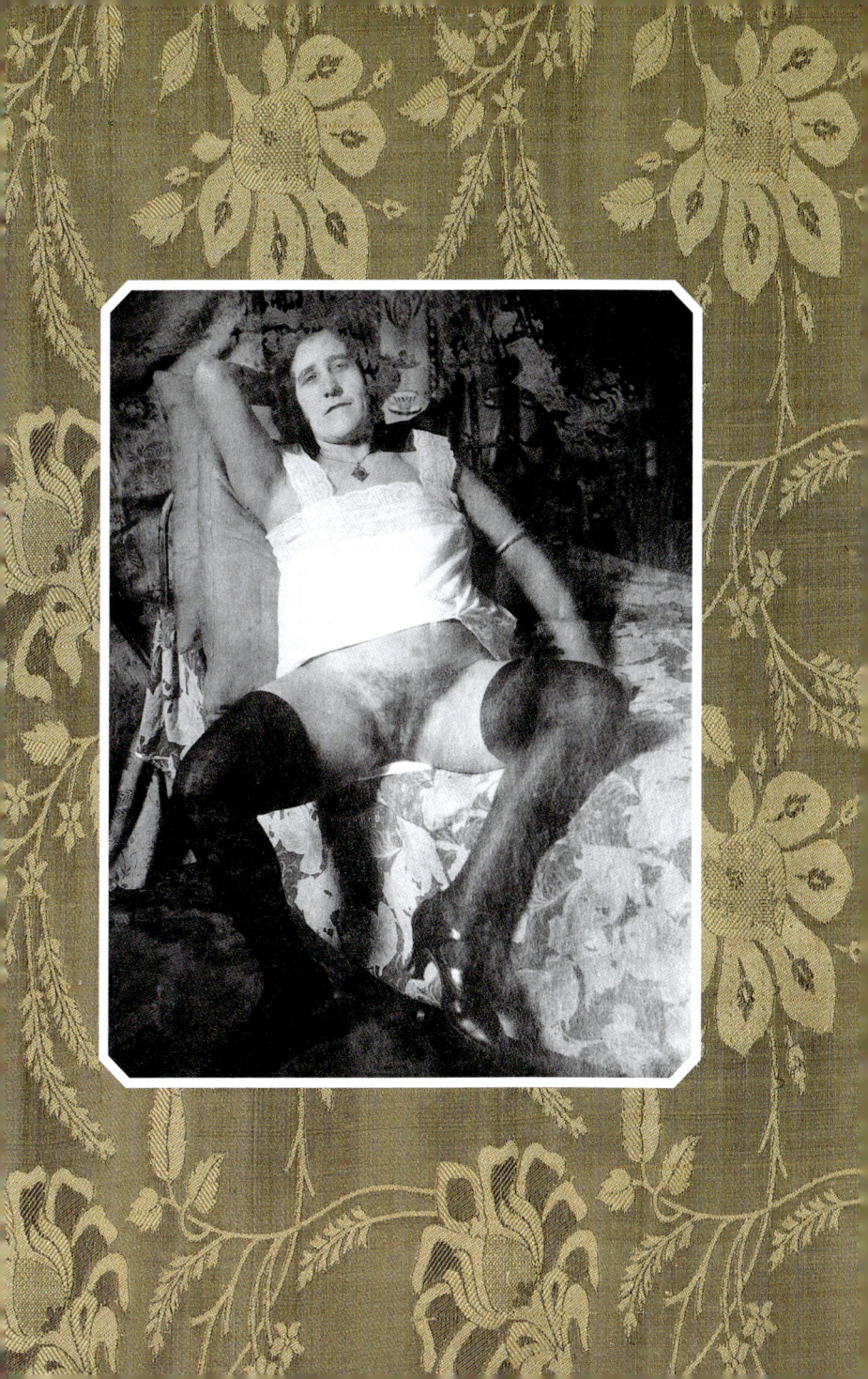

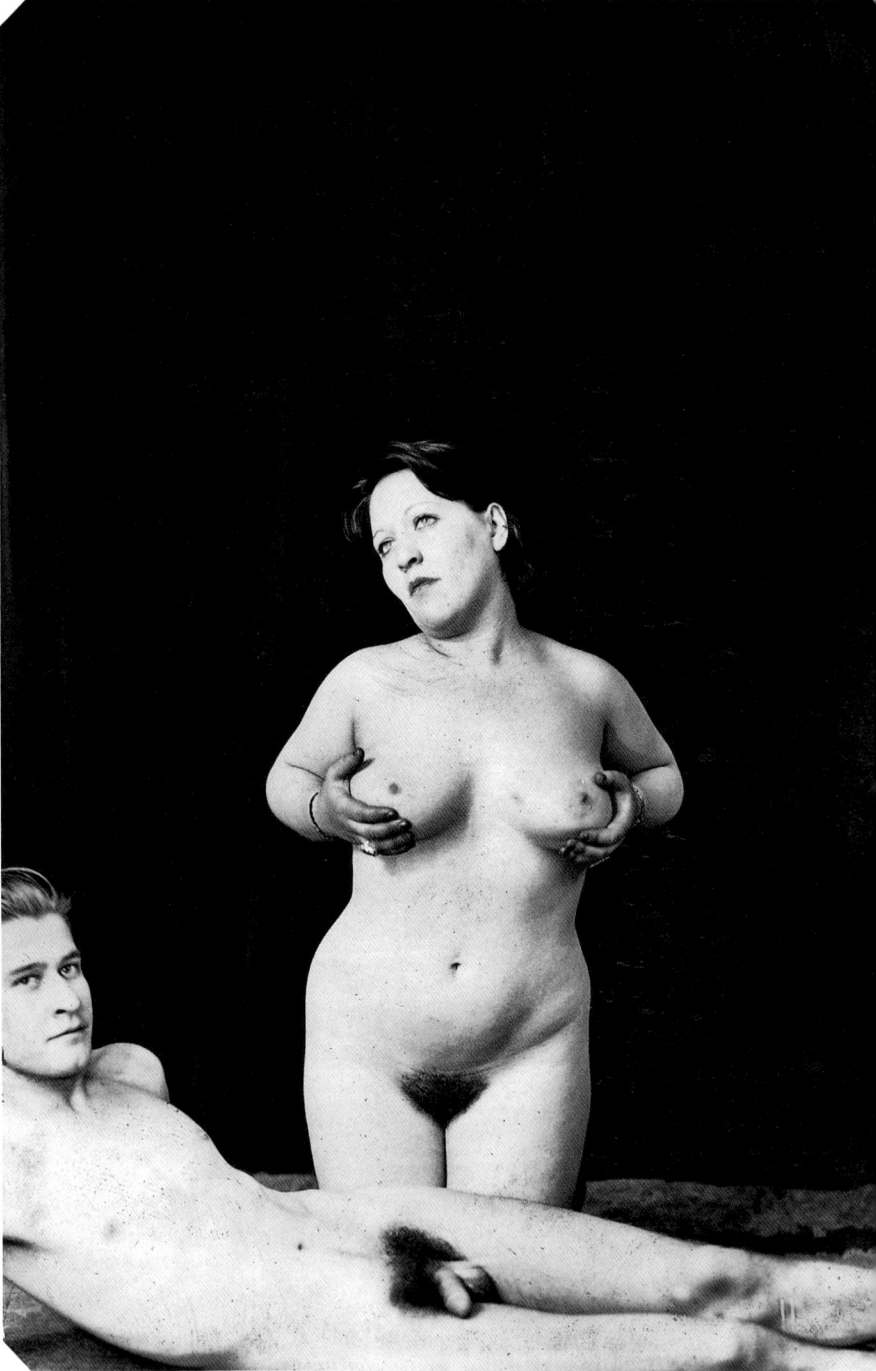

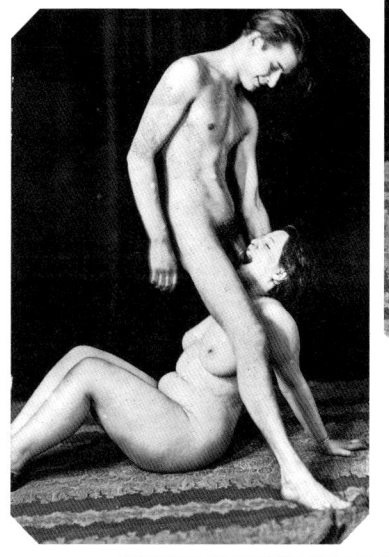

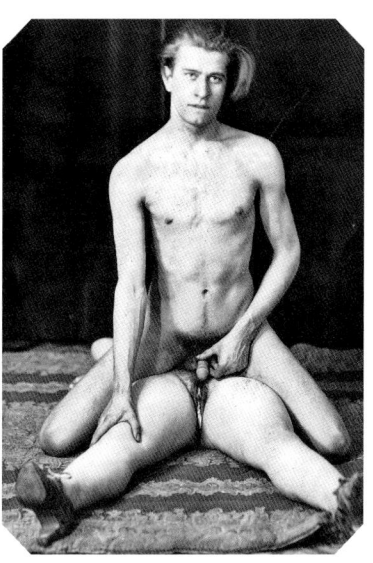

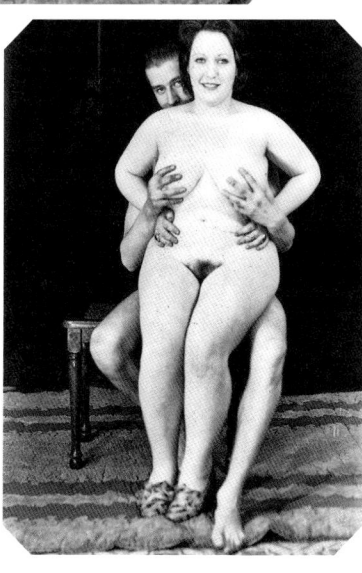

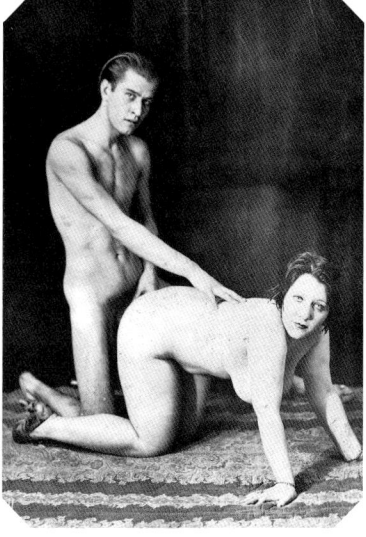

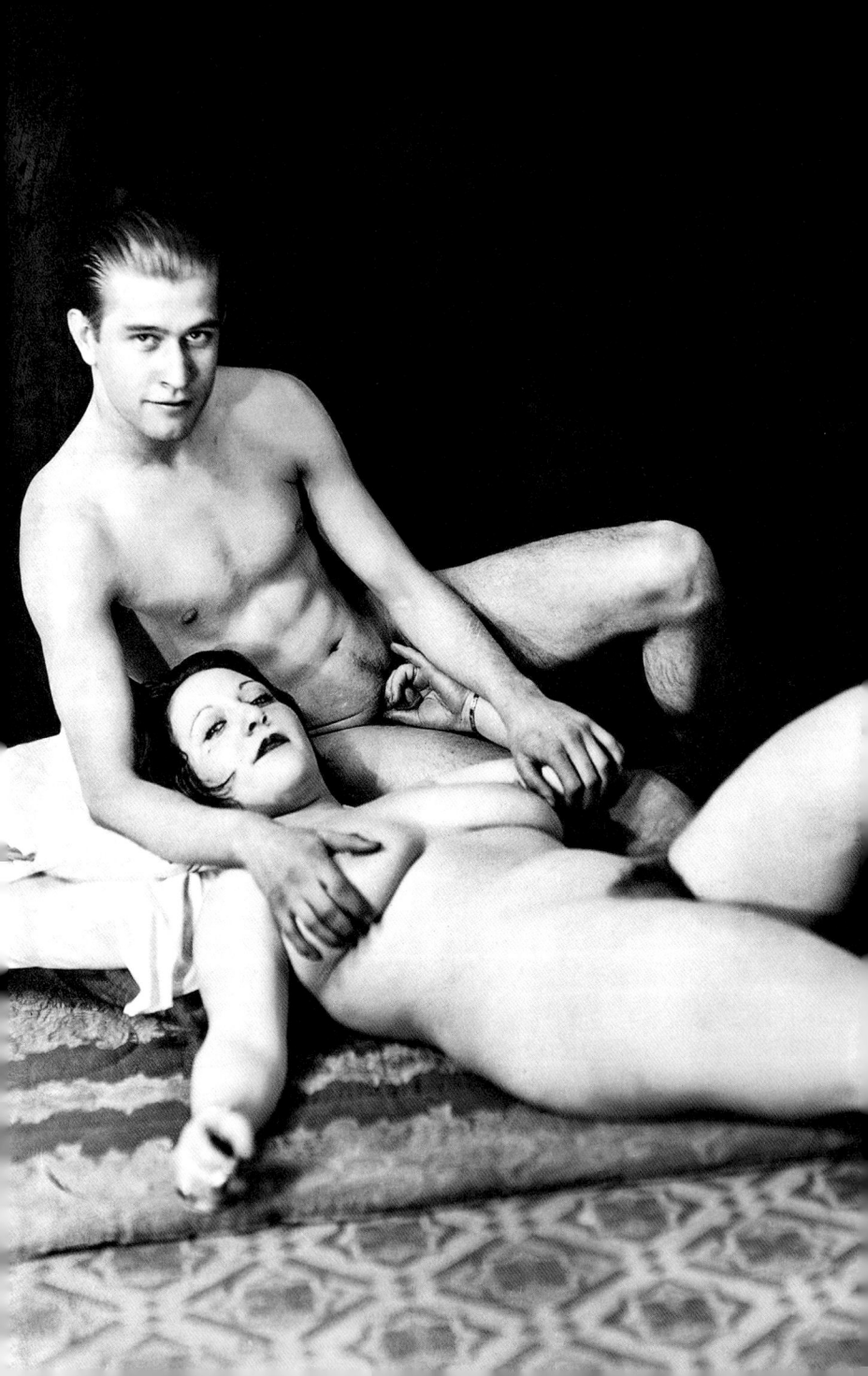

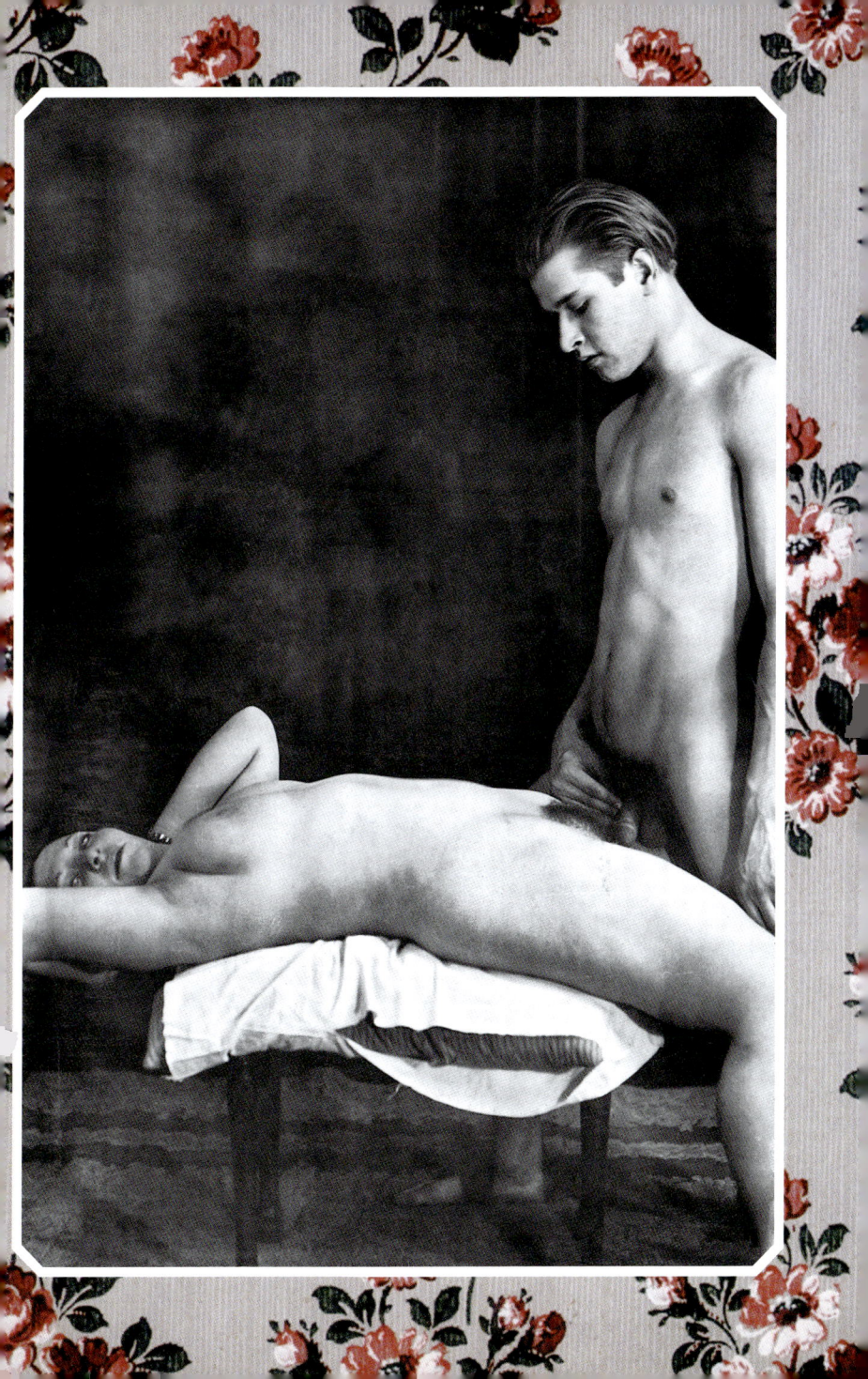

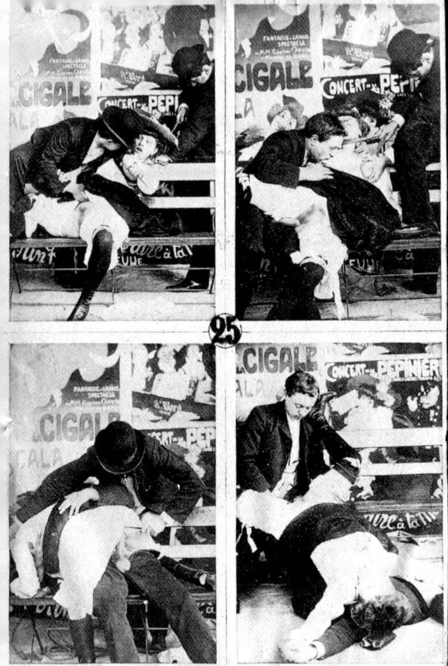

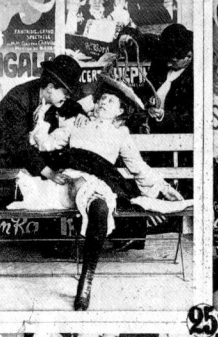

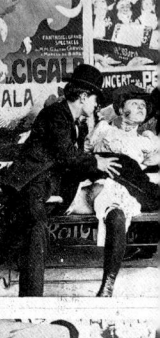

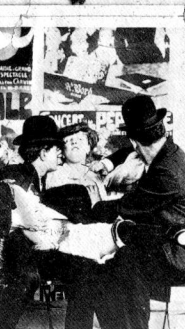

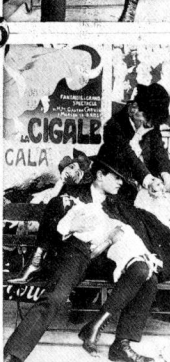

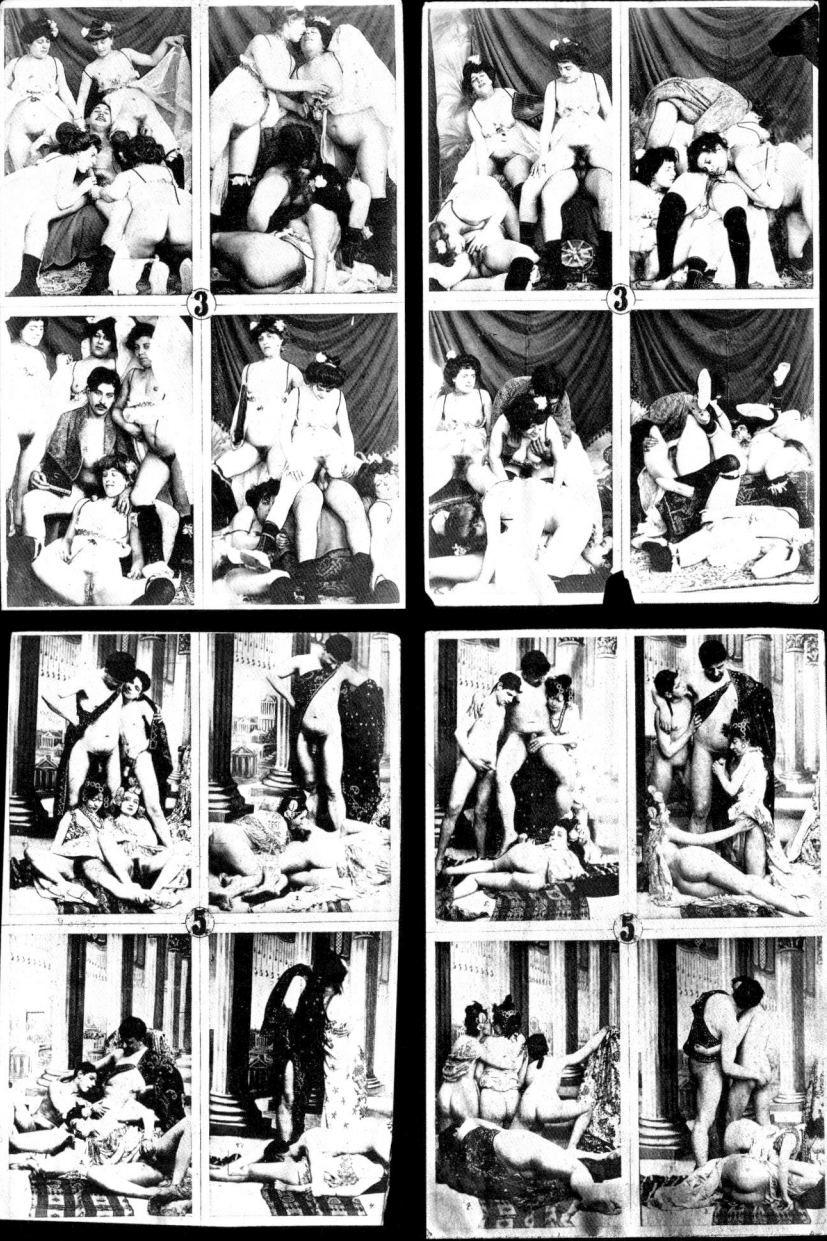

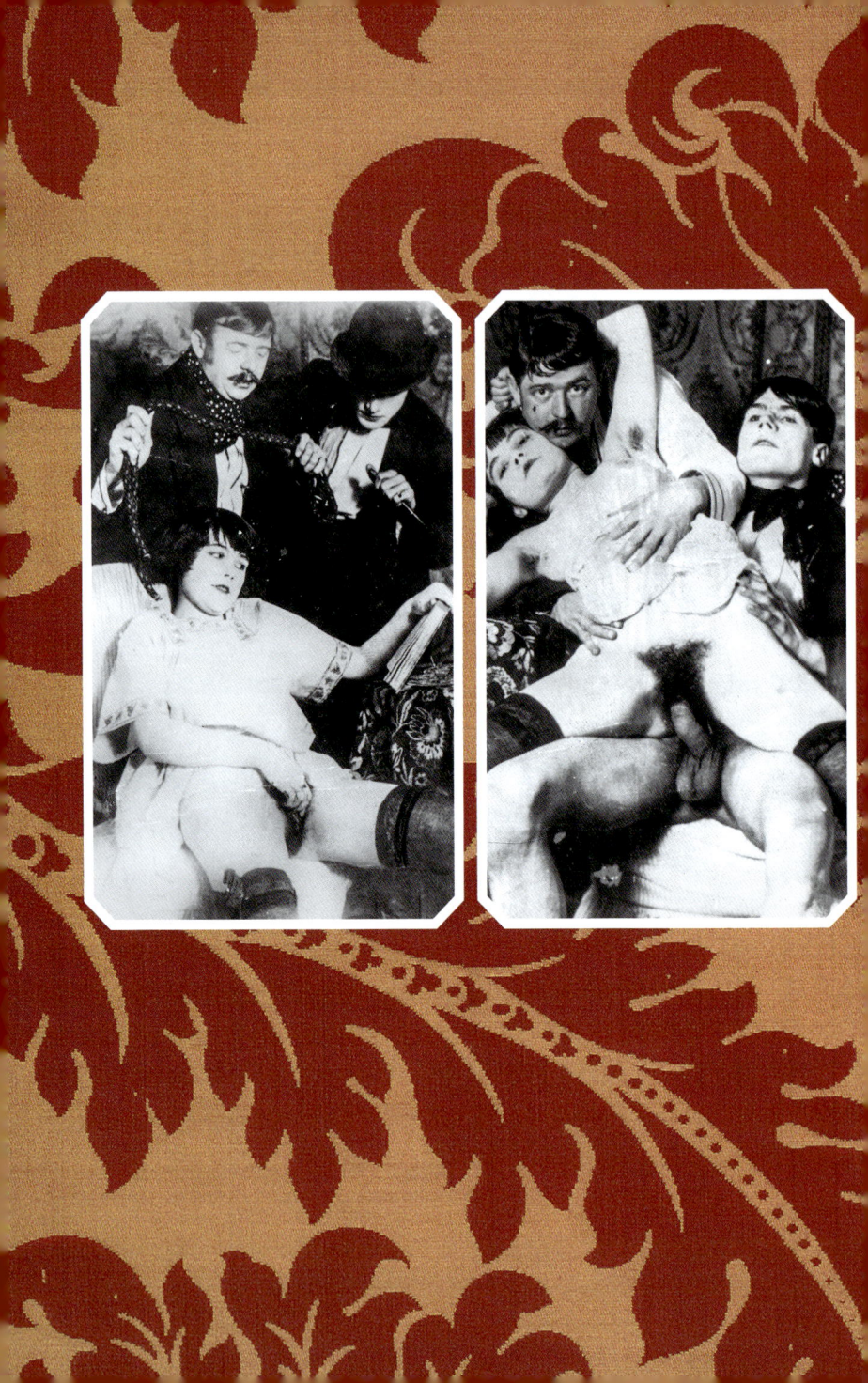

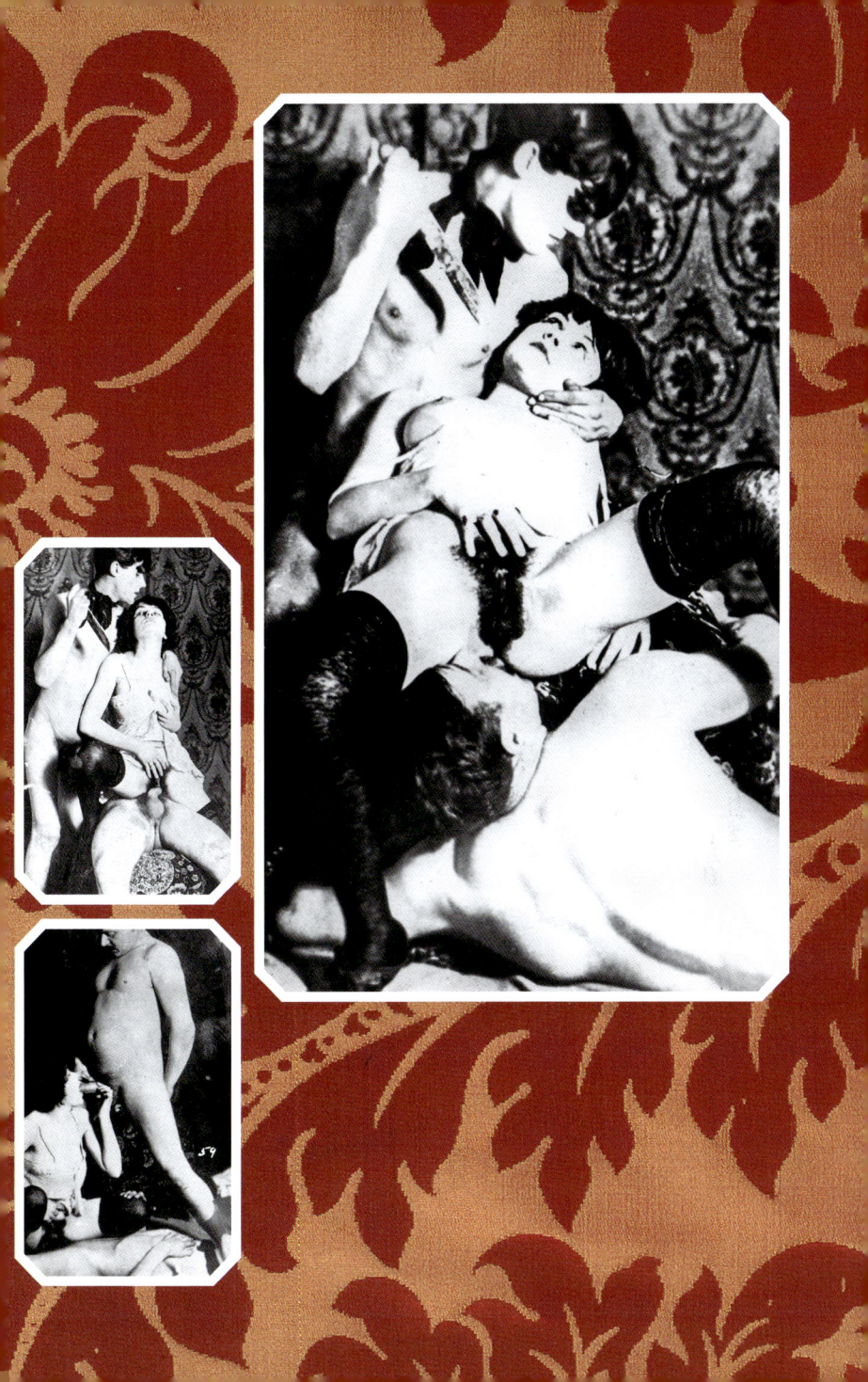

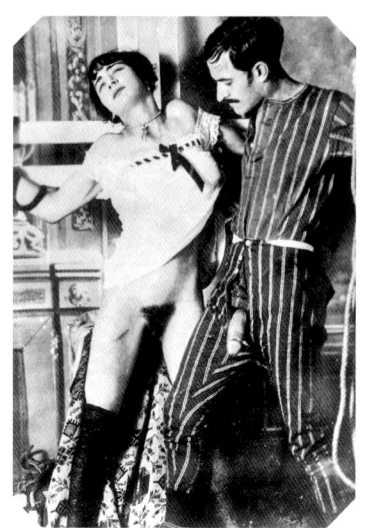
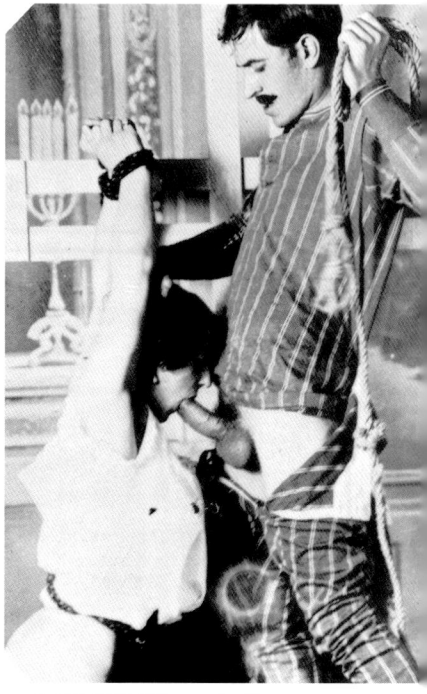
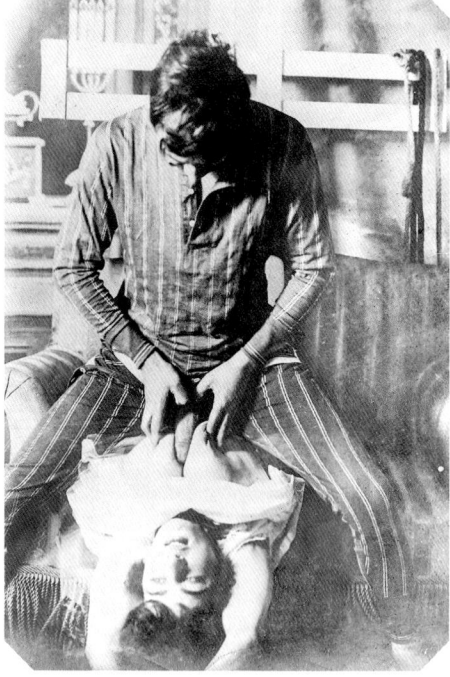
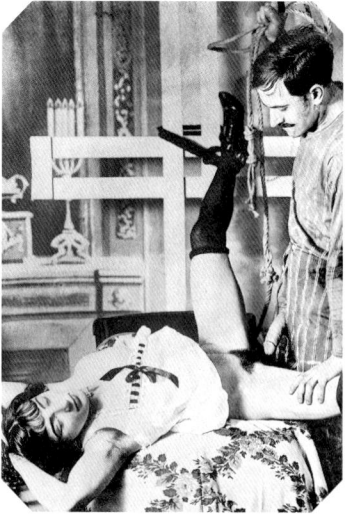

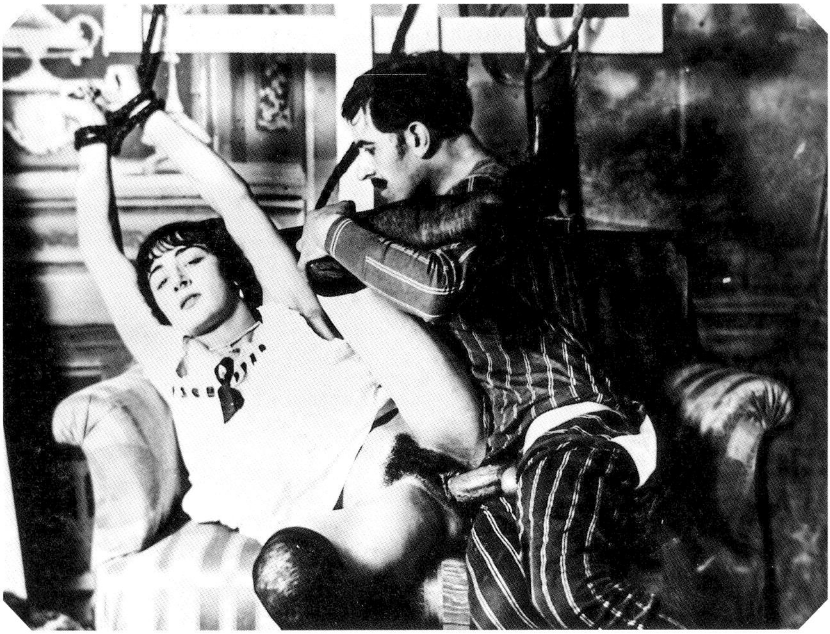

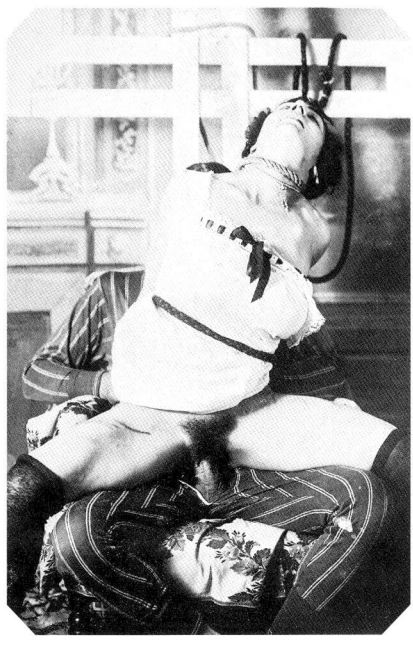

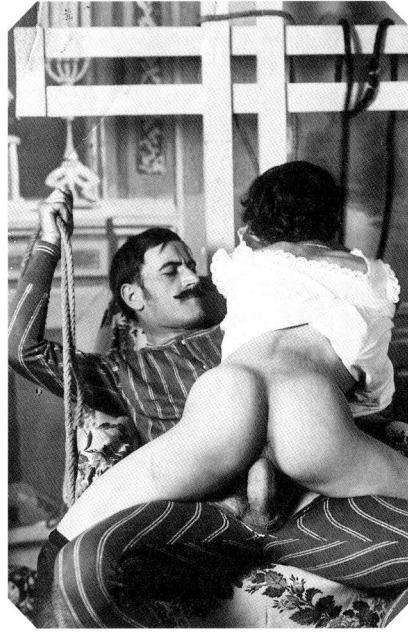

251

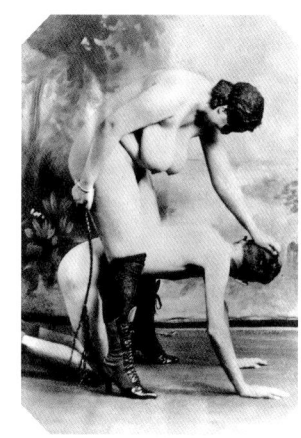
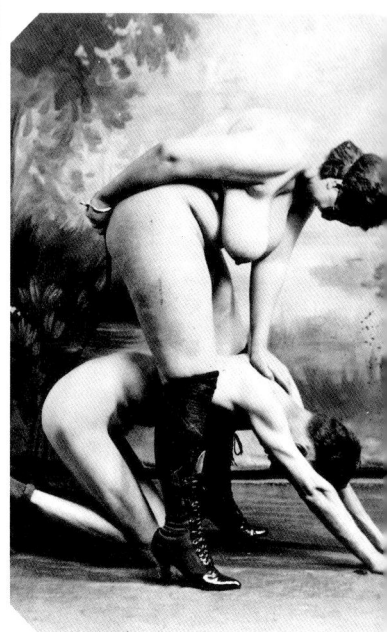
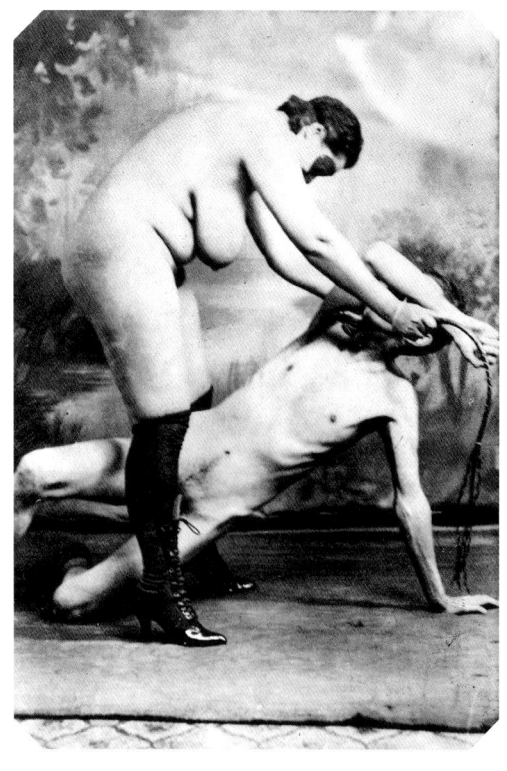

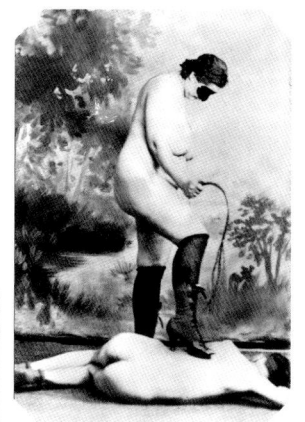

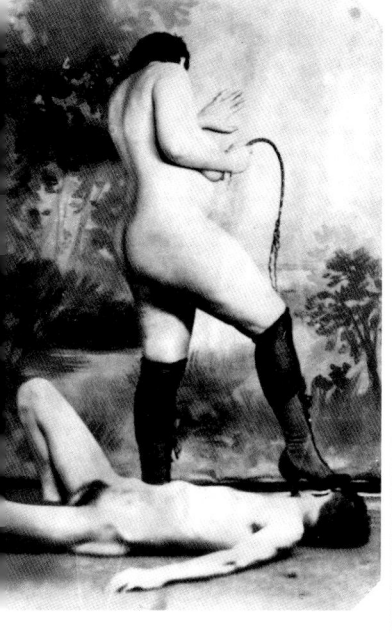

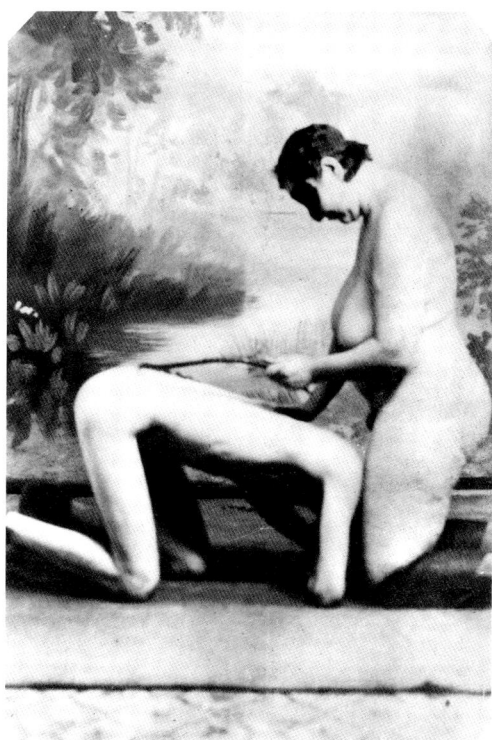

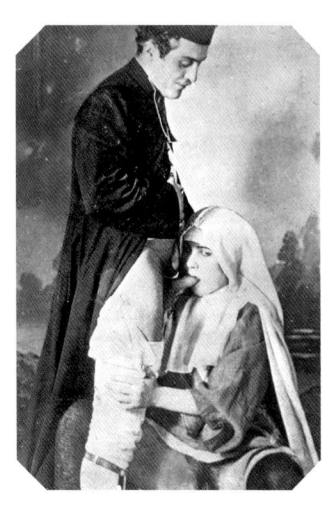
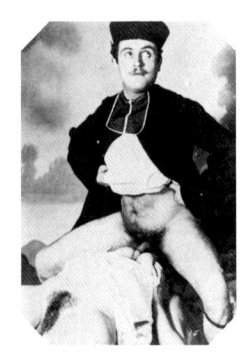
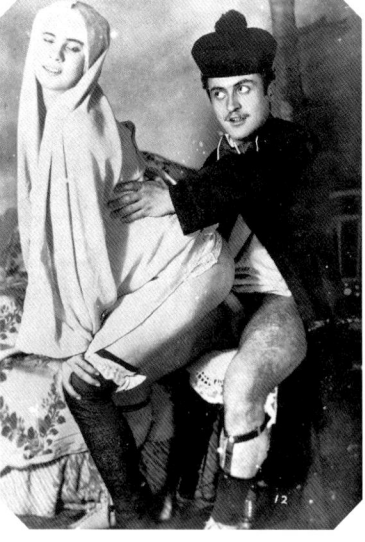
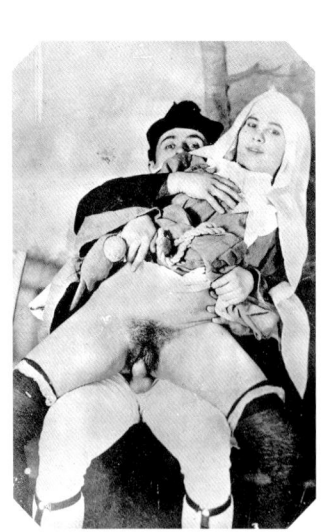
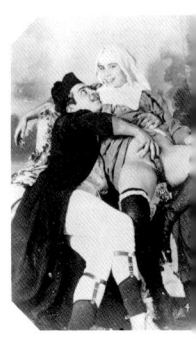

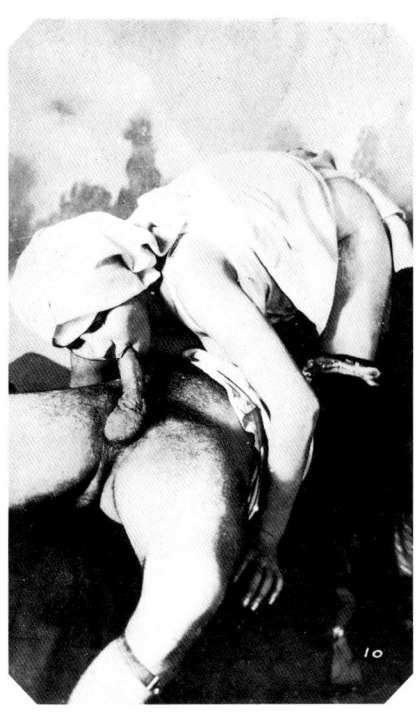
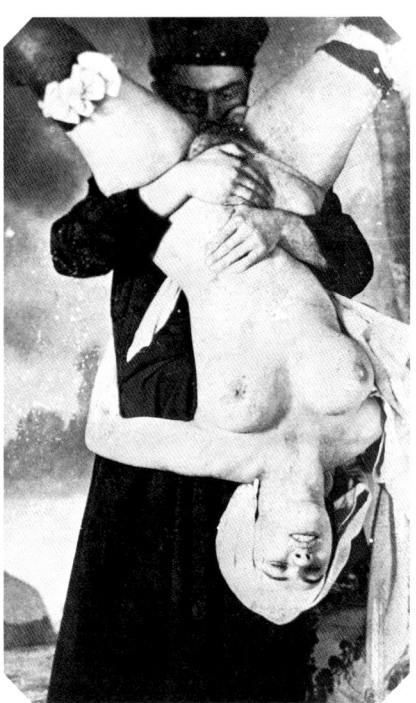

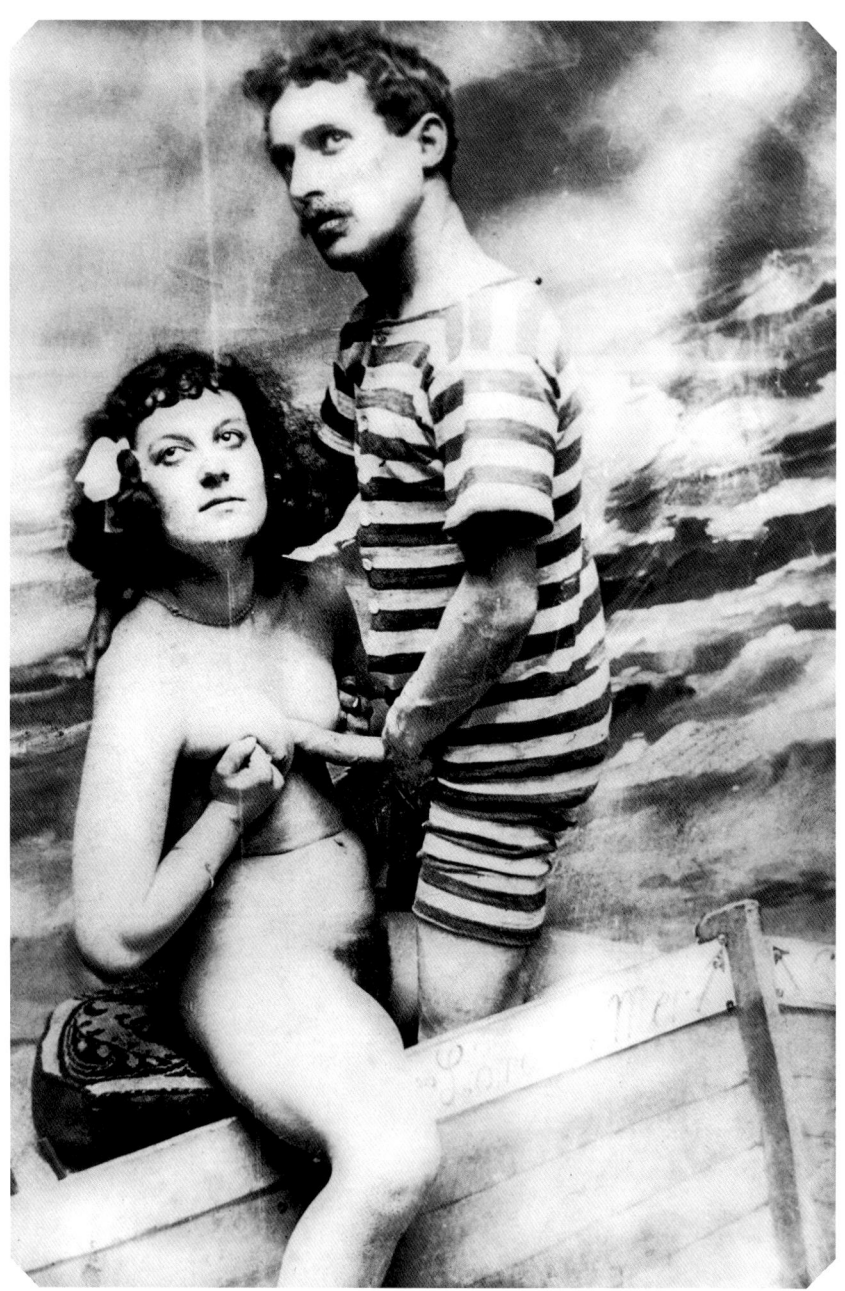

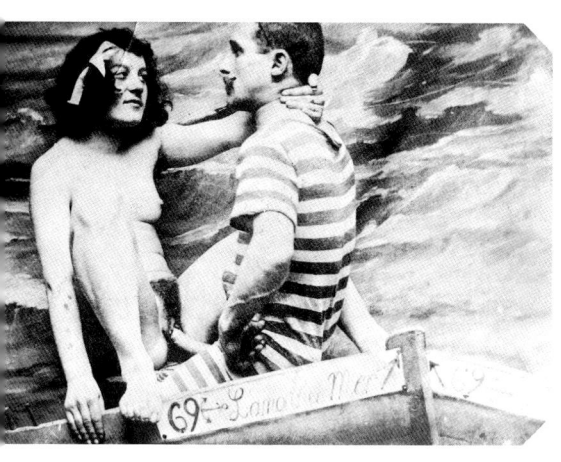

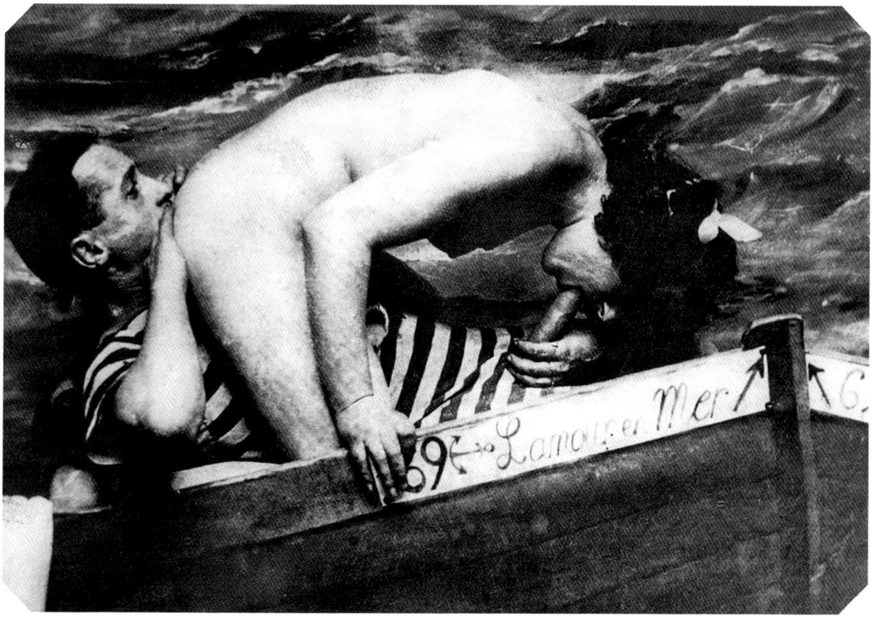

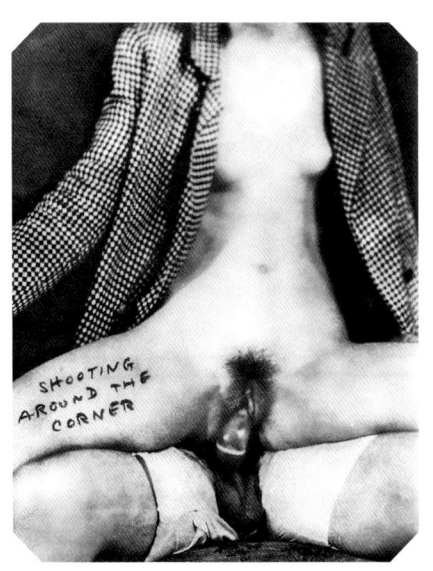

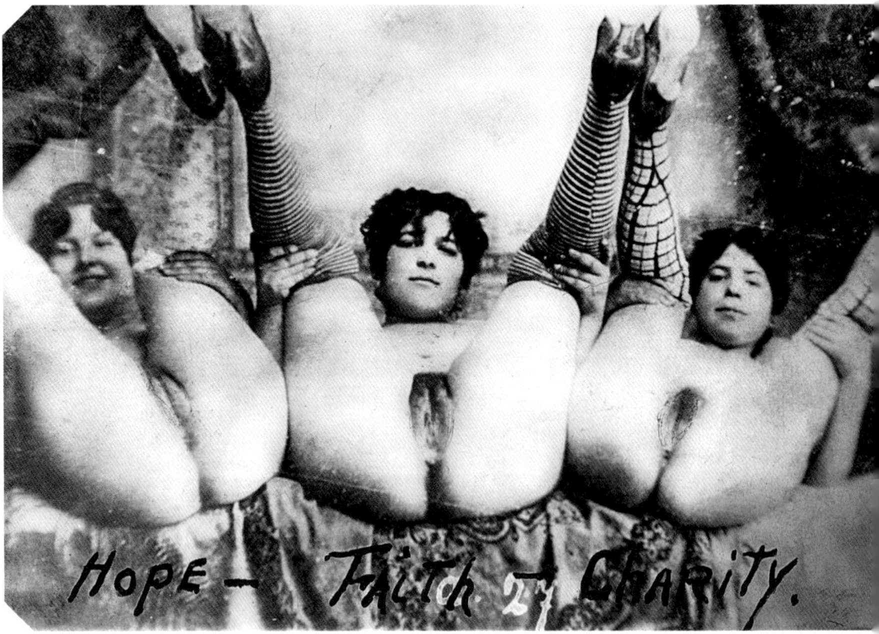

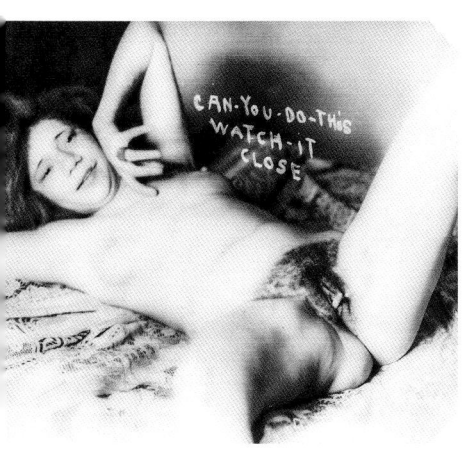

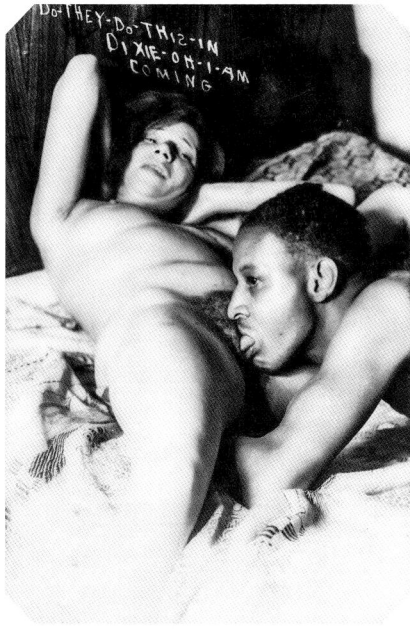

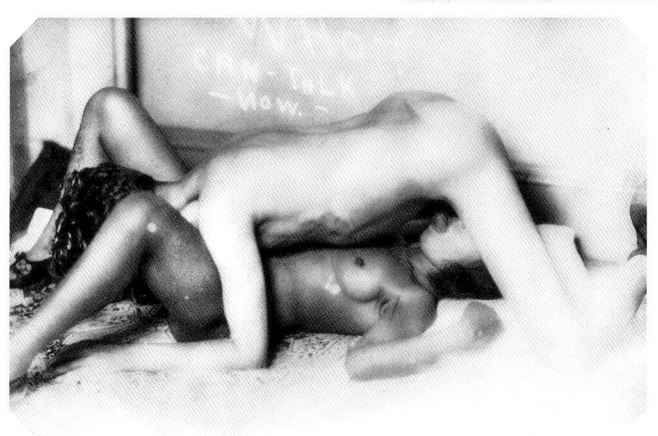

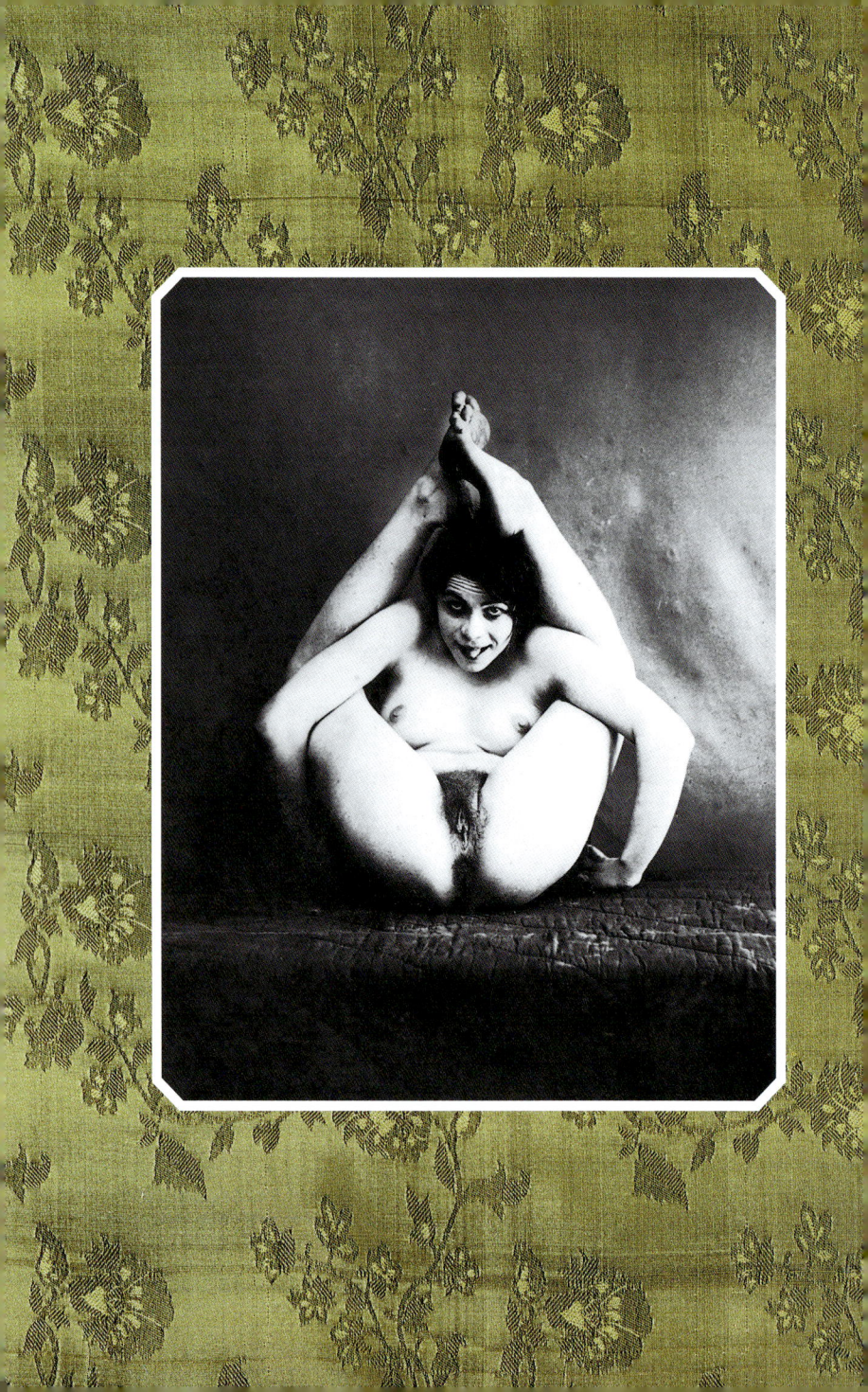

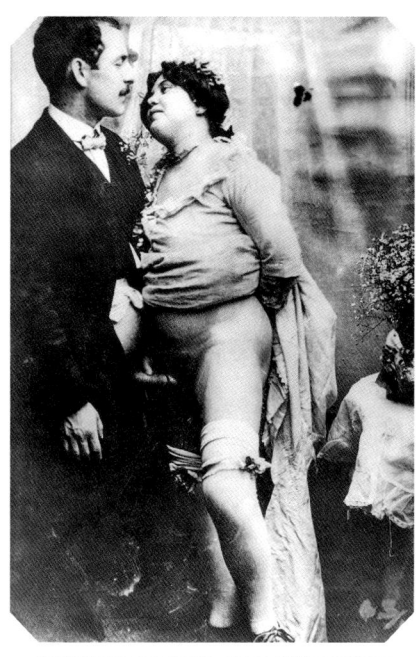
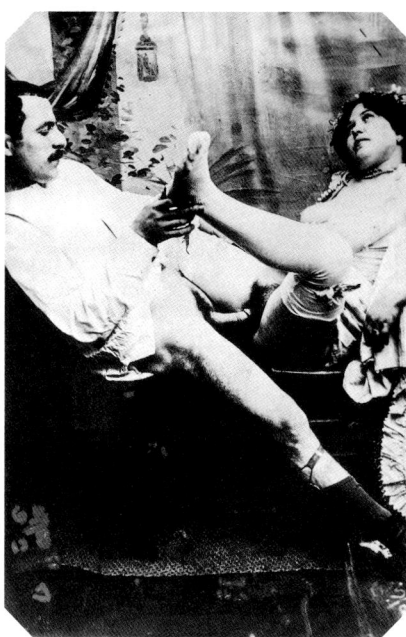
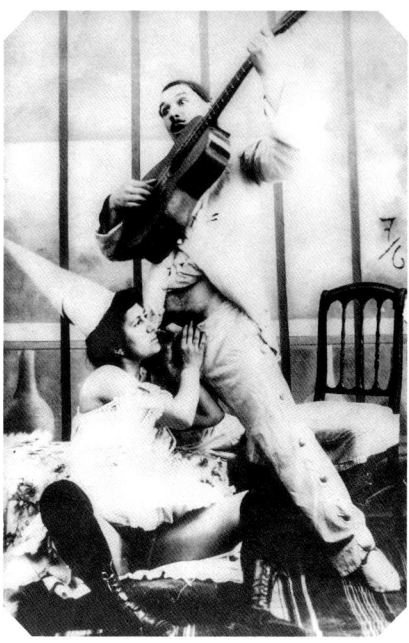
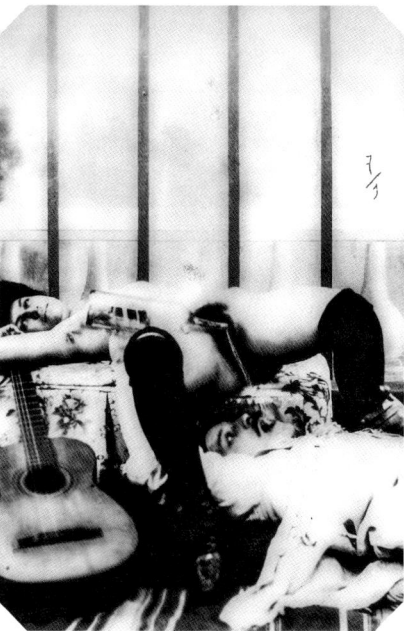

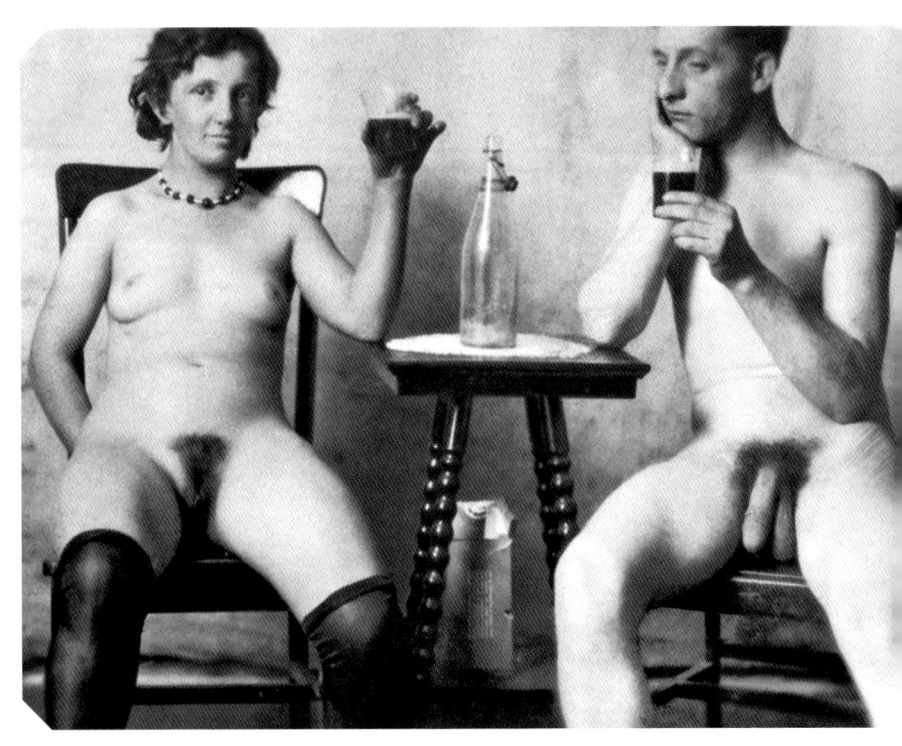

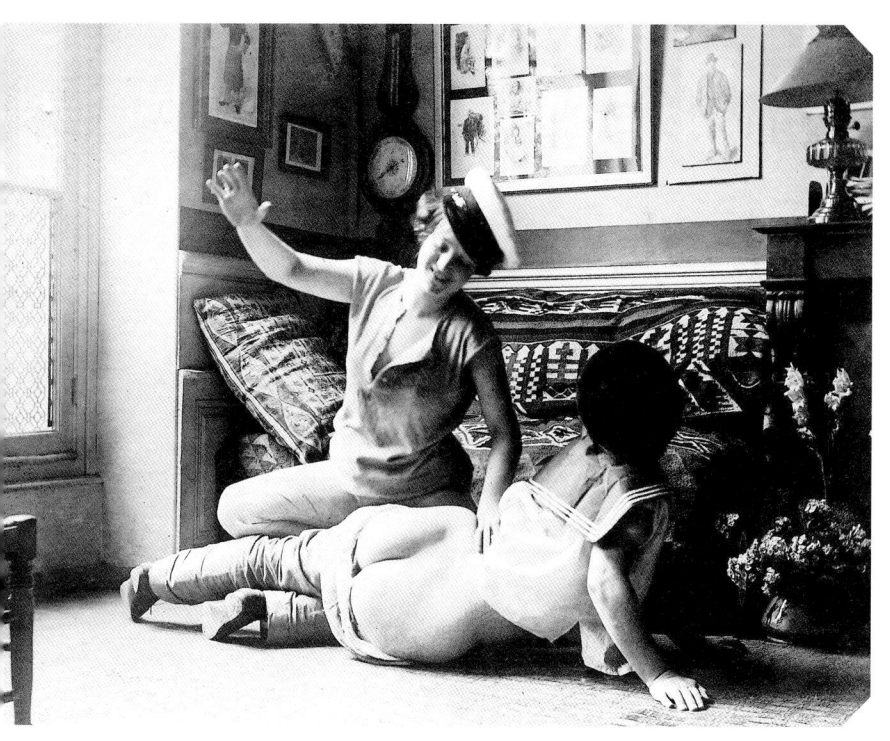

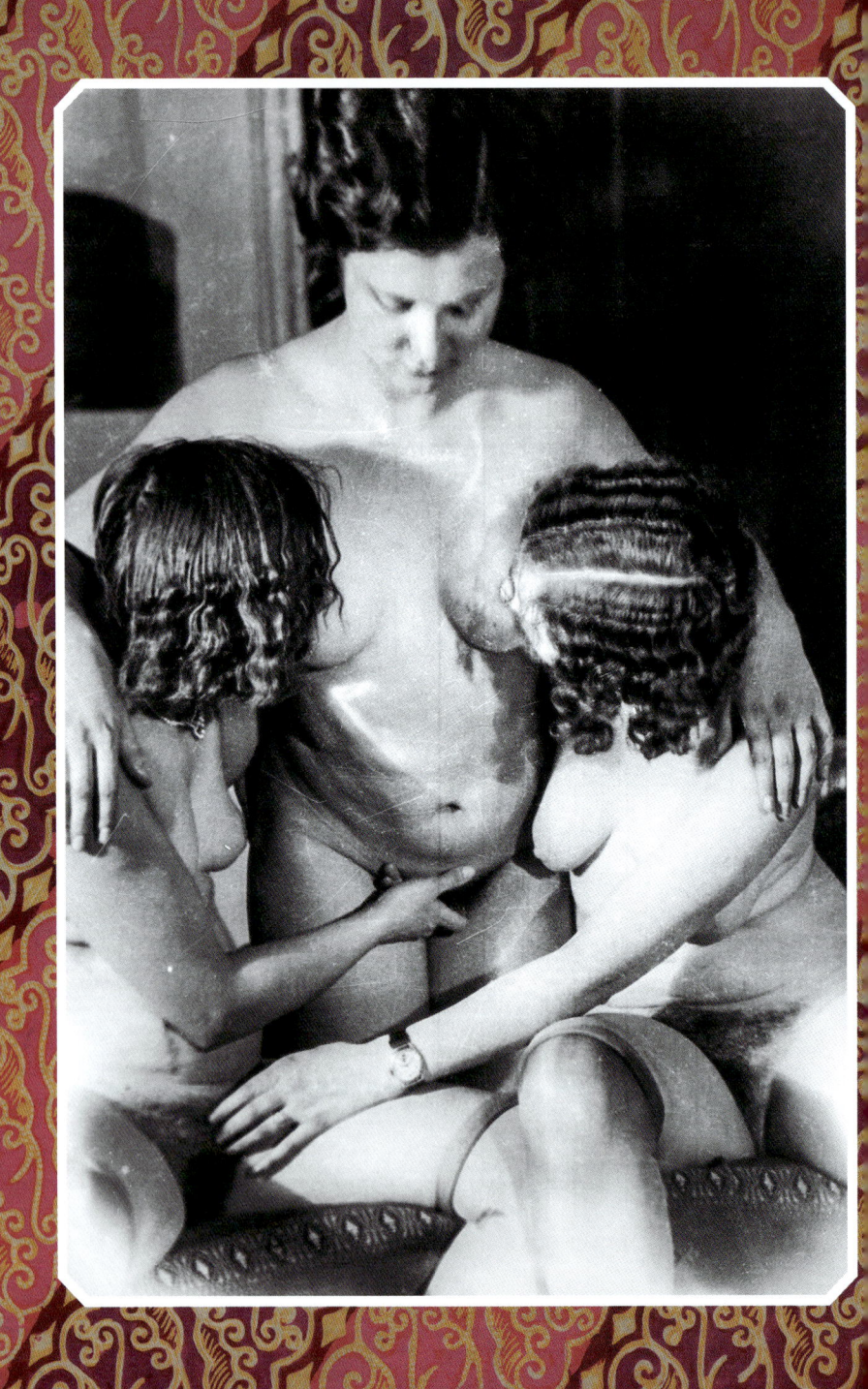

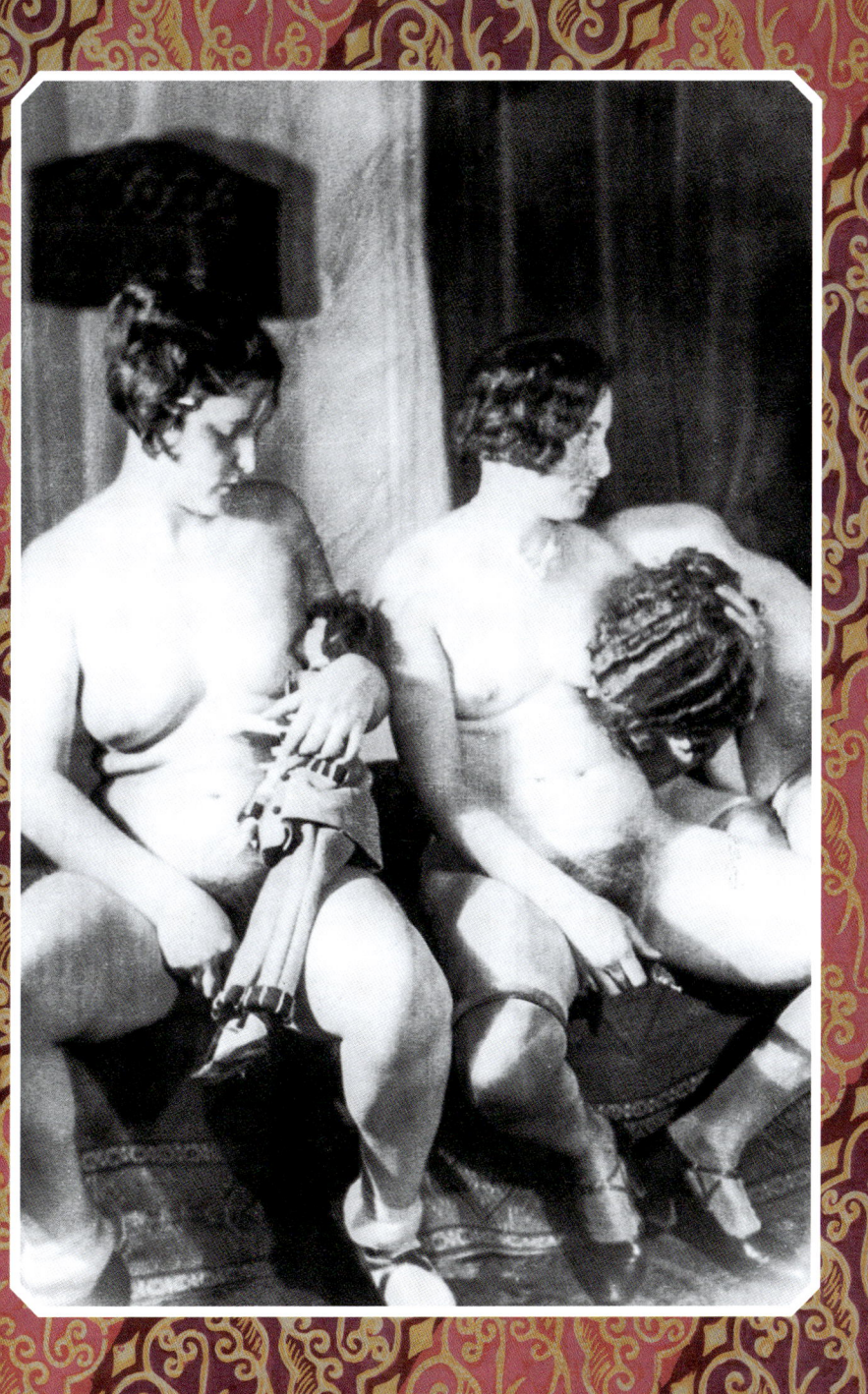

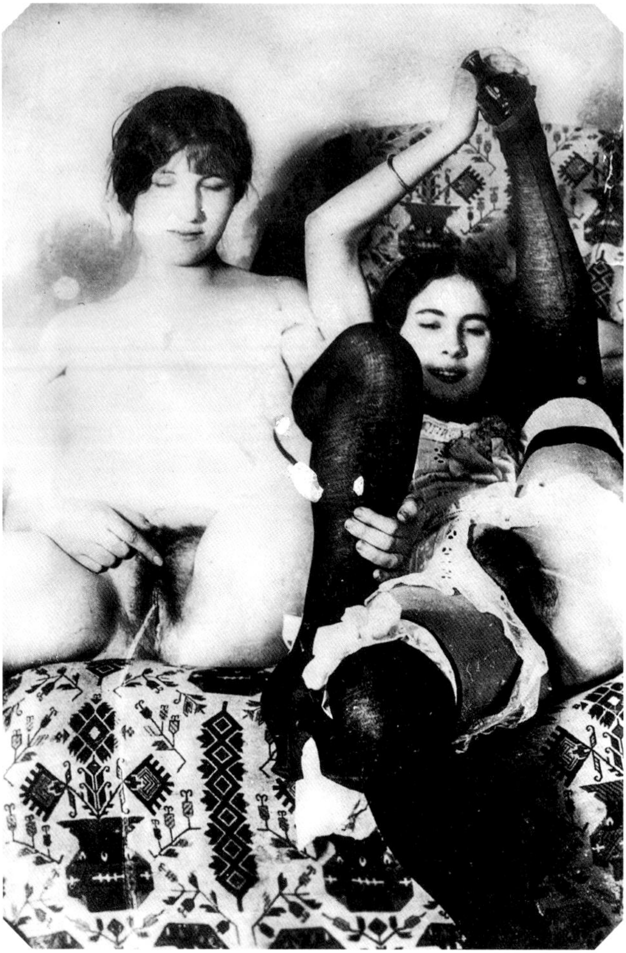

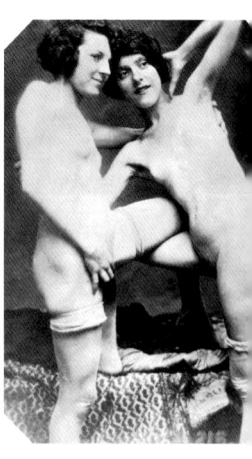

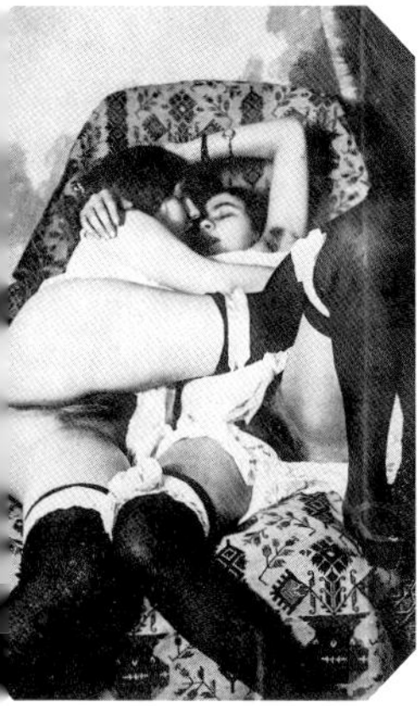

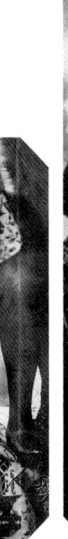

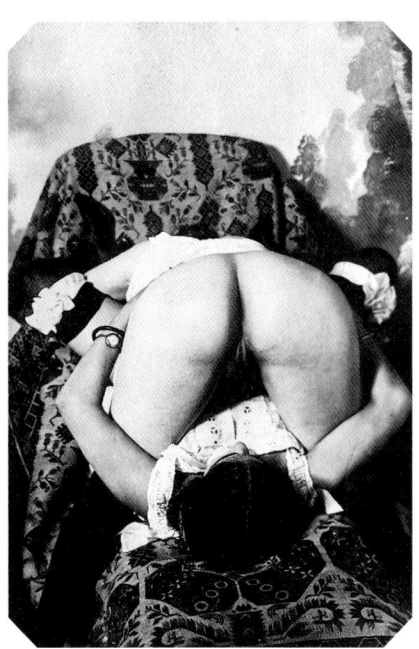

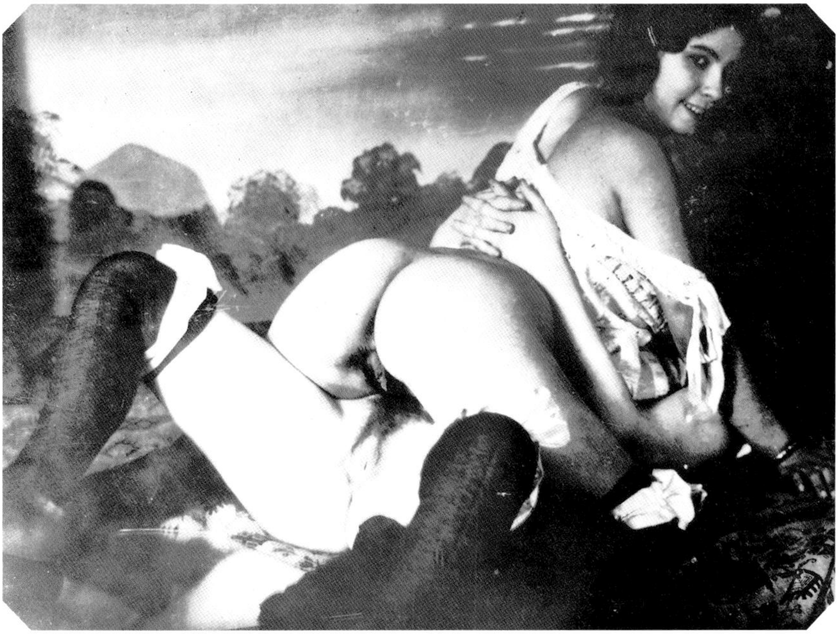

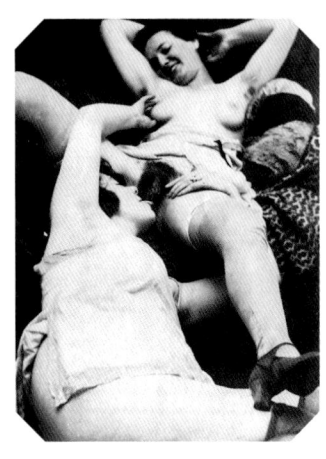
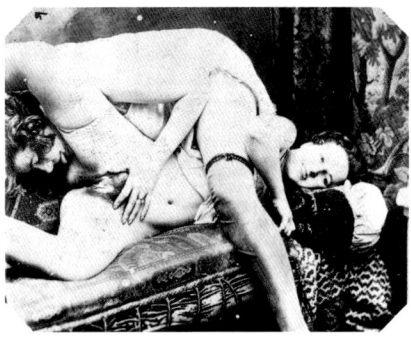

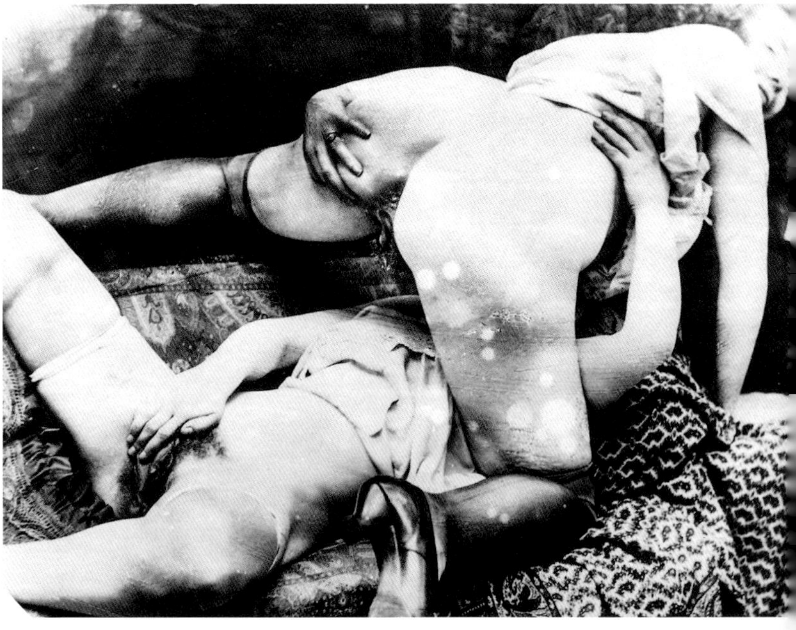

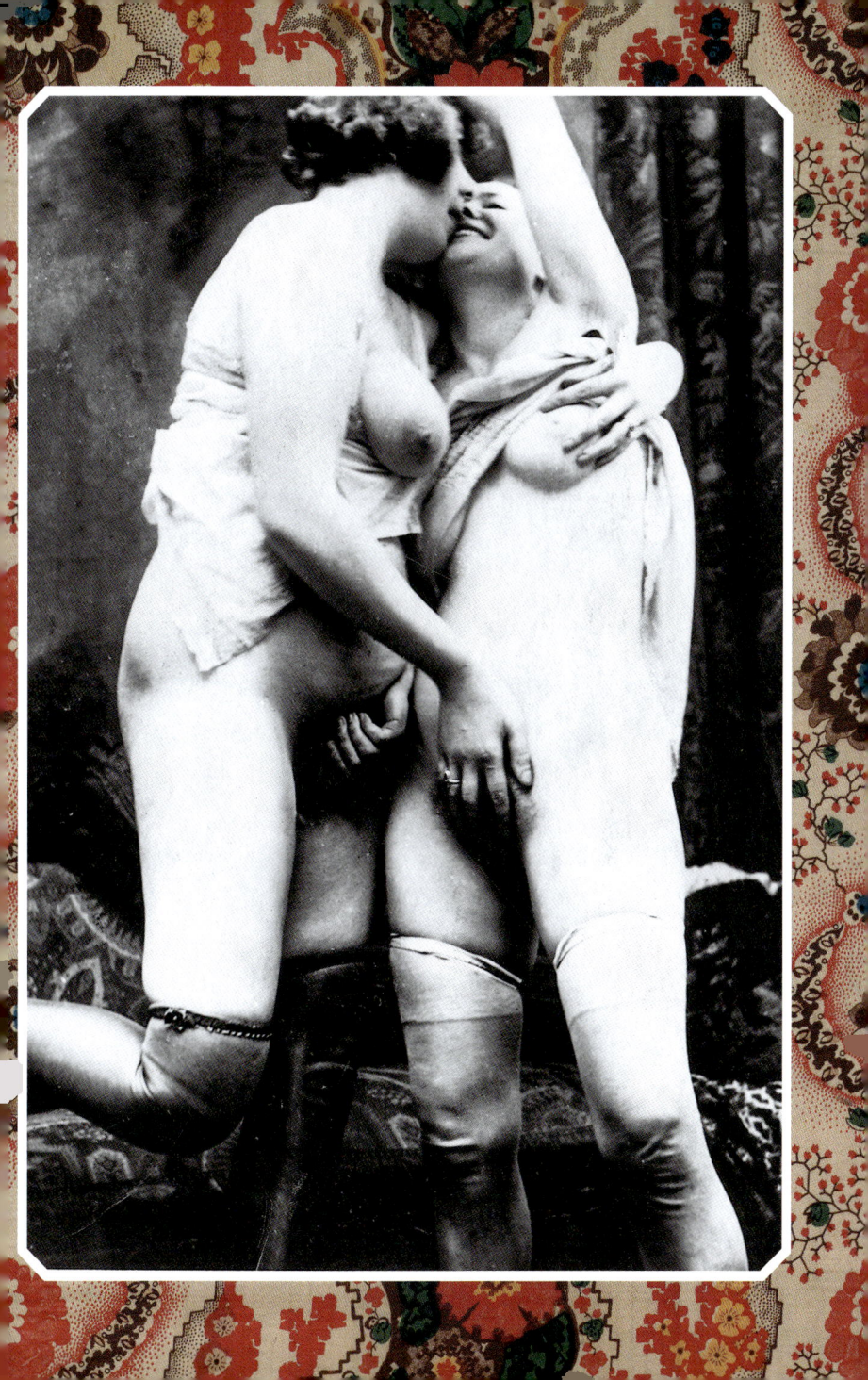

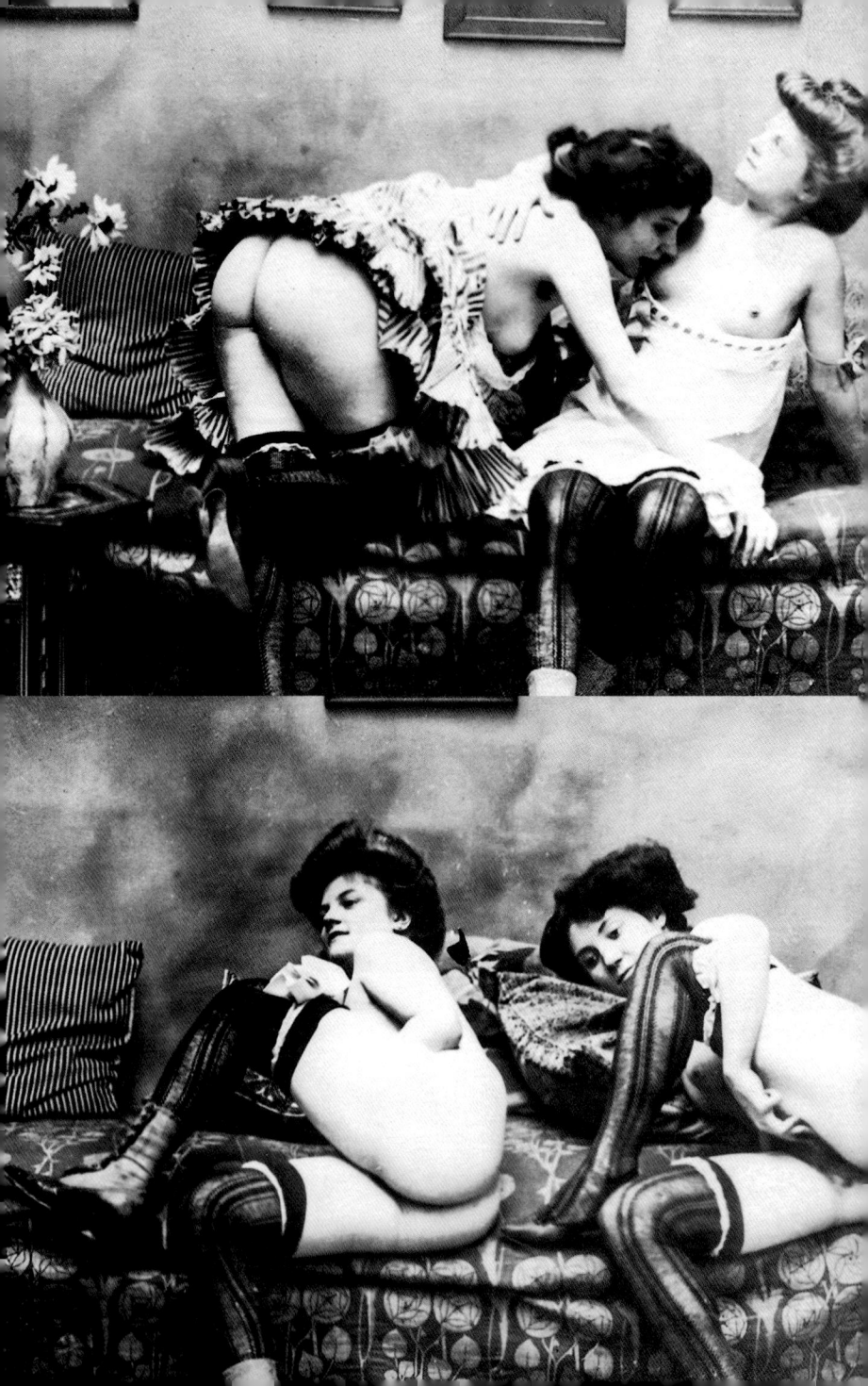

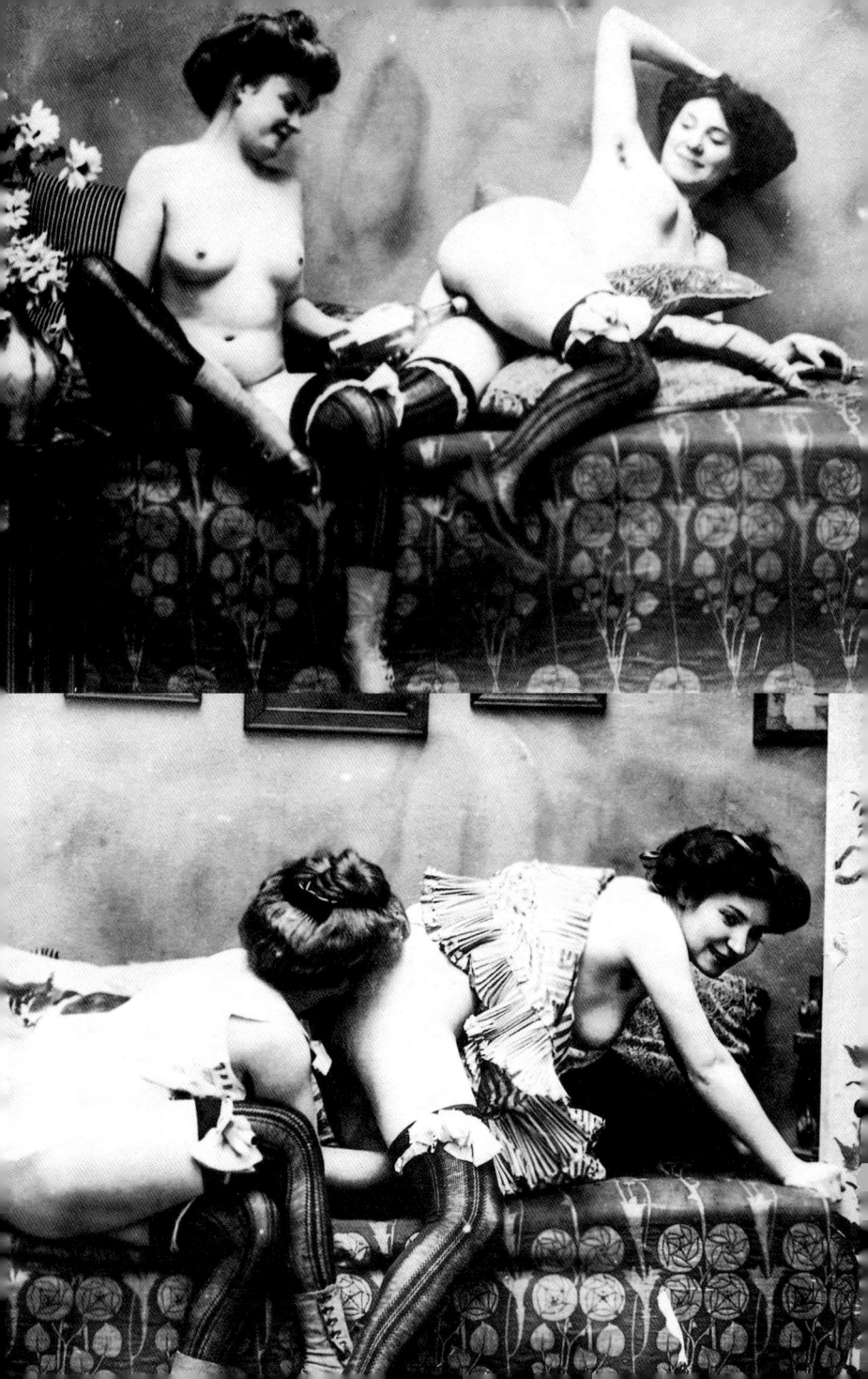

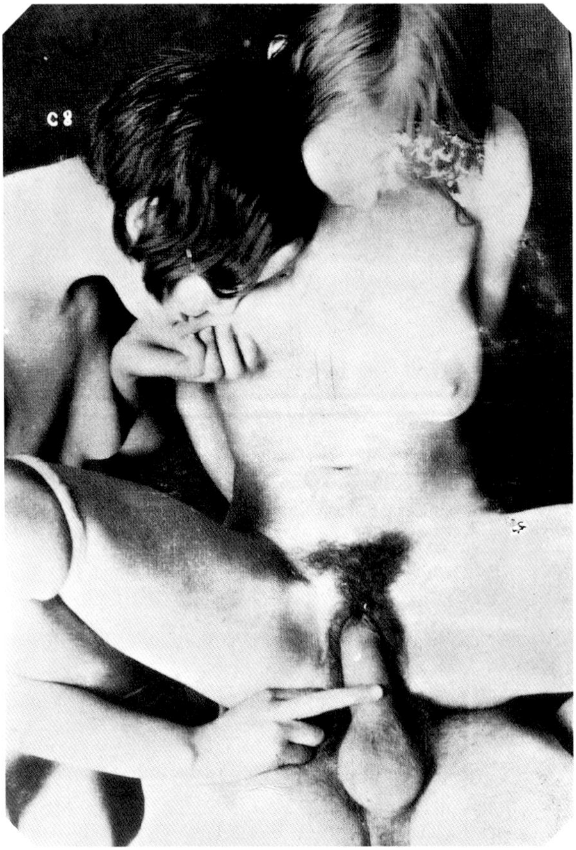

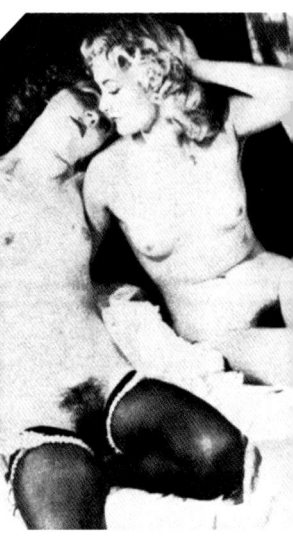
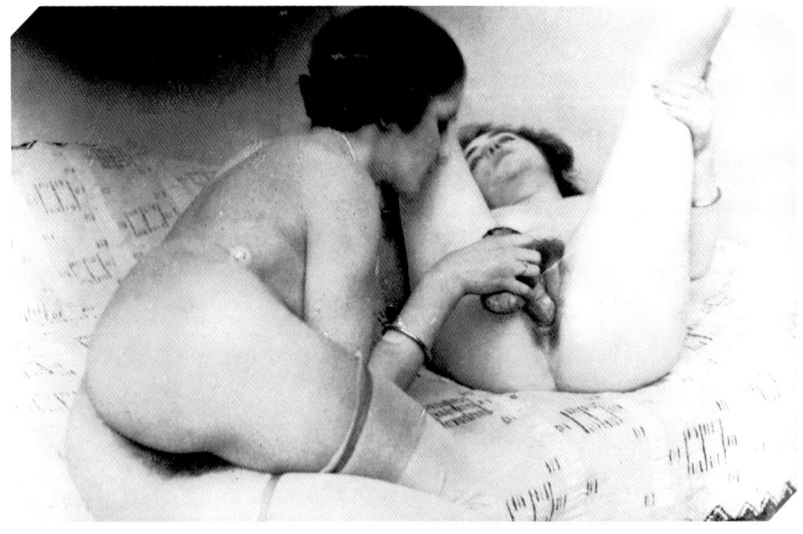

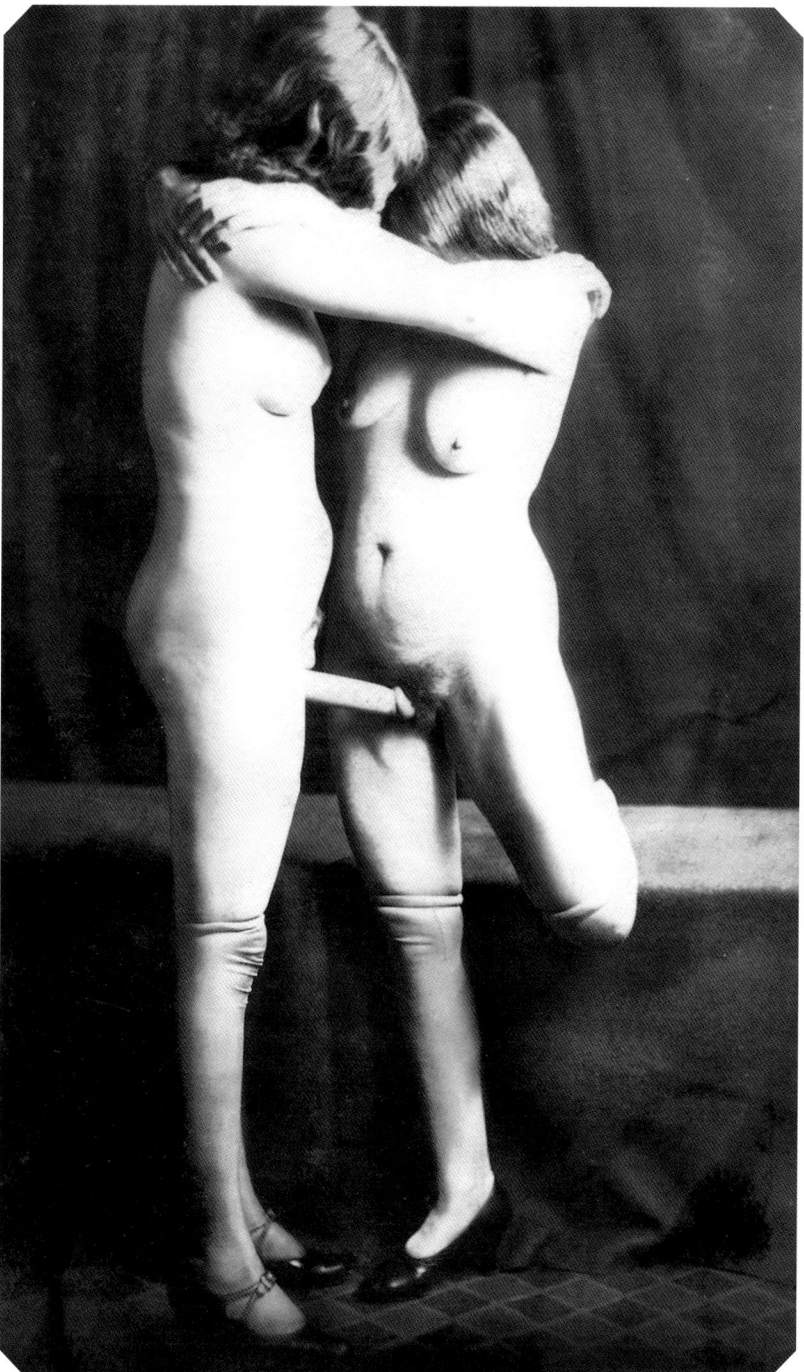

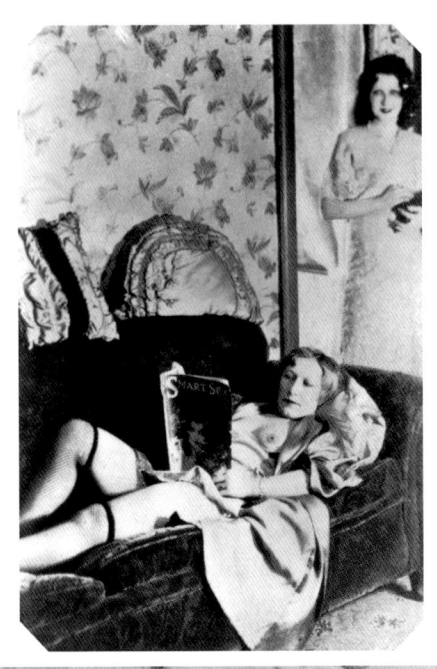

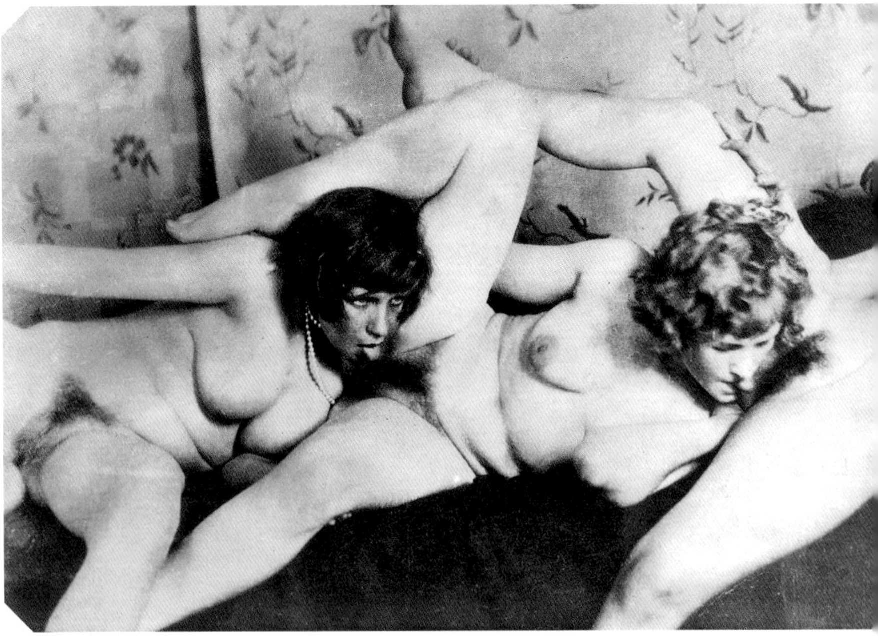

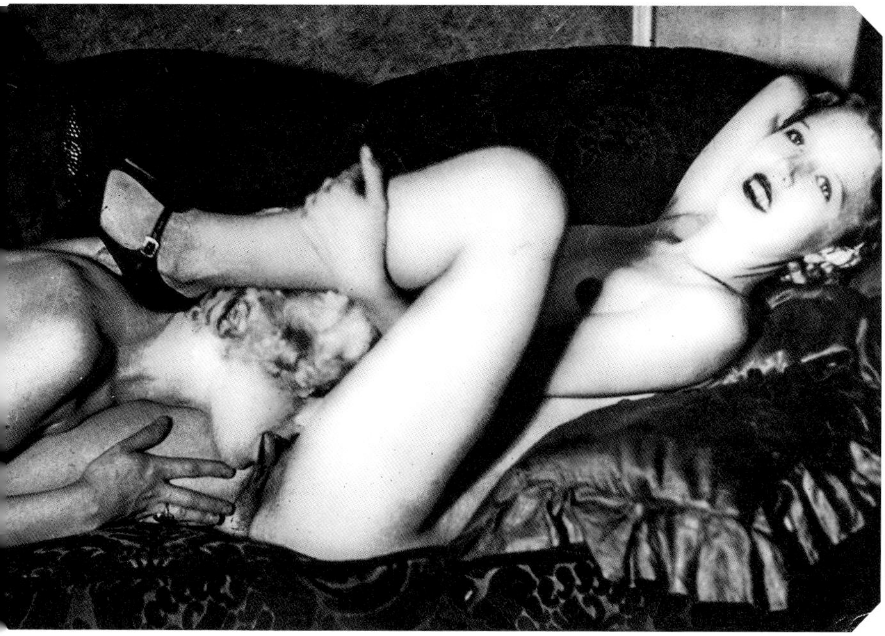

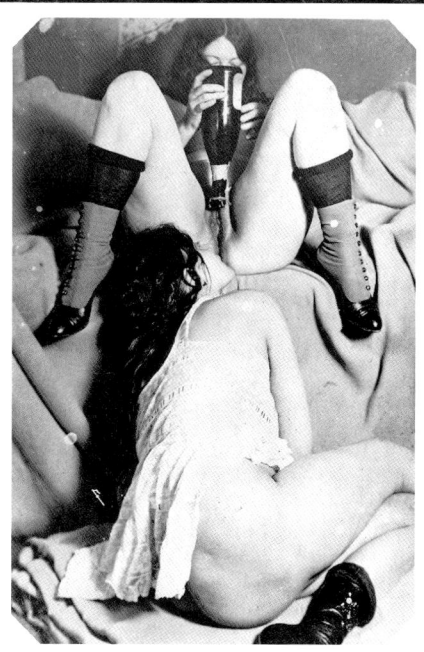

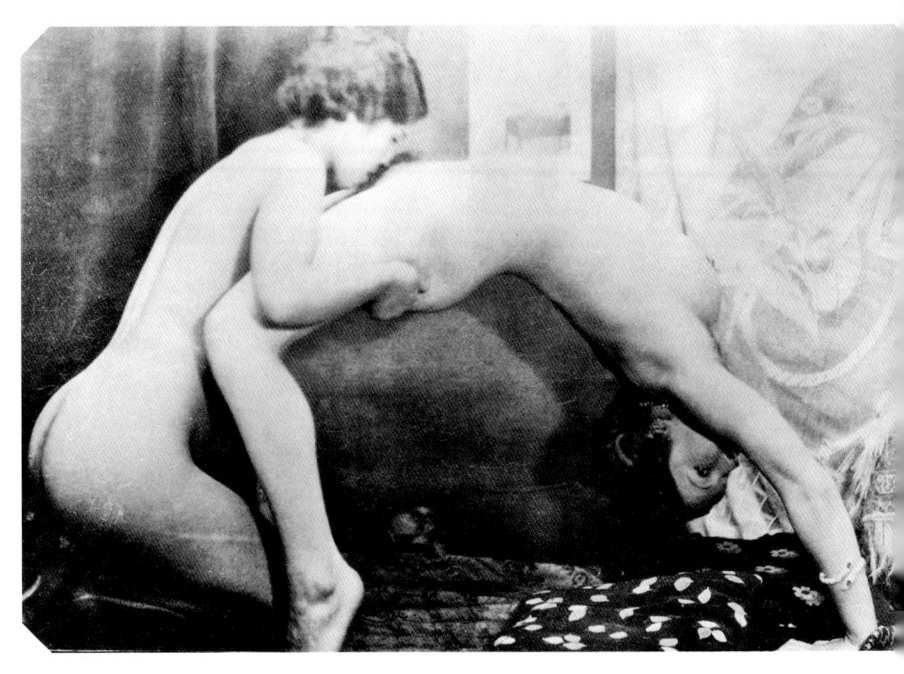

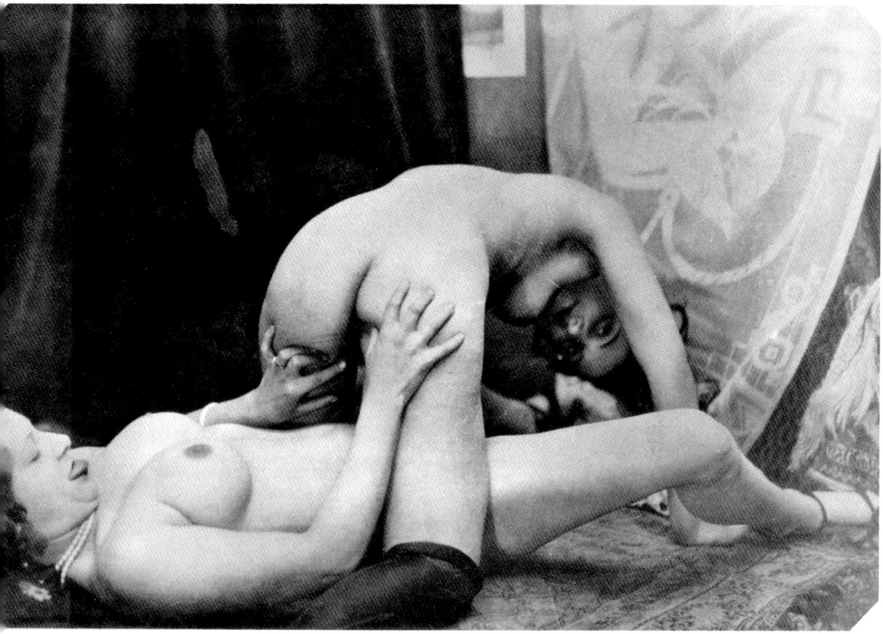

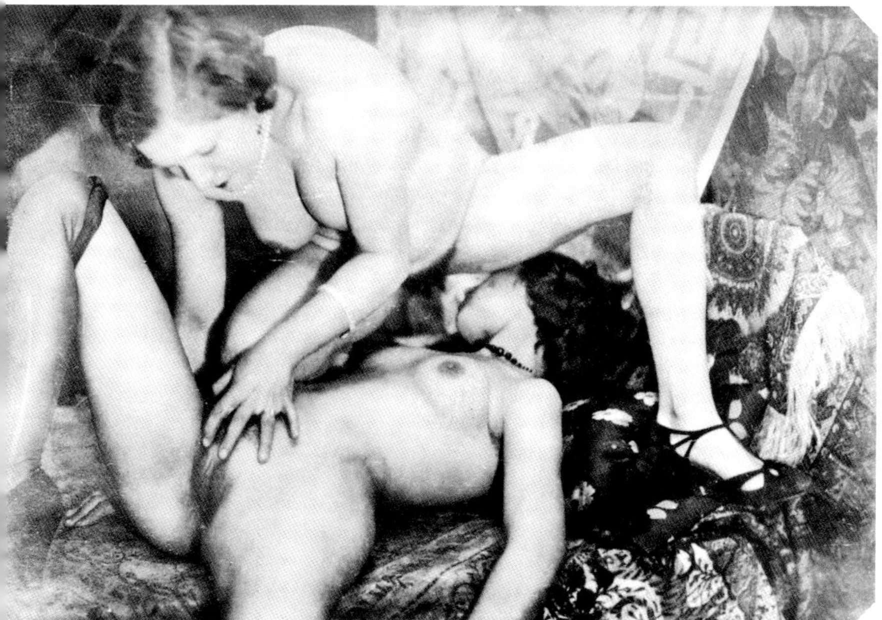

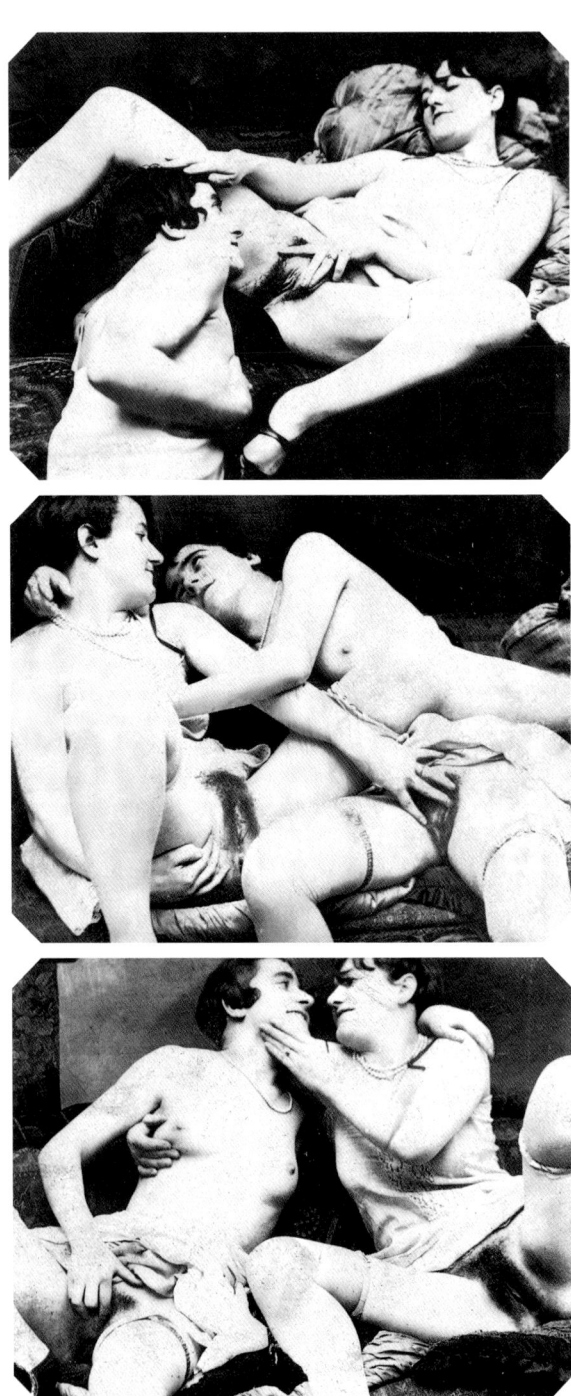

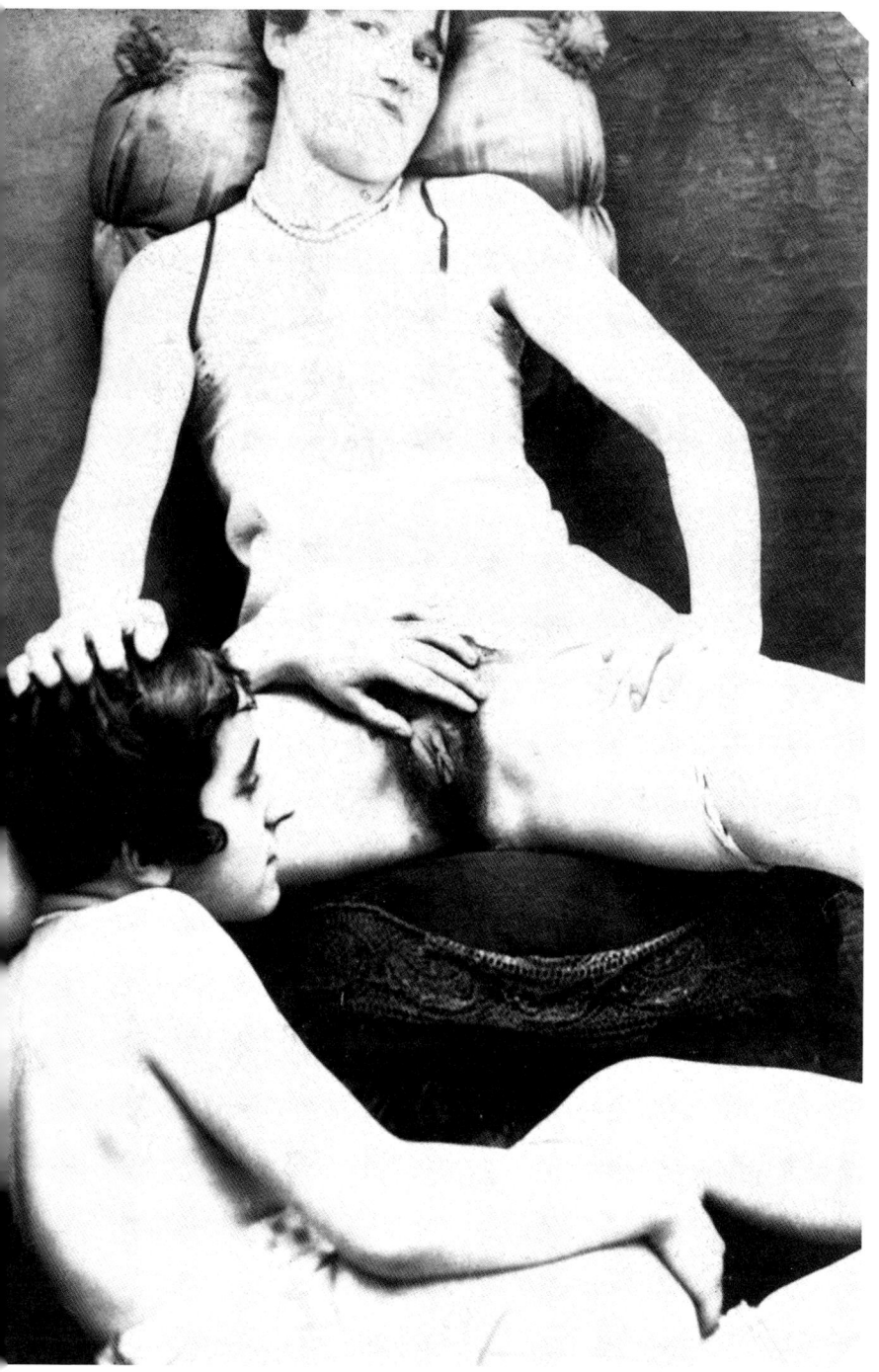

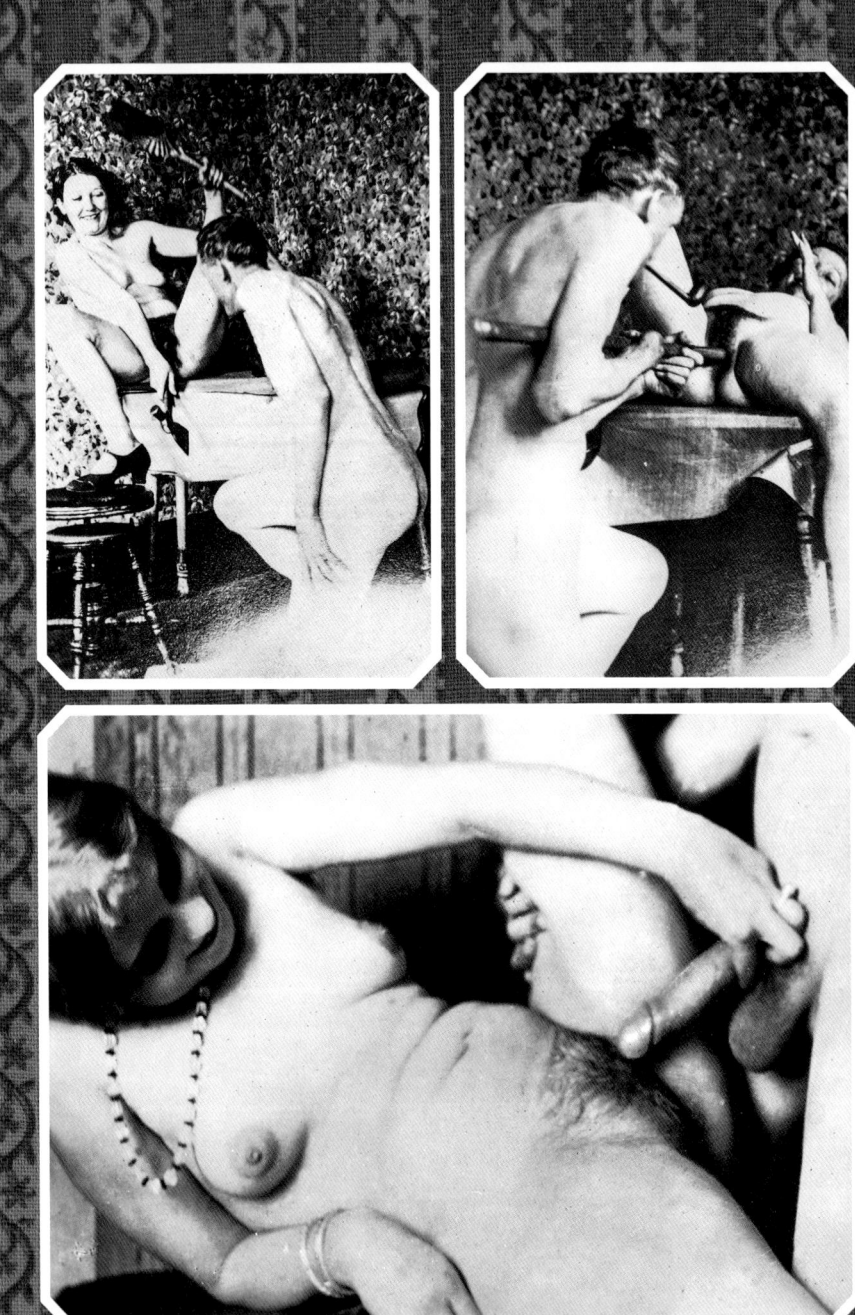

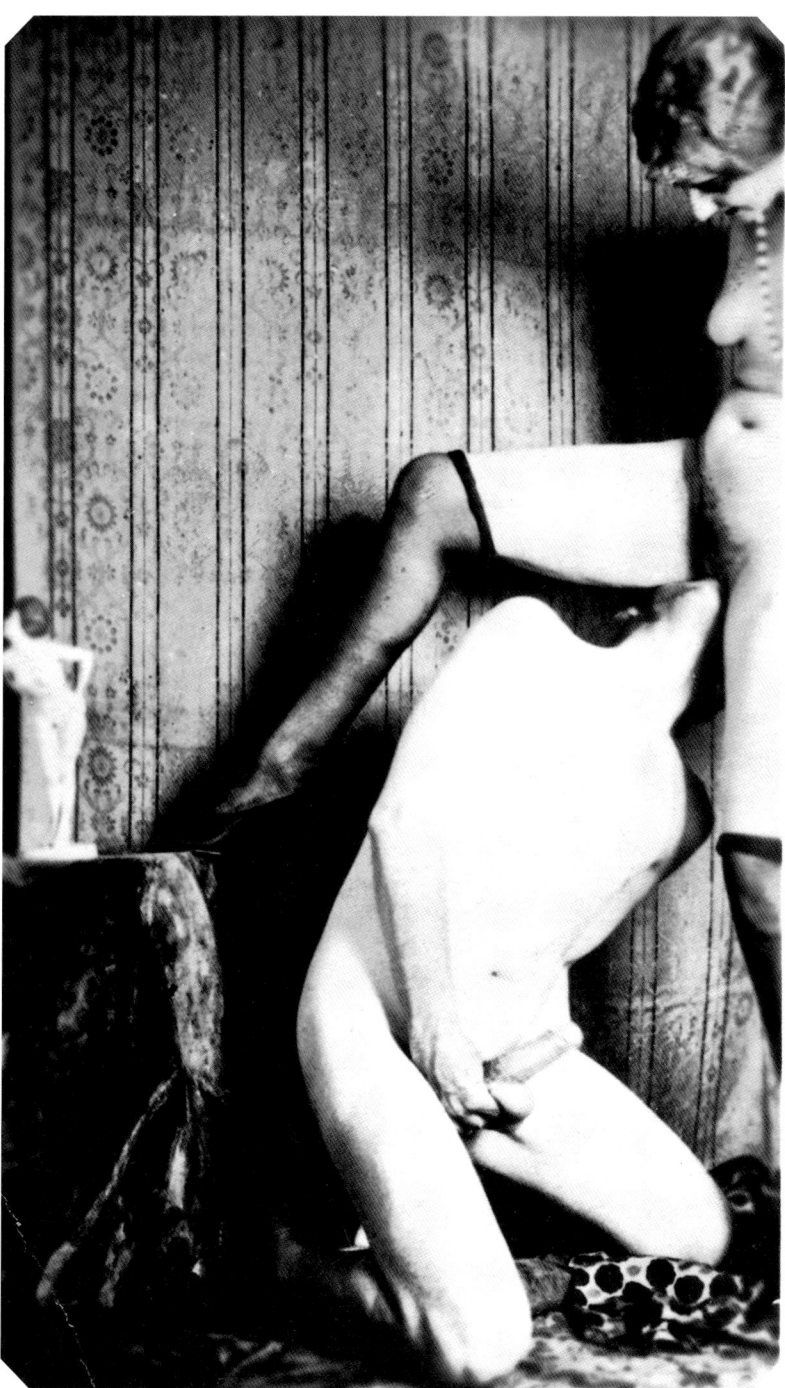

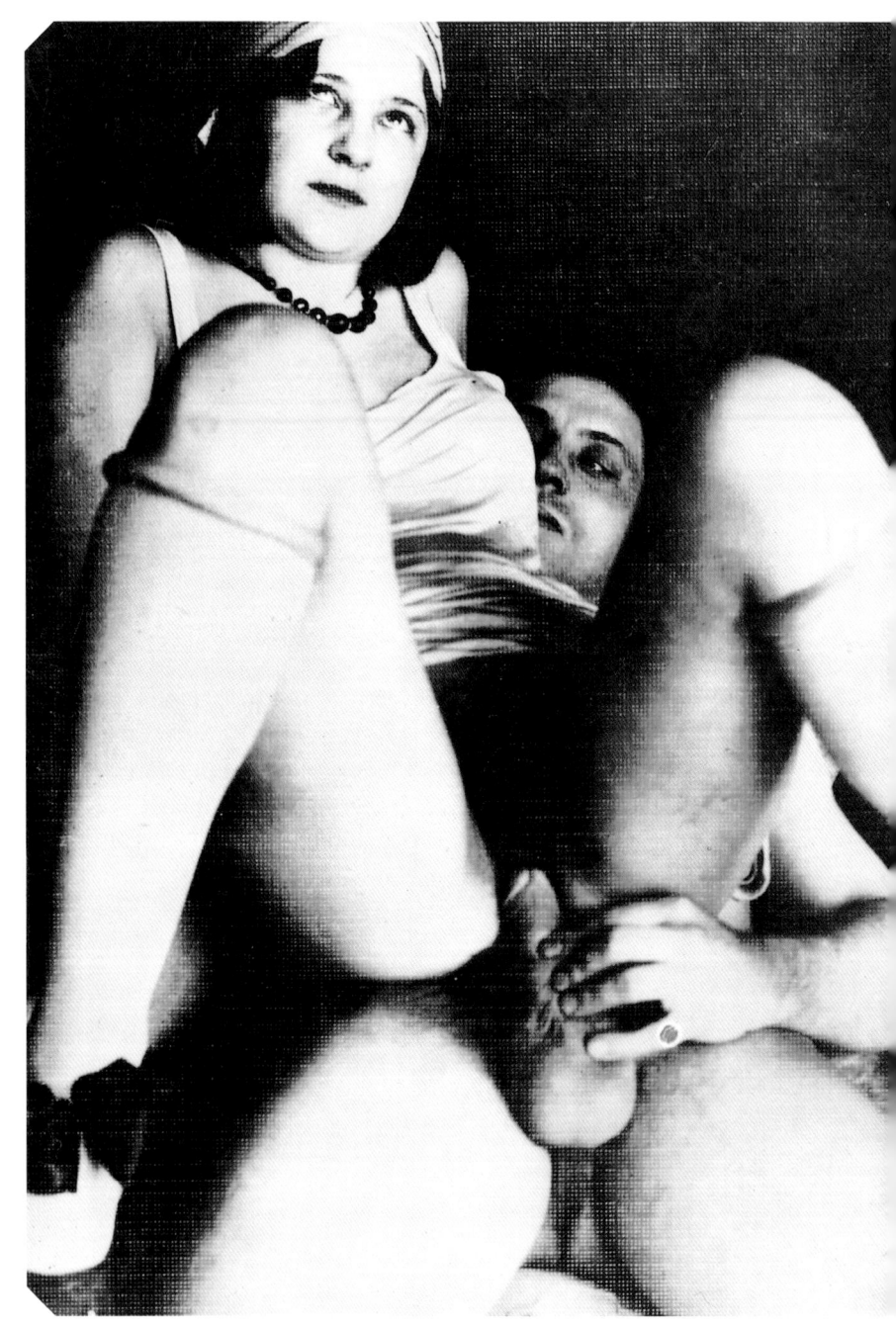

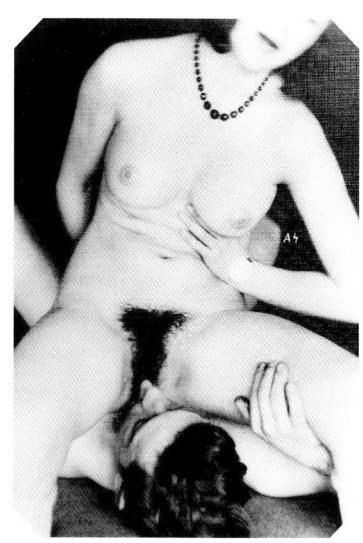

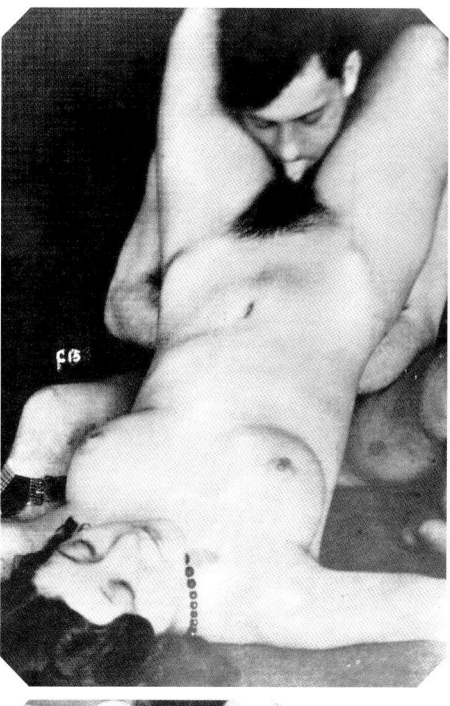

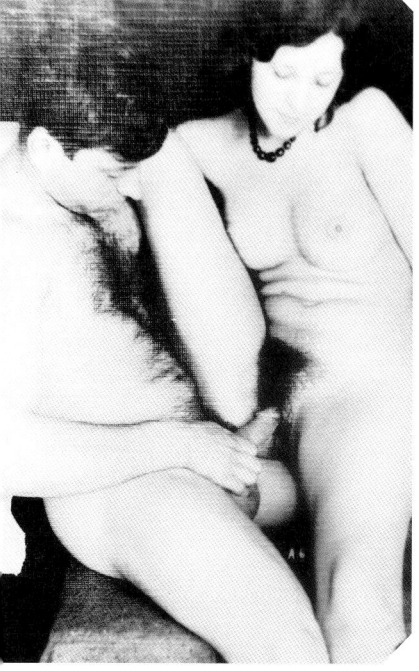

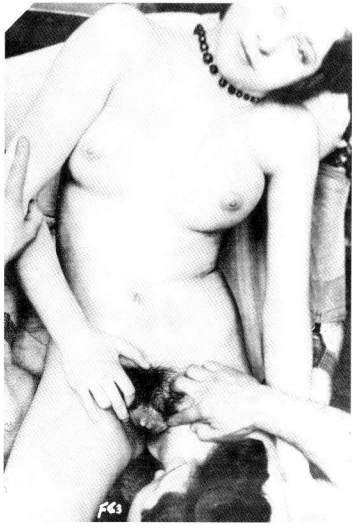

BIJOUX

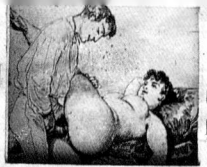

SERIE 183

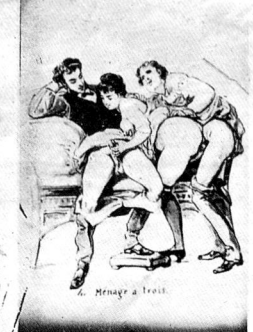

1

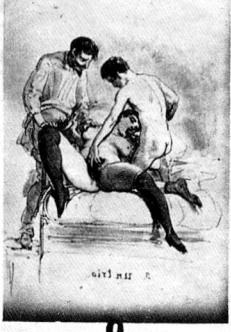

2

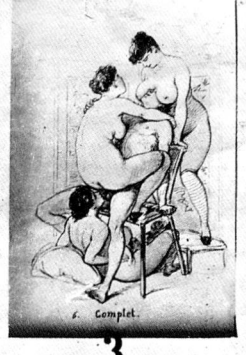

3

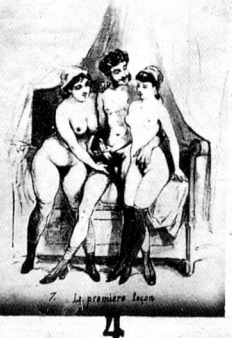

4

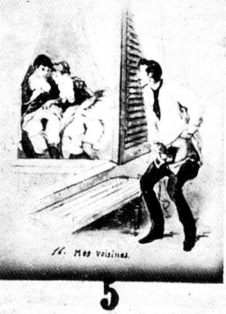

5

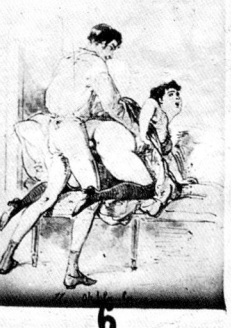

6

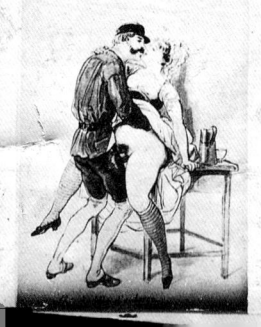

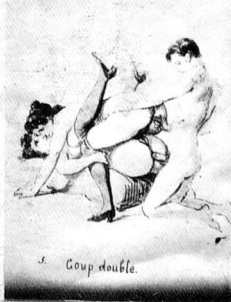

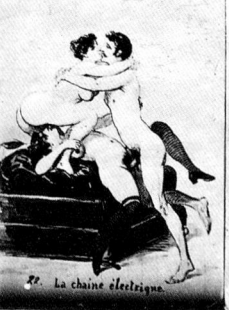

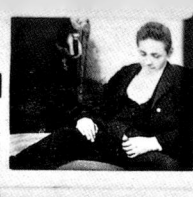

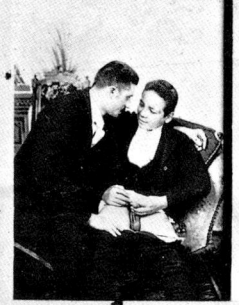

1

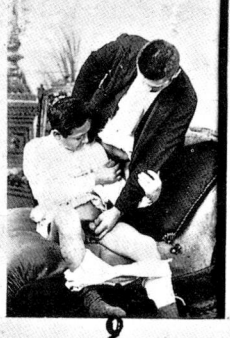

2

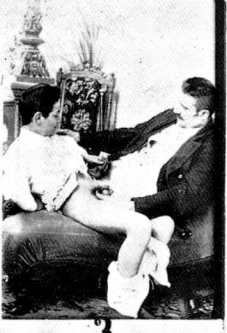

3

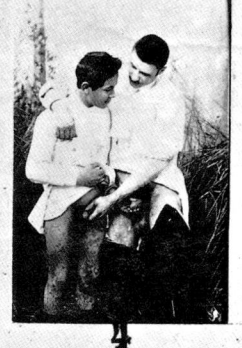

4

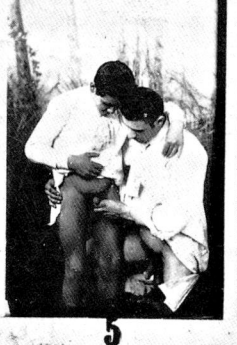

5

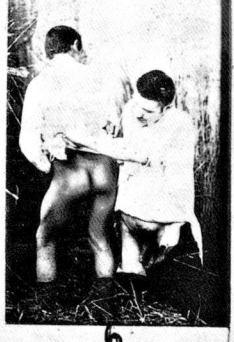

6

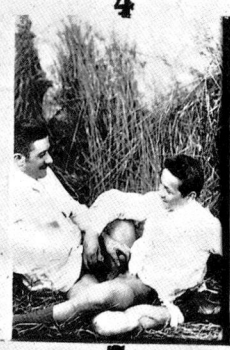

7

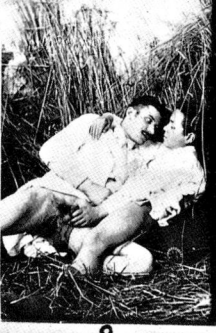

8

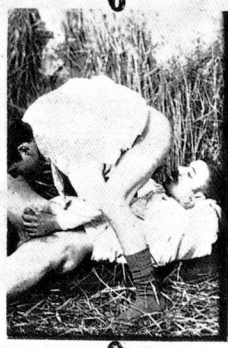

9

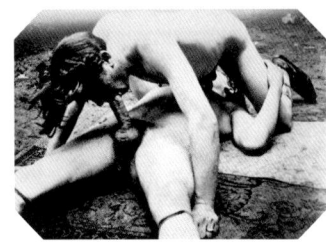

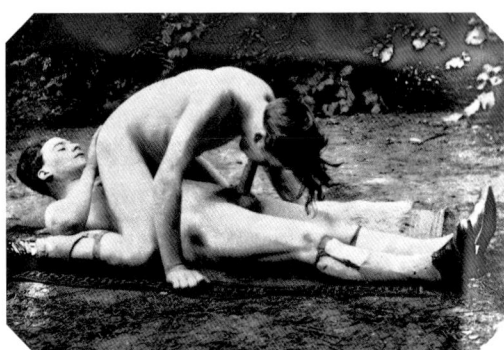

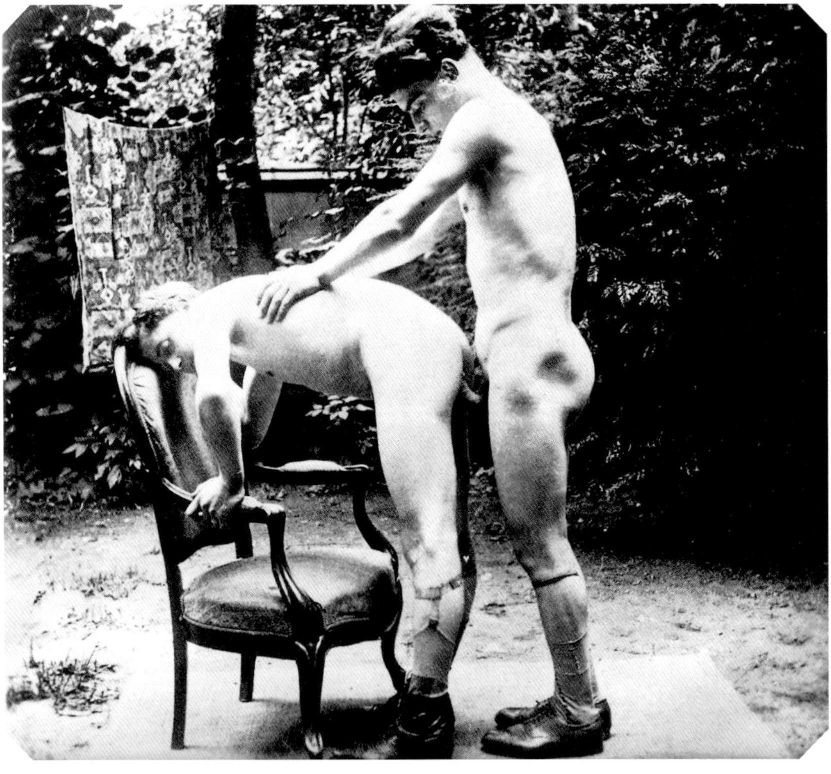

286

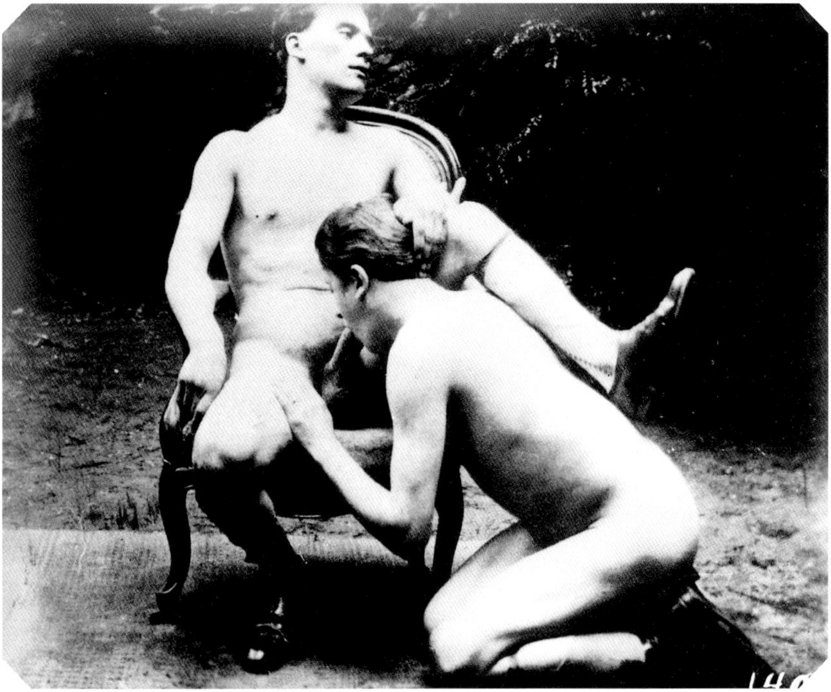

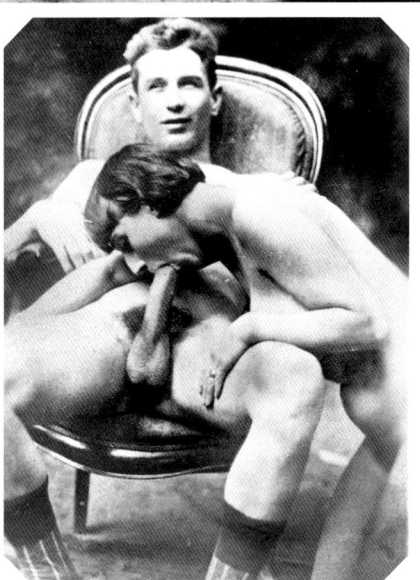
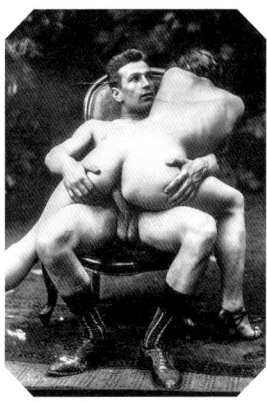

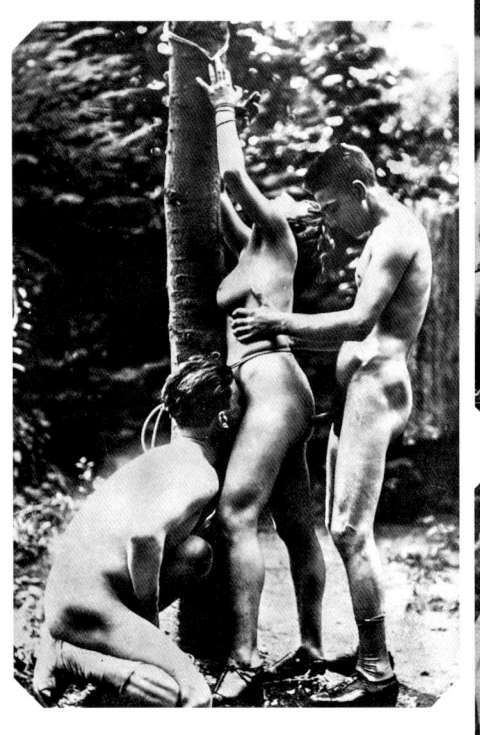
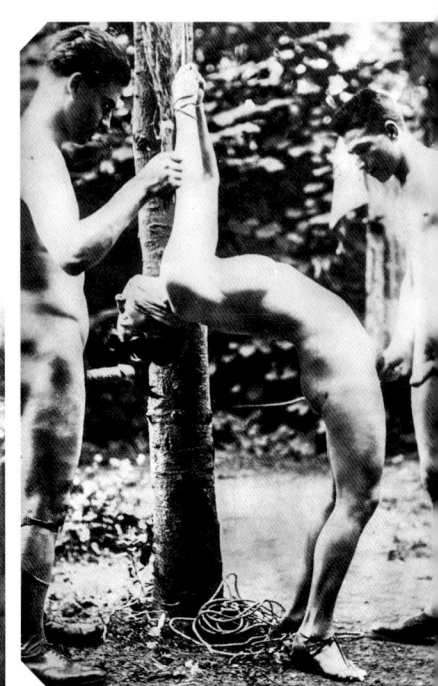
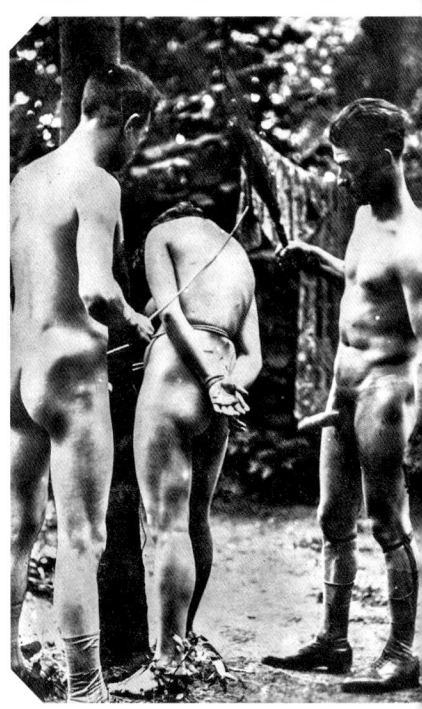

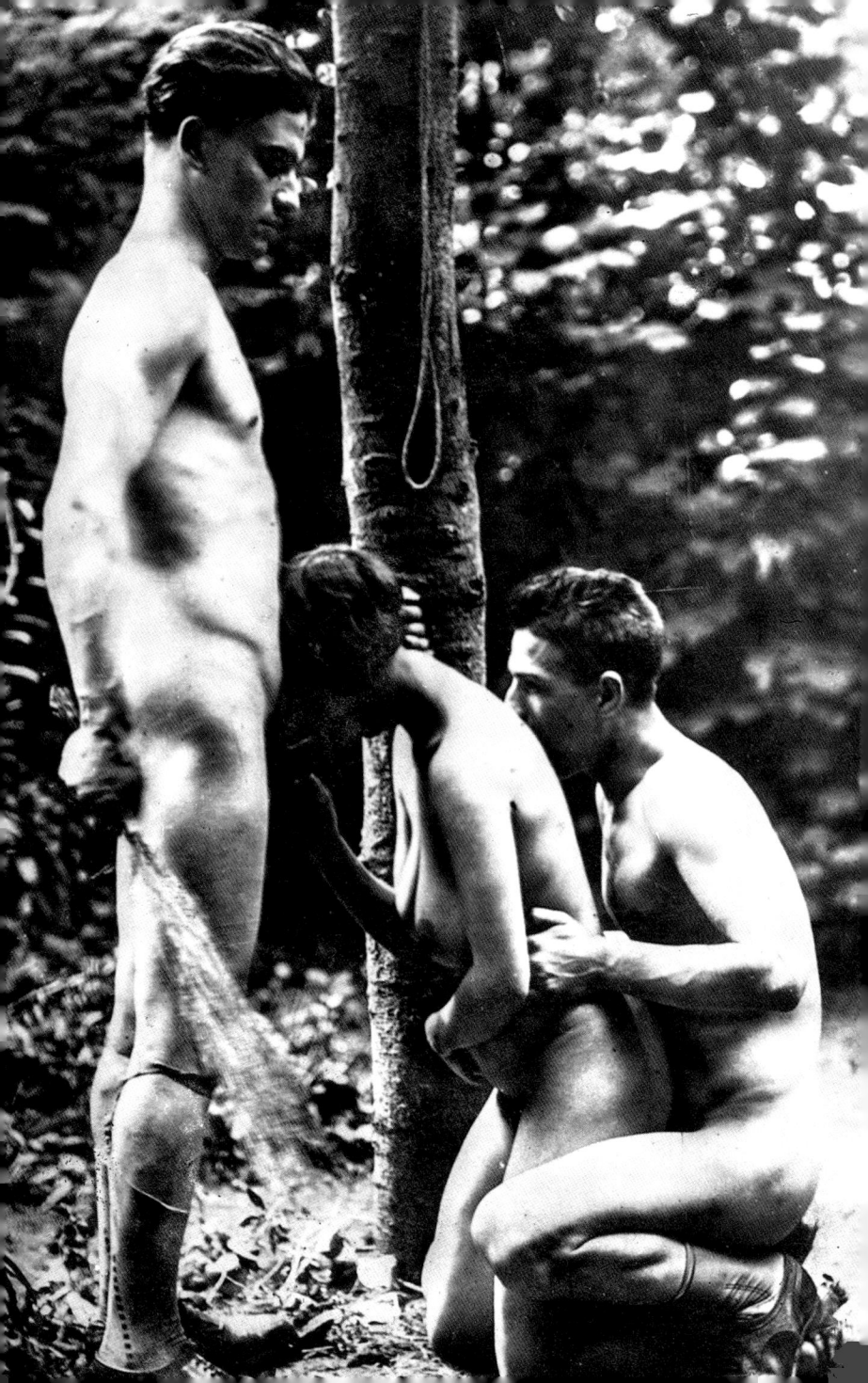

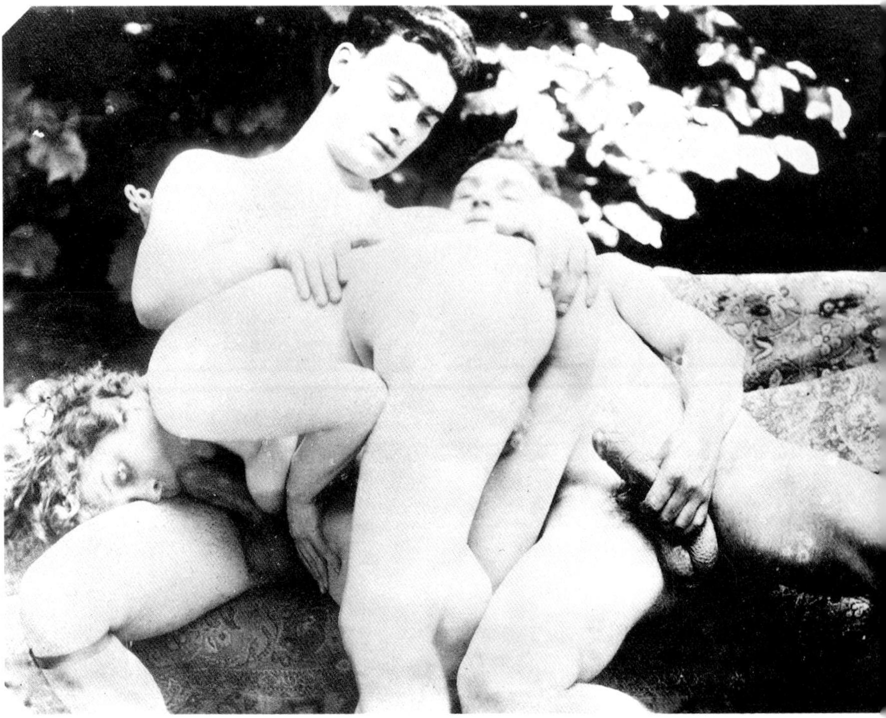

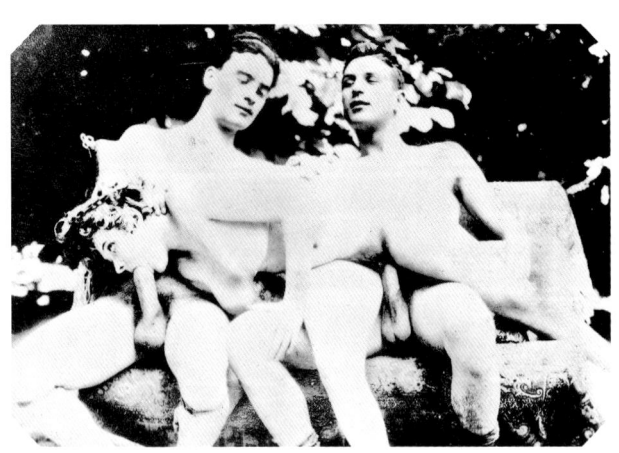

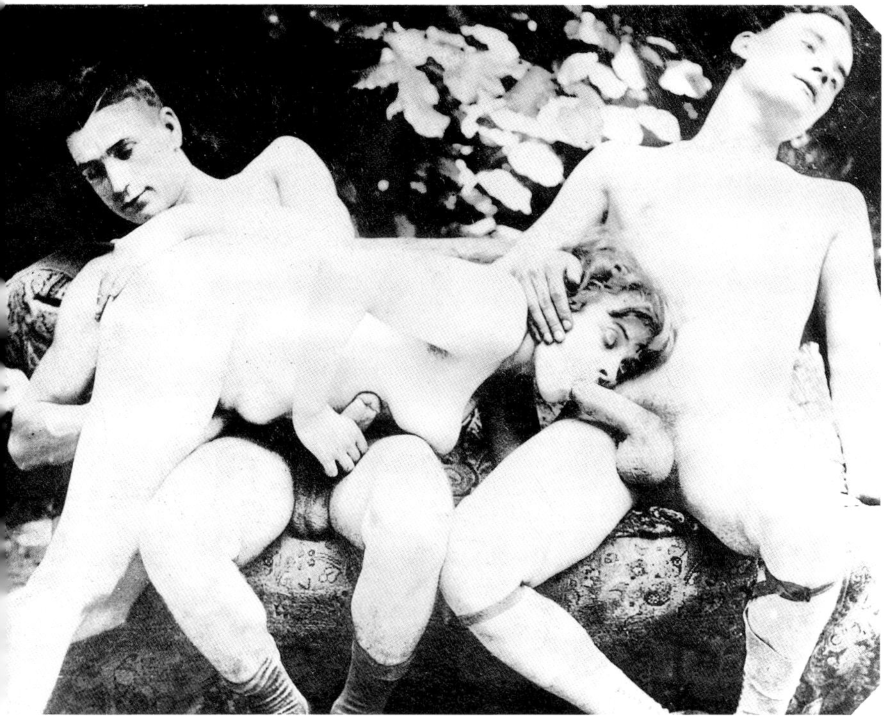

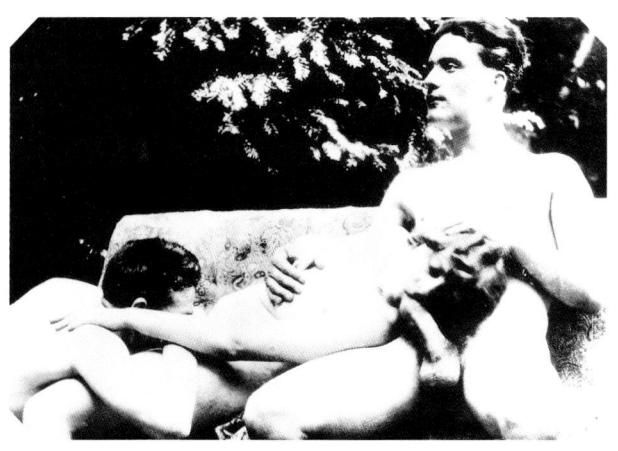

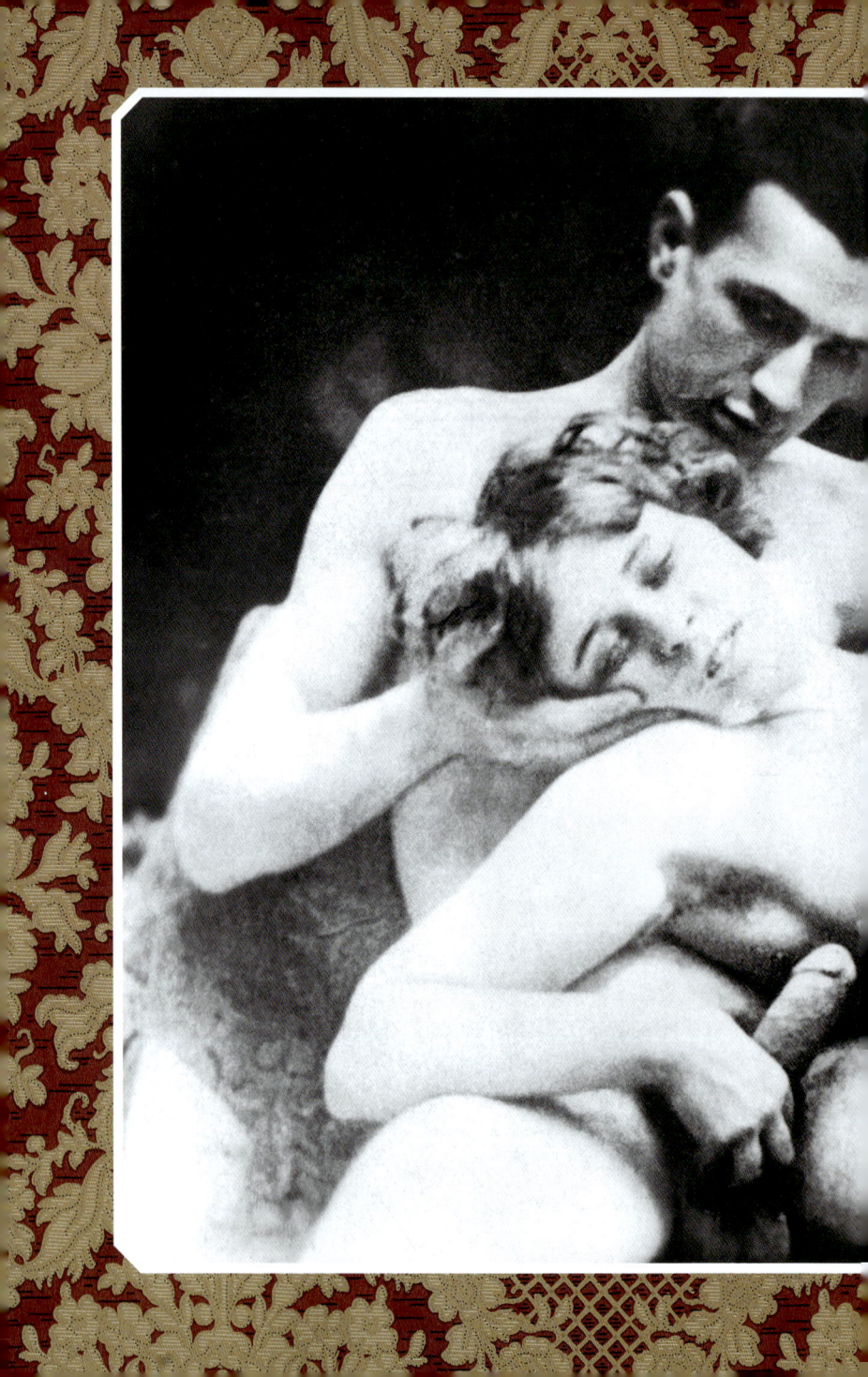

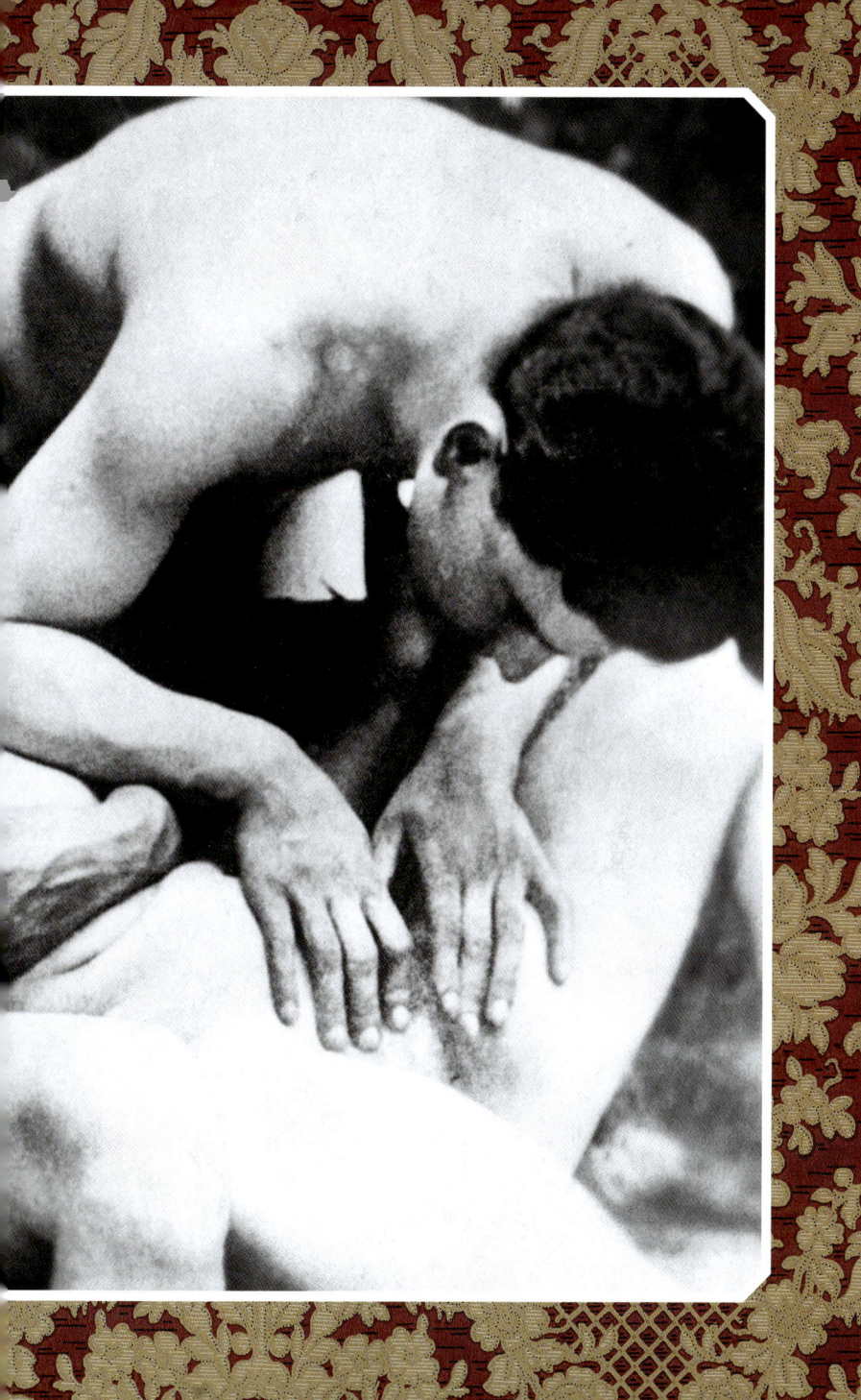

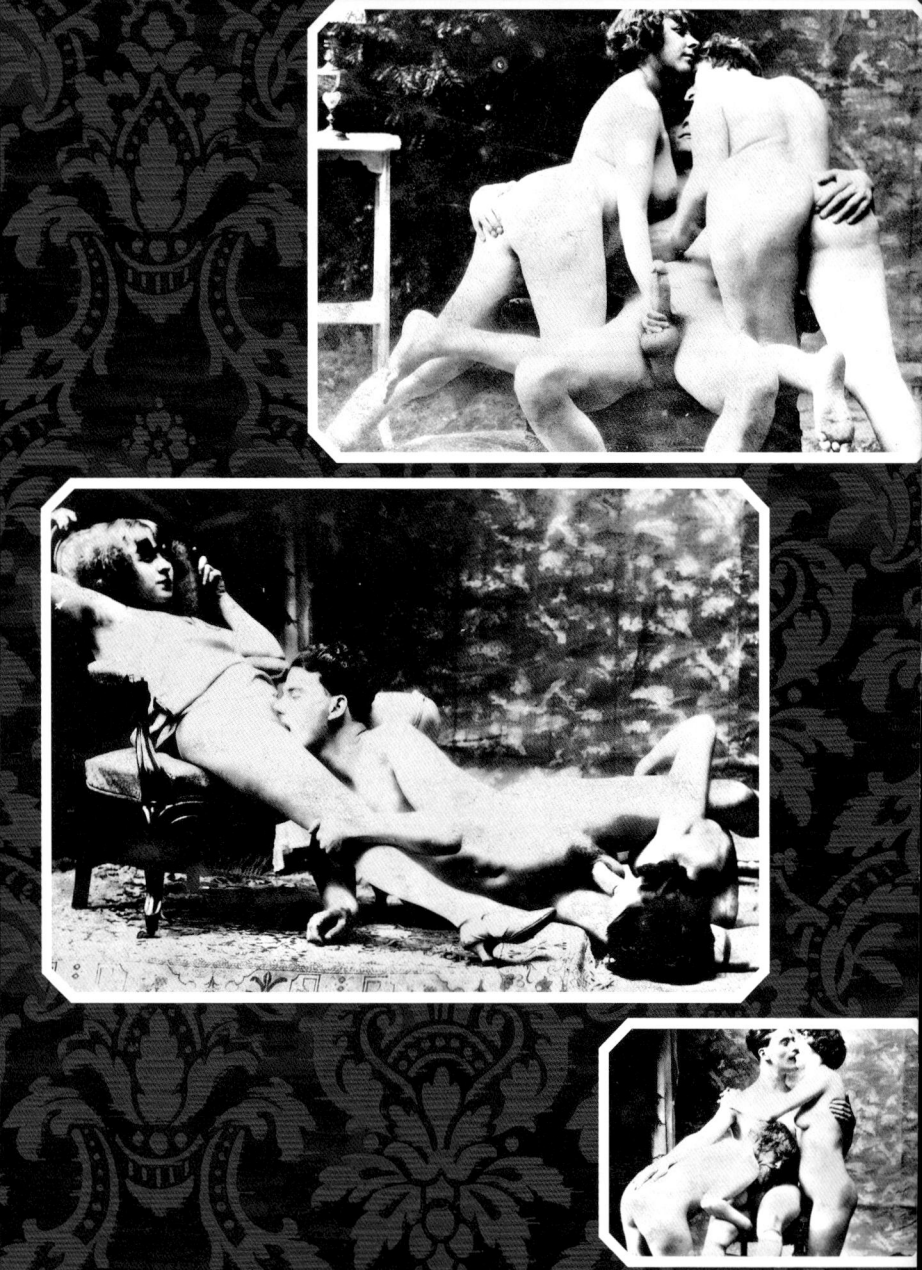

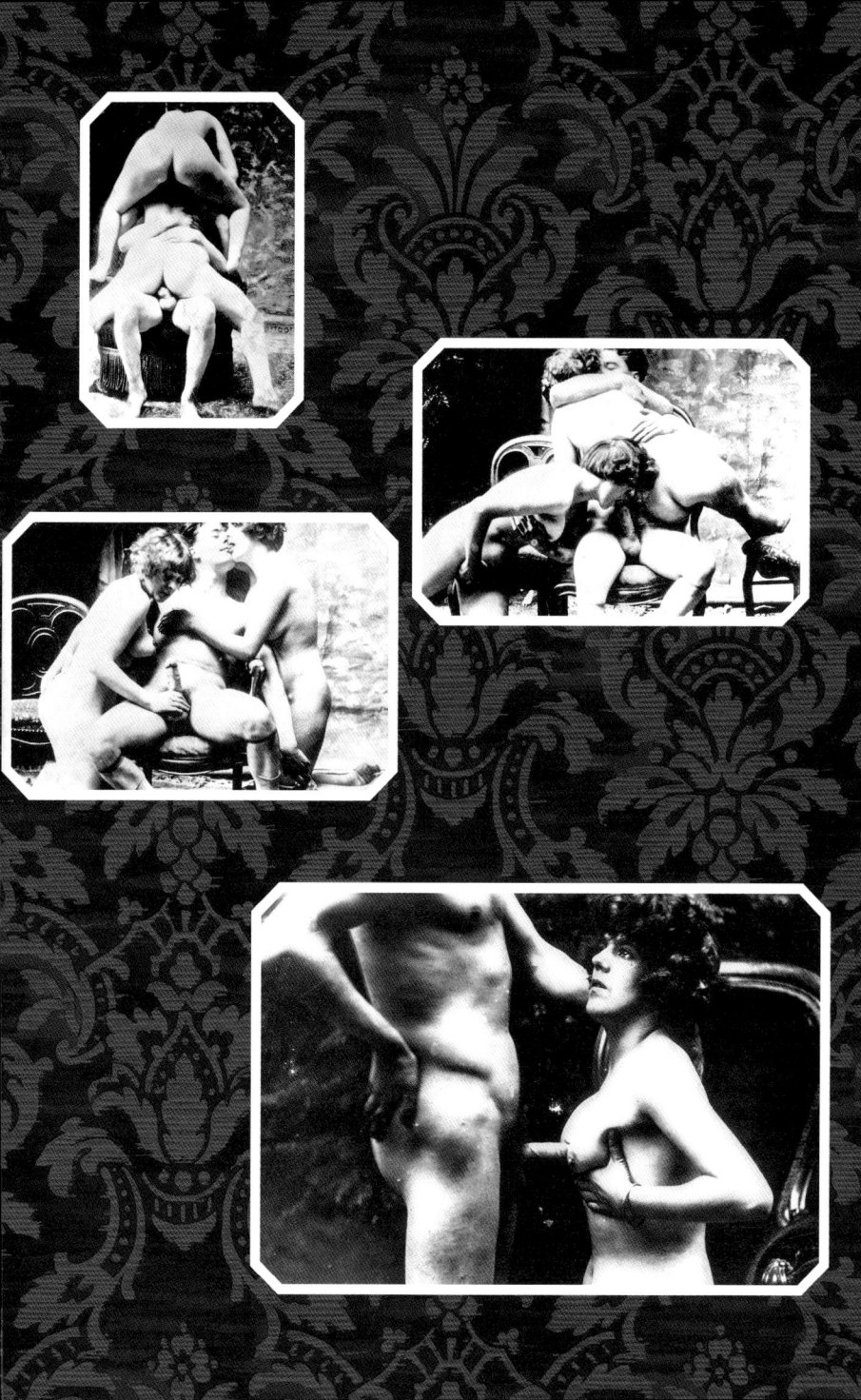

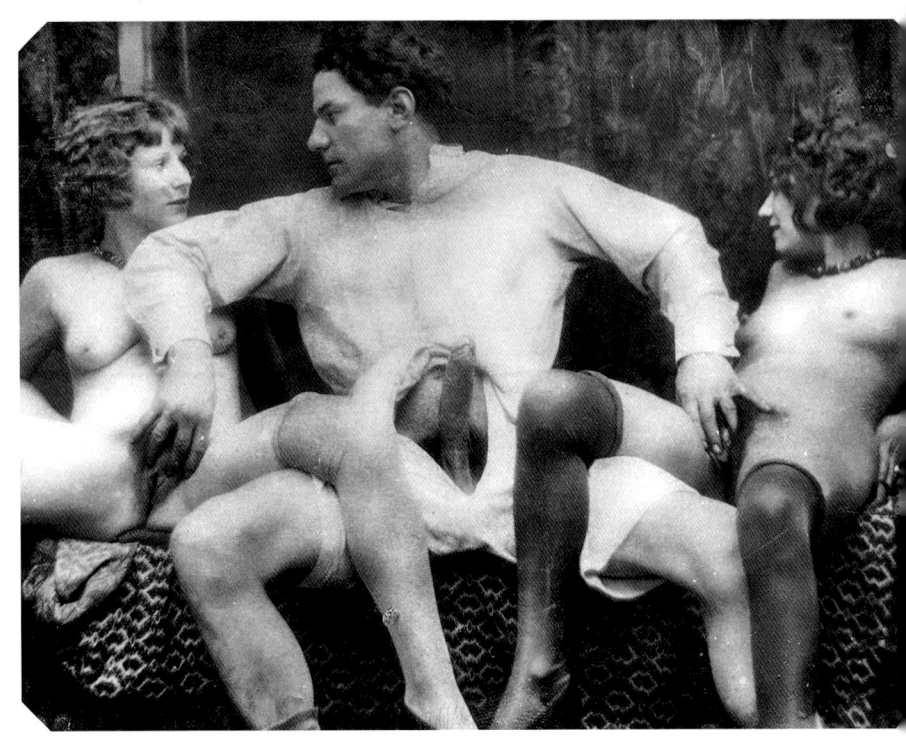

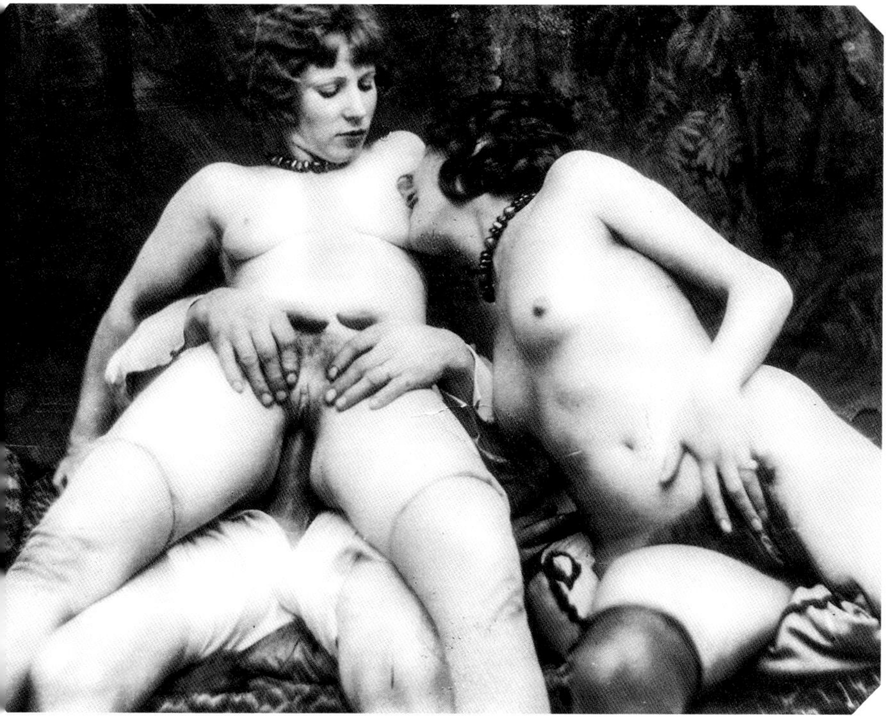

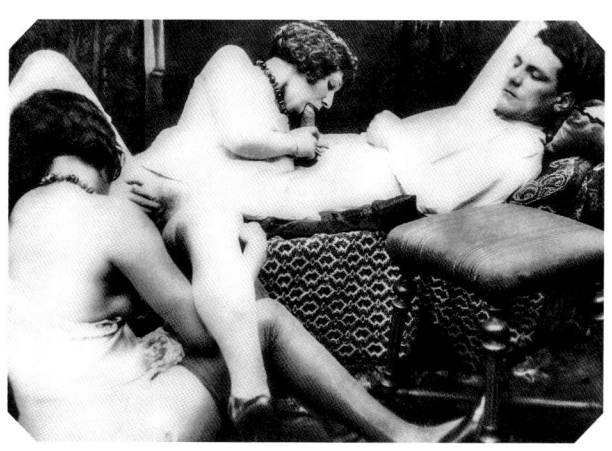

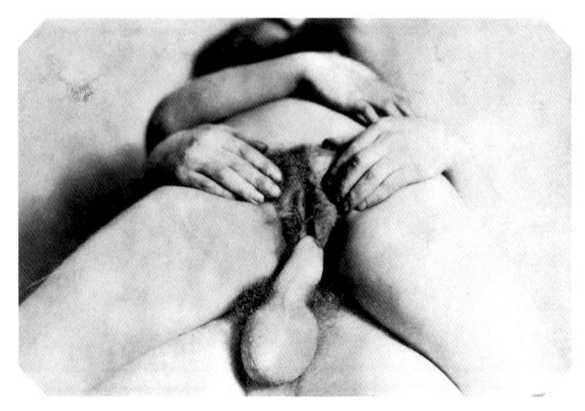

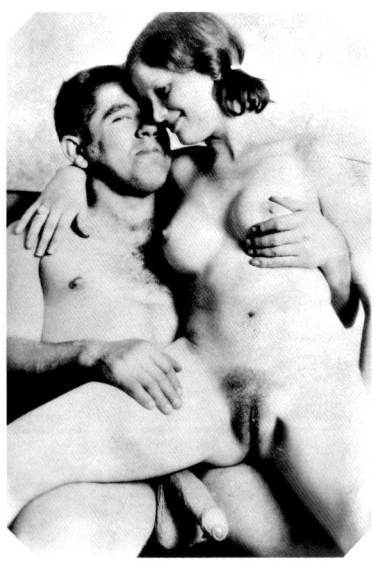

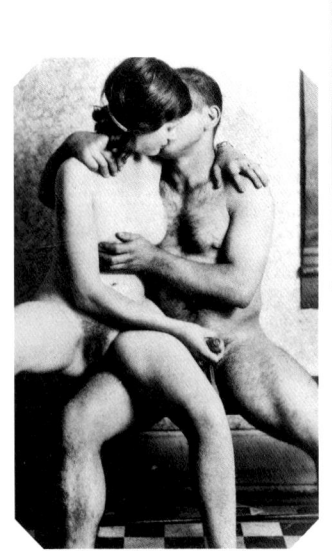

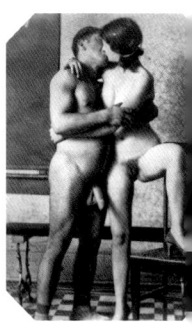

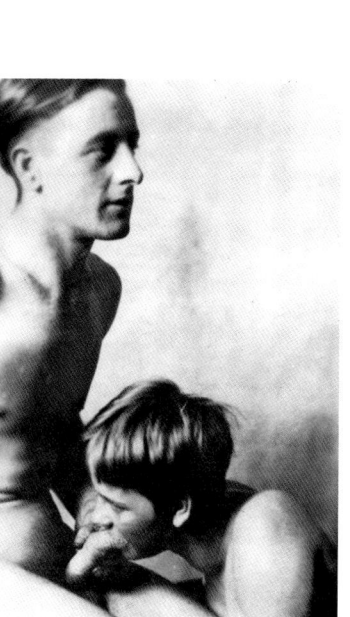

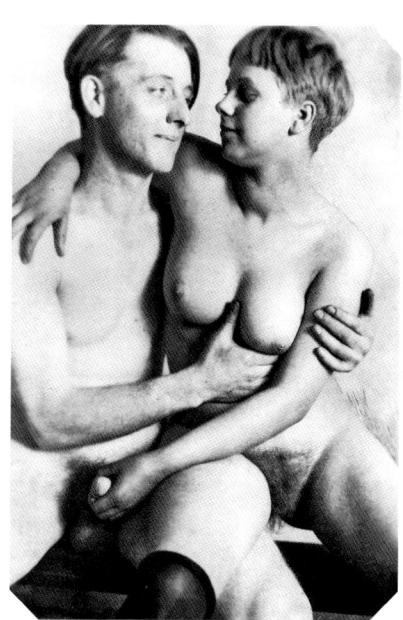

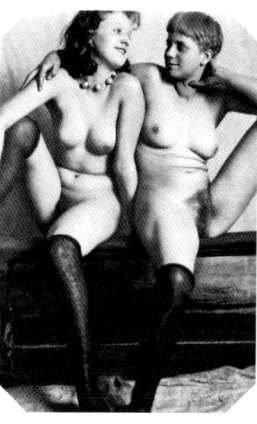

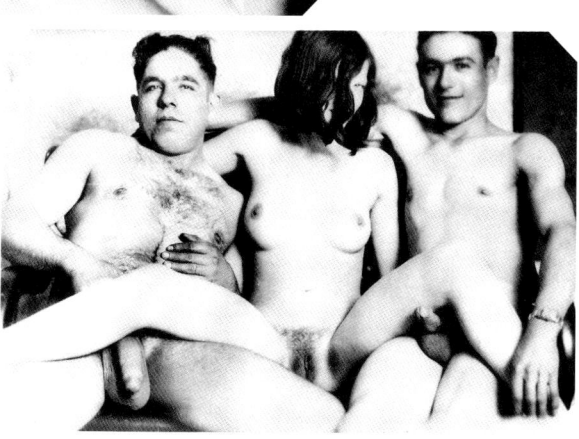

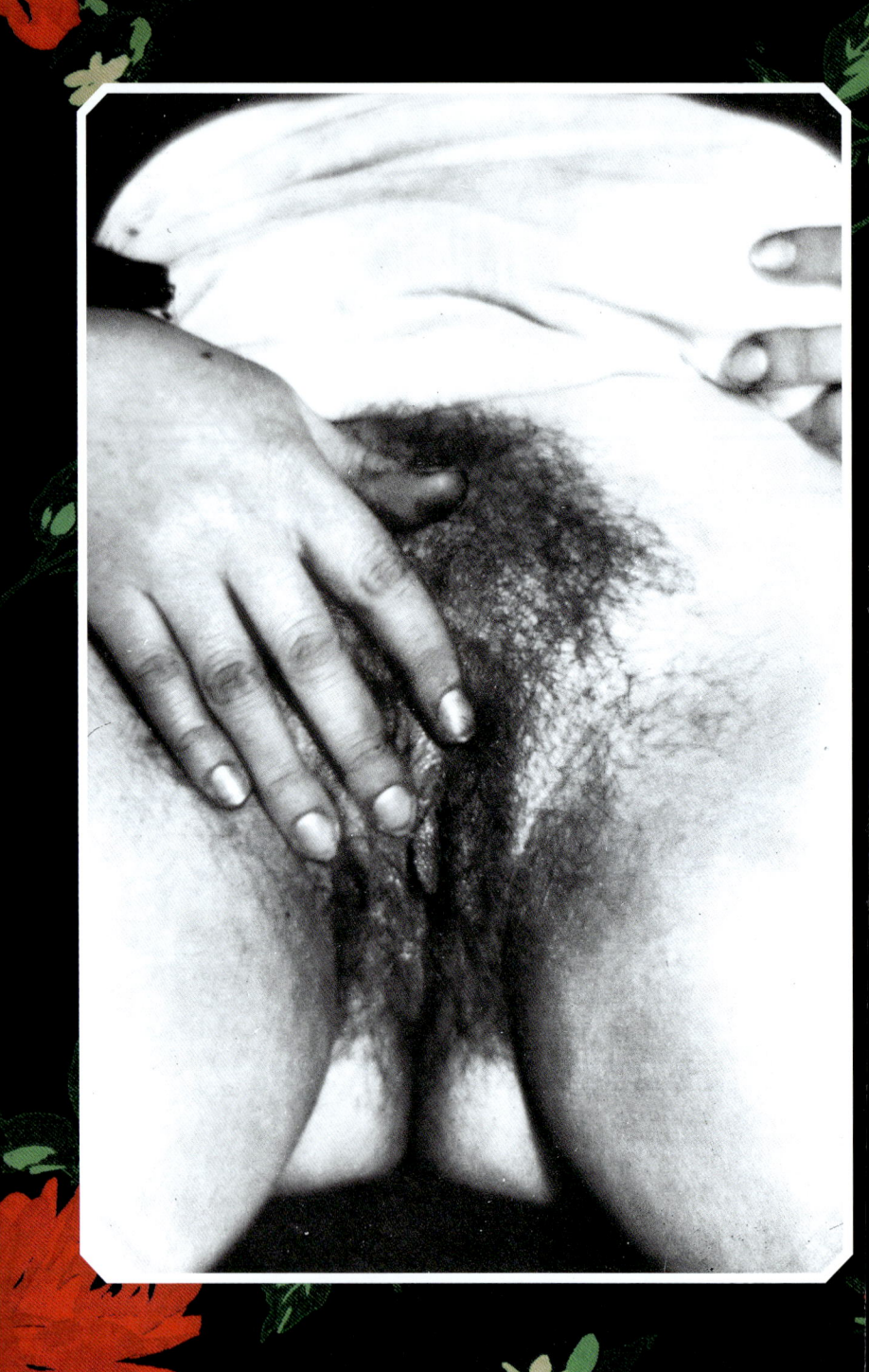

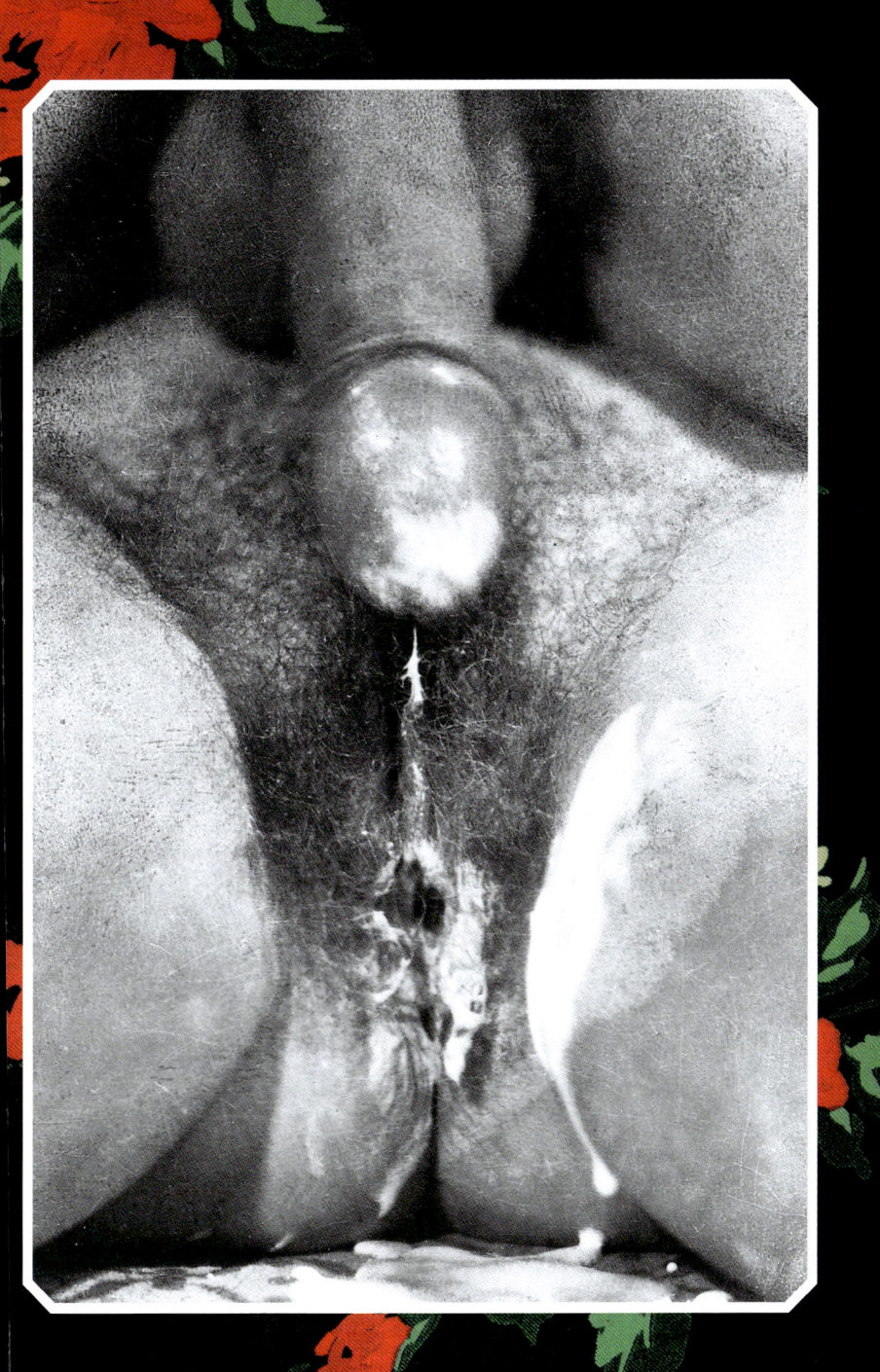

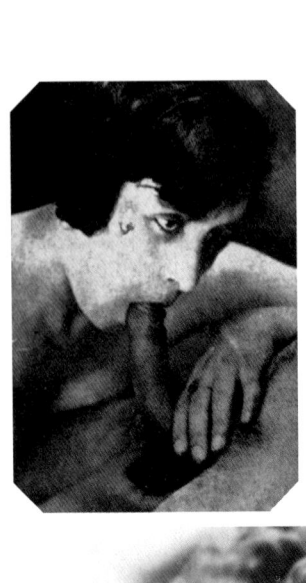

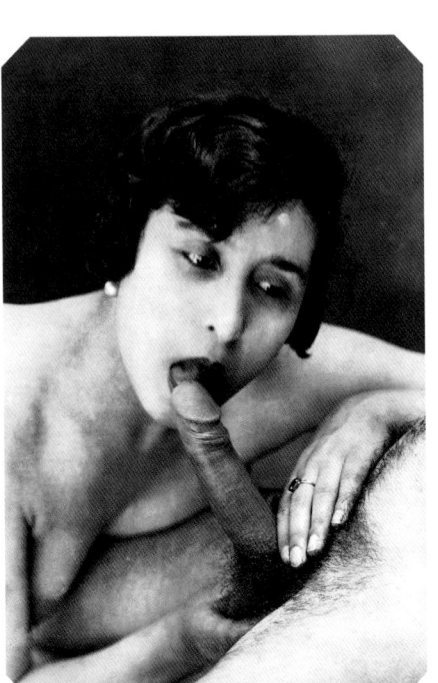

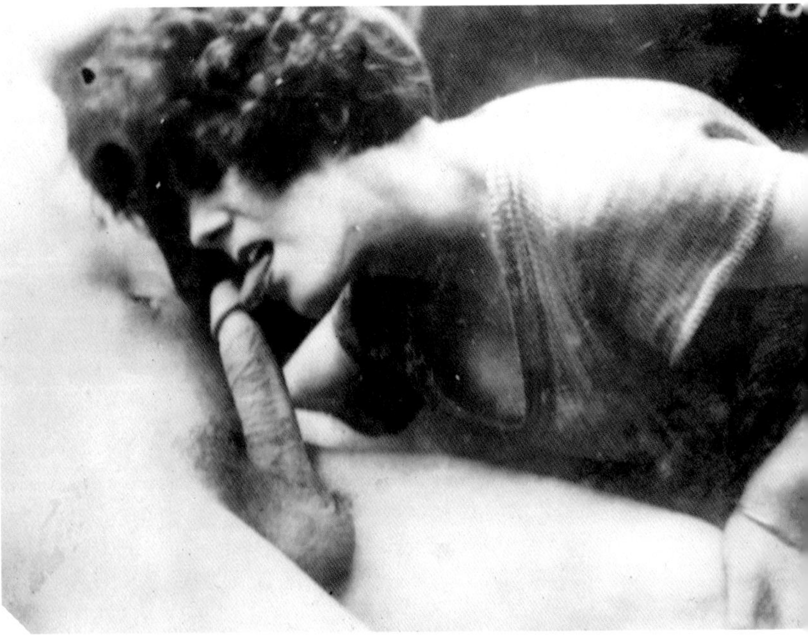

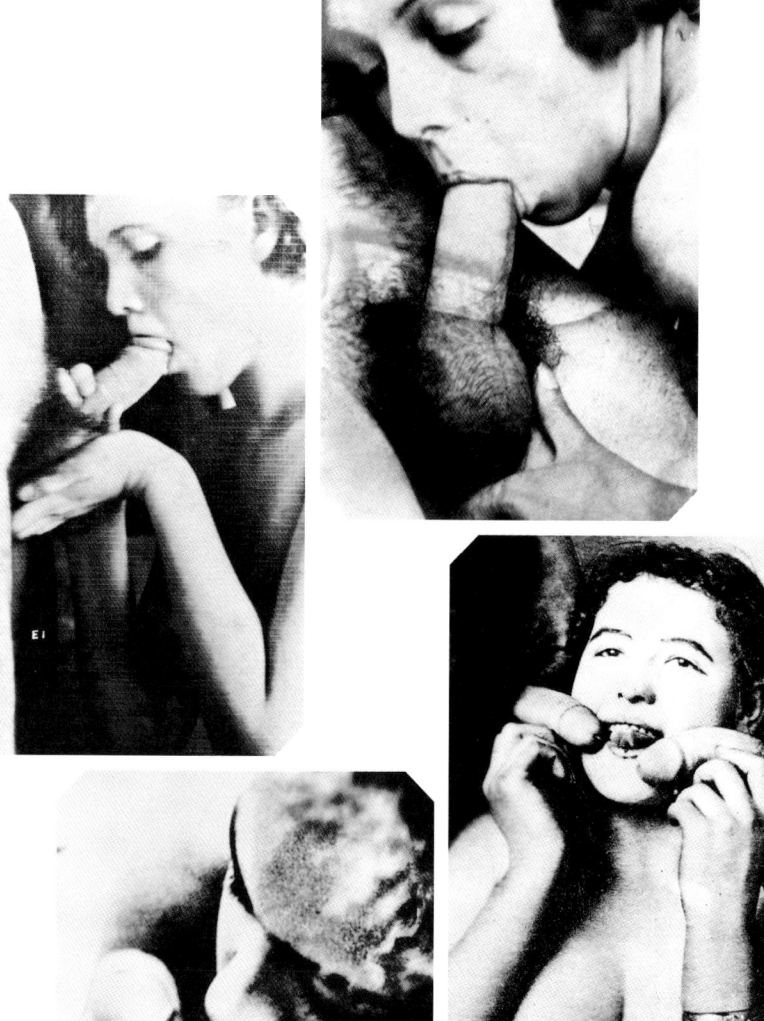

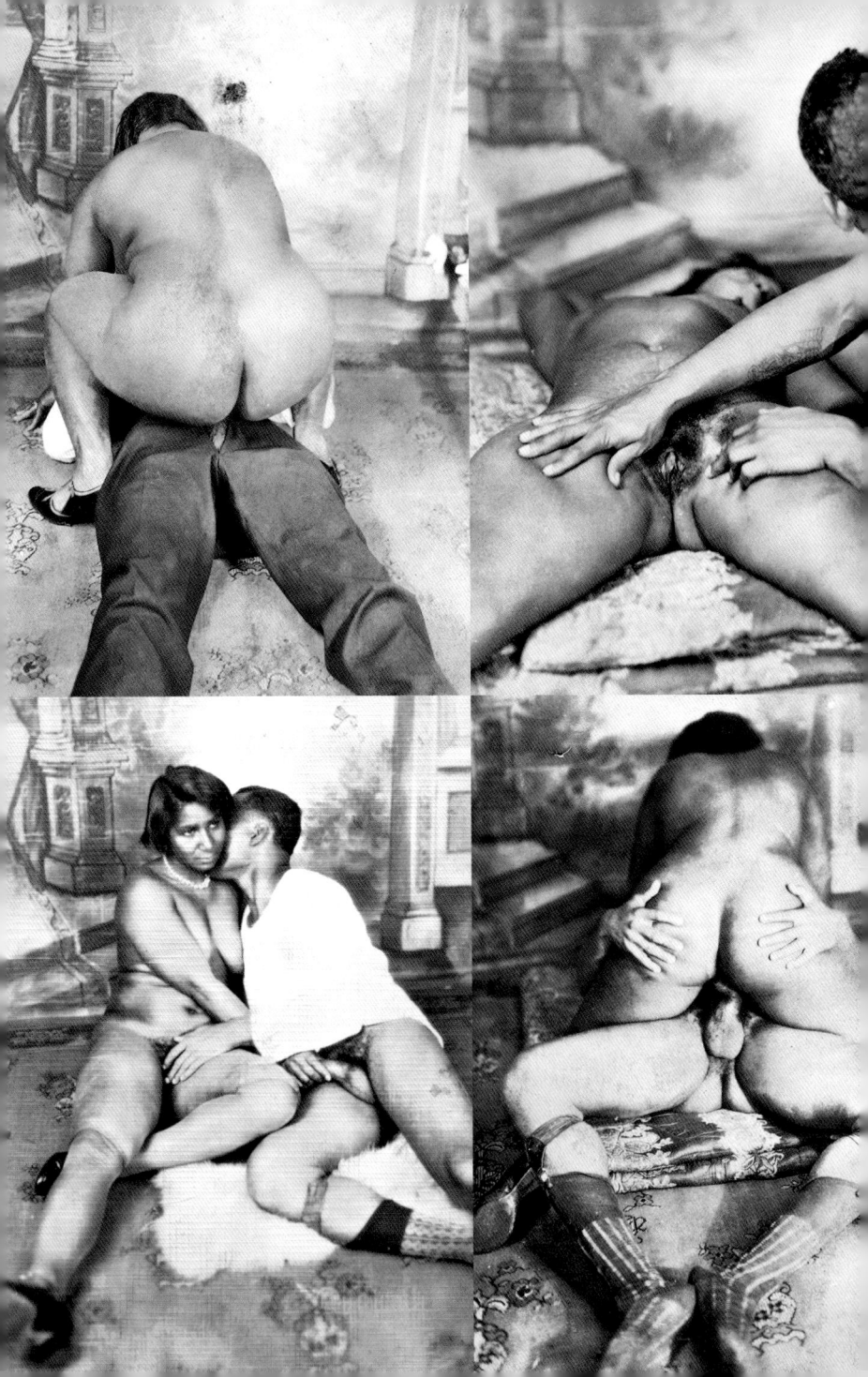

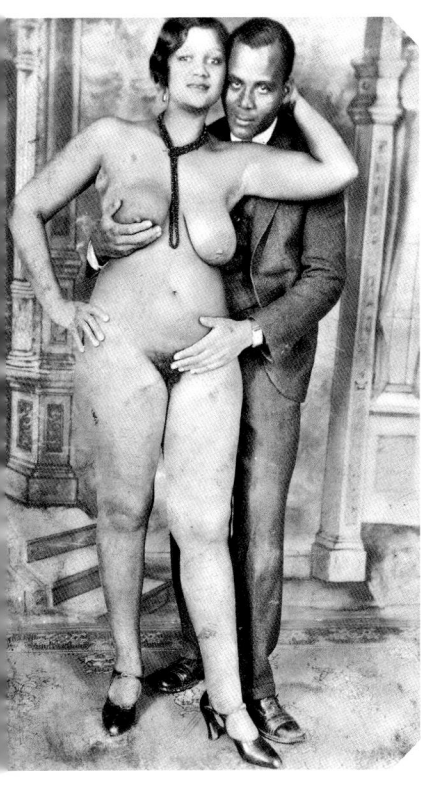

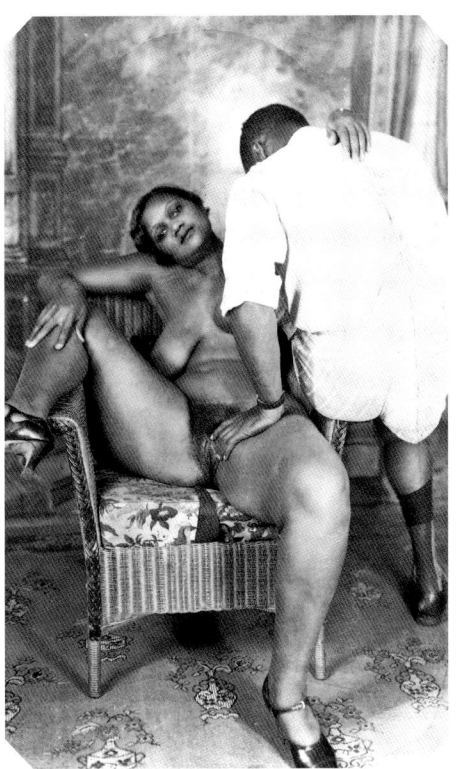

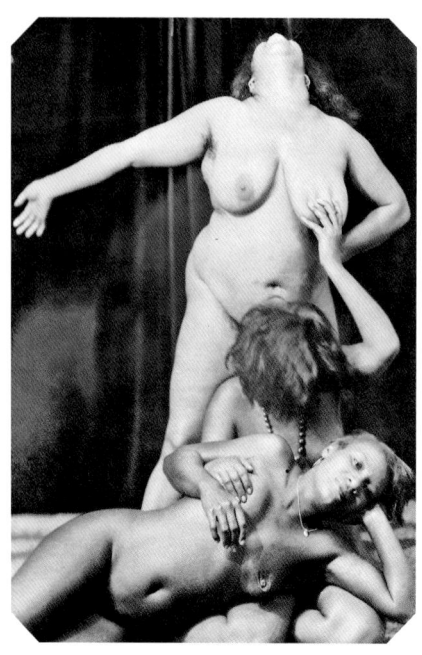
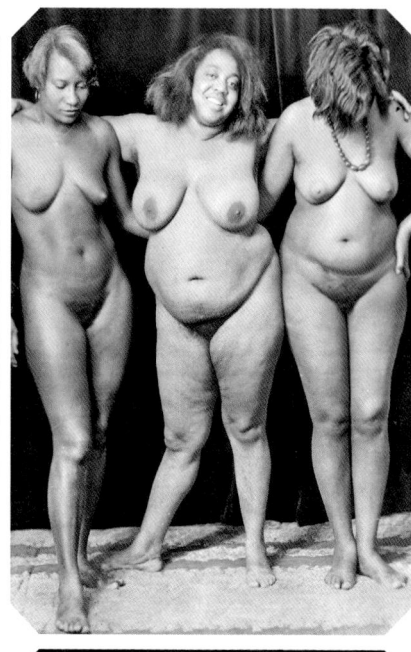
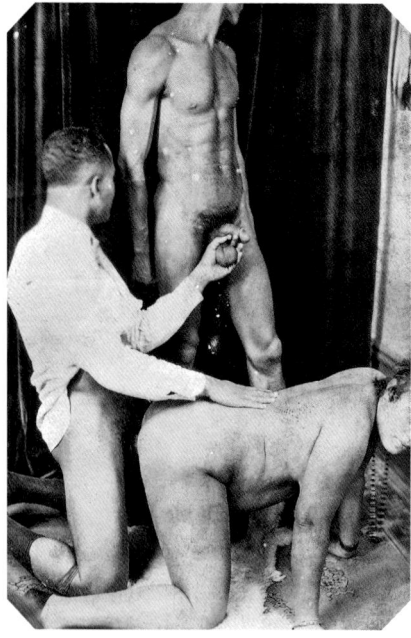
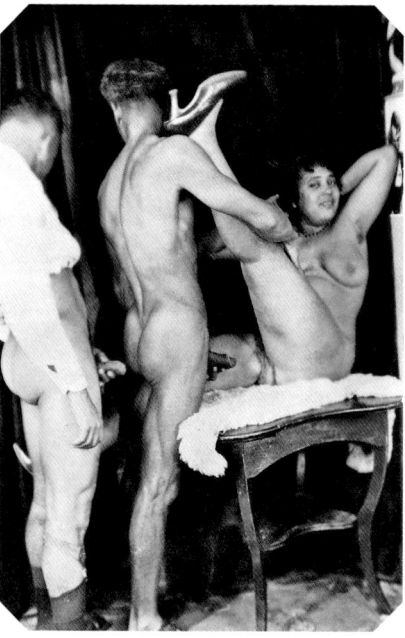

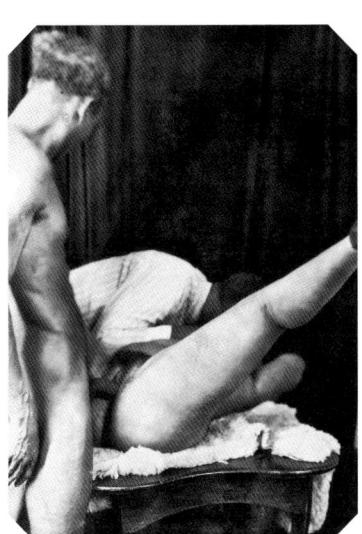

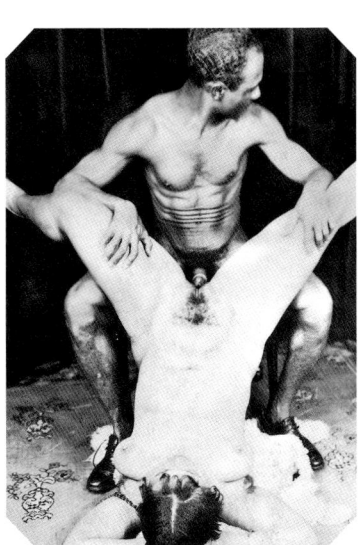

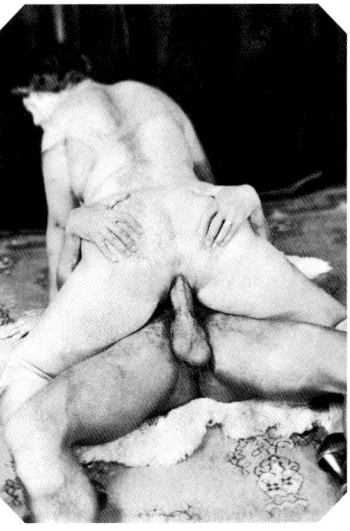

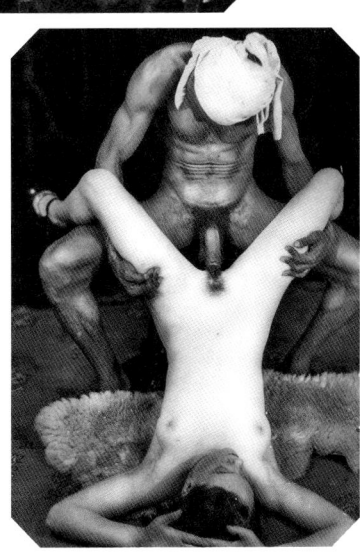

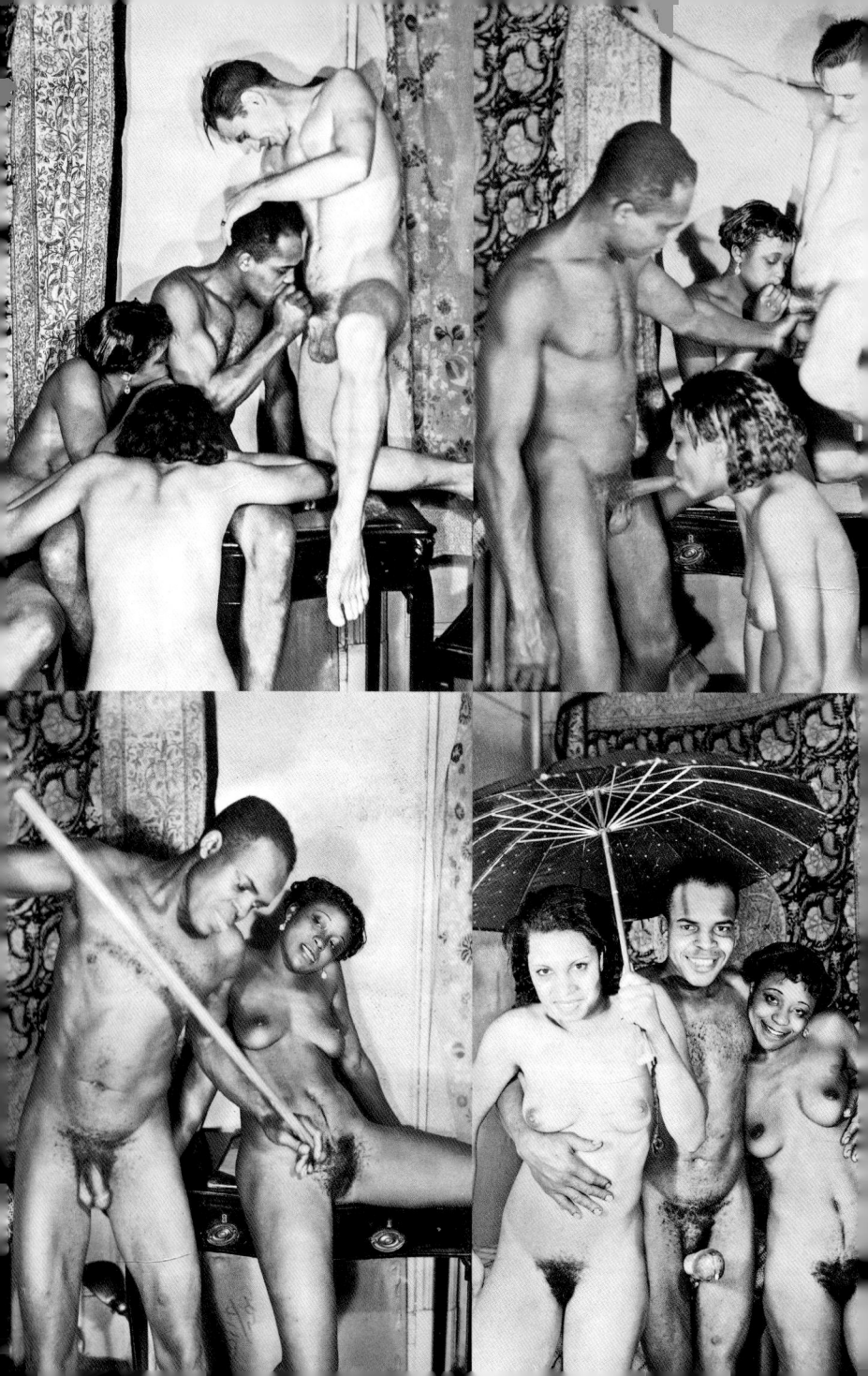

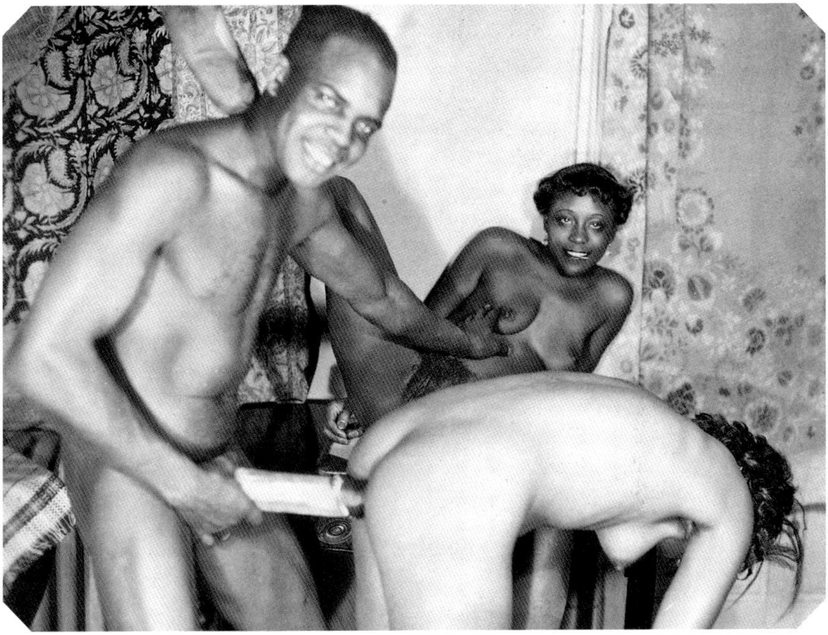

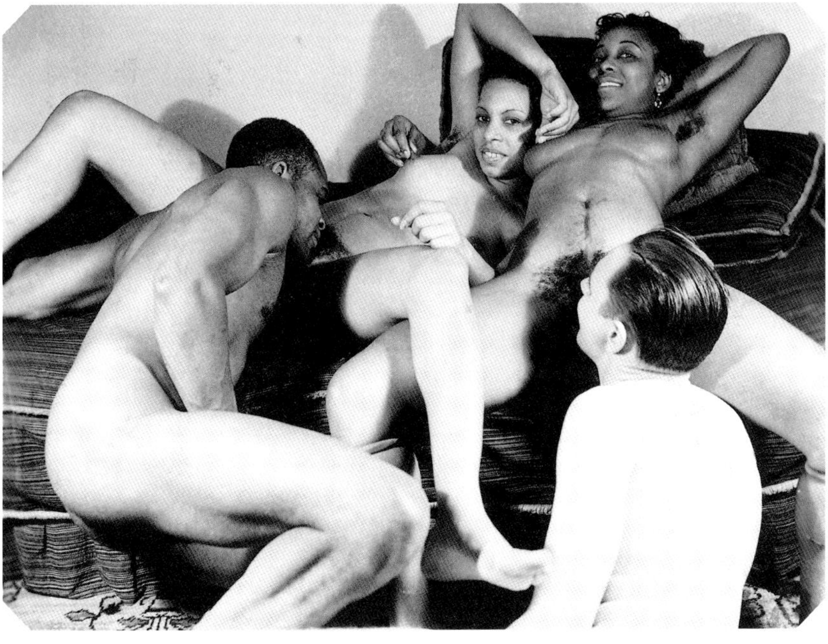

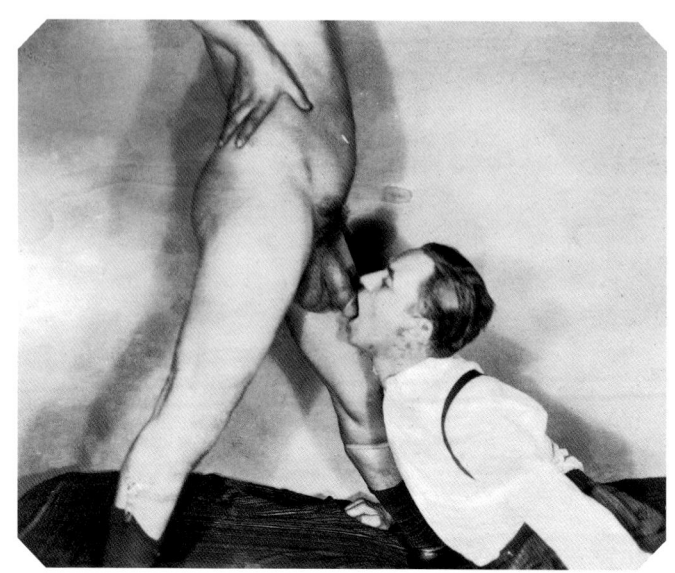

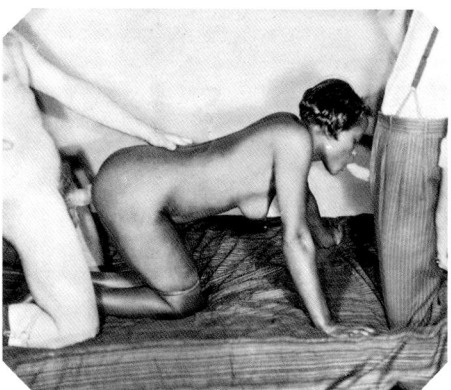

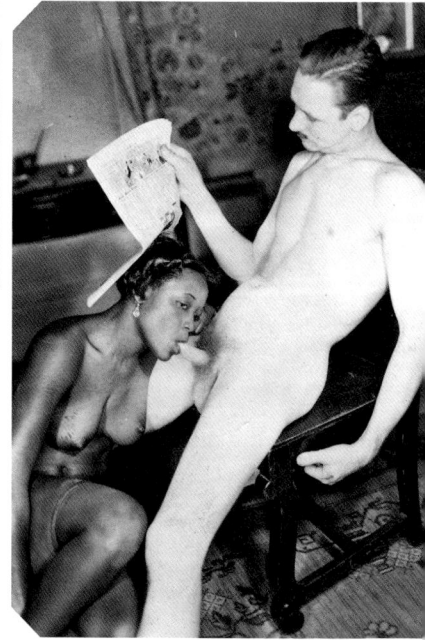

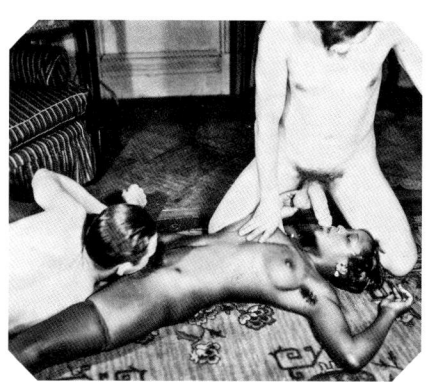

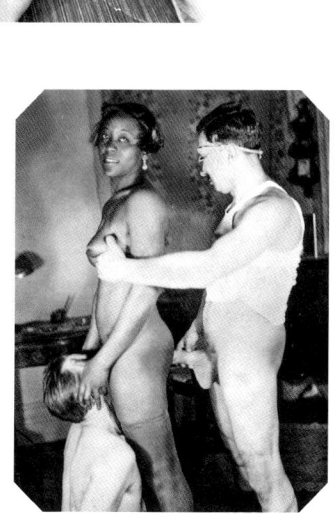

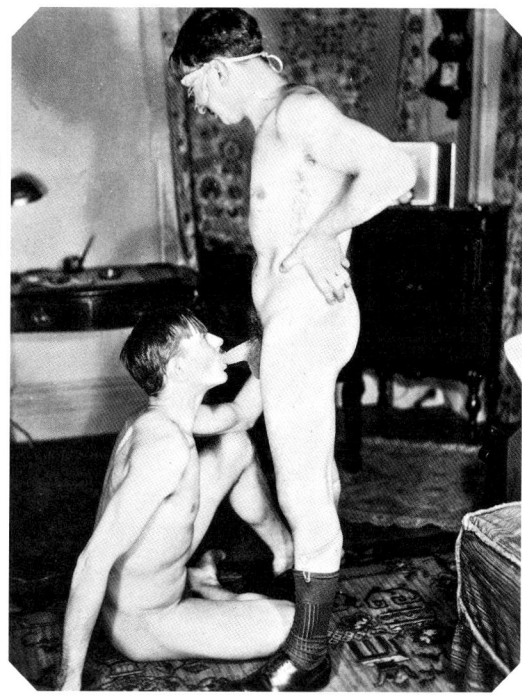

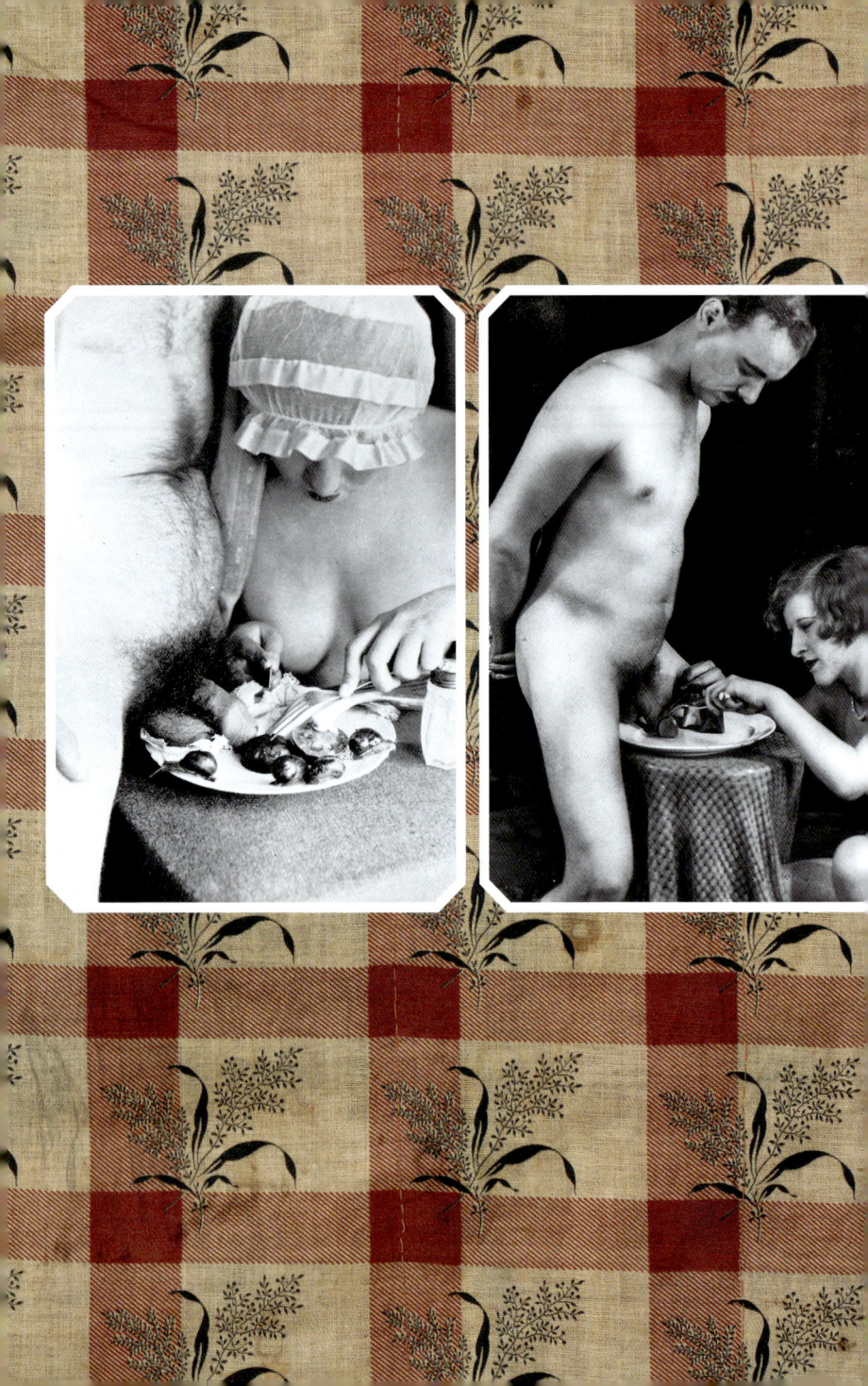

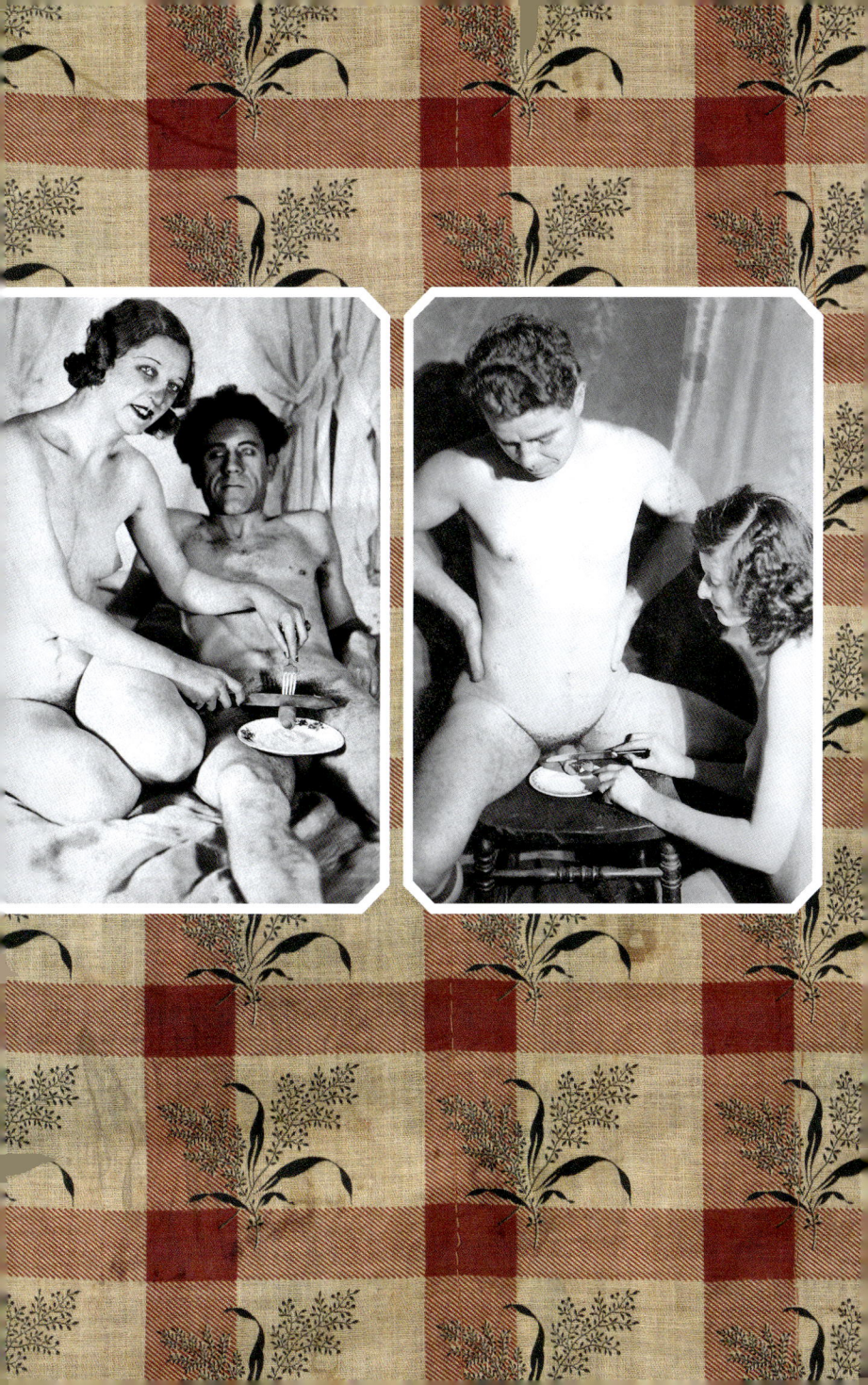

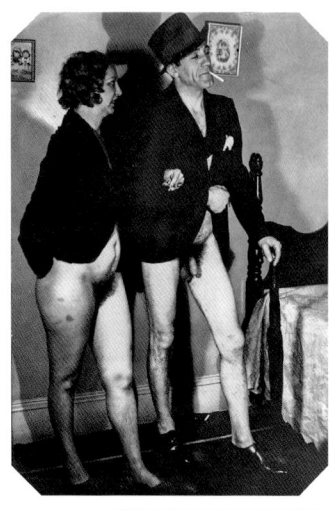
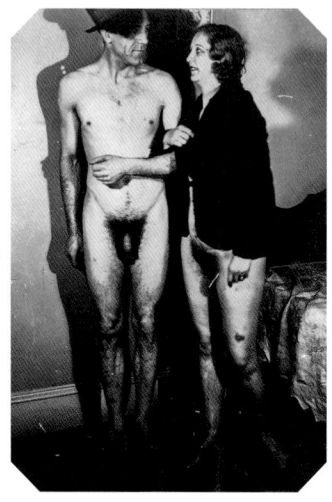
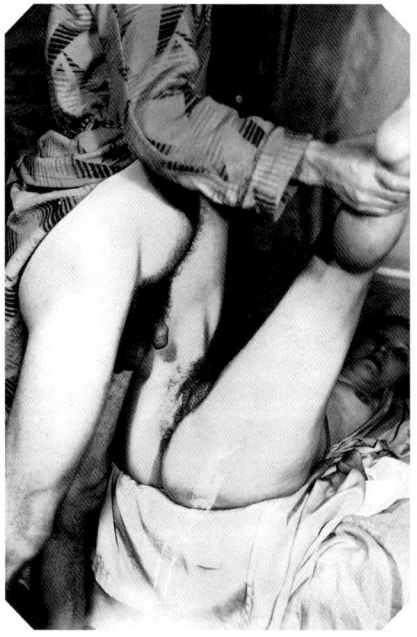
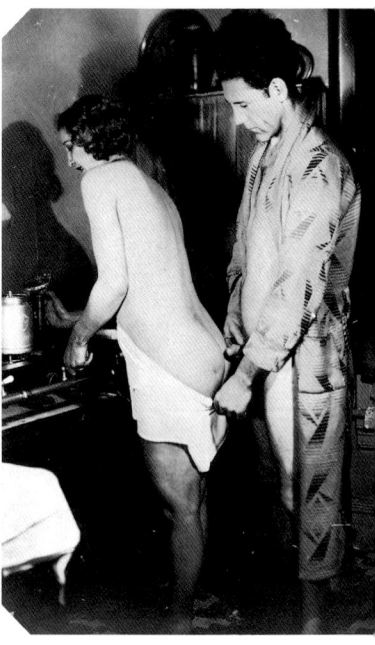

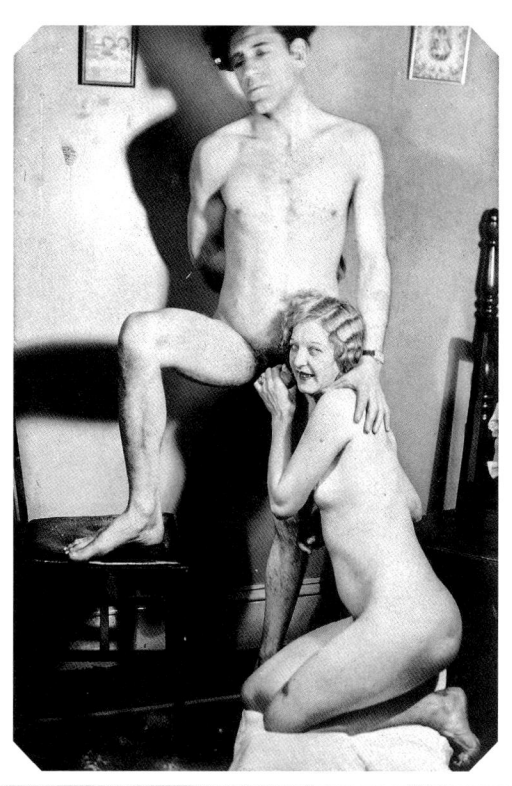

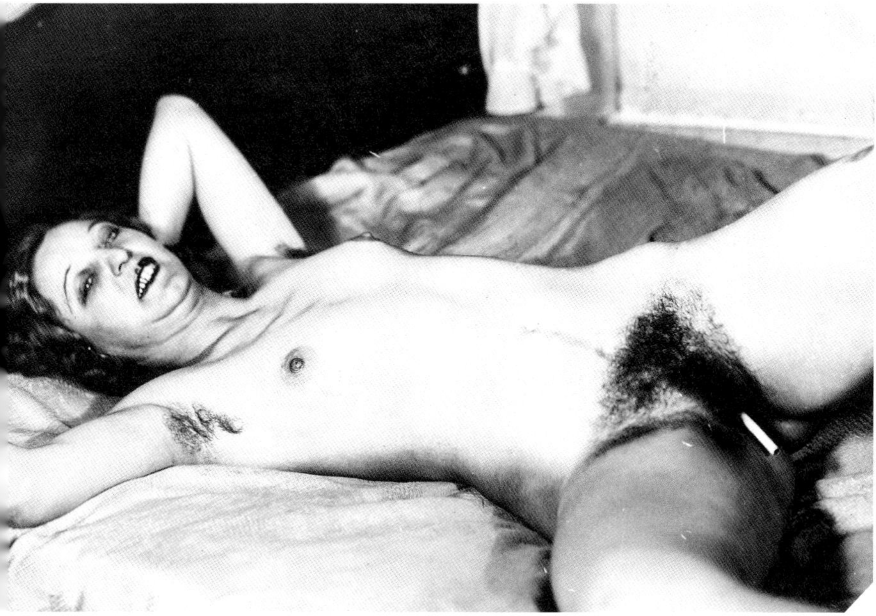

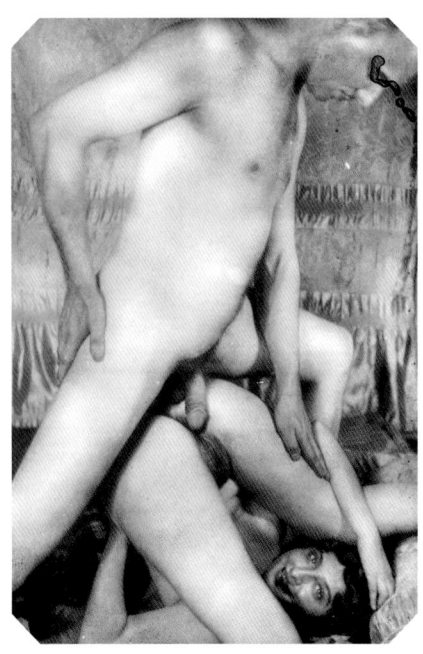
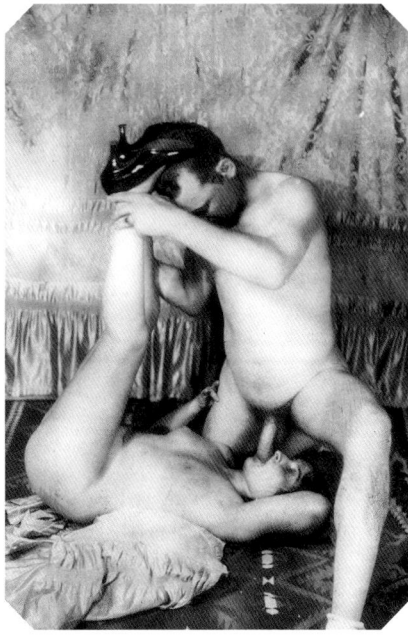
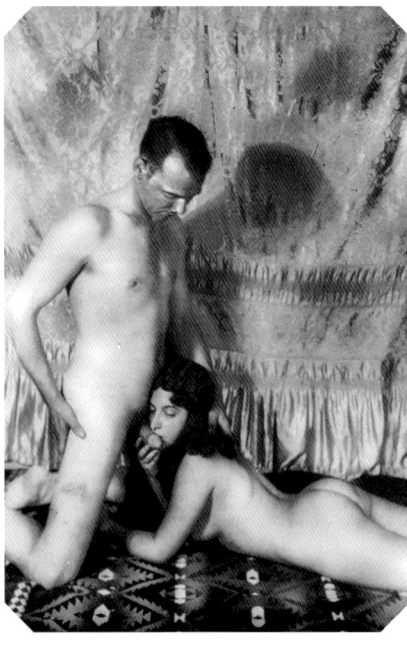
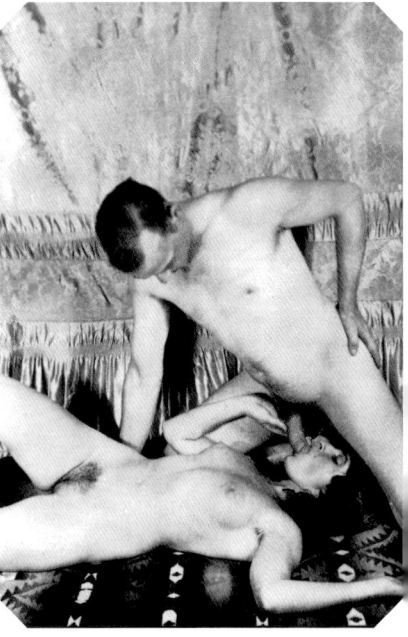

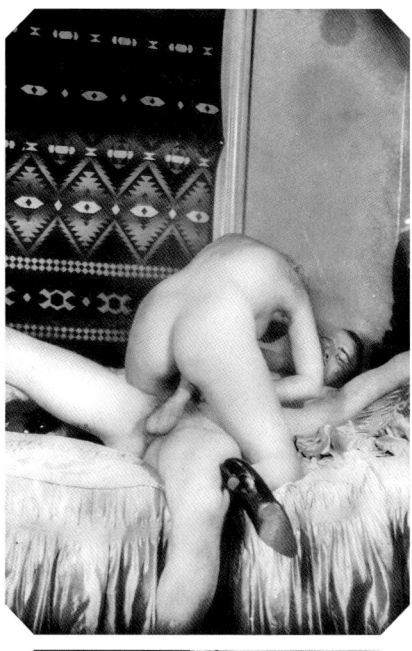
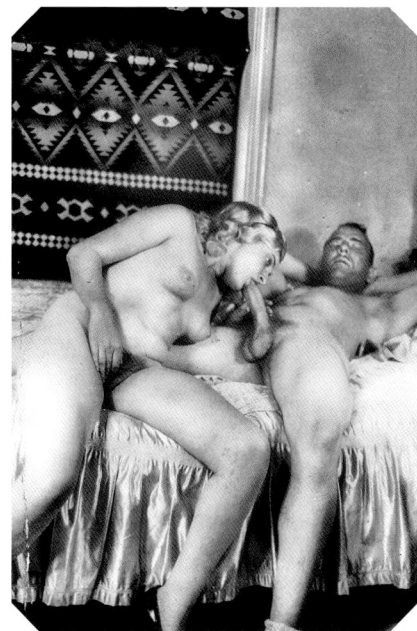
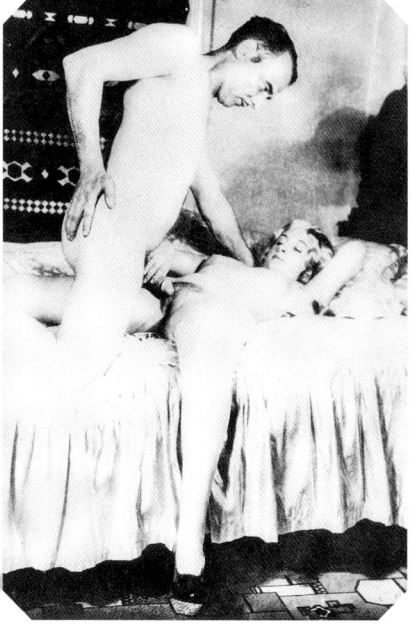
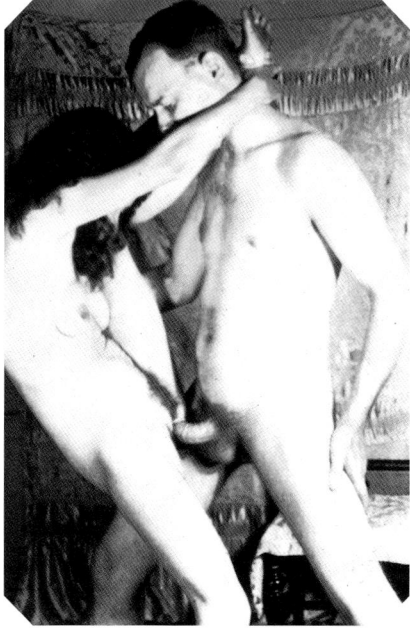

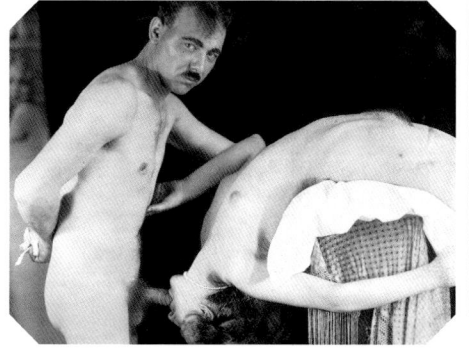

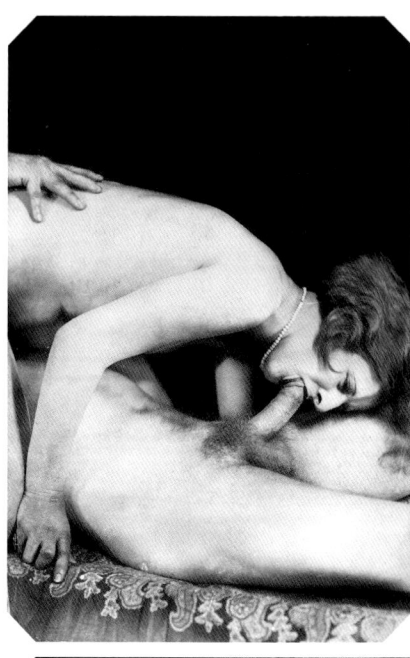

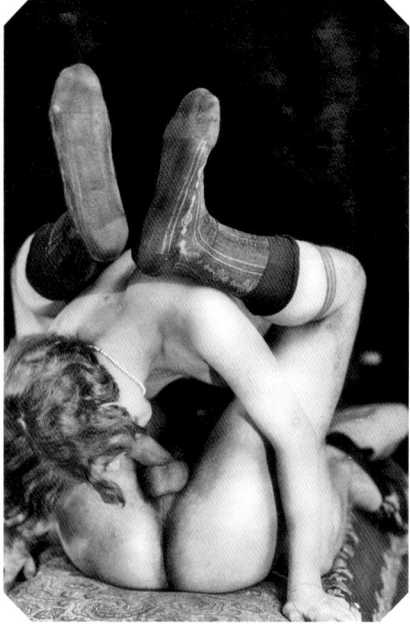

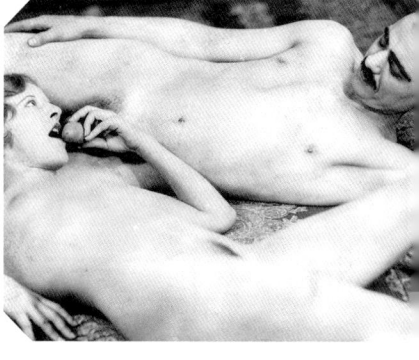

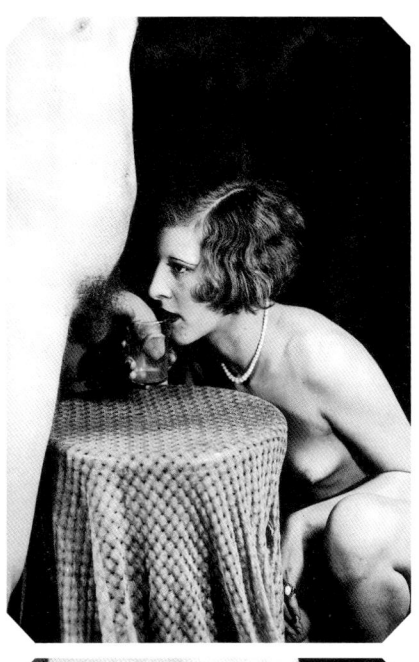
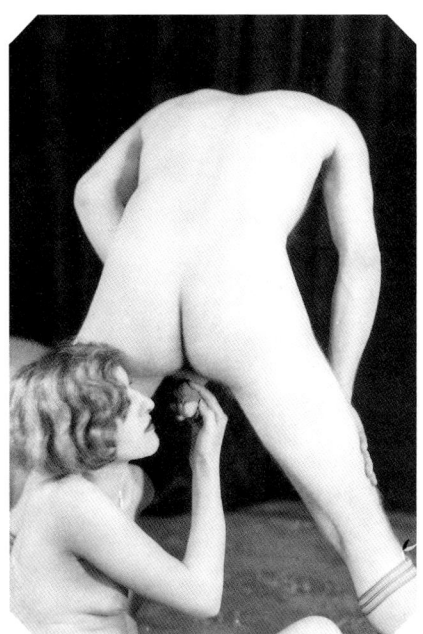
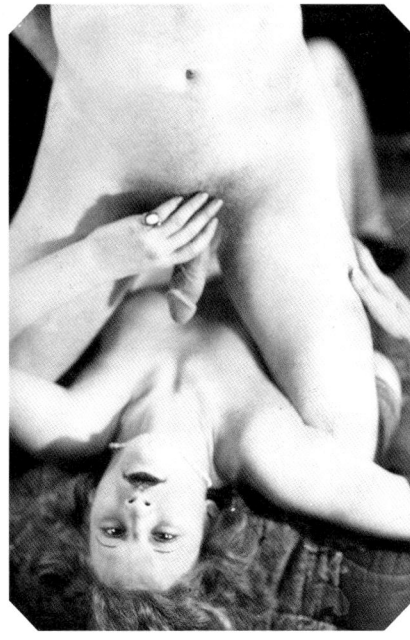
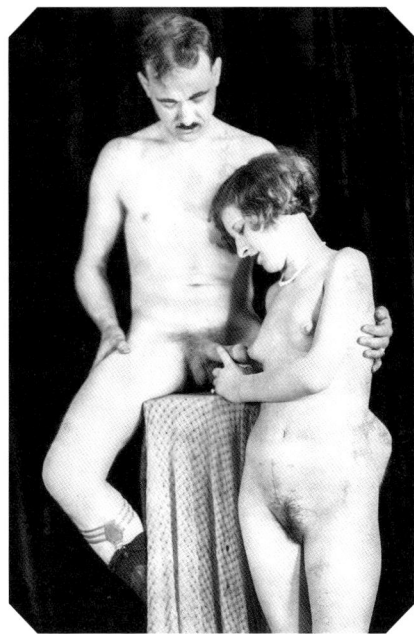

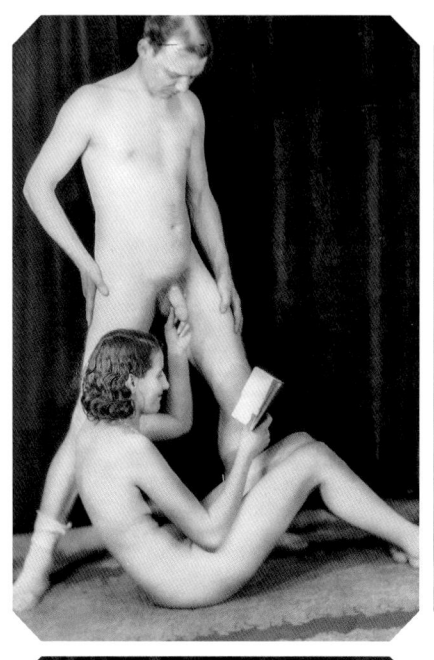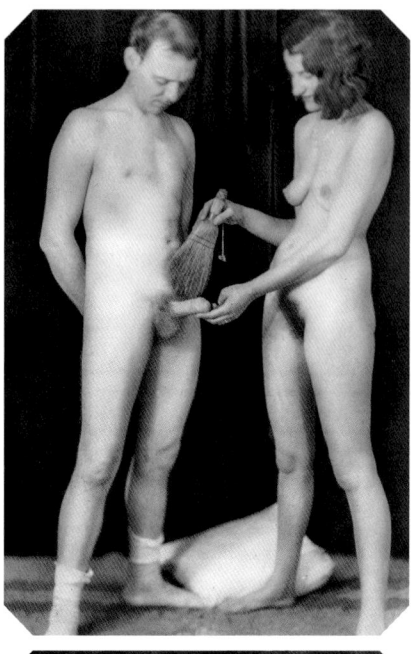

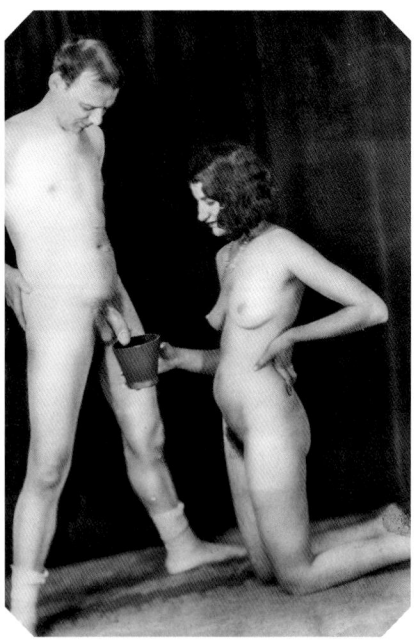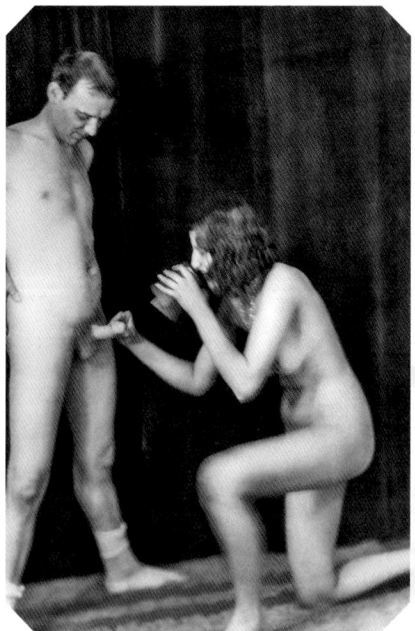

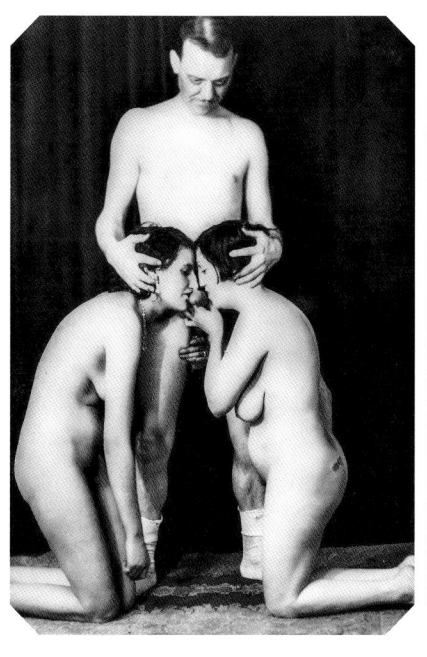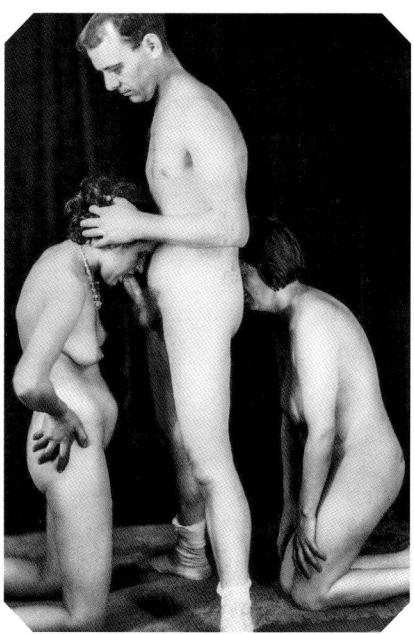

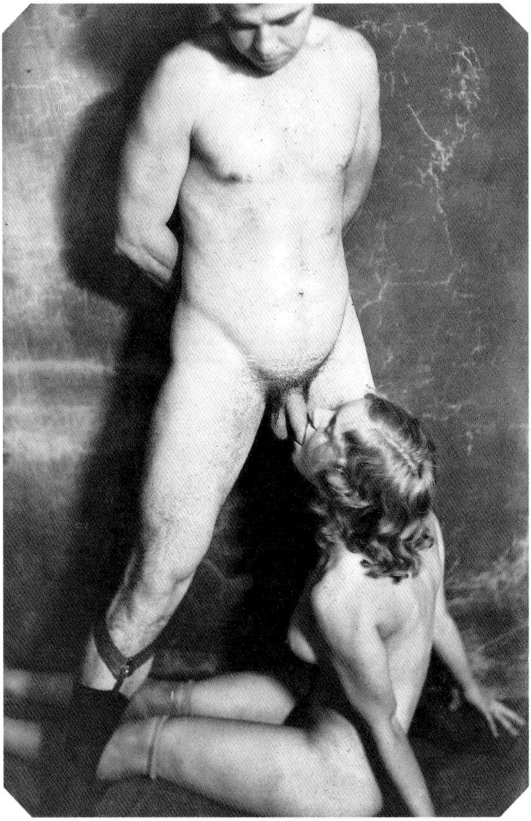

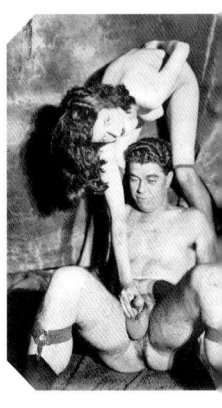

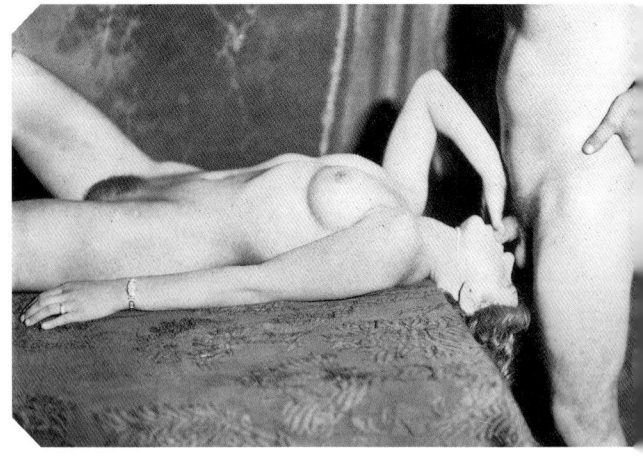

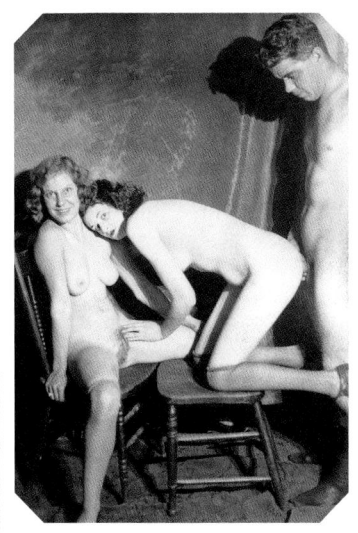

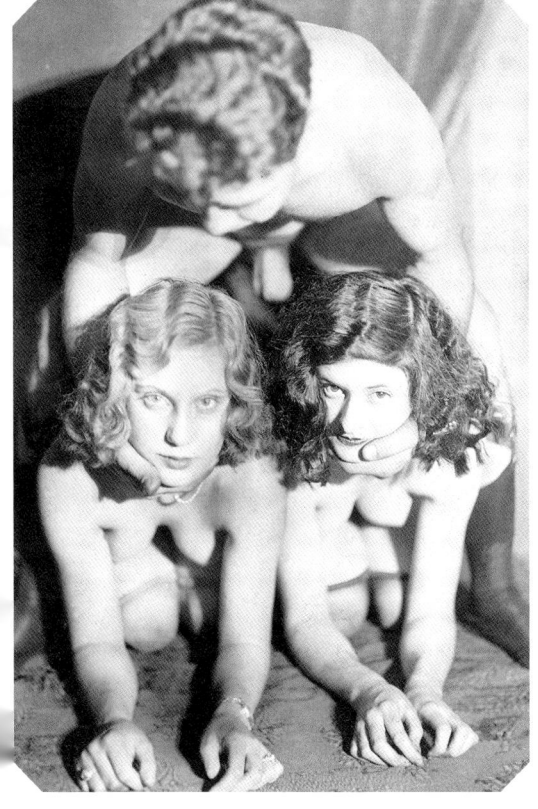

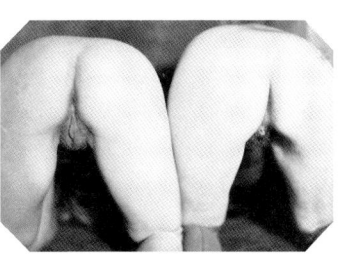

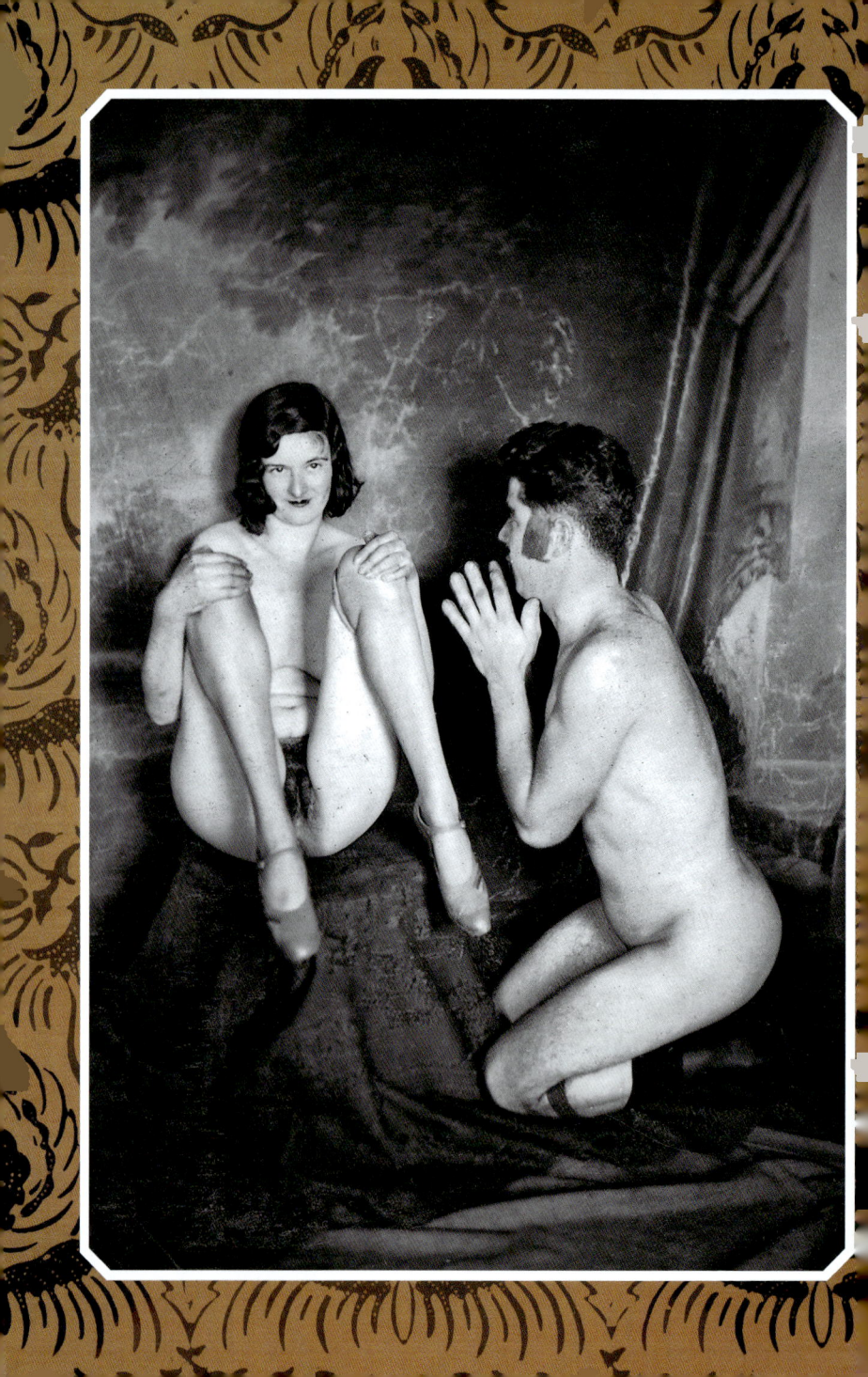

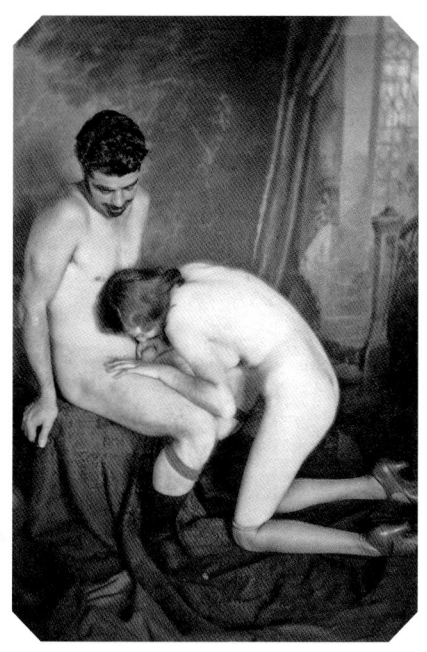
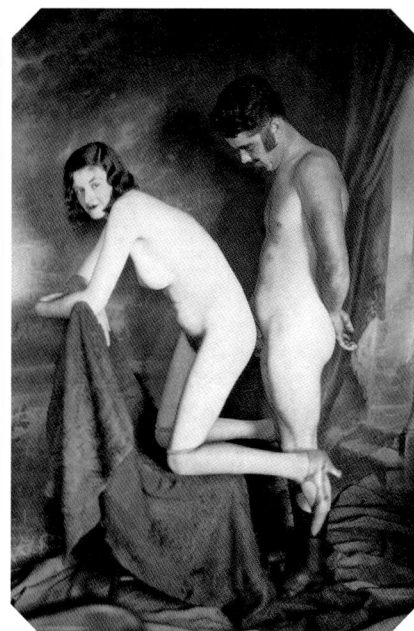

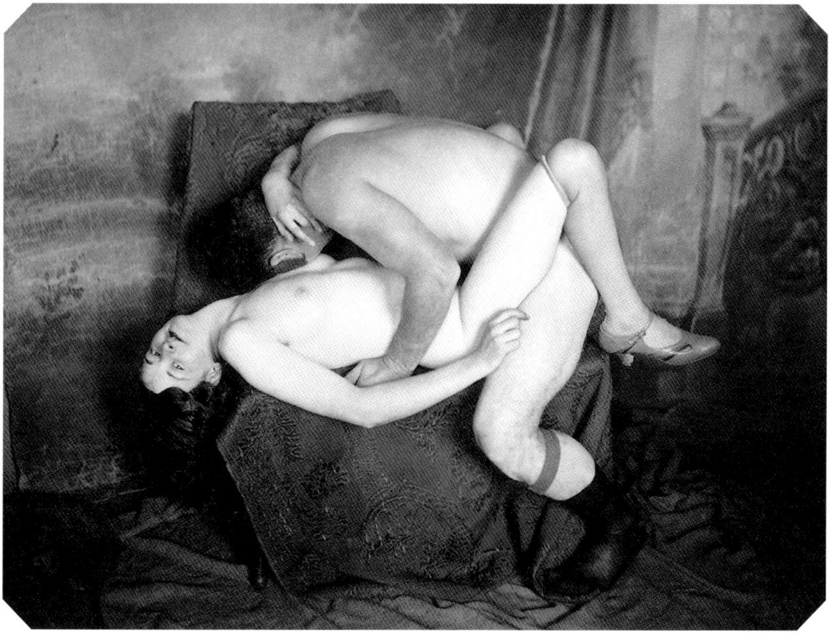

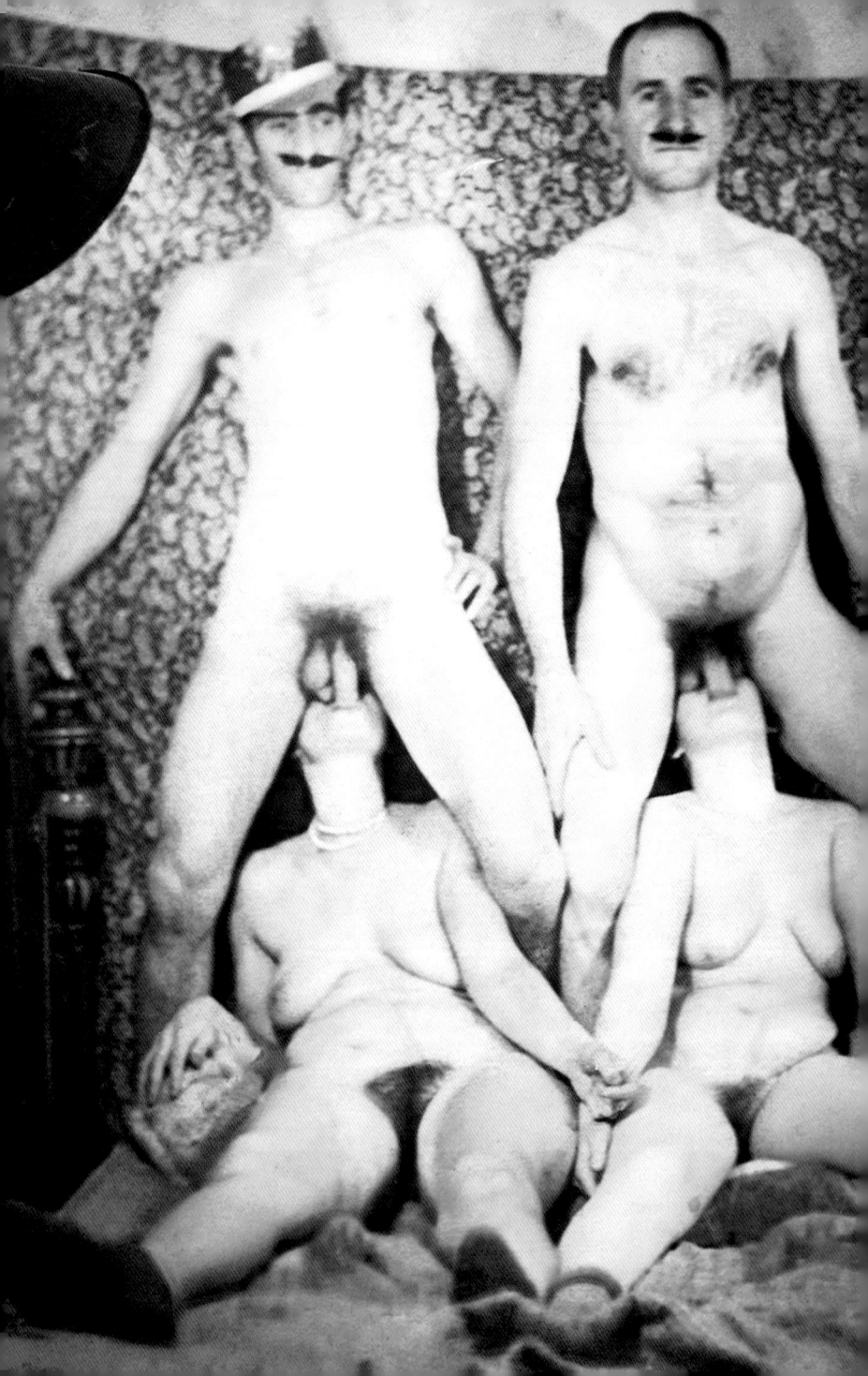

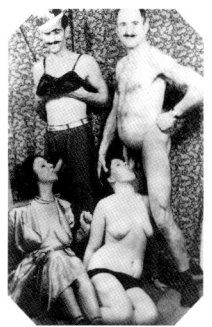

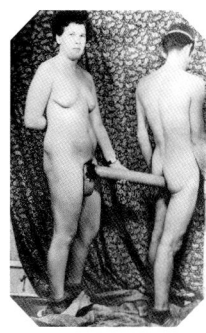

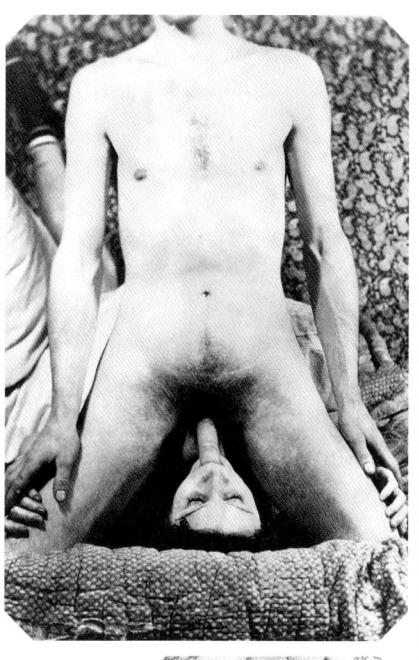

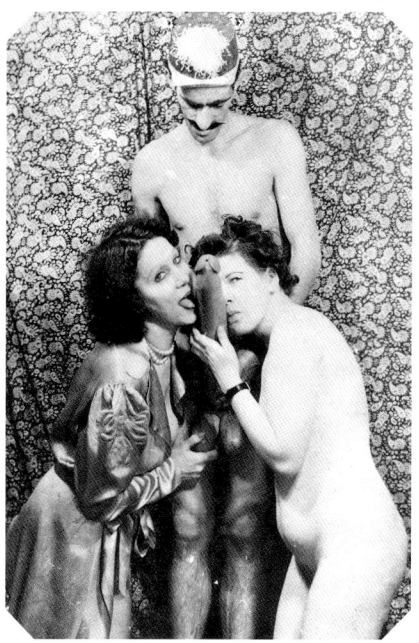

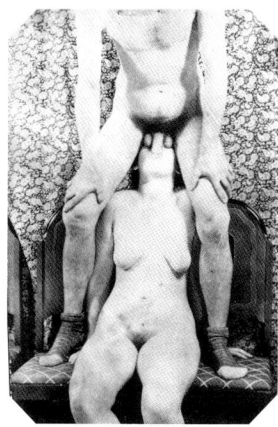

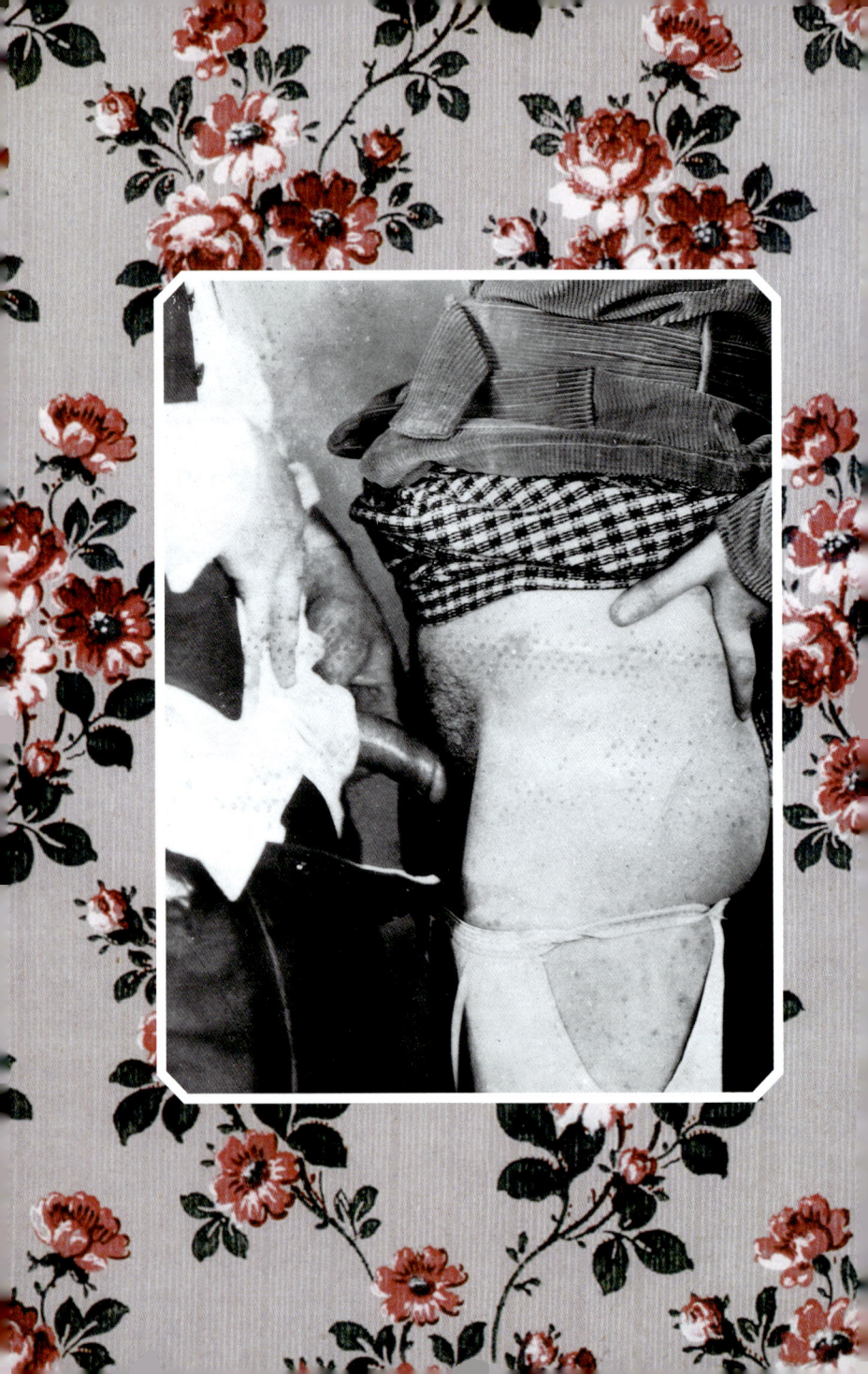

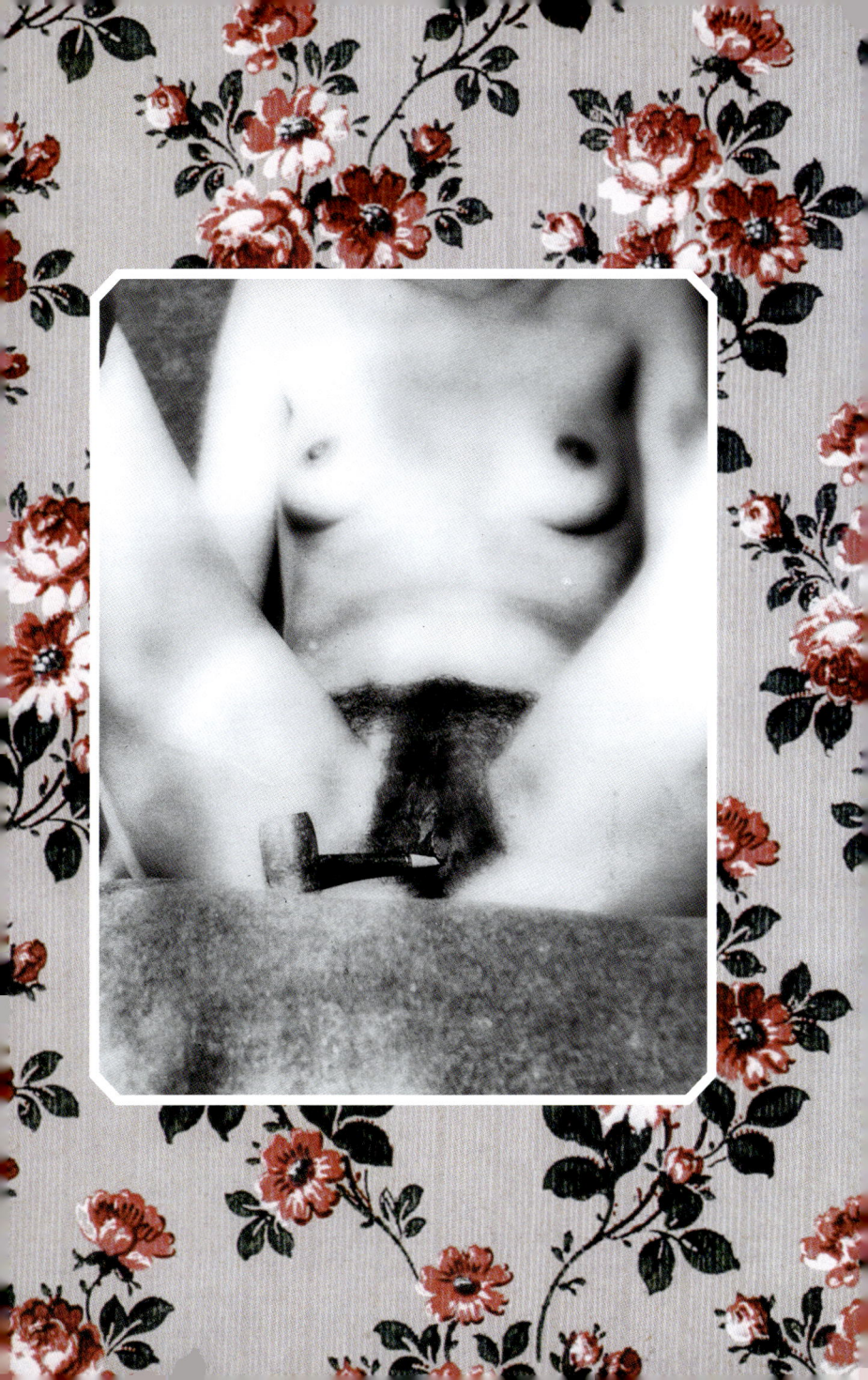

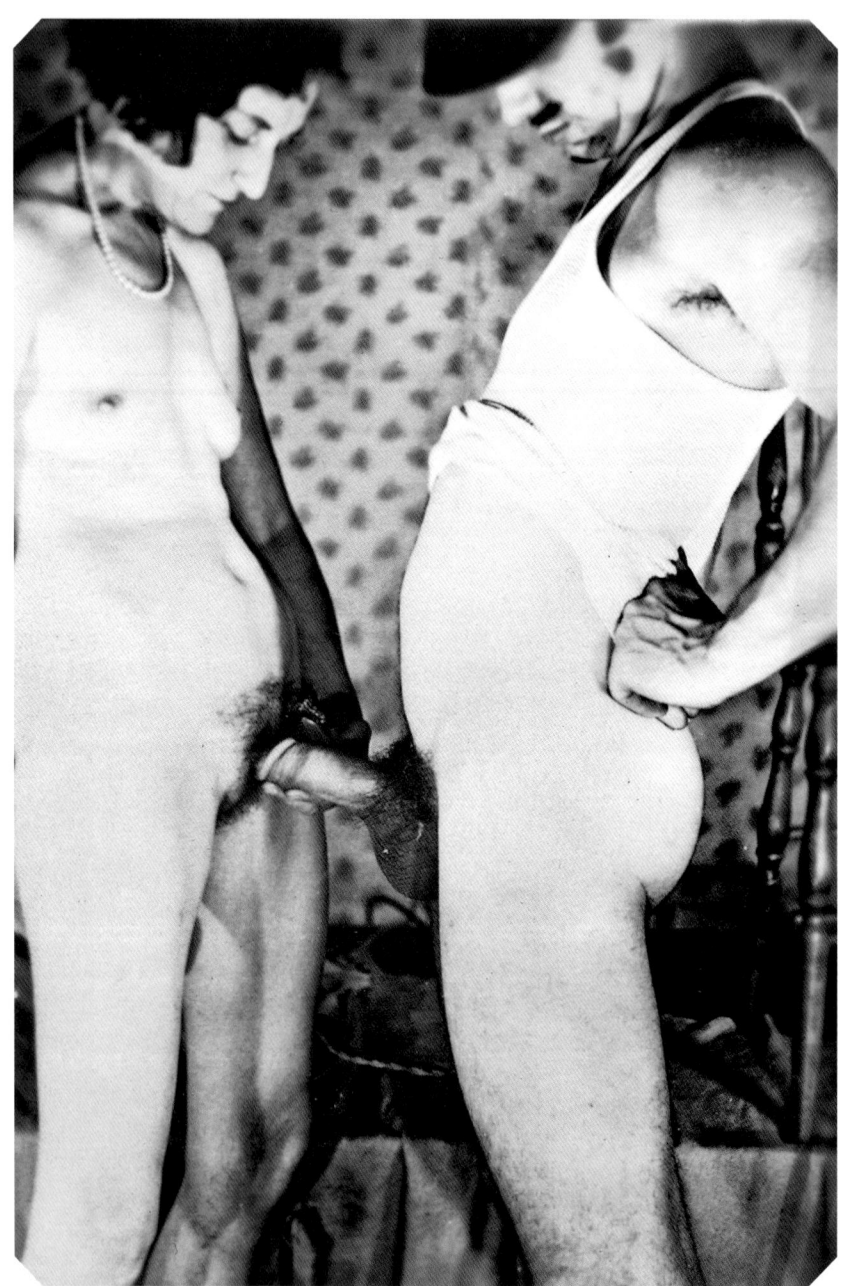

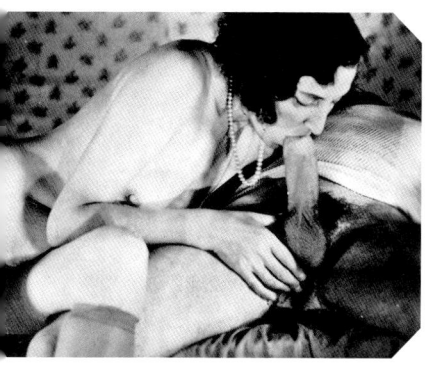

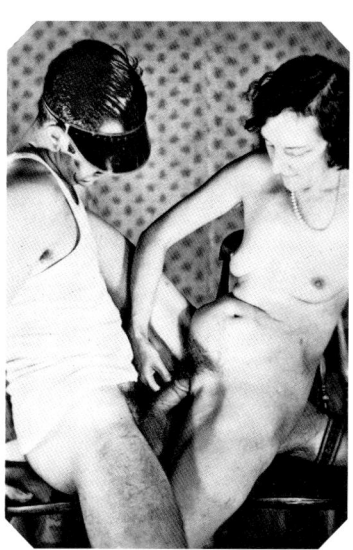

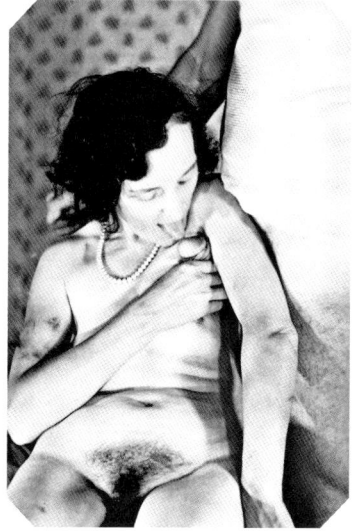

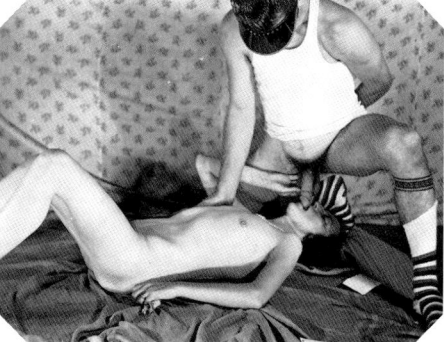

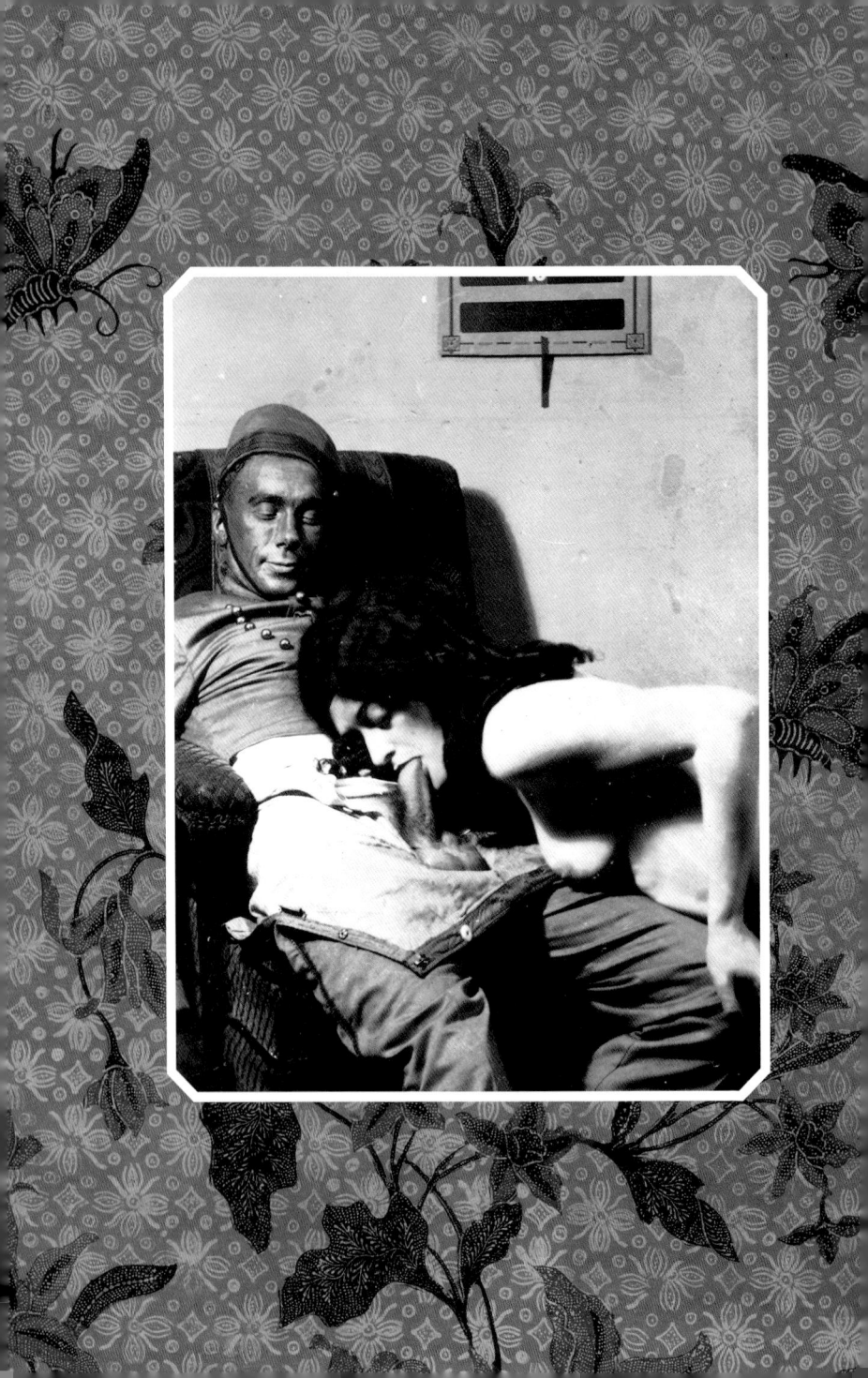

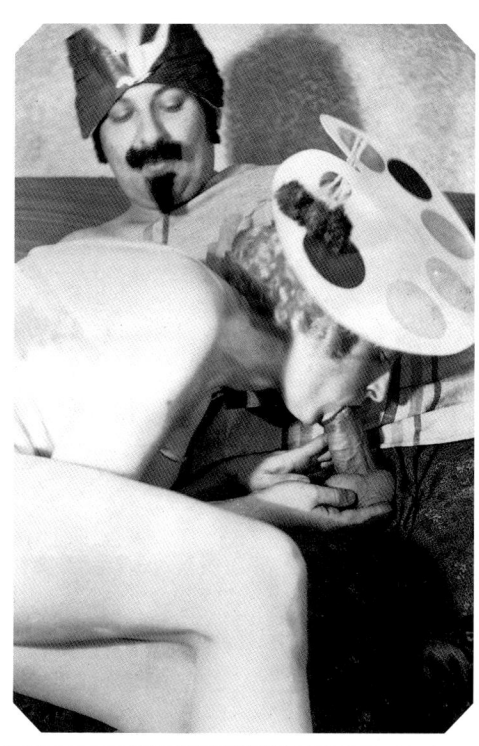

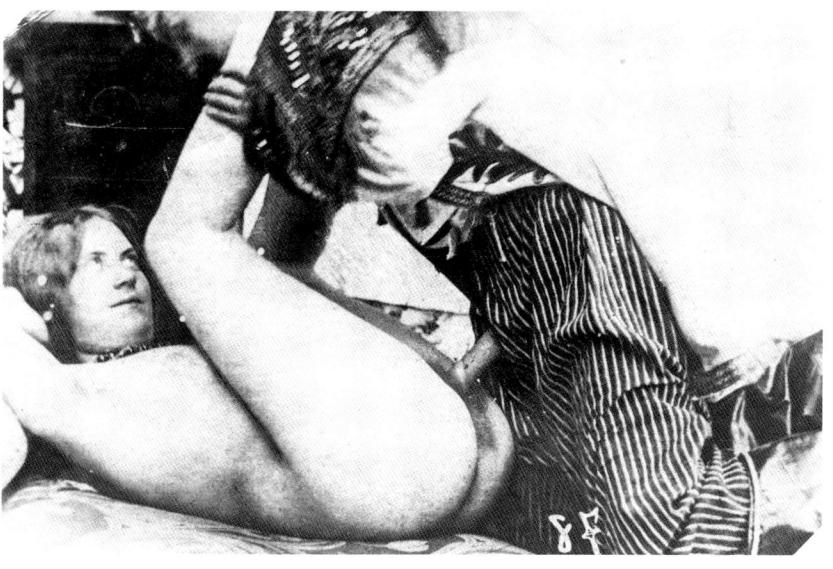

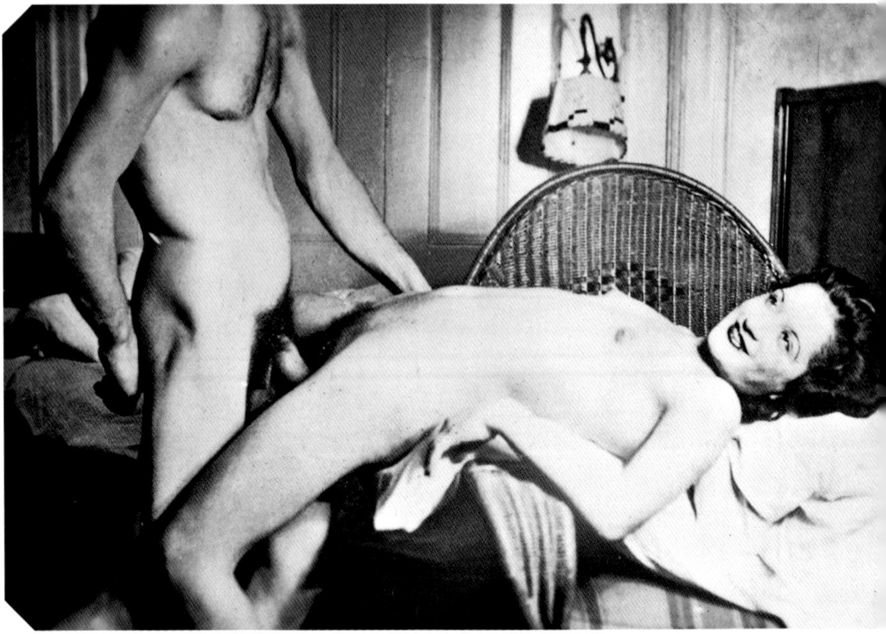

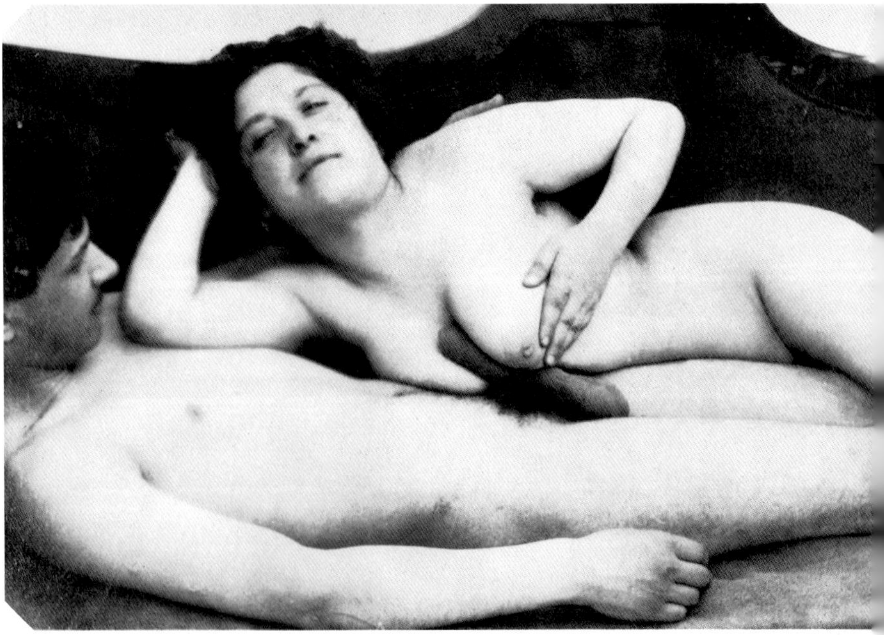

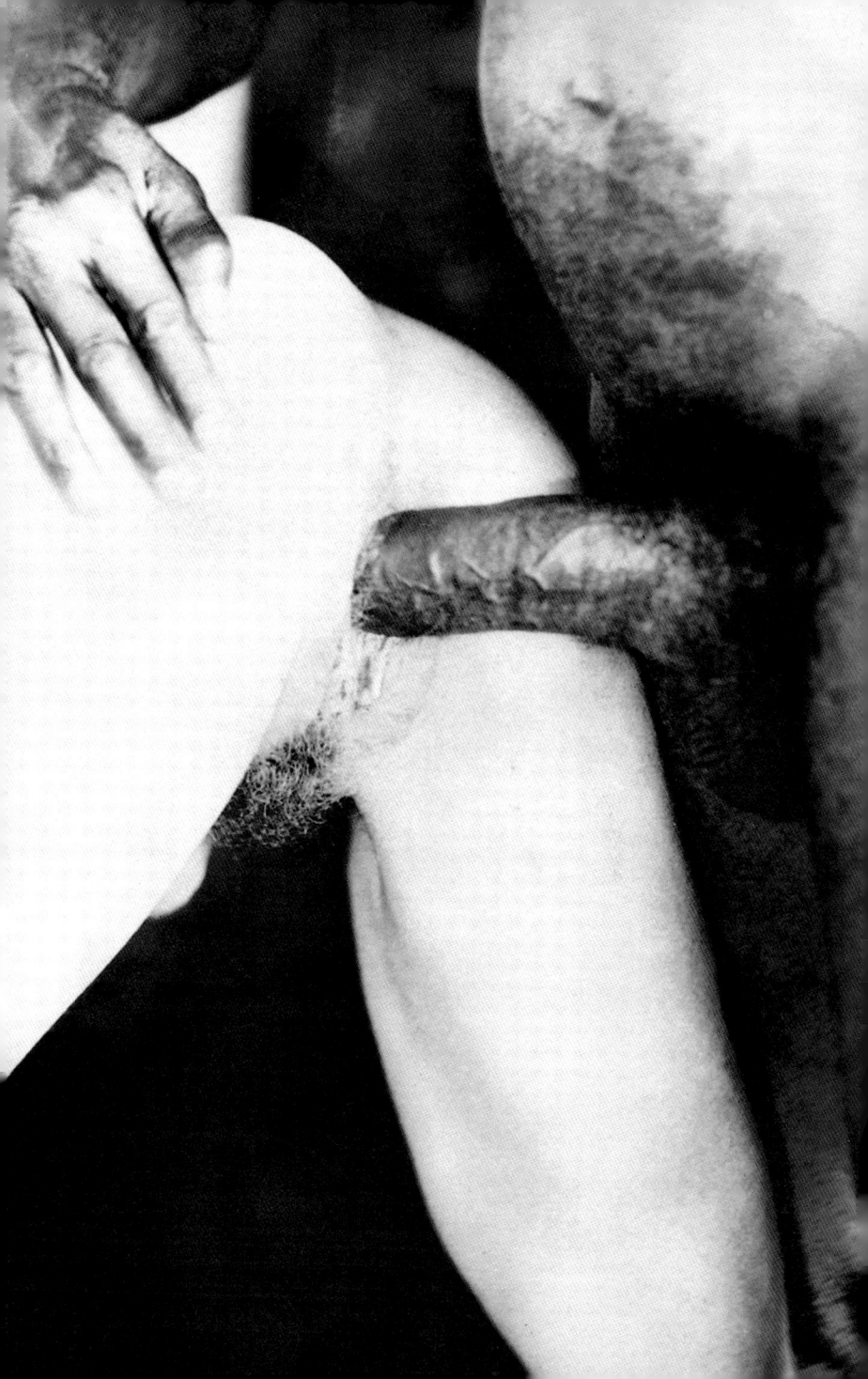

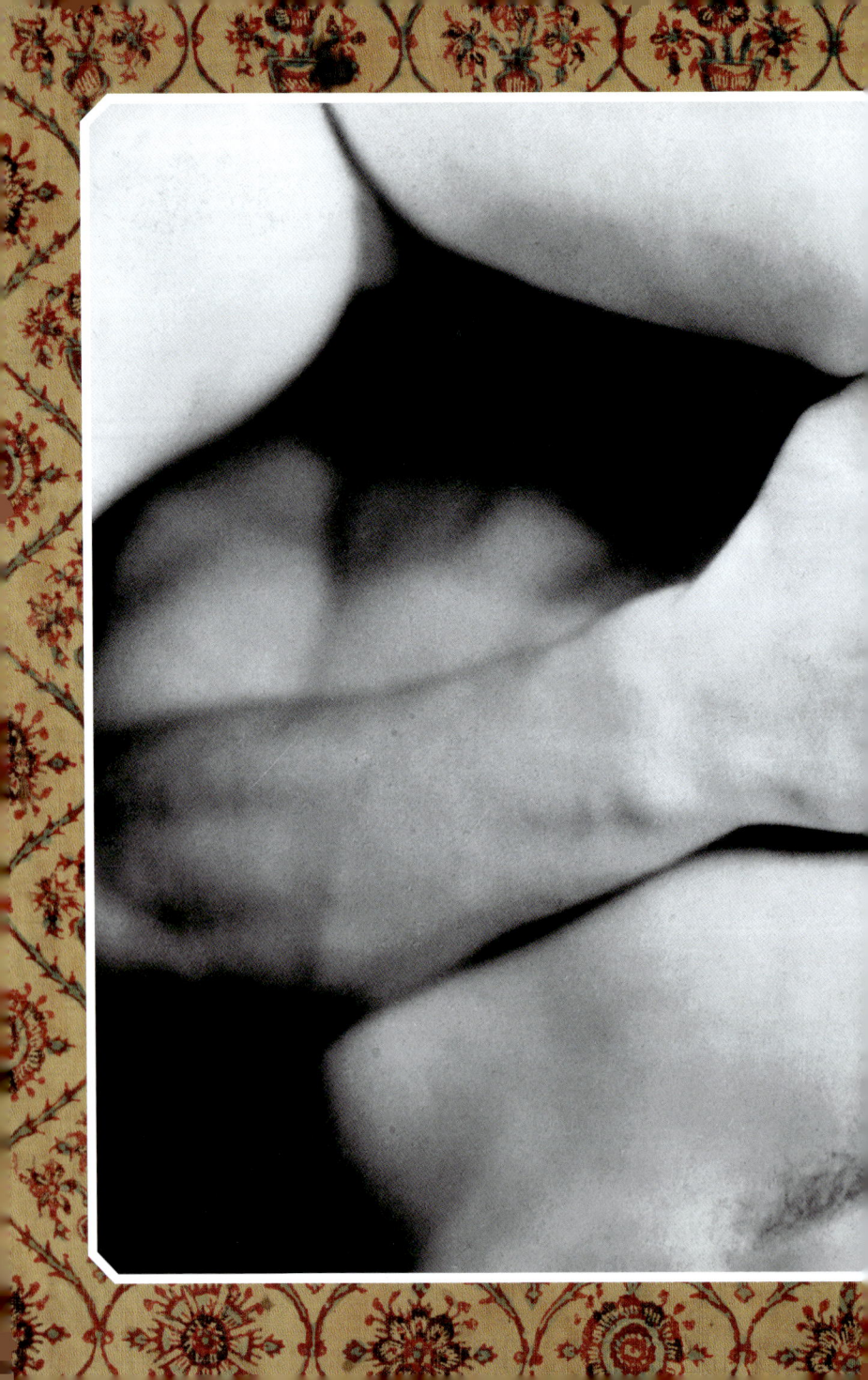

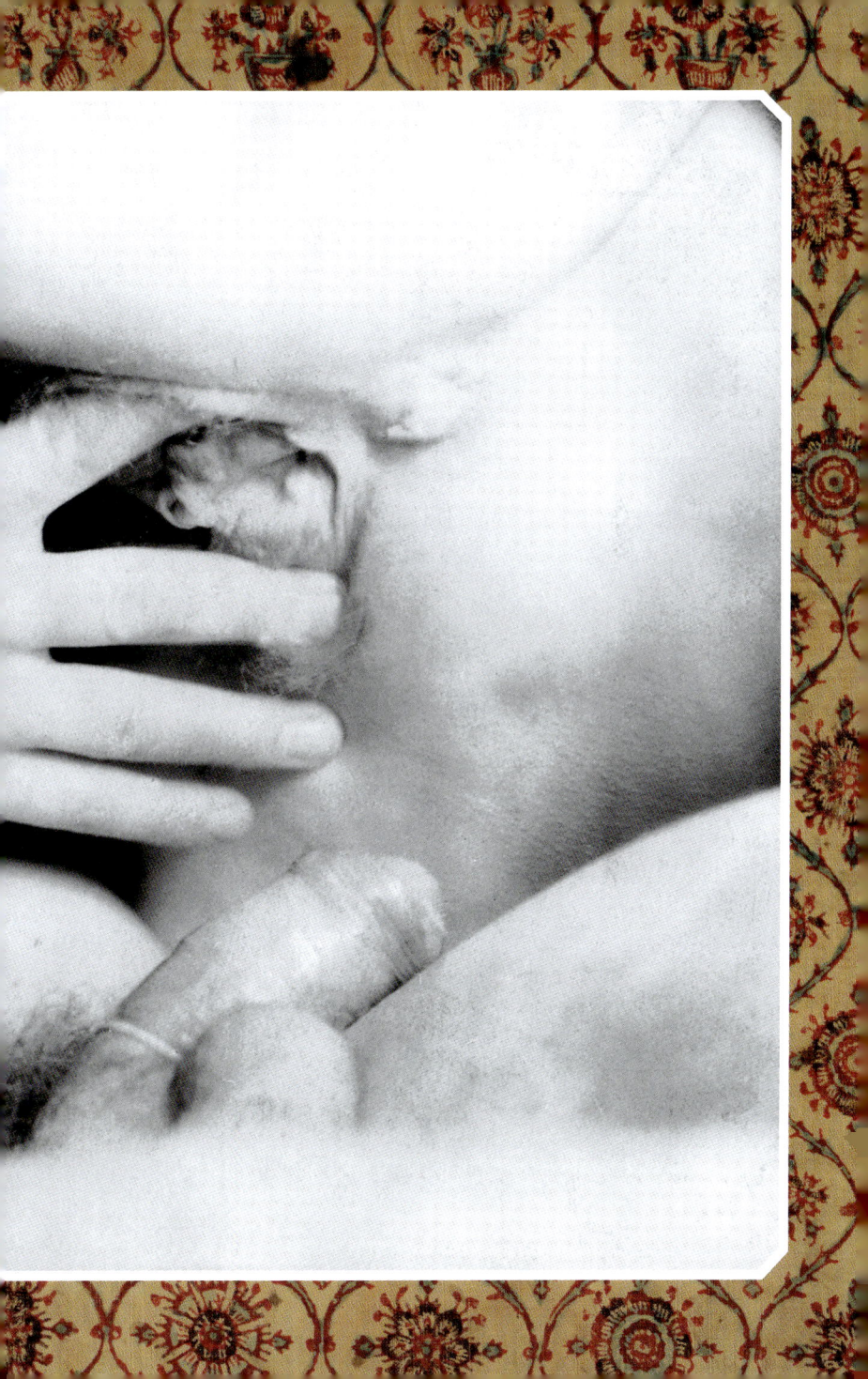

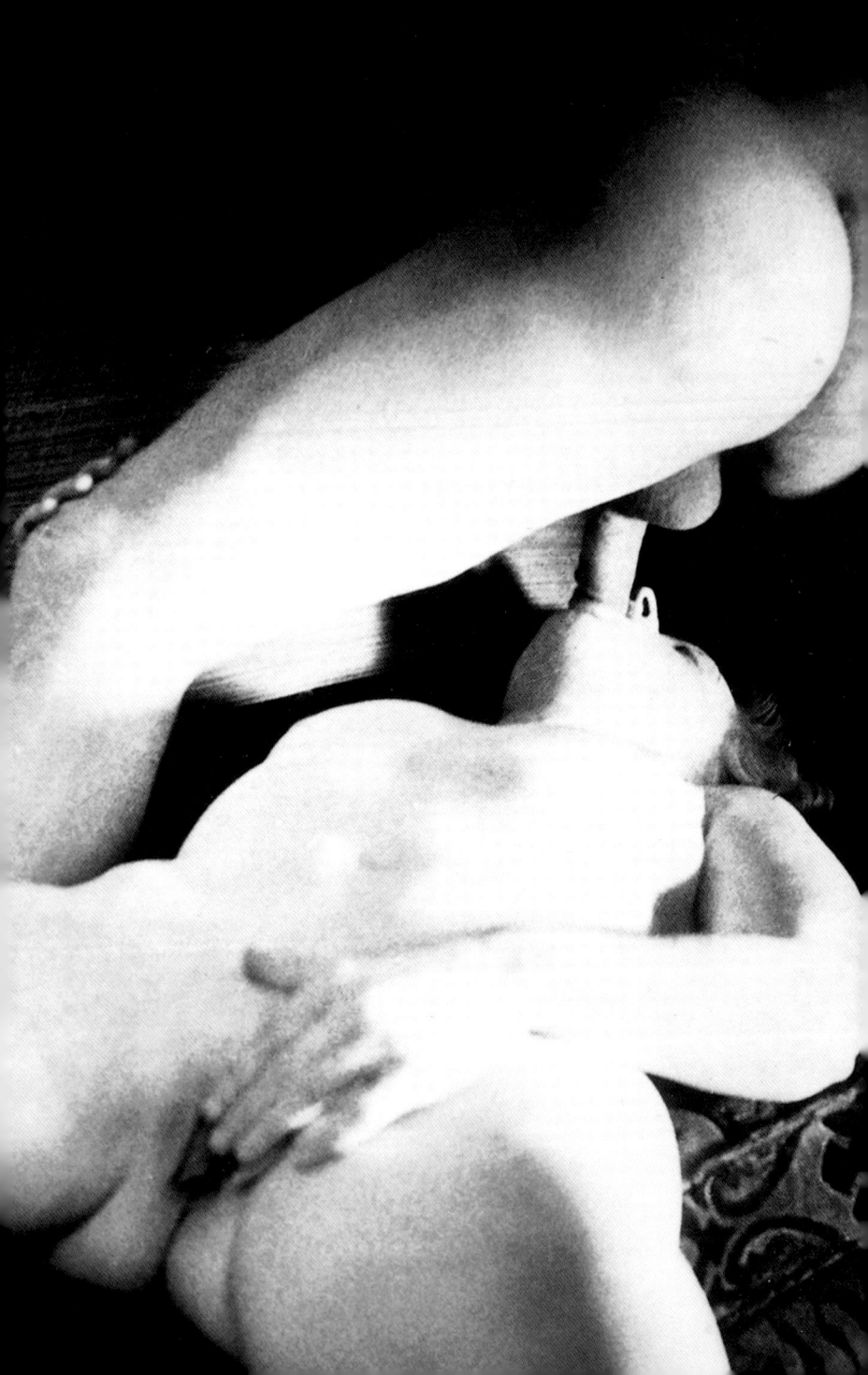

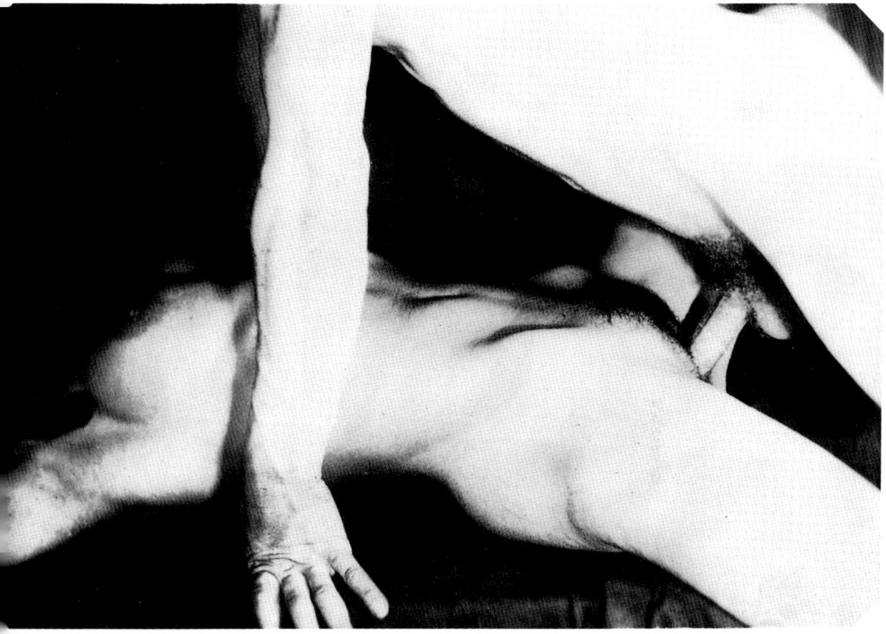

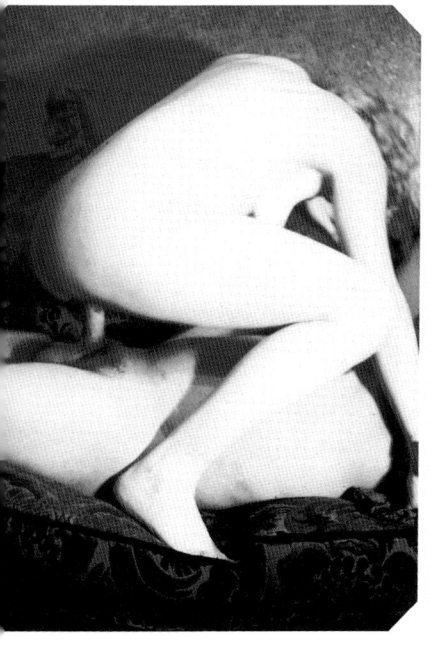
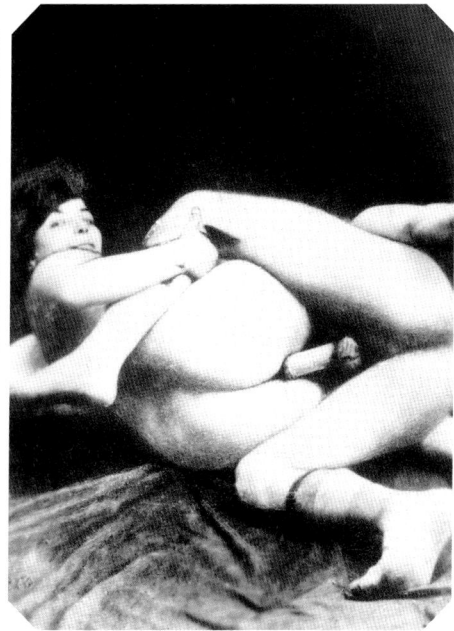

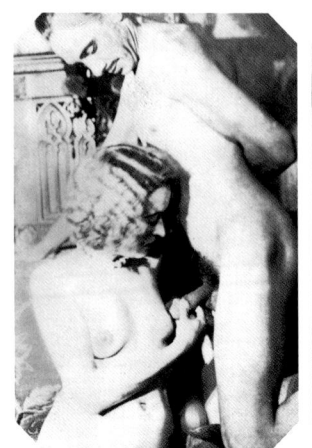
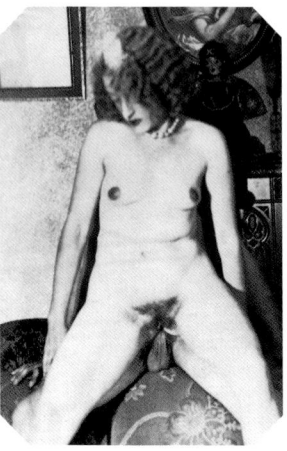
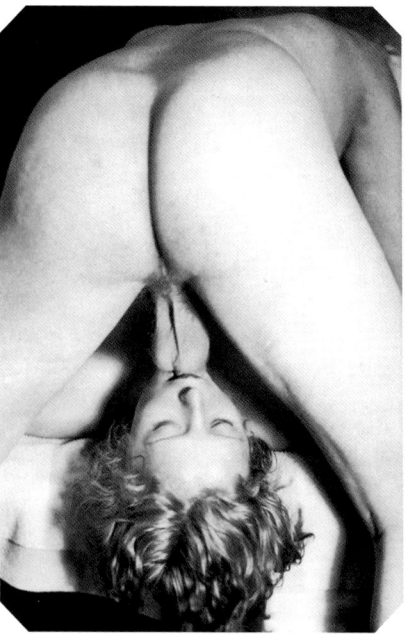
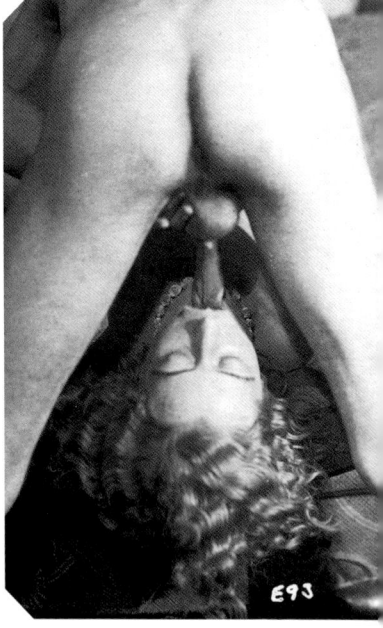

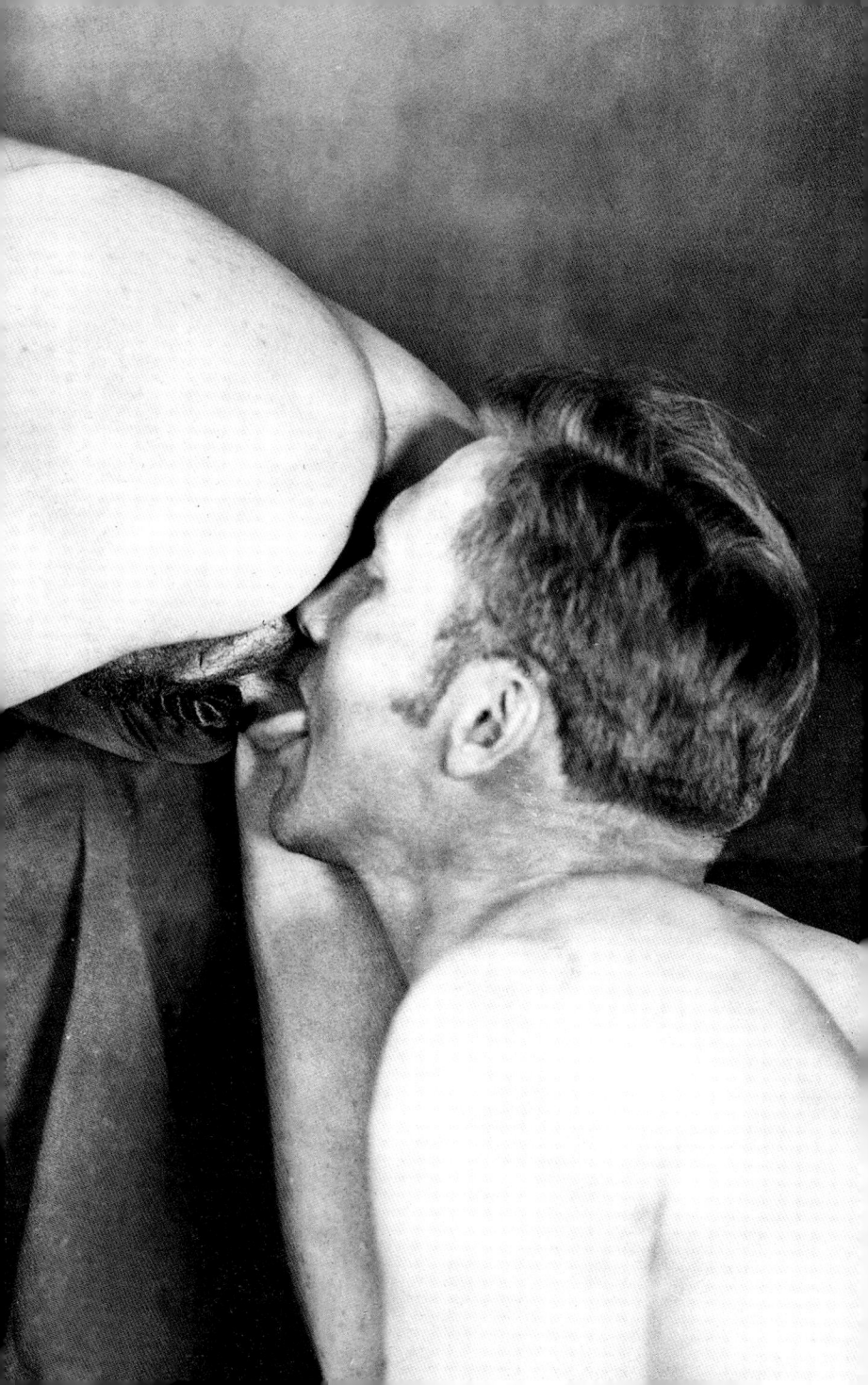

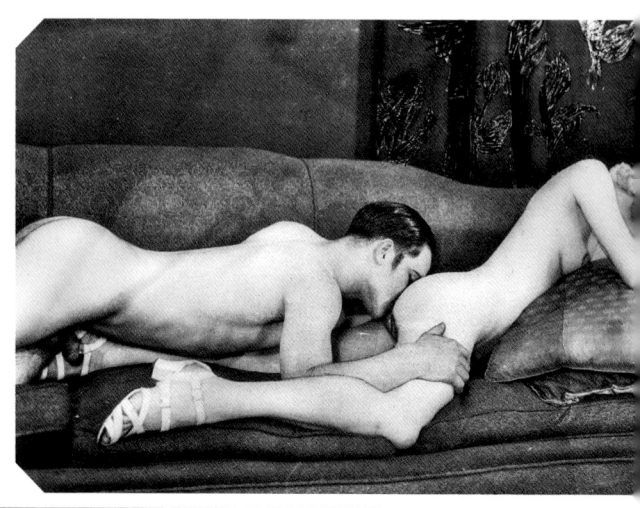

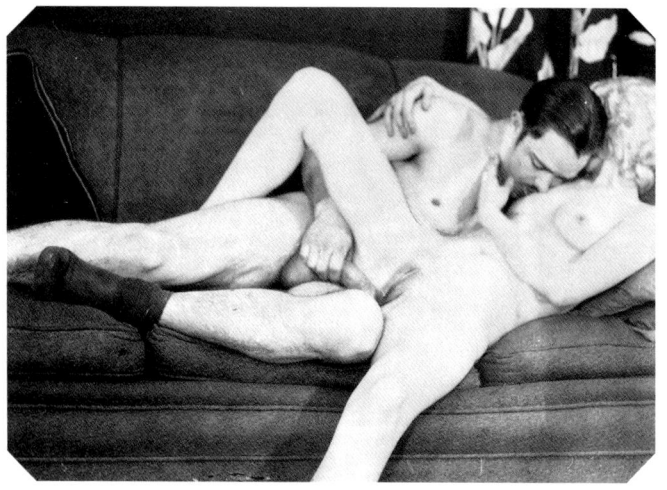

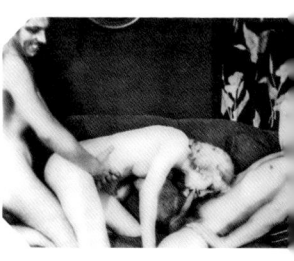

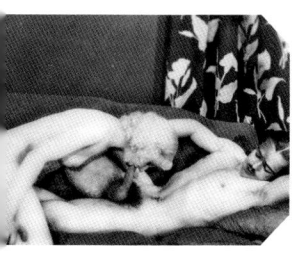

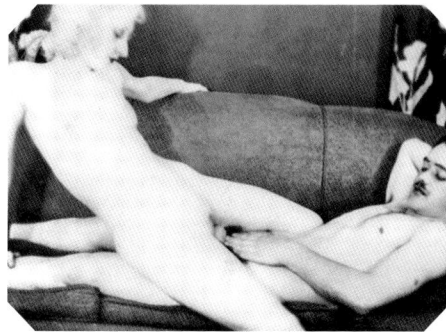

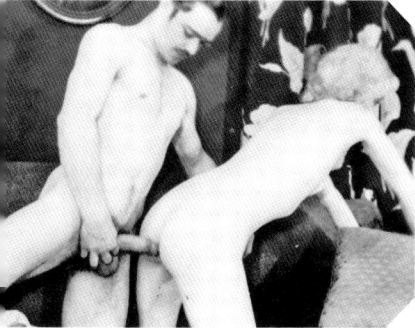

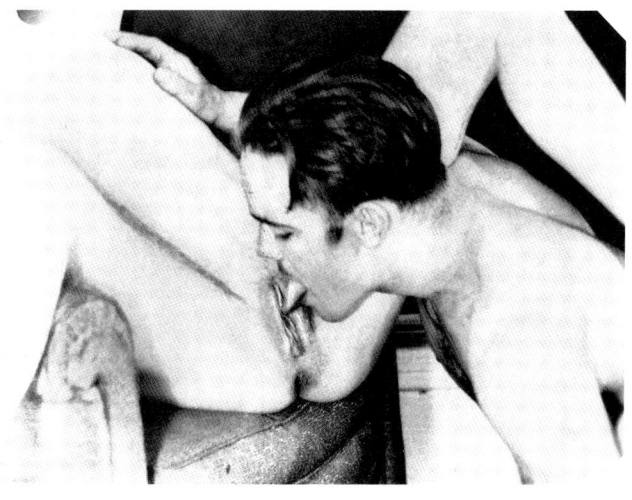

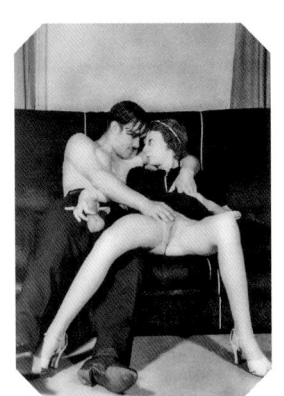

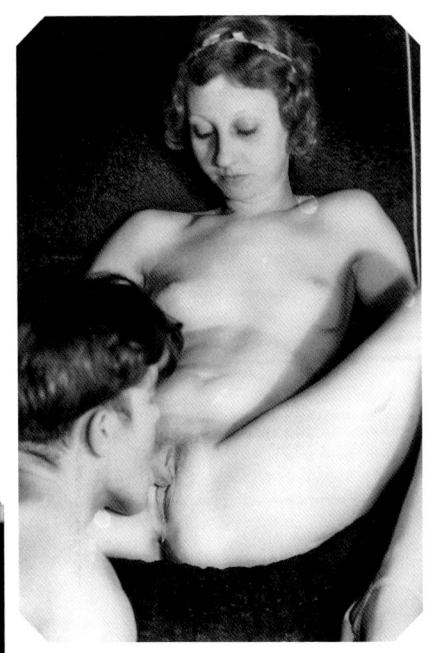

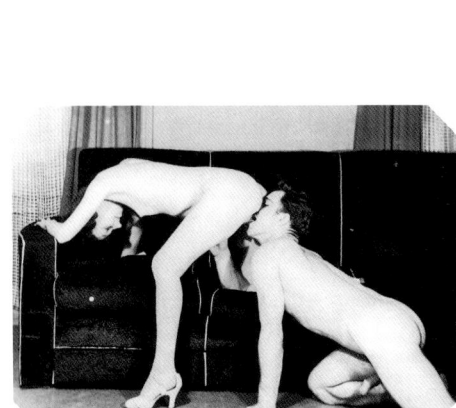

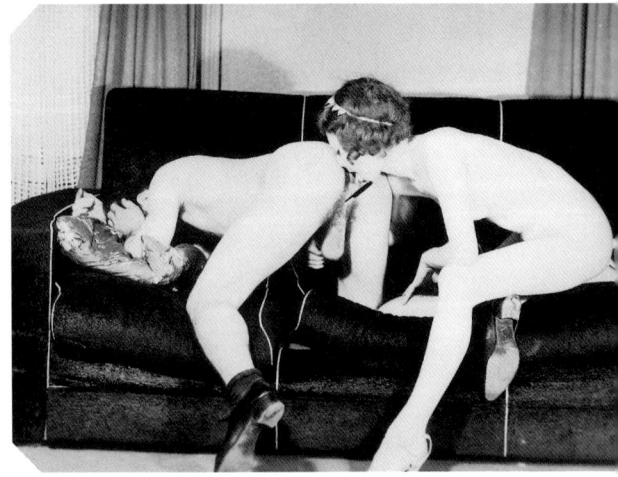

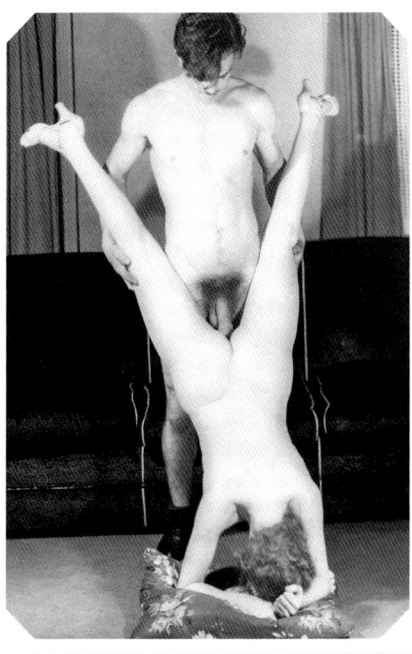
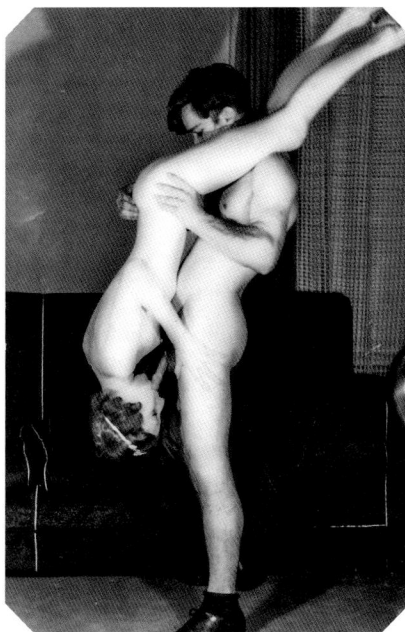

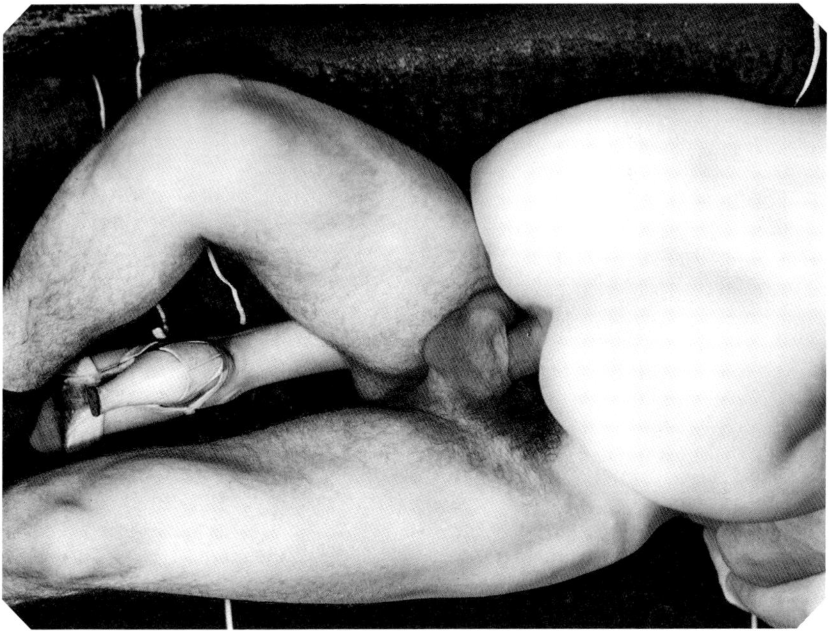

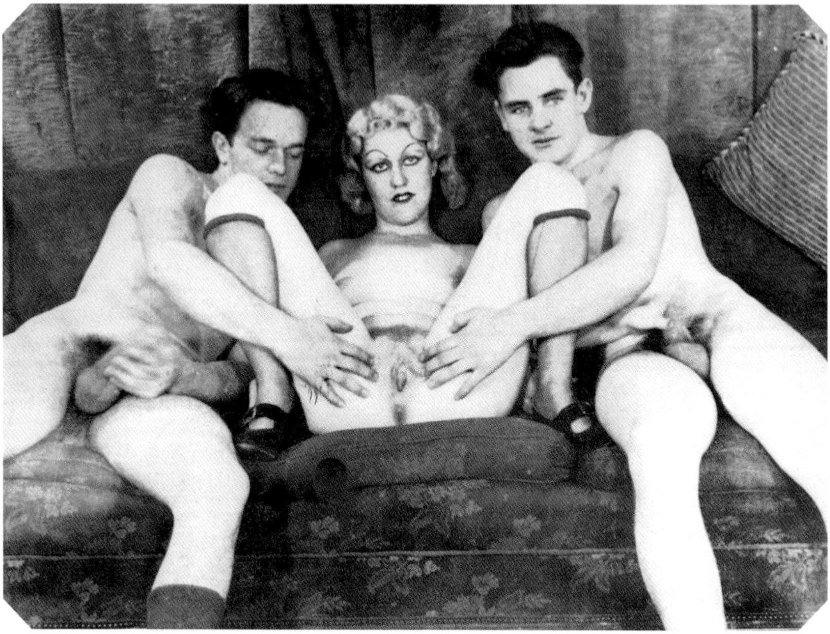

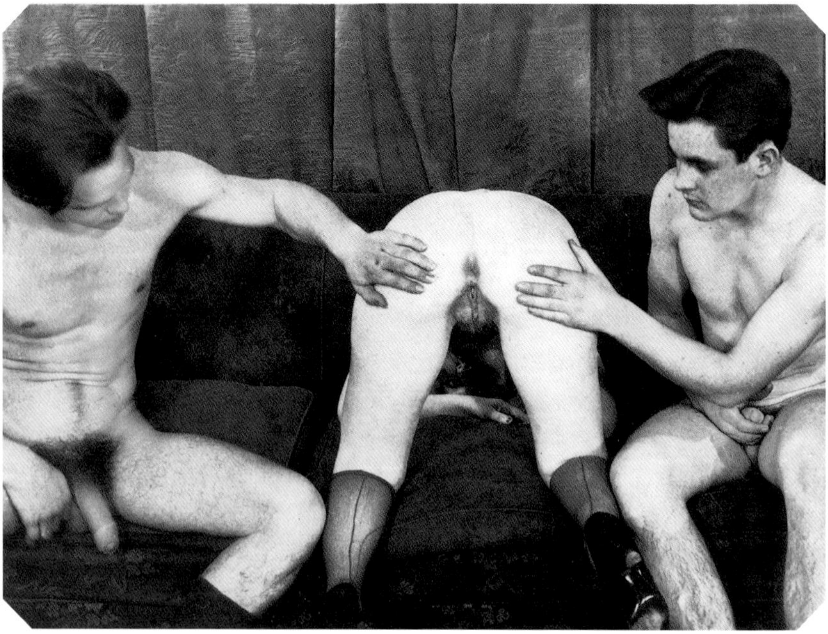

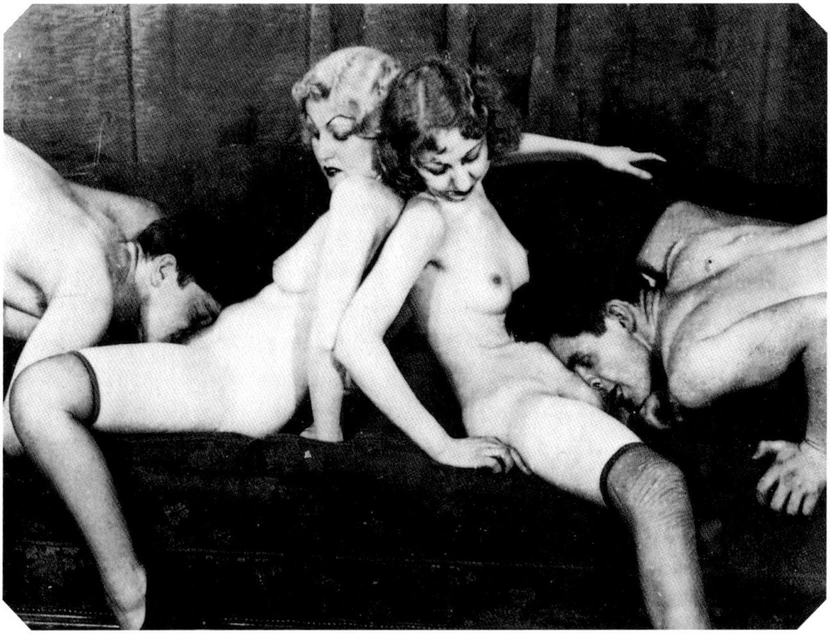

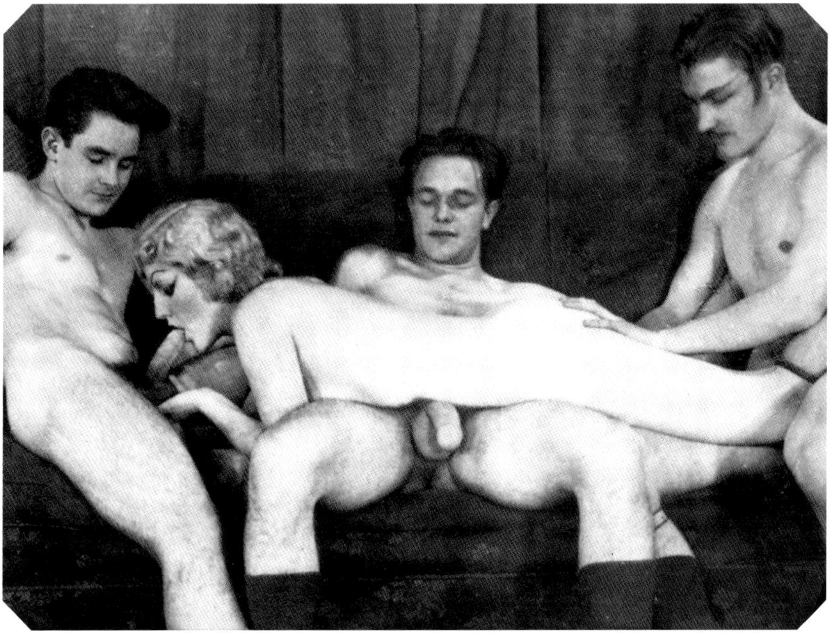

347

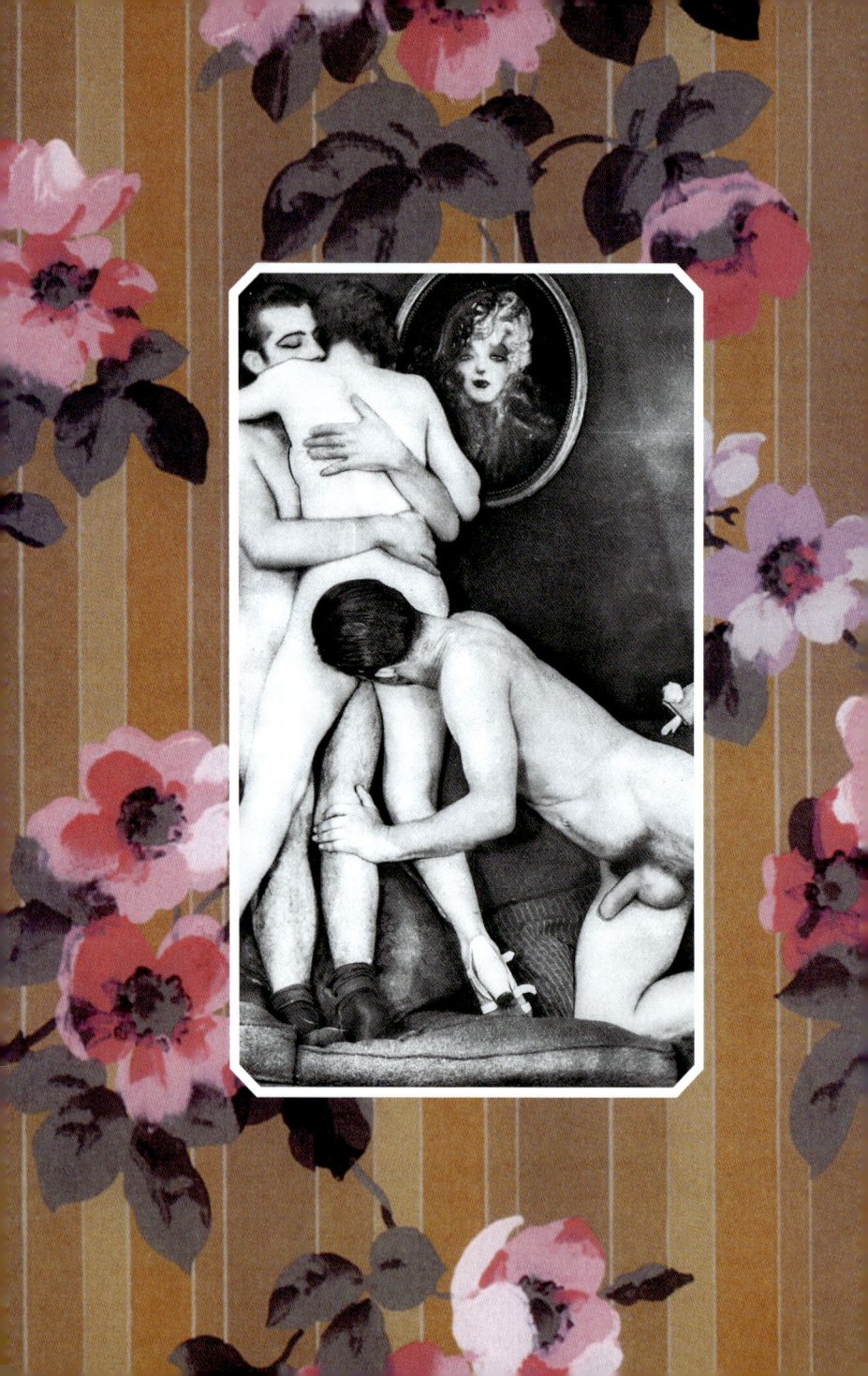

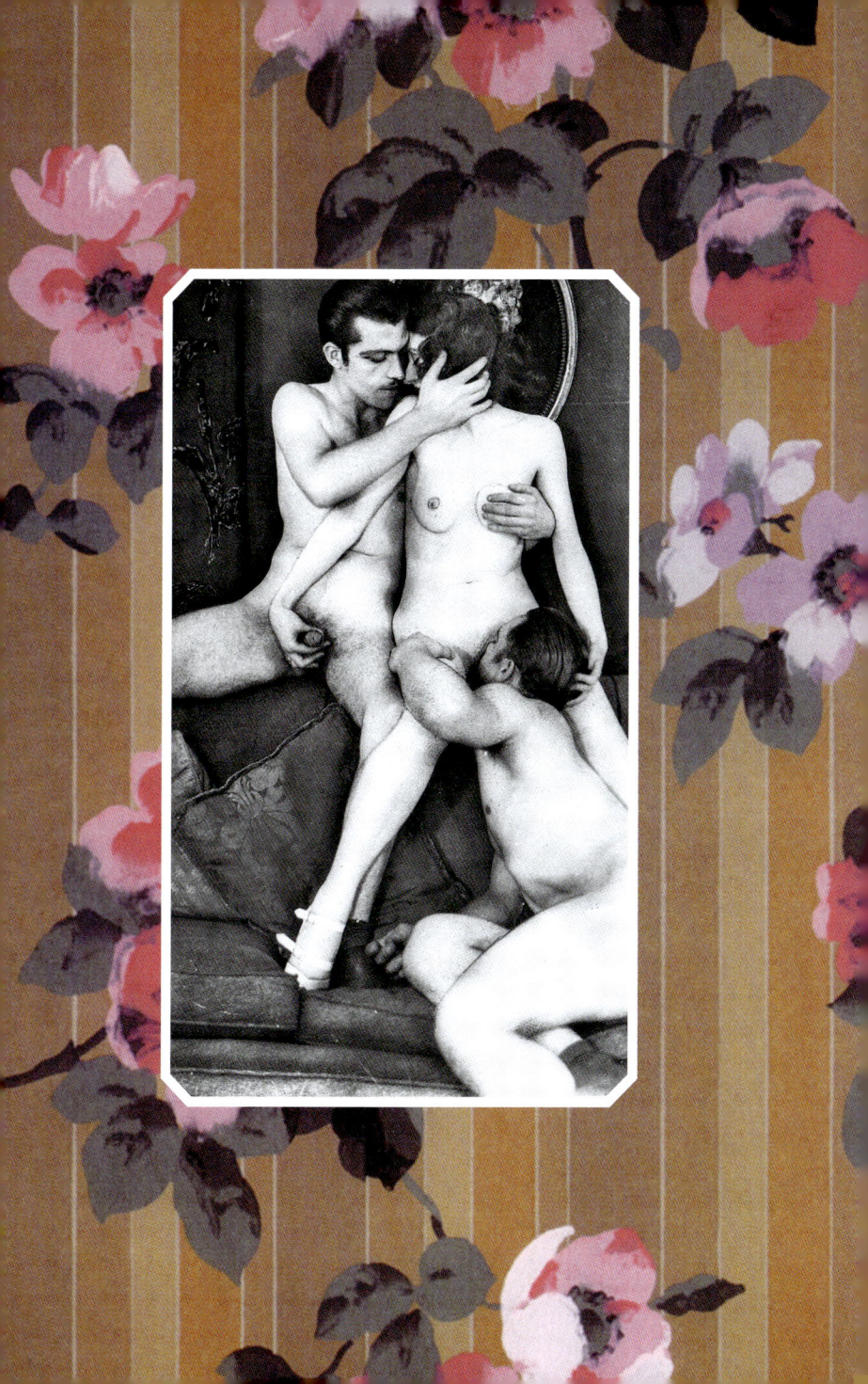

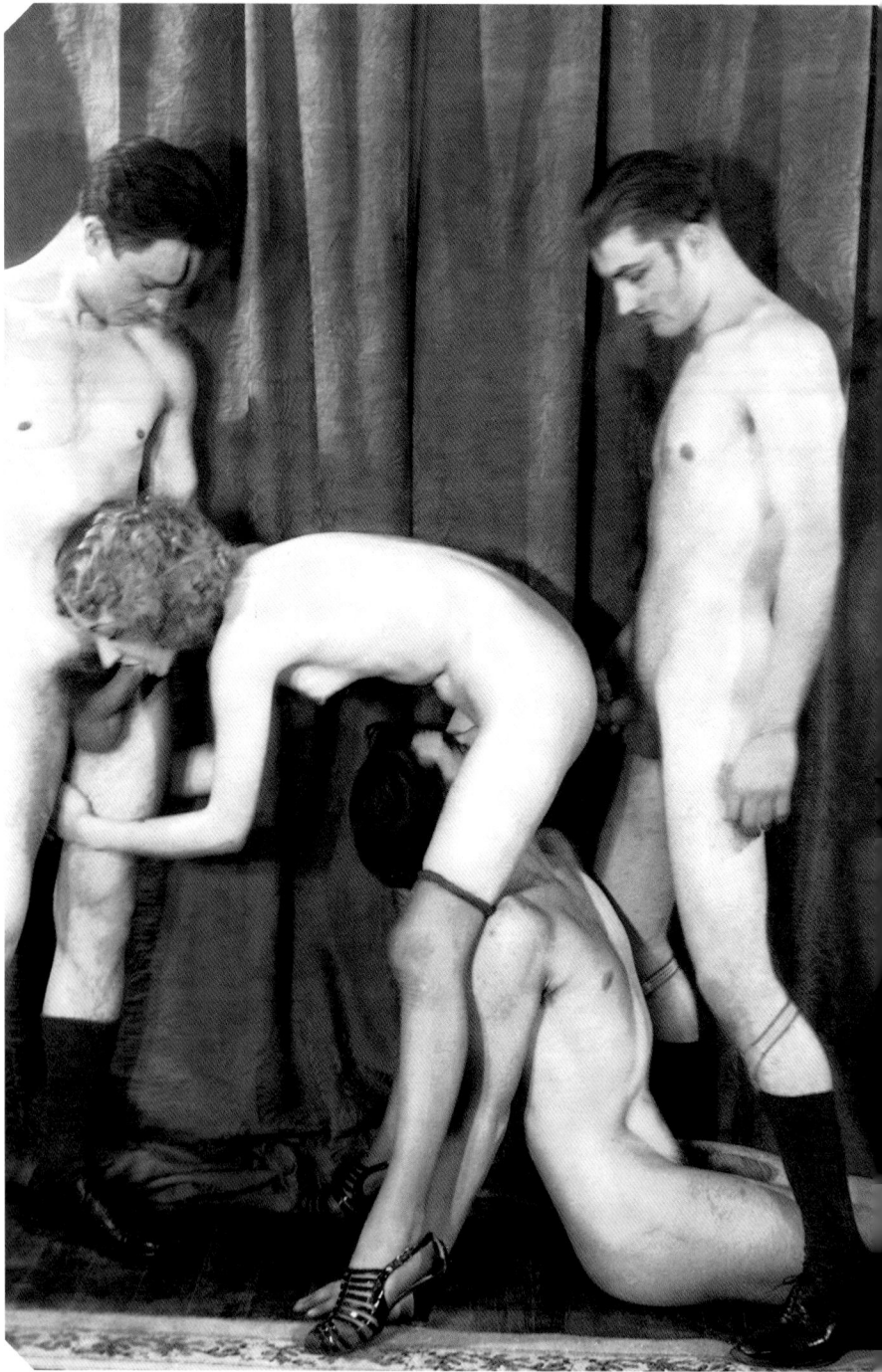

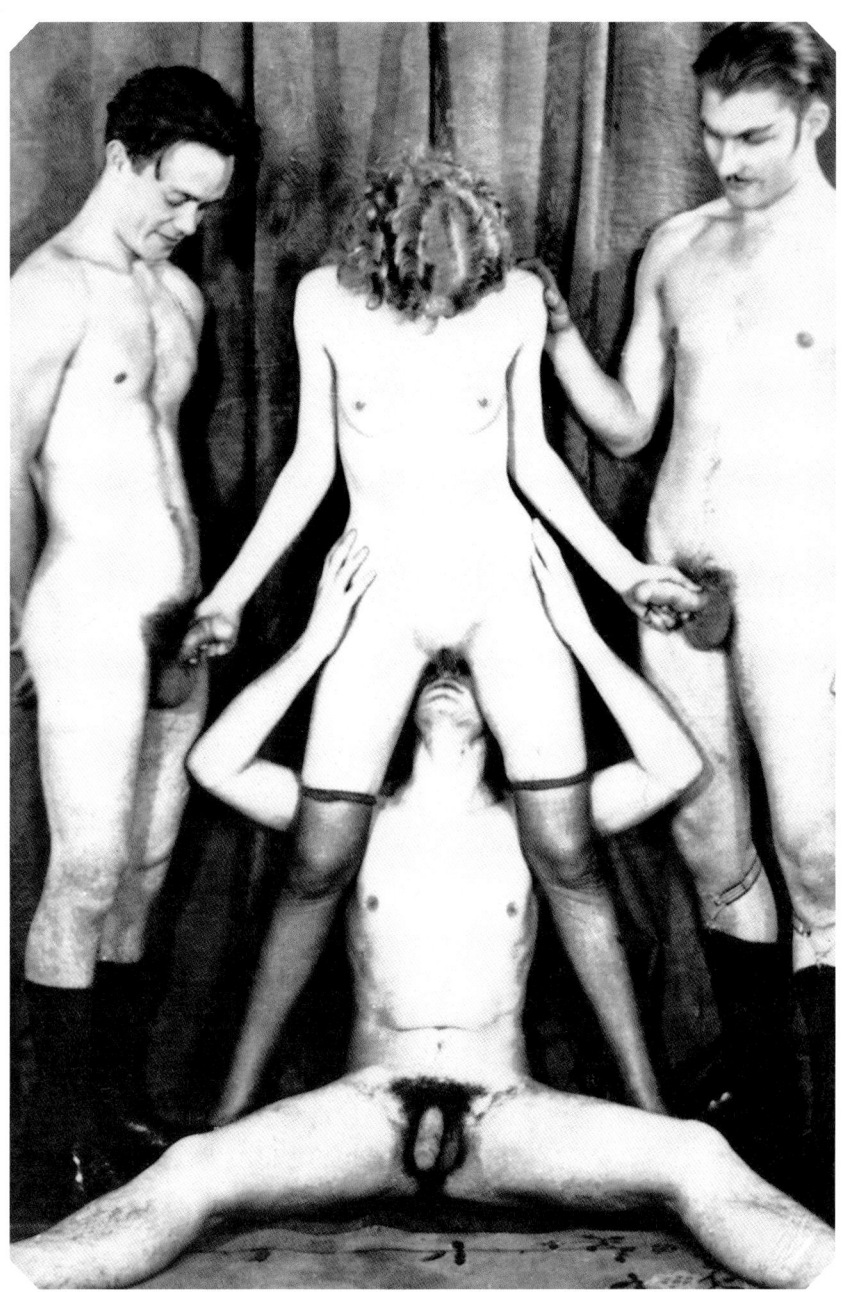

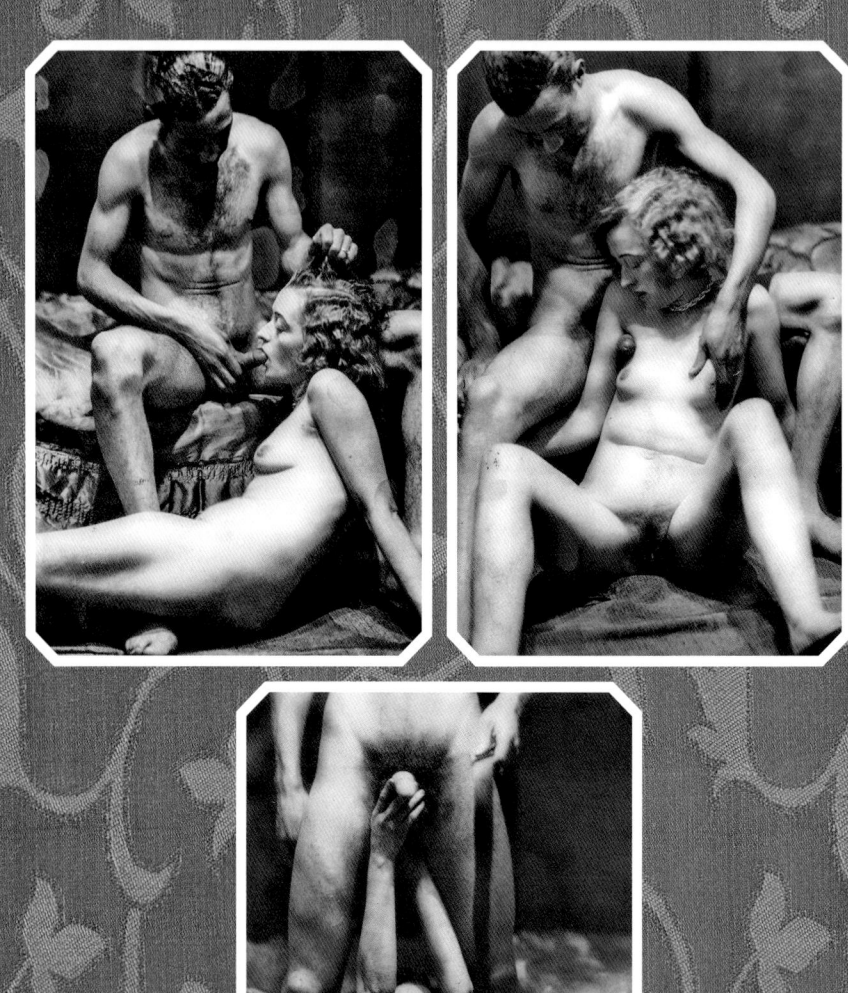

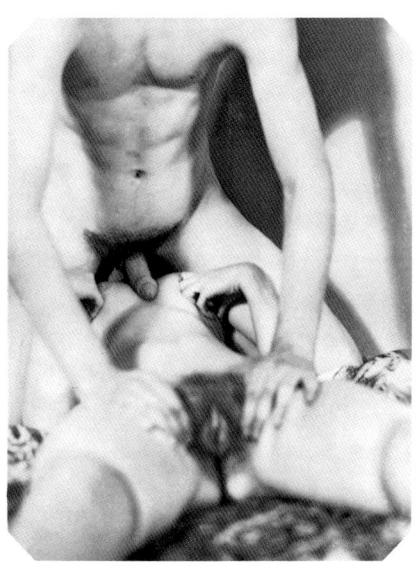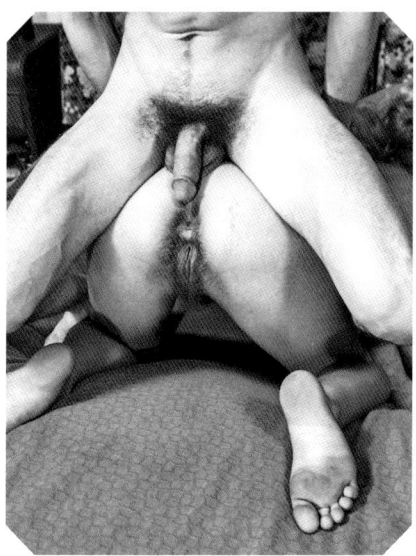

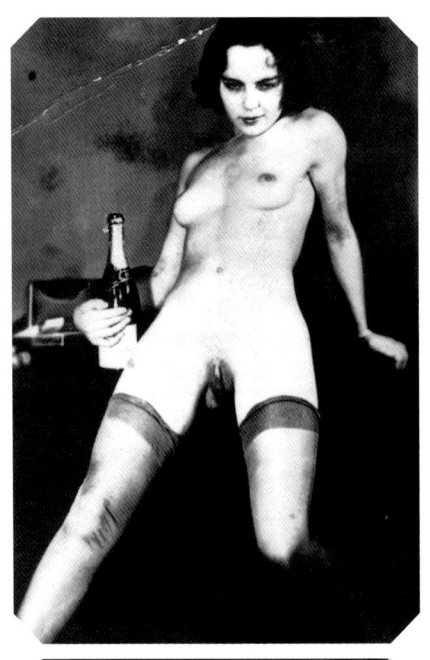
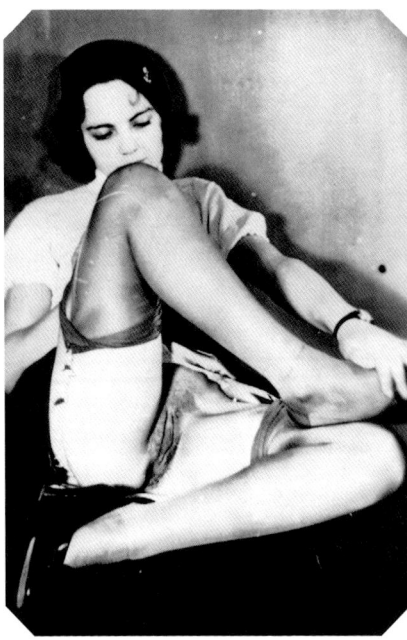
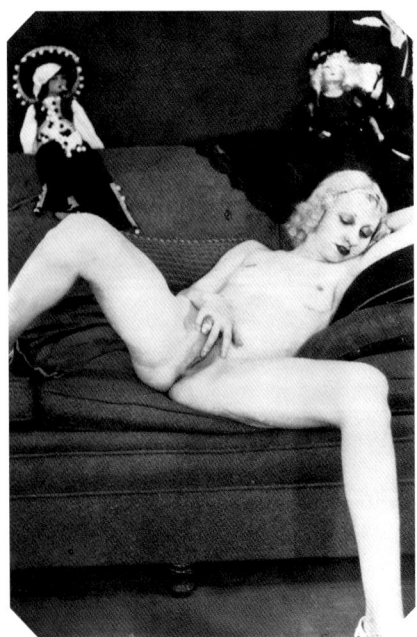
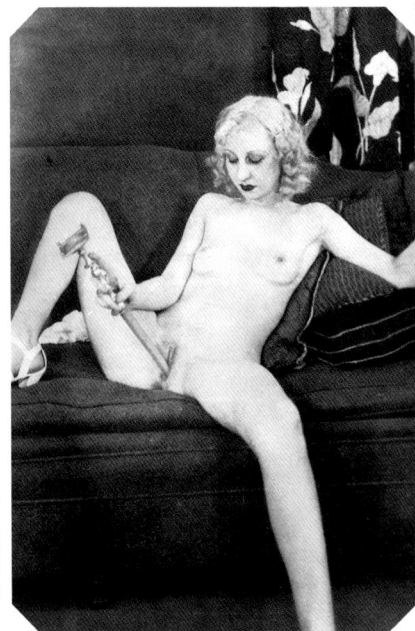

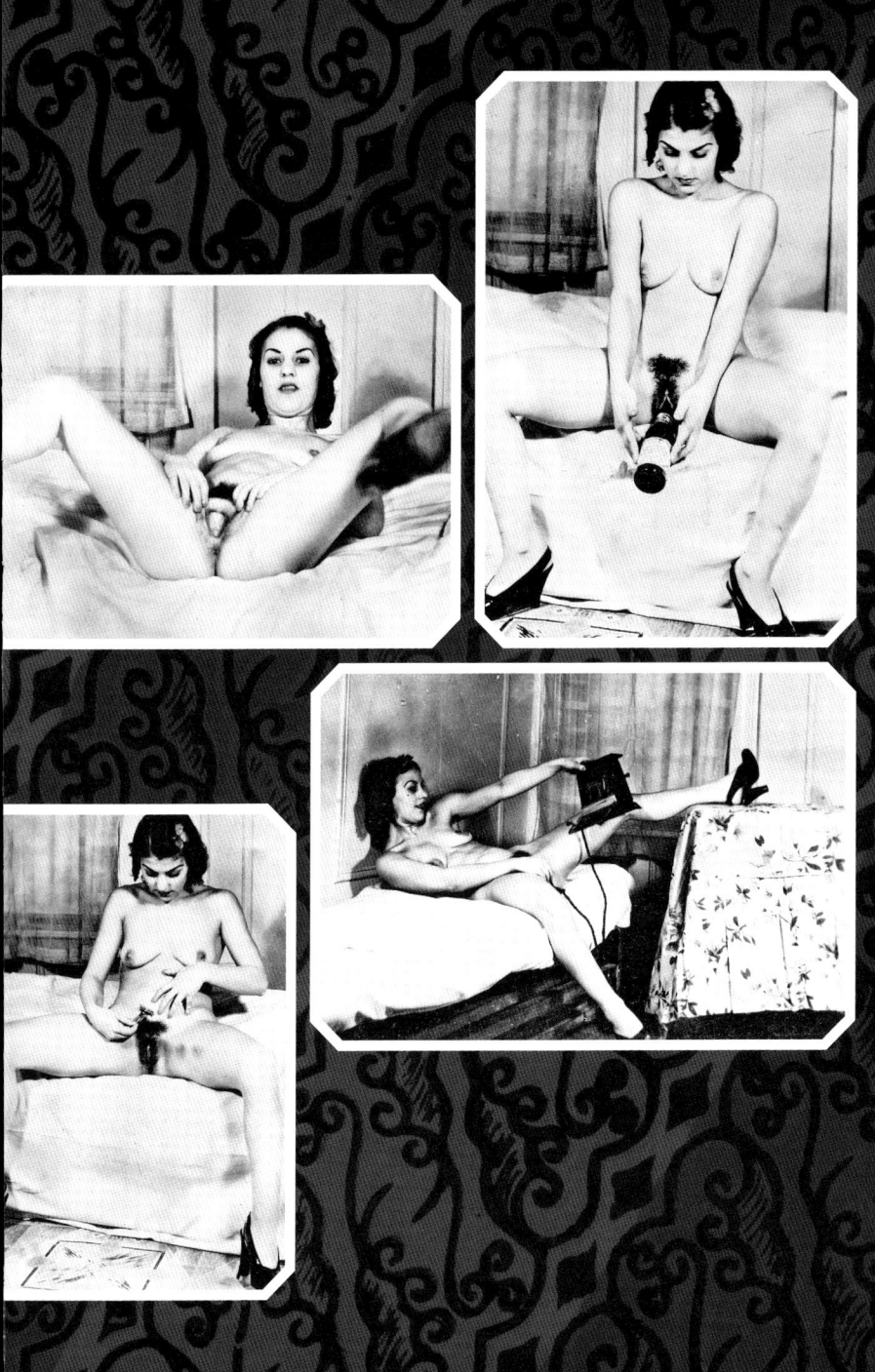

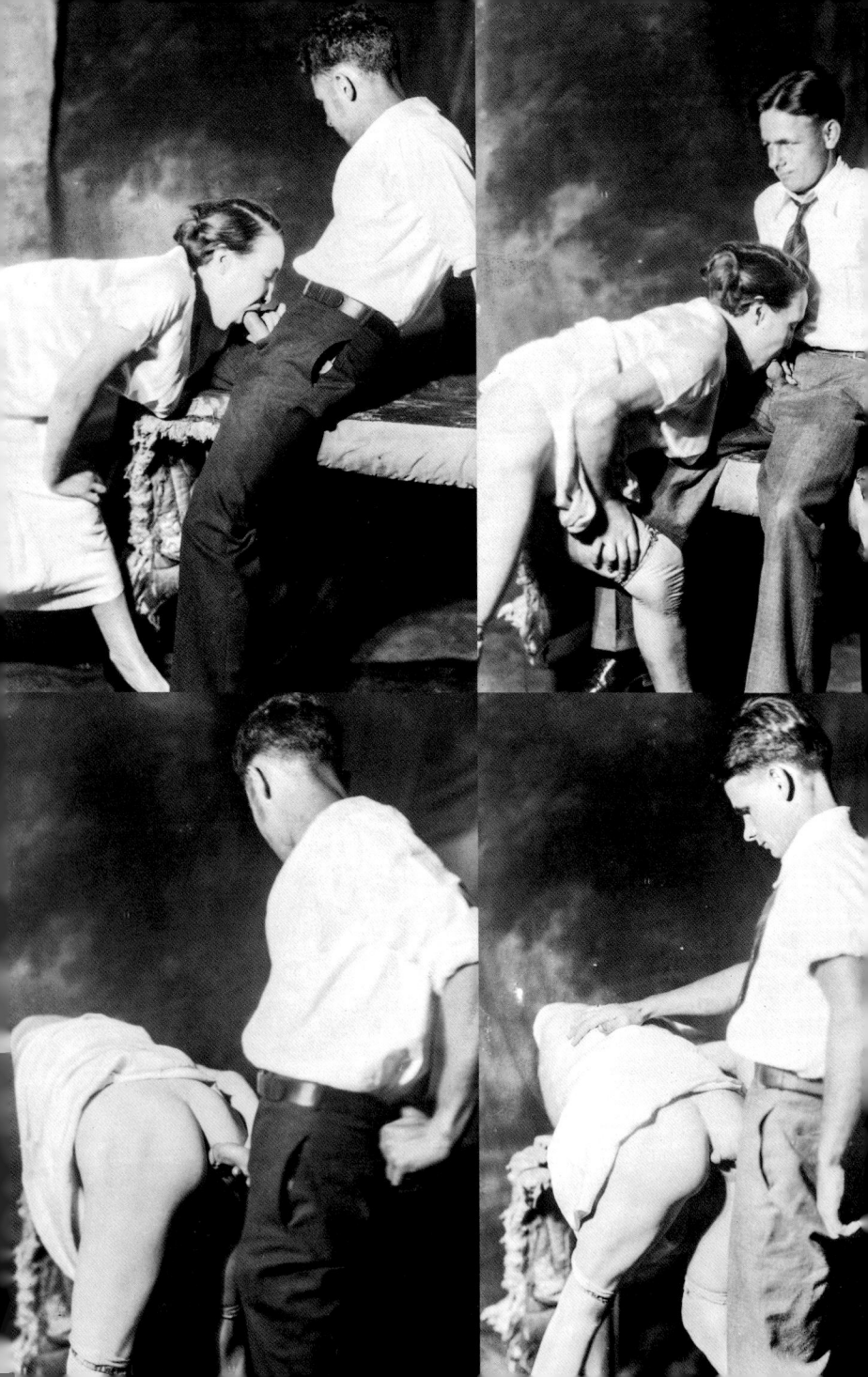

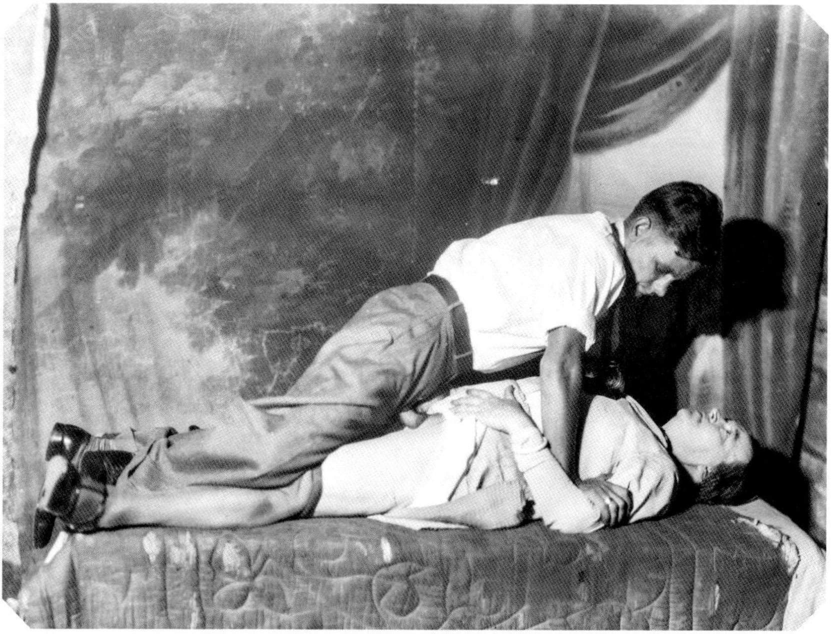

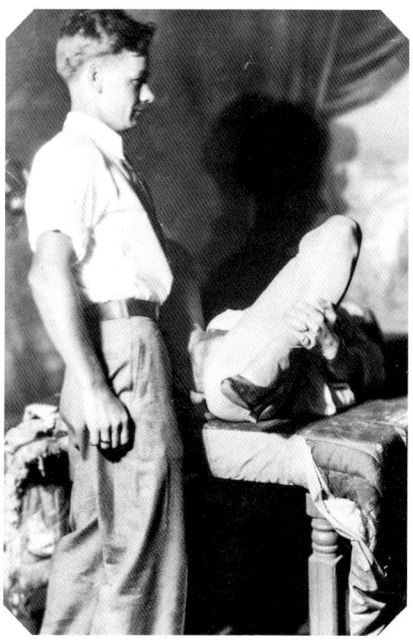

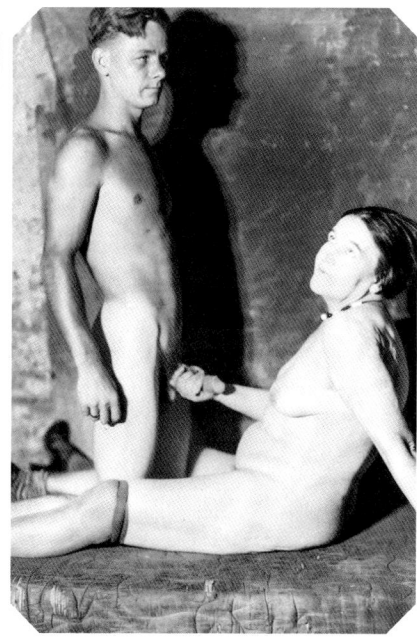

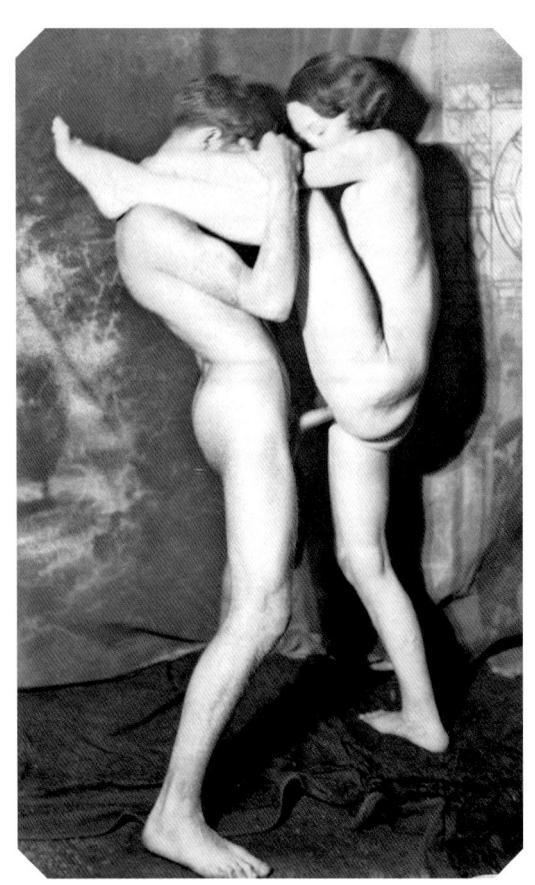

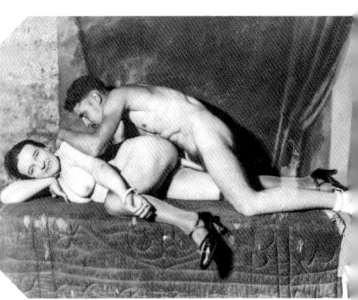

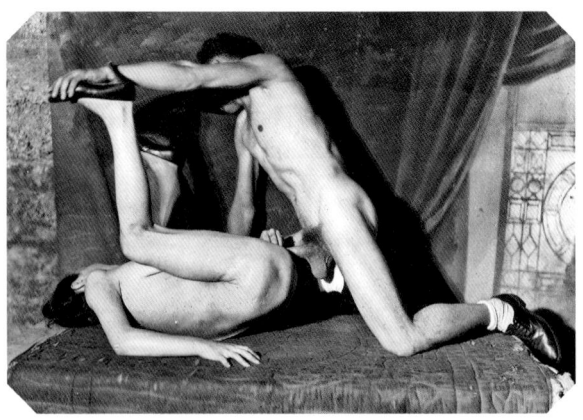

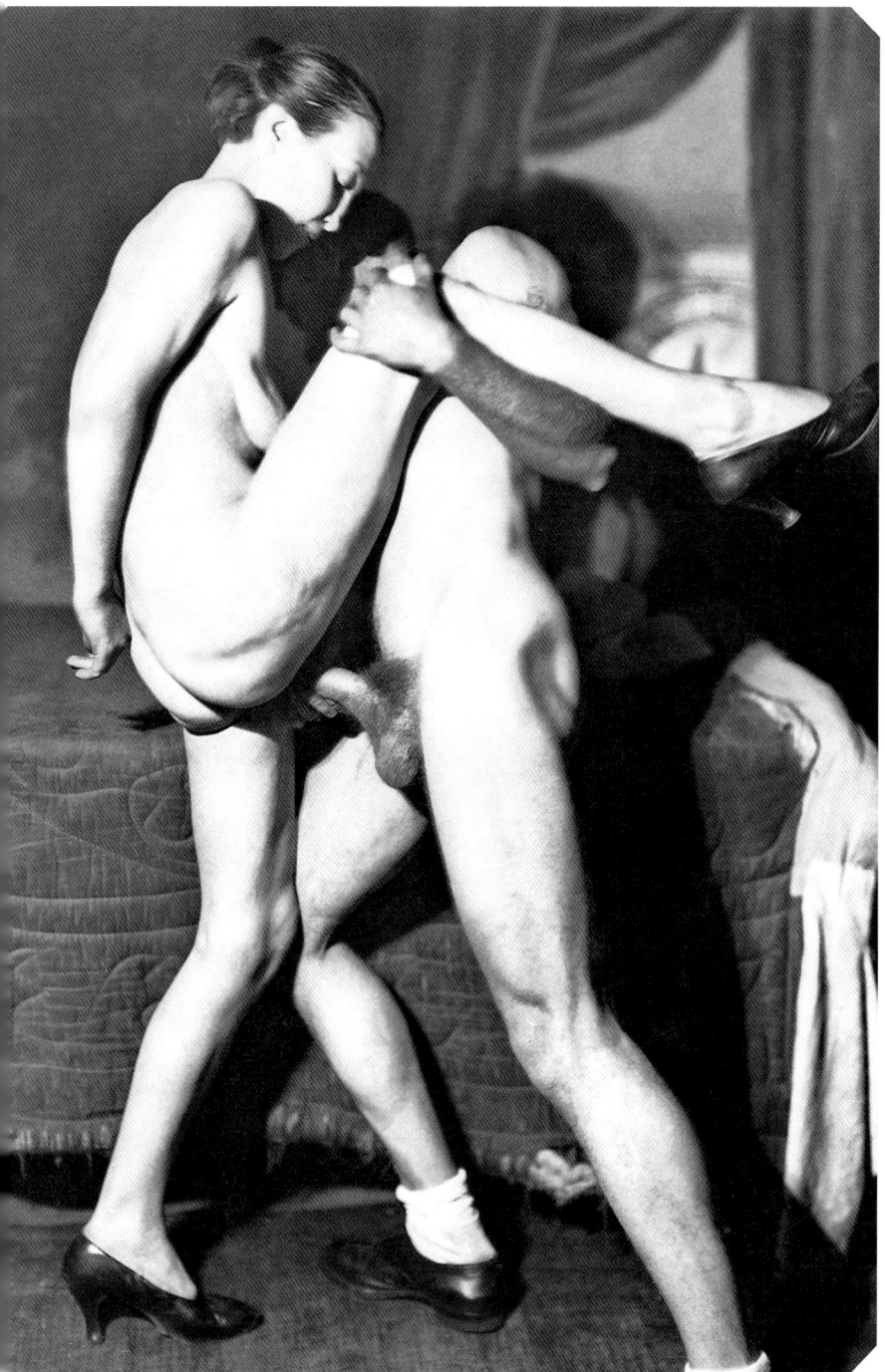

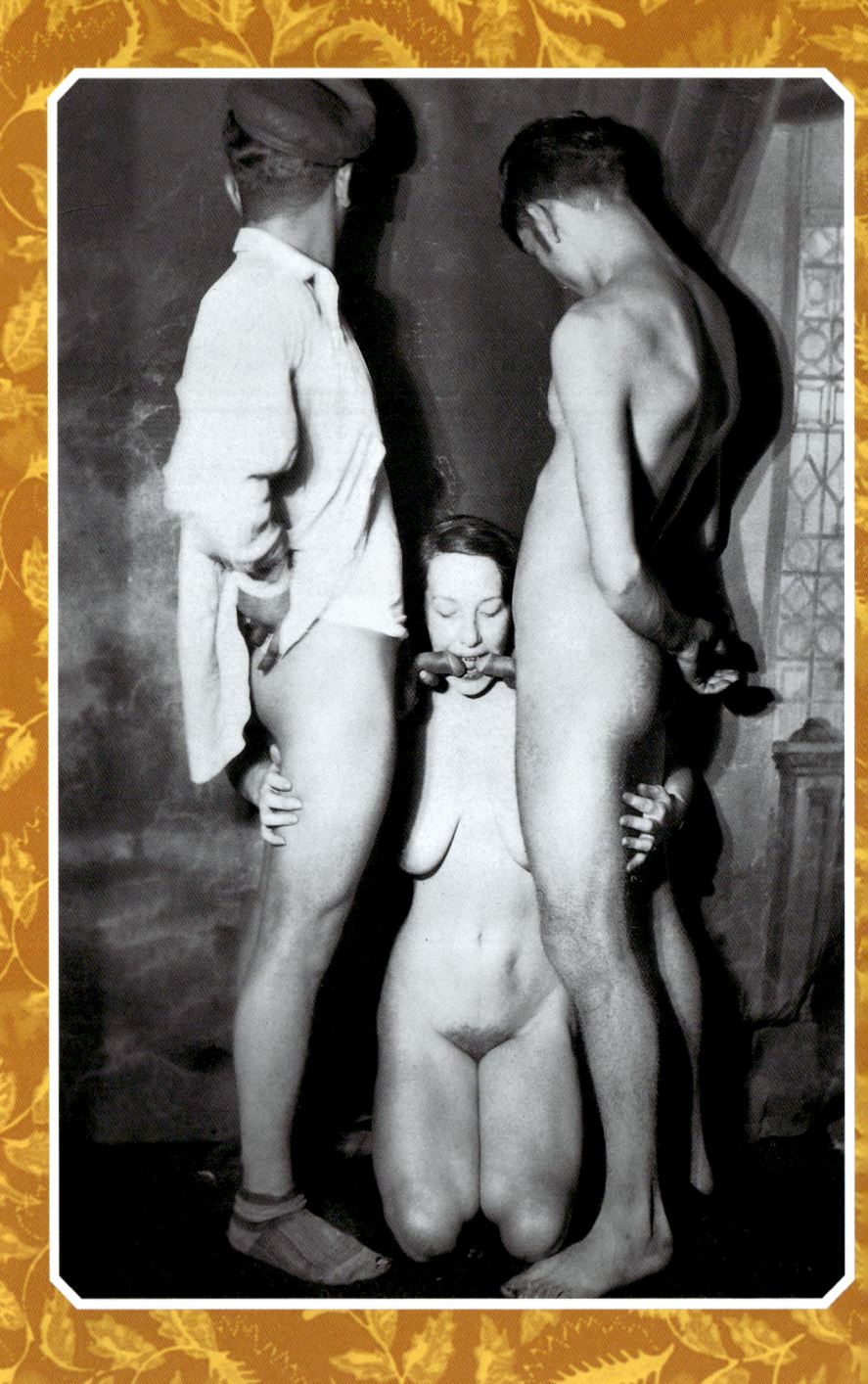

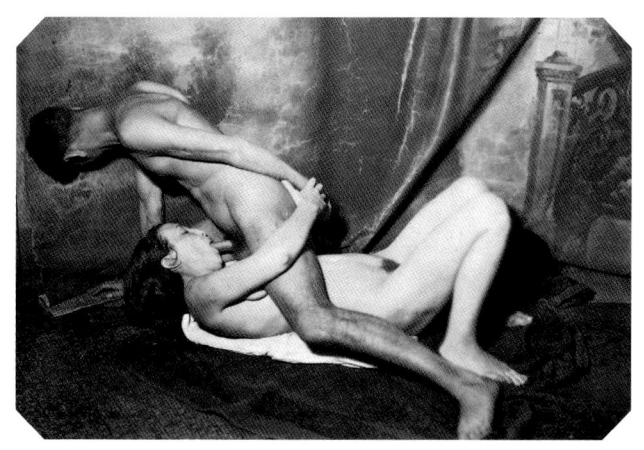

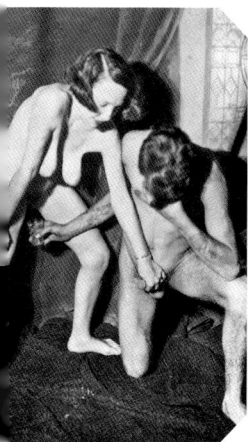

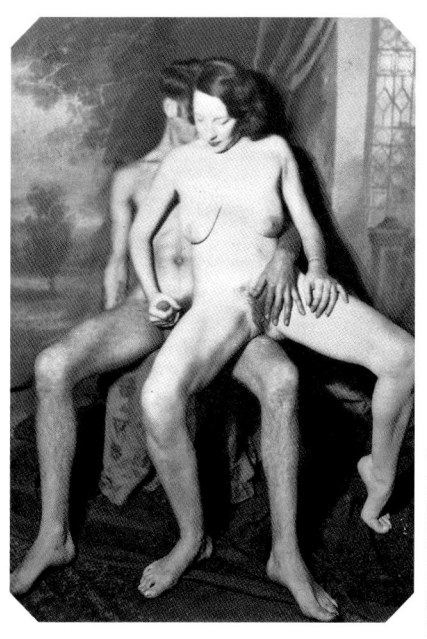

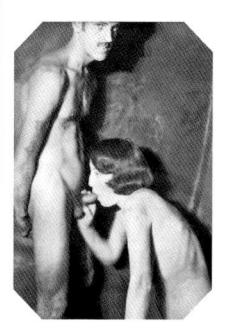

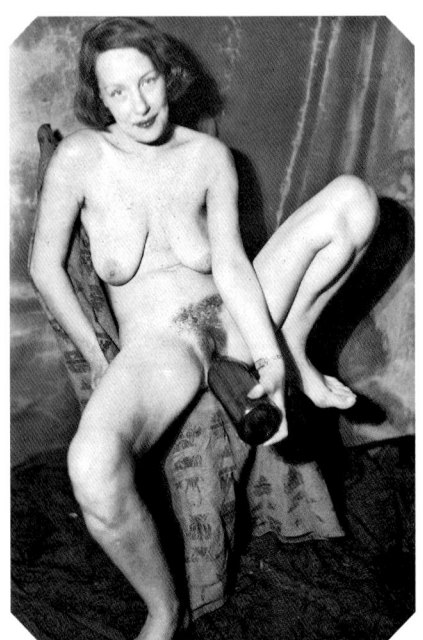
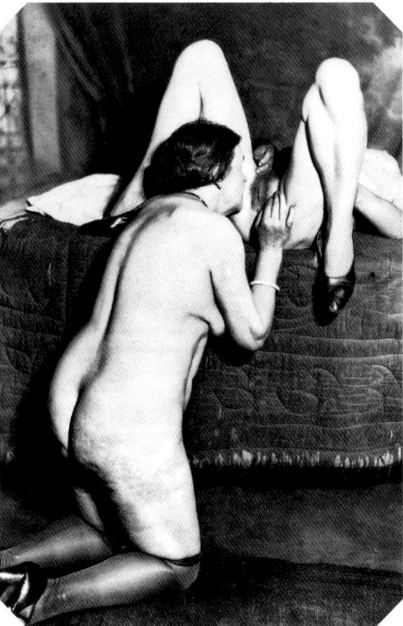

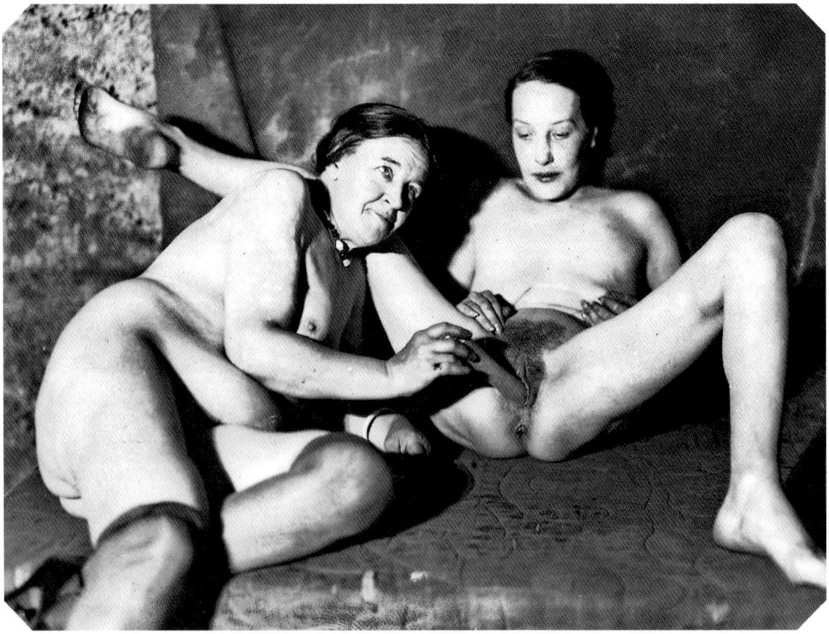

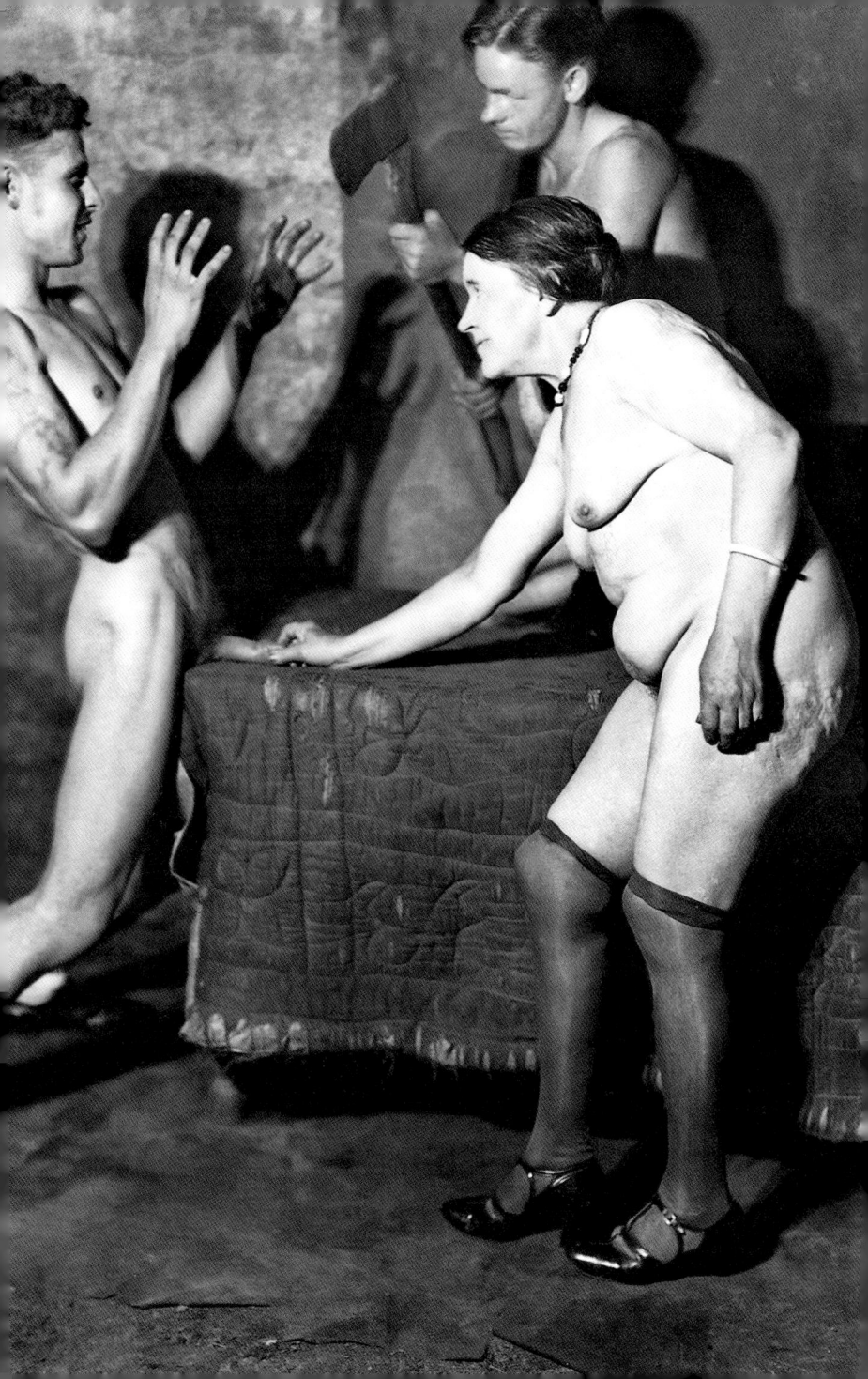

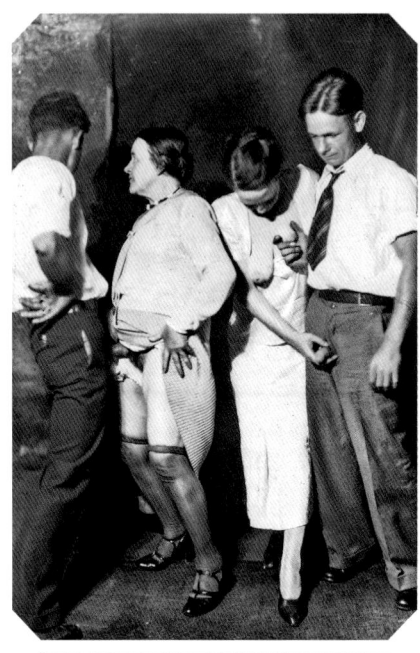
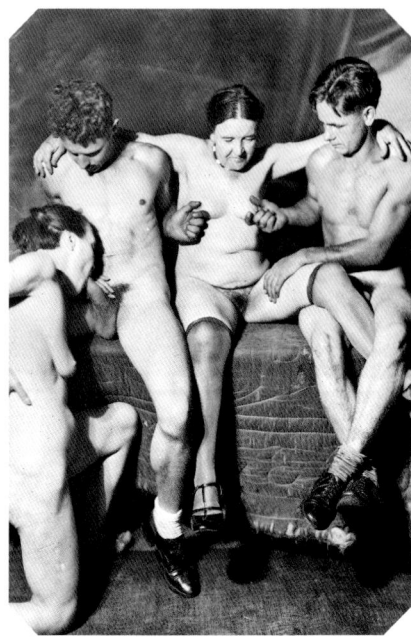
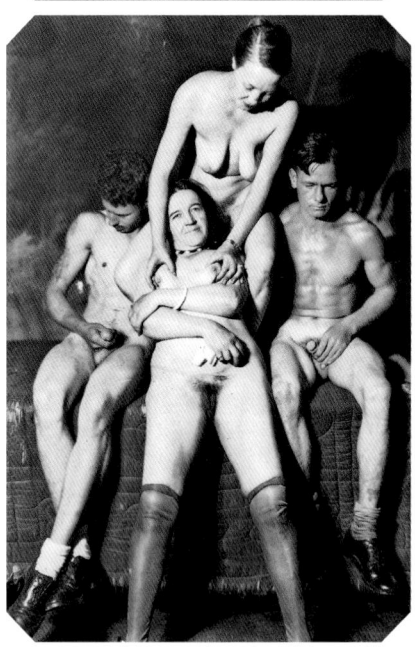
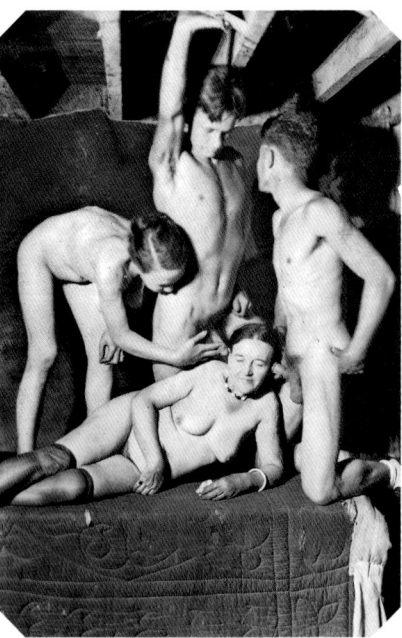

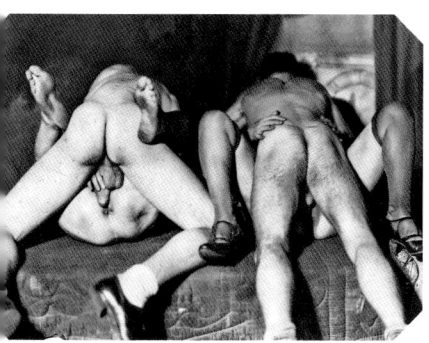

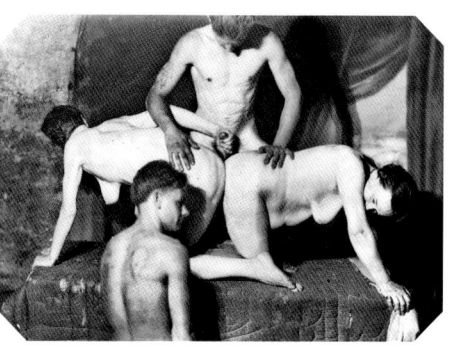

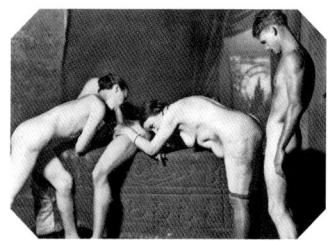

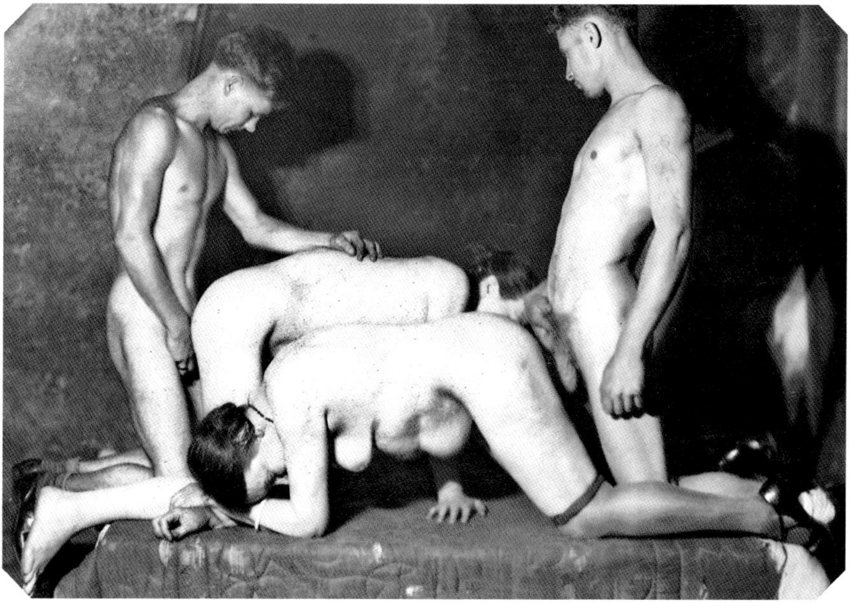

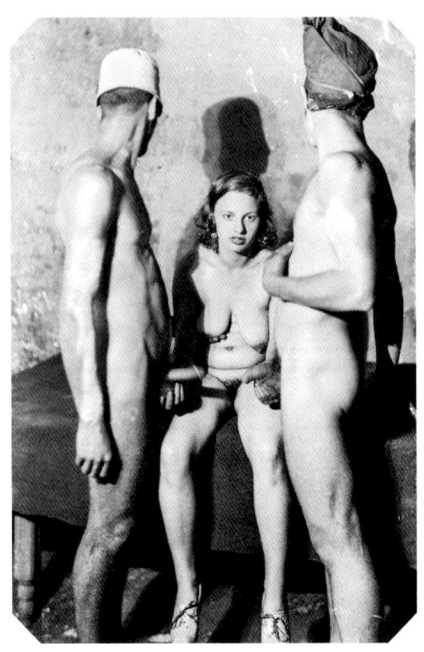 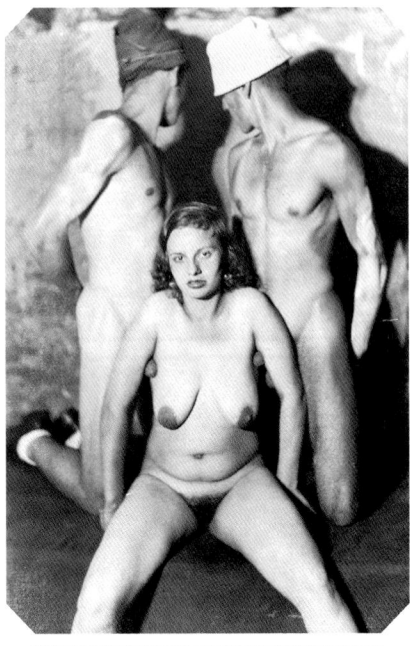

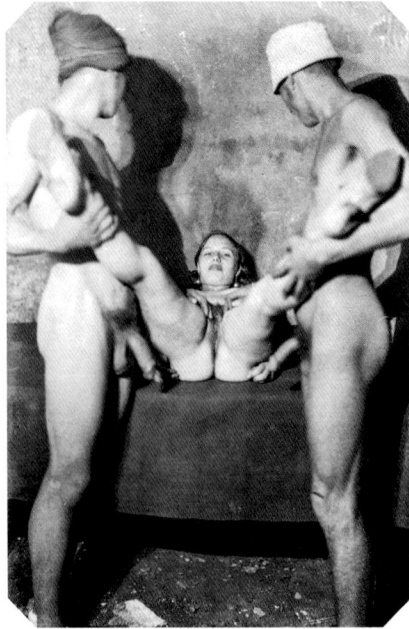 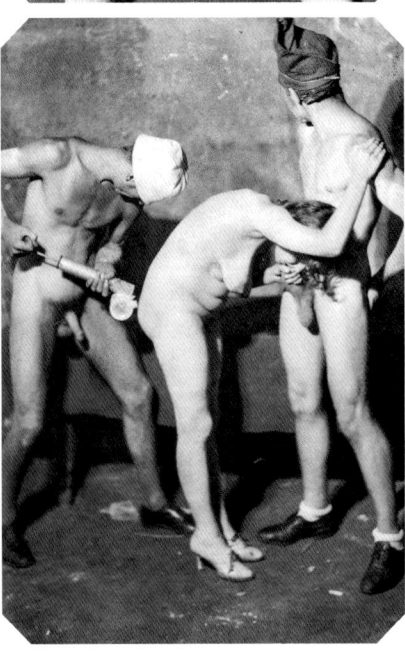

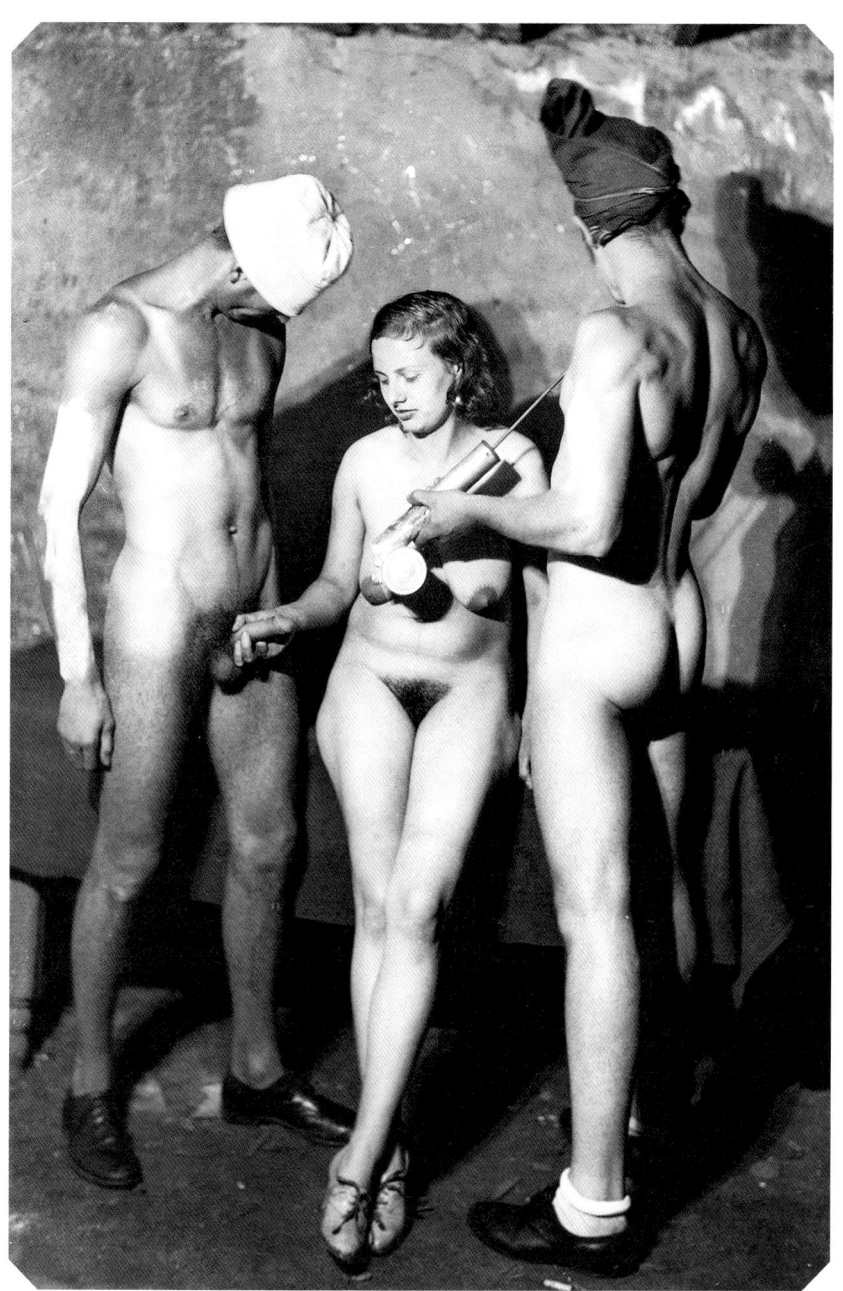

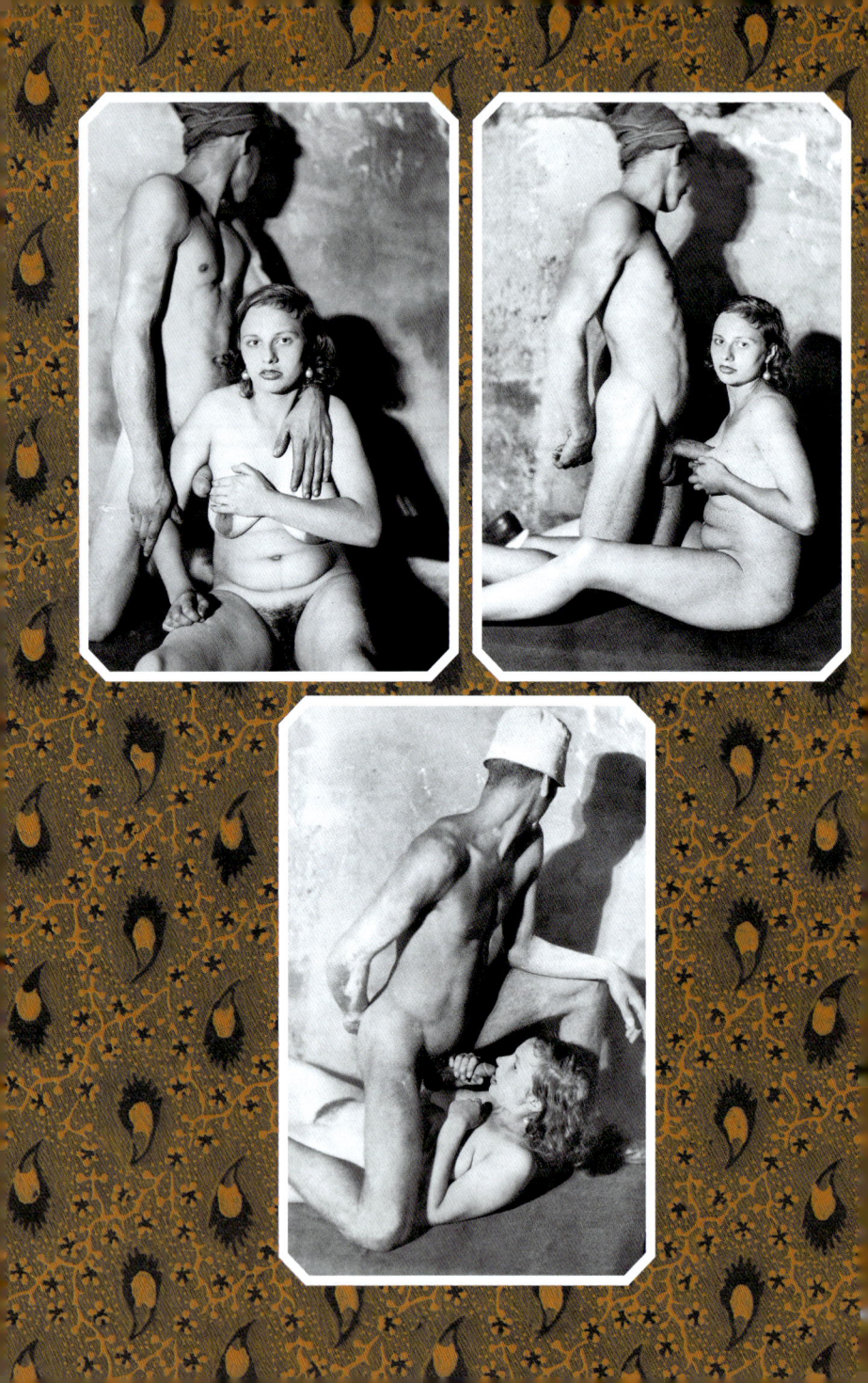

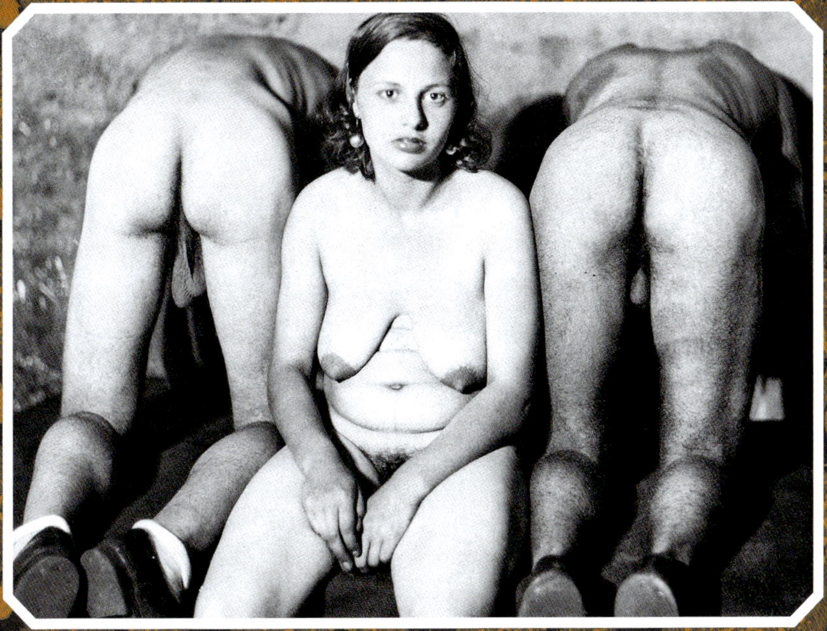

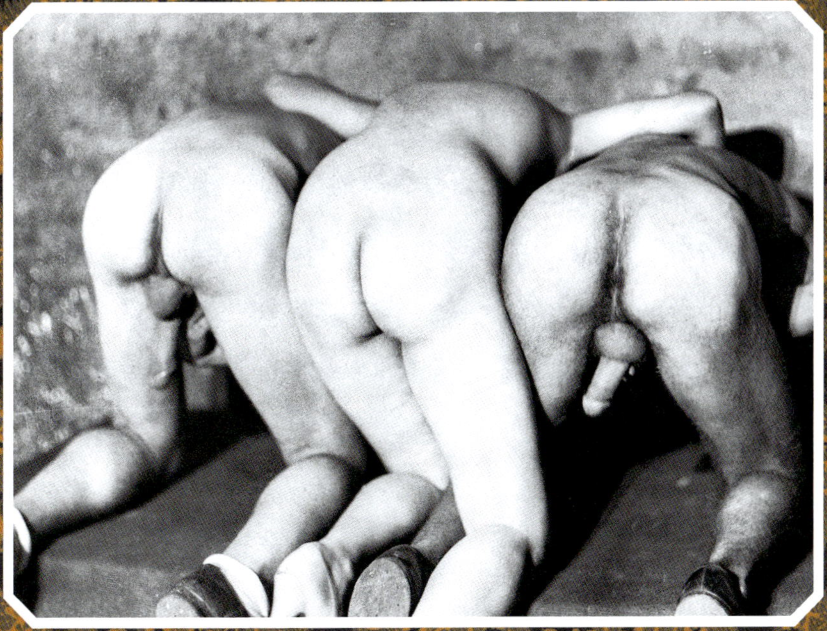

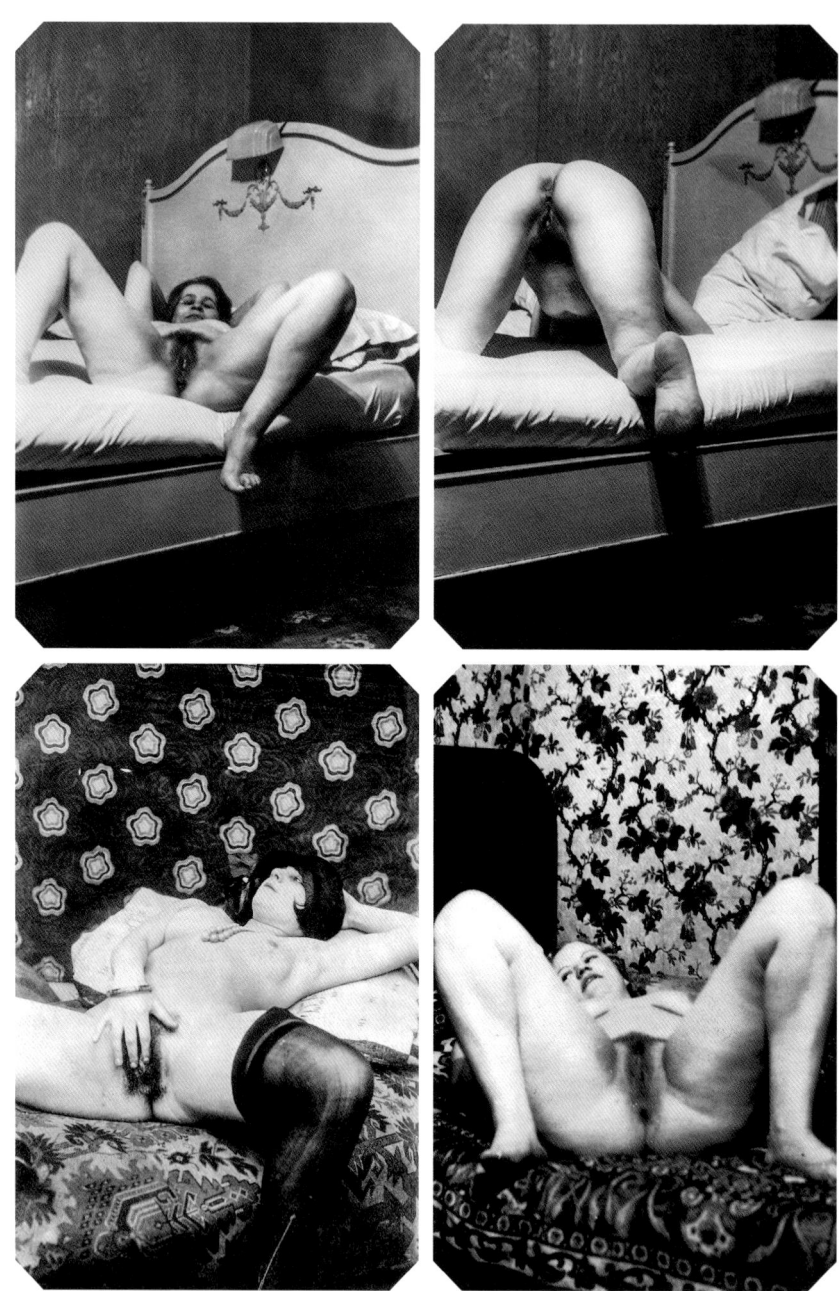

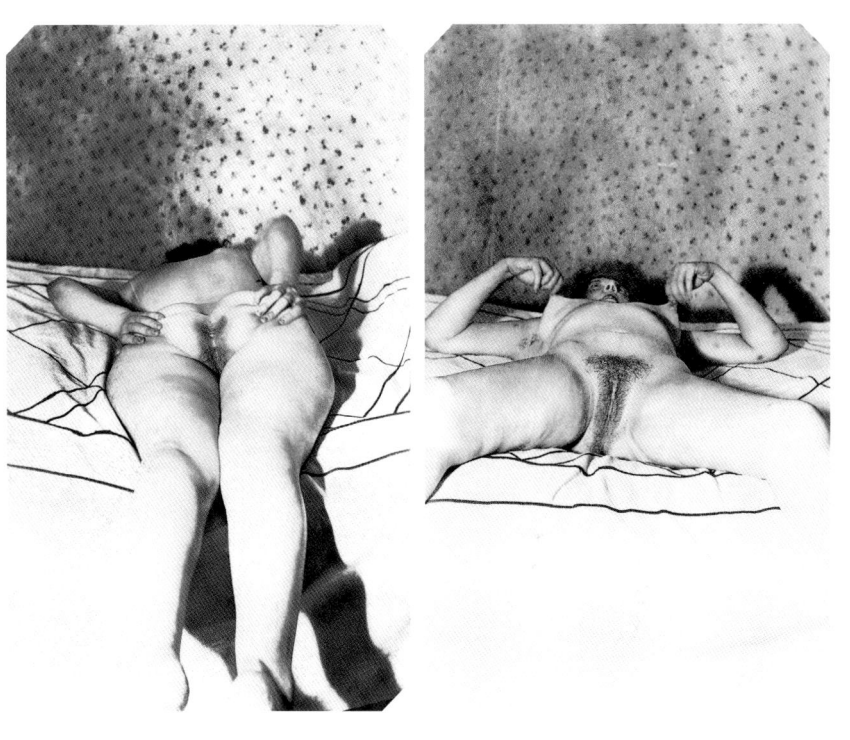

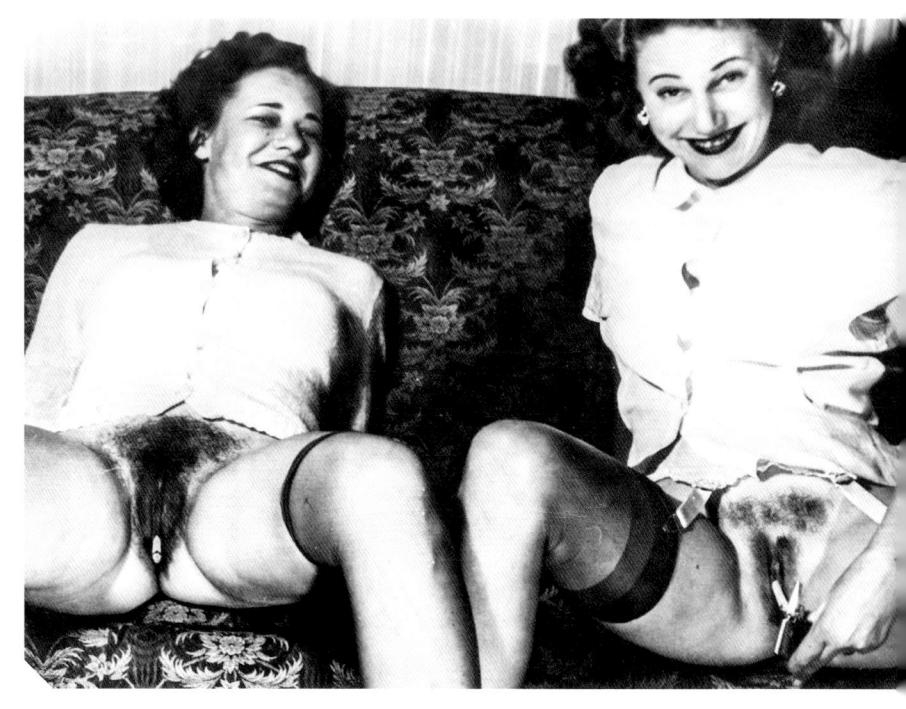

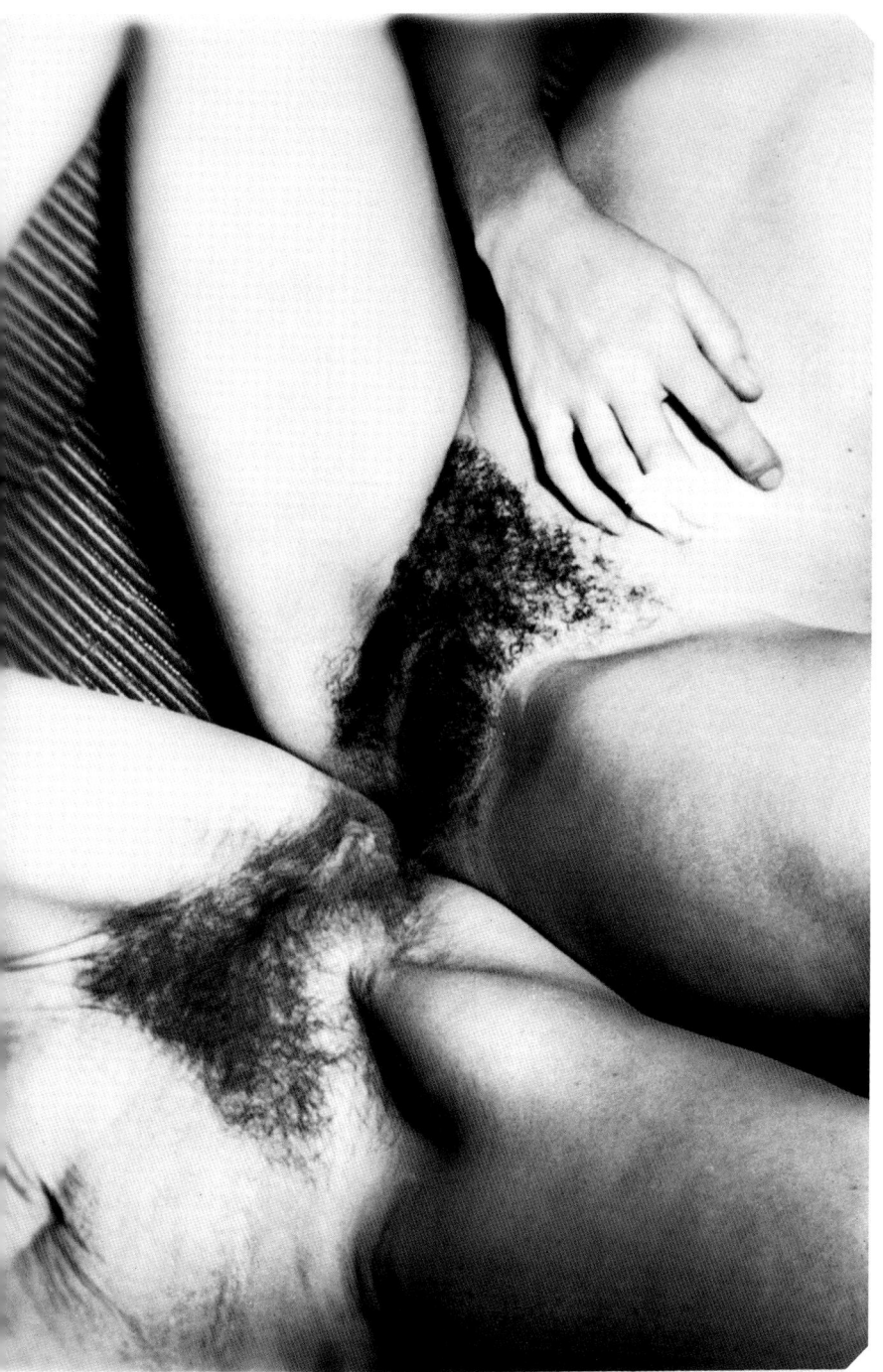

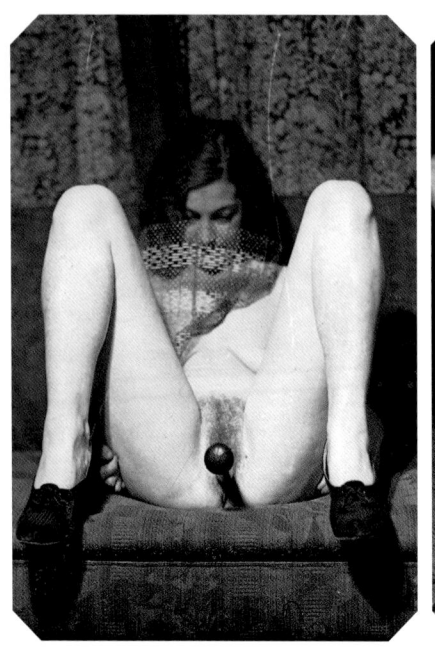
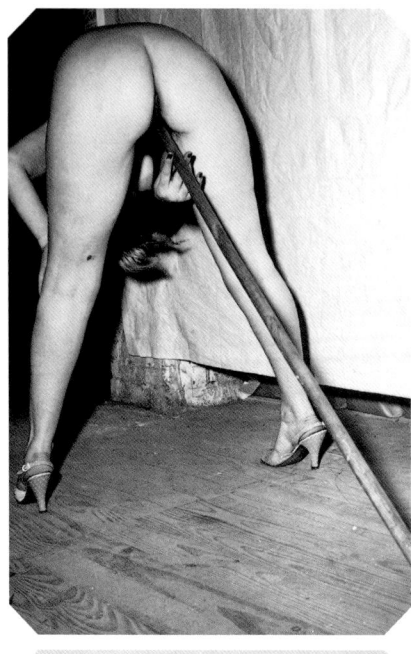
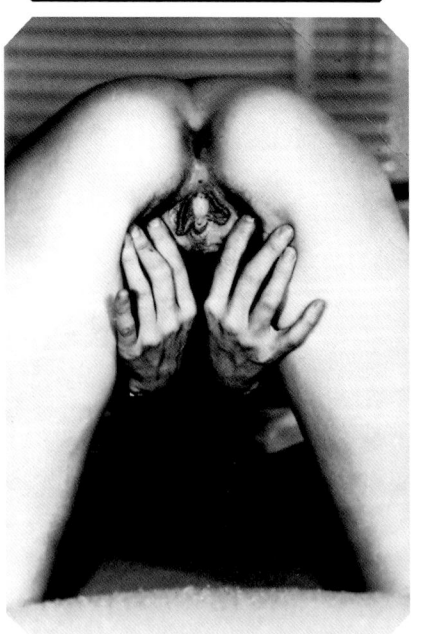
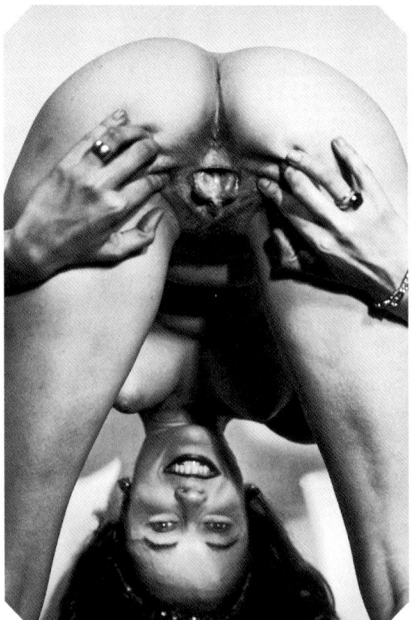

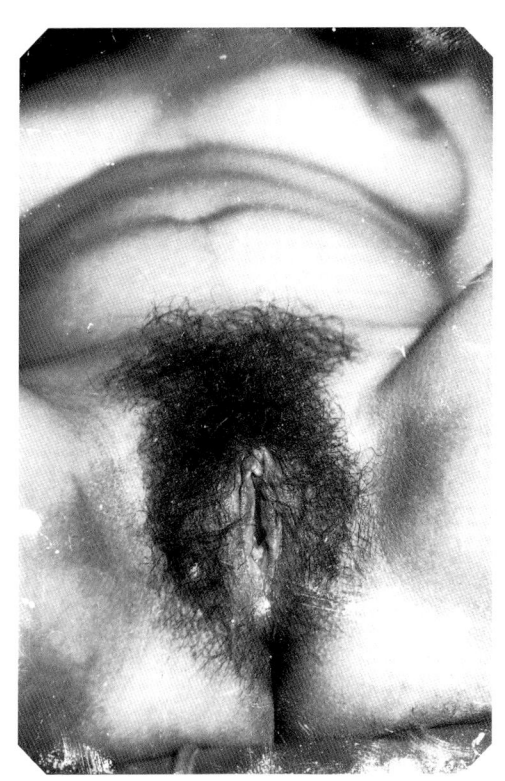

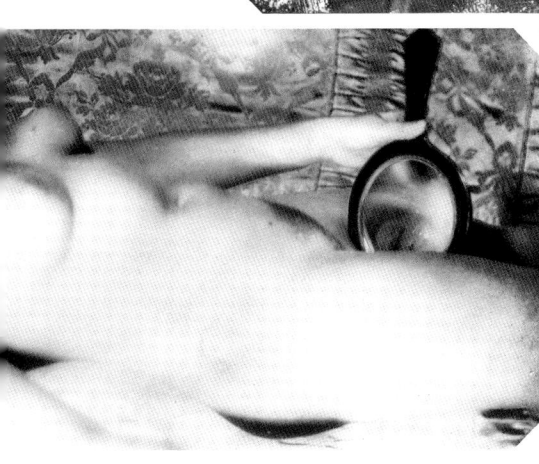

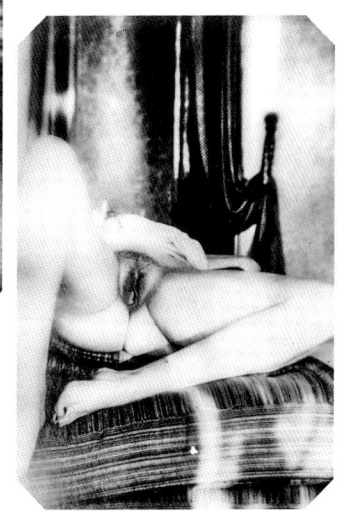

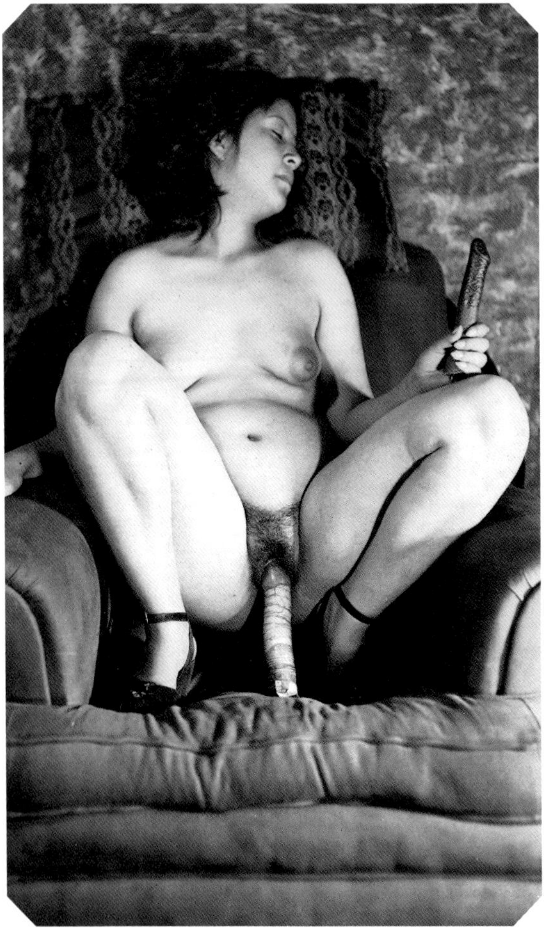

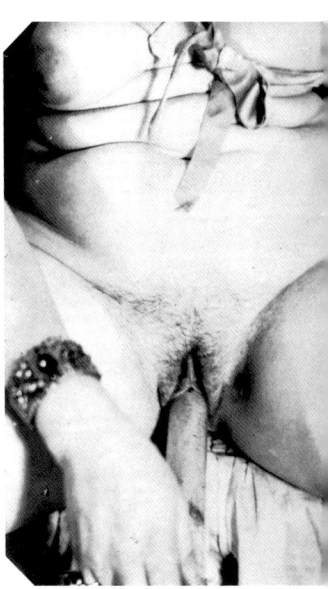

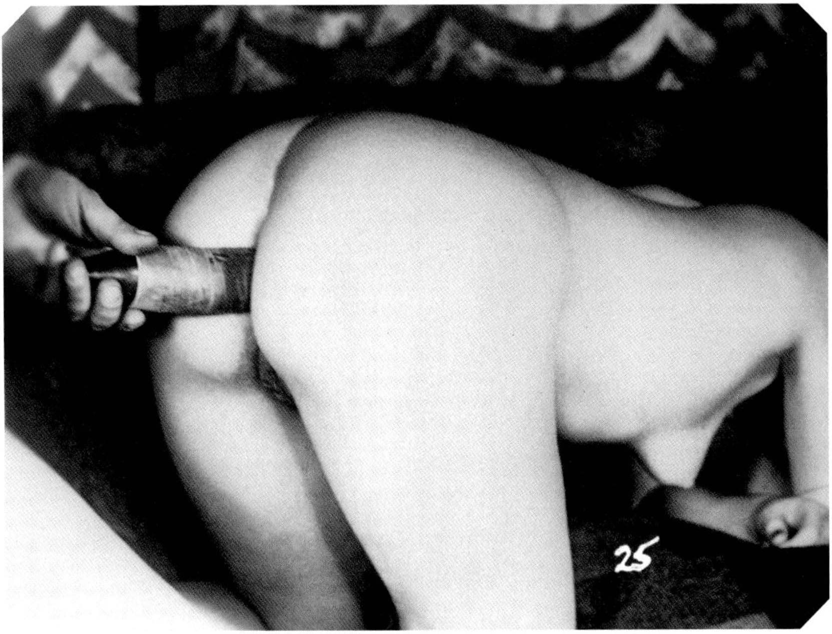

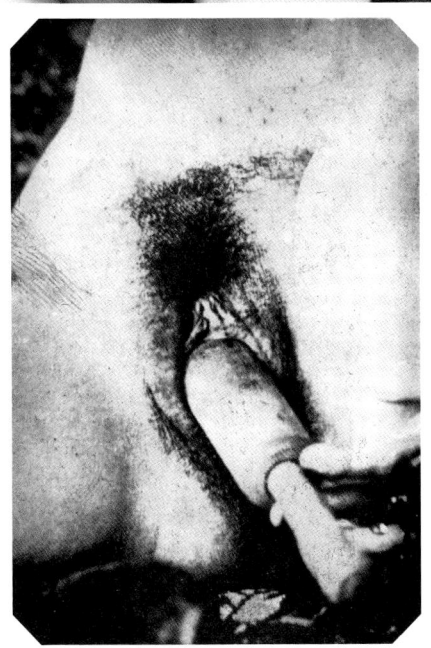

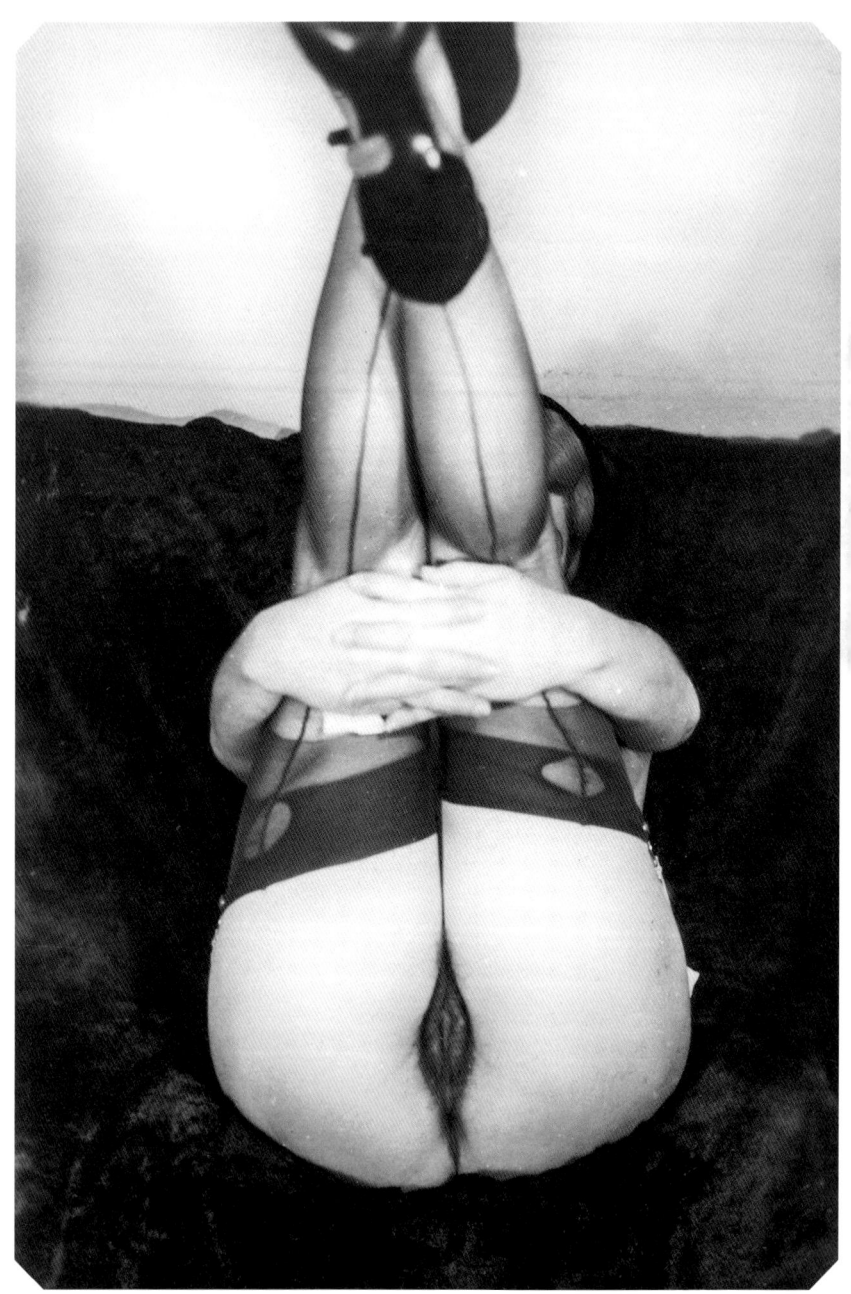

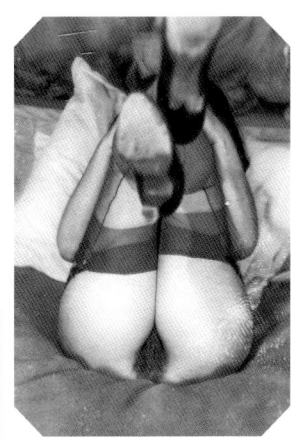

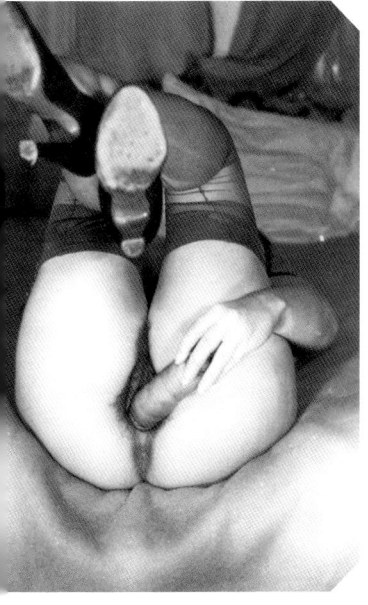

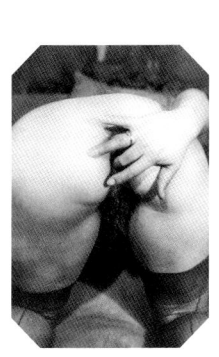

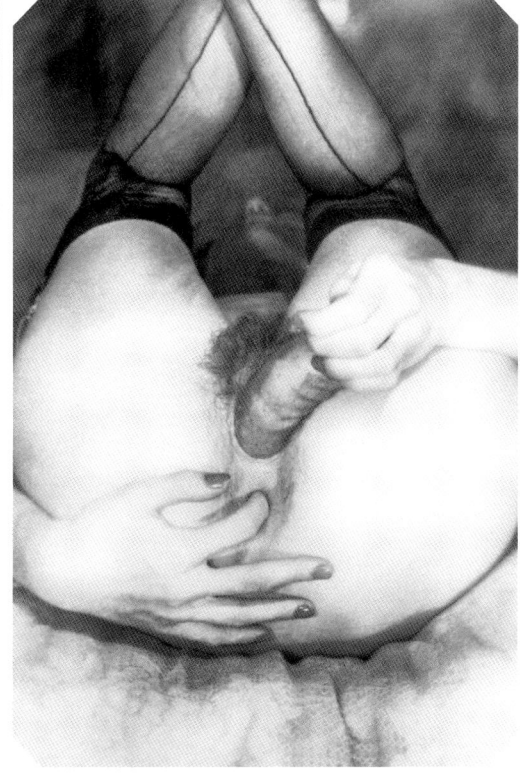

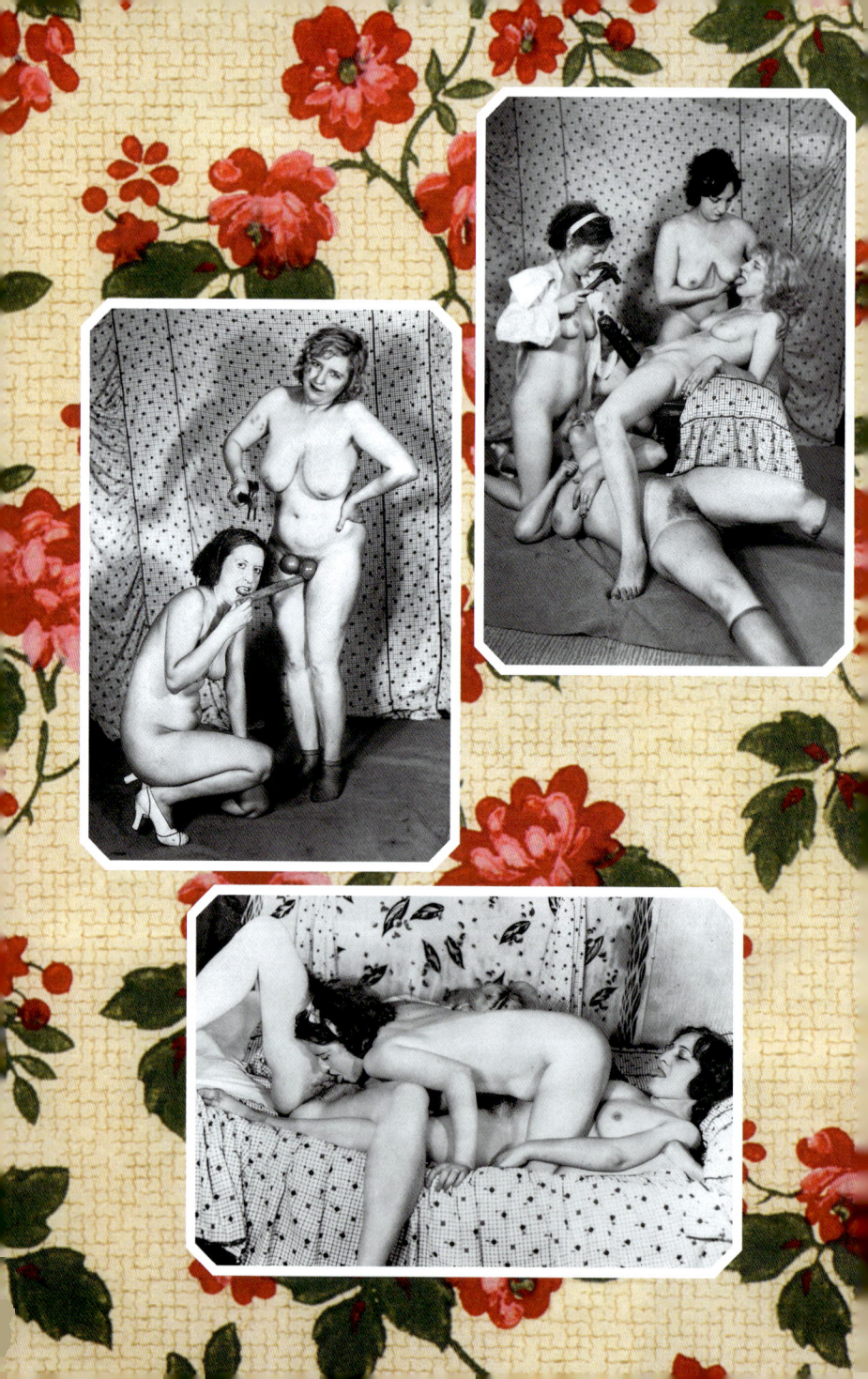

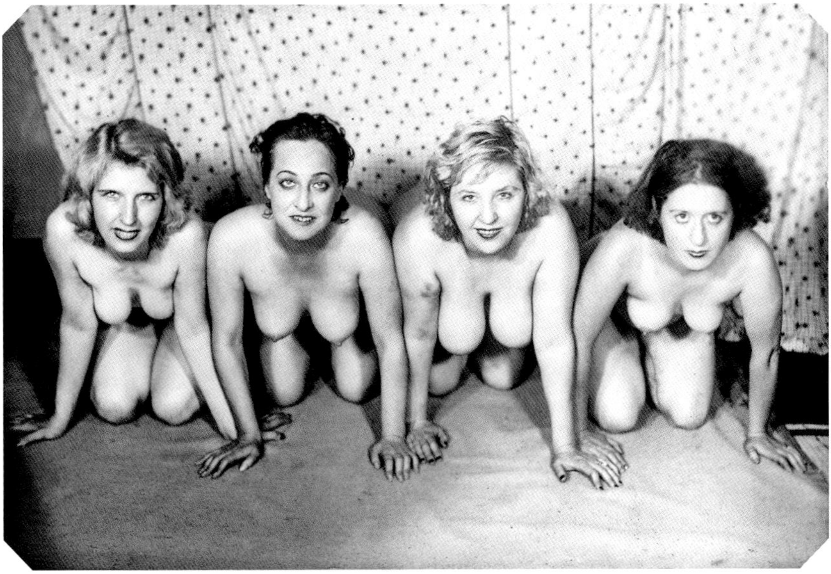

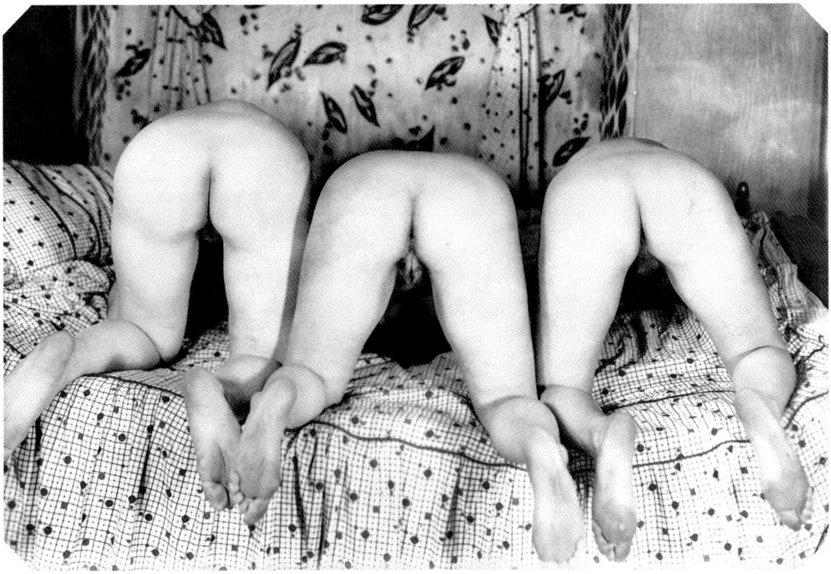

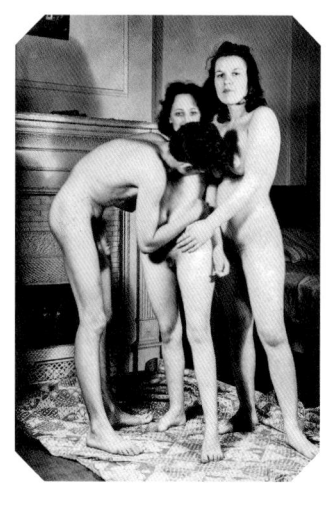

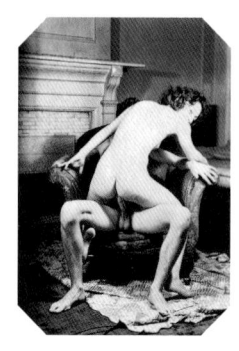

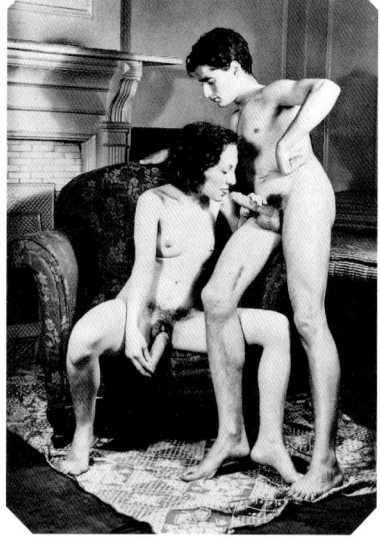

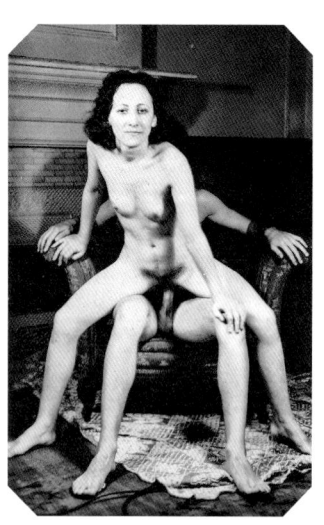

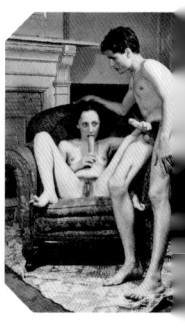

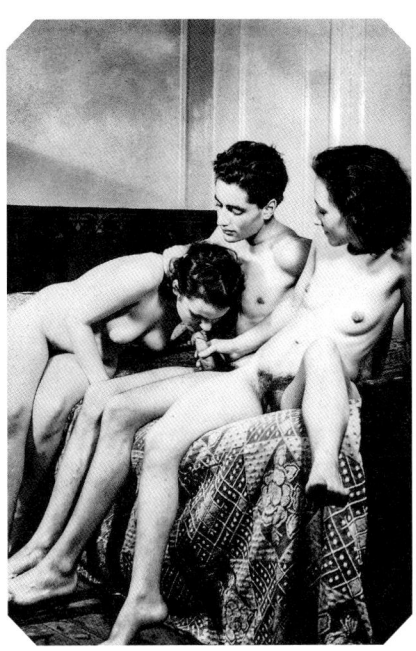
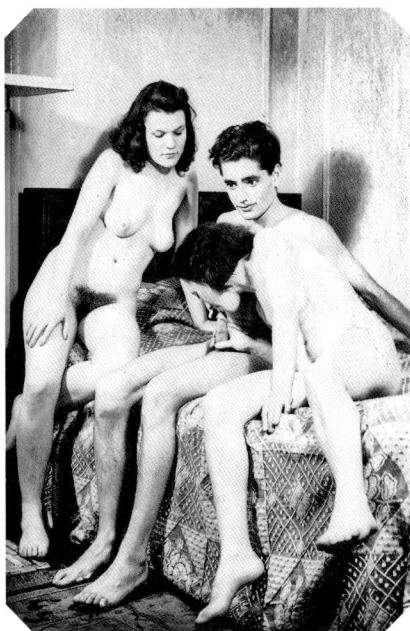

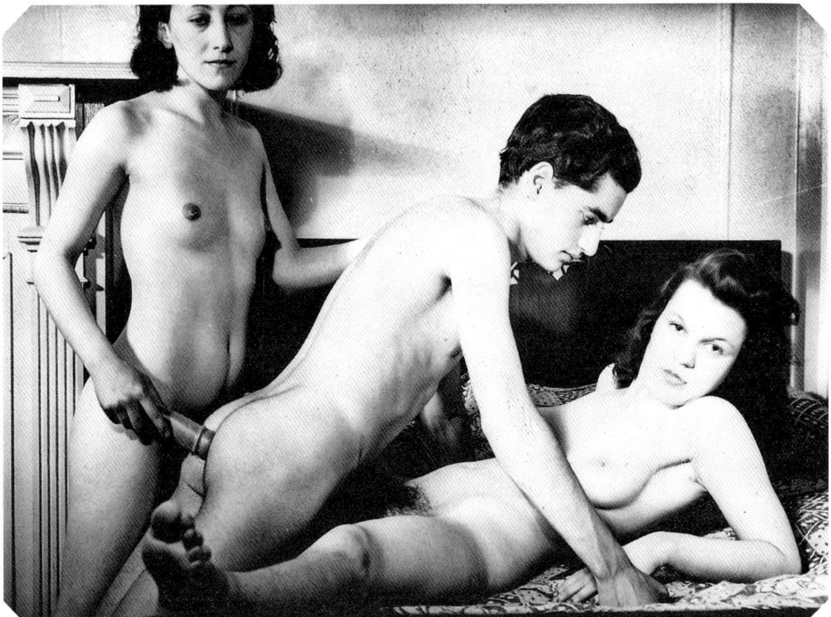

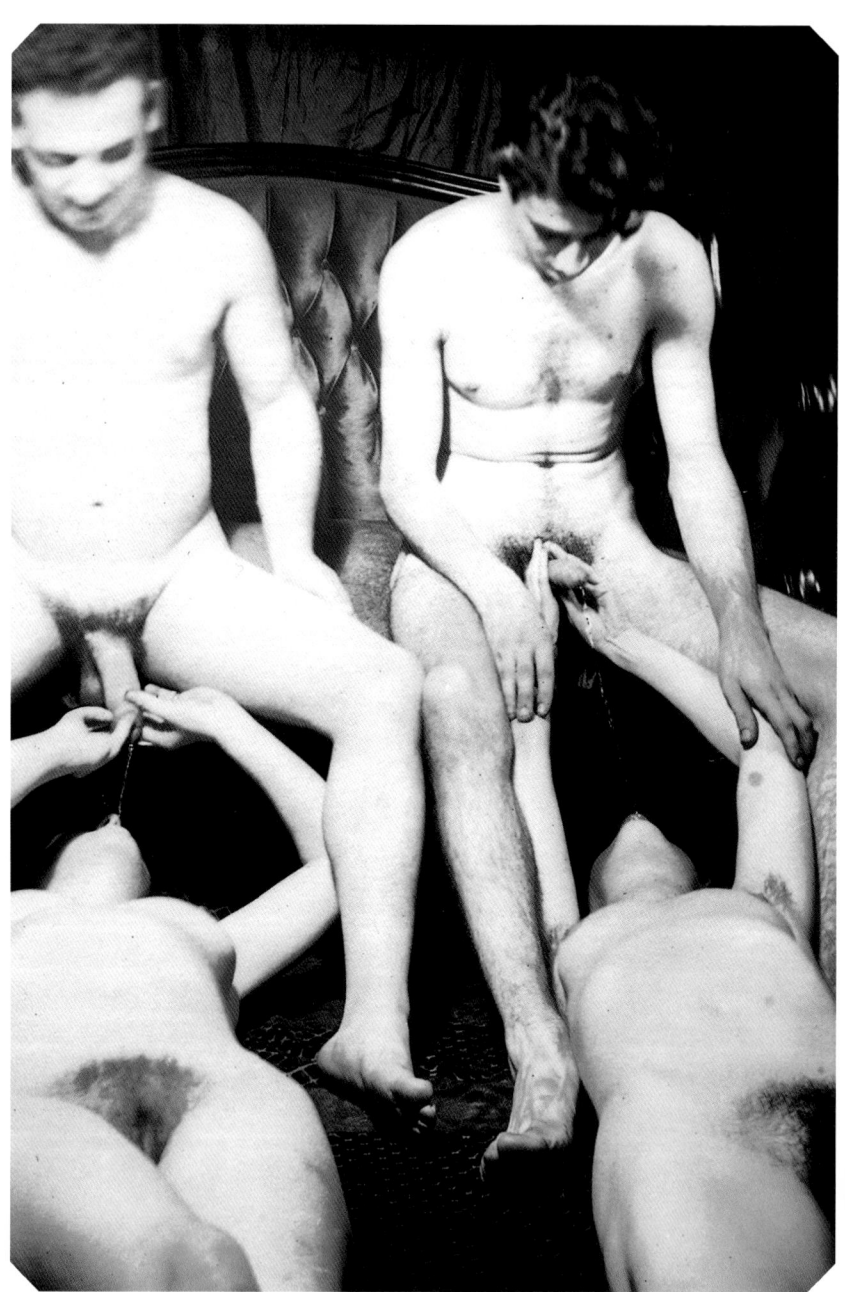

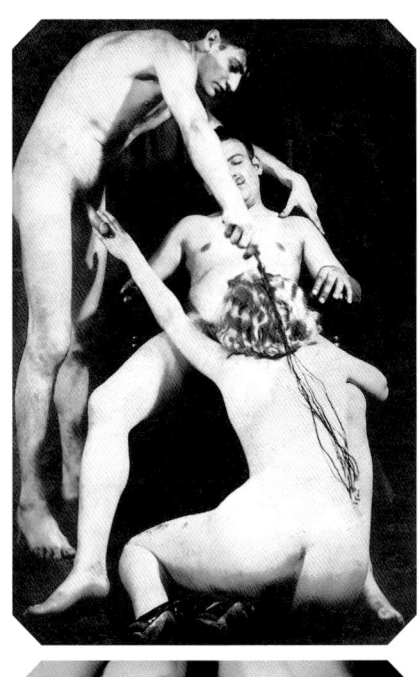
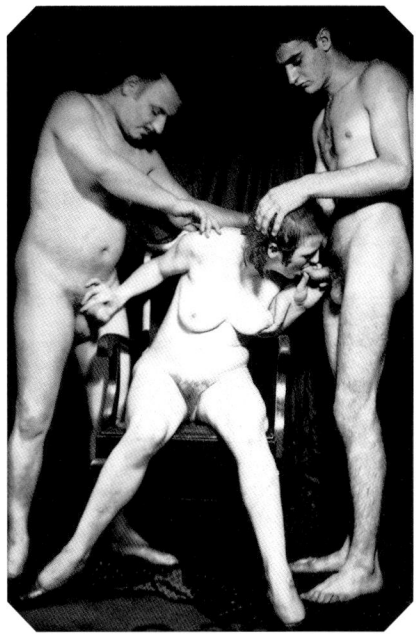
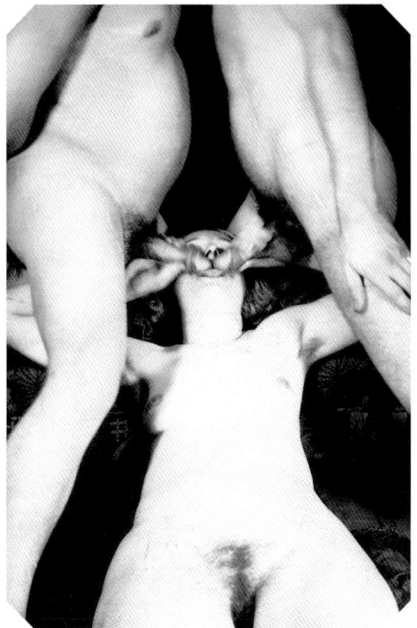
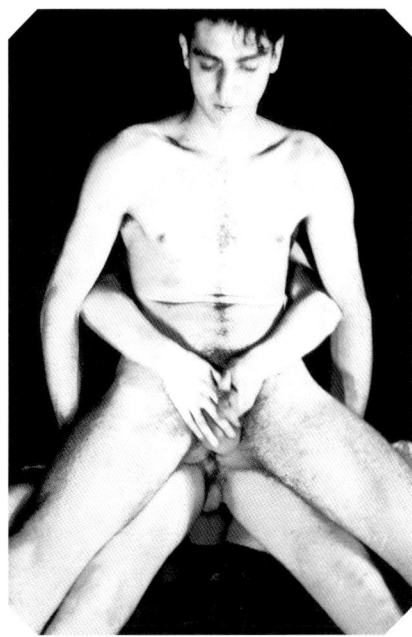

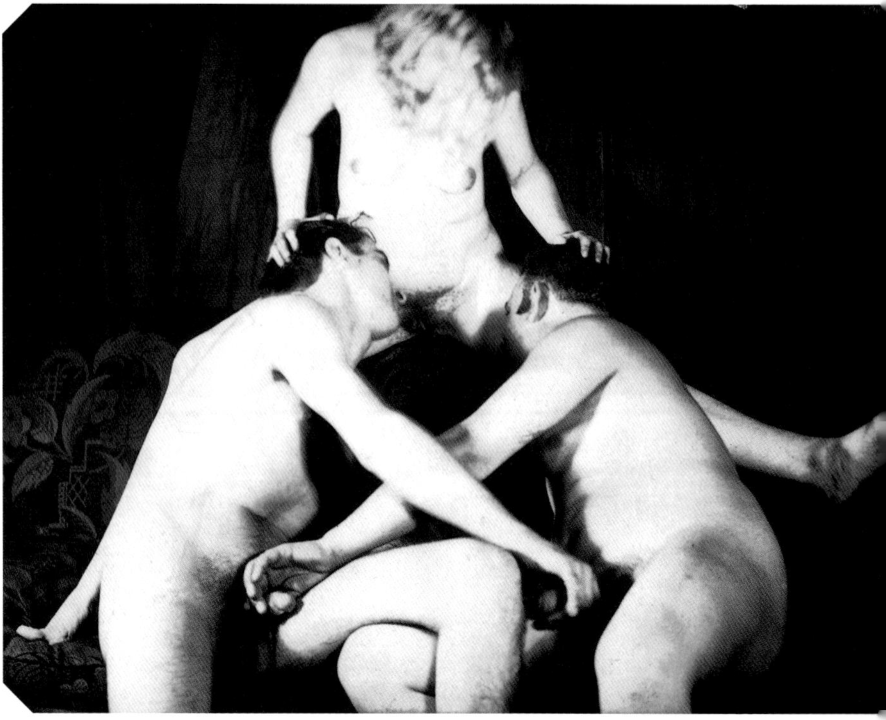

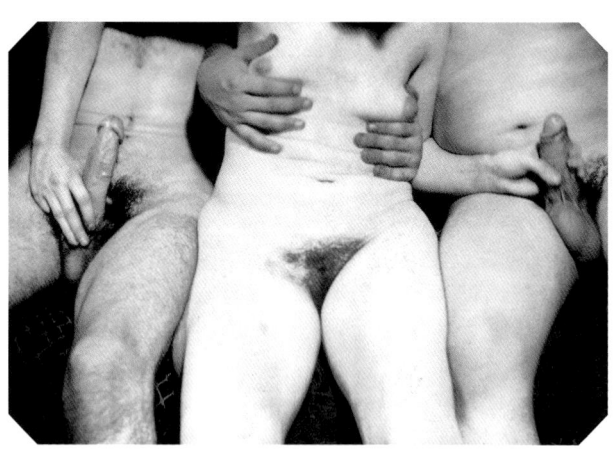

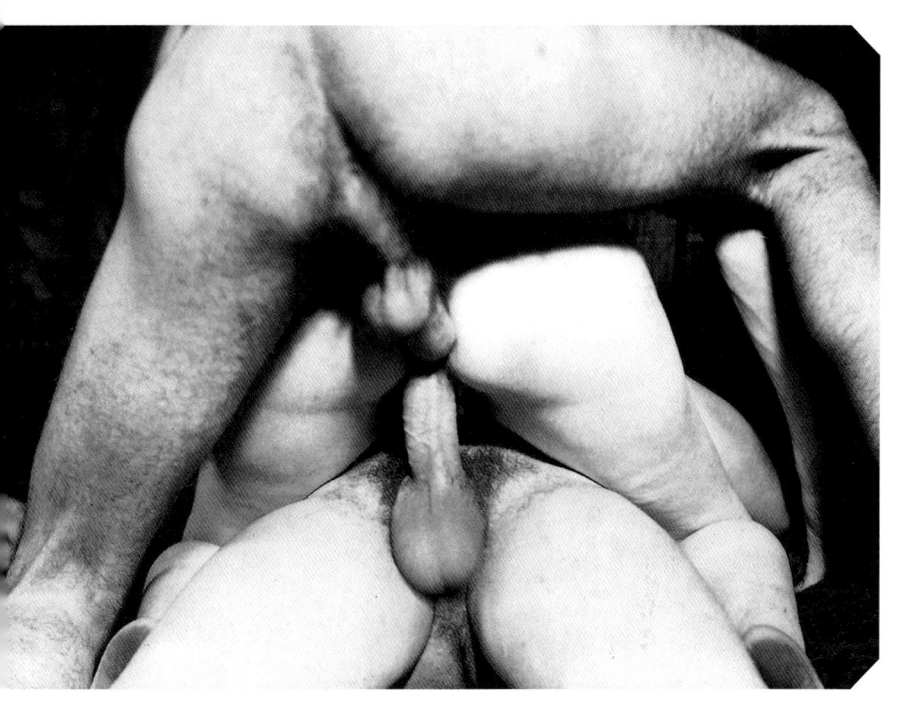

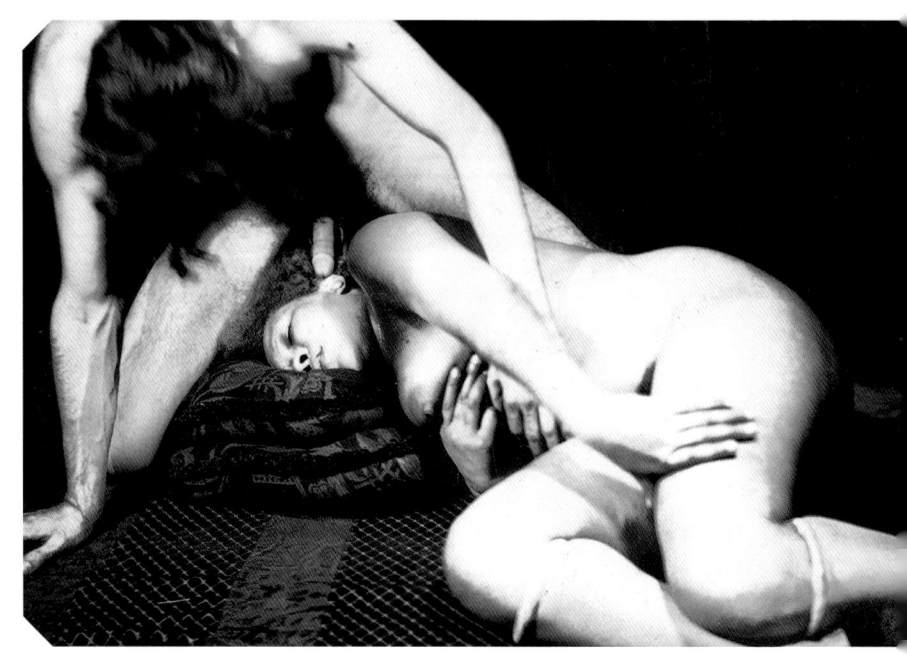

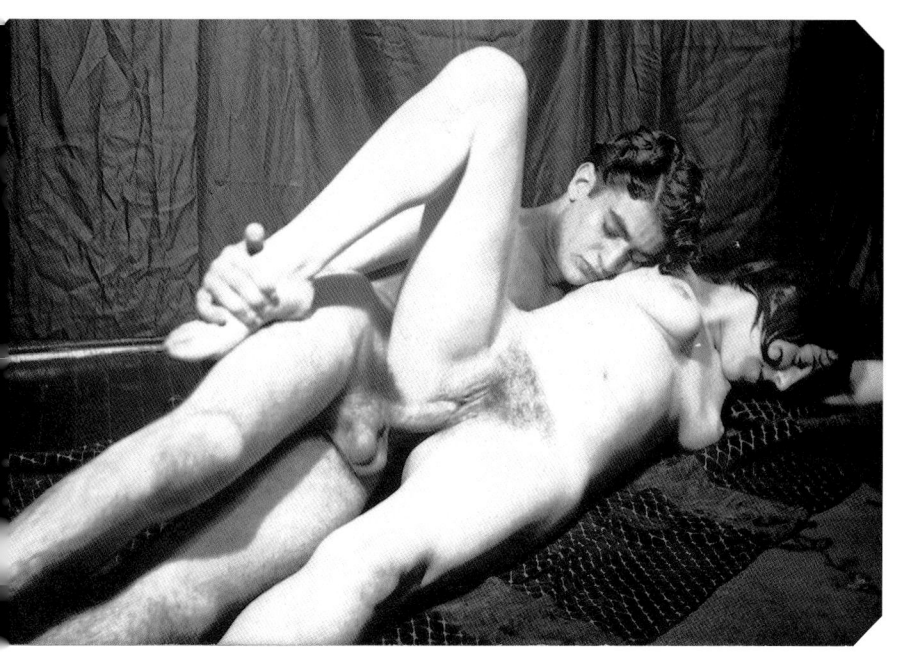

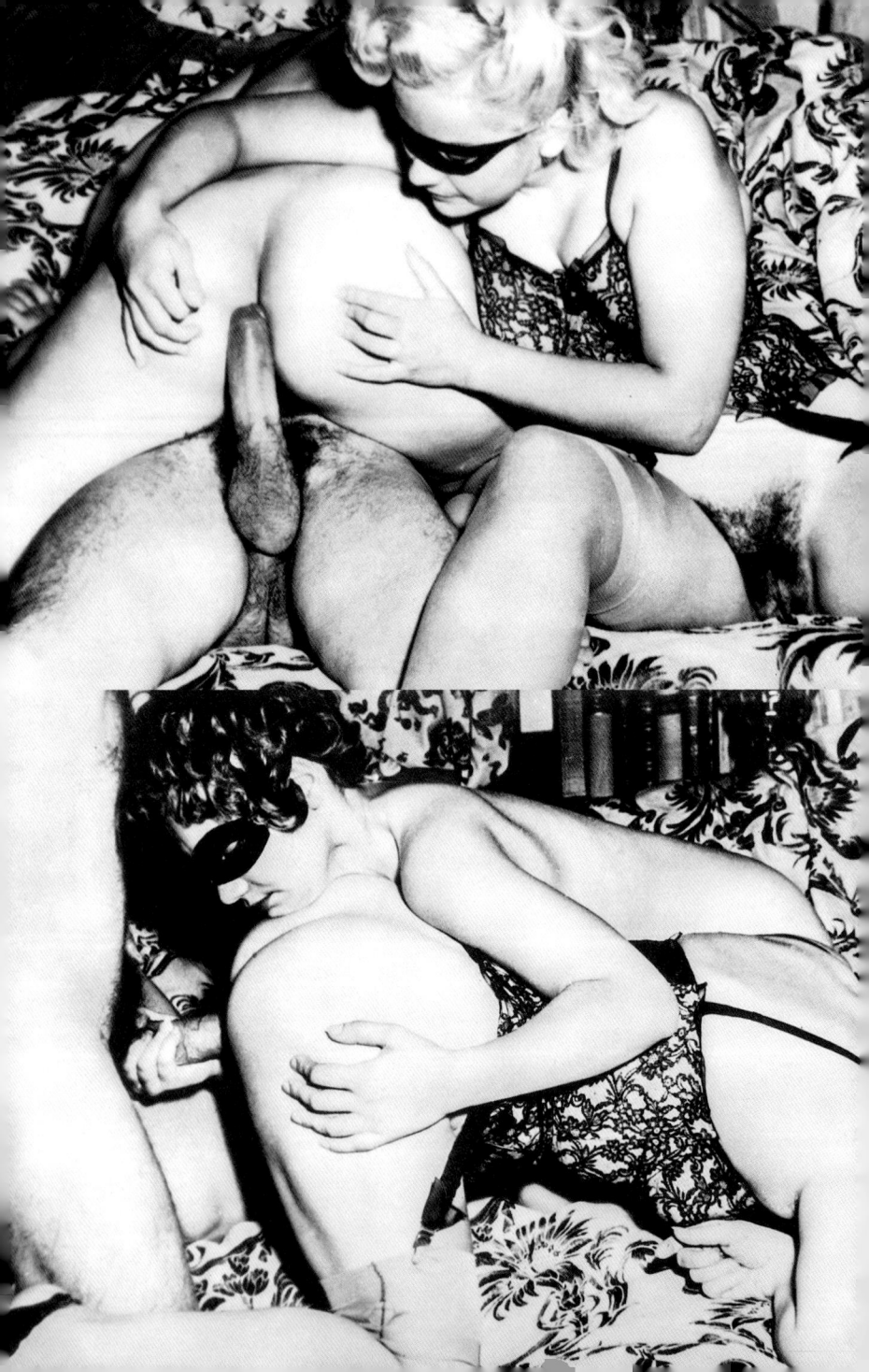

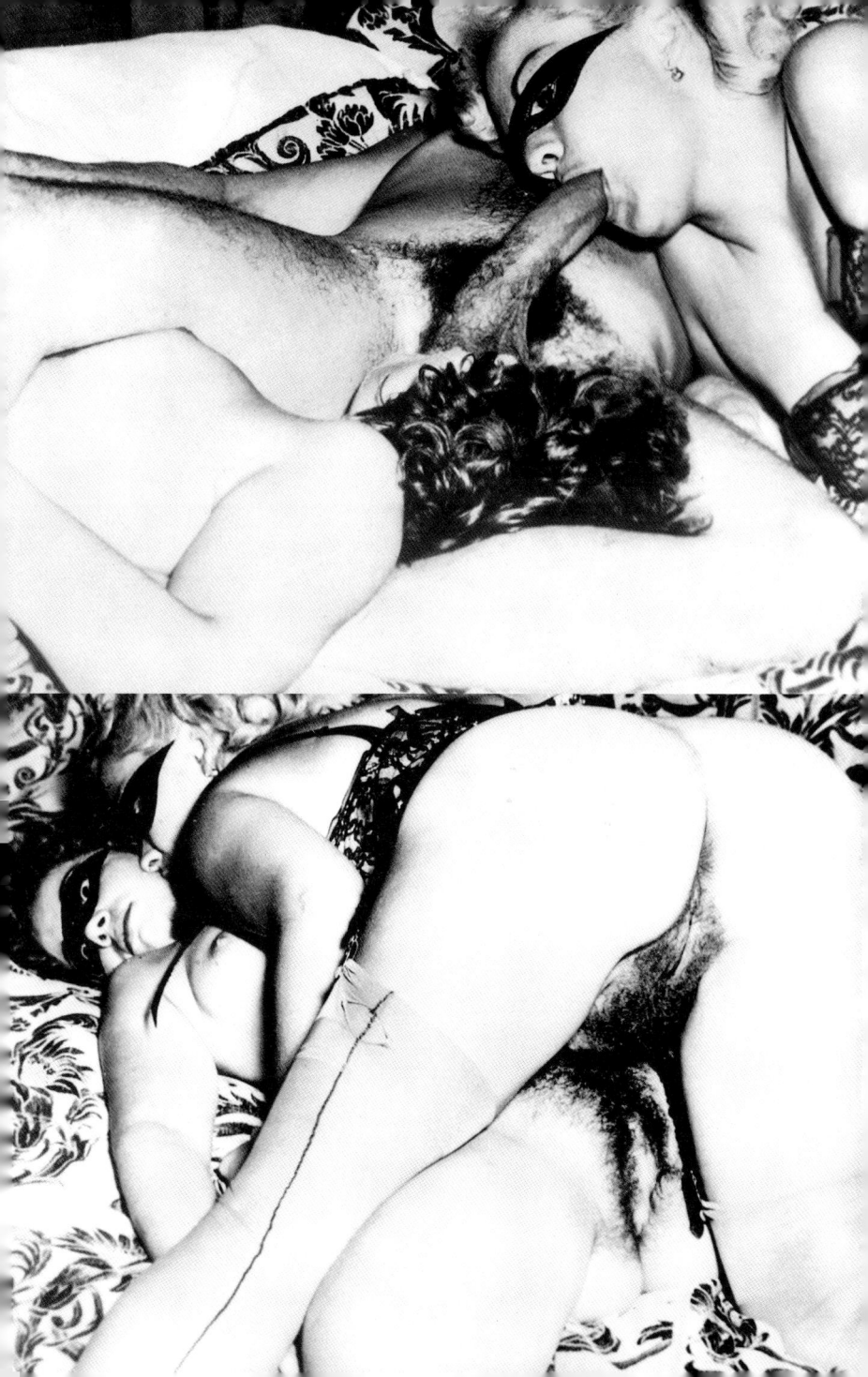

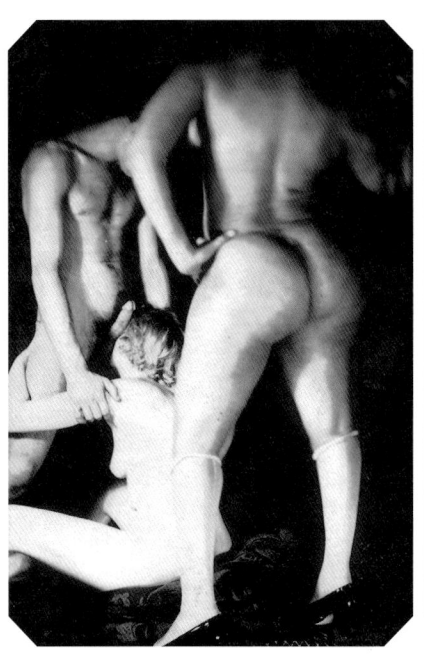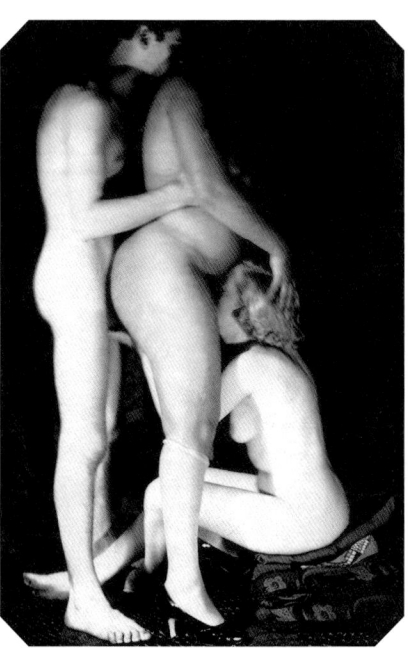

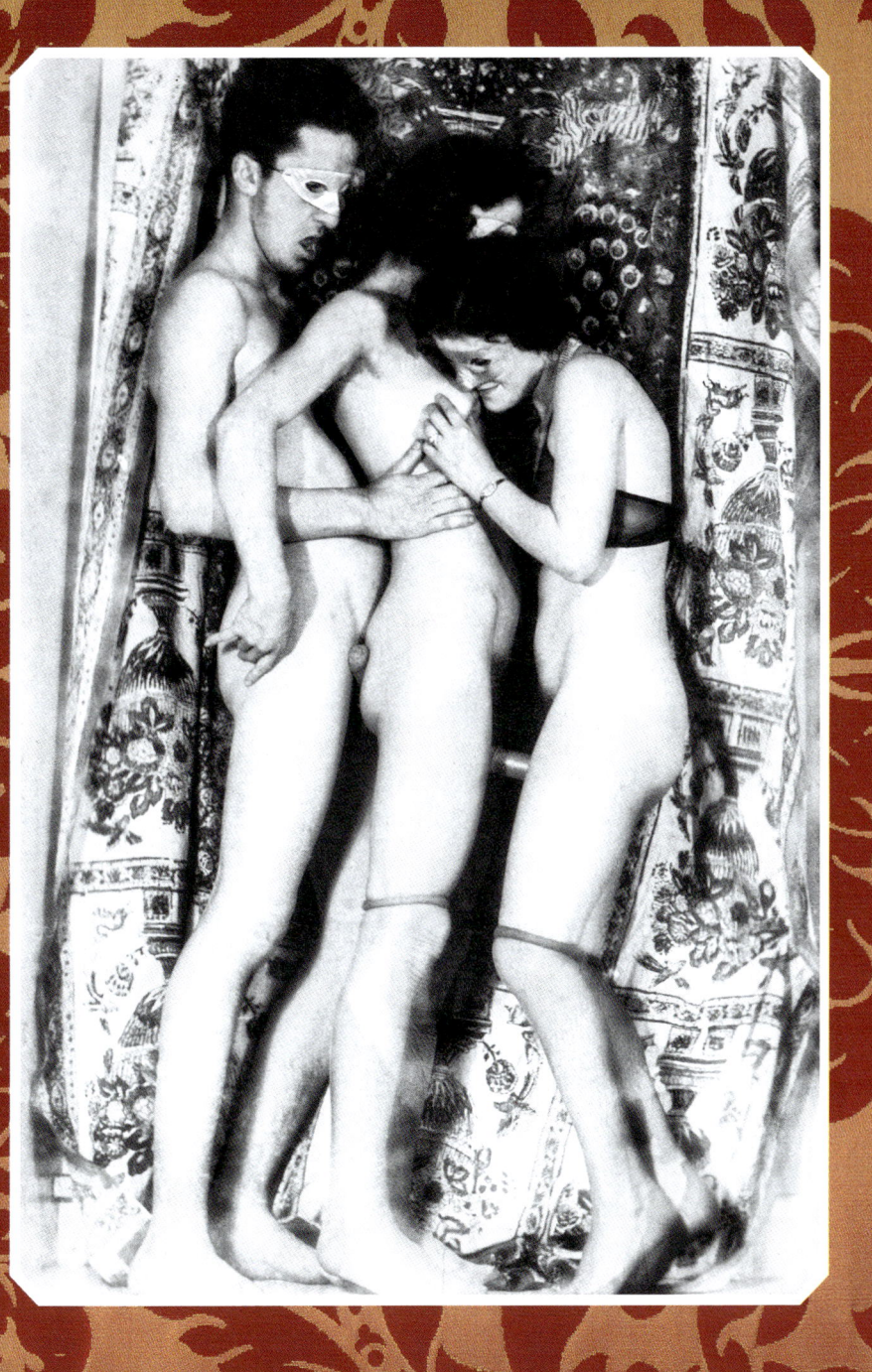

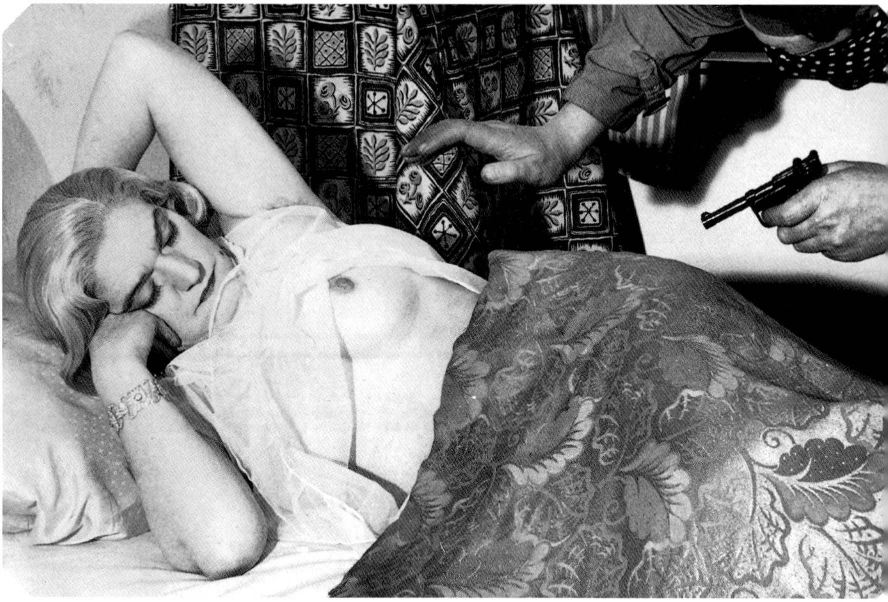

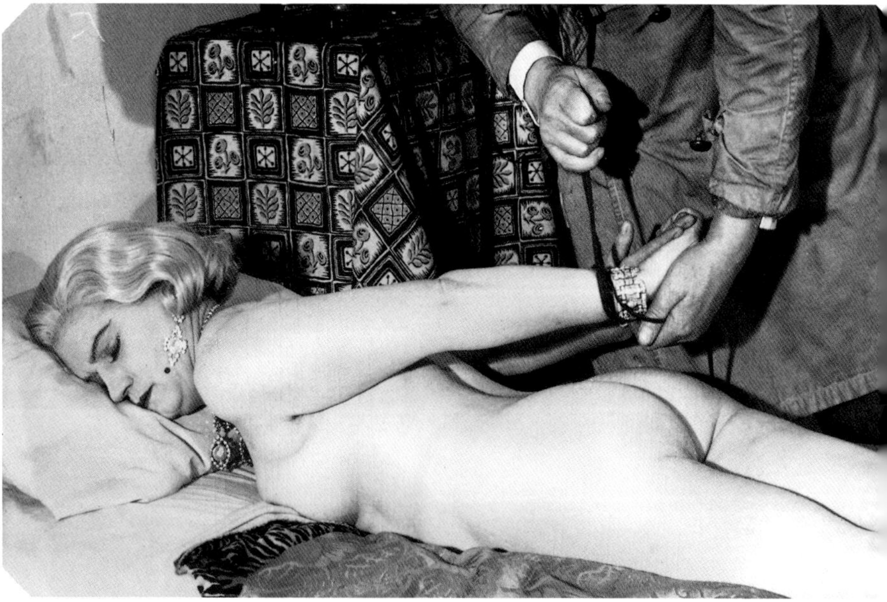

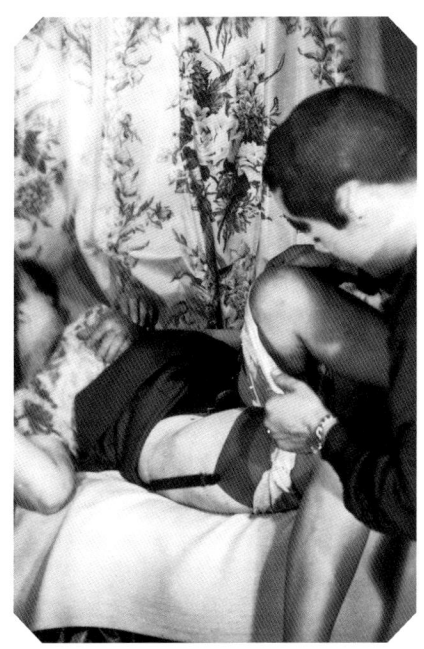
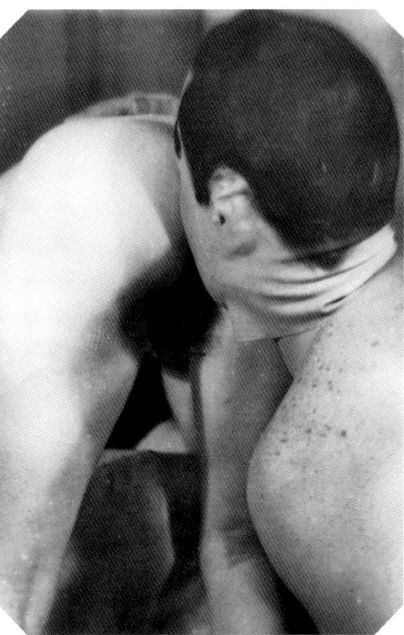

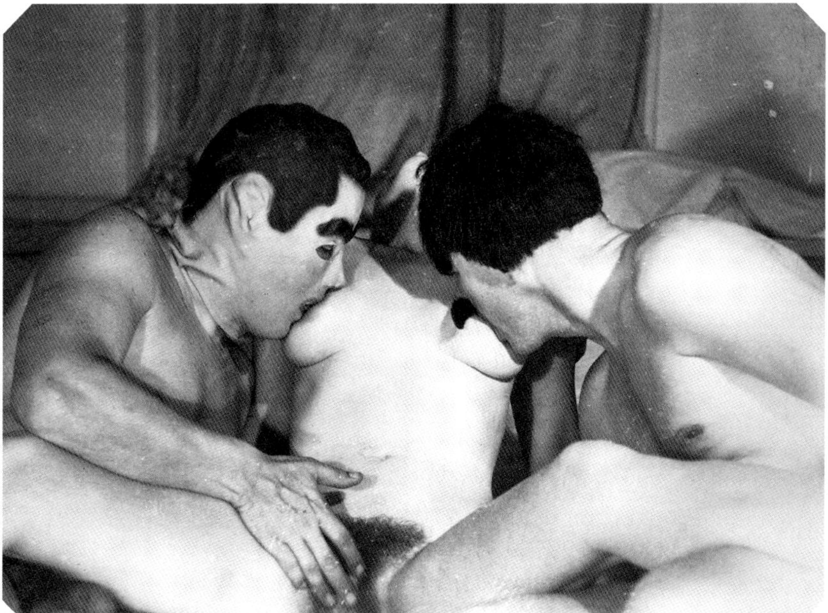

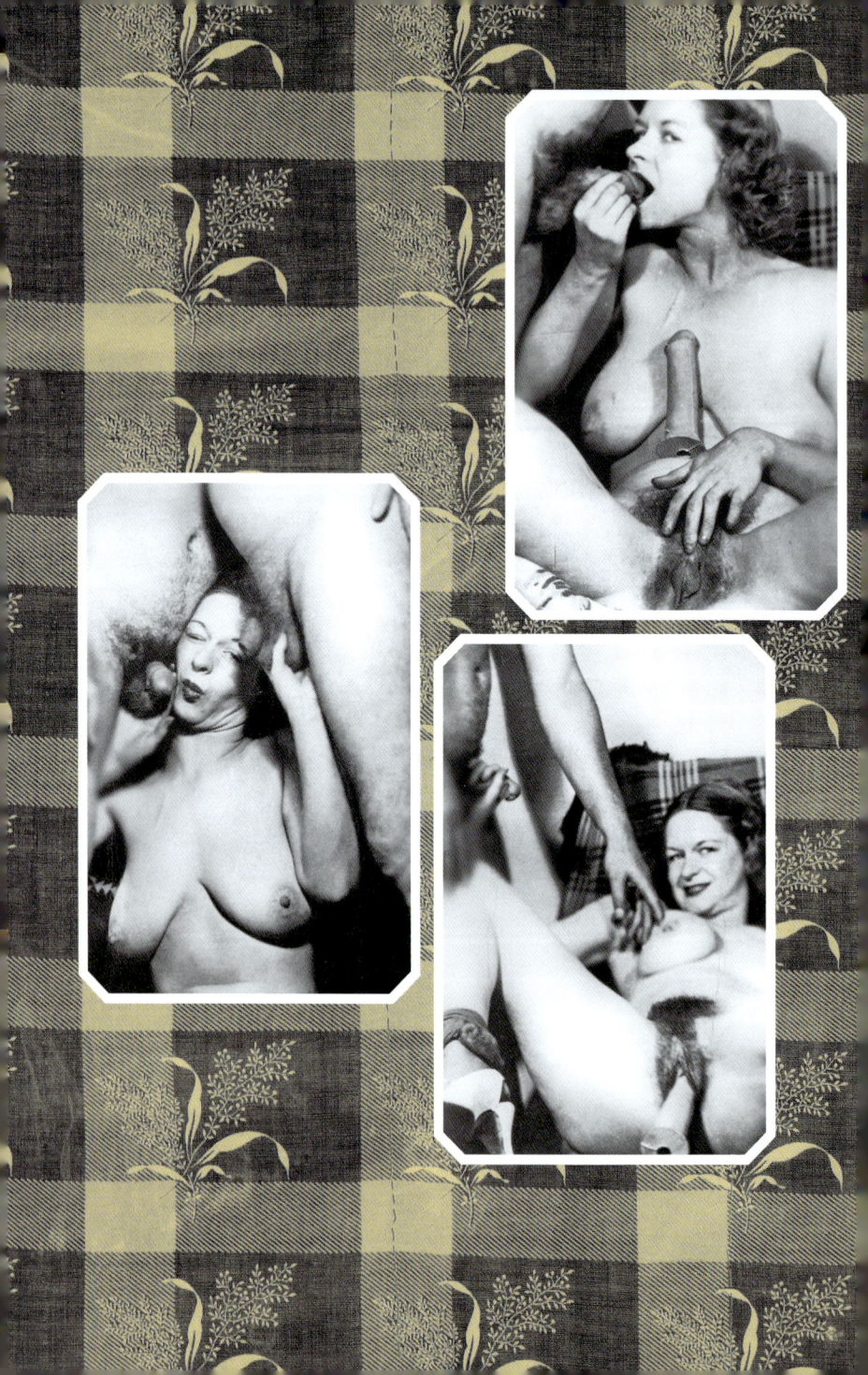

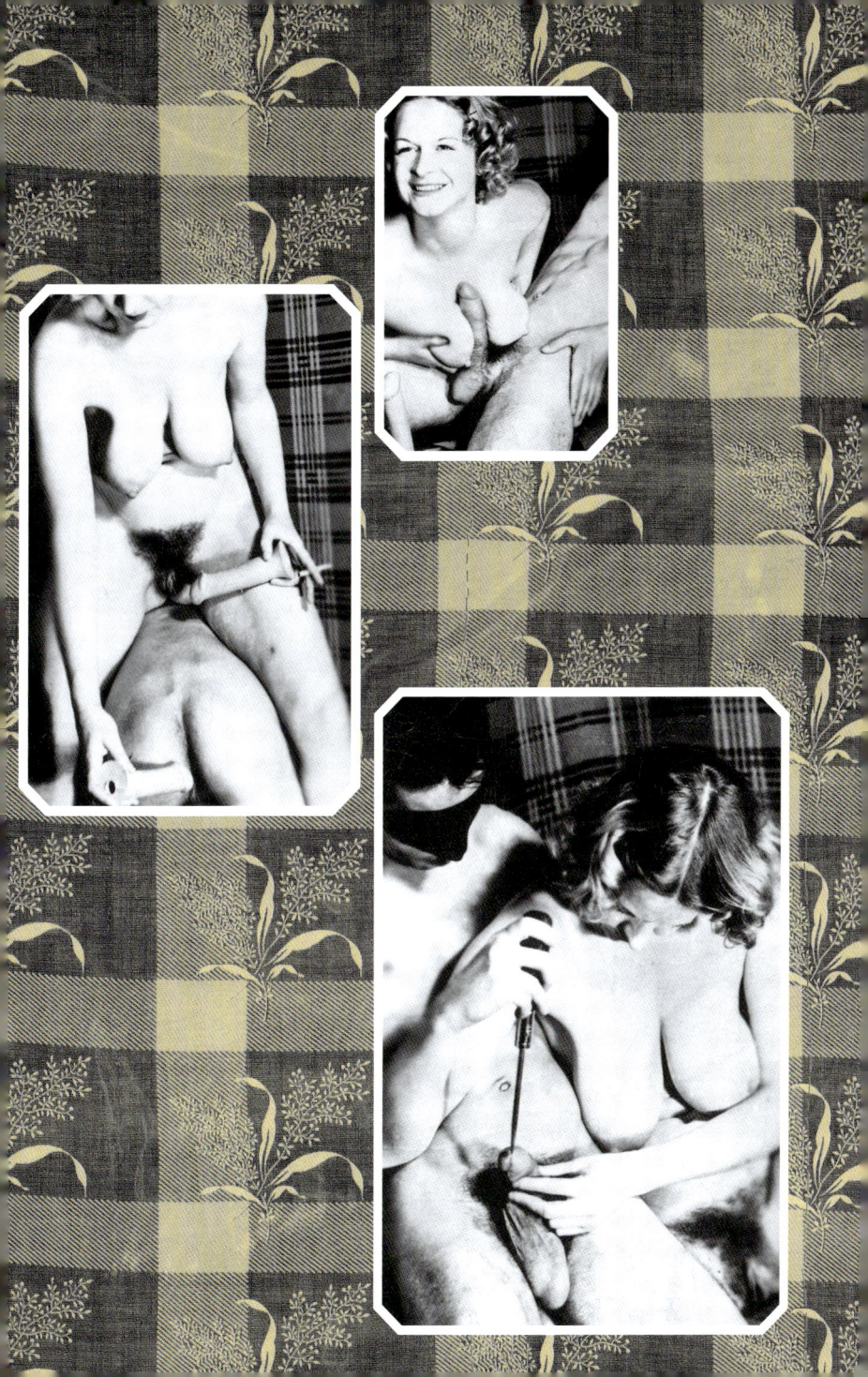

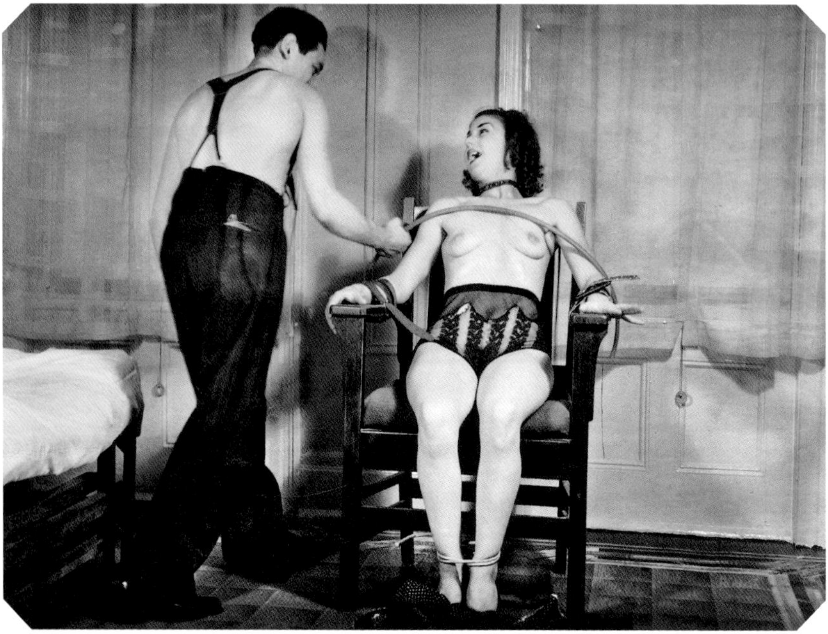

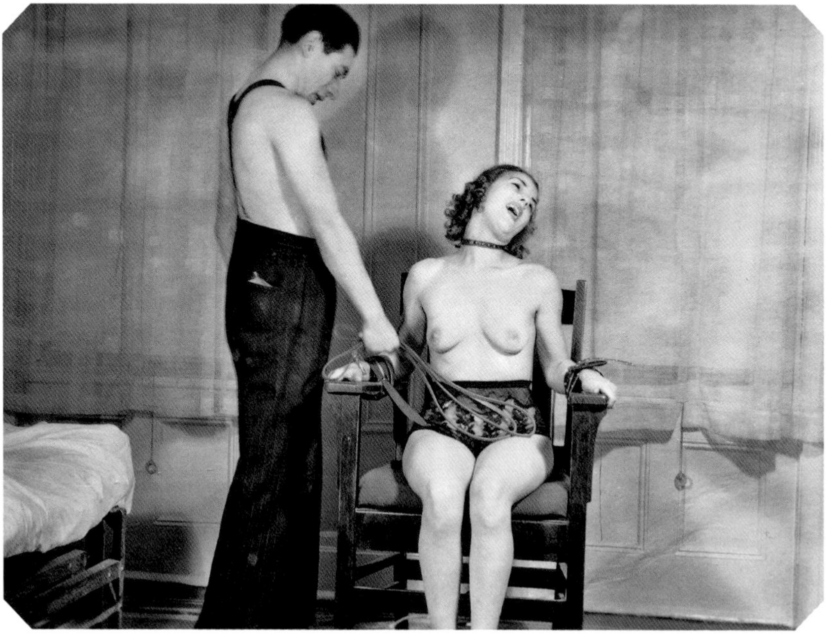

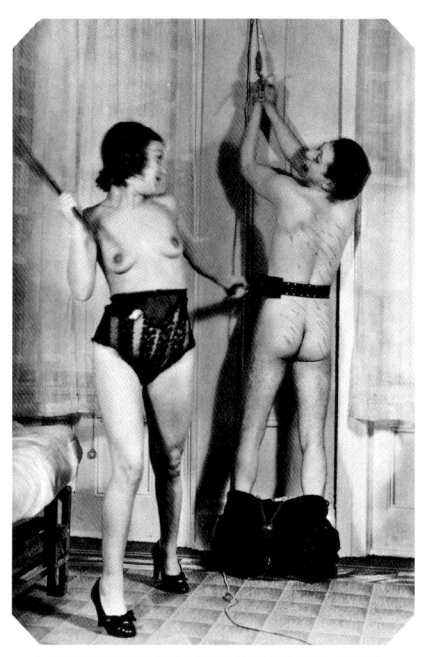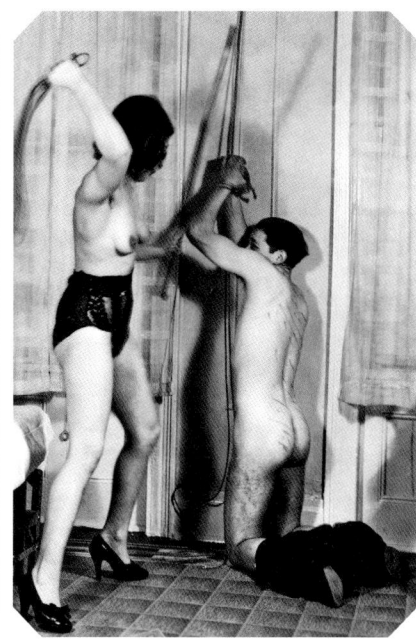
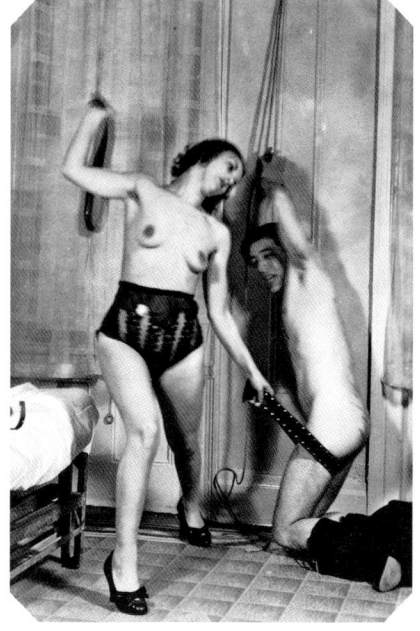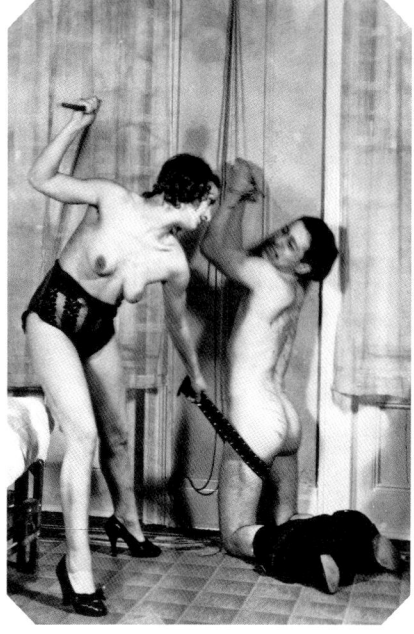

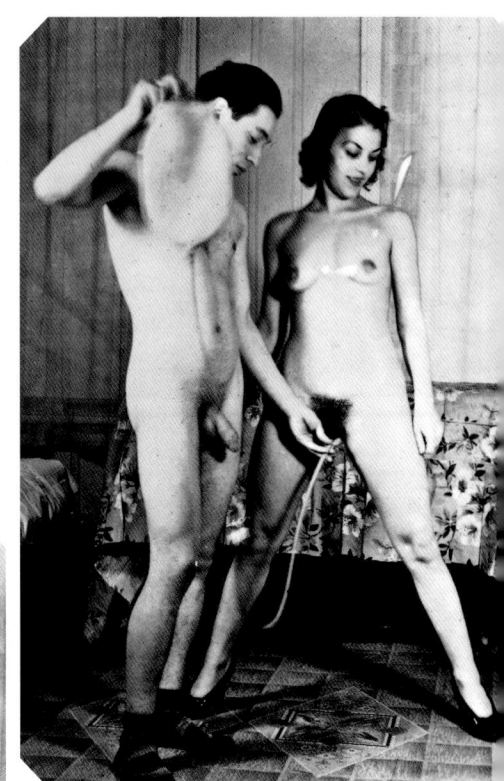

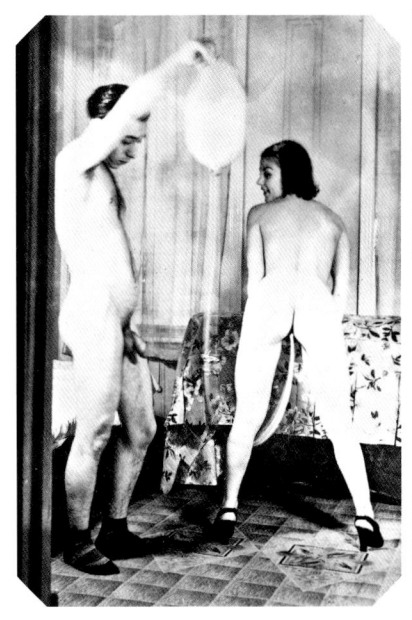

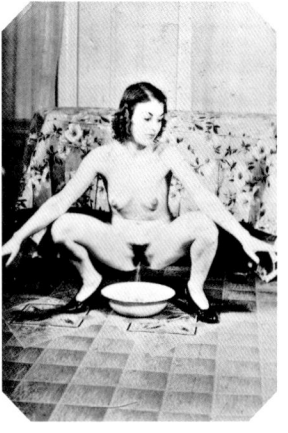

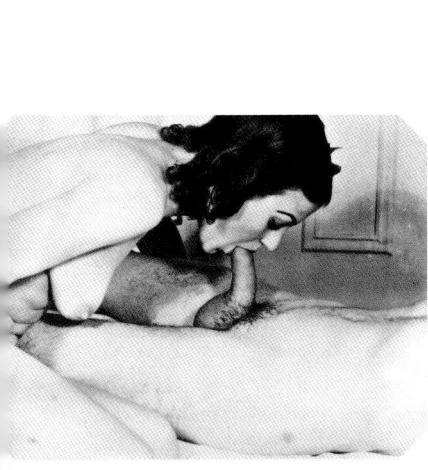

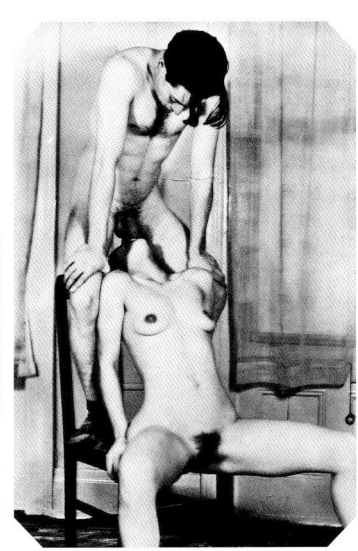

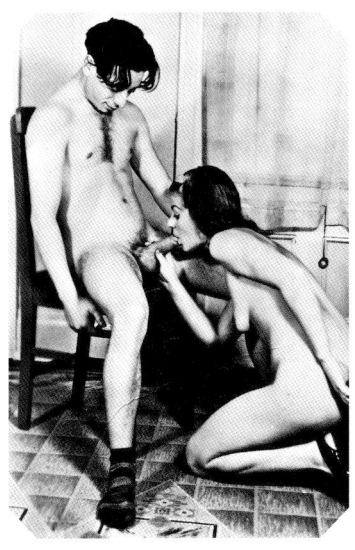

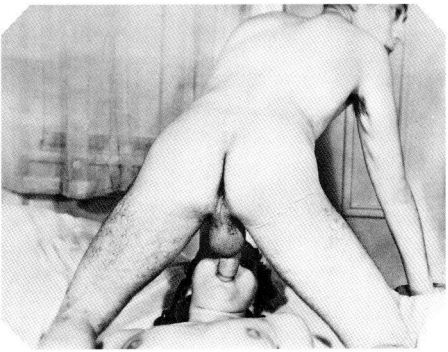

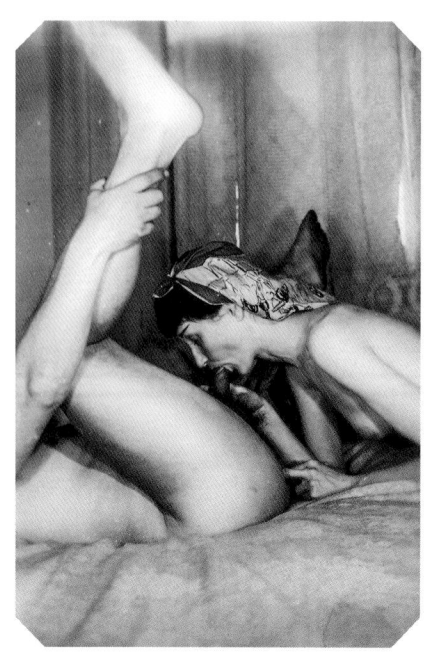
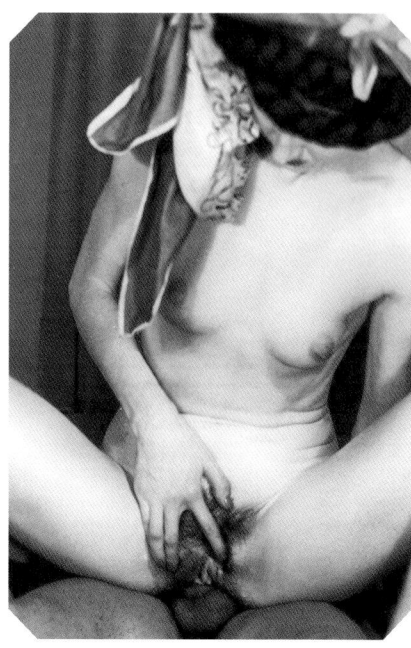
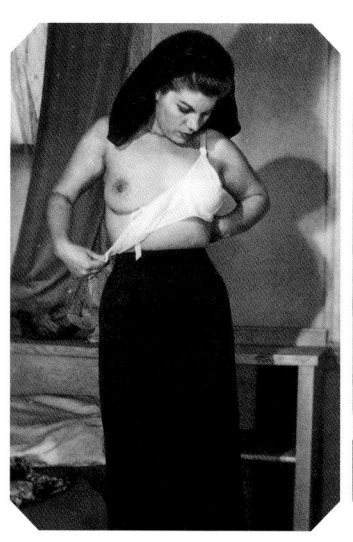
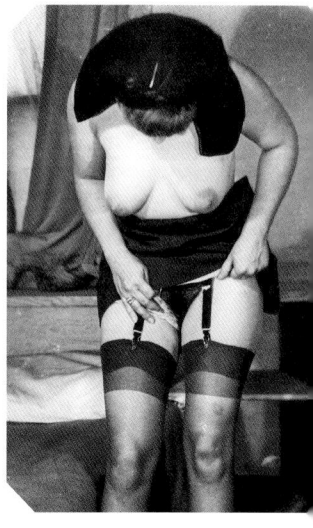

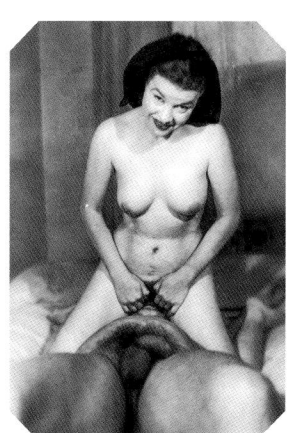
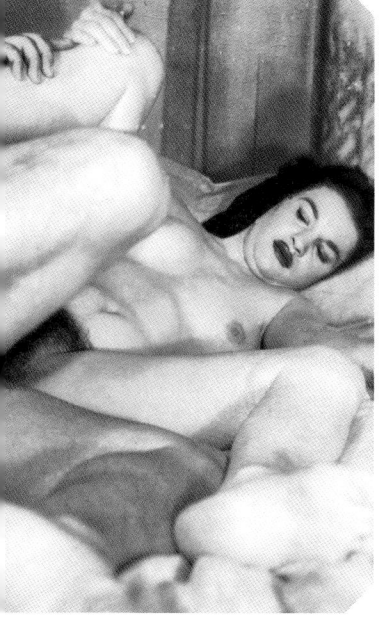
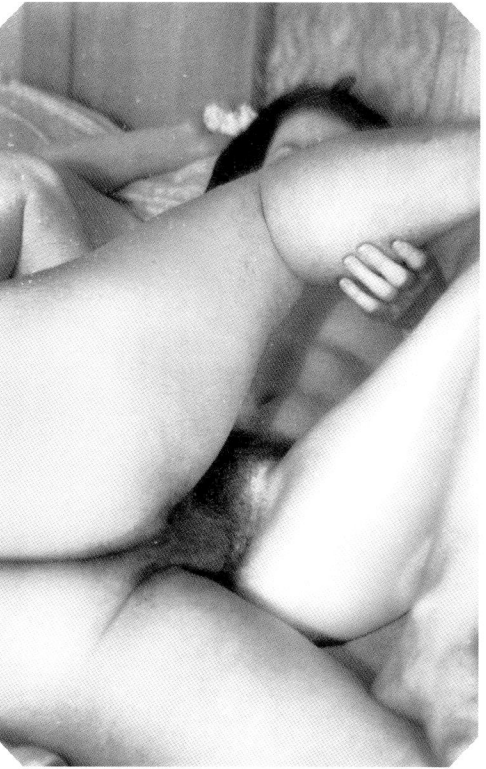

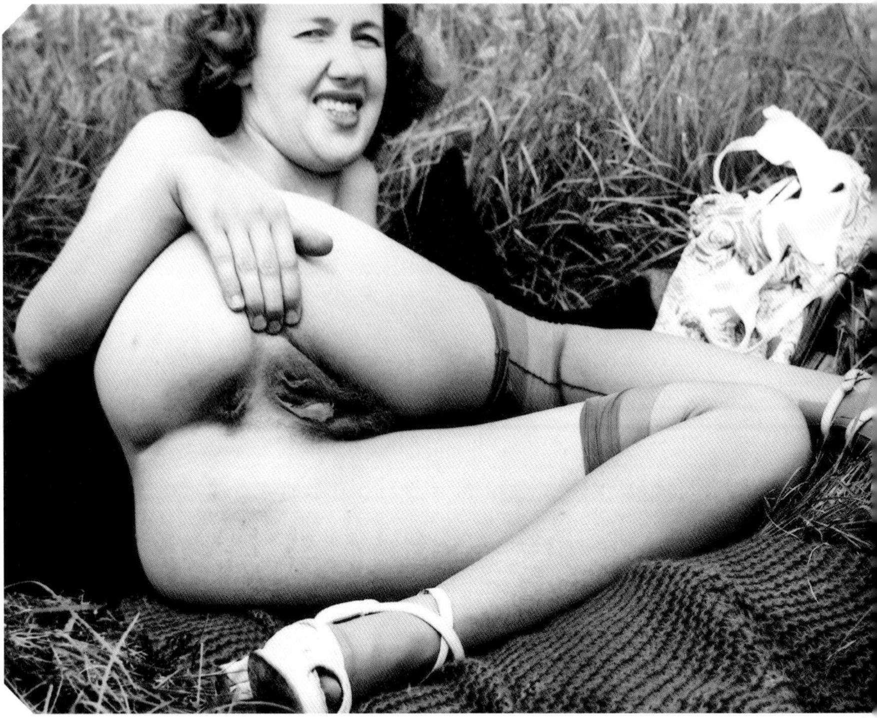

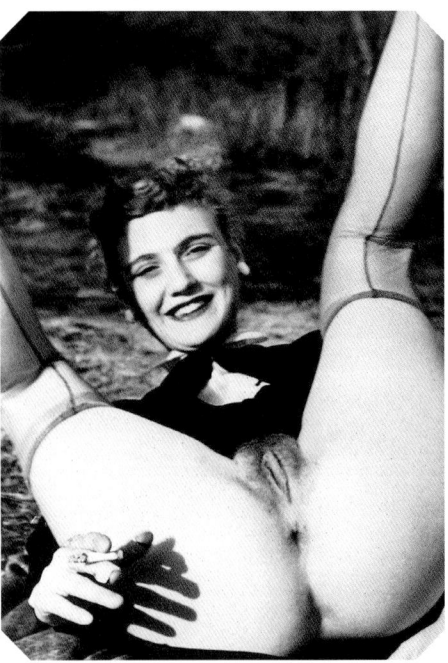
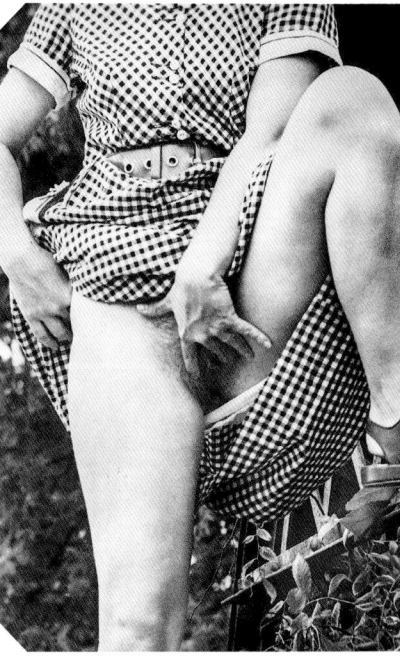

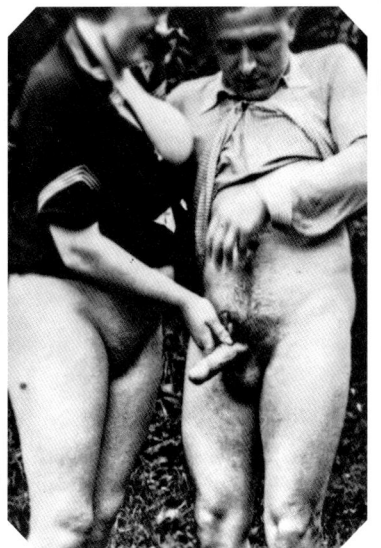

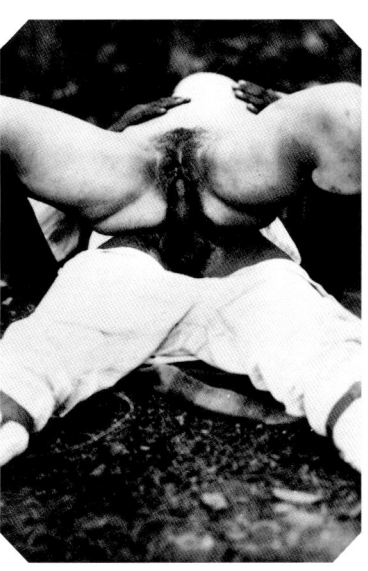

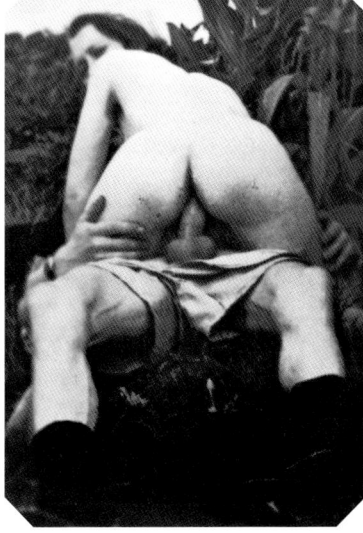

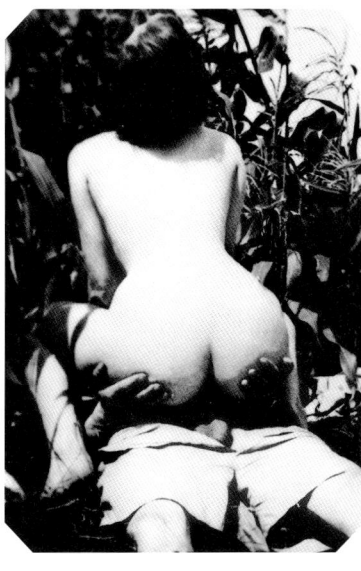

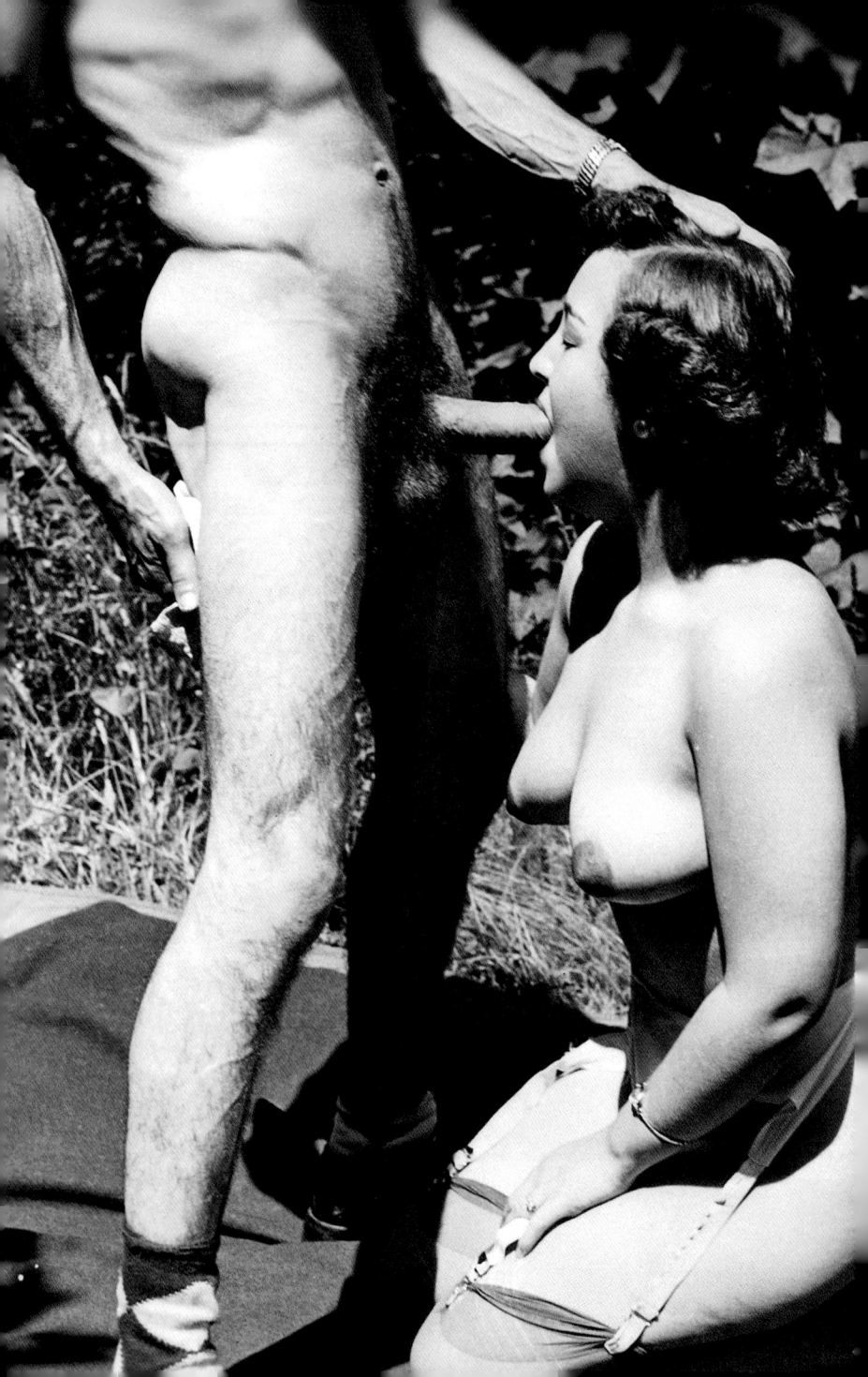

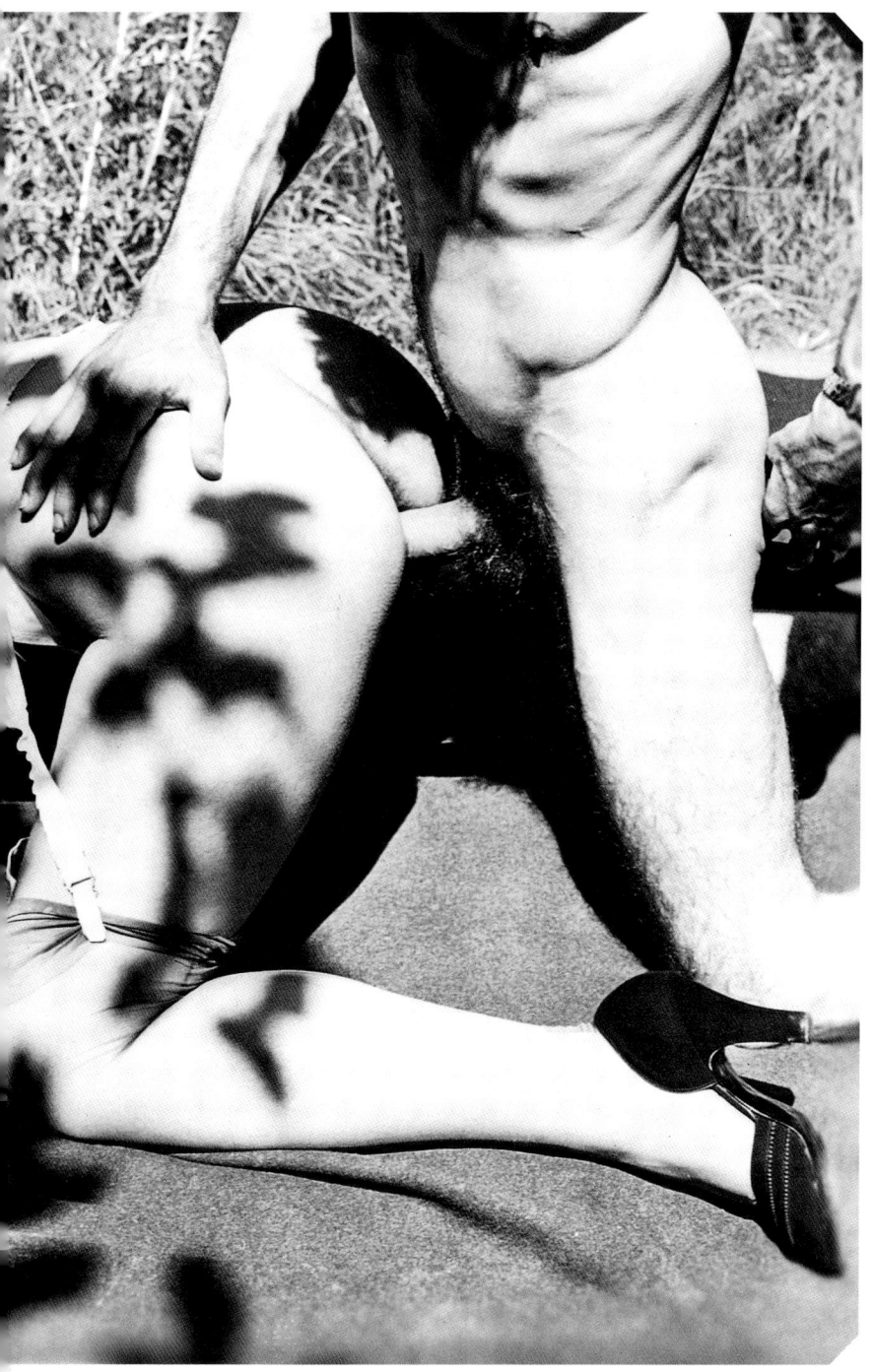

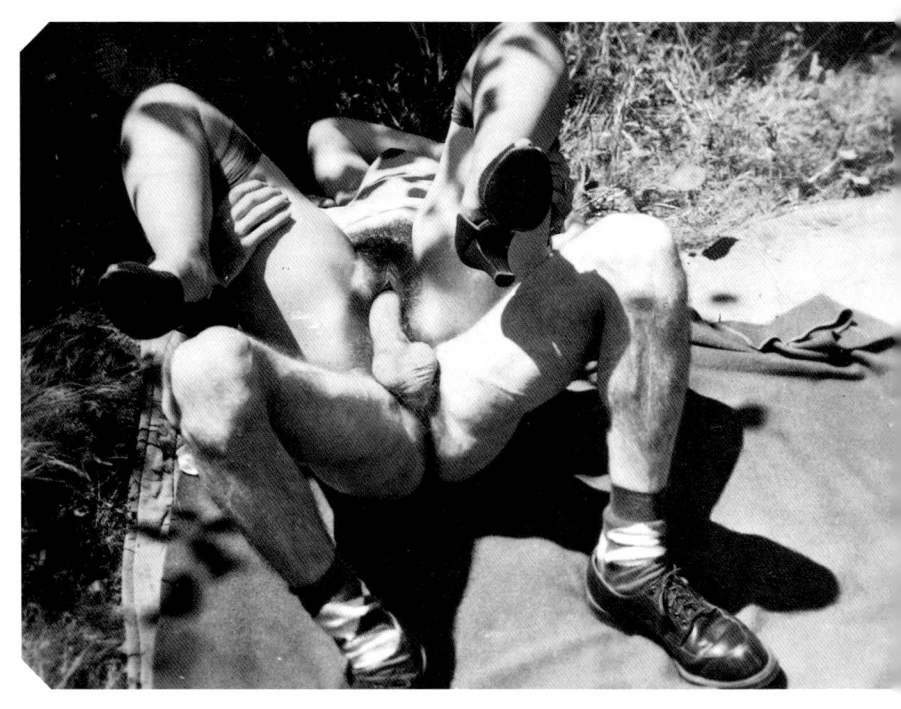

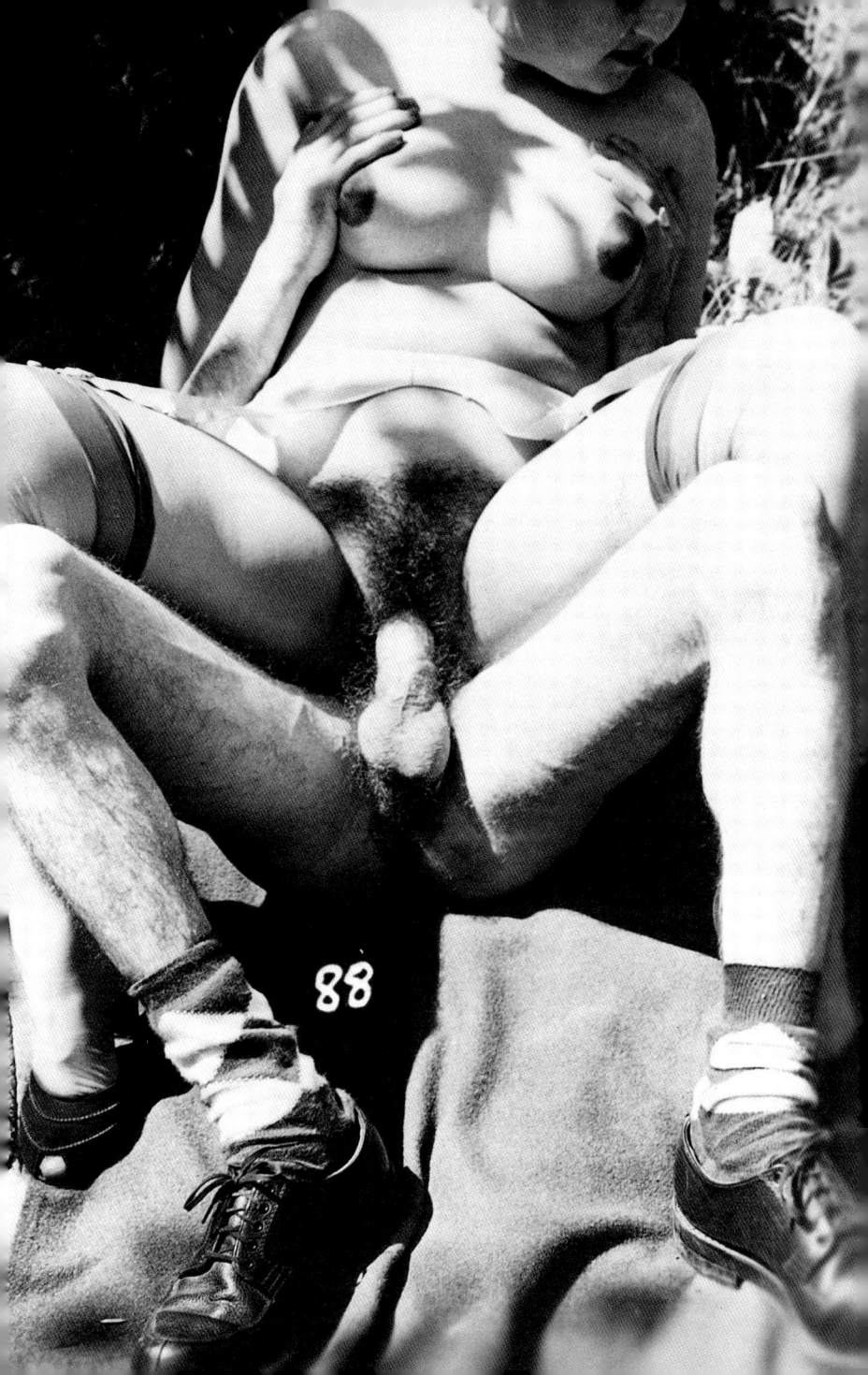

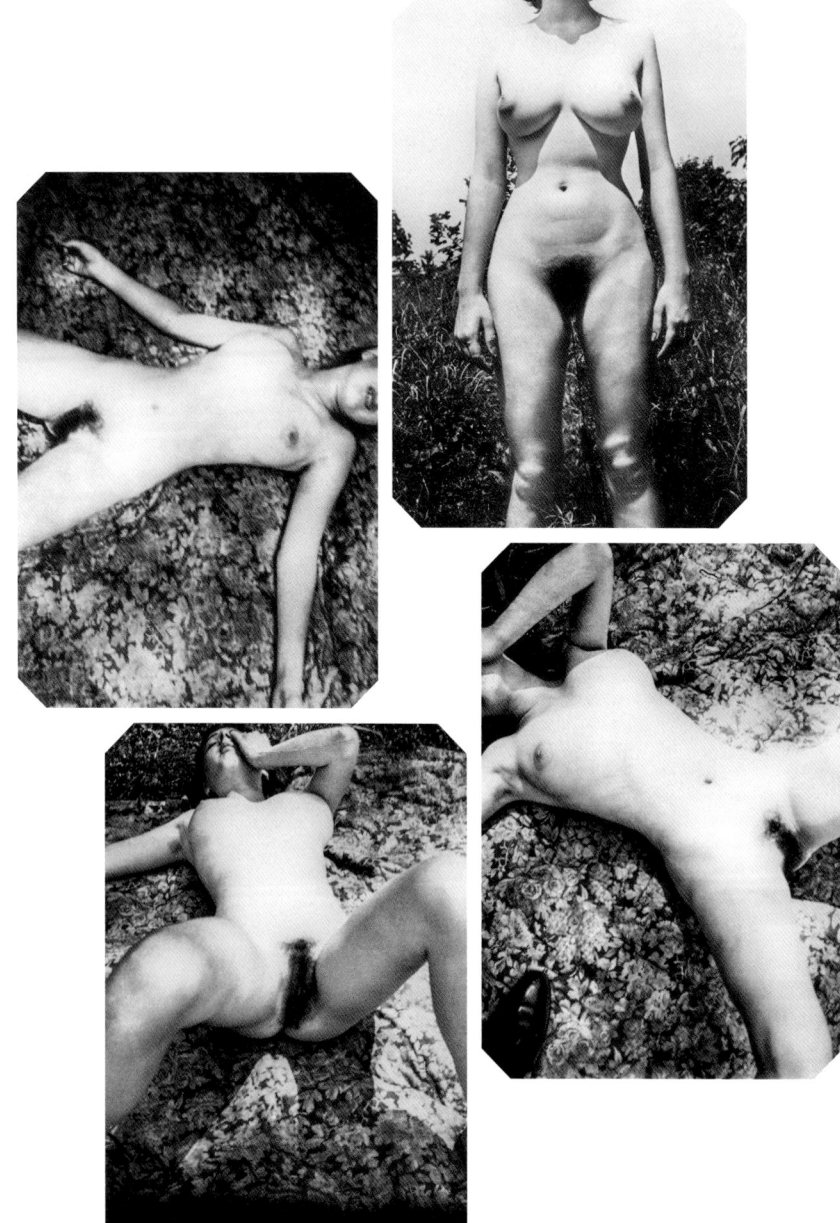

410

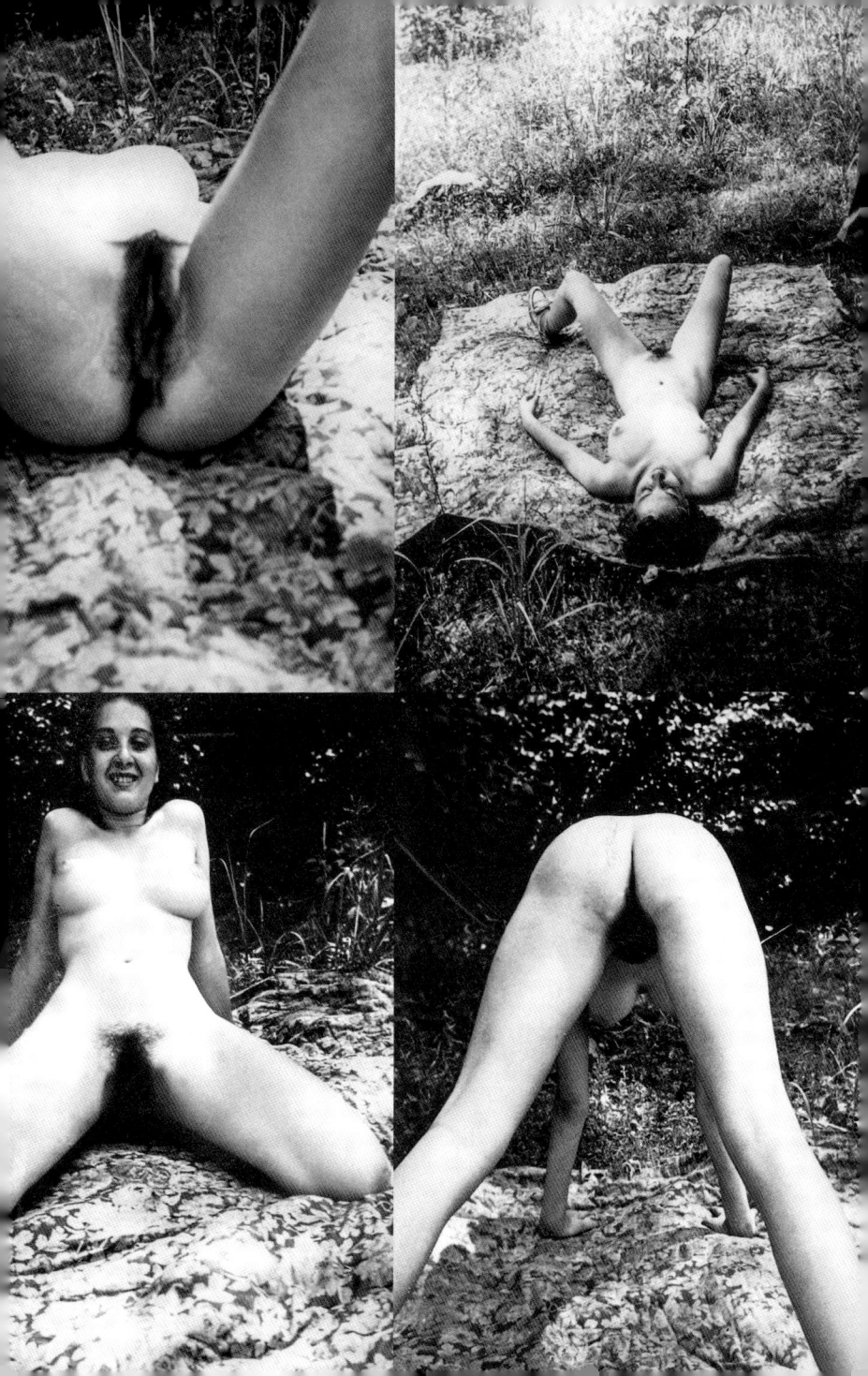

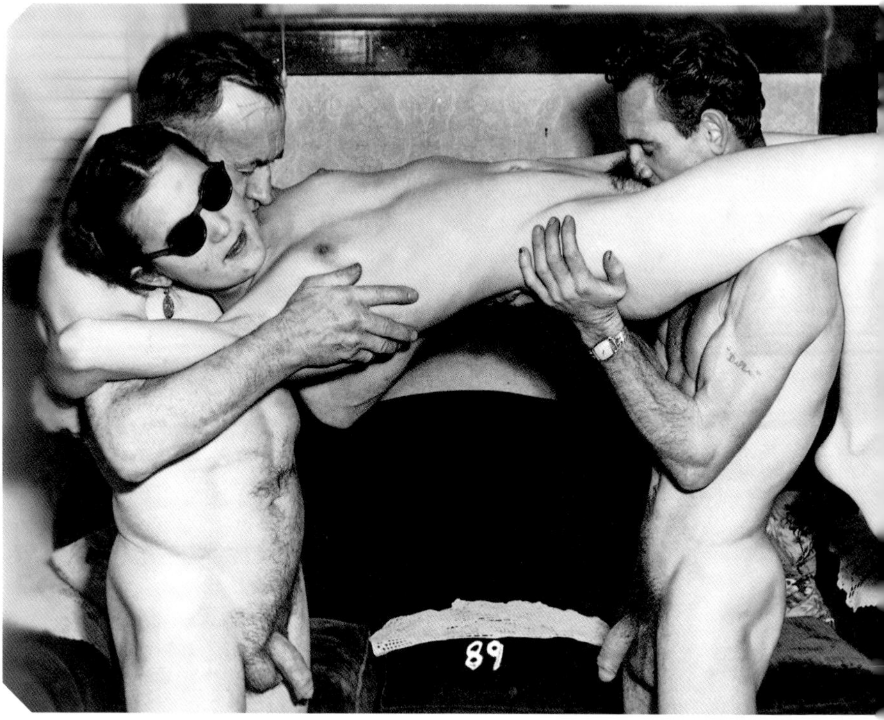

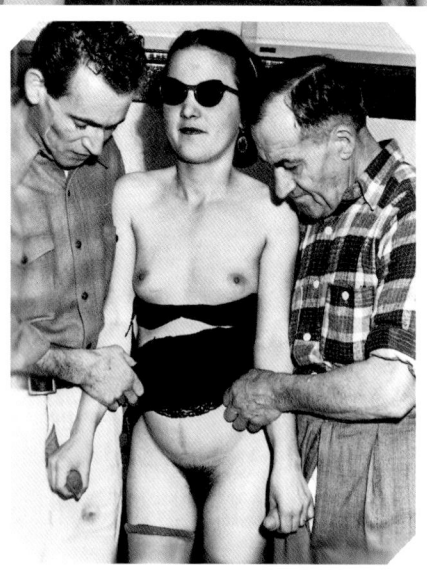

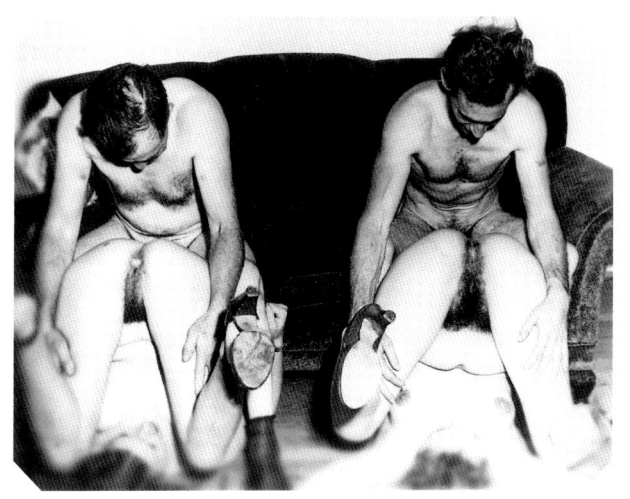

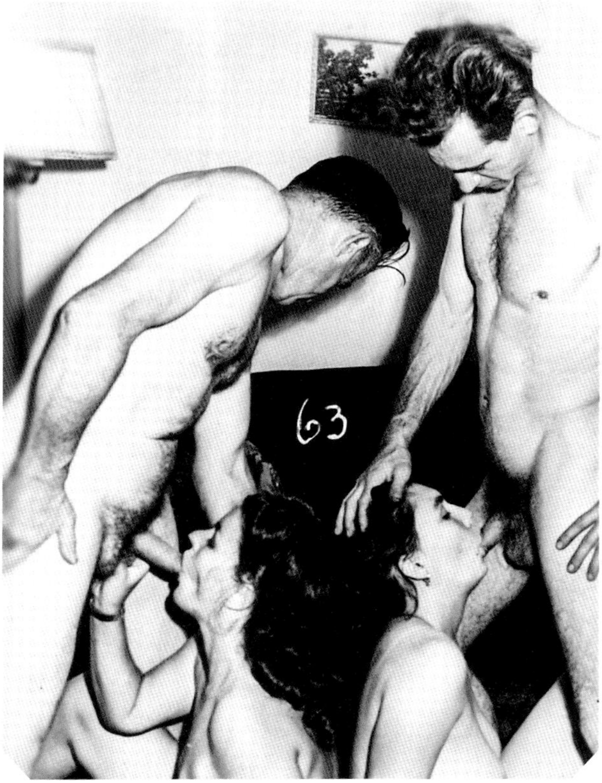

413

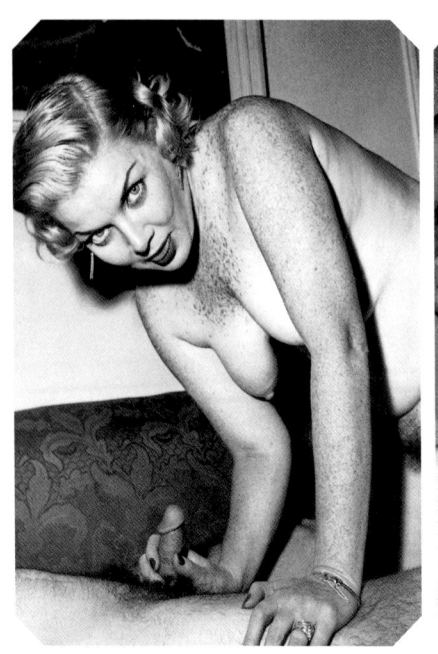
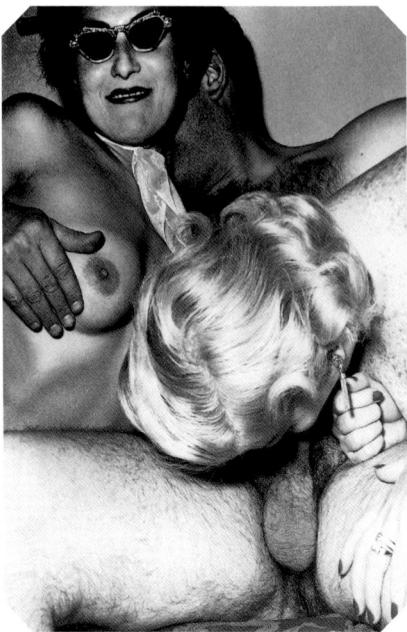

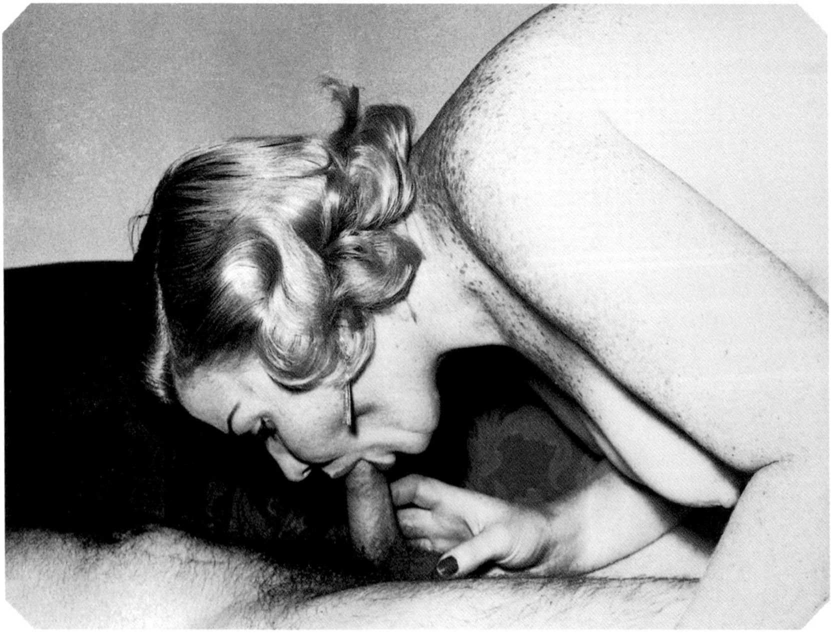

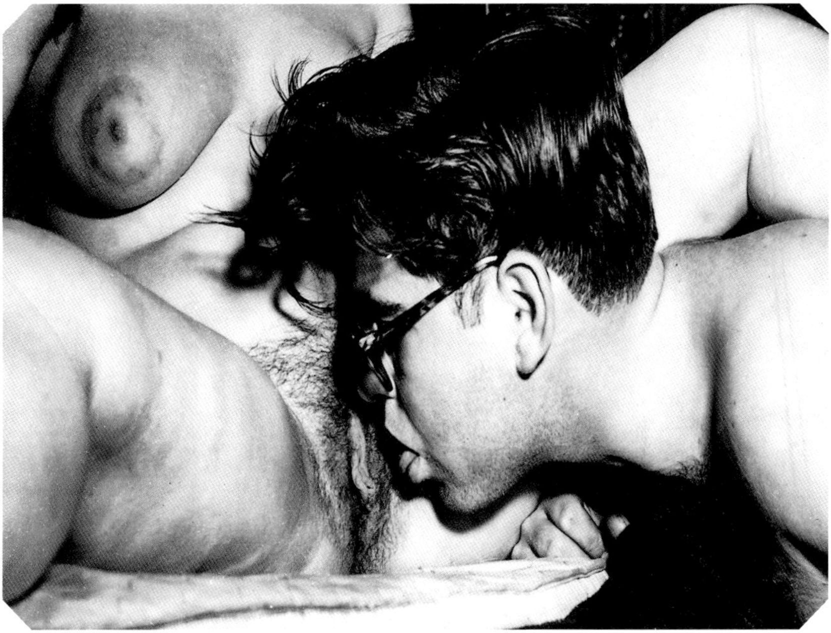

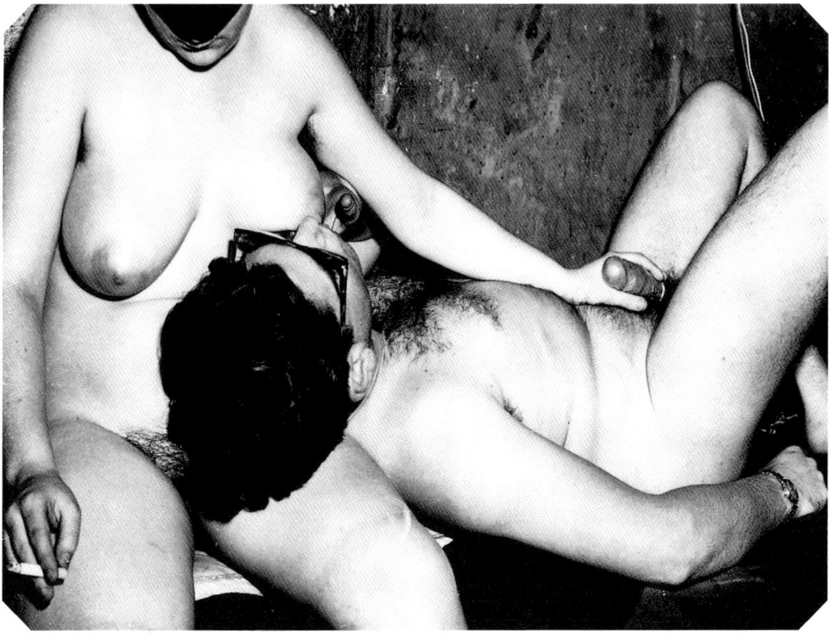

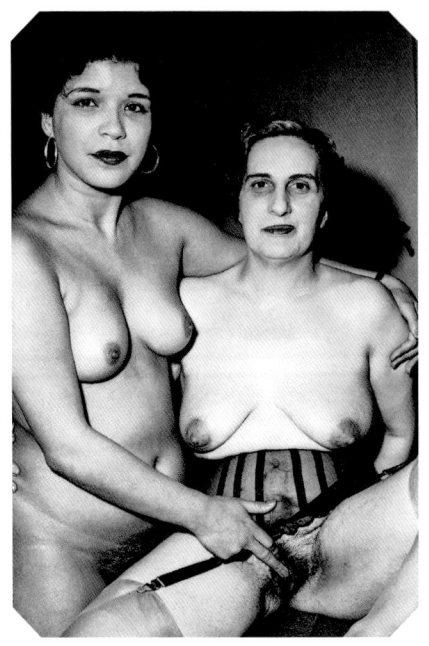
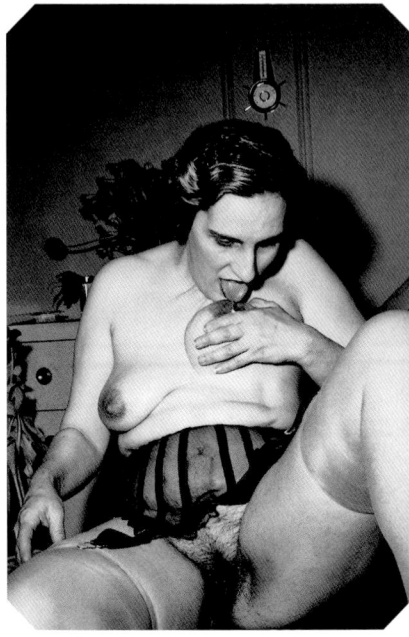
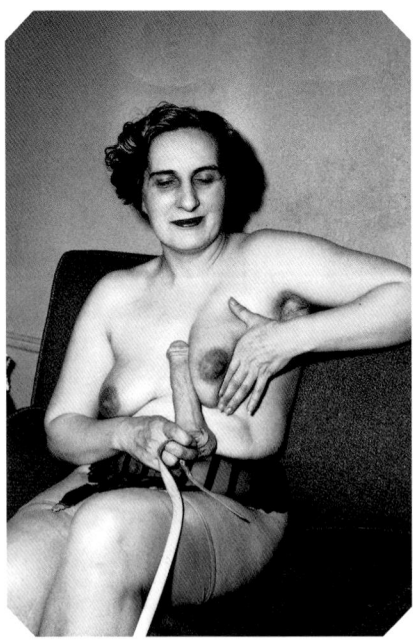
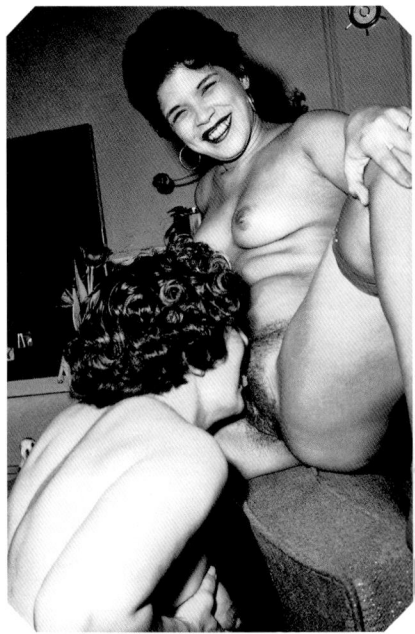

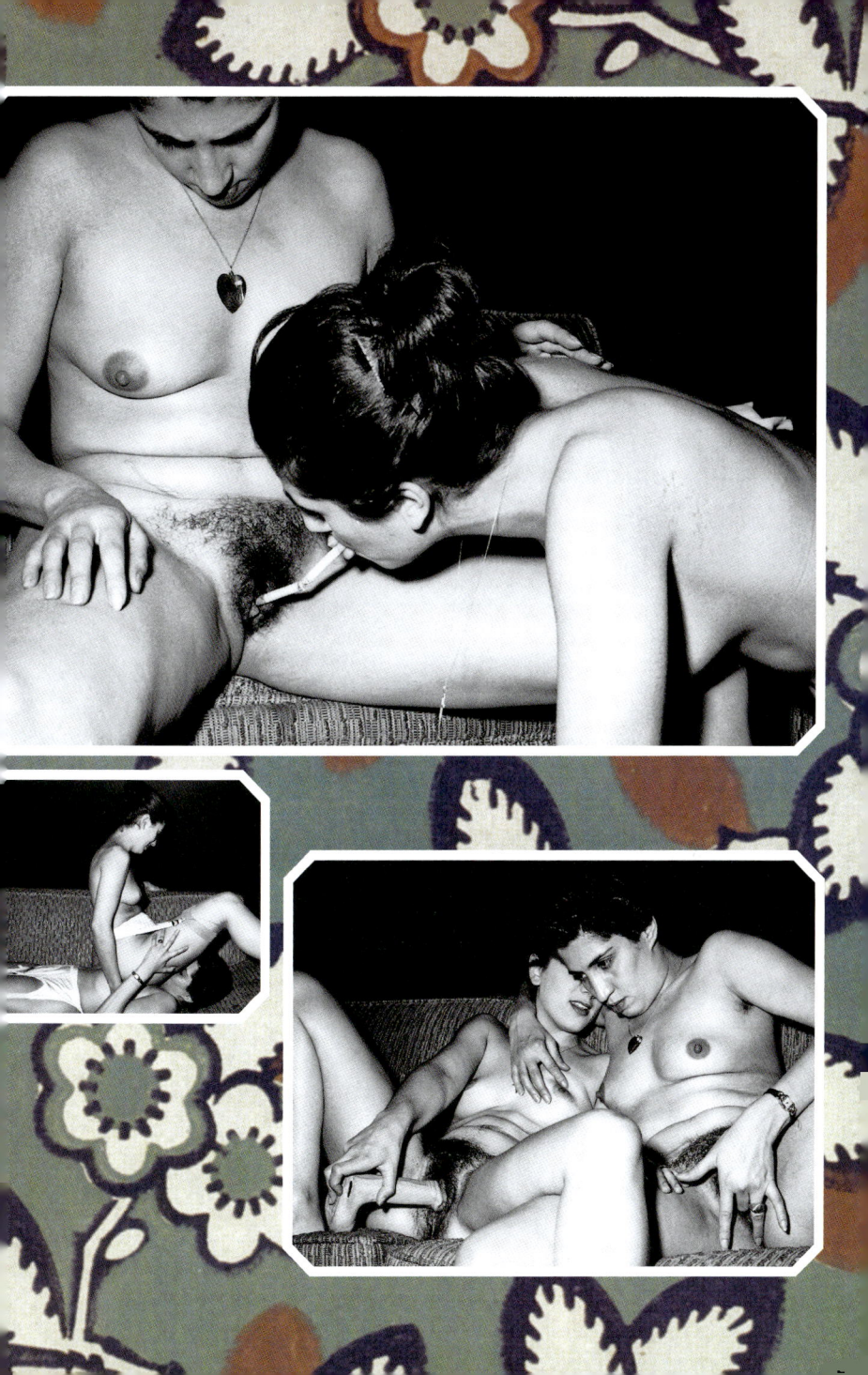

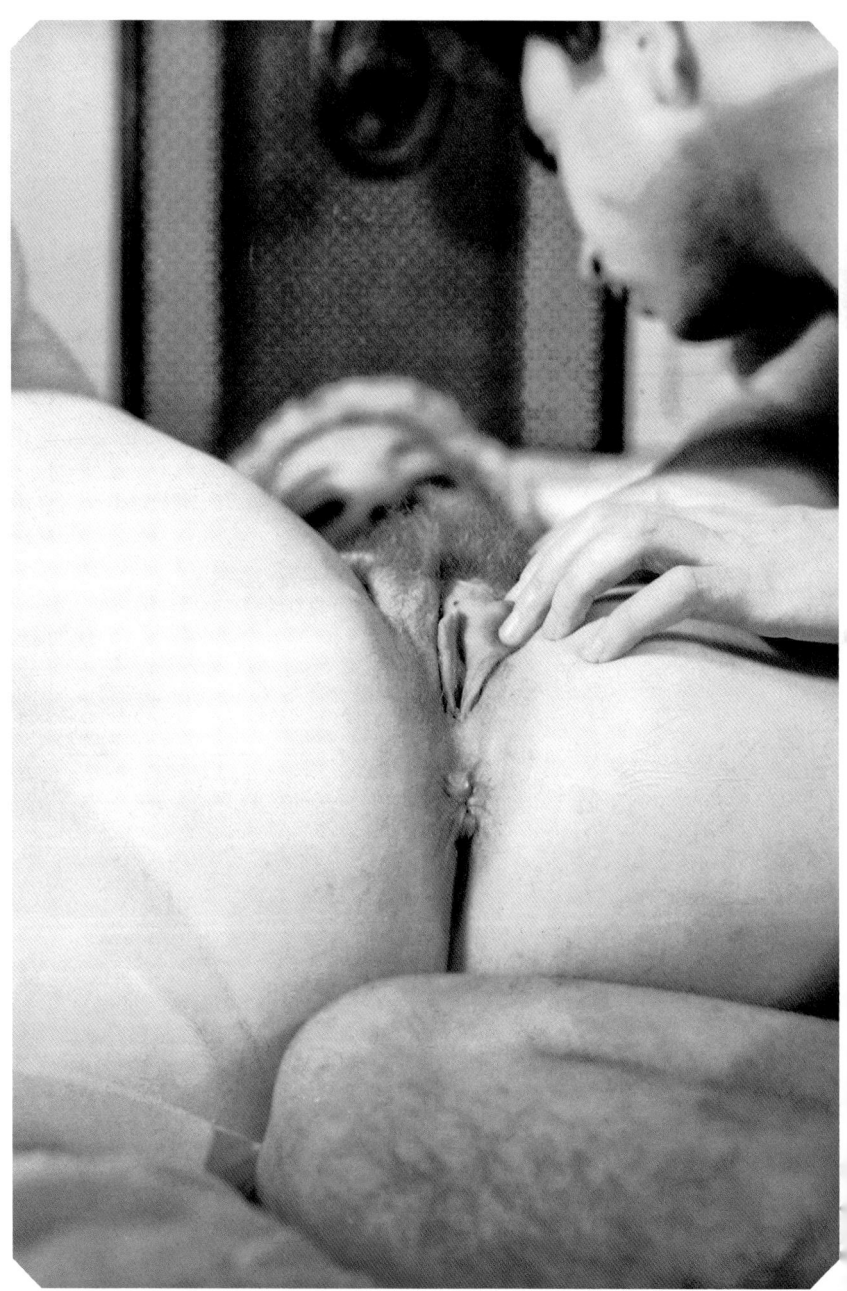

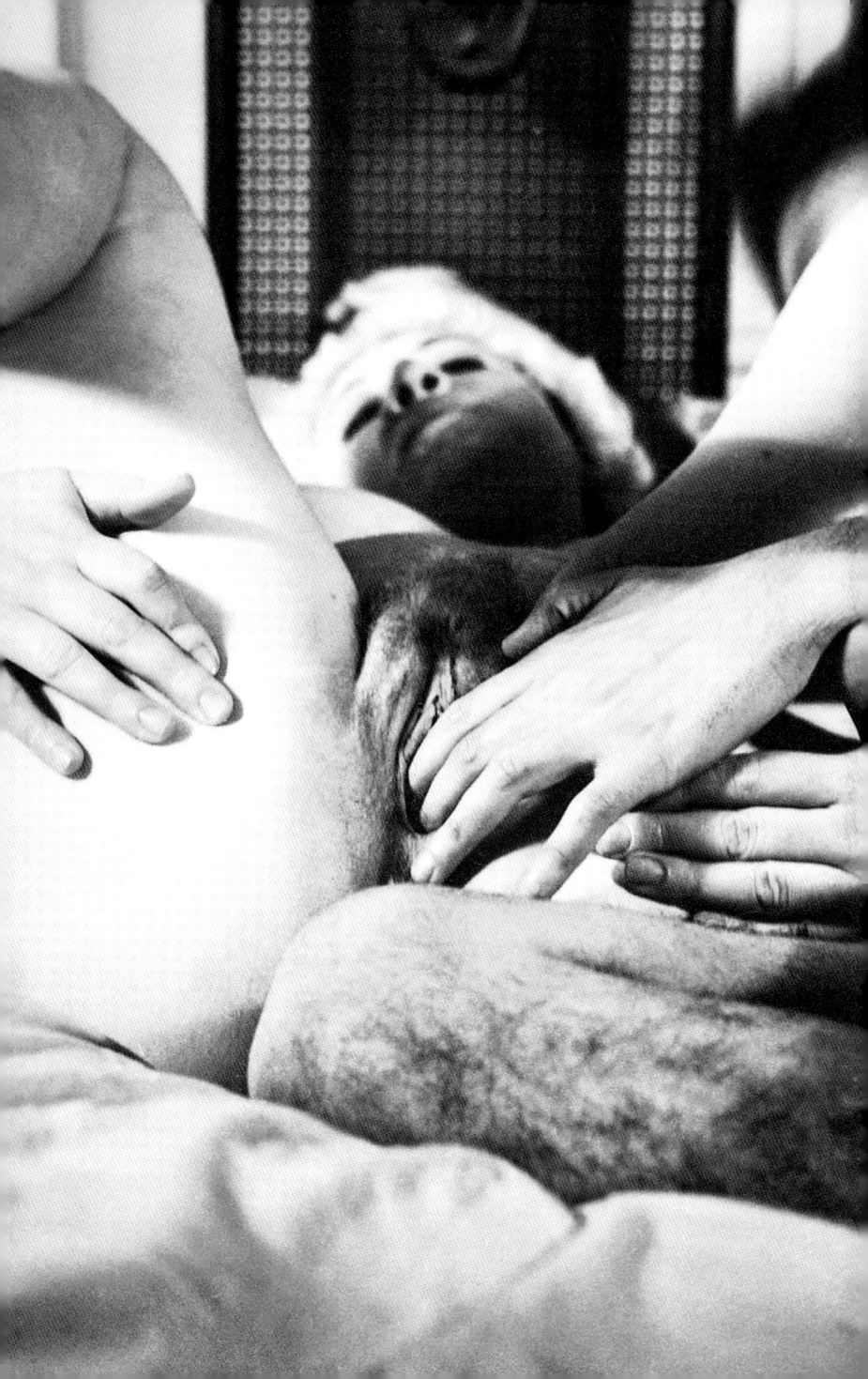

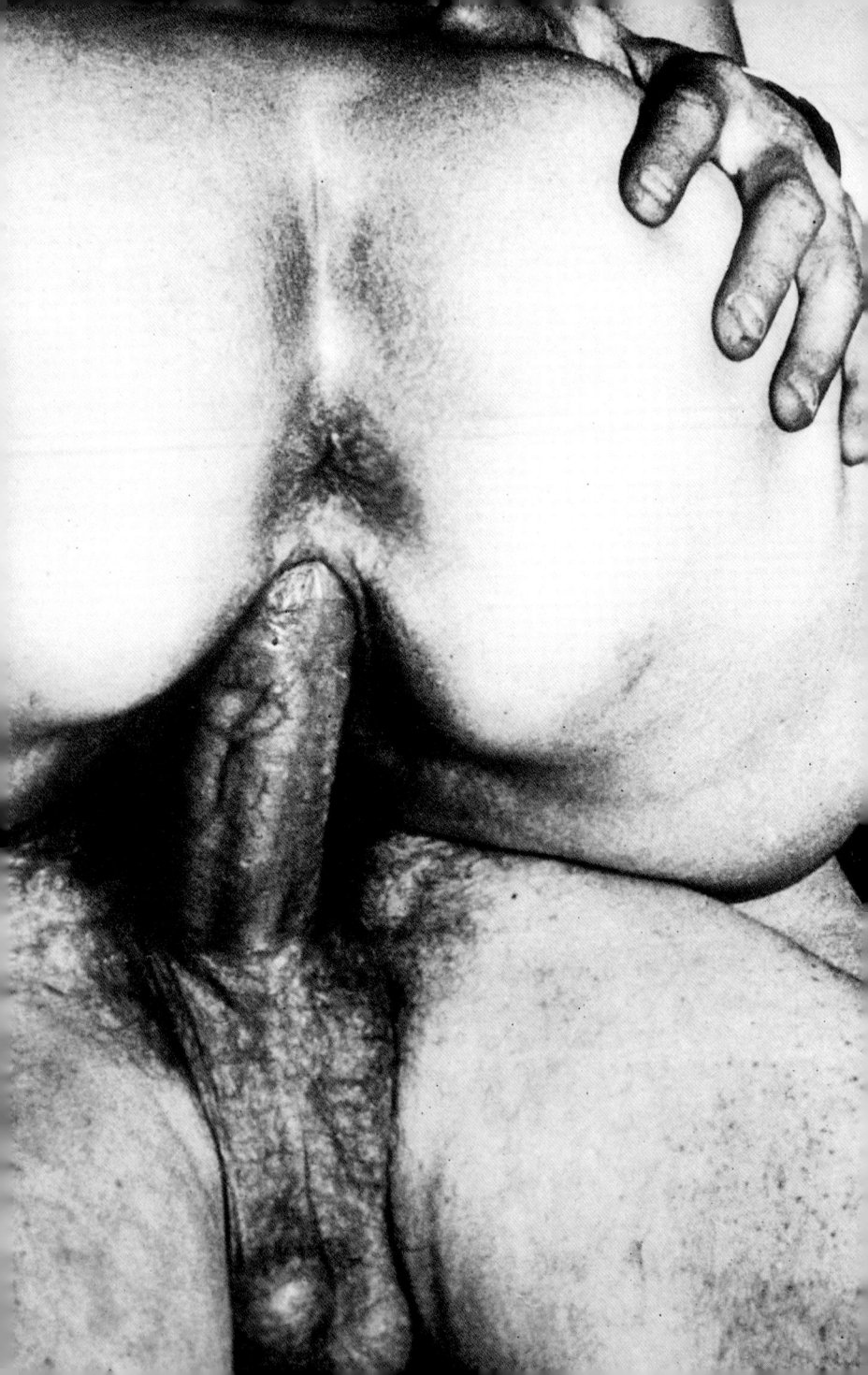

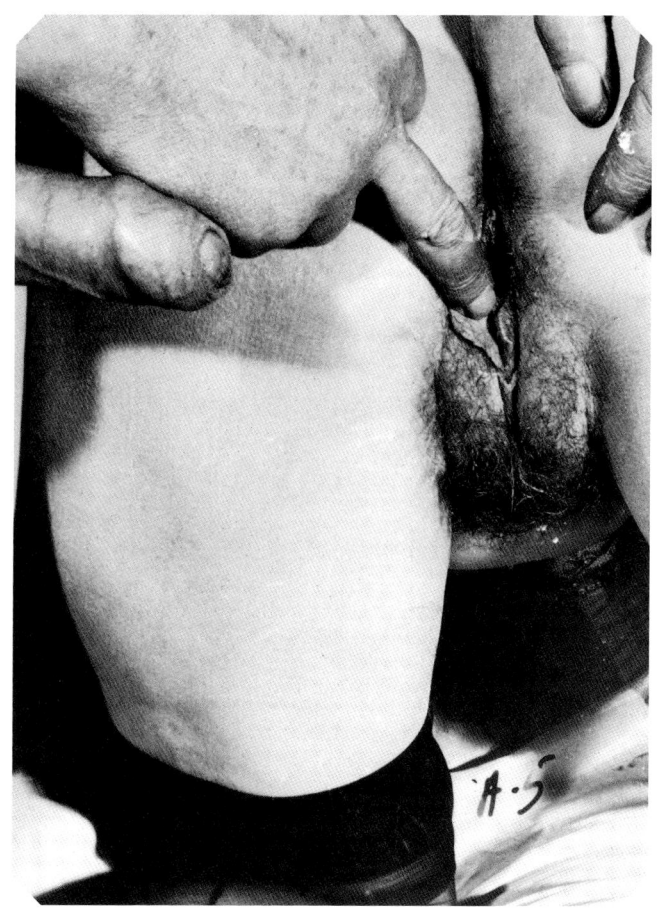

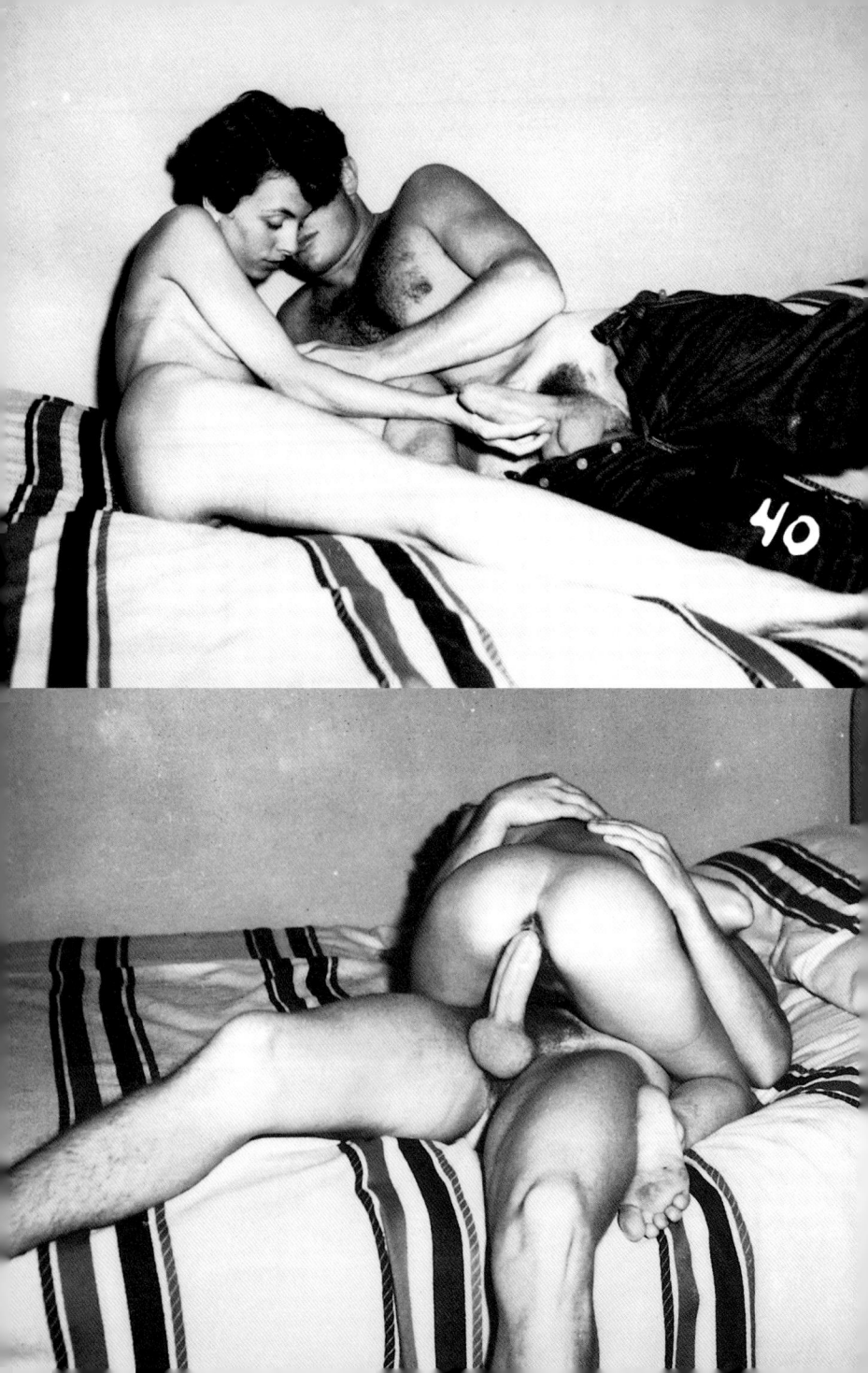

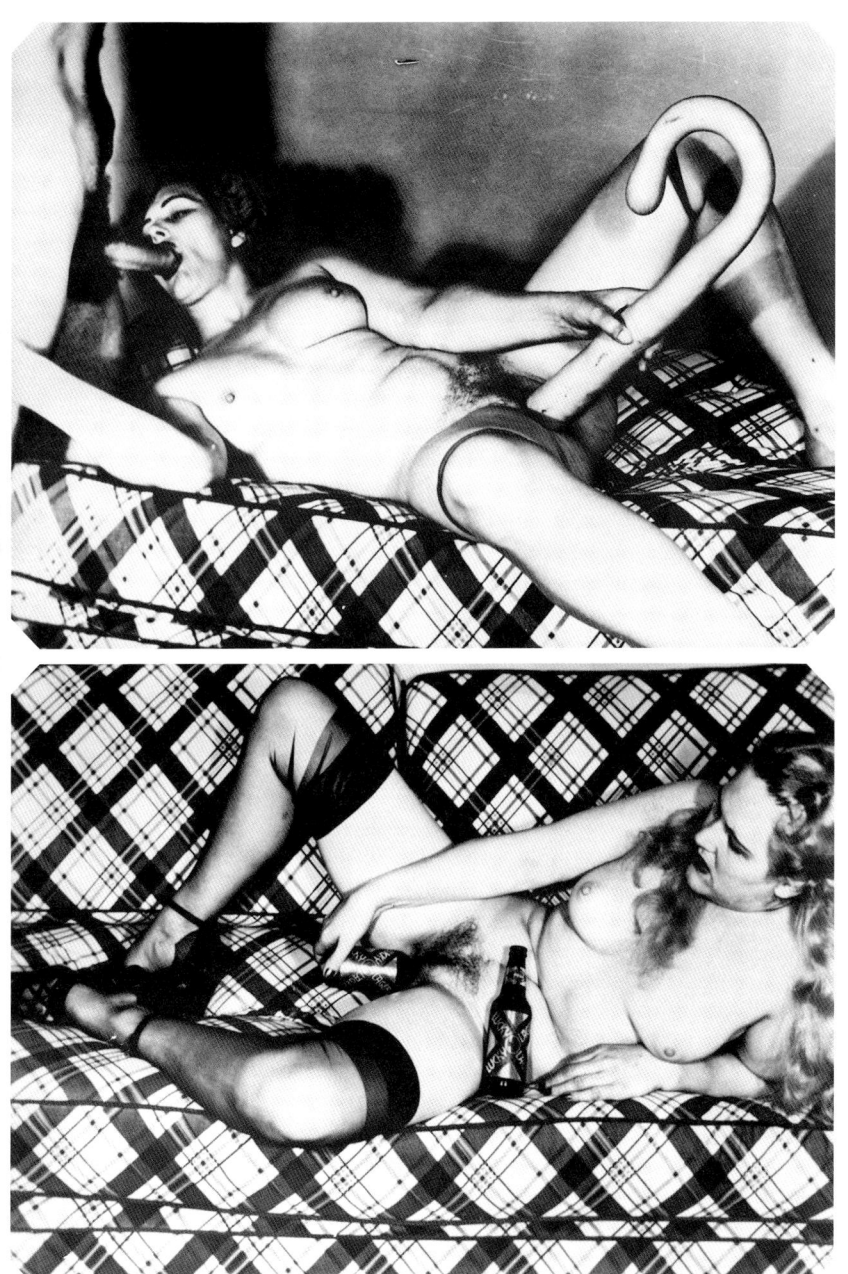

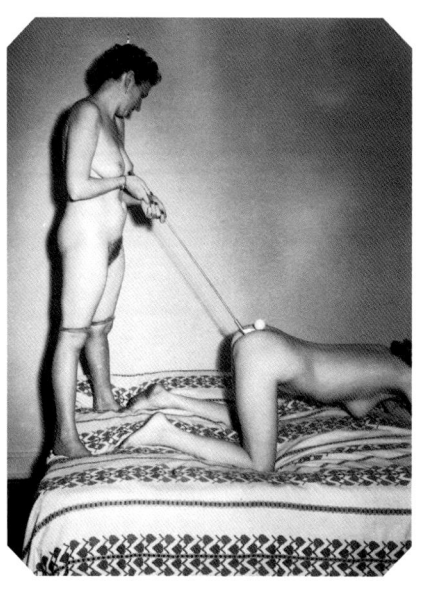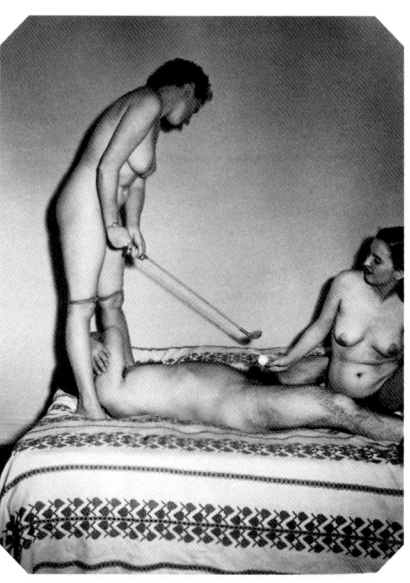

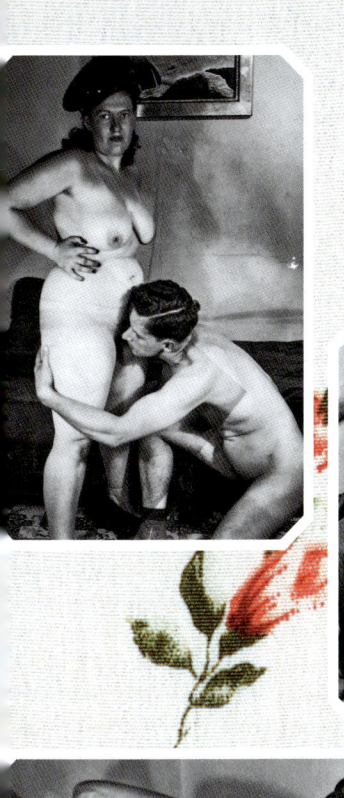

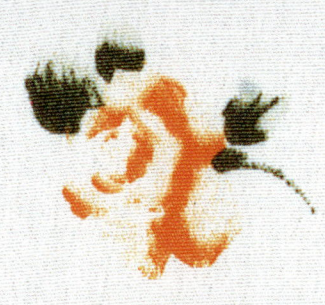

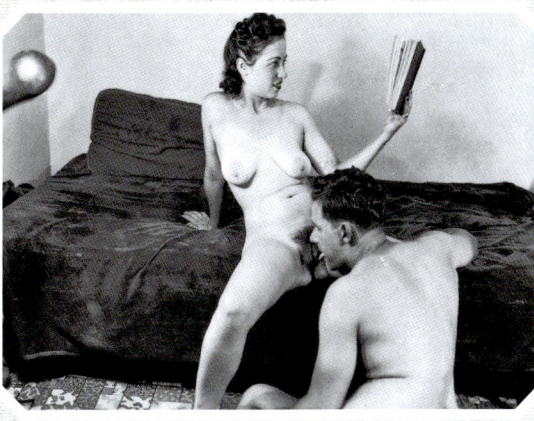

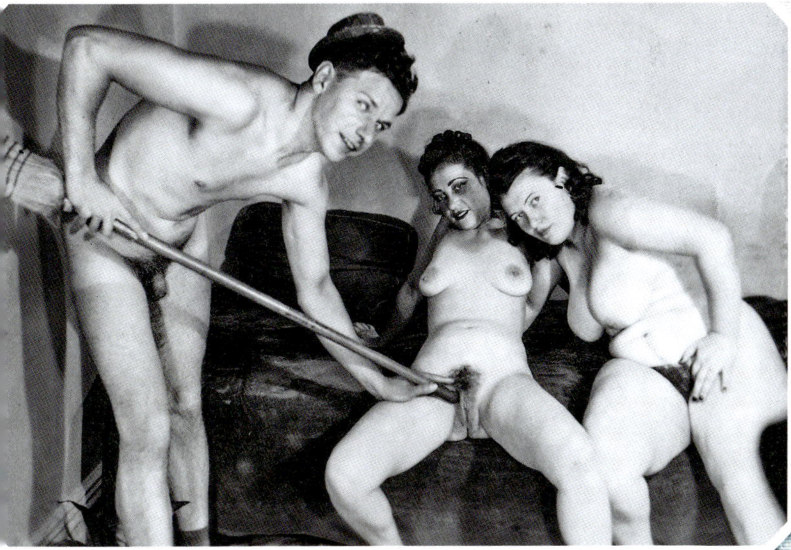

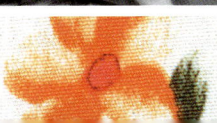

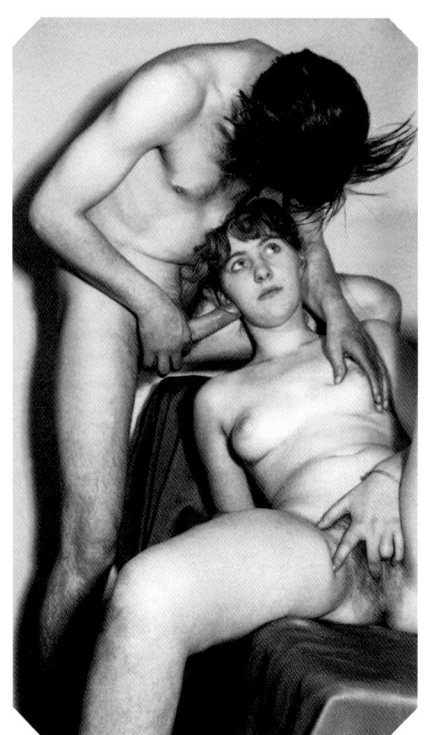
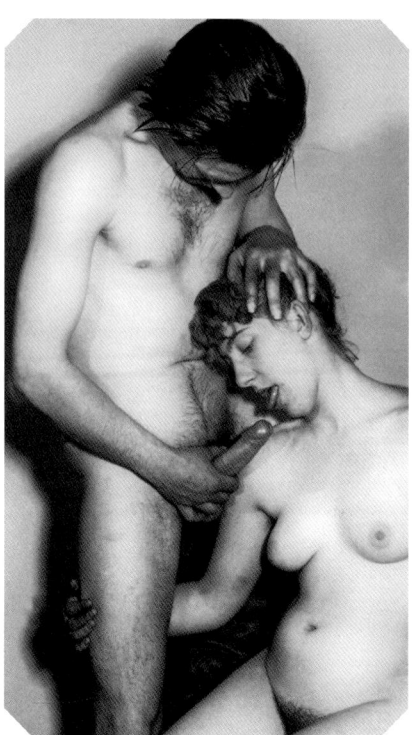
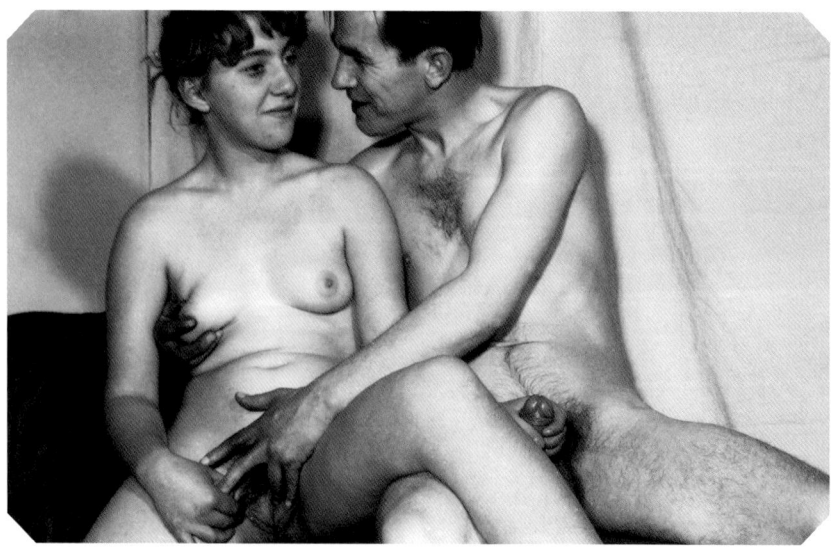

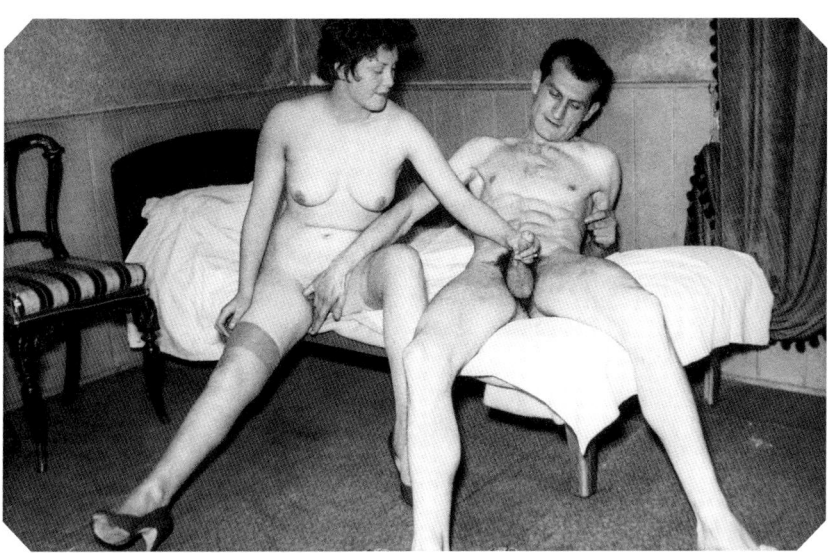

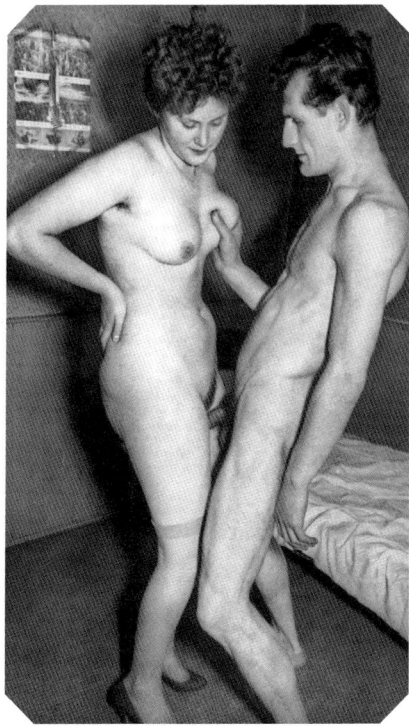

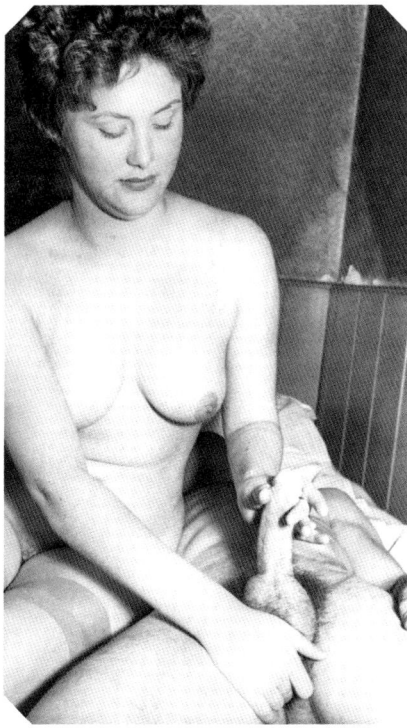

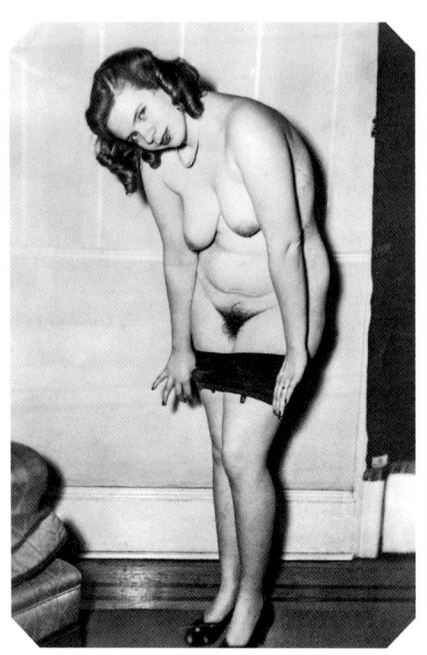
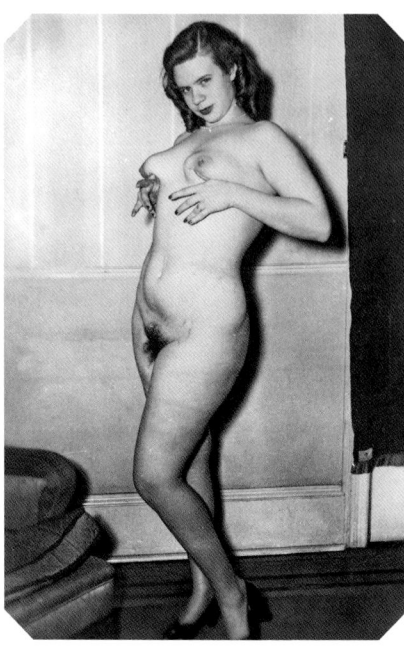
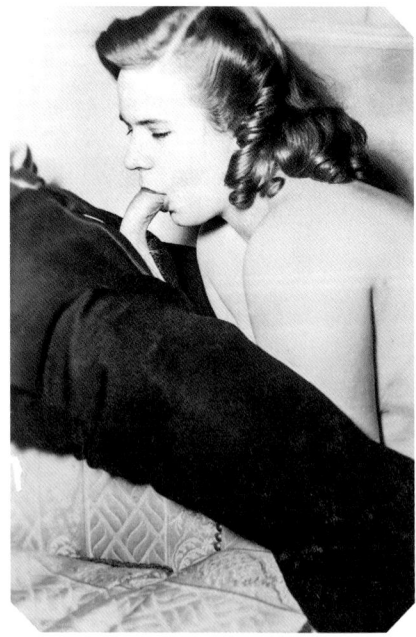
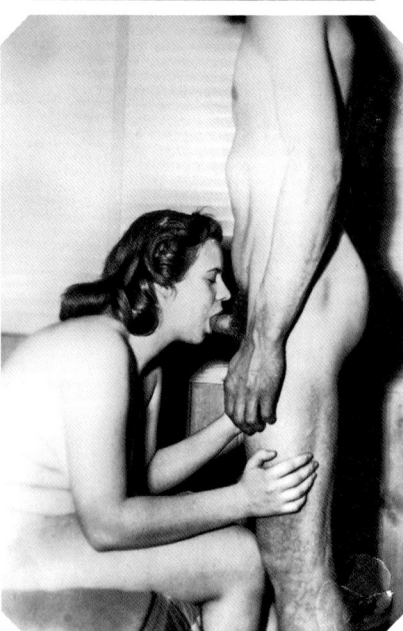

428

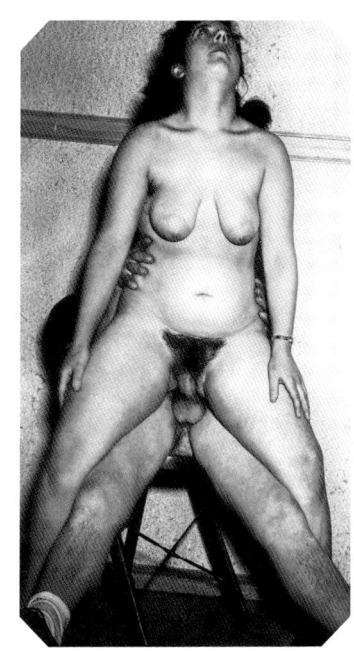
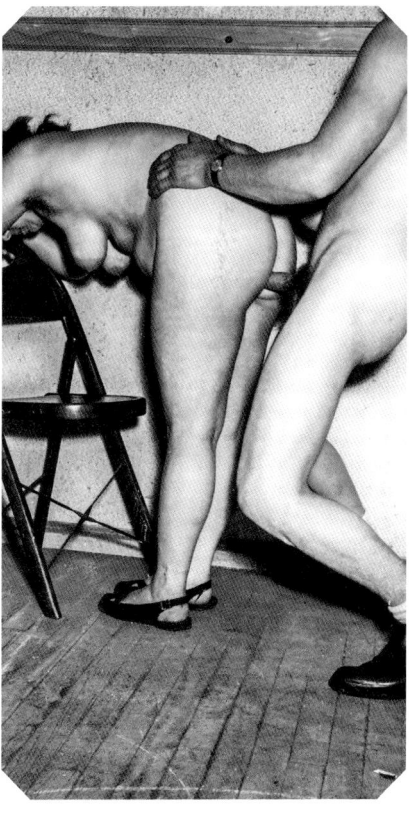
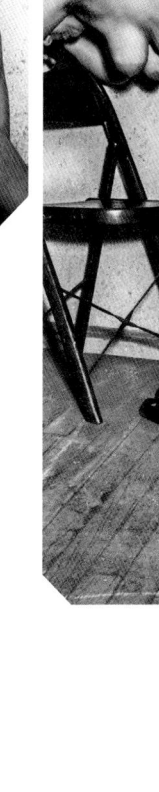

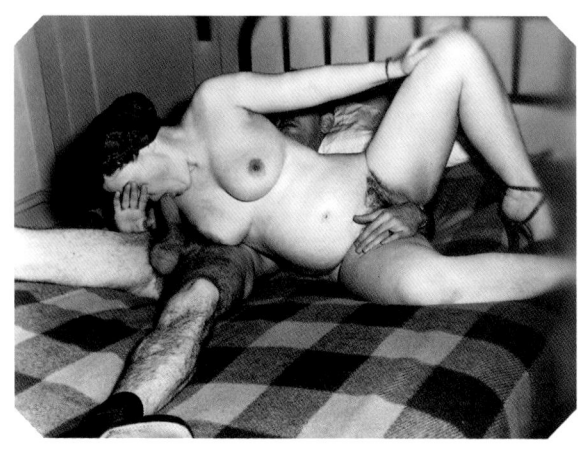

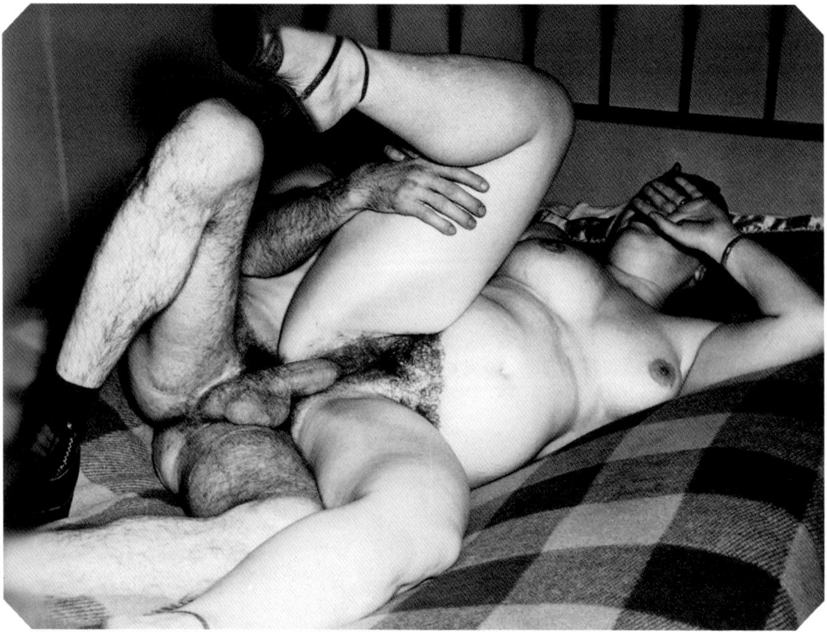

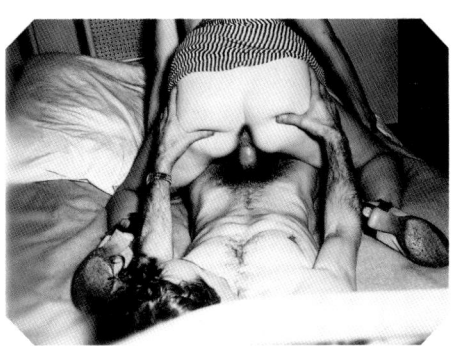

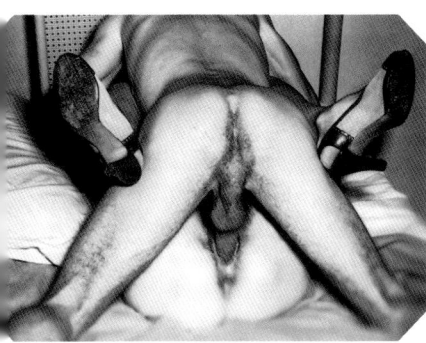

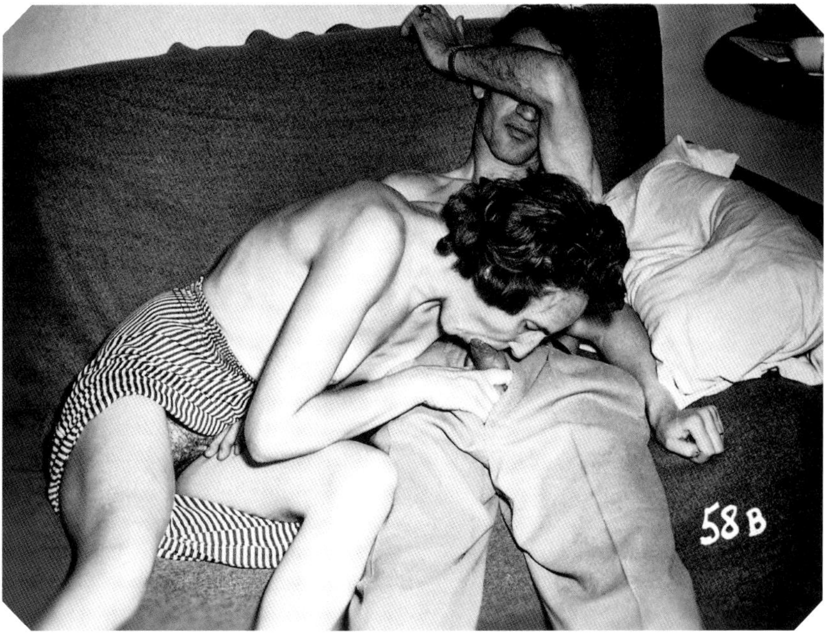

58 B

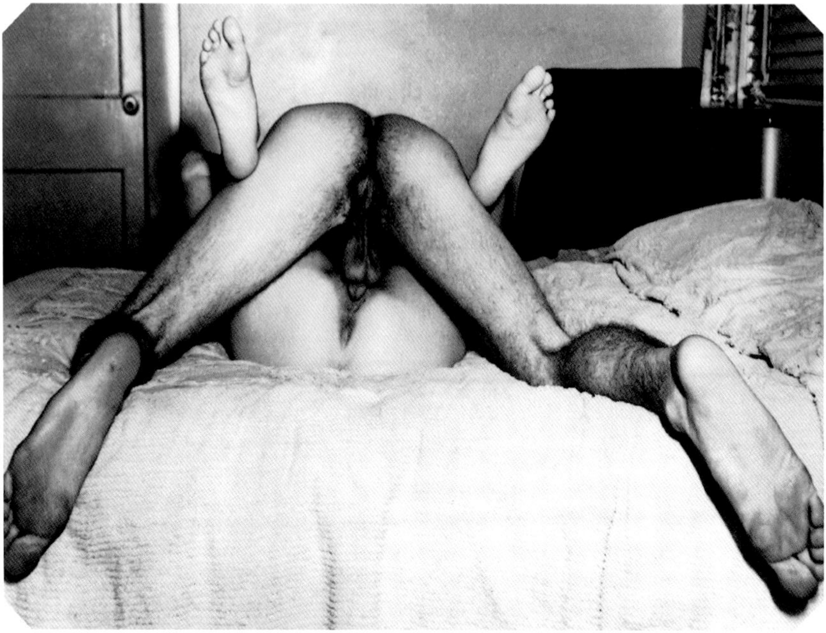

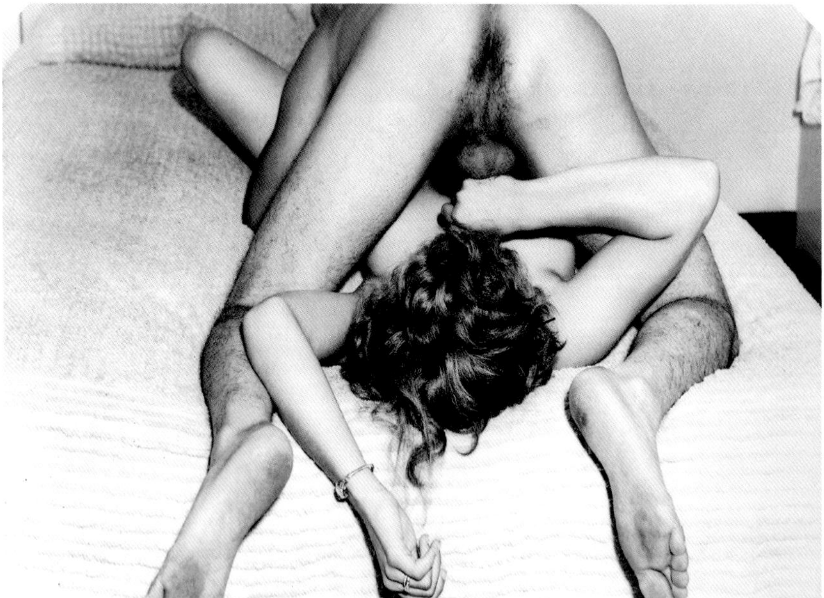

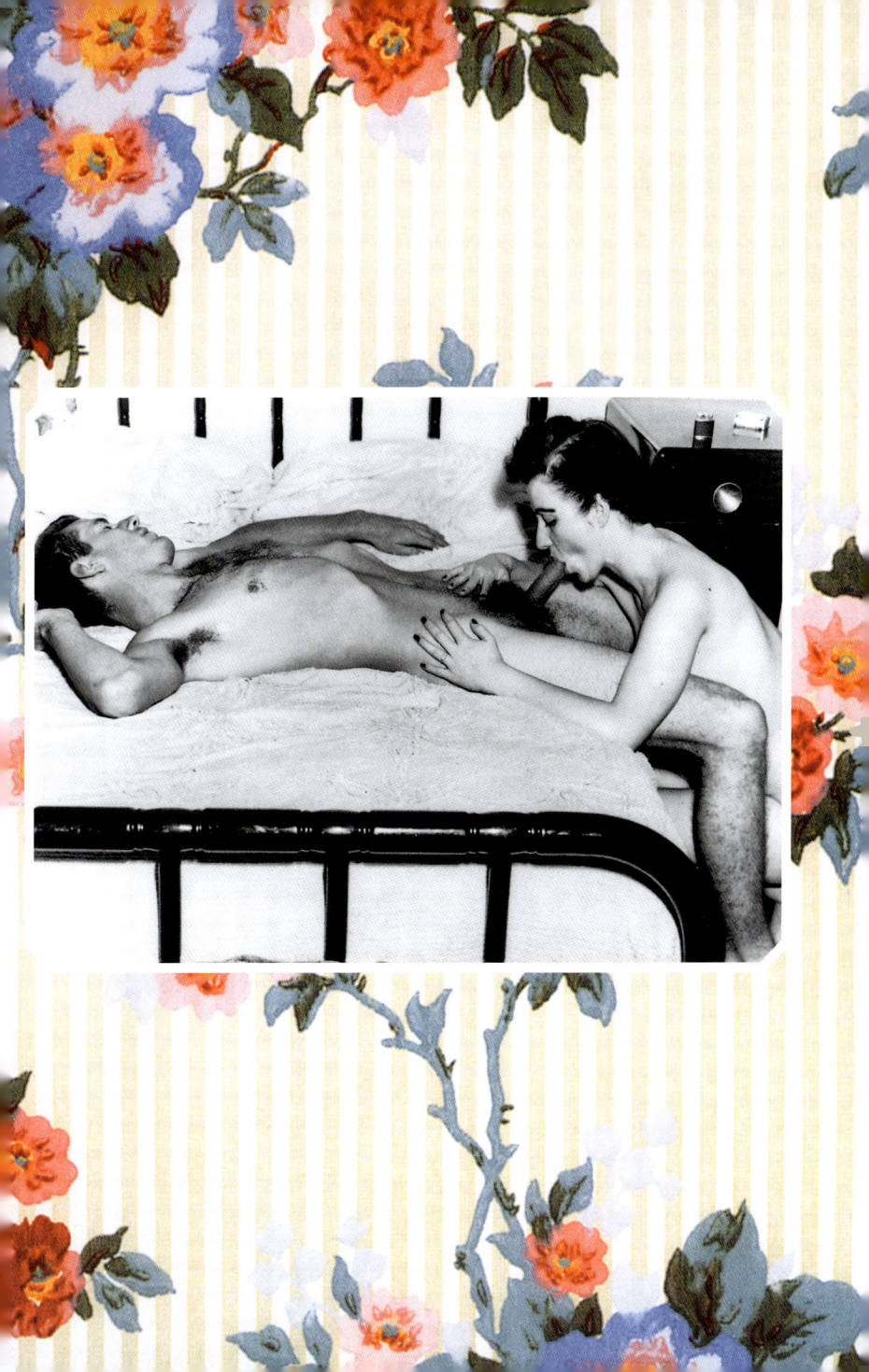

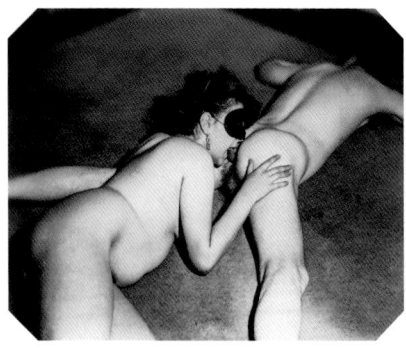
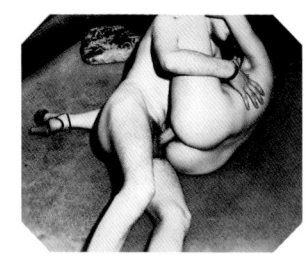
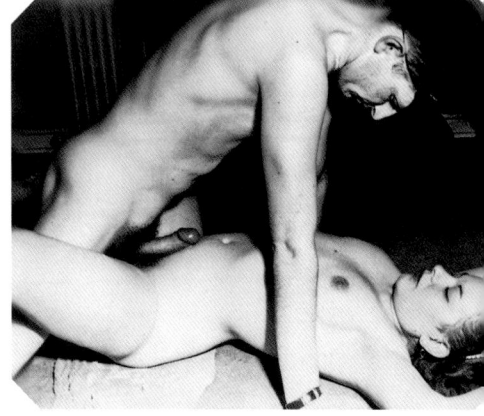

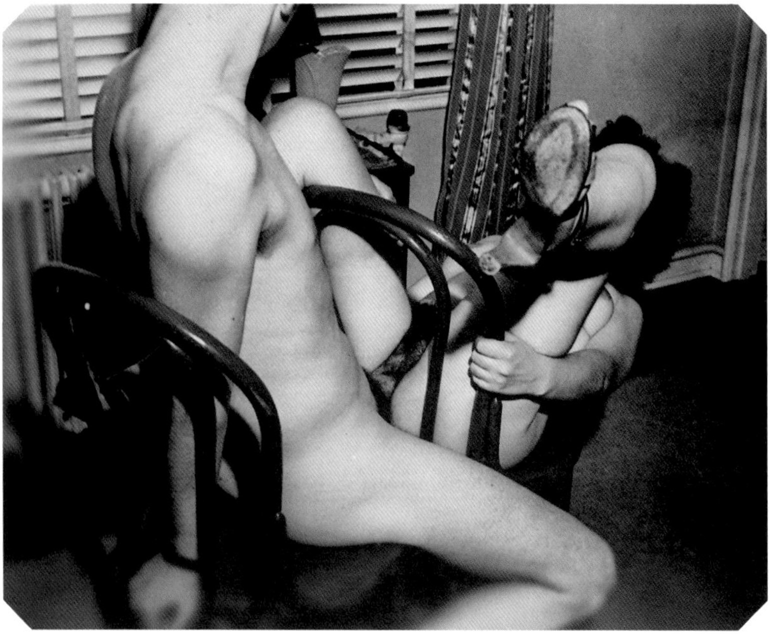

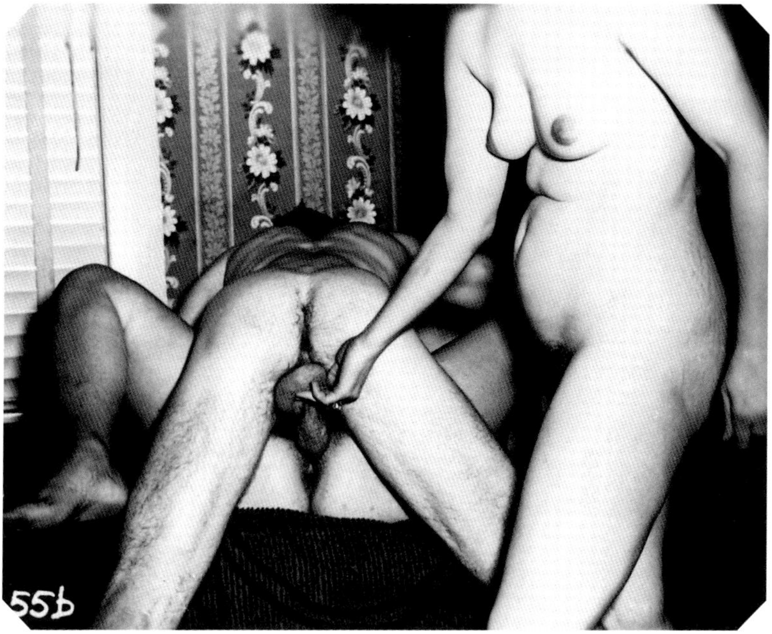

55b

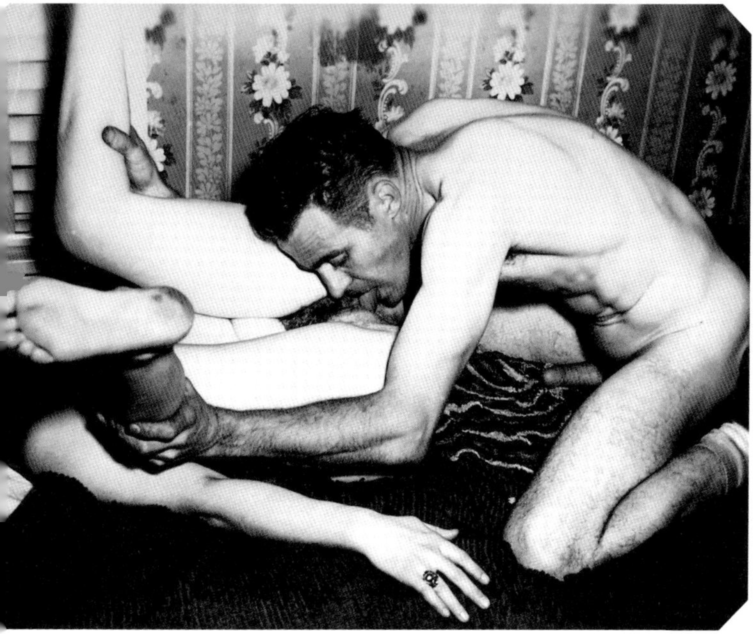

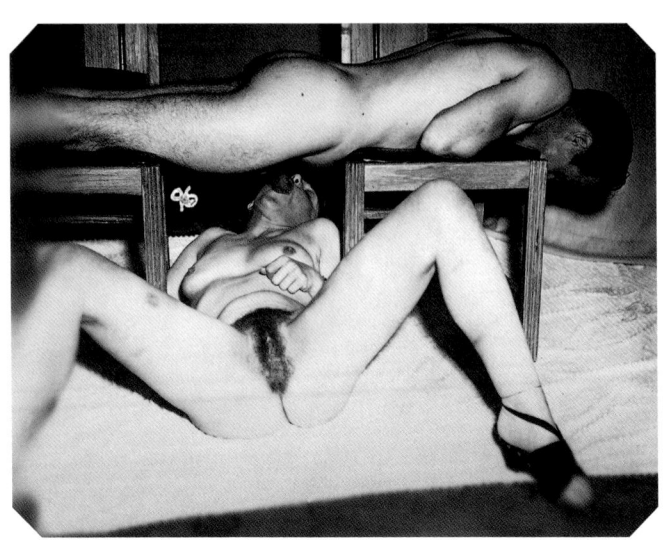

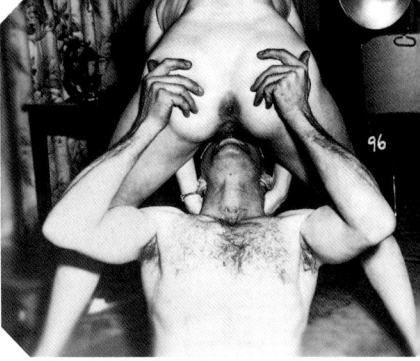

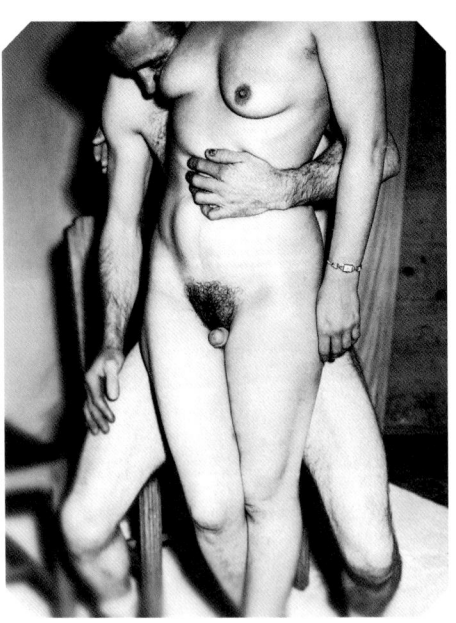

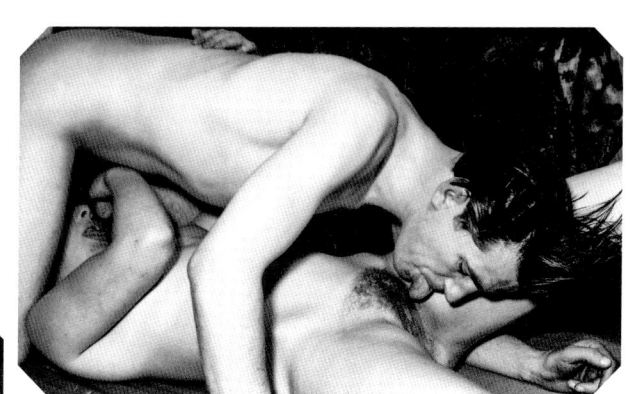

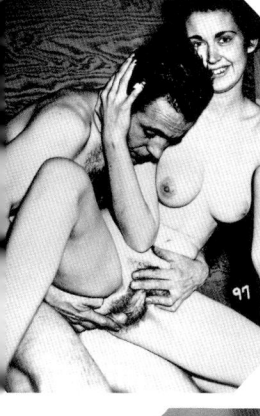

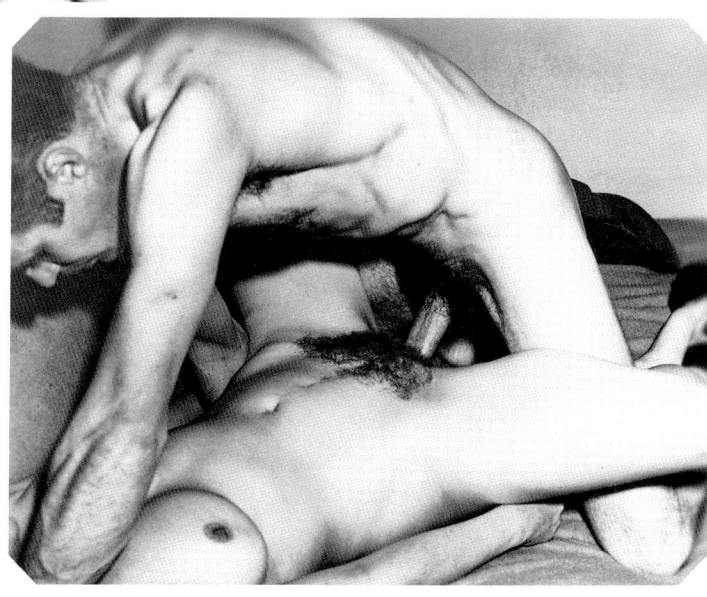

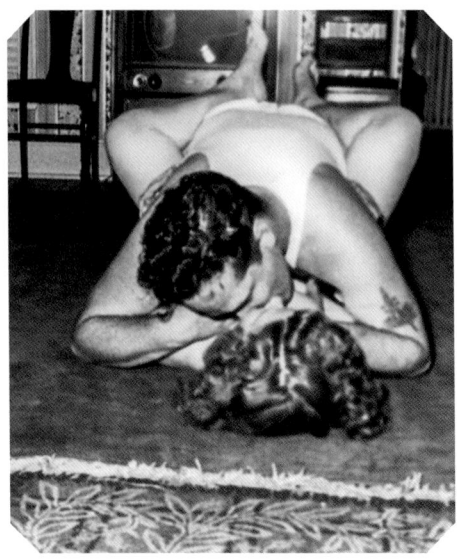
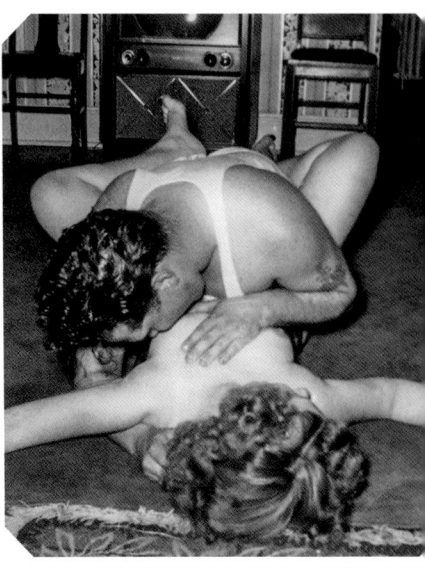
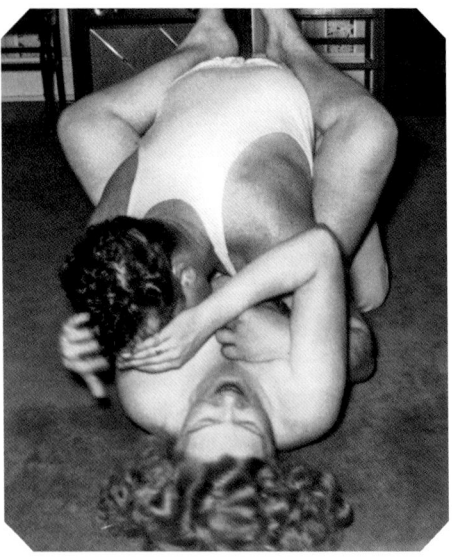
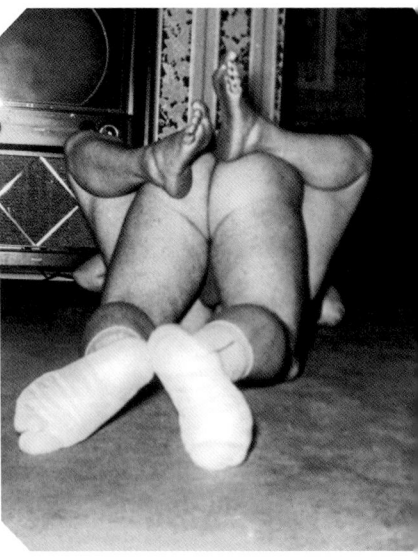

438

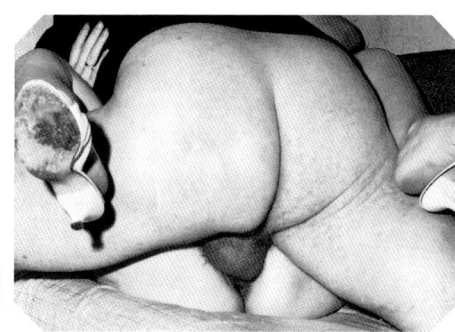

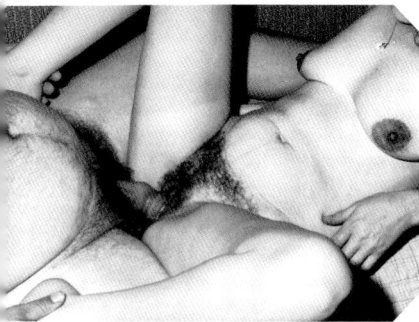

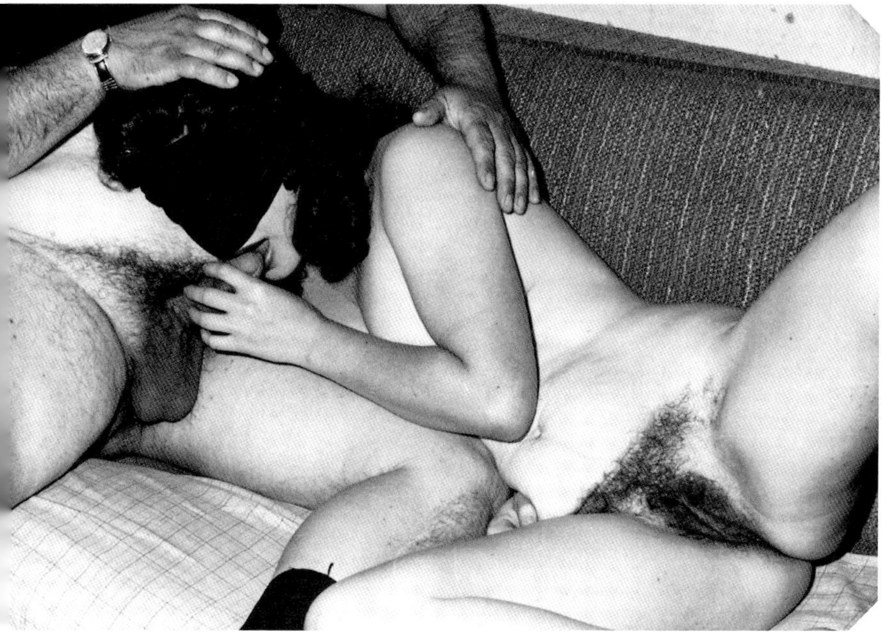

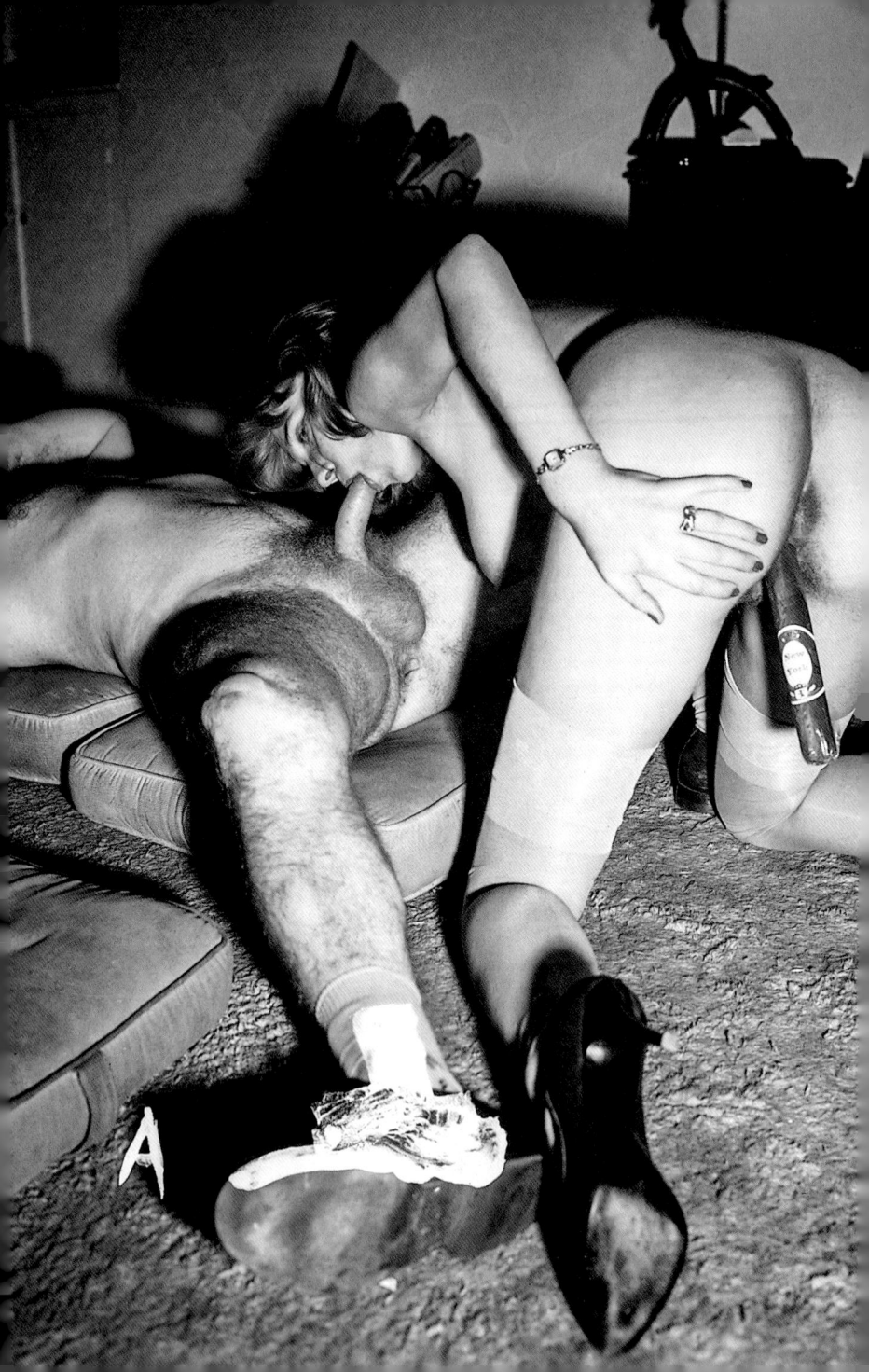

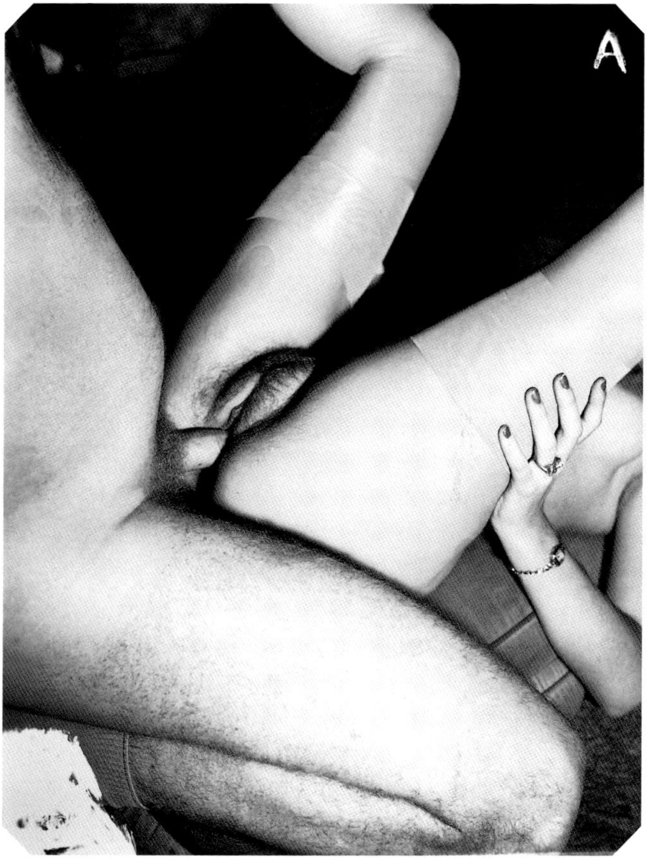

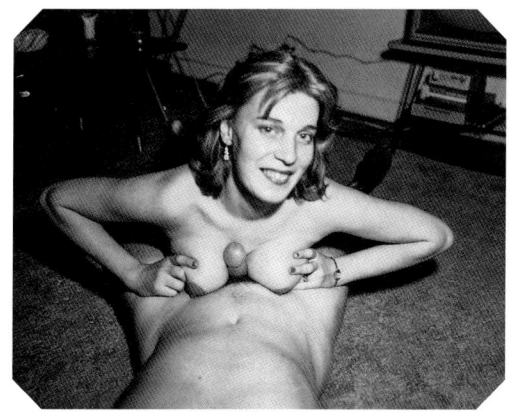

441

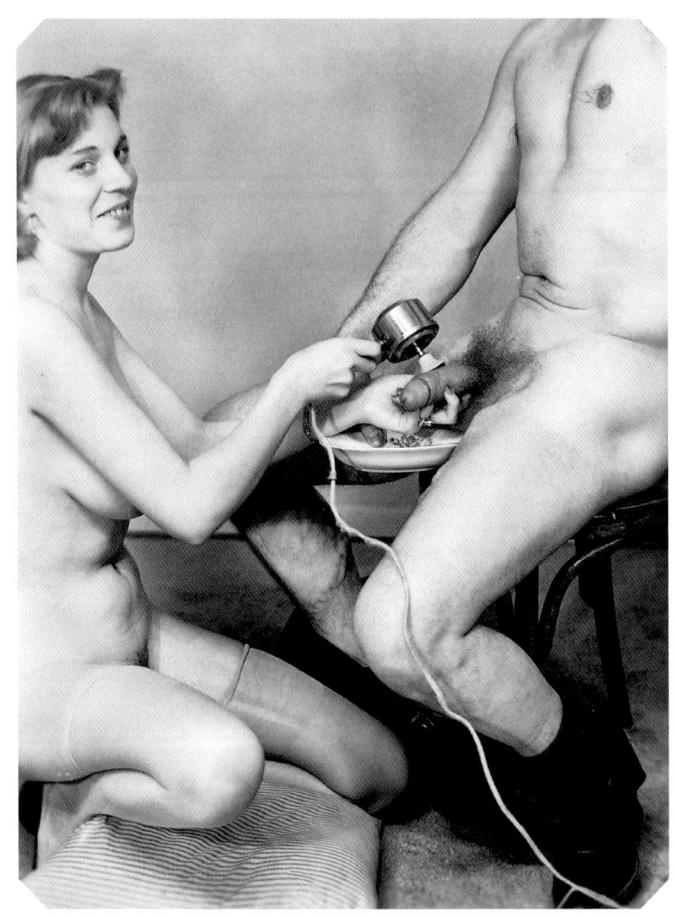

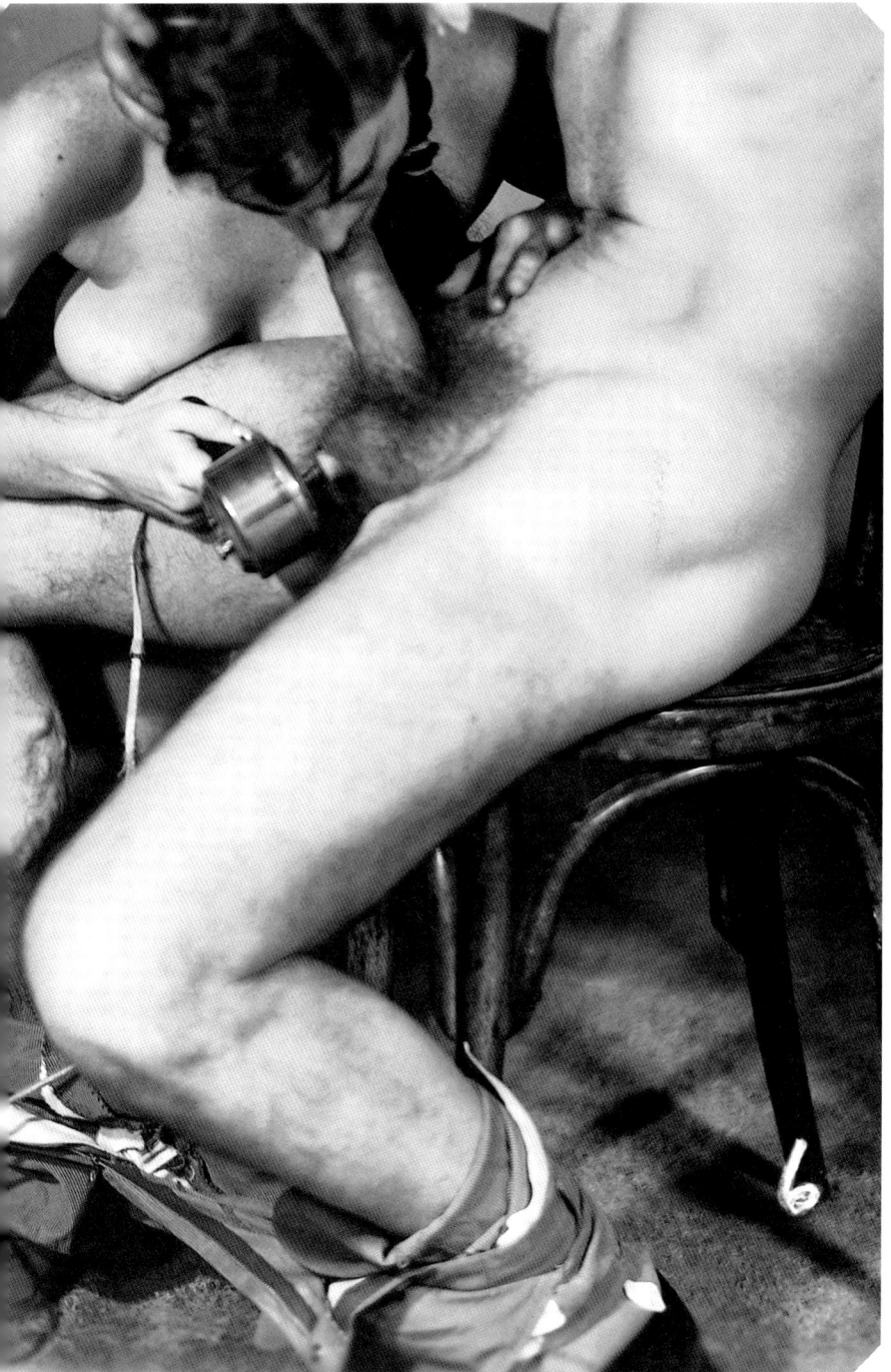

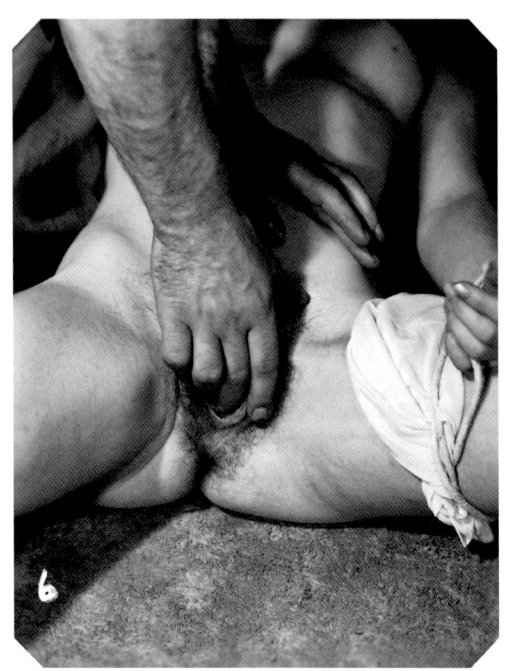

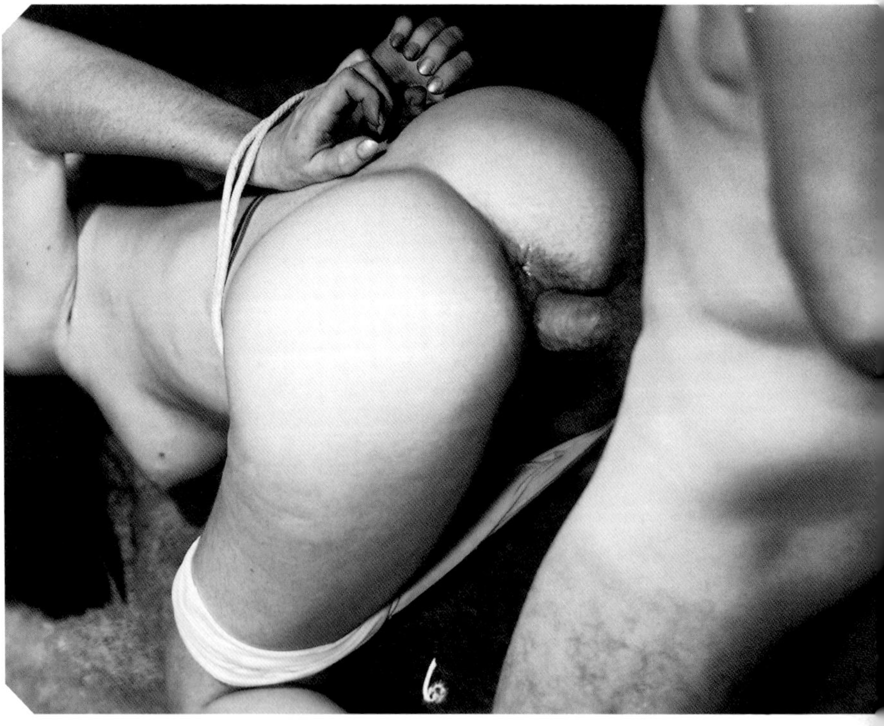

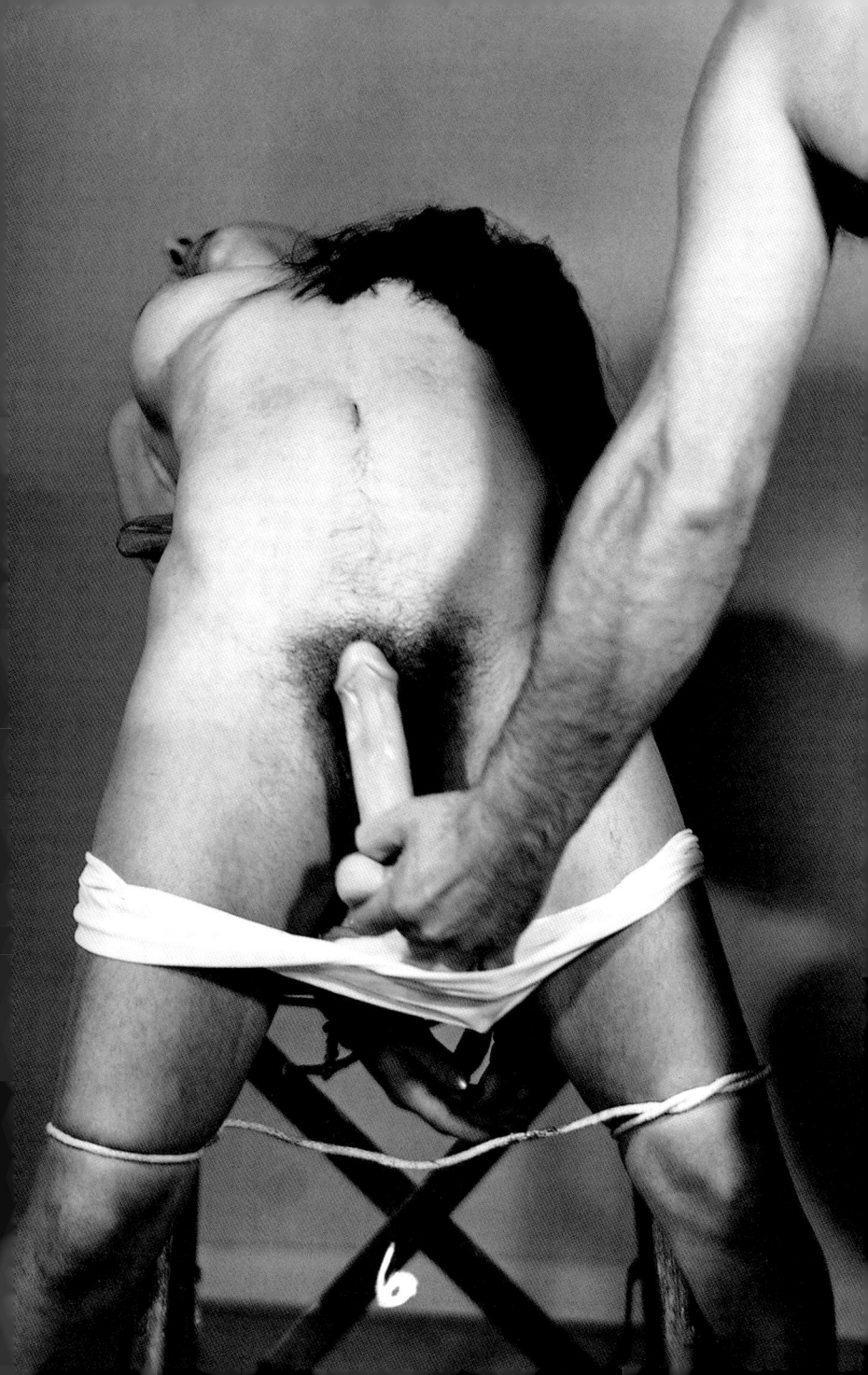

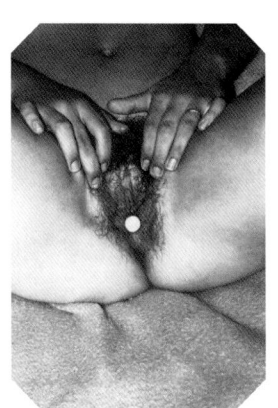

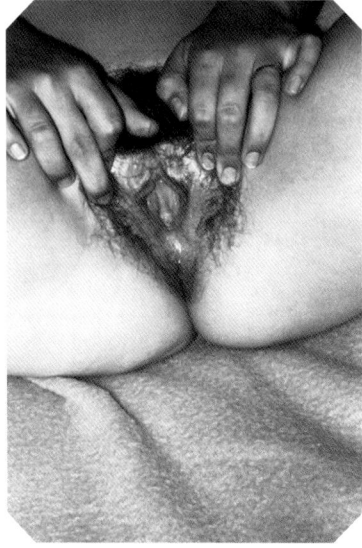

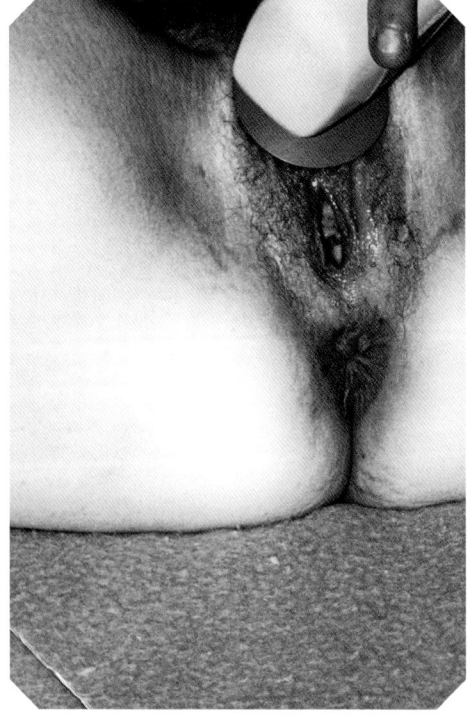

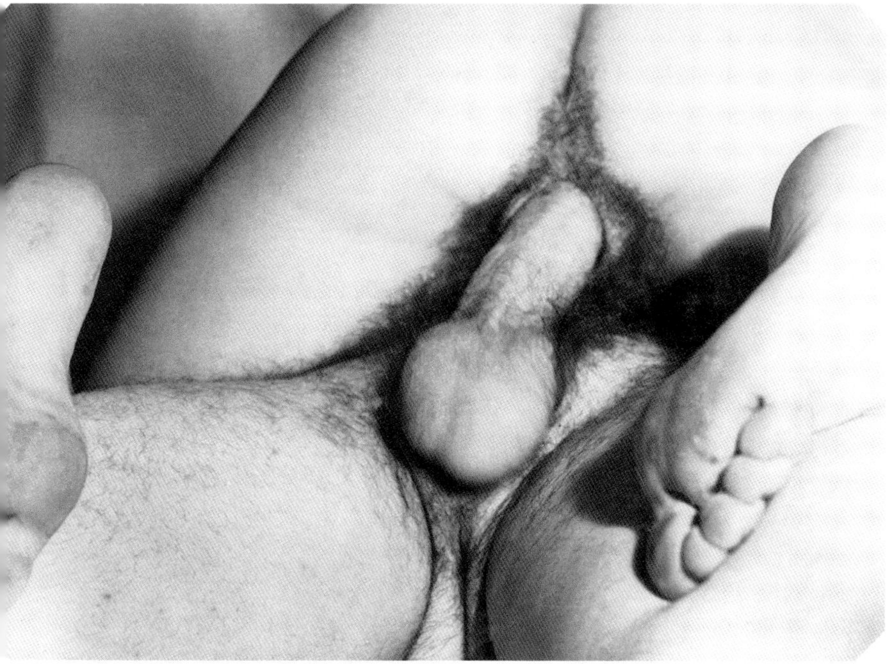

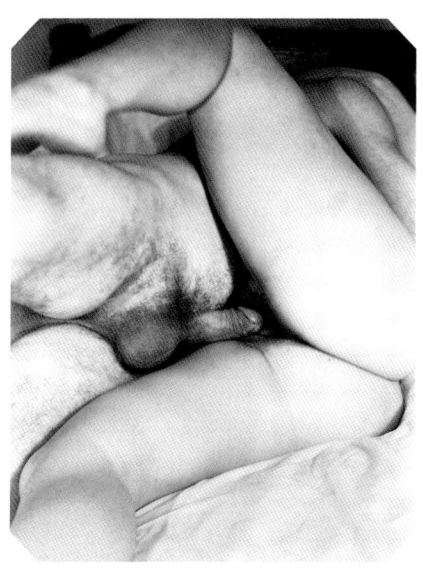

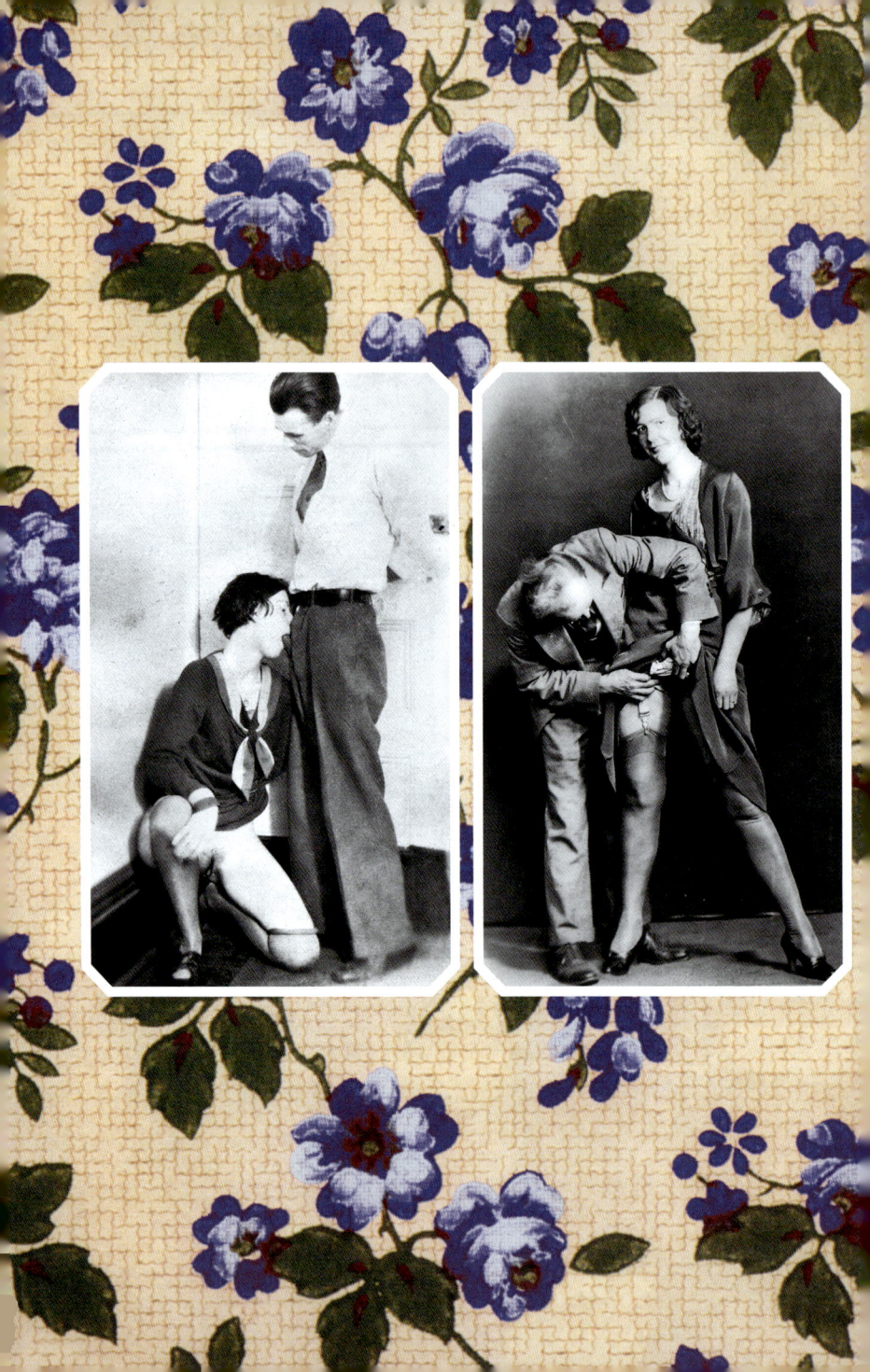

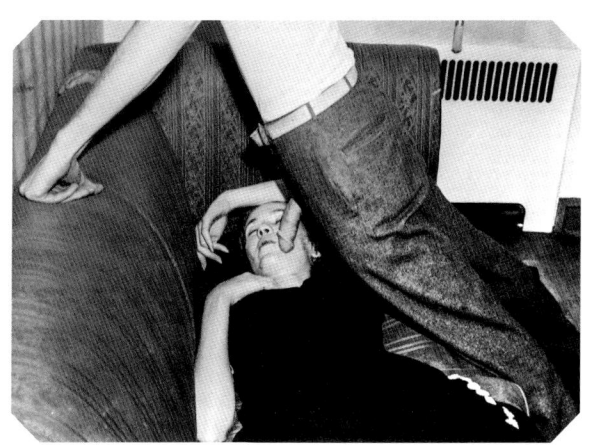

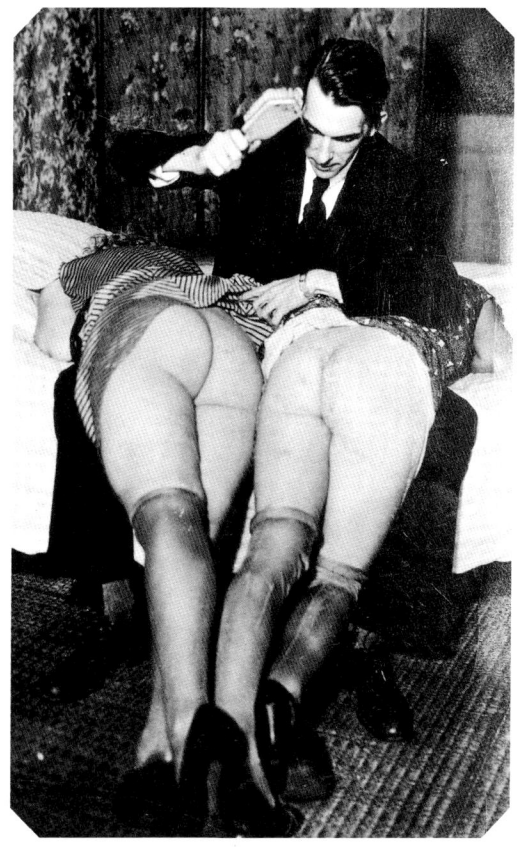

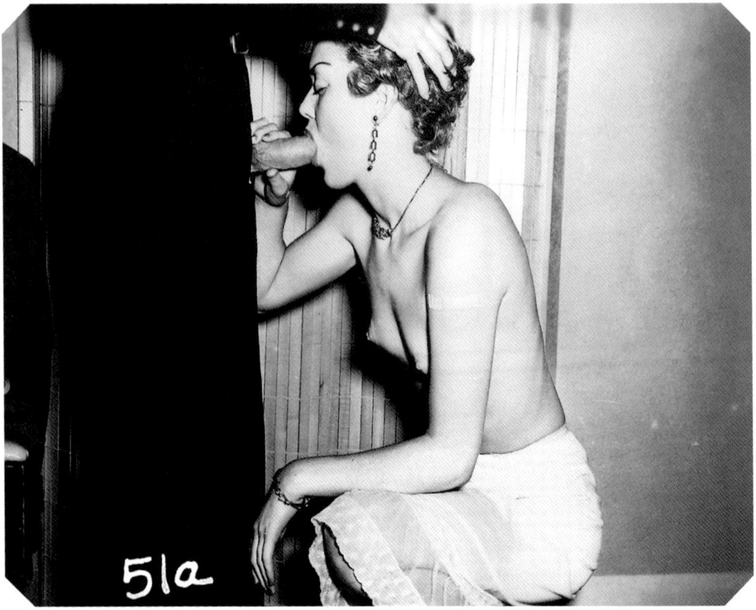

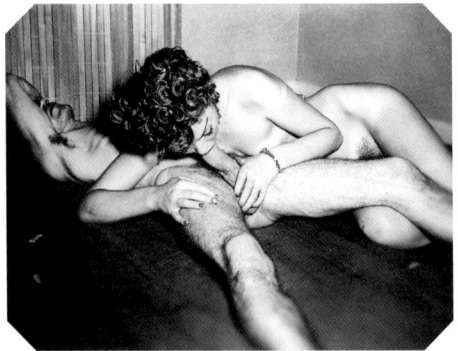

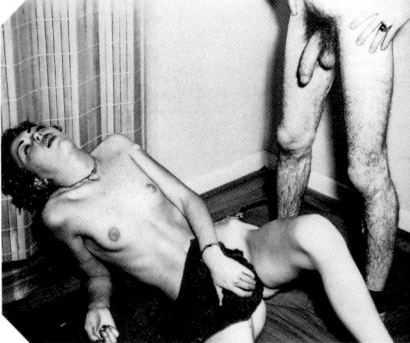

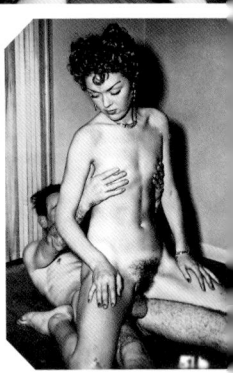

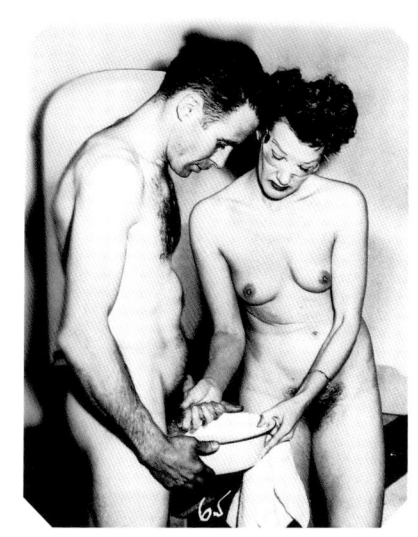

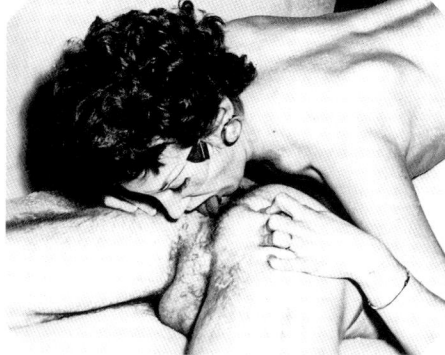

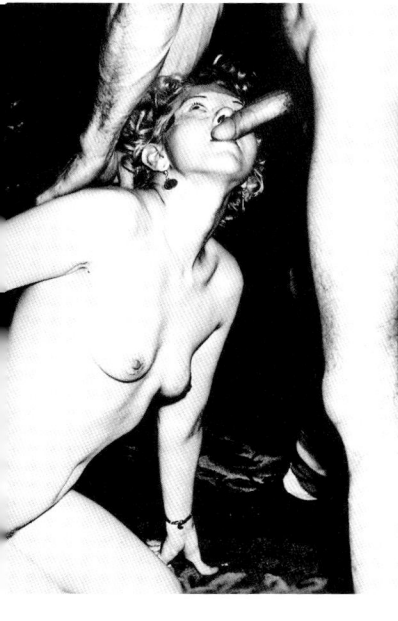

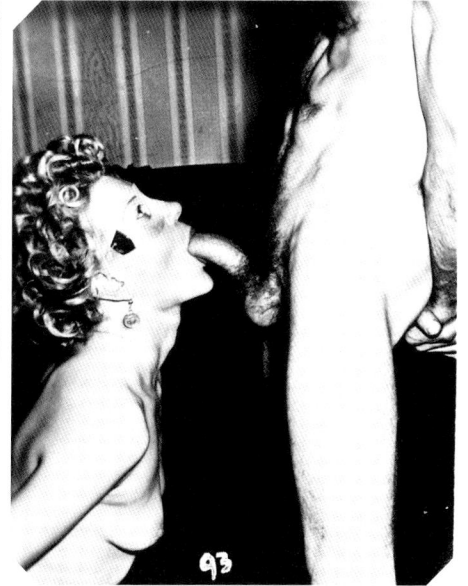

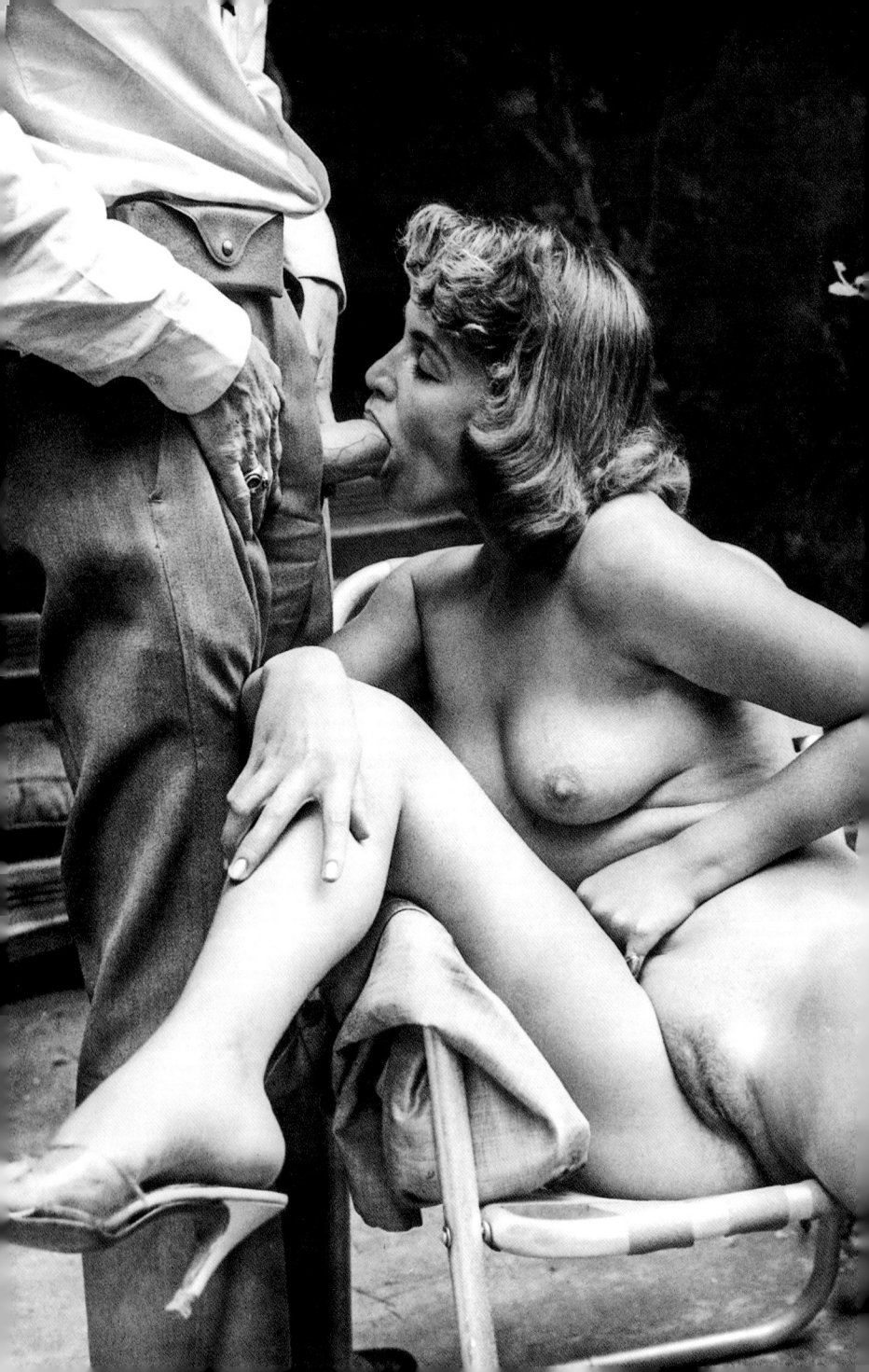

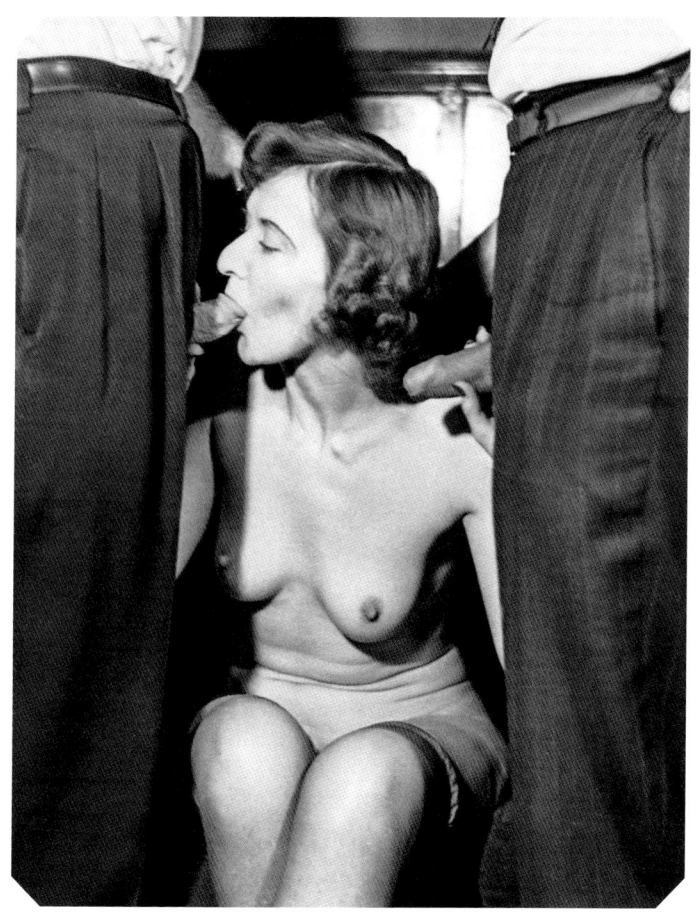

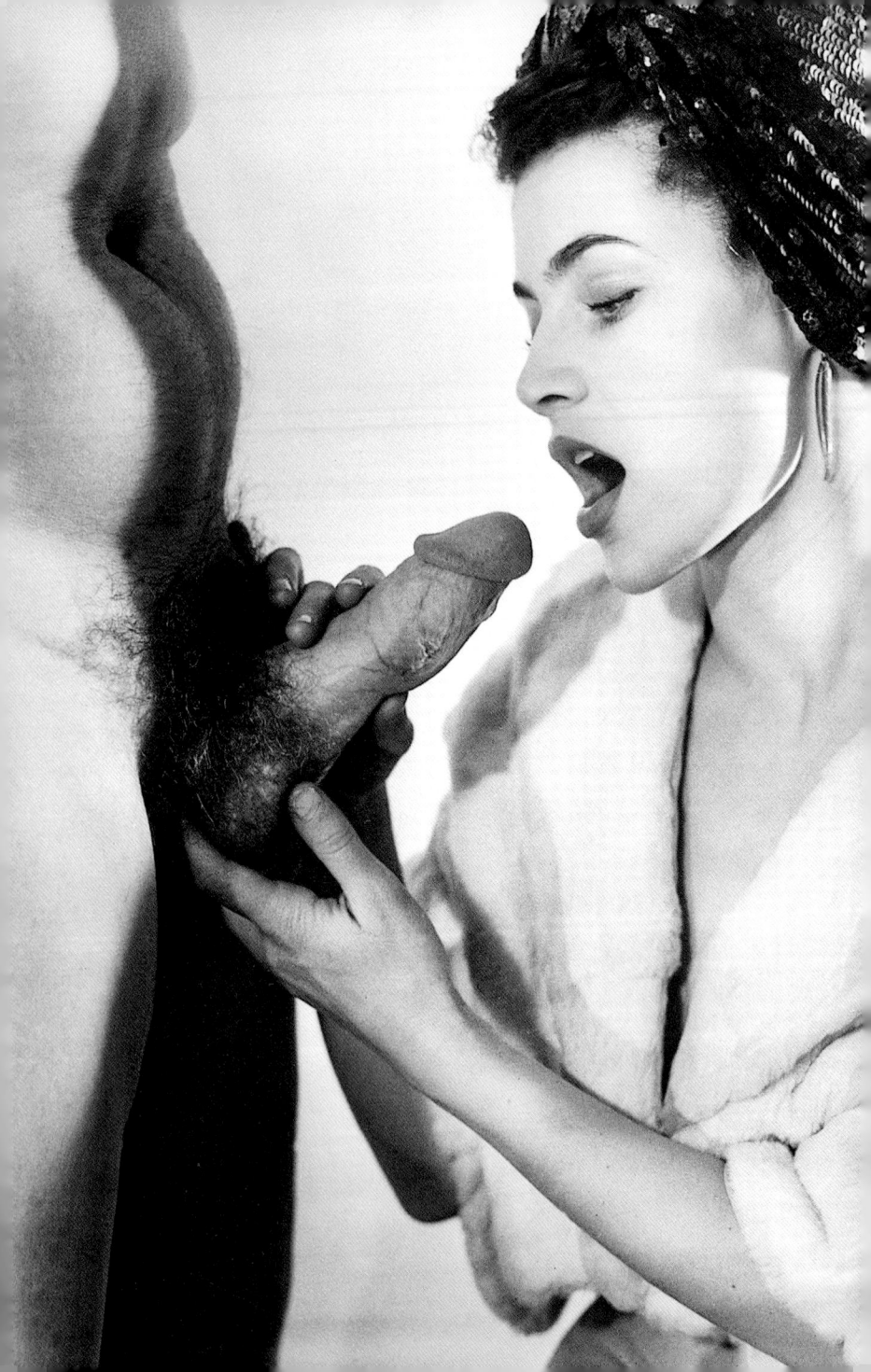

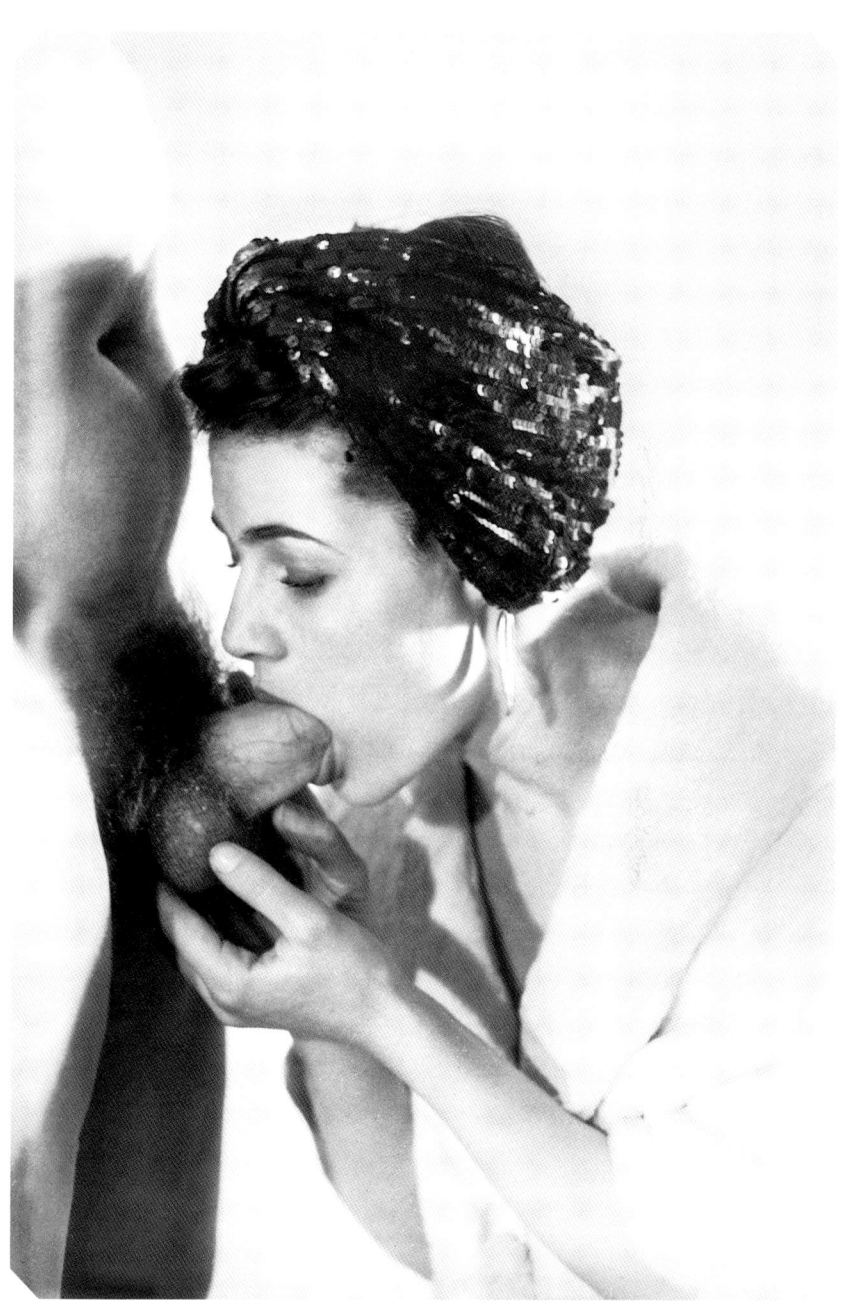

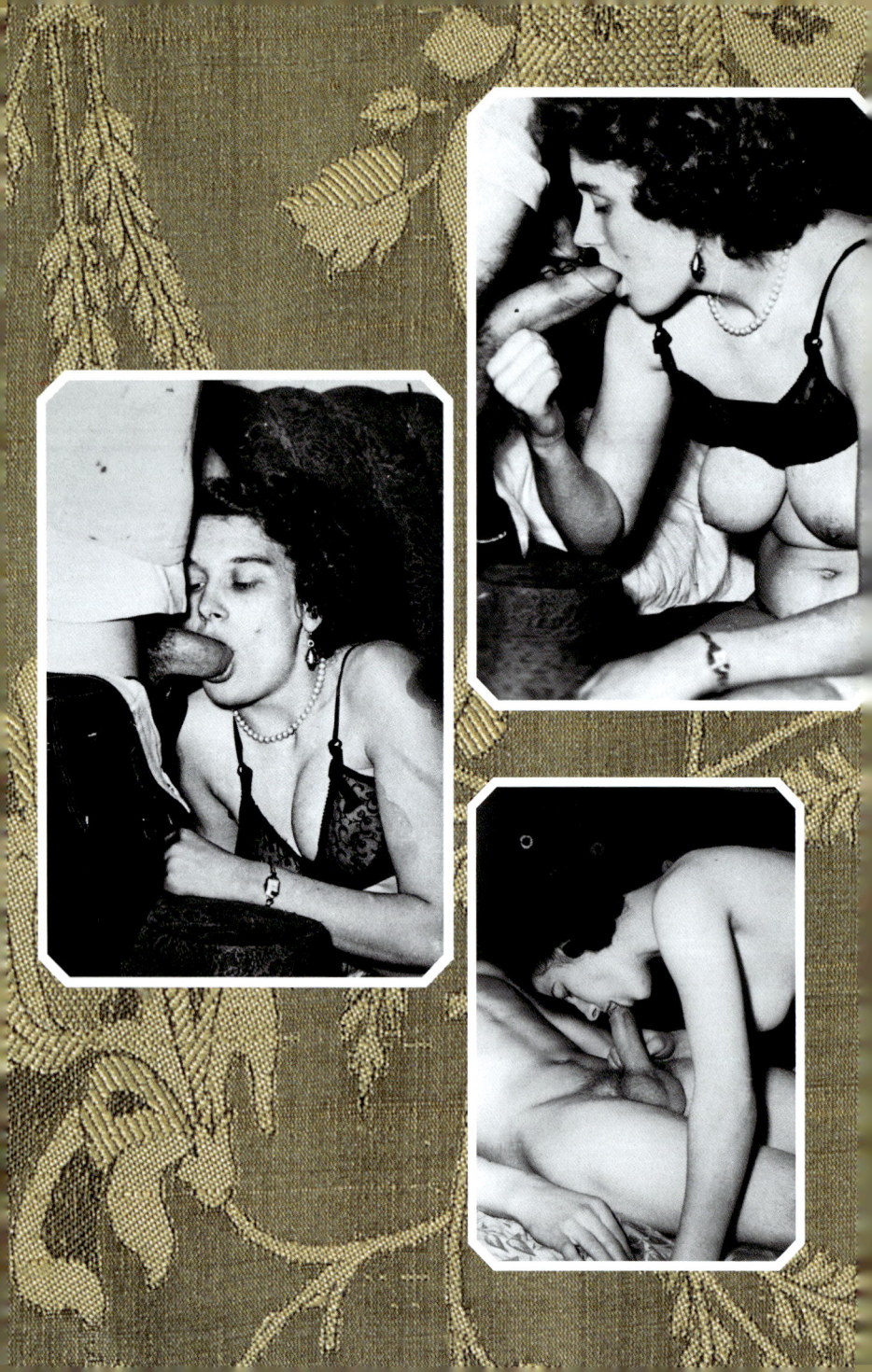

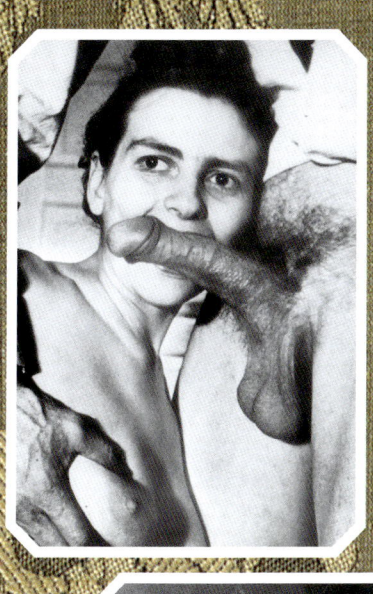
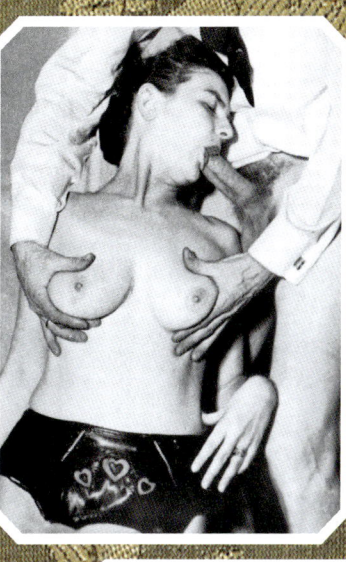
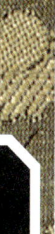
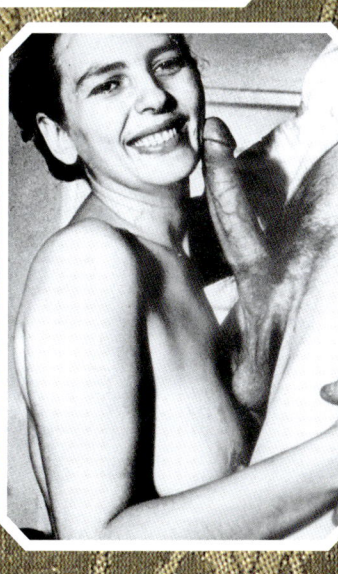
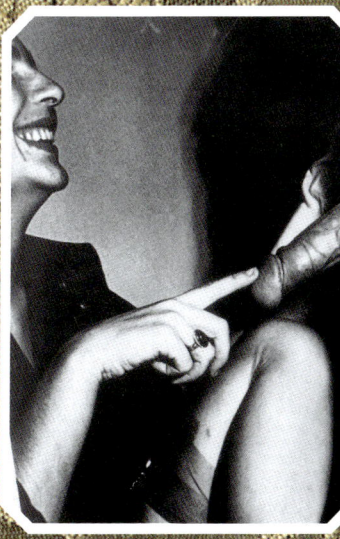

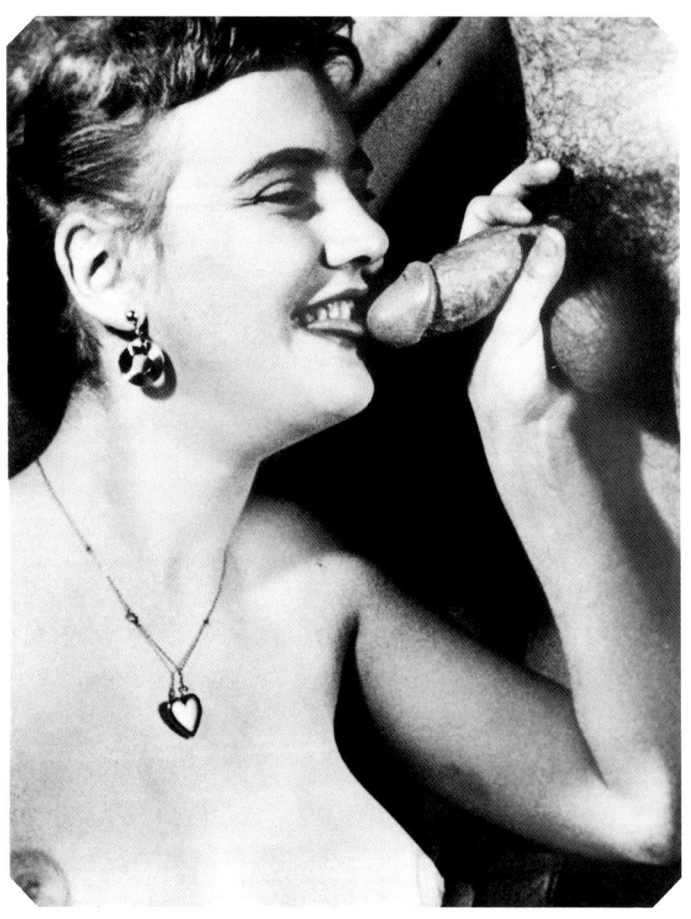

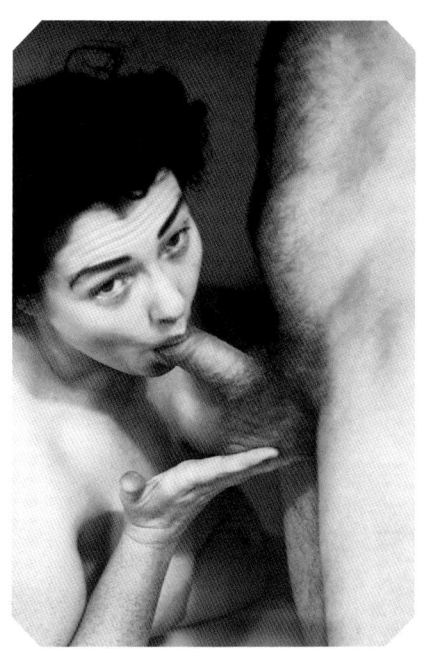
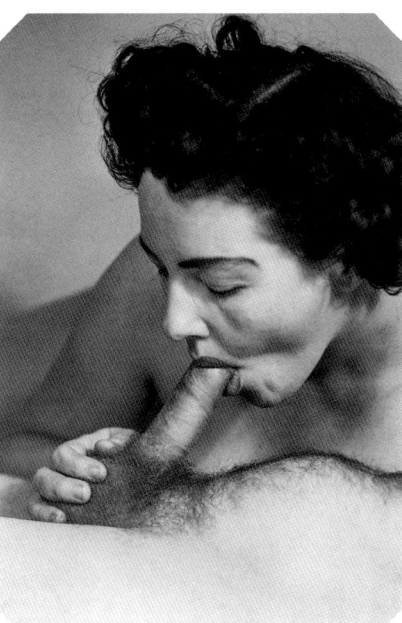

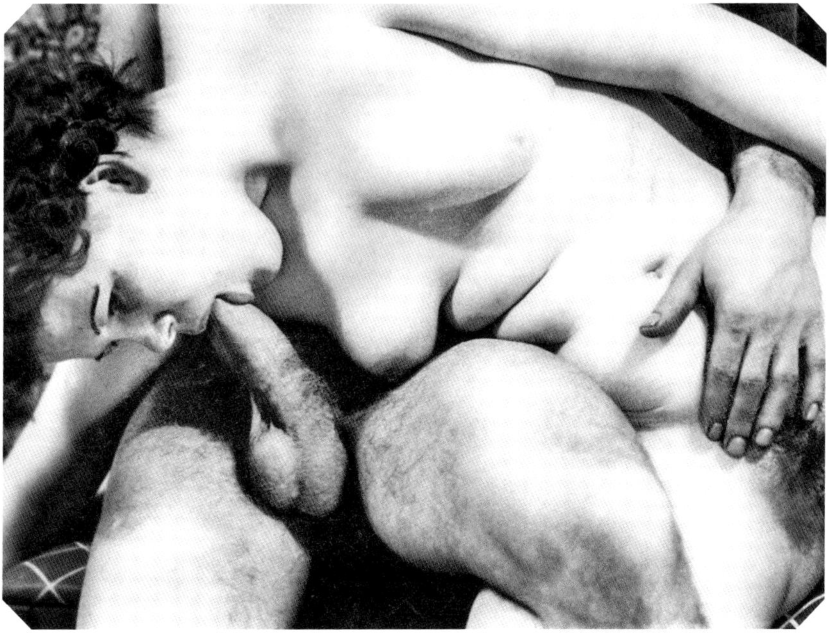

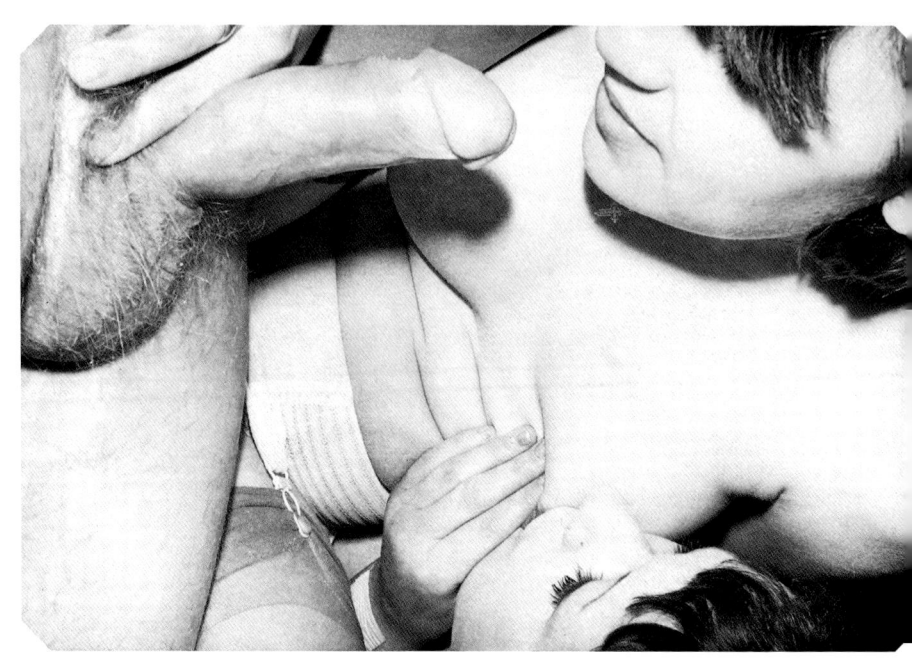

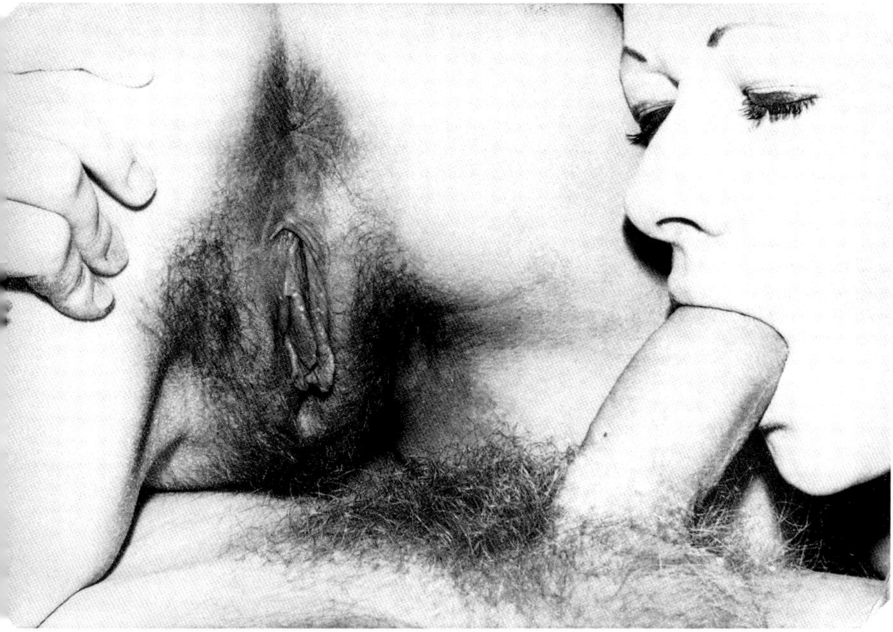

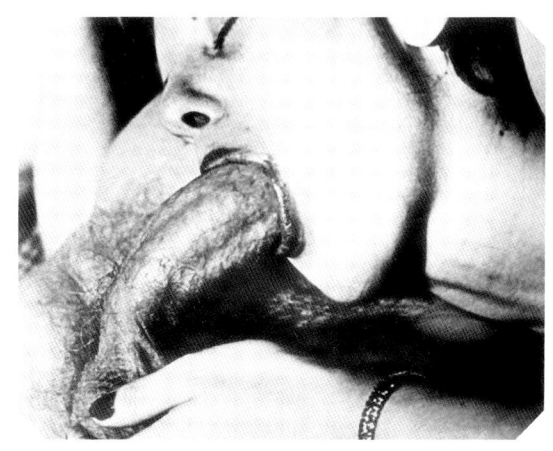

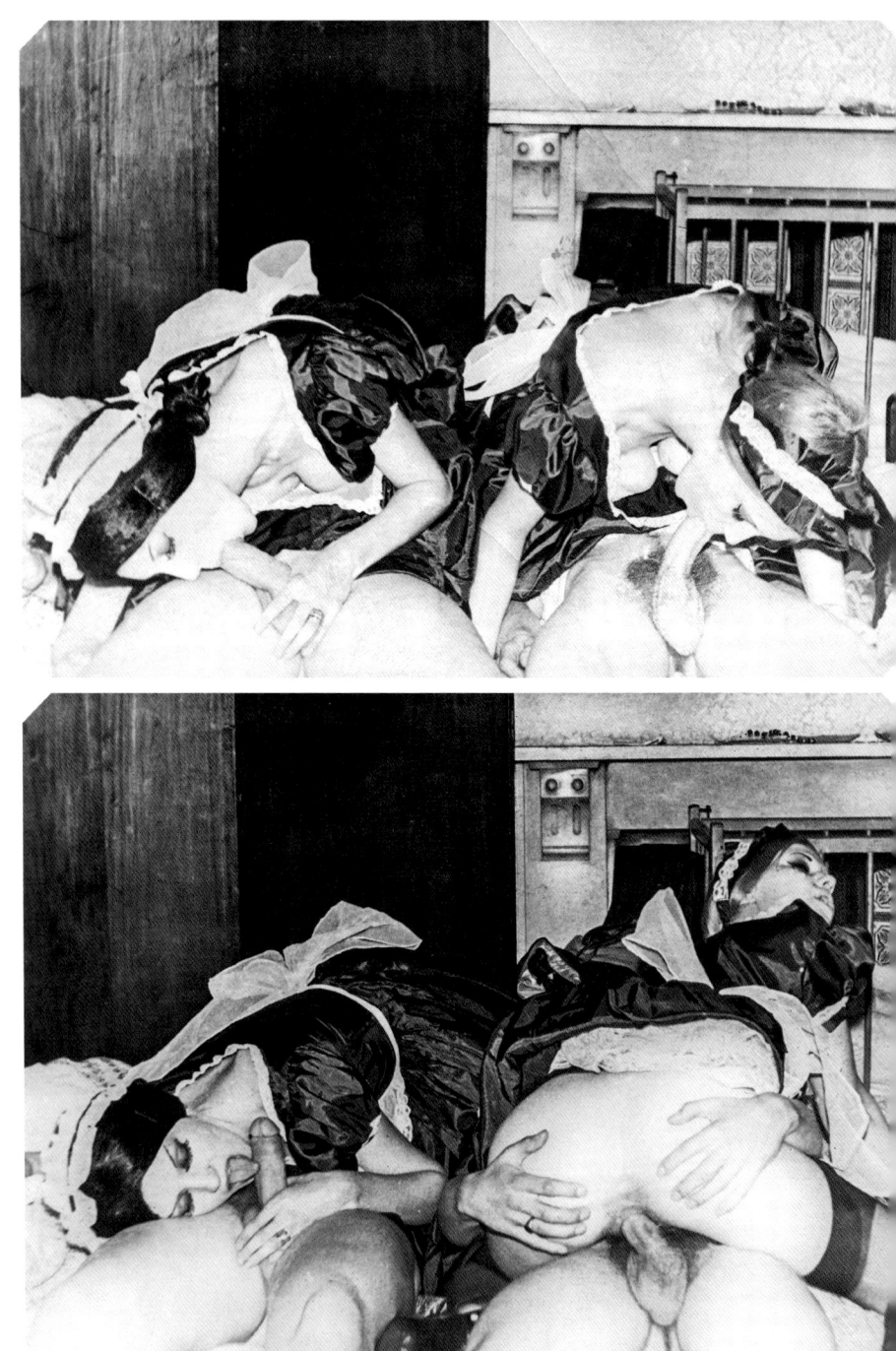

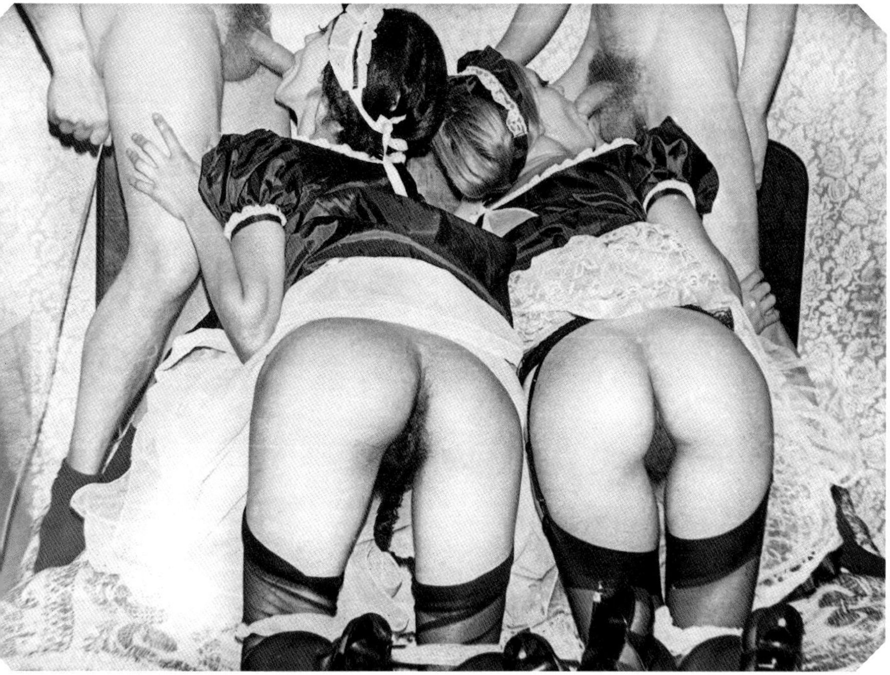

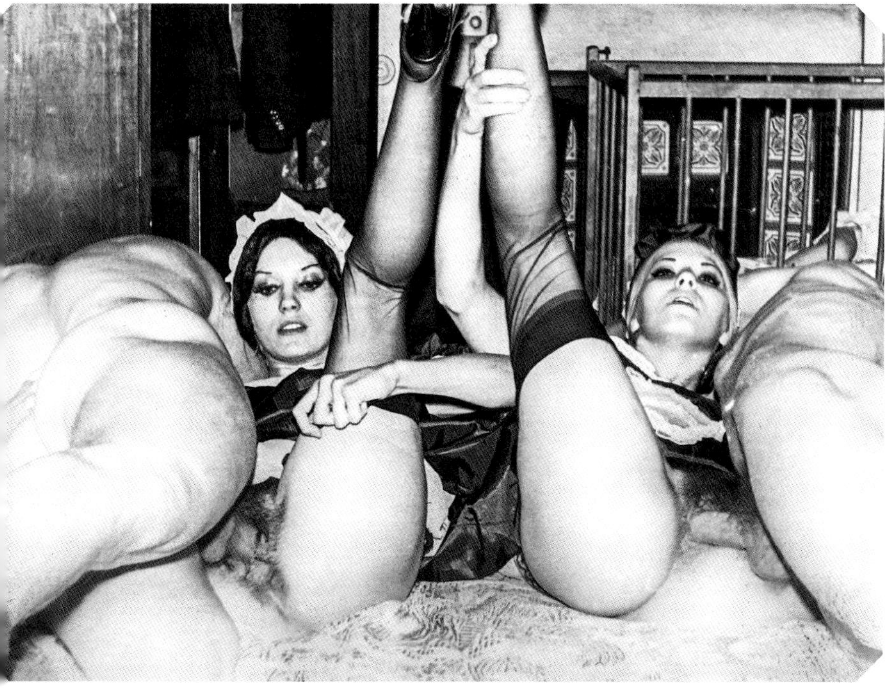

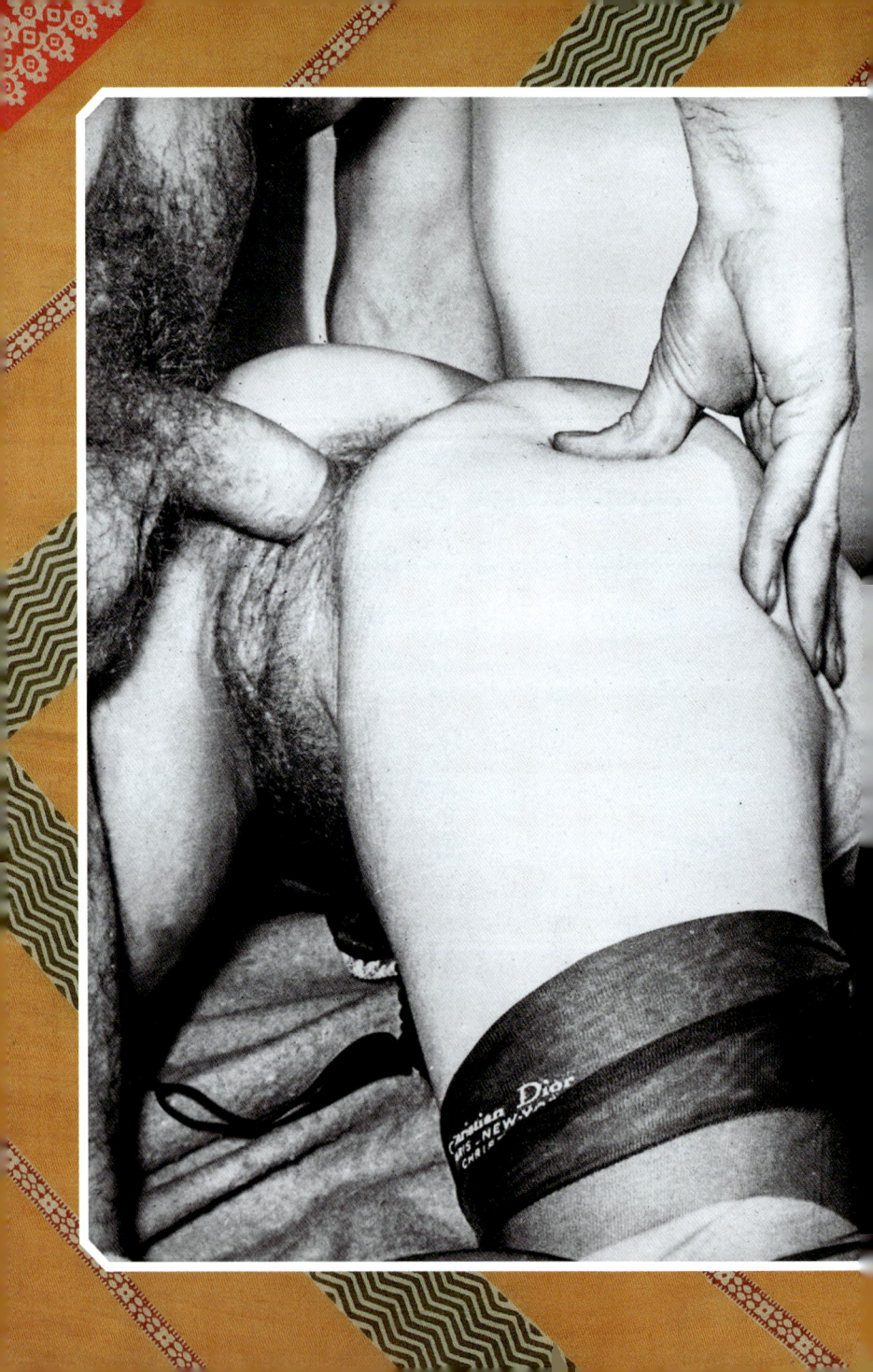

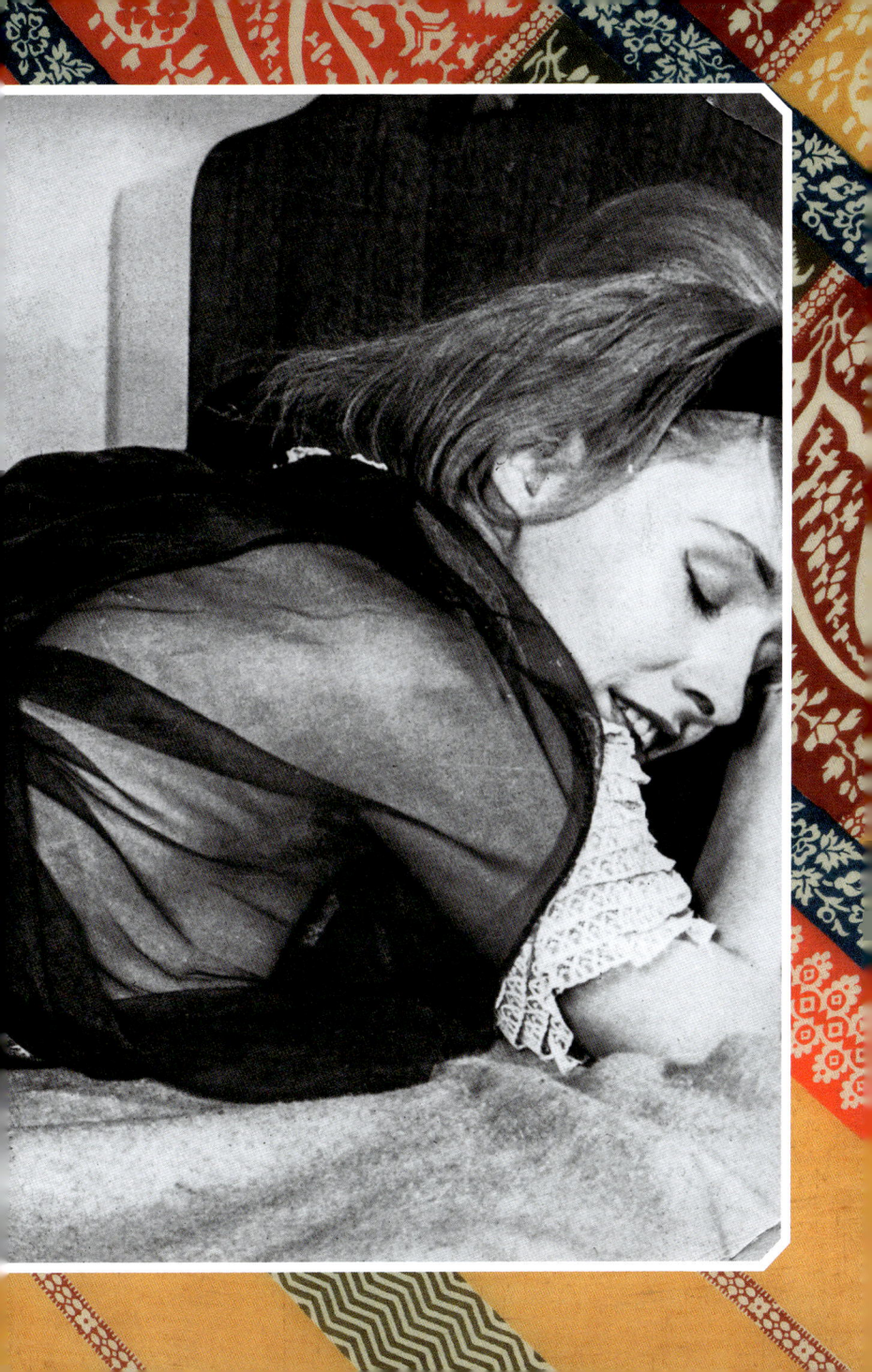

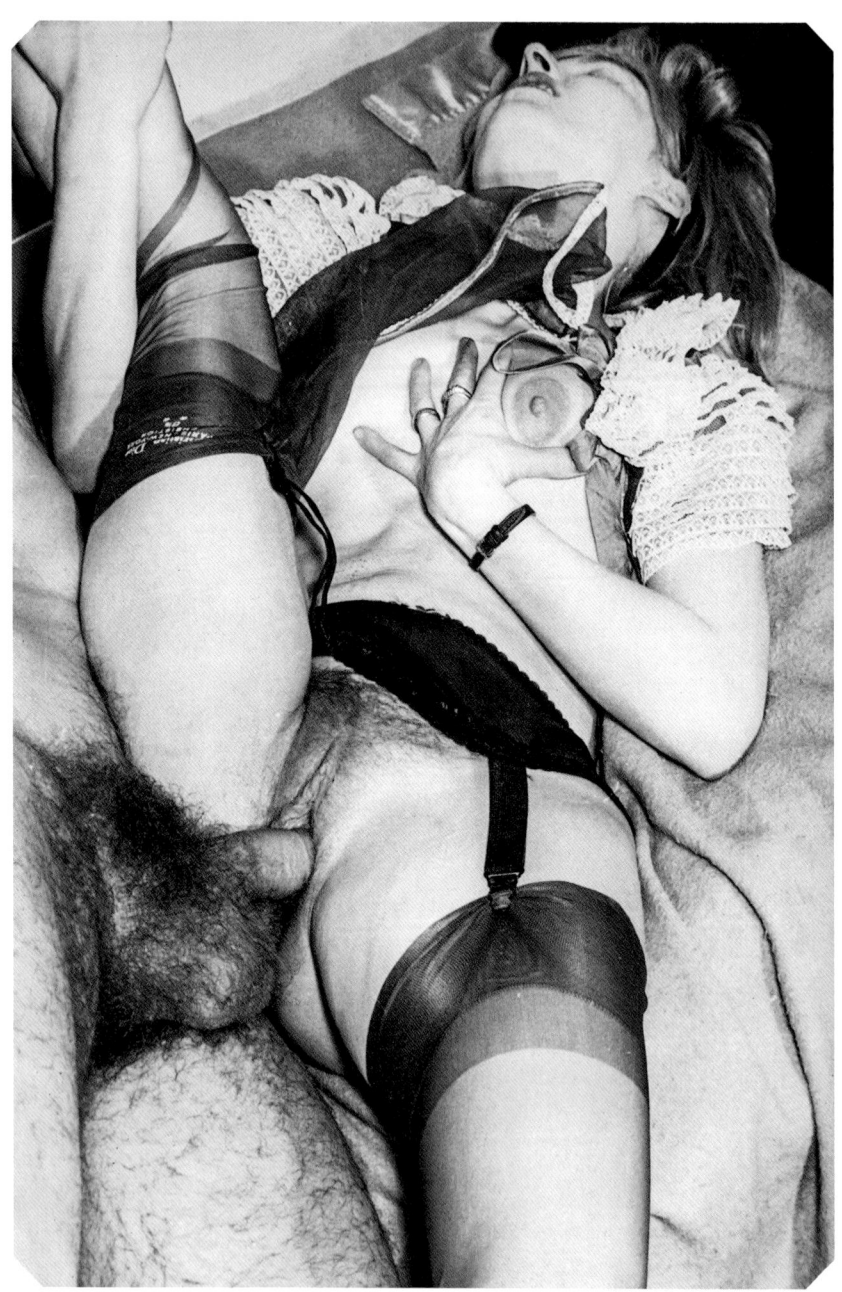

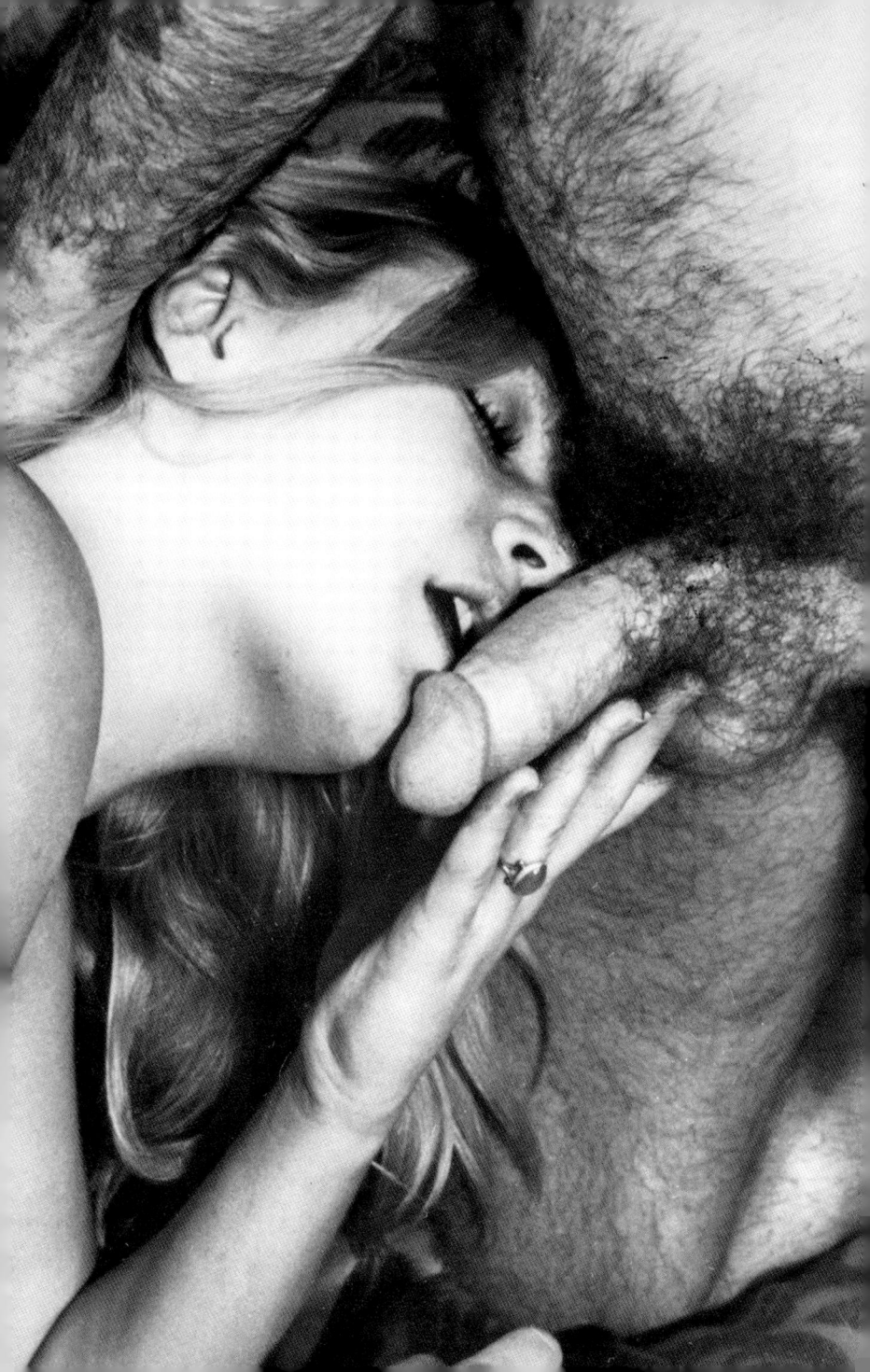

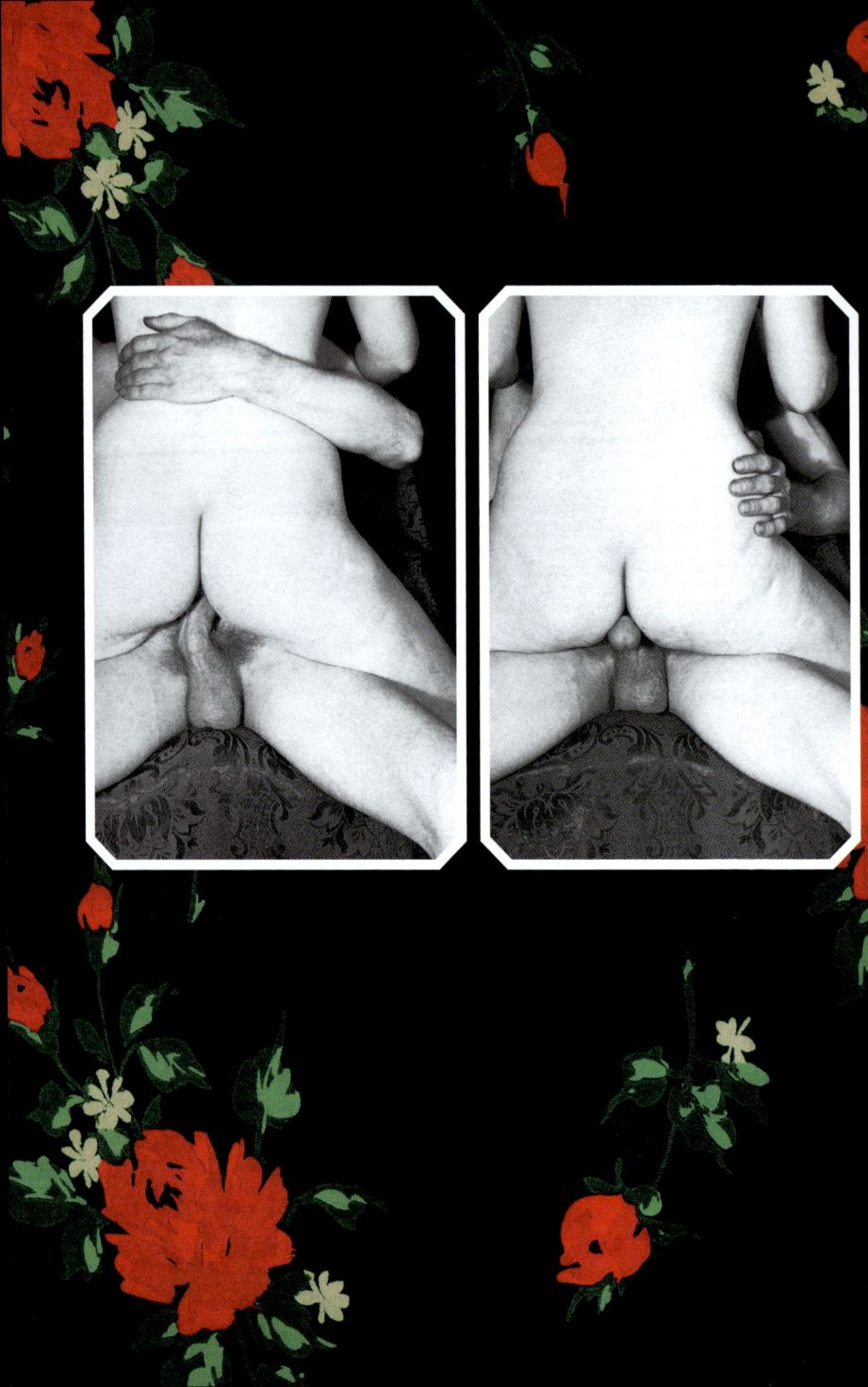

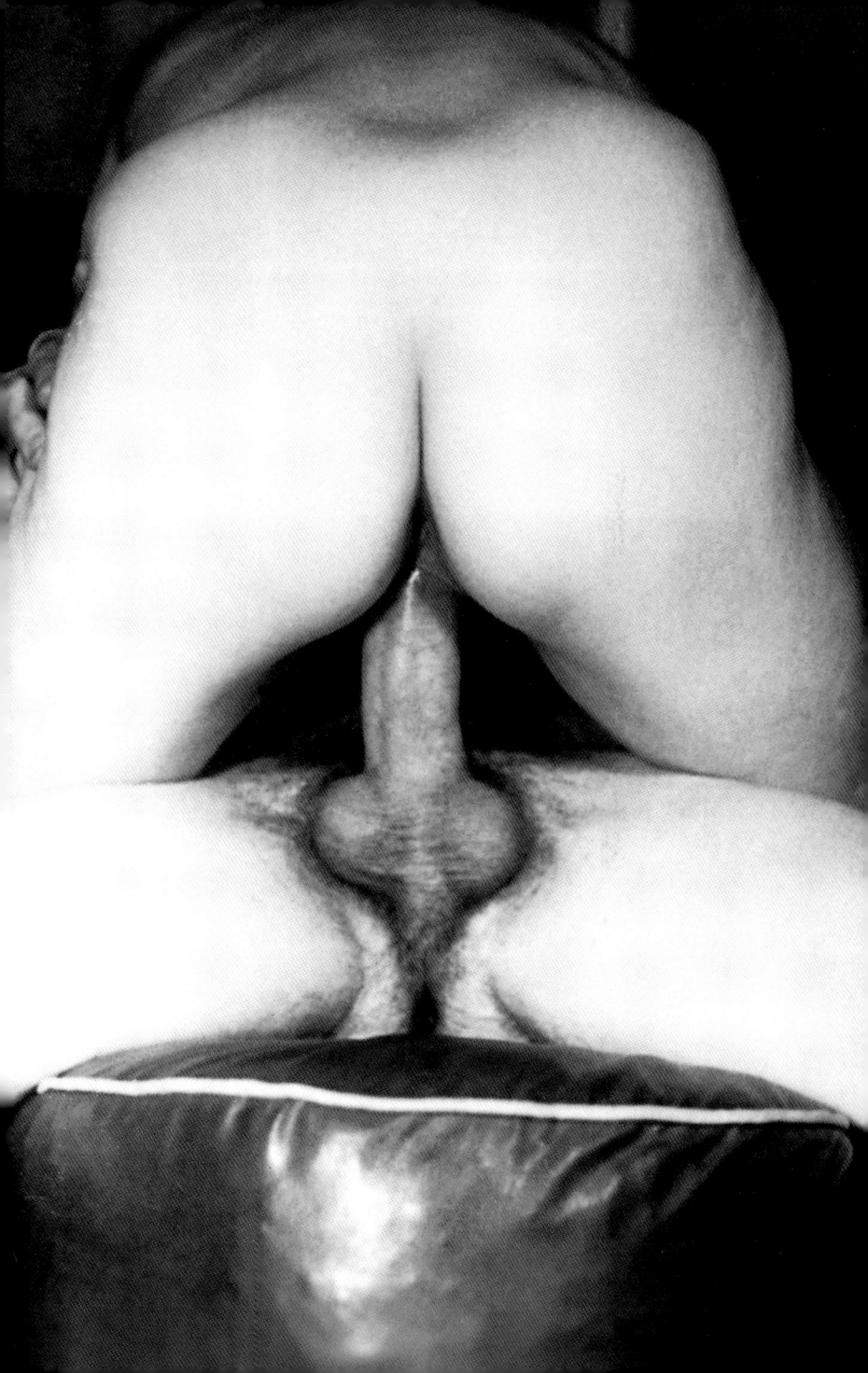

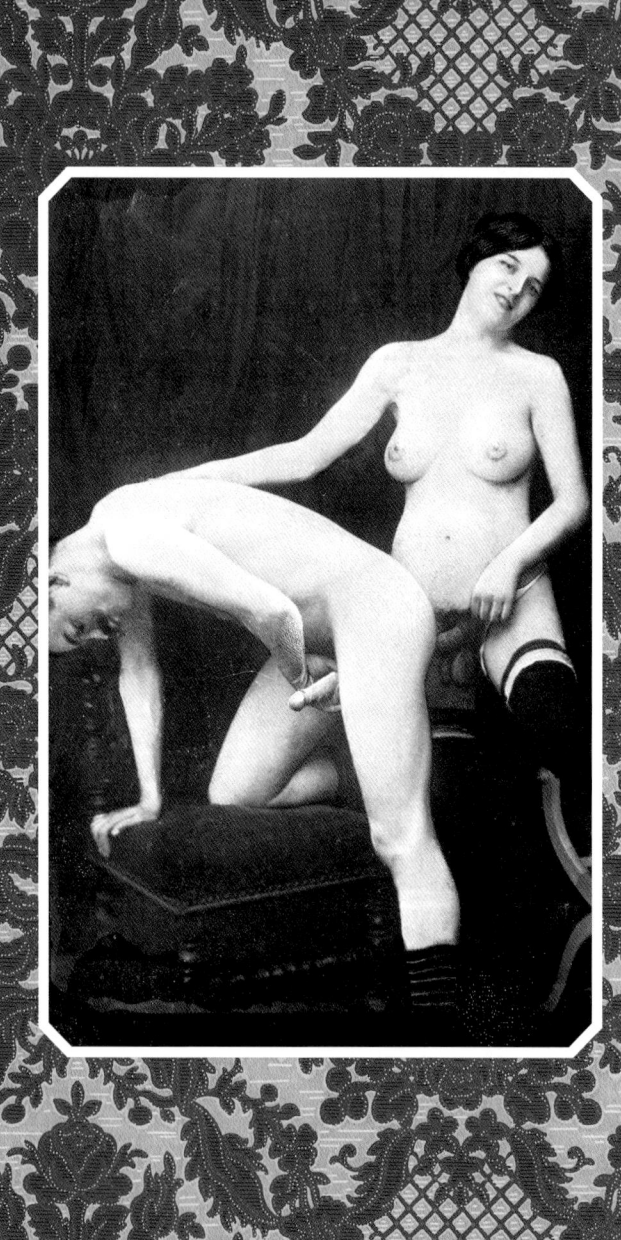

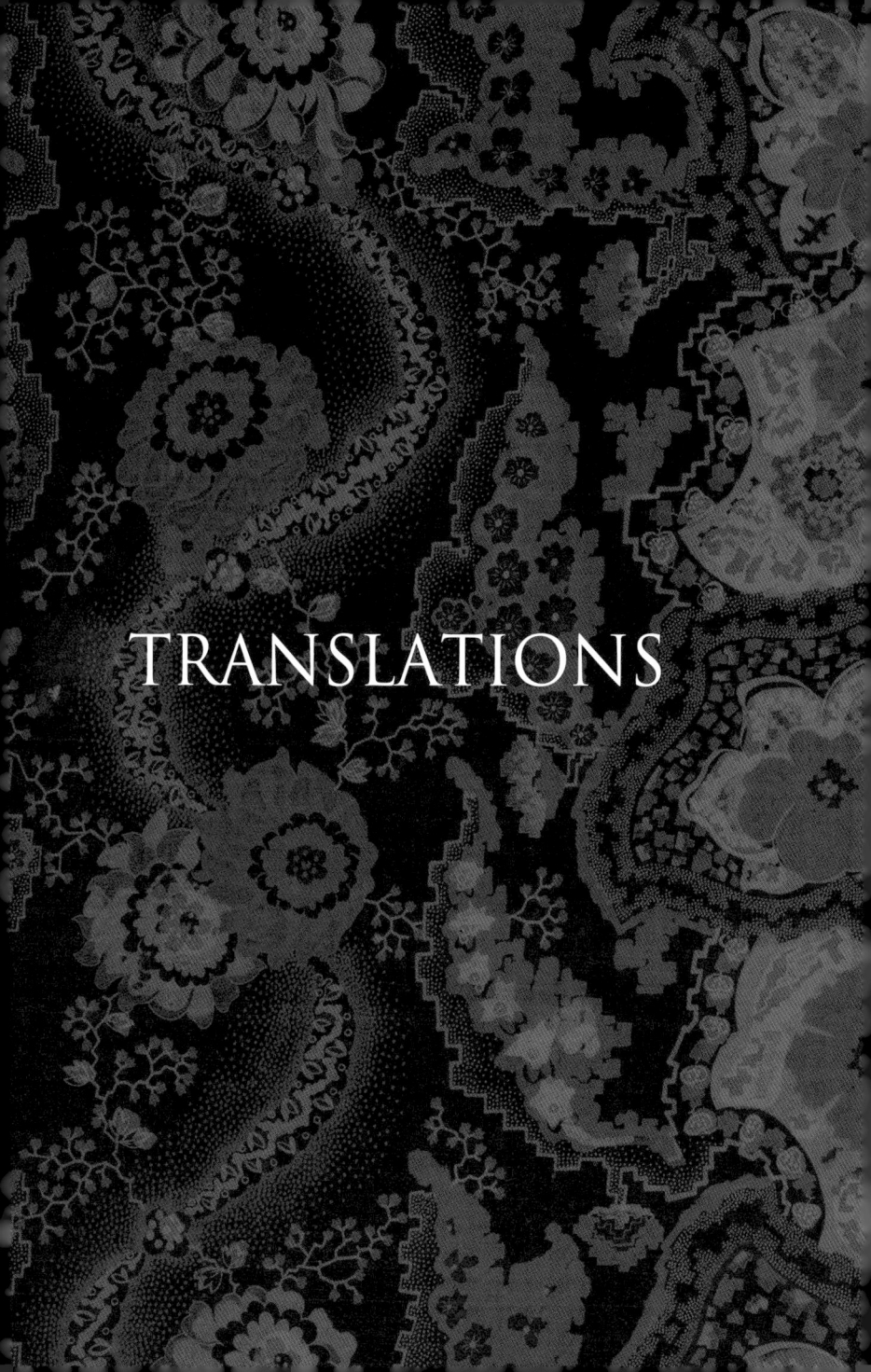

TRANSLATIONS

FORBIDDEN EROTICA: EINLEITUNG

Seit jeher zählt der Akt zu den beliebtesten Sujets der Fotografie. Wann die ersten Aktaufnahmen entstanden, lässt sich nicht mehr genau datieren, doch um 1845 tauchten Aktbilder in Gestalt kunstvoll kolorierter, kaum mehr als handtellergroßer Daguerreotypien bei Pariser Optikern, Instrumentenbauern und Kunsthändlern auf.[1] Das Spektrum reichte vom dezenten Rückenakt im Sinne der klassischen Akademien bis hin zum drastischen Herzeigen der Genitalien, von der lesbischen Liebe bis zum heterosexuellen Koitus.

Die überwiegende Mehrheit dieser Bilder wurde von Männern für Männer produziert. Sie brachten folglich die in ihrer Zeit vorherrschenden sexuellen Fantasien des Mannes zum Ausdruck, oder zumindest das, was die Fotografen dafür hielten. Um das männliche Publikum anzusprechen, zeigten viele Bilder Fellatio. Lesbische Szenen waren dezent, doch die männliche Homosexualität wurde so freizügig wie heute behandelt, obgleich sie zu jener Zeit strafrechtlich verfolgt wurde. Das beliebteste Motiv jedoch war der heterosexuelle Koitus in all seinen Spielarten. Damals wie heute ließ sich mit derartigen Aufnahmen beträchtliches Geld verdienen.

Nahezu alle Modelle der Bilder in *Forbidden Erotica* (Verbotene Fantasien) sind anonym geblieben. Viele von ihnen waren Prostituierte. Angesichts ihrer sozialen Lage – ihrem perspektivlosen Leben voller Mühsal und Not – muss es ihnen wie ein Traumjob vorgekommen sein, für pornografische Aufnahmen posieren zu dürfen. Es gibt allerdings auch Hinweise darauf, dass in einigen Fällen geistig Behinderte, die kaum begriffen, was mit ihnen geschah, für derartige Aufnahmen missbraucht wurden.

Auch die Namen der Fotografen sind nicht überliefert. Diese Fotoerotika für den Massengebrauch entstanden außerhalb eines künstlerischen Kontextes, und ihren anonym bleibenden Produzenten mangelte es in der Regel an künstlerischer Ausbildung und Fachkenntnis.

Die frühsten Aufnahmen in *Forbidden Erotica* stammen aus den siebziger und achtziger Jahren des 19. Jahrhunderts. Um diese Zeit war man in der Lage, Fotografien von Negativen abzuziehen und somit unbegrenzt zu vervielfältigen.

(Daguerreotypien, Ferro- und Ambrotypien lieferten jeweils nur ein Direktpositiv und ließen sich nicht vervielfältigen.) Die jüngsten Aufnahmen stammen aus den vierziger Jahren des 20. Jahrhunderts. In diesem Band finden sich Silbergelatineprints, Albuminabzüge, Bildpostkarten, zum Teil handkoloriert, sepiafarbene Fotografien und Fotopostkarten und eine kleine Reihe von Lithografien. Oft wurden zahllose Kopien von einer Aufnahme hergestellt. Bei einigen Bildern lässt sich deutlich erkennen, dass man einfach eine an die Wand geheftete Aufnahme neu abfotografiert hat. Neben Fotografien zeigt der Band auch eine kleine Auswahl an Postkarten mit pornografischen Illustrationen.

Die Bildpostkarte, die in den siebziger Jahren des 19. Jahrhunderts auf den Markt kam, trug wesentlich zur Verbreitung der Aktfotografie bei. Von den neunziger Jahren des 19. Jahrhunderts bis in die dreißiger Jahre des 20. Jahrhunderts waren Aktpostkarten ungemein populär. Allein in Frankreich wurden zwischen 1919 und 1939 über 20 Millionen dieser Postkarten hergestellt. Diese erotischen und pornografischen Karten waren natürlich nicht dazu gedacht, mit der Post verschickt zu werden und waren oft freizügiger als die heutige Pornografie. So war es beispielsweise nicht ungewöhnlich, dass Minderjährige auf ihnen zu sehen waren oder Frauen beim Koitus mit Hunden. Heute ist die Veröffentlichung derartiger Abbildungen gesetzlich verboten.

Von Beginn an bemühten sich die Behörden nach Kräften, die Produktion „unzüchtiger" Fotografien zu unterbinden. 1802 wurde in England die *Society for the Suppression of Vice* gegründet, um den Bürger vor blasphemischen Schriften, obszönen Büchern und Drucken sowie Bordellen zu schützen. Ein Großteil der nach 1850 entstehenden pornografischen Fotografien wurde verboten, beschlagnahmt und vernichtet. Bei einer einzigen derartigen Aktion wurden 1874 im Versandlager eines gewissen Henry Hayler in London 130 248 „unzüchtige" Bilder konfisziert.[2] In den puritanischen Vereinigten Staaten machte sich in den letzten Jahrzehnten des 19. Jahrhunderts vor allem Anthony Comstock, Sonderbeauftragter des U.S. Post Office und führender Kopf der amerikanischen „Tochterfirma" der *Society for the Suppresion of Vice*, für rigide Zensurmaßnahmen stark und sorgte dafür, dass der Vertrieb von pornografischem Material durch die Post unterbunden wurde.

Es ist kein Zufall, dass die Pornografie in Zeiten restriktiver Sexualmoral floriert. „Pornografie kann nur auf dem Boden der Prüderie gedeihen, in einer Zeit, in der der Gegensatz von Leib und Seele besonders stark empfunden wird", schreibt Paul Tabori in *Secret and Forbidden: The Moral History of the Passions of Mankind*.[3] Und Michael Koetzle ergänzt in *1000 Nudes*: „Begriffe wie ‚obszön' oder ‚unzüchtig' sind das Ergebnis einer repressiven Sexualmoral, deren Verbreitung interessanterweise mit Bekanntgabe und Rezeption der Fotografie zeitlich in etwa zur Deckung kommt."[4] *The Compact Edition of the Oxford English Dictionary* datiert die erste Erwähnung der Bezeichnung „pornography" auf 1850[5], die Fotografie wurde um 1839 erfunden.

Doch trotz aller Gesetze und Maßnahmen, ihre Produktion und Verbreitung zu unterbinden, wurden Fotografien, wie sie sich in *Forbidden Erotica* finden, zu Tausenden hergestellt und auf der ganzen Welt vertrieben. Sie waren Massenware für den Massengebrauch, und Länder wie Kuba, Frankreich, England, Japan und die Vereinigten Staaten können auf eine lange Geschichte der Produktion von Fotoerotika zurückblicken.

Die Aufnahmen in *Forbidden Erotica* stellen in ihrer überwiegenden Mehrheit das drastischste und härteste Material dar, das sich in der *Rotenberg Collection of Erotic Photography* findet. Ja, schon die Bezeichnung „erotisch", die eine verträumte, anmutige, stilvolle, kokette, bezaubernde und zurückhaltende Sexualität suggeriert, benennt eigentlich genau das, was sich in diesem Buch nicht findet. Hinter all der Prüderie der Viktorianischen Ära blühte eine geheime romantische Erotik. Hinter dieser Erotik jedoch boomte krasse Pornografie. Zwischen der künstlerischen Akt-Fotografie und dem pornografischen Bild gibt es einen deutlichen Unterschied. „Der Künstlerakt verspricht nichts, das erotische Bild manches, die obszöne oder pornographische Darstellung löst alle Versprechungen ein und wirkt dadurch auf viele Betrachter eher verstörend als anregend."[6]

Die von den Präraffaeliten und dem Jugendstil inspirierte erotische Fotografie der Belle Époque ist bereits in zahlreichen Publikationen gewürdigt worden. Die Bilder in den *Forbidden Erotica* jedoch entstammen einer anderen Welt. Sie erheben keinen künstlerischen Anspruch. Sie sind eindeutig, vielleicht schockierend und wirken auf manche möglicherweise gar erschreckend. Heutzutage sind es die meisten Menschen nicht gewohnt, Aktaufnahmen von Menschen zu sehen, die nicht den gängigen Schönheitsidealen entsprechen. Diese Bilder zeigen in nahezu unendlicher Vielfalt schlicht und einfach den sexuellen Akt. Mit den exquisiten erotischen Werken von Künstlern wie Aubrey Beardsley, Félicien Rops, Gustav Klimt oder Franz von Bayros haben sie wenig gemein. Eher schon kann man sie als Illustrationen zu zwei Klassikern der viktorianischen Pornografie verstehen, zu *My Secret Life* und *The Pearl*.

My Secret Life, ein um 1890 anonym erschienenes Buch, schildert in Tagebuchform auf unverblümte Weise die sexuellen Abenteuer eines wohlhabenden englischen Gentleman. Der Ich-Erzähler beschreibt sein Liebesleben in einer drastischen und nichts beschönigenden Sprache. Einsetzend mit frühen Erinnerungen an den sexuellen Missbrauch durch sein Kindermädchen erzählt er etwa davon, wie er die Hausmädchen beim Urinieren beobachtet, wie er trotz der Warnung seiner Mutter die sexuellen Gefälligkeiten eben dieser Dienstmädchen in Anspruch nimmt, wie er zahllose unschuldige Mädchen entjungfert und von seinen wahllosen Affären mit Bauernmädchen auf den Landstraßen. Mit zunehmendem Alter führen ihn seine Gelüste auf gefährlicheres Terrain. Er beschreibt freimütig SM-Szenen, Prostitution, Orgien, Crossdressing, Homosexualität und sogar Vergewaltigungen.

Alle Spielarten der Sexualität werden detailliert und nahezu klinisch genau geschildert: vom schlichten Geschlechtsverkehr über Fellatio und Cunnilingus (Praktiken, die der Autor „gamahuching" nennt) bis zu Sodomie, Masturbation etc. Folgende wahllos herausgegriffene Passage veranschaulicht den Tenor des Buches:

Ich legte ihn aufs Bett, nahm seinen Schwanz in den Mund und begann zu lutschen, erst noch mit der Vorhaut und dann zarter mit zurückgezogener Vorhaut … es wirkte sofort … als Sarah zurückkam, war er steif … Mit steifem Schwanz drang er sofort in sie ein … Sein Schwanz steckte bis zum Anschlag in ihrer Fotze … Ich hatte ihn dreimal gewichst, und er hatte dreimal gefickt – ich hatte sechsmal gefickt – ich hatte in seine noch warme Soße gefickt und seinen Schwanz gelutscht – Sarah war gute achtmal gefickt worden … sie sagte: „Ich bin wundgefickt." Dann bezahlte ich beide und ging.[7]

My Secret Life vermittelt den Eindruck, dass in der viktorianischen Gesellschaft die Mitglieder der Unterschicht Freiwild für die Bessergestellten waren. Bedienstete und Arme wurden zu Objekten degradiert, bisweilen wie Tiere behandelt und galten nahezu als eine andere Spezies. Des Verkehrs mit Prostituierten überdrüssig, schreibt der anonyme Verfasser von *My Secret Life*: „Ich suchte nach Abwechslung und begann mich nach einem hübschen, unverdorbenen Dienstmädchen umzusehen … Sie sind sauber, gut genährt, vollblütig, …, bereit, willig, haben Pfeffer im Arsch und sind lasziv und geil."[8] Wenn diese Frauen (und Männer) schon Freiwild waren, dann waren sie auch die perfekten Kandidaten dafür, in allen erdenklichen kompromittierenden Positionen abgelichtet zu werden.

Das Underground-Magazin *The Pearl: A Journal of Facetiae and Voluptuous Reading* erschien zwischen Juli 1879 und Dezember 1880 und behandelte ähnliche Themen wie *My Secret Life*. Allerdings unterschieden sich beide Publikation in ihrem Tenor. Während *My Secret Life* auf drastische Weise eine prosaische, hemdsärmelige Fleischeslust beschreibt, ist *The Pearl* überspitzt und sensationsheischend, originell und verspielt. Unter den Fortsetzungsgeschichten, die monatlich in dem Magazin erschienen, fanden sich etwa Titel wie „Sub-Umbra, or Sport Among the She-Noodles", „Miss Coote's Confession, or The Voluptuous Experiences of An Old Maid; In a Series of Letters to a Lady Friend", und „Lady Pokingham, or They All Do It".

Besonderes Augenmerk widmete *The Pearl* dem Flagellantismus. „Im 18. und 19. Jahrhundert," schreibt Ralph Ginzburg in *An Unhurried View of Erotica*, „wurde die Flagellomania in England in einem bis dato und auch später nicht mehr gekannten Maße kultiviert. … Auf dem Kontinent wurde diese Neigung als ‚le vice anglais' bekannt."[9] Ein Auszug aus der oben erwähnten Geschichte „Miss Coote's Confession" mag hier als Beispiel dienen:

Auf Miss Flaybums Gesicht zeichnete sich das gesamte Ausmaß ihres Unwillens ab, während ihr schwerer, korpulenter Hintern unter jedem Hieb erzitterte ... mit jedem Hieb erregten sich die Flagellatrix und ihre Freundinnen stärker an dem Schauspiel ..., (das) ihnen erlesene sinnliche Genüsse zu bereiten schien; viele der älteren Mädchen rekelten sich gemeinsam auf dem Boden oder nahmen andere wollüstige Posen ein.[10]

(Der Autor von *My Secret Life* schildert ebenfalls seine Abenteuer in einem Flagellationsstudio, dessen Besitzerin traditionell „Äbtissin" genannt wurde.)

Viele Passagen in *The Pearl* preisen die verführerische Macht des Negligés und den erst relativ neuen Reiz der Unterwäsche. (Interessanterweise ist Damenunterwäsche erst in den fünfziger Jahren des 19. Jahrhunderts in Mode gekommen, dreißig Jahre vor der ersten Ausgabe von *The Pearl*.) Der folgende Auszug belegt auch das viktorianische Faible für Frauen „eines gewissen Alters":

Maria entkleidet langsam ihre Herrin, eine attraktive, hübsche korpulente Frau in den Vierzigern. ... bald steht sie nur in Hemd und Schlüpfer da, der so prall gefüllt ist, daß er den wunderbaren Hintern darin erahnen läßt, und der unten mit kostbarer Spitze verziert ist. Darunter sieht man ein hübsches Paar draller Beine in fleischfarbenen Seidenstrümpfen und Stöckelschuhen mit juwelenbesetzten Schnallen ...[11]

My Secret Life und *The Pearl* verraten einiges über die verborgene, unterdrückte Seite der Sexualität im Viktorianischen Zeitalter. Eben diese Seite illustrieren die Abbildungen in den *Forbidden Erotica*. Sowohl der klinisch-nüchterne Tonfall aus *My Secret Life* wie auch der verspielte Stil aus *The Pearl* findet sich in diesen Aufnahmen wieder. Gewisse Fotos gehen sogar noch über den krassen Ton von *My Secret Life* hinaus. Während die meisten Modelle offenbar Spaß an der Sache haben und frech-wissend in die Kamera grinsen, starren einige mit leerem Blick in die Ferne. Der Effekt macht einen frösteln. Dann gibt es da Nahaufnahmen von klaffenden Vulven, riesige erigierte Penisse und Penetrationen, die wirklich nichts mehr der Fantasie überlassen. Sieht man von ihrer Sepiatönung und ihrem verblassten Erhaltungszustand ab, sind diese Aufnahmen durchaus zeitlos.

Vielleicht war es die Neuheit des Mediums Fotografie oder auch das Wissen, dass ihr Tun verboten war, was die frühen Fotografen beflügelte, ähnlich wie der Autor von *My Secret Life* jede erdenkliche Spielart der Sexualität zu dokumentieren. Zweifellos werden sie aber auch die finanziellen Vorteile darin entdeckt haben, so viele sexuelle Vorlieben und Obsessionen wie möglich abzudecken. Es gibt Aufnahmen von „flotten Dreiern", Sex zu viert und mit noch mehr Teilnehmern, Männer mit Männern, Frauen mit Frauen, in jeder vorstellbaren Variante. Jede Hautfarbe ist vertreten. Es gibt fantasievolle Orgien und eine überraschend große Zahl von Aufnahmen mit Fellatio und Cunnilingus – das „gamahuching" des Verfassers von *My Secret Life*.

Es finden sich Aufnahmen von vornehmen Herren, die es in der Küche mit Spülmädchen treiben. Andere wälzen sich mit Bauernmädchen im Heu. Der Betrachter darf durchs Schüsselloch zuschauen, wie drei Frauen fröhlich gemeinsam urinieren. „Pinkeln" scheint überhaupt ein Lieblingsmotiv zu sein. Auch Einläufe werden vor der Kamera verabreicht. Wie die Verfasser pornografischer Schriften lassen auch die Fotografen dieser Zeit keine Gelegenheit ungenutzt, jedes nur erdenkliche Tabu zu brechen. Ein beliebtes Motiv sind Priester und Nonnen bei verschiedensten Ausschweifungen – vom einfachen Koitus bis zur Flagellation und dem „gamahuching".

Unzählige Requisiten und Accessoires kommen zum Einsatz, vom schlichten penisförmigen Dildo (der, was einen vielleicht überraschen mag, seit Jahrtausenden gebräuchlich ist) über Zigarren, Zigaretten, Wein-, Bier- und Champagnerflaschen, Telefone, Salamis und Kürbisse bis zu Besenstielen, Billardstöcken, Hämmern, Maracás und einem Zerstäuber für Insektenspray. Als ultimativer Dildo in der Geschichte der pornografischen Postkarte darf wohl der kleine Eiffelturm gelten, der einer Frau ins Hinterteil gesteckt wird. Einige Fotos zeigen einen Mann, der seinen Golfball von der Vagina einer Frau abschlägt. Auch sexuelle Akrobatik ist ein beliebtes Motiv. Eine Frau hängt weit zurückgebeugt oder kopfunter von den Schulter eines Mannes, von einem Tisch oder Stuhl. Auf anderen Bildern steht sie auf einem Bein und hat das andere über die Schulter des Mannes gelegt. Es gibt Frauen, die einen Kopfstand machen, während der Mann sie festhält und in sie eindringt, und Frauen, deren Beine auf den Schultern eines Mannes ruhen, während sie den Kopf hängen lassen und seinen Penis in den Mund nehmen.

Wie in *My Secret Life* und *The Pearl* ist die viktorianische Faszination für SM auch auf diesen Fotografien allgegenwärtig. Das heute geläufige Erscheinungsbild der Domina mit Maske, Lederstiefeln und Peitsche war bereits im späten 19. Jahrhundert ausgeformt; eine ganze Reihe Vertreterinnen dieser Zunft findet sich in *Forbidden Erotica*. Darüber hinaus sieht man auch zahlreiche Aufnahmen von ihren mit Ketten und Handschellen gefesselten Opfern und Sklaven, die mit Peitschen, Weiden- und Birkenruten traktiert werden. Ein großer Teil der Modelle entspricht nicht der heutigen Einstellung, die sexuelle Attraktivität nur mit Jugendlichkeit assoziiert. Tatsächlich vergnügen sich auf einigen Fotos Männer mit Frauen, die gut und gerne ihre Mutter, wenn nicht ihre Großmutter sein könnten. Zahllose Modelle posieren halb entkleidet oder in Unterwäsche. Ihre rüschenbesetzten Strumpfhalter, Strümpfe, hochgeknöpften Zofenstiefel, Schnürkorsetts, Petticoats, langen, bauschigen Unterhosen und Häubchen wirkten auf den Betrachter des späten 19. und frühen 20. Jahrhunderts so erregend, wie sie heute seltsam und albern erscheinen mögen. (Man kann sich allerdings kaum vorstellen, dass Aufnahmen nackter Männer und Frauen, die mit zusammenpassenden Uniformmützen, Jacken und Stiefeln ausstaffiert sind, nicht auch damals schon Anlass zum Kichern geboten haben sollen.)

Viele „schlüpfrige Witze" wurden vor der Kamera inszeniert. So trägt etwa eine Frau nichts außer einem aufgeschlagenen Pelzmantel, der ihre buschige Vagina betont. Eine andere, smart aussehende Frau rekelt sich in ihrem Negligé und liest dabei in einem Magazin namens *Smart Sex*. Ein beliebter Ulk zeigt eine Frau, die einen Penis auf einem Teller mit Messer und Gabel wie eine Wurst zerschneidet. Drei Frauen posieren alle Viere von sich gestreckt und sind mit „Faith, Hope and Charity" (engl. Mädchennamen, dt. „Glaube, Hoffnung und Nächstenliebe") untertitelt. Eine Frau säugt eine Puppe. Es gibt einige wirklich grotesk alberne Verkleidungen: vor allem bei den Männern die lustigen Hüte und falschen Bärte à la Groucho Marx, die zum Teil mit Theaterschminke aufgemalt waren.

Interessanterweise scheinen die Modelle auf einigen der späteren Fotografien verschämter zu sein als ihre Vorgänger aus früheren Tagen. Vor allem die Männer versuchen zunehmend, ihre Identität zu verbergen. Männer wie Frauen tragen Sonnenbrillen, große Hüte, Augenbinden oder Masken oder drehen ihr Gesicht von der Kamera weg. Aber es sind in erster Linie die Männer, die ihre Anonymität wahren wollen. Da die meisten dieser Fotoerotika ein männliches Publikum ansprechen sollten, hielt man es wahrscheinlich für wichtiger, die Gesichter der weiblichen Modelle erkennen zu können. Manchmal ist es offenkundig, dass der Fotograf mutwillig den Kopf eines Modells weggelassen hat. Man kann förmlich hören, wie er zu ihm sagt: „Ehrenwort, kein Mensch wird dich erkennen."

Doch warum sollten Scham oder Befangenheit beim Modellstehen für pornografische Aufnahmen in den Jahren zwischen 1870 und 1940 zugenommen haben? Vielleicht lag es daran, dass das Medium der Fotografie nicht länger neu und aufregend war. Der Anreiz, an dieser phantastischen neuen Erfindung teilzuhaben, war dahin. Vielleicht war aber auch die Kluft zwischen den gesellschaftlichen Klassen nicht mehr so groß wie ehedem und die ökonomische Not der sozial Schwachen weniger krass. Und wenn die sozialen Bedingungen sich verbessert hatten, konnte man indirekt jedem, der sich für pornografische Fotos hergab, vorwerfen, er tue es nicht aus Not, sondern aus Verworfenheit, und habe folglich allen Grund, sich zu schämen.

Die illustrierten pornografischen Postkarten in diesem Buch unterscheiden sich deutlich von den Fotografien; sie sind verspielter und delikater. Wie Cartoons zeigen sie Szenarien, die in der Realität so nicht möglich wären. Viele beweisen einen launigen, wenngleich teuflischen Sinn für Humor. So zeigt eine Karte etwa zwei Frauen, die „Le vi-abolo" spielen (ein Wortspiel mit „Diabolo", dem Namen eines Geschicklichkeitsspiels) und dabei Penisse, die sie als Dildos benutzen, an Fäden tanzen lassen. Auf einer anderen dienen einer Frau die Penisse zweier Clowns

– eines schwarzen und eines weißen – als Zirkustrapez. Oft findet sich auf diesen Karten auch versteckte Gesellschaftskritik. So reitet etwa eine Frau auf einem riesigen Penis, der „Samen" in Form goldener Münzen in ihr Portemonnaie ejakuliert. Andere Postkarten reißen kleine Zoten. Da sieht man beispielsweise ein Bankett, bei dem die Gäste sich an Penissen gütlich tun, die mit Samenflüssigkeit beträufelt sind. Die Speise nennt sich „Asperges Sauce Blanche" (Spargel in weißer Sauce).

Während der letzten 150 Jahre wurde von den Abertausenden Fotos und Postkarten pornografischen Gehalts der größte Teil verboten, geächtet, konfisziert und vernichtet – sei es von Behörden oder von schockierten Privatpersonen. Nur wenige Exemplare sind uns erhalten geblieben. Einige von ihnen finden Sie auf den Seiten von *Forbidden Erotica*.

Laura Mirsky

Weitere Informationen finden Sie unter:
www.vintagenudephotos.com

1) Michael Koetzle, 1000 Nudes, TASCHEN, Köln 1994, S. 21.
2) Ebd., S. 229.
3) Paul Tabori, Secret and Forbidden: The Moral History of the Passions of Mankind, Signet Books, New York 1971, S. 105.
4) Koetzle, a.a.O., S. 229.
5) The Compact Edition of the Oxford English Dictionary, Band 2, Oxford University Press, USA 1971, S. 2242.
6) Koetzle, a.a.O., S. 28.
7) Anonym, My Secret Life, Grove Press, Inc., New York 1966, S. 454.

8) Anonym, „My Secret Life", in: Steven Marcus, The Other Victorians: A Study of Sexuality and Pornography in Mid-Nineteenth-Century England, Basic Books, New York 1966, S. 133.
9) Ralph Ginzburg, An Unhurried View of Erotica, The Helmsman Press, New York 1958, S. 54.
10) Anonym, The Pearl: A Journal of Facetiae and Voluptuous Reading, Grove Press, Inc., New York 1968., S. 155–156.
11) Ebd., S. 154.

FORBIDDEN EROTICA: INTERVIEW

Laura Mirsky im Gespräch mit Mark Rotenberg

L.M.: Wann und wie begannst du mit deiner Sammlung von Fotoerotika?

M.R.: Vor etwa zwanzig Jahren in Brooklyn Heights, New York, bemerkte ich, dass in meiner Nachbarschaft nur zwei Häuser weiter etwas passiert war. Ich sah, wie der Leichnam eines Mannes abtransportiert wurde. Ungefähr zwei Wochen später begannen Arbeiter im Auftrag der Stadt Sachen aus seinem Haus in einen großen Müllcontainer zu werfen. Ich schaute nach, was das war. Am ersten Tag war der Container knietief mit Girlie Magazines gefüllt. Das weckte mein Interesse. Während der nächsten Tage guckte ich immer wieder in den Müllcontainer und entdeckte alte Zeitungen aus der Zeit des Bürgerkriegs, diverse Erotika, jede Menge Fotos – alte Fotos – einige der ältesten in meiner ganzen Sammlung.

L.M.: Wie alt waren diese Fotos?

M.R.: Ich würde sagen, die ältesten Aufnahmen aus meinem damaligen Fund in dem Müllcontainer stammen aus den siebziger Jahren des 19. Jahrhunderts – alte, sepiafarbene Bilder, Albuminabzüge …

L.M.: Wie viele Fotografien hast du in dem Container entdeckt?

M.R.: Das waren um die fünfzehnhundert: von ganz frühen Aufnahmen aus den 1870ern bis zu Bildern vom Ende der 1950er, darunter auch normale Cheesecake-Fotos. Viele der sehr frühen Aufnahmen waren ausgesprochen drastisch, richtiger Hardcore. Darunter waren Kontaktabzüge und große Abzüge von den 1870ern bis in die 1930er. Nach den 1930ern wurde das Material etwas harmloser. Offensichtlich gab es von etwa 1910 bis in die zwanziger Jahre eine Phase, in der die French Postcards – normale Akte und handkolorierte Bilder – in großer Zahl hergestellt und vertrieben wurden; auch davon fand ich einige in diesem Container.

L.M.: Wie ermittelst du das Alter dieser Aufnahmen?

M.R.: Oft anhand des Stils der Aufnahmen, an den Frisuren, der Unterwäsche oder den Hintergründen. Das ist praktisch die einzige Möglichkeit, die Entstehungsperiode zu bestimmen, wenn ansonsten keine Bekleidung zu sehen ist. Manchmal entdeckt man aufgerollte Strümpfe und hochgeknöpfte Schuhe oder Stiefel ...

L.M.: Was ist, wenn die Leute auf einer Fotografie völlig unbekleidet sind? Wie bestimmst du dann die Entstehungszeit?

M.R.: Das ist sehr, sehr schwierig. Eigentlich sogar unmöglich. Es leben ja keine der Modelle mehr, um einem Auskunft zu geben, und die Fotografen sind in der Regel natürlich auch unbekannt geblieben.

L.M.: Wie ging es danach weiter?

M.R.: Nachdem ich jede Menge Fotoerotika und ein paar andere Bilder gefunden hatte, begann ich intensiv zu recherchieren.

L.M.: Wie hast du hinsichtlich der Aktfotografie recherchiert?

M.R.: Ich habe mich mit Leuten aus der New Yorker Verlagsszene unterhalten, etwa von Milky Way Productions, die das Magazin *Screw* – Al Goldsteins kleine Spielwiese – herausgeben, oder mit Leuten vom *Cheri*-Magazin ...

L.M.: Du hast dort einfach angerufen und sie gebeten, dir bei der Identifizierung der Fotos zu helfen?

M.R.: Ich habe sie angerufen, erklärt, dass ich alte Aufnahmen habe, und sie gefragt, ob sie sich die anschauen und vielleicht in ihren Blättern veröffentlichen wollen. Dann besuchte ich die Herausgeber oder Artdirektoren, und sie meinten verblüfft, so alte Aufnahmen mit diesem Sujet noch nie gesehen zu haben. Sie haben ja nur mit aktuellen Bildern zu tun. Sie waren von der Idee begeistert, meine alten Aufnahmen zu verwenden. In den Gesprächen mit diesen Leuten erfuhr ich mehr über mein Material. Ich erfuhr zum Beispiel, dass diese Fotografien tatsächlich sehr selten sind. Und dass vieles davon auf geheimen Wegen vertrieben wurde, nicht in der Öffentlichkeit und schon gar nicht im Postkartenladen, es sei denn, man kannte das Codewort.

L.M.: Und wie lautete das richtige Wort?

M.R.: Nun ja, in den USA war „French Postcards" zum Pseudonym für Erotika geworden ...

L.M.: Wer verkaufte solche Bilder und wie konnte man sie erstehen?

M.R.: Ich schätze, es gab Händler, die sie in Drugstores und später an Tankstellen verkauften. Ursprünglich gab es in Europa jedoch Postkartenhändler, die Erotika vertrieben. Sie hatten Kontaktabzüge, mit denen sie Interessenten zeigen konnten, was sie im Angebot hatten. Einige dieser Kontaktabzüge finden sich auch in diesem Buch. Auf einem kleinen handlichen Abzug sah man von vier bis zu sechzehn oder zweiunddreißig Bilder, die man sich dann als Serie oder auch einzeln kaufen konnte. So wurde viel von diesem Material an relativ öffentlichen Orten vertrieben.

L.M.: Jemand marschiert einfach in einen Postkartenladen, sagt das Zauberwort und der Verkäufer zieht diese Muster hervor?
M.R.: Ganz genau. Und dann konnte der Kunde sich die Kontaktabzüge anschauen, bestimmen, welche Sets oder – falls erhältlich – welchen Einzelabzug er haben wollte, und mit einer hübschen kleinen Sammlung nach Hause gehen und seine Fantasie stimulieren lassen.

L.M.: Wann hast du dich entschlossen, historische Fotoerotika ernsthaft zu sammeln?
M.R.: Als ich feststellte, dass die Magazine in New York meine Fotografien veröffentlichen, mich dafür bezahlen und mir dann die Originale zurückgeben wollten, erschien mir das als vernünftiger Grund, noch mehr von diesen Fotos zu sammeln. Dadurch konnte ich den Herausgebern eine breitere Auswahl zur Verfügung stellen, aus der sie dann zu bestimmten Sex- oder anderen Themen die passenden Illustrationen auswählen konnten. Ich begann, Sammlerbörsen zu besuchen, auf denen ich derartiges Material finden konnte, vor allem die Fotobörsen in New York City und Antiquariatstage in Connecticut, New York, New Jersey, Pennsylvania. Ich fragte Bekannte und Freunde, ob sie nicht jemanden kennen, der ähnliche Sachen besitzt, und schließlich begann ich auch Anzeigen in diversen Wochenblättern und Magazinen in den gesamten USA zu schalten.

L.M.: Sind dir, wenn du auf Sammlerbörsen nach diesem speziellen Material gefragt hast, je Menschen begegnet, die empört waren oder es anstößig fanden, dass du danach suchtest?
M.R.: Doch, ja. Nicht dass jemand mit mir persönlich ein Problem hatte, doch es gab durchaus Leute, die auf die Frage nach Erotika abwinkten: „Nein, nein, nein. So was führen wir nicht. So was doch nicht."

L.M.: Hast du viele alte Fotoerotika entdecken können?
M.R.: Ja. Als ich mit meiner Sammlung begann, schien es Material in Hülle und Fülle zu geben, und ich konnte auf jeder Börse, die ich besuchte, eine gute Auswahl von frühen Sachen aus den 1870ern bis zu den 1950ern finden.

L.M.: Boten die Leute es offen an?
M.R.: Einige schon, doch das meiste Material war in Kartons unter dem Tisch versteckt und wurde nur hervorgeholt, wenn ich danach fragte. Harter Stoff – also was man heute „hardcore" oder pornografisch nennt – wurde nur selten auf solchen Börsen offen angeboten. Das hat sich bis heute nicht geändert.

L.M.: Du hast deine Anzeigen erwähnt. Wie hast du die formuliert?
M.R.: „Erotika gesucht. Nur Originale in gutem Zustand: 1860 bis 1950."

L.M.: Hat sich jemals eine Zeitung geweigert, diese Anzeigen zu drucken?
M.R.: Es gab einige Blätter im Mittelwesten, die sich geweigert haben. Sie

meinten, sie würden den Handel mit solchen Dingen nicht unterstützen wollen.

L.M.: Hast du ein Echo auf diese Anzeigen bekommen?

M.R.: Oh, ja. Ich habe aus allen Teilen des Landes Antworten erhalten. Von den unterschiedlichsten Leuten: von jungen Leuten, die gerade ein Haus renovierten und einen Schuhkarton voller Erotika in einer Wand, einem alten, versiegelten Kamin, auf dem Dachboden oder in der Garage entdeckt hatten, oder von älteren Menschen, die sich von alten Sachen trennten und in der Nachttischschublade noch einen Stapel erotischer Postkarten und Spielkarten, Tijuana Bibles oder andere Erotika hatten. Ich habe von vielen unterschiedlichen Leuten Antwort bekommen – Ärzte, Rechtsanwälte, Studenten.

L.M.: Hast du auch Reisen unternommen, um dir die Sachen anzusehen?

M.R.: Ja, häufig. Ich habe viele Stunden im Auto gesessen und bin oft Hunderte von Meilen gefahren, weil mir vielversprechendes Material am Telefon beschrieben wurde oder ich per Brief Listen bekommen hatte. Die Leute haben häufig Angst davor, die Sachen mit der Post zu verschicken, weil sie glauben, das sei illegal und sie könnten wegen Verbreitung von Erotika oder Pornografie verhaftet werden.

L.M.: Ist diese Furcht begründet?

M.R.: Keineswegs. Ich suche mit meinen Anzeigen öffentlich nach diesen Dingen, und immer vorausgesetzt, dass sich unter den Aufnahmen nicht wirklich offenkundig illegales Material findet, etwa Bilder mit Minderjährigen oder Sex mit Tieren, ist praktisch alles völlig legal mit der Post zu verschicken, besonders wenn Absender und Empfänger über 21 sind.

L.M.: Ist dir eine dieser Reisen besonders im Gedächtnis geblieben?

M.R.: Vor nicht allzu langer Zeit fuhr ich ins tiefste Pennsylvania – sagen wir drei bis vier Autostunden Fahrt für jede Richtung –, um mich mit Leuten zu treffen, die mir telefonisch Aufnahmen vom Anfang des 20. Jahrhunderts angeboten hatten ...

L.M.: Wo habt ihr euch getroffen?

M.R.: Wir hatten uns auf dem Parkplatz einer McDonald's-Filiale verabredet. Jeder hatte dem anderen erklärt, nach welchem Fahrzeug er Ausschau halten sollte. Wir trafen uns zur verabredeten Zeit, der Anbieter stieg zu mir ein, und dann sahen wir uns die Bilder durch, die er verkaufen wollte ...

L.M.: Wirkte er misstrauisch dir gegenüber?

M.R.: Misstrauisch eigentlich nicht, aber jeder von uns achtete peinlich genau auf sein Verhalten und so gab es keinerlei Schwierigkeiten oder Peinlichkeiten.

L.M.: Hattest du je den Eindruck, dass jemand deine Moral in Frage stellte, weil du diese Sachen von ihm kaufen wolltest?

M.R.: Nein. Wenn mich erst mal jemand anruft oder mir schreibt, um mir dieses

Material anzubieten, dann haben wir beide diese Frage bereits hinter uns gelassen. Ich denke, dass jeder, der auf derartige Bilder stößt und ein moralisches Problem damit hat, sie sicherlich nicht weiterverbreiten oder auch nur aufbewahren will.

L.M.: Du meinst, sie werfen sie einfach weg?

M.R.: Ich bin überzeugt, dass viele dieser Aufnahmen von Menschen wiedergefunden werden, die sie nicht selbst erstanden haben, um ihren Spaß daran zu haben und sie aufzuheben. Ich glaube, dass viele Leute, die so etwas zufällig entdecken, es vernichten, indem sie es einfach in den Müll werfen. Eine Menge Leute macht lieber das, als die Bilder zu verkaufen, denn das wäre ihnen peinlich oder sie empfinden es als unmoralisch – oder beides.

L.M.: Kannst du eine Geschichte über die Entdeckung von richtig „hartem" Material erzählen?

M.R.: Aber ja. Vor einigen Jahren erzählte mir ein Sammlerkollege von einem Bekannten, der diesen Erfinder besucht hatte ...

L.M.: Es gibt also ein richtiges Netzwerk von Leuten, die diese Dinge sammeln?

M.R.: Natürlich. In den Vereinigten Staaten und wohl überall auf der Welt gibt es zahllose Sammler. Sie sammeln nicht nur alte Originalfotos, sondern auch seltene Stücke von Volkskunst, primitiver Kunst und alle möglichen Erotika – Figuren, Filme, Kalender, Magazine, Bücher, alles, was mit Erotik zu tun hat, ob in Bild oder Text. Es gibt einen enorm großen Markt für Erotika. Und sobald etwas angeboten wird, sind genügend Leute zur Stelle, die es kaufen möchten und versuchen, sich gegenseitig dabei auszustechen.

L.M.: Wie ging die Geschichte von vorhin weiter?

M.R.: Durch den Freund eines Freundes stieß ich in New Jersey also auf eine riesige Sammlung von Magazinen und Fotografien, die besagtem Mann von seinem Nachbarn geschenkt worden war. Sie umfasste die Zeit von 1870 bis in die 1930er und zählte zu den härtesten Sachen, die ich bis dato gesehen hatte. 2500 Fotos insgesamt, die alle sorgfältig in Buchhaltungsbücher geklebt worden waren, woraus man sie behutsam wieder lösen musste.

L.M.: Weißt du, wem diese Fotos ursprünglich gehörten?

M.R.: Der Mann, dem diese Magazine und Fotos von seinem Nachbarn geschenkt worden waren, erzählte mir, dass sein Nachbar sich eine eigene Werkstatt in sein Haus hatte einbauen lassen. Seine Frau und die Kinder betraten diesen Raum nie. Dort hatte er einen Schrank, in dem die Hefte und Fotos aufbewahrt wurden. Während der letzten Monate seines Lebens begriff der Mann, dass seine Familie nach seinem Tod dieses Zimmer durchsehen und diese unglaublich große Pornografiesammlung entdecken würde. Diesen Schock wollte er seiner Familie nicht zumuten, und so gab er lieber alles seinem

Nachbarn, damit der es nach Gutdünken entweder behalten, verkaufen oder vernichten könnte. So kam mein Ansprechpartner an Tausende von Magazinen und Aktaufnahmen. Die Fotos sind nun Teil meiner Sammlung.

L.M.: Wo hast du dich sonst noch mit Anbietern getroffen?
M.R.: Parkplätze sind immer ein beliebter Ort. Sie sind neutral, und man fühlt sich sicher, vor allem, wenn man in seinem eigenen Wagen bleibt.

L.M.: Es gibt also immer einen Hauch von Gefahr?
M.R.: Na ja, schließlich geht es um Erotika. Man trifft sich ja nicht, um über den Preis einer Sammlerpuppe zu verhandeln. Es geht um ein Material, das nicht jeder gerne besitzt, anschaut oder auch nur verkauft. Dem Ganzen haftet etwas Anrüchiges und – sagen wir – Verbotenes an, obwohl die Sachen eigentlich nicht verboten sind, sofern sie sich im Besitz von Erwachsenen befinden.

L.M.: Ist es schon vorgekommen, dass Leute beim Verkauf dieser Dinge übertrieben nervös waren?
M.R.: Oh, ja. Einmal hat ein Zahnarzt auf eine meiner Anzeigen geantwortet. Er erklärte, er besitze eine Reihe alter Hardcore-Fotos, Hardcore-Spielkarten und French Postcards, die er im Sockel einer alten Lampe gefunden hätte. Wir trafen uns in einem großen Einkaufszentrum im Süden New Jerseys und setzten uns an einen Tisch der zentralen Cafeteria. Er drückte mir einen Rucksack in

die Hand, und ich merkte, dass er totale Paranoia bekam. Er hatte Angst, dass – sobald ich in die Plastiktüte im Rucksack schaue –, jemand vom Sicherheitsdienst des Einkaufszentrums vorbeikommen, die Bilder sehen und uns beide wegen Besitzes von Erotika auf der Stelle verhaften könnte. Er war so paranoid, dass er nicht einmal an einem Tisch mit mir bleiben wollte. Er setzte sich zu seiner Frau, die er an einem sicheren anderen Tisch plaziert hatte, und passte auf, dass ich nicht mit den Bildern abhauen würde.

L.M.: Hast du dich schon immer für Erotika interessiert?
M.R.: Ja, schon seit meiner Kindheit. Ich habe schon mit vier Jahren gerne Mädchen geküsst und schon früh Pin-up-Magazine angeschaut ...

L.M.: Gab es die bei euch zu Hause?
M.R.: Nein, zu Hause nicht, aber mein Vater besaß einen Kiosk mit Imbiss, in dem viele Zeitschriften auslagen. Dort schaute ich mir immer die Magazine an, darunter frühe Männermagazine aus den Fünfzigern und Sechzigern. In denen gab es Aktmodelle, aber nichts Pornografisches oder auch nur vage Anstößiges. Eigentlich nur Oben-ohne-Aufnahmen, aber ziemlich nett.

L.M.: Wann hast du zum ersten Mal etwas gesehen, was du „pornografisch" nennen würdest?
M.R.: Ich muss da wohl etwa neun Jahre alt gewesen sein. Da habe ich auf dem Parkplatz vor dem Laden meines Vaters

einen Acht-Millimeter-Film gefunden, eine Rolle mit vielleicht sechs Metern Film. Ich wunderte mich, dass jemand einen Amateurfilm liegen gelassen hatte, denn ich kannte nur Filme von unserer Familie, von gemeinsamen Ausflügen und dergleichen und nahm daher an, dies wäre etwas Ähnliches. Ich nahm ihn mit, legte ihn zu Hause in unseren Projektor und sah zwei Menschen, die ausgesprochen intim miteinander waren und sich wild bewegten.

L.M.: Was hast du dabei empfunden?
M.R.: Ich spürte, dass ich da etwas sehe, was Menschen zwar machen, ich aber bis dahin noch nie gesehen hatte. Mir wurde bewusst, dass sie etwas tun, was wahrscheinlich alle tun. Das Paar wirkte glücklich bei dem, was es tat, und niemand schien es zu dieser seltsamen Haltung zu zwingen. Es sah aus, als würde es richtig Spaß machen! Ich sah etwas, dass ich vorher noch nie gesehen und wovon ich auch nichts gehört hatte! Und ich wollte mehr darüber wissen. Ich wollte wissen, worum es da ging, wie es sich anfühlte, was es bewirkte, was sein Zweck war. Am Schluss des Ganzen wirkten die beiden recht zufrieden und erschöpft. Und dann schaute ich in die Schublade des schweren Holztisches meines Vaters, ein Platz, an dem er alle möglichen privaten Dinge aufbewahrte. Dort fand ich ein paar Magazine und Fotos. Auf denen sah man Frauen, die mit gespreizten Beinen alles zeigten.

L.M.: Und wie fandest du das?
M.R.: Ich fand das toll, ich fand das absolut toll! Einige der Fotos waren richtiger Hardcore – Amateuraufnahmen. Vielleicht hat mein Vater mit seinen Magazinen den Grundstein für meine Sammlung gelegt. Andererseits war ich schon mit vier ein geiler kleiner Bengel. Filme, Magazine oder so etwas hatten nichts damit zu tun.

L.M.: Findest du Pornografie von früher aufregender als zeitgenössische Pornografie?
M.R.: Yeah. Sie ist nicht so eintönig wie moderne Pornografie. Im Gegensatz zu heute sahen die Frauen nicht alle gleich aus und waren nicht so durchgestylt. Keine hat sich mit Silikon aufgepumpt oder anderen Schönheitsoperationen unterzogen. Heute soll die Frau von Kopf bis Fuß absolut perfekt und durchtrainiert sein, superblond und mit perfekt ausrasierten Haaren. Moderne Aktaufnahmen sind langweilig im Vergleich zu den alten, auf denen die Frauen noch lange Unterhosen, aufgerollte Strümpfe, hochgeknöpfte Zofenstiefel, Schals, Hüte und Schmuck tragen konnten. Man machte Aufnahmen noch in klassischen Kulissen, vor hübschen Hintergründen mit herrlichen alten Möbeln und überall lagen schrille Teppiche oder Felle herum. Ganz anders als heute.

L.M.: Was ist mit den Modellen auf diesen alten Aufnahmen? Findest du sie attraktiv?
M.R.: Einige waren attraktiv, andere nicht, wie im wirklichen Leben halt. Wenn man die Straße langgeht, sieht auch nicht jede Frau wie Pamela Anderson Lee aus. Gott sei Dank! Aber wenn

man sich zeitgenössische Erotika ansieht, vor allem die Magazine, dann gleicht ein Modell dem anderen.

L.M.: Was, glaubst du, werden die meisten Menschen von den Bildern in diesem Buch halten?

M.R.: Ich hoffe, es verschlägt ihnen die Sprache! Selbst wenn ich mit meinen Aufnahmen zu den Zeitschriftenverlegern gehe, versammeln sich sofort die Leute um mich. Sie stehen da und staunen. Die glauben mitunter, Erotika wären etwas relativ Neues, etwas, das für sie und von ihnen erfunden worden ist. Was frühe Fotoerotika anbelangt, haben sie nur sehr wenig Ahnung.

L.M.: Und wie wird deiner Meinung nach der Durchschnittsleser auf diese Fotosammlung reagieren?

M.R.: Wenn sie Aufnahmen sehen, die siebzig, achtzig, neunzig, hundert Jahre oder noch älter sind als sie selbst, werden sie verblüfft sein! Es wird ihnen die Sprache verschlagen! Im Laufe der Jahre habe ich über hunderttausend Fotos gesammelt. Im Geheimen und Verborgenen gibt es solche Fotos seit der Erfindung der Fotografie. Seit zum ersten Mal ein Kameraverschluss geklickt hat, sind alle sexuellen Sitten und Praktiken fotografisch dokumentiert worden: auf Daguerreotypien, Salzpapierabzügen, Kalotypien, Ferrotypien, Projektionsbildern der Laterna magica, räumlichen Stereobildern, ob auf Glasplatten oder Fotopapier, auf Ansichtskarten, Dias oder Film. Mit jedem fotografischen Verfahren wurde auch ein beträchtlicher Teil an Aktaufnahmen und Pornografie hergestellt.

L.M.: Wie unterscheidest du zwischen erotischer und pornografischer Fotografie?

M.R.: Ich schätze, Pornografie ist die passende Bezeichnung für alles Material, das das Blut in Wallung bringt. Wenn dein Puls schneller schlägt und dir heiß wird, dann kann man es Pornografie nennen.

L.M.: Würdest du den Großteil der Aufnahmen in diesem Buch pornografisch nennen?

M.R.: Ja. Ich möchte denjenigen sehen, der sich dieses Buch anschauen kann, ohne irgendeine Reaktion bei sich zu verspüren.

FORBIDDEN EROTICA: INTRODUCTION

Le nu est, et a toujours été, un des thèmes les plus populaires de la photographie. Personne ne sait exactement quand les premières photos de nu ont été prises mais elles semblent avoir fait leur entrée en scène à Paris, vers 1845, chez des opticiens, des fabricants d'instruments et des marchands d'art[1]. Le contenu de ces images était des plus variés, allant des nus présentés décemment de dos, à la manière des « études académiques » classiques, à l'exhibition éhontée des organes génitaux, des rapports sexuels entre lesbiennes au coït hétérosexuel.

La grande majorité de ces images était produite par des hommes, pour des hommes. Elles étaient donc représentatives de l'imagination érotique masculine générale, ou, du moins, de l'idée que s'en faisaient les photographes. Pour séduire un public masculin, de nombreux clichés montraient des fellations. Les scènes de lesbianisme étaient moins fréquentes qu'aujourd'hui, mais les rapports homosexuels entre hommes étaient présentés aussi explicitement qu'ils le sont de nos jours, même si l'homosexualité masculine était alors considérée comme un crime. Naturellement, le sujet le plus populaire était les rapports hétérosexuels dans toutes leurs combinaisons possibles et imaginables. Le photographe qui parvenait à fixer de telles scènes, pouvait, comme c'est encore le cas aujourd'hui, se faire beaucoup d'argent.

On connaît l'identité de très peu, voire aucun, des modèles ayant posé pour les photos présentées dans *Forbidden Erotica* (« Voluptés interdites »). Un grand nombre d'entre elles étaient des prostituées. Compte tenu de la situation dans laquelle la plupart se trouvaient, condamnées à une vie de souffrances, de privations et d'asservissement, poser pour des pornographes devait leur paraître une aubaine. Il semblerait également qu'un petit nombre des modèles était des patients d'asiles psychiatriques qui ne se rendaient même pas compte de ce qu'ils faisaient en posant pour des photos.

Les noms des photographes ayant pris ces photos n'ont pas survécu non plus. Les photos étaient produites en dehors du cadre formel de ce qui était admis en matière artistique et étaient destinées à une consommation populaire. Leurs auteurs, souvent anonymes, n'étaient pas des artistes professionnels avec une formation et une pratique rigoureuse.

Les photos les plus anciennes de *Forbidden Erotica* datent des années 1870 et 1880. À cette époque, on avait déjà inventé des procédés pour développer les clichés à partir de négatifs, permettant leur production en masse. (Les formats antérieurs, tels que les daguerréotypes, les ferrotypes et les ambrotypes, étaient des positifs uniques qui ne pouvaient être reproduits à grande échelle.) Les images les plus récentes datent des années 1940. Les formats des clichés de cet album incluent des tirages sur gélatine argentée, des tirages sur papier albuminé, des photographies tirées en cartes postales, des photographies et cartes postales en ton sépia, ainsi qu'un petit nombre de lithographies. De nombreuses générations de duplicatas ont été réalisées à partir des mêmes originaux. Sur certaines copies, on peut même voir que l'original a été punaisé sur un mur puis re-photographié. L'album présente également une petite sélection de cartes postales pornographiques illustrées.

La carte postale photographiée, qui fit son apparition vers 1870, accéléra la popularisation et la propagation de la photographie érotico-pornographique. Elle connut son apogée entre les années 1890 et les années 1930. Rien qu'en France, entre 1919 et 1939, on produisit plus de 20 millions de cartes postales de nu. Ces cartes postales érotiques et pornographiques, qui n'avaient jamais été destinées à être acheminées par la poste, sont souvent plus explicites que la pornographie d'aujourd'hui. Il n'était pas rare, par exemple, de voir des mineurs participant à des scènes érotiques et de nombreuses cartes postales montrent des femmes s'accouplant avec des chiens. Les lois modernes interdisent la publication de telles images.

Dès le début, les autorités firent tout leur possible pour empêcher la production de photographies «obscènes». En 1802, la Society for the Suppression of Vice (Société pour la répression du vice) fut créée en Grande-Bretagne pour protéger le public des parutions blasphématoires, des bordels, des livres et des gravures obscènes. Une grande partie de la photographie pornographique produite après 1850 fut interdite, confisquée et détruite. Pour ne citer qu'un exemple, en 1874, dans le hangar d'expédition d'un certain Henry Hayler, la police londonienne découvrit 130 248 images «pornographiques» qui furent aussitôt confisquées[2]. À la fin du 19e siècle, les États-Unis, enracinés dans le puritanisme depuis leur fondation, trouvèrent leur principal chantre de la censure en la personne d'Anthony Comstock, agent spécial des services postaux et secrétaire de la New York Society for the Supression of Vice. Comstock joua un rôle déterminant dans l'adoption de mesures strictes sur la diffusion de la pornographie via les services postaux des États-Unis.

Ce n'est pas un hasard si la production pornographique ne fut jamais aussi florissante que pendant une époque particulièrement répressive. Comme l'explique Paul Tabori dans *Secret and Forbidden: The Moral History of the Passions of Mankind*, «la pornographie ne peut s'épanouir que dans un sol nourri par la pruderie et à un âge où le contraste entre l'esprit et la chair est le plus intense »[3]. De fait, « les concepts d'‹ obscène › ou de ‹ pornographique › sont les fruits d'une morale sexuelle répressive. Il est d'ailleurs intéressant de noter que cette morale commença justement à perdre de son influence à partir de la diffusion de la photographie et de son accueil par le public »[4]. *Le Petit Robert* fait remonter l'apparition du mot « pornographie » à 1842[5], la photographie ayant été inventée en 1839.

Même ainsi, en dépit des lois qui les interdisaient et des tentatives pour faire cesser leur production et leur distribution, des photos comme celles des *Forbidden Erotica* étaient réalisées par milliers et vendues dans le monde entier. Manifestement, ces photographies étaient produites à grande échelle pour un marché de masse. Cuba, la France, l'Angleterre, le Japon et les États-Unis ont une longue histoire bien documentée concernant leur production.

Les images de *Forbidden Erotica* comptent parmi les plus crues et les plus explicites de la collection de photographies érotiques de Rotenberg. De fait, le terme « érotique », qui suggère une sexualité diaphane, voilée, gracieuse, élégante, coquette, charmante, délicate et réservée, décrit tout ce que les photos de ce livre ne sont pas. En marge de la pudibonderie victorienne, un érotisme romantique et discret s'épanouit. En marge de cet érotisme, la pornographie *hard* explosa littéralement. Il y a une énorme différence entre un photographe artistique, érotique et pornographique. « Le nu artistique ne fait aucune promesse, la photo érotique en suggère certaines, et la photo pornographique les comble toutes, exerçant sur beaucoup de spectateurs un effet plus dérangeant qu'excitant. »[6]

On a publié de nombreuses collections de photographies érotiques de la Belle Époque, inspirées par les préraphaélites et l'Art nouveau. Les photos de *Forbidden Erotica* ont été prises un peu plus loin dans les coulisses. Elles ne prétendent en aucun cas être de l'art. Elles sont explicites, parfois choquantes, et peut-être même effrayantes pour certaines. Aujourd'hui, la plupart des gens ne sont pas habitués à voir des photographies de personnes nues qui ne sont pas forcément belles. Elles montrent la vérité simple et crue de l'acte sexuel, dans une variété qui paraît infinie. Elles ont peu en commun avec les œuvres érotiques sophistiquées d'artistes de la Belle Époque tels qu'Aubrey Beardsley, Félicien Rops, Gustav Klimt ou Franz von Bayros. Elles pourraient plutôt illustrer deux classiques de la littérature pornographique victorienne : *My Secret Life* et *The Pearl*.

My Secret Life (« Ma vie secrète »), œuvre anonyme publiée vers 1890, est le journal sexuel particulièrement détaillé d'un riche gentleman anglais. L'auteur y décrit toutes ses aventures galantes dans un langage qui n'est ni expurgé ni embelli. Commençant par ses premiers souvenirs d'attouchements sexuels de la part de sa gouvernante, il raconte ensuite comment il épiait les femmes de chambre pendant qu'elles urinaient, comment il jouit plus tard de leurs faveurs en dépit de l'ordre de sa mère de les laisser tranquilles, comment il dépucela d'innombrables vierges et comment il s'accouplait avec des filles de ferme rencontrées au hasard de ses promenades dans la campagne. En grandissant, ses appétits le menèrent vers des territoires plus aventureux. Il fournit des descriptions assez crues de scènes de ligotage, de domination, de flagellation, de prostitution, d'orgies, de travestissement, d'homosexualité et même de viol.

Toutes sortes d'activités sexuelles sont restituées avec moult détails et une précision presque clinique : de la simple pénétration, à la fellation, au cunnilingus, à la masturbation, à la sodomie, etc. L'extrait suivant, un passage parmi tant d'autres du même acabit, traduit assez bien la teneur de *My Secret Life* :

Je le couchai sur le lit et, ayant pris sa bite dans ma bouche, me mis à la sucer, d'abord avec le prépuce, puis, délicatement, avec ce dernier retroussé… l'effet fut instantané… elle était bien dure le temps que Sarah revienne… La queue dressée, il la monta aussitôt… enfonçant sa bite raide dans sa chatte jusqu'à la garde… Je l'avais déjà enculé trois fois et il me l'avait mise trois fois… J'avais baisé six fois. Je m'étais branlé dans son foutre et je lui avais sucé la bite… Sarah avait été baisée au moins huit fois… (Elle) déclara : « Me voilà baisée de fond en comble. » Puis, après les avoir payées, je partis.[7]

Dans *My Secret Life*, il semble couler de source que les classes inférieures devaient se prêter sans rechigner à l'exploitation sexuelle par ceux qui leur étaient « supérieurs », à savoir les riches de la société victorienne. Les domestiques et les pauvres étaient considérés comme des objets. Ils étaient parfois traités comme des animaux et presque vus comme une espèce à part. Lassé des rapports avec des prostituées, l'auteur anonyme de *My Secret Life* écrit : « Souhaitant un changement, je me mis à la recherche d'une gentille servante bien fraîche… Elles sont propres, bien nourries, en bonne santé… prêtes, soumises. Elles ont le feu au cul, sont vicieuses et lubriques à souhait. »[8] Pour ce qui était de la séduction ou du viol pur et simple de ces femmes – et de ces hommes –, la chasse était ouverte toute l'année. Il était donc naturel qu'ils soient considérés comme de parfaits spécimens à photographier dans toutes sortes de postures compromettantes.

La revue clandestine *The Pearl: A Journal of Facetiae and Voluptuous Reading* (« La perle : Journal de facéties et lectures voluptueuses »), publiée de juillet 1879 à décembre 1880, couvrait un territoire semblable à celui de *My Secret Life*, mais dans un style très différent. Tandis que *My Secret Life* décrit froidement une sexualité débridée au jour le jour, *The Pearl* est emphatique et dramatique, humoristique et fantaisiste. La revue publiait plusieurs récits sous forme de feuilletons, avec des titres du genre « Sub-Umbra ou du sport chez les femmes nouilles », « Les confessions de Mlle du Mont-Chauve ou les expériences voluptueuses d'une vieille fille ; conversations épistolaires avec une charmante amie » ou « Madame du Pieu-Charnu ou toutes les mêmes ».

The Pearl semblait attacher une importance particulière à la flagellation. Dans *An Unhurried View of Erotica*, Ralph Ginzburg écrit : « La flagellomanie dans l'Angleterre du 18ᵉ et 19ᵉ siècles avait été élevée à un rang sans précédent et jamais égalé depuis dans l'histoire de l'humanité… Ce violon d'Ingres était connu sur le continent comme ‹ le vice anglais ›. »[9] Un extrait de *The Pearl*, pris dans « Les confessions de Mlle du Mont-Chauve » nous servira d'illustration :

Le visage de Miss Flaybum témoigne de l'intensité de son indignation tandis que son derrière gras et dodu se tortille à chaque coup… La flagellatrice et ses amis commencent à être sérieusement échauffés par le spectacle… (qui) semble leur procurer des sensations d'une volupté exquise. Bon nombre des filles plus âgées sont étendues ensemble sur le sol, ou dans d'autres positons de plaisir sensuel.[10]

(L'auteur de *My Secret Life* relate également des aventures lors d'une visite dans un salon de flagellation, dont les propriétaires étaient traditionnellement appelés des « abbesses ».)

De nombreux passages de *The Pearl* attestent également du pouvoir affriolant du déshabillé et de l'attrait relativement récent des sous-vêtements. (Il est intéressant de noter que les sous-vêtements féminins n'avaient fait leur apparition que dans les années 1850, soit une trentaine d'années avant la première parution de *The Pearl*.) L'extrait suivant témoigne également de la fascination toute victorienne pour les femmes « d'un certain âge ».

Maria déshabille progressivement sa maîtresse, qui appartient à la catégorie des belles quadragénaires bien grasses… Elle se tient à présent en chemise et culotte, cette dernière si bien remplie qu'on entrevoit la promesse d'une croupe splendide, ses pans superbement ourlés de luxueuses dentelles, sous lesquelles on aperçoit une belle paire de jambes dodues dans des bas couleur chair et des souliers à hauts talons ornés de boucles en bijoux…[11]

À eux deux, *The Pearl* et *My Secret Life* en disent long sur la sexualité secrète et réprimée de l'époque victorienne. Les images de *Forbidden Erotica* constituent autant d'illustrations photographiques de cette sexualité. On y retrouve à la fois le ton clinique de *My Secret Life* et l'esprit ludique de *The Pearl*. Certaines images reproduisent et même surpassent le côté austère et froid de *My Secret Life*. Si la plupart des modèles semblent prendre du plaisir à poser, souriant ou lançant des regards entendus vers l'objectif, d'autres ont le regard vide et perdu au loin. L'effet vous donne froid dans le dos. Puis il y a les gros plans de vulves béantes et désincarnées, d'énormes verges en érection, de pénétrations qui ne laissent rien à l'imagination. Si ce n'est pour leurs tons sépia et fanés, ces images n'ont pas d'âge.

Inspirés sans doute par la nouveauté de la photographie, ou par le fait que leur sujet était interdit, les premiers photographes semblent avoir été déterminés, comme l'auteur de *My Secret Life*, à saisir toutes les combinaisons possibles d'actes sexuels. Ils avaient probablement également découvert les avantages financiers qu'ils avaient à gagner en satisfaisant tous les fantasmes et les fétichismes inimaginables. On trouve des images de ménages à trois, à quatre et plus, des hommes avec des hommes, des femmes avec des femmes, dans toutes les permutations possibles. Toutes les races sont représentées. On trouve également des collages sophistiqués d'orgies, et une abondance d'images de fellations et de cunnilingus.

On voit des gentlemen coinçant des filles de cuisine dans l'office, d'autres culbutant de jeunes paysannes dans le foin. Le spectateur peut regarder « par le petit trou », comme on dit, trois femmes urinant gaiement côte à côte. La « pissette » semble avoir été un sujet favori. Des lavements sont également administrés devant l'objectif. Les premiers photographes pornographes, comme les auteurs de littérature pornographique, semblent avoir sauté sur toutes les occasions de transgresser un tabou. Autre thème de prédilection : le clergé, notamment les prêtres et les bonnes sœurs, réalisant toutes sortes d'actes licencieux, du simple coït à la flagellation et à la fellation.

Des myriades d'accessoires et de jouets sexuels étaient utilisés, du simple godemiché en forme de pénis (qui, certains seront peut-être surpris de l'apprendre, existe depuis des millénaires) aux cigares, cigarettes, bouteilles de vin, de champagne, de bière, téléphones, saucisses, calebasses, balais, queues de billards, marteaux, maracas et même un vaporisateur d'insecticide. Le godemiché le plus « in » de l'histoire de la carte postale dite « française » est sans doute la mini tour Eiffel insérée dans le derrière d'une dame. Plusieurs clichés montrent un homme exerçant son swing avec une balle de golf posée sur le vagin d'une femme. Les acrobaties sexuelles étaient également très populaires. Une femme fait le pont en arrière ou le poireau sur les épaules d'un homme, une table, une chaise. Elle se tient sur une jambe, l'autre passée par-dessus l'épaule de son partenaire. Elle se tient sur la tête tandis qu'il la pénètre en lui tenant les chevilles. Ou encore, elle pose les jambes sur les épaules de l'homme et, la tête en bas, prend son pénis dans sa bouche.

Comme dans *My Secret Life* et *The Pearl*, la fascination des Victoriens pour le ligotage, la domination et la flagellation est largement représentée dans les photographies. L'iconographie actuelle de la dominatrice, avec son masque en cuir, ses cuissardes et son fouet, était déjà bien établie à la fin du 19e siècle. On trouvera plusieurs de ses ancêtres dans *Forbidden Erotica*. Il y avait également beaucoup d'images de victimes, enchaînées, menottées et battues avec des fouets, des cravaches ou des baguettes de bouleau. Un grand nombre des modèles ne correspond pas à l'obsession actuelle de l'attrait érotique de la jeunesse. De fait, certaines photographies montrent des femmes batifolant avec des hommes qui pourraient être leurs fils, voire leurs petits-fils. De nombreux modèles posent à demi dévêtus ou en sous-vêtements. Leurs jarretières à froufrous, leurs bas, leurs bottines, leurs corsets en dentelle, leurs jupons, leurs culottes bouffantes et leurs bonnets devaient être aussi affriolants à la fin du 19e siècle et au début du 20e siècle, qu'ils nous apparaissent désuets et un tantinet ridicules aujourd'hui (bien qu'on ait du mal à imaginer que les images d'hommes et de femmes attifés de coiffes, de vestes et de chaussures militaires – et rien d'autre – ne cherchaient pas à provoquer quelques gloussements de rire, même à l'époque).

De nombreuses «grivoiseries» étaient mises en scène devant l'objectif. Une femme porte un manteau au col en fourrure, ouvert sur son corps nu et assorti à la fourrure de son sexe. Une élégante en déshabillé est allongée nonchalamment, lisant un magazine intitulé *Smart Sex* («Le Sexe chic»). Un des canulars les plus populaires montre une femme s'apprêtant à planter son couteau et sa fourchette dans le pénis qui repose dans son assiette (une saucisse humaine, bien sûr). Trois femmes posent côte à côte, les cuisses grandes ouvertes. Elles se nomment «la Foi, l'Espérance et la Charité». Une femme allaite une poupée. Certains déguisements sont d'une absurdité hilarante, notamment les chapeaux de clown, les fausses moustaches des hommes et les grimages au cambouis appliqués à la Groucho Marx.

Il est intéressant de constater que les modèles des photos les plus récentes semblent plus honteux que leurs prédécesseurs. En tout cas, ils sont plus nombreux à tenter de cacher leur identité, surtout les hommes. Les deux sexes portent souvent des lunettes noires, des chapeaux, des loups ou des masques, ou détournent simplement la tête. Il semble qu'il y ait beaucoup plus d'hommes que de femmes qui tiennent à conserver leur anonymat. La plupart de ces photos étant prises pour le plaisir des hommes, on considérait sans doute qu'il était plus important de pouvoir voir le visage des femmes. Parfois, on voit nettement que le photographe a fait exprès de laisser le visage des modèles hors du champ. On peut presque l'entendre promettre : «Je te jure que personne ne saura que c'est toi.»

Pourquoi la gêne ou la honte de poser pour de la pornographie aurait-elle augmenté entre les années 1870 et 1940 ? Peut-être parce que la photographie elle-même n'était plus aussi nouvelle et excitante. L'attrait de participer à une merveilleuse nouvelle invention était passé. À moins que l'écart entre les classes ne fût plus aussi marqué qu'autrefois et la situation économique des pauvres moins dramatique. La vie étant moins dure, le fait de poser pour des photos pornographiques ne signifiait plus que vous étiez dans la misère, mais dépravé, et par conséquent, que vous devriez avoir honte.

Les cartes postales illustrées présentées dans ce livre sont très différentes des photographies. Elles sont plus légères et délicates. Comme des dessins animés, elles suivent des scénarios non réalistes. Un grand nombre d'entre elles font preuve d'un sens de l'humour espiègle et diabolique. Une carte montre deux femmes jouant au «vi-abolo» (un jeu de mots sur le diabolo), faisant rebondir des pénis sur des fils et les utilisant comme godemichés. Sur une autre, une femme fait du trapèze en se tenant aux pénis de deux clowns, un noir et un blanc. Ces cartes servent également de toile de fond à des commentaires ironiques sur la société. Sur l'une d'entre elles, on voit une femme chevaucher un pénis géant qui crache son « sperme » sous la forme de pièces d'or tombant directement dans son sac. D'autres cartes postales présentent des calembours. L'une d'entre elles montre un banquet où les convives savourent des « asperges en sauce blanche », à savoir des phallus arrosés de sperme.

Au cours des 150 dernières années, la plupart des milliers de ces anciennes photos et cartes postales pornographiques ont été interdites, saisies et détruites par les autorités – ou par des particuliers qui les réprouvaient – jusqu'à ce qu'elles aient pratiquement disparu. Quelques rares exemples ont survécu. Certains figurent dans les pages de *Forbidden Erotica*.

Laura Mirsky

Pour de plus amples informations merci de contacter :
www.vintagenudephotos.com

1) Michael Koetzle, 1000 Nudes, TASCHEN, Cologne 1994, p. 31.
2) Ibid., p. 230.
3) Paul Tabori, Secret and Forbidden: The Moral History of the Passions of Mankind, Signet Books, New York 1971, p. 105.
4) Koetzle, op. cit., p. 230.
5) Le Petit Robert 1, Le Robert, Paris 1996, p. 1728.
6) Koetzle, op. cit., p. 40.
7) Anonyme, My Secret Life, Grove Press, Inc., New York 1966, p. 454.

8) Anonyme, My Secret Life, dans : Steven Marcus, The Other Victorians: A Study of Sexuality and Pornography in Mid-Nineteenth-Century England, Basic Books, New York 1966, p. 133.
9) Ralph Ginzburg, An Unhurried View of Erotica, The Helmsman Press, New York 1958, p. 54.
10) Anonyme, The Pearl: A Journal of Facetiae and Voluptuous Reading, Grove Press, Inc., New York 1968, pp. 155–156.
11) Ibid., p. 154.

FORBIDDEN EROTICA: ENTRETIEN

Cet entretien avec Mark Rotenberg a été réalisé par Laura Mirsky.

L.M. : Comment as-tu commencé ta collection d'images érotiques et pornographiques ?

M.R. : C'était il y a une vingtaine d'années, dans le quartier de Brooklyn Heights, à New York. J'ai remarqué du remue-ménage devant une maison à deux pas de chez moi et j'ai vu qu'on emmenait le corps d'un homme. Environ deux semaines plus tard, des employés municipaux ont commencé à balancer les affaires qui se trouvaient dans la maison dans une immense benne à ordures. Je suis allé voir ce qu'ils jetaient. Le premier jour, elle était à moitié remplie de magazines de filles nues. Ma curiosité était piquée. Au cours des jours suivants, j'ai continué à fouiller le contenu de la benne. J'y ai trouvé des journaux datant de la guerre de Sécession et des images érotiques. Il y avait beaucoup de photos, de vieilles photos, certaines parmi les plus anciennes de ma collection.

L.M. : Anciennes à quel point ?

M.R. : Les plus anciennes que j'ai repêchées dans cette benne devaient dater des années 1870. C'étaient de vieux clichés sépia, des tirages sur papier albuminé…

L.M. : Combien de photos y avait-il dans cette benne ?

M.R. : Environ mille cinq cents, datant des années 1870 jusqu'à la fin des années 1950. Certaines étaient de simples photos de « cheesecake » mais un grand nombre des plus anciennes étaient très crues, ce qu'on appelle du « hard ». Il y avait des feuilles d'échantillons et des tirages originaux datant des années 1870 à 1930. À partir des années 1930, les images devenaient un peu plus pudiques. Il y a manifestement eu une période dans les années 1910 et 1920 où les cartes postales françaises ont été produites et distribuées à grande échelle. Il y en avait beaucoup dans cette benne à ordures.

L.M. : Comment peux-tu déterminer l'âge d'une photographie ?

M.R. : Le plus souvent à partir des éléments de style qu'on voit sur l'image, qu'il s'agisse des coiffures, de la lingerie ou des toiles de fond. Quand il y a très peu de vêtements sur lesquels se baser, ce sont à peu près les seuls indices dont on dispose pour identifier la période à laquelle la photo a été prise. Parfois, on voit des bas roulés, des bottines, des bottes…

L.M. : Comment fais-tu quand les gens sur l'image sont complètement nus ? À partir de quoi détermines-tu l'âge de la photo ?

M.R. : C'est très, très difficile. On n'a pas vraiment de moyens de le savoir. Il est peu probable que les modèles soient encore de ce monde pour témoigner et on ignore l'identité des photographes de la plupart des clichés présentés dans ce livre.

L.M. : Poursuis ton histoire de benne à ordures.

M.R. : Après avoir récupéré beaucoup de matériel érotique et tout un tas d'images plus ou moins artistiques, j'ai commencé à faire des recherches approfondies…

L.M. : Où as-tu fait des recherches sur la photo de nu ?

M.R. : Je suis allé voir les gens de l'édition à New York… MilkyWay Productions, qui publie le magazine *Screw*, le petit monde d'Al Goldstein, les gens de la revue *Cheri*…

L.M. : Tu leur as simplement téléphoné en leur demandant s'ils pouvaient t'aider à identifier les photos ?

M.R. : Je les ai appelés en leur disant que j'avais des clichés anciens et je leur ai demandé s'ils voulaient les voir pour éventuellement les utiliser dans leurs publications. Puis j'ai rendu visite aux rédacteurs en chef et aux directeurs artistiques de ces revues. Ils ont poussé des « Ah ! » et des « Oh ! » admiratifs et ont déclaré qu'ils n'avaient jamais vu des images de ce type aussi anciennes. Ils ne publiaient que du matériel récent. L'idée d'utiliser des photos anciennes les a beaucoup séduits. C'est en parlant avec eux que j'en ai appris de plus en plus sur ces images et que ce matériel, par exemple, était très rare. J'ai appris qu'à l'époque, il était en grande partie distribué sous le manteau, pas publiquement et certainement pas chez les marchands de cartes postales, à moins que le client ne connaisse le mot magique…

L.M. : Quel était le mot magique ?

M.R. : Aux États-Unis, le terme « carte postale française » devint sans doute synonyme d'image érotique.

L.M. : Qui vendait ces images ? Comment se les procurait-on ?

M.R. : On en trouvait probablement dans certains drugstores puis, plus tard, dans les stations-service. Mais, à l'origine, en Europe, je sais que les marchands de cartes postales vendaient également des images érotiques. Ils montraient à leurs clients des échantillons des différentes images qu'ils avaient en stock. Certains de ces échantillons sont publiés dans ce livre. C'était une feuille de la taille d'une photo standard, qui pouvait présenter entre quatre et seize, parfois jusqu'à trente-deux clichés qu'on pouvait acheter soit par séries soit individuellement. C'est ainsi que la plupart du matériel était distribué dans les lieux publics.

L.M. : On entrait dans une boutique de cartes postales, on prononçait le mot magique et le marchand vous sortait ces feuilles d'échantillons ?

M.R. : Oui, c'est ça. Le client ou la cliente examinait les échantillons pour choisir la série, ou les séries, qu'il ou elle voulait acheter, à moins qu'ils n'optent pour des images individuelles présentées sur la feuille. Puis ils s'en allaient avec sous le bras la jolie petite collection qui avait titillé leur imagination.

L.M. : Quand as-tu décidé de te mettre sérieusement à collectionner les images érotiques anciennes ?

M.R. : Dès que j'ai montré les images que j'avais récupérées à divers bureaux d'édition à New York et que j'ai compris qu'ils étaient prêts à me payer pour les utiliser puis à me restituer les originaux. Ça m'a paru une bonne raison de continuer mes recherches. Je voulais pouvoir leur présenter un échantillonnage plus vaste afin qu'ils puissent monter des projets spécifiques à partir de n'importe quel thème érotique. J'ai commencé à faire toutes les foires où je savais que ce genre de matériel serait disponible, notamment les foires de photographies à New York, et les brocantes spécialisées dans les œuvres sur papier dans le Connecticut, l'État de New York, le New Jersey et la Pennsylvanie. J'ai demandé à mes amis s'ils avaient dans leurs relations des gens susceptibles de posséder ce genre de photos et j'ai passé des annonces dans divers hebdomadaires et mensuels publiés un peu partout aux États-Unis.

L.M. : Lorsque tu allais dans ces foires à la recherche de ce genre de matériel, as-tu rencontré des gens scandalisés ou choqués par ce que tu cherchais ?

M.R. : Oui. Personne ne s'en est pris à moi personnellement mais je rencontrais souvent des gens qui, quand je leur demandais s'ils avaient des images érotiques, répondaient : « Non, non, non, non ! Nous ne faisons pas ce genre de chose. Nous ne vendrions jamais ça ! »

L.M. : Tu as trouvé beaucoup d'images érotiques ?

M.R. : Oui. Quand j'ai commencé ma collection, les sources semblaient inépuisables. Dans chaque foire où j'allais, j'étais sûr de repartir avec un bel assortiment d'images datant des années 1870 aux années 1950.

L.M. : Les marchands les présentaient ouvertement ?

M.R. : Certains, oui. Mais le plus souvent, ils me sortaient une boîte de sous une table après que je leur ai demandé ce qu'ils avaient. Les images les plus osées, celles qu'on qualifierait de hard ou de pornographiques, étaient rarement présentées aux yeux de tous. D'ailleurs, c'est encore le cas aujourd'hui.

L.M. : Tu as dit que tu avais passé des annonces. Que disaient-elles ?

M.R. : « Recherche images érotiques. Originaux des années 1860 à 1950. Bon état important. »

L.M. : Les revues acceptaient toutes de passer tes annonces ?
M.R. : Certaines publications du Midwest ont refusé. Elles m'ont répondu qu'elles ne voulaient pas encourager le commerce de ce genre d'images.

L.M. : Tu as eu des réponses à tes annonces ?
M.R. : Oui, oui. Je recevais régulièrement des réponses de toutes sortes de gens habitant aux quatre coins du pays. Des jeunes qui venaient d'emménager dans une maison et avaient découvert une vieille boîte à chaussures dans un mur, une vieille cheminée murée, le grenier ou le garage. Des gens plus âgés qui avaient décidé de se débarrasser de leurs vieilleries et avaient retrouvé un petit paquet de cartes coquines, des *Bibles de Tijuana* ou d'autres images érotiques, des jeux de cartes oubliés au fond du tiroir d'une table de nuit… J'ai été contacté par des gens très, très différents, des médecins, des avocats, des étudiants…

L.M. : Tu te déplaçais pour rencontrer ces gens ?
M.R. : Oui, très souvent. J'ai passé des heures en voiture à parcourir des centaines de kilomètres, surtout quand on m'avait décrit une grande quantité de matériel au téléphone ou dans une lettre. Très souvent, les gens n'osent pas envoyer ce genre de photos par la poste. Ils ont peur de faire quelque chose d'illégal et d'être arrêtés pour diffusion de matériel érotique ou pornographique.

L.M. : C'est vrai que c'est illégal ?
M.R. : Non, pas du tout. Les annonces que je passe dans la presse sont très claires et, à partir du moment où les photos ne montrent rien d'illégal, comme des mineurs ou de la zoophilie, tout le reste est acceptable et peut être acheminé par la poste, surtout si l'expéditeur et le destinataire sont majeurs.

L.M. : Tu te souviens d'un voyage en particulier ?
M.R. : Il n'y a pas très longtemps, je me suis rendu en Pennsylvanie, ce qui représente quatre heures de route dans un sens puis dans l'autre. Je suis allé rencontrer des gens qui m'avaient contacté par téléphone au sujet d'images du 20e siècle.

L.M. : Où les as-tu rencontrés ?
M.R. : On s'était donné rendez-vous à une heure donnée sur le parking d'un McDonald. Chacun avait décrit sa voiture à l'autre et on s'est reconnus comme convenu. Je suis resté assis dans ma voiture tandis que cette personne prenait place à côté de moi et me montrait les images qu'elle avait à vendre.

L.M. : Elle était méfiante ?
M.R. : Non, pas vraiment, en tout cas pas vis-à-vis de moi, mais chacun faisait très attention à se comporter de la manière la plus neutre possible. Il n'y avait rien d'inconvenant, rien de déplacé.

**L.M. : As-tu déjà eu l'impression que les

gens qui te vendaient des images portaient un jugement moral sur toi ?

M.R. : Non. Une fois que les gens ont franchi le pas et décidé de m'appeler ou de m'écrire pour me proposer du matériel, c'est qu'ils sont déjà passés au-delà du jugement moral. Ceux qui tombent par hasard sur ce genre de photos et sont moralement choqués n'ont certainement pas envie, à mon avis, de les laisser circuler ni même de les laisser continuer à exister.

L.M. : Ils les jettent purement et simplement ?

M.R. : Je suis sûr que la plupart des gens qui tombent sur ce genre d'images par hasard, c'est-à-dire sans les avoir achetées dans le but de les regarder, de s'en délecter et de les préserver, les détruisent, ou les jettent simplement à la poubelle. Beaucoup de gens préfèrent ça plutôt que de les vendre, parce qu'ils sont gênés, qu'ils les réprouvent moralement ou les deux.

L.M. : Tu as des anecdotes concernant des trouvailles particulièrement « salaces » ?

M.R. : Oui, bien sûr. Il y a plusieurs années, un ami qui collectionne lui aussi des magazines et des photos m'a rapporté qu'un ami à lui, autre collectionneur, lui avait raconté qu'un autre ami collectionneur s'était rendu dans la maison d'un inventeur…

L.M. : Il existe des réseaux de gens qui collectionnent ce genre de choses ?

M.R. : Naturellement. Partout aux États-Unis et, je suppose, dans le monde entier, il y a de nombreux collectionneurs de matériel érotique, pas seulement de photos originales mais également de gadgets, d'art folklorique, d'art primitif, de toutes sortes d'objets, des statuettes aux films en passant par les calendriers, les magazines, les livres, tout ce qui peut avoir un thème érotique, qu'il s'agisse d'images, de textes imprimés, d'illustrations… Il y a un grand marché pour l'érotisme. Chaque fois qu'il y a quelque chose à vendre, il y a des acheteurs potentiels, parfois luttant âprement les uns contre les autres pour en devenir acquéreurs.

L.M. : O.K. Reprenons notre histoire.

M.R. : Par l'intermédiaire de l'ami d'un ami habitant dans une zone urbaine du New Jersey, j'ai su qu'il y avait une grande collection de magazines et de photos à vendre. Son propriétaire les avait hérités de son voisin. Elle contenait certaines des images les plus pornographiques que j'ai vues à ce jour, datant des années 1870 aux années 1930. Il y en avait deux mille cinq cents en tout, soigneusement collées dans des cahiers de comptabilité, d'où il a fallu tout décoller.

L.M. : Tu sais à qui elles avaient appartenu à l'origine ?

M.R. : Après avoir rencontré l'homme qui avait hérité de tous ces magazines et de ces photos, j'ai appris qu'il tenait toute la collection de son voisin, qui s'était fait construire un atelier privé dans sa maison. Une pièce où sa femme et ses enfants n'avaient pas le droit d'entrer. Dans cet atelier se trouvait un cabinet où il enfermait tous ses magazines et ses photos. Au cours des derniers mois de sa vie, il s'est rendu compte qu'après sa mort, sa famille fouillerait sûrement son atelier et tomberait sur ce matériel dont elle ignorait l'existence. Ne voulant pas qu'elle soit choquée en découvrant qu'il possédait cette incroyable collection de pornographie, il a décidé de la donner à son voisin, en lui laissant le choix de la conserver, de la vendre ou de la détruire. Ce voisin est l'homme que j'ai rencontré. Il avait des milliers de magazines et de photos. Ces dernières sont à présent dans mes archives.

L.M. : Peux-tu nous parler d'autres endroits où tu es allé pour rencontrer des gens ?
M.R. : Les parkings sont parfaits pour les rendez-vous. Ils sont neutres et on ne se sent pas coincé, surtout quand on reste dans sa voiture.

L.M. : Ça veut dire qu'il y a toujours une sensation de danger ?
M.R. : Il s'agit de matériel érotique. Ce n'est pas comme si on rencontrait quelqu'un pour discuter de la vente d'une poupée de collection. Ce n'est pas un matériel que tout le monde est ravi de posséder, de voir ou de vendre. Il y a toujours un petit quelque chose de scandaleux et, disons… de clandestin, même s'il ne s'agit que d'une impression, car le matériel lui-même n'a rien d'illégal tant qu'il est entre les mains d'adultes.

L.M. : As-tu déjà rencontré des gens qui avaient peur de te vendre ce type de matériel ?
M.R. : Oh oui ! Je me souviens d'un dentiste qui m'avait contacté après avoir lu une de mes petites annonces. Il affirmait posséder de vieilles photos et des cartes à jouer pornographiques ainsi que des cartes postales coquines qu'il avait trouvées dans le socle d'une vieille lampe. On s'est donné rendez-vous dans un grand centre commercial de banlieue dans le sud du New Jersey, en plein milieu, dans un grand espace couvert, une sorte d'aire de pique-nique où on pouvait s'asseoir. On s'est assis à une table et il m'a tendu un sac à dos. Et là, j'ai assisté à une crise de paranoïa aiguë comme j'en ai rarement vue. Mon vendeur était terrorisé à l'idée que, quand j'ouvrirais la sacoche en plastique à l'intérieur du sac, une des patrouilles de vigiles du centre commercial passerait par là, nous surprendrait avec les photos et nous arrêterait sur-le-champ pour possession de matériel érotique. Il était très, très paranoïaque, au point qu'il est allé s'asseoir à une autre table où l'attendait sa femme et ils m'ont surveillé de loin tandis que j'examinais les photos, craignant sans doute que je m'enfuie avec ou que je fasse je ne sais quoi.

L.M. : Tu t'es toujours intéressé à l'érotisme ?
M.R. : Oui, depuis que je suis tout petit. J'embrassais déjà les filles à l'âge de quatre ans et je feuilletais les premiers magazines érotiques de pin-up…

L.M. : Il y en avait chez toi ?
M.R. : Non, pas à la maison mais mon père tenait un petit café où il vendait des confiseries, de la papeterie et des journaux. C'est là que je feuilletais les revues, parmi lesquelles certains des premiers

magazines pour hommes des années 1950 et 1960. On y voyait des femmes nues, mais il n'y avait rien de pornographique là-dedans, ce n'était même pas salace. C'était juste des modèles photographiés les seins nus… elles étaient très jolies.

L.M. : Quand as-tu vu pour la première fois de la pornographie ?

M.R. : Je devais avoir dans les neuf ans, je crois. Je me souviens d'avoir découvert un bout de pellicule 8 mm sur le parking devant le café de mon père. Il devait y en avoir deux mètres cinquante, encore enroulés sur une bobine. Je trouvais étrange que quelqu'un ait oublié là ce que je pensais être un film amateur, parce que les seuls films en 8 mm que j'avais vus jusque-là étaient ceux qu'on tournait en famille, à la maison ou en vacances. Je l'ai emporté chez nous et je l'ai mis sur notre projecteur. Et là, sur l'écran, j'ai vu deux personnes très, très étroitement enlacées et s'agitant frénétiquement.

L.M. : Qu'est-ce que tu as ressenti en voyant cela ?

M.R. : Que je voyais quelque chose de naturel mais que je n'avais jamais vu auparavant. Il m'est tout de suite venu à l'esprit que c'était probablement quelque chose que tout le monde faisait. Le couple avait l'air plutôt heureux et, apparemment, personne ne les avait forcés à prendre cette position bizarre. Cela me paraissait très excitant ! Je me demandais pourquoi je n'avais jamais vu ça avant. Je crois même que je n'en avais jamais entendu parler. Je voulais en savoir plus. Je voulais savoir ce qu'ils faisaient au juste, quel effet cela faisait, ce qu'on ressentait et pourquoi. Une fois qu'ils ont eu cessé de gigoter, l'homme et la femme paraissaient satisfaits et fatigués. Je me souviens aussi d'avoir fouillé dans un tiroir sous l'établi de mon père, où il gardait toutes sortes de choses. C'était plus ou moins son domaine privé. J'y ai trouvé des magazines et des photos. Certains montraient des nus de face, avec des femmes aux cuisses écartées, dévoilant tous leurs charmes.

L.M. : Qu'est-ce que tu as ressenti en les voyant pour la première fois ?

M.R. : Je les ai trouvées fantastiques, fantastiques ! Certaines photos étaient vraiment pornographiques. C'était des clichés amateurs. Je devrais sans doute remercier mon père d'être à l'origine de ma collection d'images érotiques et d'avoir vendu tous ces magazines dans son magasin. D'un autre côté, j'étais déjà un sacré petit vicieux dès l'âge de quatre ans. Cela n'avait rien à voir avec les magazines ou le film ou quoi que ce soit.

L.M. : Tu trouves ces photos pornographiques anciennes plus excitantes que la pornographie moderne ?

M.R. : Oui. Elles sont moins uniformes que la pornographie moderne. Les modèles ne se ressemblent pas tous, contrairement à aujourd'hui. Les filles ne sont pas du tout artificielles comme elles le sont maintenant. Elles ne sont pas siliconées. Elles n'ont pas d'implants un peu partout dans leur corps. Aujourd'hui, chaque centimètre carré du corps de la femme doit être le plus gonflé, le plus lisse, le plus impeccable, le plus blond, le plus rasé possible. La photo érotique d'aujourd'hui est ennuyeuse par rapport aux photos anciennes, où les femmes pouvaient porter des culottes bouffantes, des bas à jarretelles, des bottines, des châles, des chapeaux et des bijoux. On prenait les photos dans des décors classiques, avec de jolis fonds, de beaux meubles anciens, de somptueux tapis, des peaux de bêtes jetées un peu partout. Ça fait une très grosse différence.

L.M. : Et les modèles sur ces vieilles photos ? Tu les trouves belles ?

M.R. : Certaines, oui, d'autres moins, comme dans la vie de tous les jours. Quand on marche dans la rue, on ne s'attend pas à ce que tout le monde ressemble à Pamela Anderson. Dieu merci ! Mais quand on regarde des photos érotiques modernes, notamment dans les magazines, chaque fille est identique à celle de la page précédente.

L.M. : À ton avis, comment réagiront la plupart des gens en voyant ta collection dans ce livre ?

M.R. : J'espère qu'ils en resteront bouche bée ! Même dans le cercle d'éditeurs avec lesquels je travaille, chaque fois que j'apporte des photos anciennes, il y a immédiatement un attroupement qui se forme autour de moi. Les gens n'en croient pas leurs yeux. Ils s'imaginent que l'érotisme a été inventé hier, pour eux, par eux dans certains cas. Ils ne connaissent pratiquement rien des débuts de la photo érotique.

L.M. : Comment crois-tu que le citoyen moyen réagira en voyant cette collection de photographies ?

M.R. : Lorsqu'ils voient des images qui ont soixante-dix, quatre-vingts, quatre-vingt-dix, cent ans de plus qu'eux, voire plus, les gens sont estomaqués ! Estomaqués ! Au fil des ans, j'ai rassemblé plus de cent mille photos. Dès le jour où la première photo a été prise, il s'est formé un mouvement secret, privé, clandestin, répertoriant toutes les facettes du comportement sexuel. Cela a existé dès le premier claquement d'obturateur. Daguerréotypes, tirages sur papier salé, calotypes, ferrotypes, diapositives de lanterne magique, vues stéréoscopiques, qu'il s'agisse d'images sur verre, sur papier, sur cartes, sur transparents ou sur pellicule : sous tous les formats de photographies, on trouve des images érotiques et pornographiques.

L.M. : Comment distingues-tu l'érotisme de la pornographie ?

M.R. : Pour moi, la pornographie désigne le matériel qui te met l'eau à la bouche. Si tu commences à avoir un peu trop chaud et que ta tension artérielle grimpe d'un cran ou deux, en d'autres termes, s'il se produit quelques modifications de tes liquides internes, alors c'est de la pornographie.

L.M. : Tu considères que cet album est en grande partie pornographique ?

M.R. : Oui. Je défie quiconque de le feuilleter sans avoir une réaction visible d'une manière ou d'une autre.

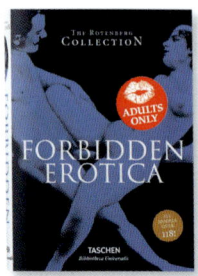

Forbidden Erotica

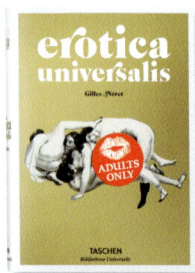

Erotica Universalis

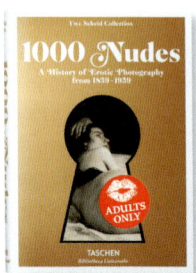

1000 Nudes

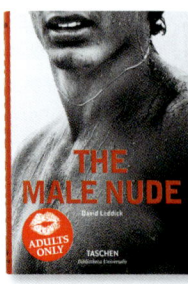

The Male Nude

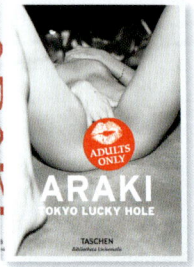

Araki.
Tokyo Lucky Hole

Bookworm's delight:
never bore, always excite!

TASCHEN
Bibliotheca Universalis

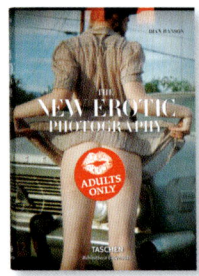

The New Erotic
Photography

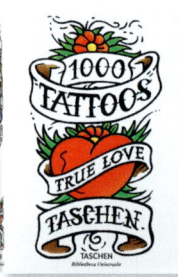

1000 Tattoos

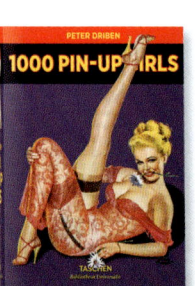

1000 Pin-Up Girls

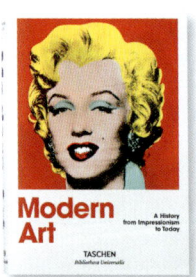

Modern Art

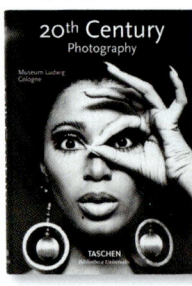

20th Century Photography

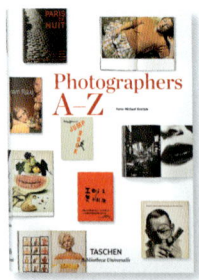

Photographers A–Z

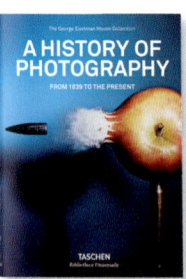

A History of Photography

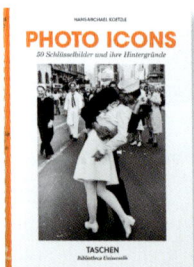

Photo Icons

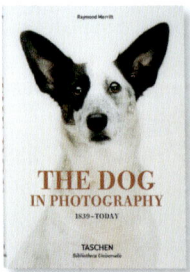

The Dog in Photography

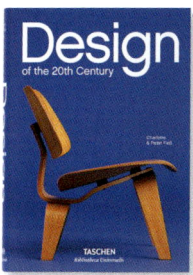

Design of the 20th Century

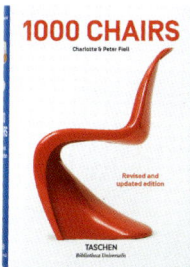

1000 Chairs

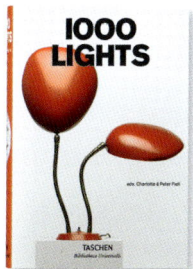

1000 Lights

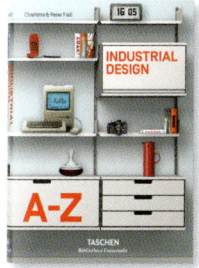

Industrial Design A–Z

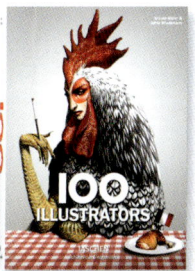

100 Illustrators

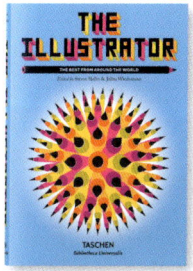

The Illustrator

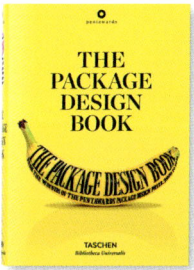

The Package Design Book

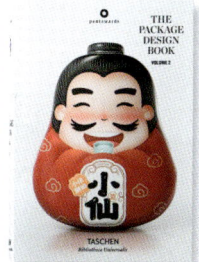

The Package Design Book. Volume 2

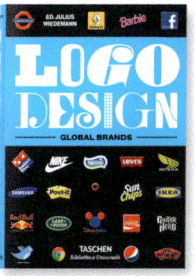

Logo Design. Global Brands

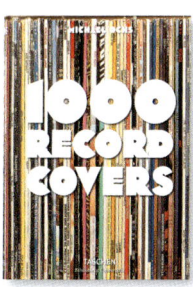

1000 Record Covers

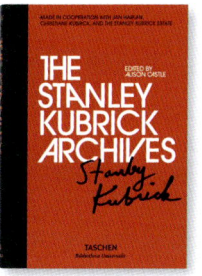

The Stanley Kubrick Archives

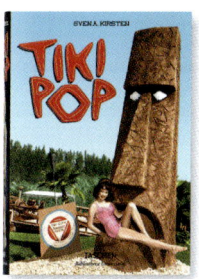

Tiki Pop

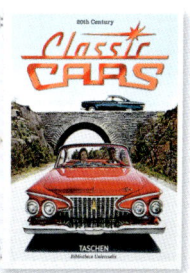

20th Century Classic Cars

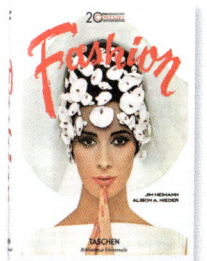

20th Century Fashion

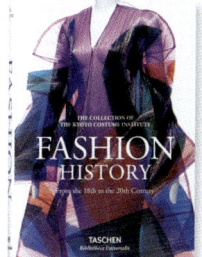

Fashion History

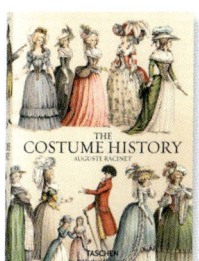

Racinet. The Costume History

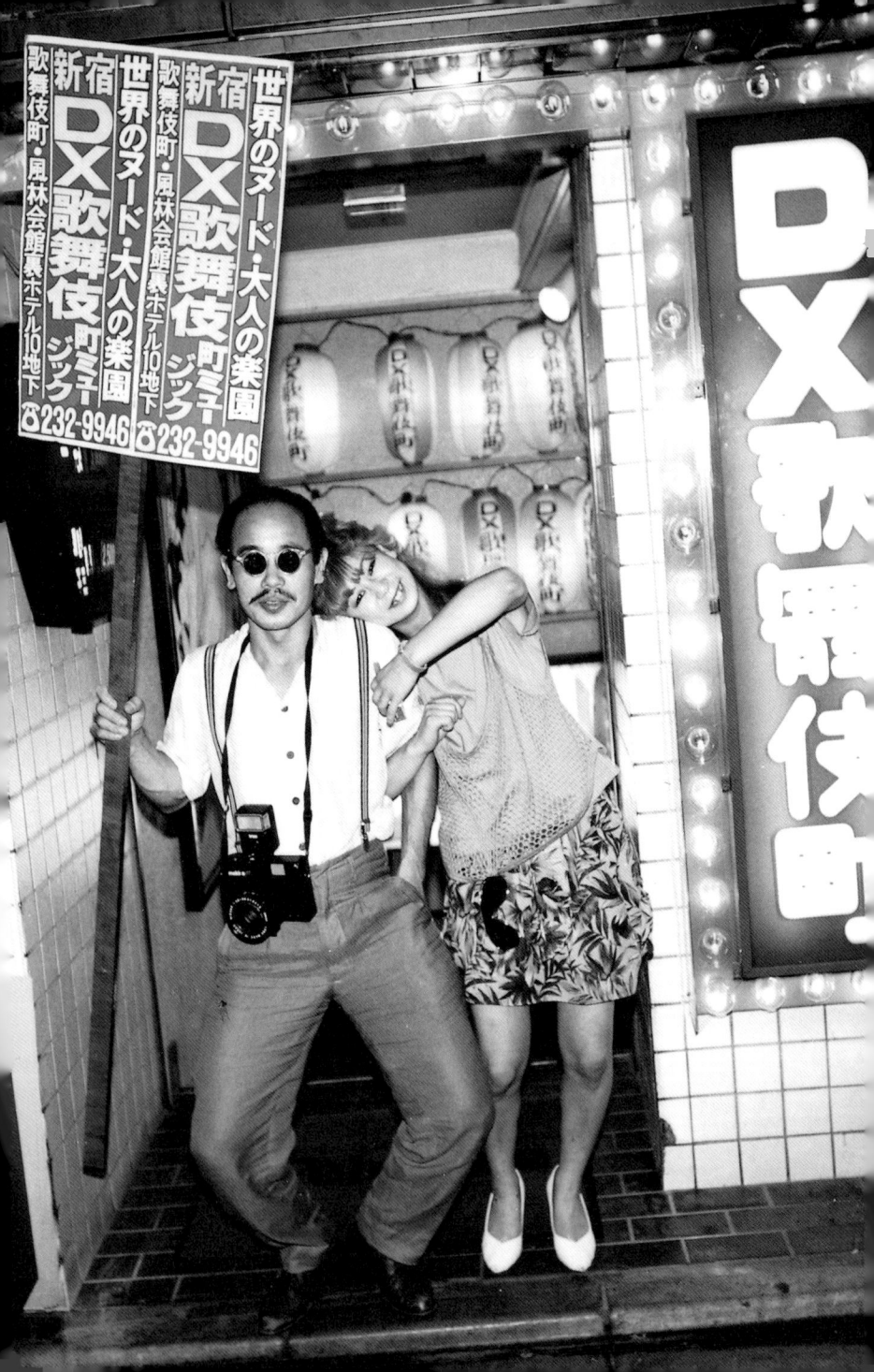

Pleasure parlors

Araki's tour of an erotic underworld

Taking the "Lucky Hole" as his title, Nobuyoshi Araki captures Japan's sex industry in full flower, documenting in more than 800 photos the pleasure-seekers and providers of Tokyo's Shinjuku neighborhood before the February 1985 New Amusement Business Control and Improvement Act closed down many of the country's sex locales. Through mirrored walls and bed sheets, we witness the bondage and the orgies, making this the last word on an age of bacchanalia, infused with moments of humor, poetry, and questioning interjections.

"Without obscenity, our cities are dreary places and life is bleak."

— Nobuyoshi Araki

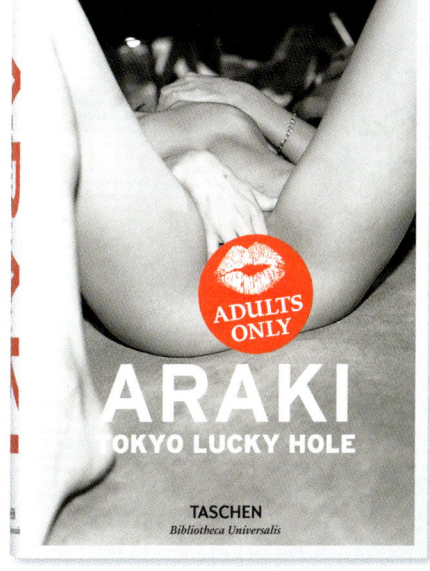

Araki. Tokyo Lucky Hole
Nobuyoshi Araki
704 pages
TRILINGUAL EDITION IN:
ENGLISH / DEUTSCH / FRANÇAIS

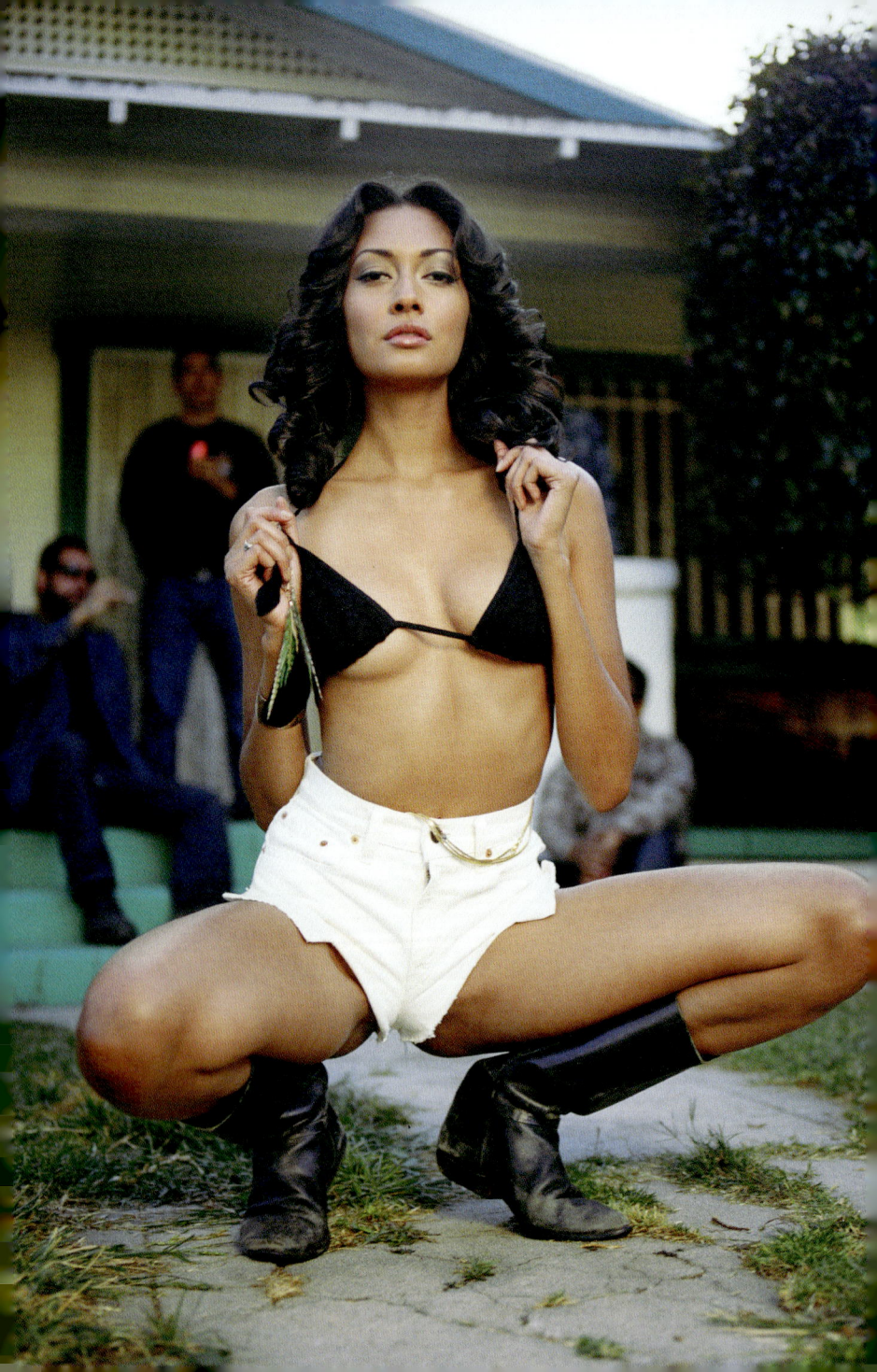

International sex appeal

62 photographers take on the nude female form

In 2007 TASCHEN released *The New Erotic Photography*, followed in 2012 by *The New Erotic Photography 2*. Each book featured hundreds of fresh and provocative images from the world's most intriguing erotic talents. Now the best of both books is available in *The New Erotic Photography*, featuring 62 photographers from 10 countries, exploring the global variations of erotic photography, as well as the evolution of photographic media over the last decade. The featured photographers include new names Gregory Bojorquez, Jo Schwab, Tomohide Ikeya, Frédéric Fontenoy, Andrew Pashis, and Jan Hronsky, as well as established artists Guido Argentini, Bruno Bisang, Eric Kroll, and the late Bob Carlos Clarke. It all adds up to an awful lot of nudes for a tantalizingly low price.

"The ultimate collection of contemporary erotic photography."
— *British Journal of Photography*, London

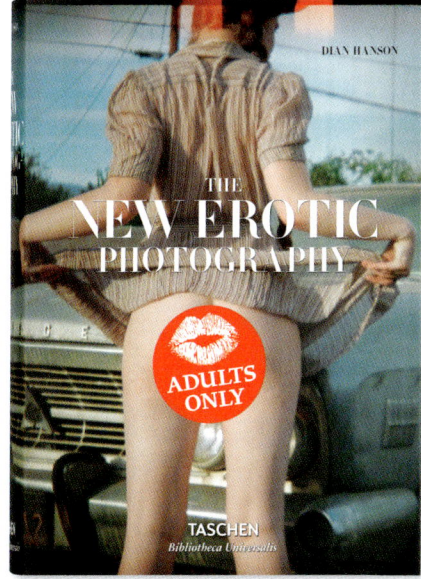

The New Erotic Photography
Dian Hanson
592 pages
TRILINGUAL EDITION IN:
ENGLISH / DEUTSCH / FRANÇAIS

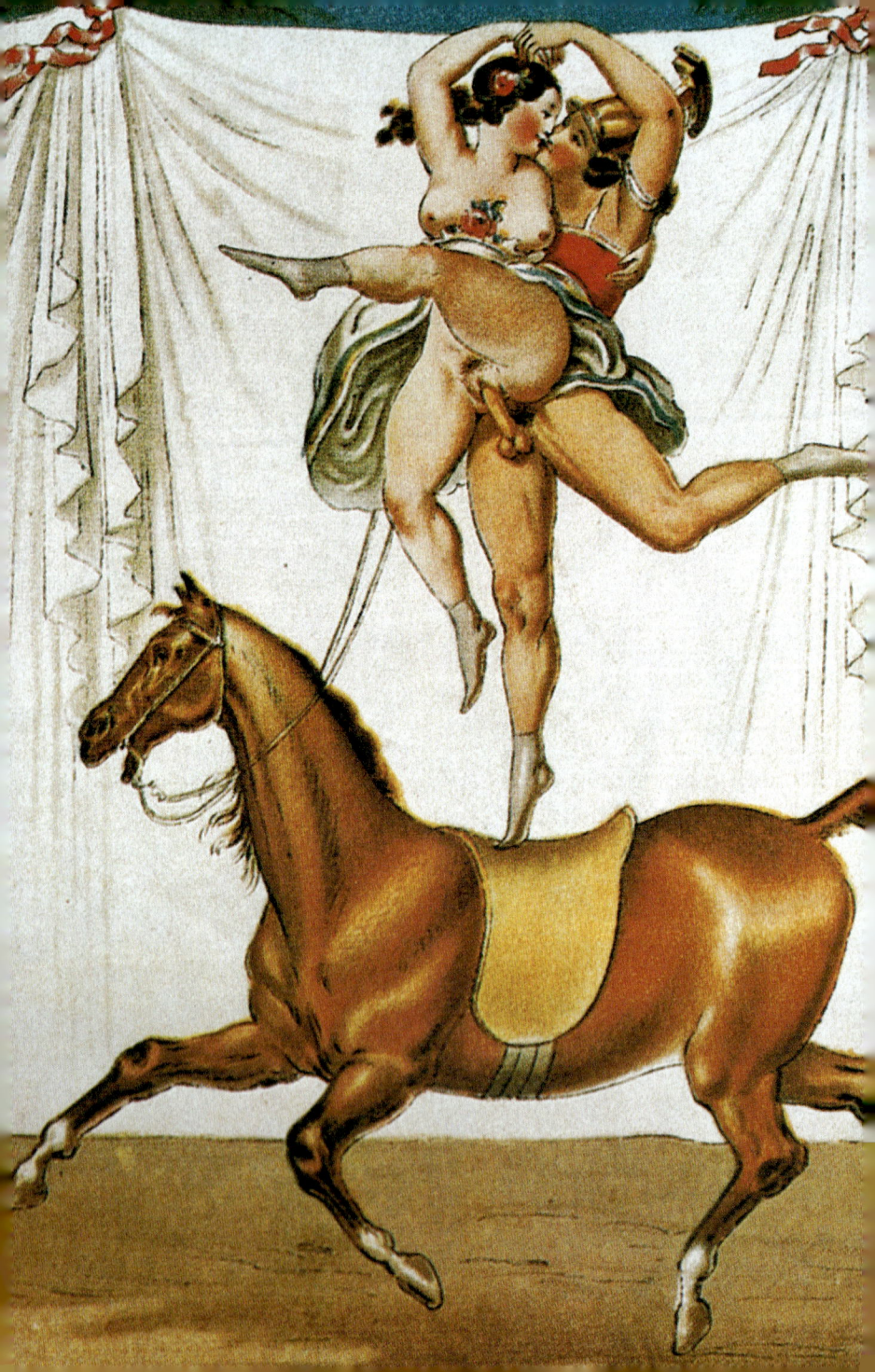

The art of pleasure

An erotic history of humanity

From the dawn of time, ever since Adam and Eve, artists of every age — whether the Egyptian, Greek, or Roman artists of Antiquity, or more recent famous names such as Rembrandt, Courbet, Degas, or Picasso — have succumbed to their fantasies, obsessions, and libido, and produced erotic works that the censors have taken good care to keep hidden from the public. For *Erotica Universalis*, we surface from the subterranean realms of the museums to enter those of our national and private libraries. Here we discover that not only did most of our famous authors write erotic texts that bordered on indecency, but also that great artists like Boucher, Fragonard, Dalí, and Matisse were inspired to provide suitable illustrations for these naughty books.

"*Erotica Universalis* outlines the blush-worthy history of erotic art, surveying icons – from Egypt's Golden Empire to present day – with a knack for translating sexual fantasies into master works of art."
— *The Huffington Post*, New York

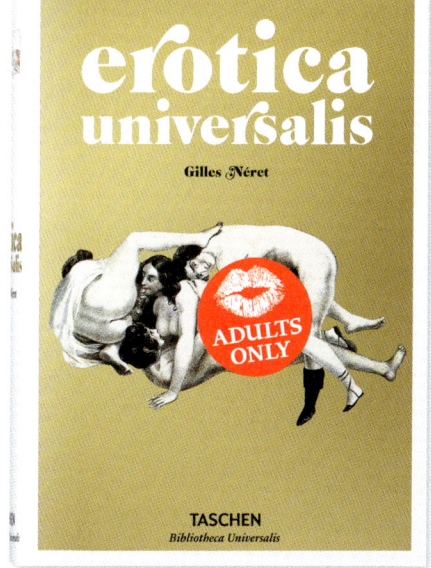

Erotica Universalis
Gilles Néret
576 pages
TRILINGUAL EDITION IN:
ENGLISH / DEUTSCH / FRANÇAIS

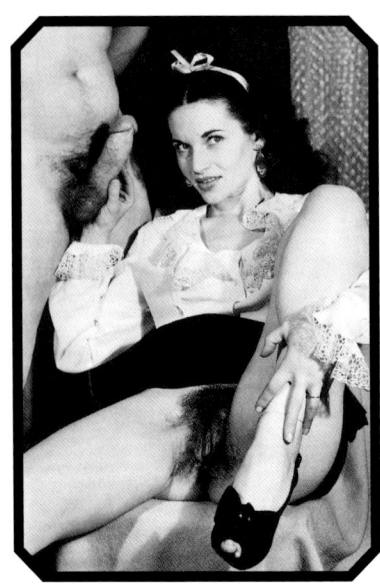

EACH AND EVERY TASCHEN BOOK PLANTS A SEED!
TASCHEN is a carbon neutral publisher. Each year, we offset our annual carbon emissions
with carbon credits at the Instituto Terra, a reforestation program in Minas Gerais, Brazil,
founded by Lélia and Sebastião Salgado. To find out more about this ecological partnership,
please check: www.taschen.com/zerocarbon
Inspiration: unlimited. Carbon footprint: zero.

To stay informed about TASCHEN and our upcoming titles, please subscribe to our
free magazine at www.taschen.com/magazine, follow us on Instagram and Facebook,
or e-mail your questions to contact@taschen.com.

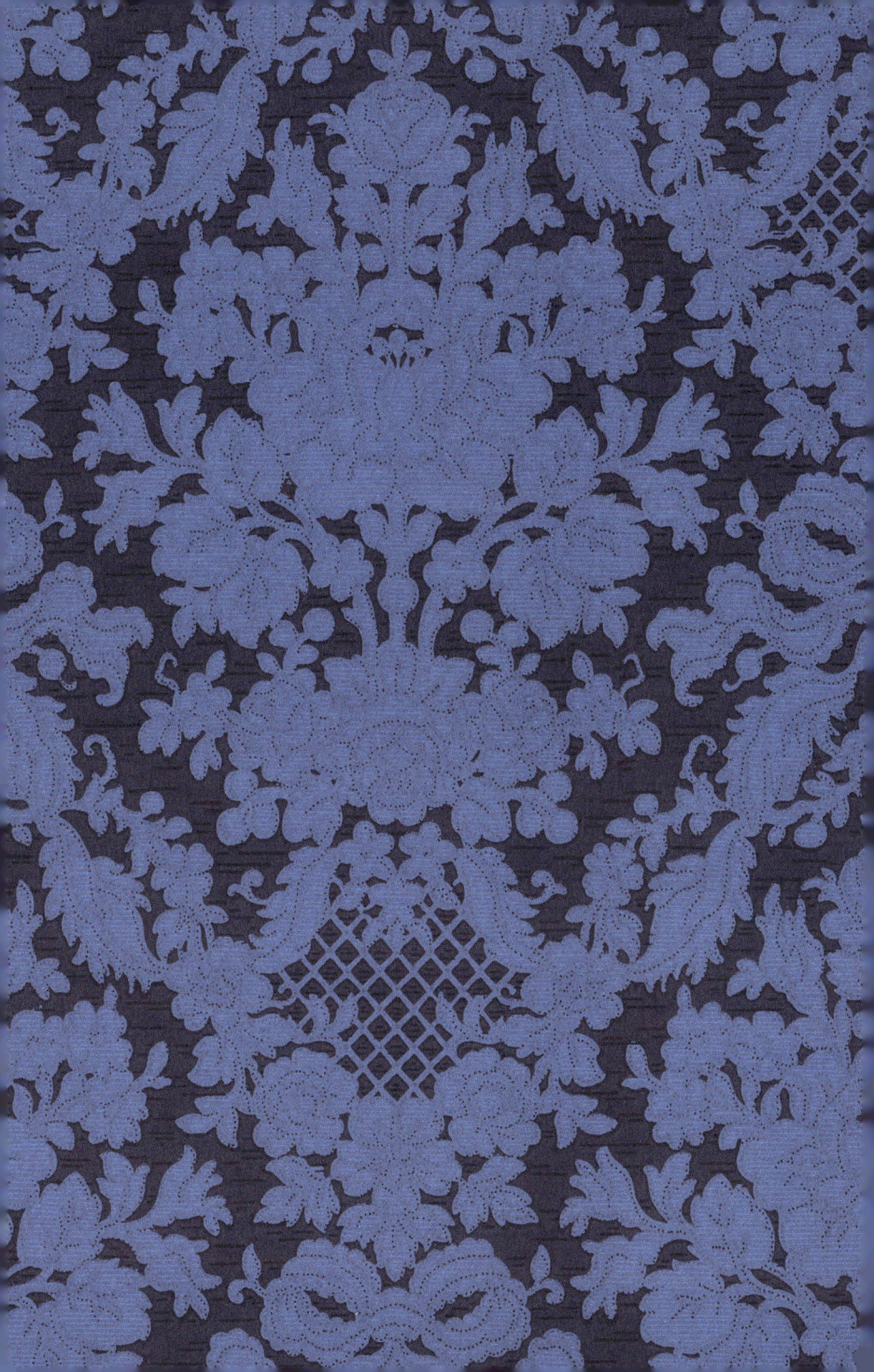

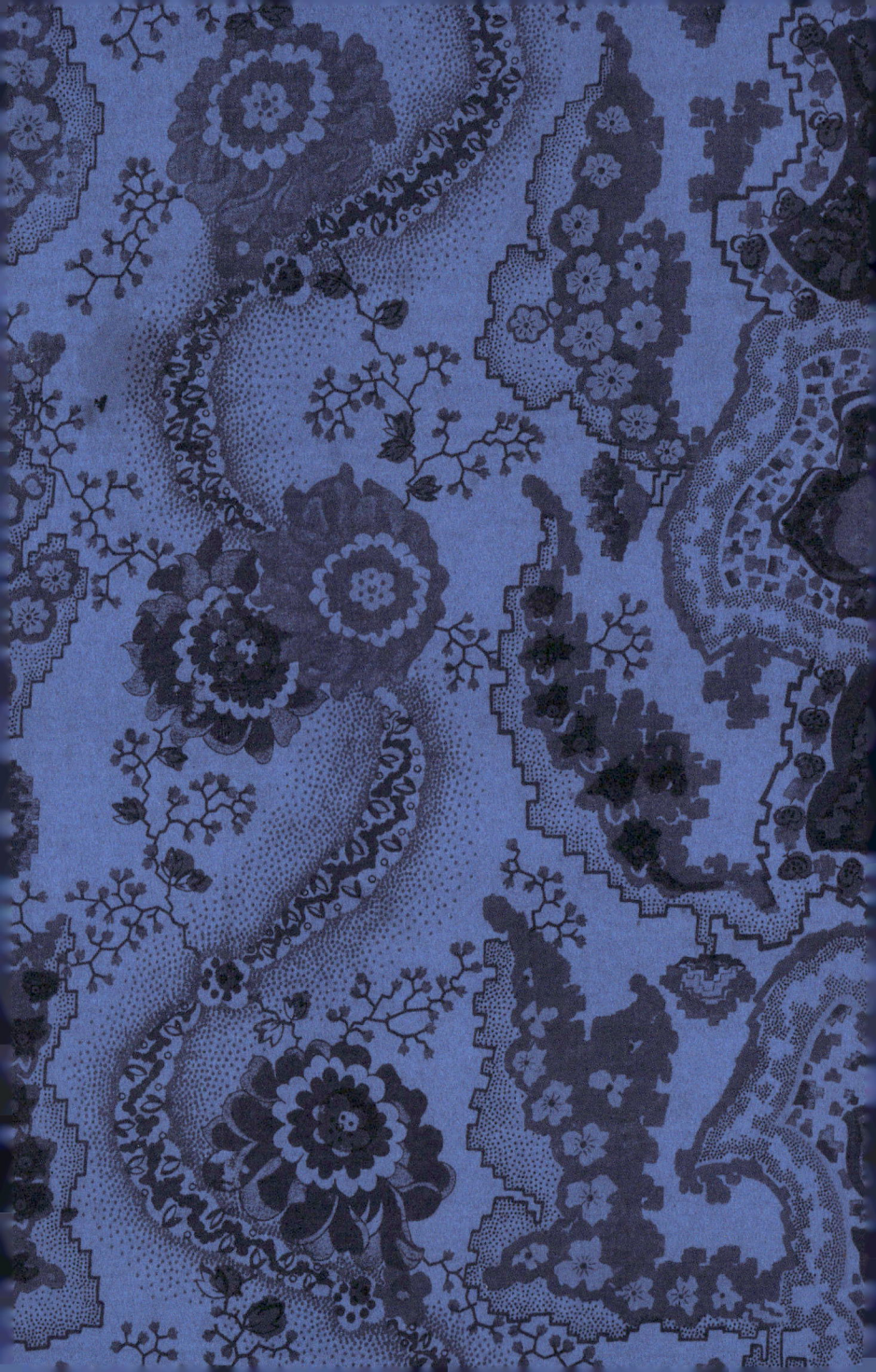